Reiner Hähnle · Wil van der Aalst (Eds.)

Fundamental Approaches to Software Engineering

22nd International Conference, FASE 2019
Held as Part of the European Joint Conferences on Theory and Practice of Software, ETAPS 2019
Prague, Czech Republic, April 6–11, 2019
Proceedings

Editors
Reiner Hähnle
Technische Universität Darmstadt
Darmstadt, Germany

Wil van der Aalst
RWTH Aachen University
Aachen, Germany

https://doi.org/10.1007/978-3-030-16722-6

LNCS Sublibrary: SL1 – Theoretical Computer Science and General Issues

ETAPS Foreword

Welcome to the 22nd ETAPS! This is the first time that ETAPS took place in the Czech Republic in its beautiful capital Prague.

ETAPS 2019 was the 22nd instance of the European Joint Conferences on Theory and Practice of Software. ETAPS is an annual federated conference established in 1998, and consists of five conferences: ESOP, FASE, FoSSaCS, TACAS, and POST. Each conference has its own Program Committee (PC) and its own Steering Committee (SC). The conferences cover various aspects of software systems, ranging from theoretical computer science to foundations to programming language developments, analysis tools, formal approaches to software engineering, and security.

Organizing these conferences in a coherent, highly synchronized conference program enables participation in an exciting event, offering the possibility to meet many researchers working in different directions in the field and to easily attend talks of different conferences. ETAPS 2019 featured a new program item: the Mentoring Workshop. This workshop is intended to help students early in the program with advice on research, career, and life in the fields of computing that are covered by the ETAPS conference. On the weekend before the main conference, numerous satellite workshops took place and attracted many researchers from all over the globe.

ETAPS 2019 received 436 submissions in total, 137 of which were accepted, yielding an overall acceptance rate of 31.4%. I thank all the authors for their interest in ETAPS, all the reviewers for their reviewing efforts, the PC members for their contributions, and in particular the PC (co-)chairs for their hard work in running this entire intensive process. Last but not least, my congratulations to all authors of the accepted papers!

ETAPS 2019 featured the unifying invited speakers Marsha Chechik (University of Toronto) and Kathleen Fisher (Tufts University) and the conference-specific invited speakers (FoSSaCS) Thomas Colcombet (IRIF, France) and (TACAS) Cormac Flanagan (University of California at Santa Cruz). Invited tutorials were provided by Dirk Beyer (Ludwig Maximilian University) on software verification and Cesare Tinelli (University of Iowa) on SMT and its applications. On behalf of the ETAPS 2019 attendants, I thank all the speakers for their inspiring and interesting talks!

ETAPS 2019 took place in Prague, Czech Republic, and was organized by Charles University. Charles University was founded in 1348 and was the first university in Central Europe. It currently hosts more than 50,000 students. ETAPS 2019 was further supported by the following associations and societies: ETAPS e.V., EATCS (European Association for Theoretical Computer Science), EAPLS (European Association for Programming Languages and Systems), and EASST (European Association of Software Science and Technology). The local organization team consisted of Jan Vitek and Jan Kofron (general chairs), Barbora Buhnova, Milan Ceska, Ryan Culpepper, Vojtech Horky, Paley Li, Petr Maj, Artem Pelenitsyn, and David Safranek.

The ETAPS SC consists of an Executive Board, and representatives of the individual ETAPS conferences, as well as representatives of EATCS, EAPLS, and EASST. The Executive Board consists of Gilles Barthe (Madrid), Holger Hermanns (Saarbrücken), Joost-Pieter Katoen (chair, Aachen and Twente), Gerald Lüttgen (Bamberg), Vladimiro Sassone (Southampton), Tarmo Uustalu (Reykjavik and Tallinn), and Lenore Zuck (Chicago). Other members of the SC are: Wil van der Aalst (Aachen), Dirk Beyer (Munich), Mikolaj Bojanczyk (Warsaw), Armin Biere (Linz), Luis Caires (Lisbon), Jordi Cabot (Barcelona), Jean Goubault-Larrecq (Cachan), Jurriaan Hage (Utrecht), Rainer Hähnle (Darmstadt), Reiko Heckel (Leicester), Panagiotis Katsaros (Thessaloniki), Barbara König (Duisburg), Kim G. Larsen (Aalborg), Matteo Maffei (Vienna), Tiziana Margaria (Limerick), Peter Müller (Zurich), Flemming Nielson (Copenhagen), Catuscia Palamidessi (Palaiseau), Dave Parker (Birmingham), Andrew M. Pitts (Cambridge), Dave Sands (Gothenburg), Don Sannella (Edinburgh), Alex Simpson (Ljubljana), Gabriele Taentzer (Marburg), Peter Thiemann (Freiburg), Jan Vitek (Prague), Tomas Vojnar (Brno), Heike Wehrheim (Paderborn), Anton Wijs (Eindhoven), and Lijun Zhang (Beijing).

I would like to take this opportunity to thank all speakers, attendants, organizers of the satellite workshops, and Springer for their support. I hope you all enjoy the proceedings of ETAPS 2019. Finally, a big thanks to Jan and Jan and their local organization team for all their enormous efforts enabling a fantastic ETAPS in Prague!

February 2019

Joost-Pieter Katoen
ETAPS SC Chair
ETAPS e.V. President

Preface

This volume contains the papers presented at the 22nd International Conference on Fundamental Approaches to Software Engineering (FASE 2019) held during April 9–11, 2019, in Prague. FASE 2019 was organized as part of the annual European Joint Conferences on Theory and Practice of Software (ETAPS 2019). ETAPS is the most important and visible annual European event related to software sciences.

As usual, the papers submitted to FASE focus on the foundations on which software engineering is built. The papers submitted covered topics such as software engineering, requirements engineering, software architectures, specification, software quality, validation, verification of functional and non-functional properties, model-driven development and model transformation, model transformations, software processes, and software evolution.

We received 94 abstract submissions of which 74 were turned into full submissions (63 research papers, five tool papers, and six demo papers). We had submissions from the following countries (sorted based on the number of submissions): Germany, France, Canada, Estonia, USA, Argentina, UK, Norway, Spain, Brazil, China, South Korea, Australia, Czechia, Austria, Denmark, Italy, Japan, the Netherlands, Pakistan, South Africa, Tunisia, India, Poland, Portugal, Romania, Turkey, Belgium, Colombia, Macedonia, Malta, Sweden, and Ukraine.

Of the 74 submitted papers, 24 papers were accepted after reviewing and discussions among the Program Committee (PC) members (20 research papers, two tool papers, and two demo papers). This corresponds to a 32% acceptance rate. Beside the 30 PC members, there were 100 external reviewers. For the fourth time, FASE used a double-blind reviewing process. Overall the reviewing process was smooth and it was possible to have consensus on all decisions. We thank the PC members and reviewers for doing a great job!

Apart from thanking the authors, we also thank Marsha Chechik (University of Toronto) for contributing a paper based on her plenary ETAPS 2019 invited talk, which is also included in these proceedings. The title of Marsha's talk was "Software Assurance in an Uncertain World." She discussed the problem that software systems are deeply rooted in uncertainty since most complex open-world functionality is either not completely specifiable or it is not cost-effective to do so. Moreover, these systems are placed in an uncertain ever-evolving environment.

This volume shows that, despite the rapid progress in software engineering, there are still many open problems. These problems are important for the way we do business, the way we govern, and the way we socialize. We depend on complex software artifacts, yet we still need to fully understand how to best develop and maintain them. The papers in this volume help to progress the state of the art and hopefully inspire and influence future work.

We thank the ETAPS 2019 organizers, in particular, Jan Kofron and Jan Vitek (general chairs), Barbora Buhnova (publicity chair), Vojtech Horkey and Arten

Pelnisyn (web chairs), and David Safranek (publications chair). We also thank Joost-Pieter Katoen, the ETAPS SC chair, for managing the whole process, and Gabriele Taentzer, the FASE SC chair, for swift feedback on several questions.

We hope that you will enjoy reading the volume.

February 2019

Wil van der Aalst
Reiner Hähnle

Organization

Program Committee

Christel Baier	TU Dresden, Germany
Stefano Berardi	University of Turin, Italy
Mario Bravetti	University of Bologna, Italy
Jordi Cabot	Open University of Catalonia, Spain
Ana Cavalcanti	University of York, UK
Marsha Chechik	University of Toronto, Canada
Ferruccio Damiani	University of Turin, Italy
Ewen Denney	NASA Ames Research Center, USA
Dilian Gurov	KTH Royal Institute of Technology, Sweden
Ludovic Henrio	CNRS, France
Reiner Hähnle	TU Darmstadt, Germany
Gerti Kappel	Vienna University of Technology, Austria
Ekkart Kindler	Technical University of Denmark, Denmark
Martin Leucker	University of Lübeck, Germany
Jun Pang	University of Luxembourg, Luxembourg
André Platzer	Carnegie Mellon University, USA
Bernhard Rumpe	RWTH Aachen University, Germany
Alessandra Russo	Imperial College London, UK
Rick Salay	University of Toronto, Canada
Ina Schaefer	Technische Universität Braunschweig, Germany
Andy Schürr	TU Darmstadt, Germany
Perdita Stevens	The University of Edinburgh, UK
Mariëlle Stoelinga	University of Twente, The Netherlands
Jun Sun	Singapore University of Technology and Design, Singapore
Gabriele Taentzer	Philipps-Universität Marburg, The Netherlands
Silvia Lizeth Tapia Tarifa	University of Oslo, Norway
Maurice H. Ter Beek	ISTI-CNR, Pisa, Italy
Wil M. P. van der Aalst	RWTH Aachen University, Germany
Heike Wehrheim	Paderborn University, Germany
Yingfei Xiong	Peking University, China

Additional Reviewers

Aspinall, David
Bafrani, Mahsa
Baxter, James
Berti, Alessandro
Bettini, Lorenzo
Bill, Robert
Bozzano, Marco
Bubel, Richard
Canovas Izquierdo, Javier Luis
Cerone, Andrea
Chen, Yifan
Ciancia, Vincenzo
Cordwell, Katherine
Dalibor, Manuela
Dashevskyi, Stanislav
Din, Crystal Chang
Drave, Imke Helene
Ed-Douibi, Hamza
Escobar, Santiago
Ferrari, Alessio
Fritsche, Lars
Fulton, Nathan
Gadyatskaya, Olga
Gario, Marco
Gerhold, Marcus
Gerking, Christopher
Giannini, Paola
Girault, Alain
Guanciale, Roberto
Gómez, Abel
Habermehl, Peter
Haglund, Jonas
Henderson, Robbie
Herda, Mihai
Hillemacher, Steffen
Johnsen, Einar Broch
Kamburjan, Eduard
Kharraz, Karam
Knüppel, Alexander
Kosiol, Jens
König, Jürgen
Lange, Felix Dino
Laurent, Jonathan
Leroy, Dorian
Lidström, Christian
Lienhardt, Michael
Lindner, Andreas
Lischke, Sabrina
Lochau, Malte
Lu, Sirui
Luthmann, Lars
Martínez, Salvador
Mauro, Jacopo
Mazzanti, Franco
Meijer, Jeroen
Mereuta, Radu
Michael, Judith
Mitsch, Stefan
Miyazawa, Alvaro
Mover, Sergio
Najafzadeh, Mahsa
Nassar, Nebras
Netz, Lukas
Oortwijn, Wytse
Palmskog, Karl
Paolini, Luca
Papadakis, Michail
Papadakis, Mike
Pedro, Andre
Petrocchi, Marinella
Pozzato, Gian Luca
Raco, Deni
Ren, Luyao
Ribeiro, Pedro
Ruijters, Enno
Ruland, Sebastian
Runge, Tobias
Schivo, Stefano
Schlatte, Rudolf
Schlie, Alexander
Schmalzing, David
Schmitz, Malte
Sharma, Arnab
Shumeiko, Igor
Sogokon, Andrew
Spagnolo, Giorgio Oronzo
Sproston, Jeremy
Steffen, Martin
Thoma, Daniel
Thüm, Thomas
Toews, Manuel
Tomaszek, Stefan
Tveito, Lars
Wally, Bernhard
Wang, Bo
Wang, Guancheng
Zacchiroli, Stefano
Zawadzki, Erik
Zhang, Yuhao
Zhu, Qihao

Contents

FASE Invited Talk

Software Assurance in an Uncertain World

Marsha Chechik(✉), Rick Salay, Torin Viger, Sahar Kokaly, and Mona Rahimi

University of Toronto, Toronto, Canada
chechik@cs.toronto.edu

Abstract. From financial services platforms to social networks to vehicle control, software has come to mediate many activities of daily life. Governing bodies and standards organizations have responded to this trend by creating regulations and standards to address issues such as safety, security and privacy. In this environment, the compliance of software development to standards and regulations has emerged as a key requirement. Compliance claims and arguments are often captured in assurance cases, with linked evidence of compliance. Evidence can come from testcases, verification proofs, human judgment, or a combination of these. That is, experts try to build (safety-critical) systems carefully according to well justified methods and articulate these justifications in an assurance case that is ultimately judged by a human. Yet software is deeply rooted in uncertainty; most complex open-world functionality (e.g., perception of the state of the world by a self-driving vehicle), is either not completely specifiable or it is not cost-effective to do so; software systems are often to be placed into uncertain environments, and there can be uncertainties that need to be We argue that the role of assurance cases is to be the grand unifier for software development, focusing on capturing and managing uncertainty. We discuss three approaches for arguing about safety and security of software under uncertainty, in the absence of fully sound and complete methods: assurance argument rigor, semantic evidence composition and applicability to new kinds of systems, specifically those relying on ML.

1 Introduction

From financial services platforms to social networks to vehicle control, software has come to mediate many activities of daily life. Governing bodies and standards organizations have responded to this trend by creating regulations and standards to address issues such as safety, security and privacy. In this environment, the compliance of software development to standards and regulations has emerged as a key requirement.

Development of safety-critical systems begins with *hazard analysis*, aimed to identify possible causes of harm. It uses severity, probability and controllability of a hazard's occurrence to assign the Safety Integrity Levels (in the automotive industry, these are referred to as ASILs [35]) – the higher the ASIL level,

R. Hähnle and W. van der Aalst (Eds.): FASE 2019, LNCS 11424, pp. 3–21, 2019.
https://doi.org/10.1007/978-3-030-16722-6_1

the more rigor is expected to be put into identifying and mitigating the hazard. Mitigating hazards therefore becomes the main requirement of the system, with system safety requirements being directly linked to the hazards. These requirements are then refined along the LHS of the V until individual modules and their implementation can be built. The RHS includes appropriate testing and validation, used as supporting evidence in developing an argument that the system adequately handles its hazards, with the expectation that the higher the ASIL level, the stronger the required justification of safety is.

Assurance claims and arguments are often captured by *assurance cases*, with linked evidence supporting it. Evidence can come from testcases, verification proofs, human judgment, or a combination of these. Assurance cases organize information allowing argument unfolding in a comprehensive way and ultimately allowing safety engineers to determine whether they trust that the system was adequately designed to avoid systematic faults (before delivery) and adequately detect and react to failures at runtime [35].

Yet software is deeply rooted in uncertainty; most complex open-world functionality (e.g., perception of the state of the world by a self-driving vehicle), is either not completely specifiableor it is not cost-effective to do so [12]. Software systems are often to be placed into uncertain environments [48], and there can be uncertainties that need to be considered at the design phase [20]. Thus, we believe that the role of assurance cases is to *explicitly capture and manage uncertainty coming from different sources, assess it and ultimately reduce it to an acceptable level, either with respect to a standard, company processes, or assessor judgment.* The various software development steps are currently not well integrated, and uncertainty is not expressed or managed explicitly in a uniform manner. Our claim in this paper is that *an assurance case is the unifier among the different software development steps, and can be used to make uncertainties explicit, which also makes them manageable. This provides a well-founded basis for modeling confidence about satisfaction of a critical system quality (security, safety, etc.) in an assurance case, making assurance cases play a crucial role in software development.* Specifically, we enumerate sources of uncertainty in software development. We also argue that organizing software development and analysis activities around the assurance case as a *living document* allows all parts of the software development to explicitly articulate uncertainty, steps taken to manage it, and the degree of confidence that artifacts acting as evidence have been performed correctly. This information can then help potential assessors in checking that the development outcome adequately satisfies the software desired quality (e.g., safety).

The area of system dependability has produced a significant body of work describing how to model assurance cases (e.g., [4,5,14,38]), and how to assess reviewer's confidence in the argument being made (e.g., [16,31,45,59,60]). There is also early work on assessing the impact of change on the assurance argument when the system undergoes change [39]. A recent survey [43] provides a comprehensive list of assurance case tools developed over the past 20 years and an analysis of their functionalities including support for assurance case creation, assessment and maintenance. We believe that the road to truly making assurance cases the grand unifier for software development for complex high-assurance systems has many challenges. One is to be able to successfully argue about safety and security of software under uncertainty, without fully sound and complete methods. For that, we believe that *assurance arguments must be rigorous* and that we need to properly understand how to perform *evidence composition* for traditional systems, but also for *new kinds of systems*, specifically those relying on ML. We discuss these issues below.

Rigor. To be validated or reused, assurance case structures must be as rigorous as possible [51]. Of course, assurance arguments ultimately depend on human judgment (with some facts treated as "obvious" and "generally acceptable"), but the structure of the argument should be fully formal so as to allow to assess its completeness. Bandur and McDermid called this approach "formal modulo engineering expertise" [1].

Evidence Composition. We need to effectively combine the top-down process of uncertainty reduction with the bottom-up process of composing evidence, specifically, evidence obtained from applying testing and verification techniques.

Applicability to "new" kinds of systems. We believe that our view – rigorous, uncertainty-reduction focused and evidence composing – is directly applicable to systems developed using machine learning, e.g., self-driving cars.

This paper is organized as follows: In Sect. 2, we briefly describe syntax of assurance cases. In Sect. 3, we outline possible sources of uncertainty encountered as part of system development. In Sect. 4, we describe the benefits of a rigorous language for assurance cases by way of example. In Sect. 5, we describe, again by way of example, a possible method of composing evidence. In Sect. 6, we develop a high-level assurance case for a pedestrian detection subsystem. We conclude in Sect. 7 with a discussion of possible challenges and opportunities.

2 Background on Assurance Case Modeling Notation

The most commonly used representation for safety cases is the graphical Goal Structuring Notation (GSN) [30], which is intended to support the assurance of critical properties of systems (including safety). GSN is comprised of six core elements – see Fig. 1. Arguments in GSN are typically organized into a tree of the core elements shown in Fig. 1[1]. The root is the overall goal to be satisfied by the system, and it is gradually decomposed (possibly via strategies) into sub-goals and finally into solutions, which are the leaves of the safety case. Connections between goals, strategies and solutions represent *supported-by* relations, which indicate inferential or evidential relationships between elements. Goals and strategies may be optionally associated with some contexts, assumptions and/or justifications by means of *in-context-of* relations, which declare a contextual relationship between the connected elements.

[1] In this paper, we use both diamond and triangle shapes interchangeably to depict an "undeveloped" element.

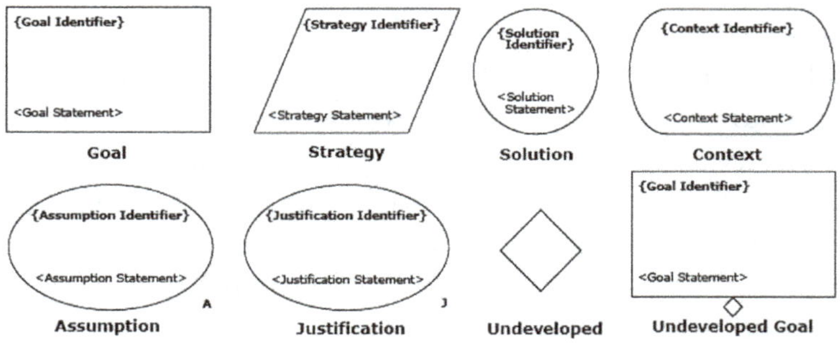

Fig. 1. Core GSN elements from [30].

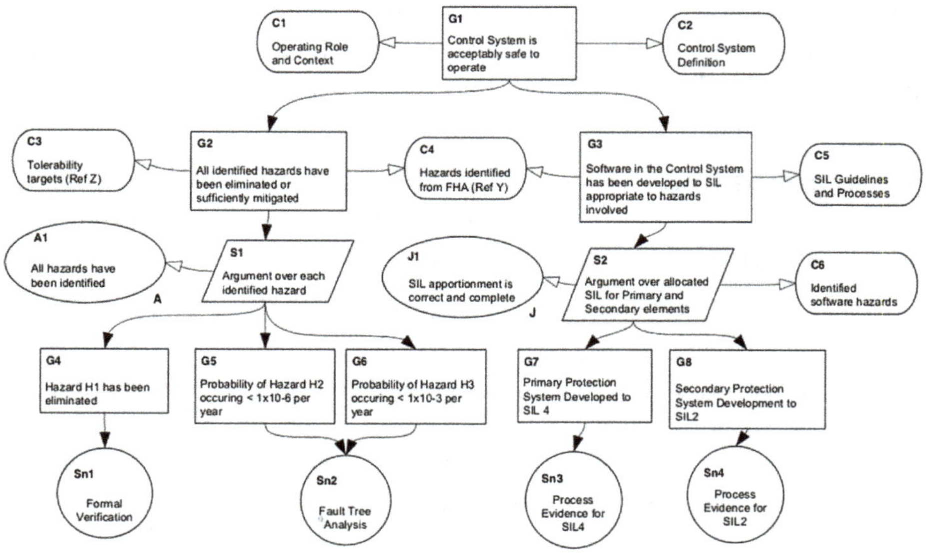

Fig. 2. Example safety case in GSN (from [30]).

For example, consider the safety case in Fig. 2. The overall goal **G1** is that the "Control System is acceptably safe to operate" given its role, context and definition, and it is decomposed into two sub-goals: **G2**, for eliminating and mitigating all identified hazards, and **G3**, for ensuring that the system software is developed to an appropriate ASIL. Assuming that all hazards have been identified, **G2** can in turn be decomposed into three sub-goals by considering each hazard separately (**S1**), and each separate hazard is shown to be satisfied using evidence from formal verification (**Sn1**) or fault tree analysis (**Sn2**). Similarly, under some specific context and justification, **G3** can be decomposed into two sub-goals, each of which is shown to be satisfied by the associated evidence.

3 Sources of Uncertainty in Software Development

In this section, we briefly survey uncertainty in software development, broadly split into the categories of uncertainties about the specifications, about the environment, about the system itself, and about the argument of its safety. For each part, we aim to address how building an assurance case is related to understanding and mitigating such uncertainties.

Uncertainty in Specifications. Software specifications tend to suffer from incompleteness, inconsistency and ambiguity [42,46]. Specification uncertainty stems from a misunderstanding or an incomplete understanding of how the system is supposed to function in early phases of development; e.g., miscommunication and inability of stakeholders to transfer knowledge due to differing concepts and vocabularies [2,13]; unknown values for sets of known events (a.k.a. the *known unknowns*); and the unknown and unidentifiable events (a.k.a. the *unknown unknowns*) [57].

Recently, machine-learning approaches for interactively learning the software specifications have become popular; we discuss one such example, of pedestrian detection, in Sect. 6. Other mitigations of specification uncertainties, suggested by various standards and research, are identification of edge cases [36], hazard and obstacle analysis [55] to help identify unknown unknowns [35], step-wise refinement to handle partiality in specifications, ontology- [9] and information retrieval-driven requirements engineering approaches [21], as well as generally building arguments about addressing specification uncertainties.

Environmental Uncertainty. The system's environment can refer to adjacent agents interacting with the system, a human operator using the system, or physical conditions of the environment. Sources of environmental uncertainties have been thoroughly investigated [19,48]. One source originates from unpredictable and changing properties of the environment, e.g., assumptions about actions of other vehicles in the autonomous vehicle domain or assuming that a plane is on the runway if its wheels are turning. Another uncertainty source is input errors from broken sensors, missing, noisy and inaccurate input data, imprecise measurements, or disruptive control signals from adjacent systems. Yet another source might be when changes in the environment affect the specification. For example, consider a robotic arm that moves with the expected precision but the target has moved from its estimated position.

A number of techniques have been developed to mitigate environmental uncertainties, e.g., runtime monitoring systems such as RESIST [10], or machine-learning approaches such as FUSION [18] which self-tune the adaptive behavior of systems to unanticipated changes in the environment. More broadly, environmental uncertainties are mitigated by a careful requirements engineering process, by principled system design and, in assurance cases, by an argument that they had been adequately identified and adequately handled.

System Uncertainties. One important source of uncertainty is faced by developers who do not have sufficient information to make decisions about their system during development. For example, a developer may have insufficient information to choose a particular implementation platform. In [19,48], this source of uncertainty is referred to as *design-time uncertainty*, and some approaches to handling it are offered in [20]. Decisions made while resolving such uncertainties are crucial to put into an assurance argument, to capture the context, i.e., a particular platform is selected because of its performance, at the expense of memory requirements.

Another uncertainty refers to correctness of the implementation [7]. This uncertainty lays in the V&V procedure and is caused by whether the implementation of the tool can be trusted, whether the tool is used appropriately (that is, its assumptions are satisfied), and in general, whether a particular verification technique is the right one for verifying the fulfillment of the system requirements [15]. We address some of these uncertainties in Sect. 5.

Argument Uncertainty. The use of safety arguments to demonstrate safety of software-intensive systems raises questions such as the extent to which these arguments can be trusted. That is, how confident are we that a verified, validated software is actually safe? How much evidence and how thorough of an argument do we require for that?

To assess uncertainties which may affect the system's safety, researchers have proposed techniques to estimate confidence in structured assurance cases, either through qualitative or quantitative approaches [27,44]. The majority of these are based on the Dempster-Shafer Theory [31,60], Josang's Opinion Triangle [17], Bayesian Belief Networks (BNNs) [16,61], Evidential Reasoning (ER) [45] and weighted averages [59]. The approaches which use BBNs treat safety goals as nodes in the network and try to compute their conditional probability based on given probabilities for the leaf nodes of the network. Dempster-Shafer Theory is similar to BBNs but is based on the *belief function* and its *plausibility* which is used to combine separate pieces of information to calculate the probability. The ER approach [45] allows the assessors to provide individual judgments concerning the trustworthiness and appropriateness of the evidence, building a separate argument from the assurance case.

These approaches focus on assigning and propagating confidence measures but do not specifically address uncertainty in the argument. They also focus on aggregating evidence coming from multiple sources but treat it as a "black box", instead of how a piece of evidence from one source might compose with another. We look at these questions in Sects. 4 and 5, respectively.

4 Formality in Assurance Cases

As discussed in Sect. 1, we believe that the ultimate goal of an assurance case is to explicitly capture and manage uncertainty, and ultimately reduce it to an acceptable level. Even informal arguments improve safety, e.g., by making people decompose the top level goal case-wise, and examine the decomposed parts critically. But the decomposed cases tend to have an ad hoc structure dictated by experience and preference, with under-explored completeness claims, giving both developers and regulators a false sense of confidence, no matter how confidence is measured, since they feel that their reasoning is rigorous even though it is not [58]. Moreover, as assurance cases are produced and judged by humans, they are typically based on *inductive arguments*. Such arguments are susceptible to fallacies (e.g., arguing through circular reasoning, using justification based

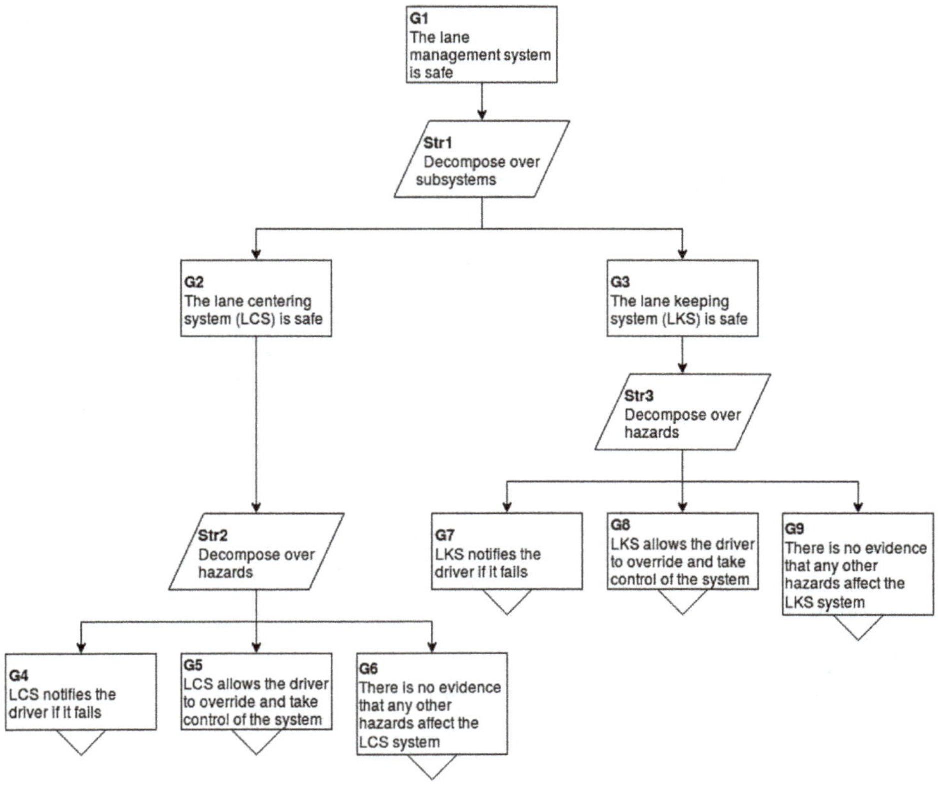

Fig. 3. A fragment of the Lane Management (LMS) Safety case.

on false dichotomies), and evaluations by different reviewers may lead to the discovery of different fallacies [28].

There have been several attempts to improve credibility of an argument by making the argument structure more formal. [25] introduces the notion of confidence maps as an explicit way of reasoning about sources of doubt in an argument, and proposes justifying confidence in assurance arguments through *eliminative induction* (i.e., an argument by eliminating sources of doubt). [29] highlights the need to model both evidential and argumentation uncertainties when evaluating assurance arguments, and considers applications of the formally evaluatable extension of Toulmin's argument style proposed by [56]. [11] details VAA – a method for assessing assurance arguments based on Dempster-Shafer theory. [51] is a proponent of completely deductive reasoning, narrowing the scope of the argument so that it can be formalized and potentially formally checked, using automated theorem provers, arguing that this would give a modular framework for assessing (and, we presume, reusing) assurance cases. [1] relaxes Rushby's position a bit, aiming instead at formal assurance argumentation "modulo engineering expertise", and proof obligations about consistency of arguments remain valid even for not fully formal assurance arguments. To this end, they provided a specific formalization of goal validity given validity of subgoals and contexts/context assumptions, resulting in such rules as

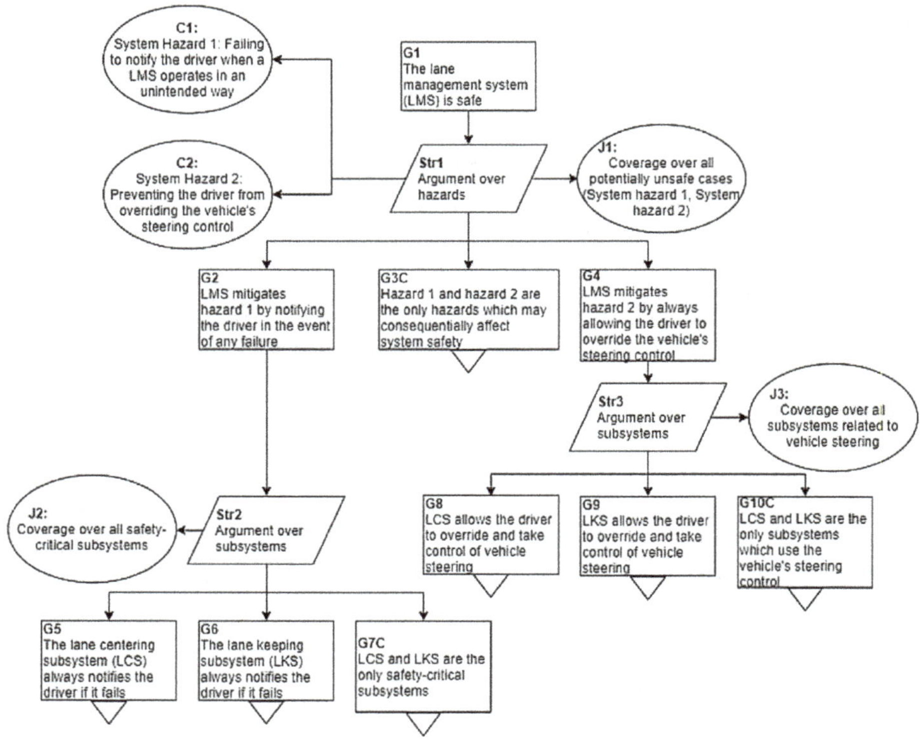

Fig. 4. An alternative representation of the same LMS fragment.

"assumptions on any given element must not be contradictory nor contradict the context assumed for that goal" [1].

Our Position. We believe that a degree of formality in assurance cases can go a long way not only towards establishing its validity, identifying and framing implicit uncertainties and avoiding fallacies, but also supporting assurance case modularity, refactoring and reuse. We illustrate this position on an example.

Example. Consider two partially developed assurance cases that argue that the lane management system (LMS) of a vehicle is safe (Figs. 3 and 4). The top-level safety goal **G1** in Fig. 3 is first decomposed by the strategy **Str1** into a set of subgoals which assert the safety of the LMS subsystems. An assessor can only trust that goals **G2** and **G3** imply **G1** by making an implicit assumption that the system safety is completely determined by the safety of its individual subsystems. Neither the need for this assumption nor the credibility of the assumption itself are made explicit in the assurance case, which weakens the argument and complicates the assessment process. The argument is further weakened by the absence of a completeness claim that all subsystems have been covered by this decomposition.

Strategies **Str2** and **Str3** in Fig. 3 decompose the safety claims about each subsystem into arguments over the relevant hazards. Yet the hazards themselves are never explicitly stated in the assurance case, making the direct relevance of each decomposed goal to its corresponding parent goal, and thus to the argument as a whole, unclear. While goals **G6** and **G9** attempt to provide completeness claims for their respective decompositions, they do so by citing lack of negative evidence without describing efforts to uncover such evidence. This justification is fallacious and can be categorized as "an argument from ignorance" [28].

Now consider the assurance case in Fig. 4 which presents a variant of the argument in Fig. 3, refined with context nodes, justification nodes and completeness claims. The top-level goal **G1** is decomposed into a set of subgoals asserting that particular hazards have been mitigated, as well as a completeness claim **G3C** stating that hazards **H1** and **H2** are the only ones that may be prevalent enough to defeat claim **G1**. Context nodes **C1** and **C2** define the hazards themselves, which clarifies the relevance of each hazard-mitigating goal. The node **J1** provides a justification for the validity of **Str1** by framing the decomposition as a proof by (exhaustive) cases. That is, **Str1** is justified by the statement that if **H1** and **H2** are the only hazards that could potentially make the system unsafe, then the system is safe if **H1** and **H2** have been adequately mitigated. This rigorous argument can be represented by the logical expression $\mathbf{G3C} \implies ((\mathbf{G2} \wedge \mathbf{G4}) \implies \mathbf{G1})$, and if completeness holds then **G2** and **G4** are sufficient to show **G1**. We now have a rigorous argument step that our confidence in **G1** is a direct consequence of confidence in its decomposed goals **G2**, **G3C** and **G4**, even though there may still be uncertainty in the evidential evaluation of **G2**, **G3C** and **G4**. That is, uncertainty has been made explicit and can be reasoned about at the evidential level. By removing argumentation uncertainty and explicating implicit assumptions, we get a more comprehensive framework for assurance case evaluation, where the relation between all reasoning steps is formally clear. Note that if the justification provides an inference rule, then the argument becomes deductive. Otherwise, it is weaker (the justification node can be used to quantify just *how* weaker) but still rigorous.

While the completeness claim **G3C** in Fig. 4 may be directly supported by evidence, the goals **G2** and **G4** are further decomposed by the strategies **Str2** and **Str3**, respectively, which represent decompositions over subsystems. These strategies are structured similarly to **Str1**, and can be expressed by the logical expressions $\mathbf{G7C} \implies ((\mathbf{G5} \wedge \mathbf{G6}) \implies \mathbf{G2})$ and $\mathbf{G10C} \implies ((\mathbf{G8} \wedge \mathbf{G9}) \implies \mathbf{G4})$, respectively. In Fig. 3, a decomposition by subsystems was applied directly to the top-level safety goal which necessitated a completeness claim that the safety of all individual subsystems implied safety of the entire system. Instead, the argument in Fig. 4 only needs to show that the set of subsystems in each decomposition is complete w.r.t. a particular hazard, which may be a more feasible claim to argue. This ability to transform an argument into a more easily justifiable form is another benefit of arguing via rigorous reasoning steps.

5 Combining Evidence

Evidence for assurance cases can come from a variety of sources: results from different testing and verification techniques, human judgment, or their combination. Multiple testing and verification techniques may be used to make the evidence more complete. A verification technique *complements* another if it is able

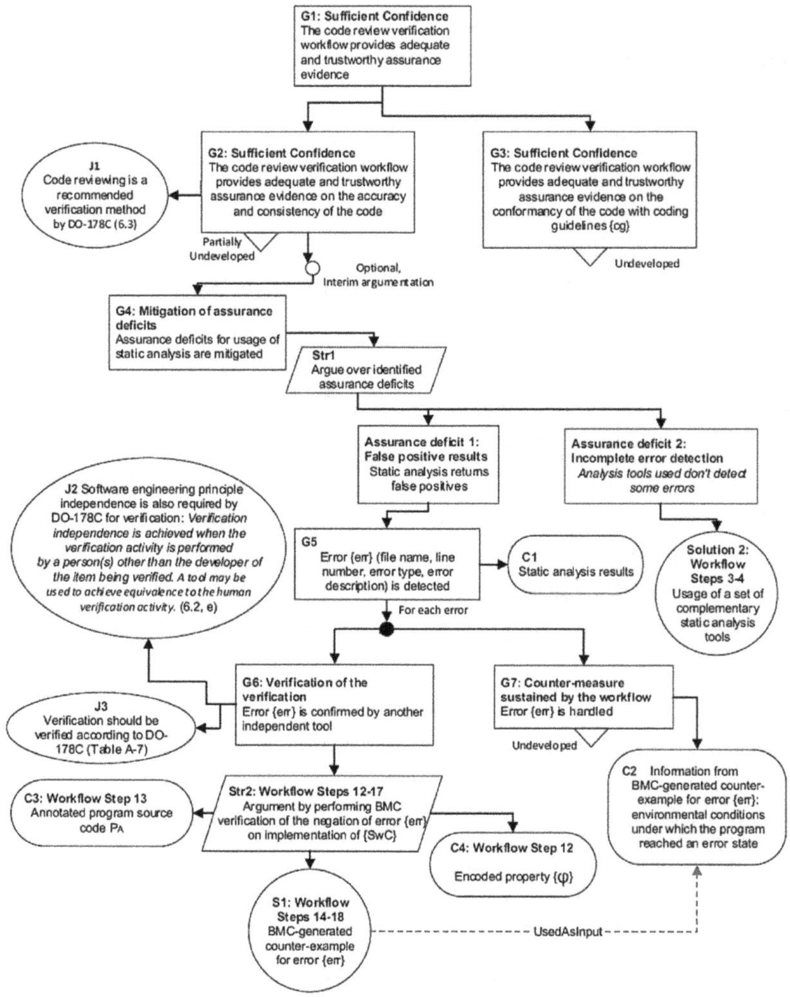

Fig. 5. Confidence argument for code review workflow (from [6]).

to verify types of requirements which cannot be verified by the other technique. For example, results of verification of properties via a bounded model checker (BMC) are complemented by additional test cases [8]. A verification technique *supports* another if it is used to detect faults in the other's verification results, thus providing backing evidence [33]. For example, a model checking technique may support a static analysis technique by verifying the faults detected [6]. Note that these approaches are principally different from just aggregating evidence treating it as a blackbox!

Habli and Kelly [32] and Denney and Pai [15] present safety case patterns for the use of formal method results for certification. Bennion et al. [3] present a safety case for arguing the compliance of a particular model checker, namely, the Simulink Design Verifier for DO-178C. Gallina and Andrews [23] argue about adequacy of a model-based testing process, and Carlan et al. [7] provide a safety pattern for choosing and composing verification techniques based on how they contribute to the identification or mitigation of systematic faults known to affect system safety.

Our Position. We, as a community, need to figure out the precise conditions under which particular testing and verification techniques "work" (e.g., modeling floating-point numbers as reals, making a small model hypothesis to justify sufficiency of a particular loop unrolling, etc.), and how they are intended to be composed in order to reduce uncertainty about whether software satisfies its specification. We illustrate a particular composition here.

Example. In this example, taken from [6], a model checker supports static analysis tools (that produce false negatives) by verifying the detected faults [6]. The assurance case is based on a workflow (not shown here) where an initial review report is constructed, by running static analysis tools and possibly peer code reviews. Then the program is annotated with the negation of each potential erroneous behavior as a desirable property for the program, and given to a model-checker. If the model-checker is able to verify the property, it is removed from the initial review report and not considered as an error. If the model-checker finds a violation, the alleged error is confirmed. In this case, a weakest-precondition generation mechanism is applied to find out the environmental conditions (external parameters that are not under the control of the program) under which the program shows the erroneous behavior. These conditions and the error trace are then added to the error description.

The paper [6] presents both the assurance case and the confidence argument for the code review workflow. We reproduce only the latter here (see Fig. 5), focusing on reducing uncertainty about the accuracy and consistency of the code property (goal **G2**). False positives generated by static analysis are mitigated using BMC – a method with a completely different verification rationale, thus implementing the safety engineering principle of independence (**J2**). Strategy (**Str2**) explains how errors can be confirmed or dismissed using BMC (goal **G6**). The additional information given by BMC can be used for the mitigation of the error (**C2**).

This approach takes good steps towards mitigating particular assurance deficits using a composition of verification techniques but leaves open several problems: how to ensure that BMC runs under the same environmental conditions as the static analysis tools? how deeply should the loops be unrolled? what to do with cases when the model-checker runs out of resources without giving a conclusive answer? and in general, what are the conditions under which it is safe to trust the "yes" answers of the model-checker.

6 Assurance Cases for ML Systems

Academia and industry are actively building systems using AI and machine learning, including a rapid push for ML in safety-critical domains such as medical devices and self-driving cars. For their successful adoption in society, we need to ensure that they are trustworthy, including obtaining confidence in their behavior and robustness.

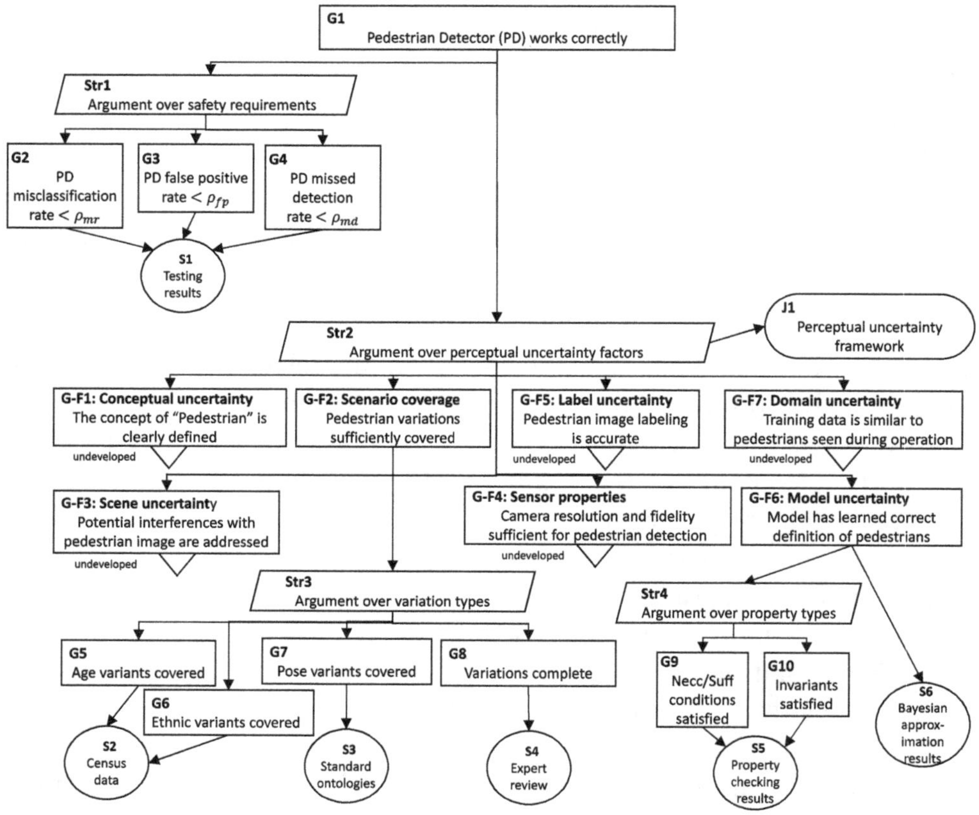

Fig. 6. A partially developed GSN safety case of pedestrian detector example.

Significant strides have already been made in this space, from extending mature testing and verification techniques to reasoning about neural networks [24,37,47,54] for properties such as safety, robustness and adequate handling of adversarial examples [26,34]. There is active work in designing systems that balance learning under uncertainty and acting safely, e.g., [52] as well as the broad notion of fairness and explainability in AI, e.g., [49].

Our Position. We believe that assurance cases remain a unifying view for ML-based systems just as much as for more conventional systems, allowing us to understand how the individual approaches fit into the overall goal of assuring safety and reliability and where there are gaps.

Example. We illustrate this idea with an example of a simple pedestrian detector (PD) component used as part of an autonomous driving system. The functions that PD supports consist of detection of objects in the environment ahead of the vehicle, classification of an object as a *pedestrian* or *other*, and localization of the position and extent of the pedestrian (indicated by bounding box). We assume that PD is implemented as a convolutional deep neural network with various stages to perform feature extraction, proposing regions containing objects and classification of the proposed objects. This is a typical approach for two-stage object detectors (e.g., see [50]).

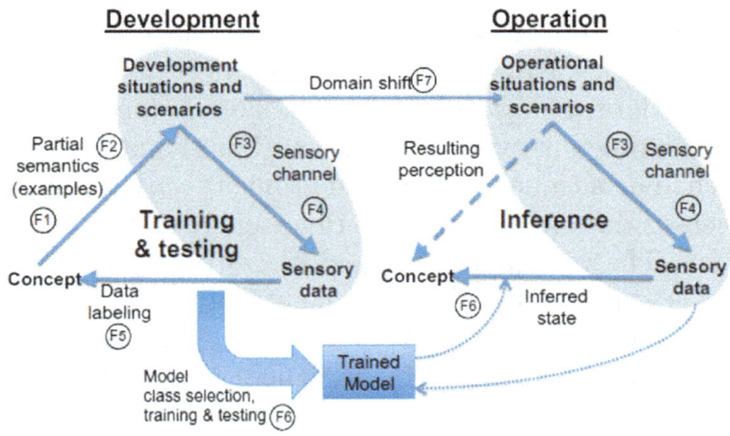

Fig. 7. A framework for factors affecting perceptual uncertainty (source: [12]).

As part of a safety critical system, PD contributes to the satisfaction of a top-level safety goal requiring that the vehicle always maintain a safe distance from all pedestrians. Specific safety requirements for PD can be derived from this goal, such as (RQ1) PD misclassification rate (i.e., classifying a pedestrian as "other") must be less than ρ_{mc}, (RQ2) PD false positive rate (i.e., classifying any non-pedestrian object or non-object as "pedestrian") must be less than ρ_{fp}, and (RQ3) PD missed detection rate (i.e., missing the presence of pedestrian) must be less than ρ_{md}. Here, the parameters ρ_{mc}, ρ_{fp} and ρ_{md} must be derived in conjunction with the control system that uses the output from PD to plan the vehicle trajectory.

The partially developed safety case for PD is shown in Fig. 6. The three safety requirements are addressed via the strategy **Str1** and, as expected, testing results are given as evidence of their satisfaction. However, since testing can only provide limited assurance about the behaviour of PD in operation, we use an additional strategy, **Str2**, to argue that a rigorous method was followed to develop PD. Specifically, we follow the framework of [12] for identifying the factors that lead to uncertainty in ML-based perceptual software such as PD.

The framework is defined at a high level in Fig. 7. The left "perception triangle" shows how the perceptual concept (in the case of PD, the concept "pedestrian") can occur in various scenarios in the world, how it is detected using sensors such as cameras, and how this can be used to collect and label examples in order to train an ML component to learn the concept. The perception triangle on the right is similar but shows how the trained ML component can be used during the system operation to make inferences (e.g., perform the pedestrian detection). The framework identifies seven factors that could contribute to uncertainty in the behaviour of the perceptual component. A safety case demonstrating a rigorous development process should provide evidence that each factor has been addressed.

In Fig. 6, strategy **Str2** uses the framework to argue that the seven factors are adequately addressed for PD. We illustrate development of two of these factors here. Scenario coverage (Goal **G-F2**) deals with the fact that the training data must represent the concept in a sufficient variety of scenarios in which it could occur in order for the training to be effective. The argument here first decomposes this goal into different types of variation (**Str3**) and provides appropriate evidence for each. The adequacy of age and ethnicity variation in the data set is supported by census data (**S2**) about the range of these dimensions of variation in the population. The variation in the pedestrian pose (i.e., standing, leaning, crouching, etc.) is supplied by a standard ontology of human postures (**S3**). Finally, evidence that the types are adequate to provide sufficient coverage of variation (completeness) is provided by an expert review (**S4**).

Another contributing factor developed in Fig. 6 is model uncertainty (Goal **G-F6**). Since there is only finite training data, there can be many possible models that are equally consistent with the training data, and the training process could produce any one of them, i.e., there is residual uncertainty whether the produced model is in fact correct. The presence of model uncertainty means that while the trained model may perform well on inputs similar to the training data, there is no guarantee that it will produce the right output for other inputs. Some evidence of good behaviour here can be gathered if there are known properties that partially characterize the concept and can be checked. For example, a reasonable necessary condition for PD is that the object being classified as a pedestrian should be less than 9 ft tall. Another useful property type is an invariant, e.g., a rotated pedestrian image is still a pedestrian. Tools for property checking of neural networks (e.g., [37]) can provide this kind of evidence (**S5**). Another way to deal with model uncertainty is to estimate it directly. Bayesian deep learning approaches [22] can do this by measuring the degree of disagreement between multiple trained models that are equally consistent with the training data. The more the models are in agreement are about how to classify a new input, the less model uncertainty is present and the more confident one can be in the prediction. Using this approach on a test data set can provide evidence (**S6**) about the degree of model uncertainty in the model. This approach can also be used during the operation to generate a confidence score in each prediction and use a fault tolerance strategy that takes a conservative action when the confidence falls below a threshold.

7 Summary and Future Outlook

In this paper, we tried to argue that an assurance case view on establishing system correctness provides a way to unify different components of the software development process and to explicitly manage uncertainty. Furthermore, although our examples came from the world of safety-critical automotive systems, the assurance case view is broadly applicable to a variety of systems, not just those in the safety-critical domain and includes those constructed by non-traditional means such as ML. This view is especially relevant to much of the research activity being conducted by the ETAPS community since it allows, in principle, to understand how each method contributes to the overall problem of system assurance.

Most traditional assurance methods aim to build an informal argument, ultimately judged by a human. However, while these are useful for showing compliance to standards and are relatively easy to construct and read, such arguments may not be rigorous, missing essential properties such as completeness, independence, relevance, or a clear statement of assumptions [51]. As a result, fallacies in existing assurance cases are present in abundance [28]. To address this weakness, we argued that building assurance cases should adhere to systematic principles that ensure rigor. Of course, not all arguments can be fully deductive since relevance and admissibility of evidence is often based on human judgment. Yet, an explicit modeling and management of uncertainty in evidence, specifications and, assumptions as well as the clear justification of each step can go a long way toward making such arguments valid, reusable, and generally useful in helping produce high quality software systems.

Challenges and Opportunities. Achieving this vision has a number of challenges and opportunities. In our work on impact assessment of model change on assurance cases [39,40], we note that even small changes to the system may have significant impact on the assurance case. Because creation of an assurance case is costly, this brittleness must be addressed. One opportunity here is to recognize that assurance cases can be refactored to improve their qualities without affecting their semantics. For example, in Sect. 4, we showed that the LMS safety claim could either be decomposed first by hazards and then by subsystems or vice versa. Thus, we may want to choose the order of decomposition based on other goals, e.g., to minimize the impact of change on the assurance case by pushing the affected subgoals lower in the tree. Another issue is that complex systems yield correspondingly complex assurance cases. Since these must ultimately be judged by humans, we must manage the cognitive load the assurance case puts on the assessor. This creates opportunities for mechanized support, both in terms of querying, navigating and analyzing assurance cases as well as in terms of modularization and reuse of assurance cases.

Evidence composition discussed in Sect. 5 also presents significant challenges. While standards such as DO-178C and ISO26262 give recommendations on the use of testing and verification, it is not clear how to compose partial evidence or how to use results of one analysis to support another. Focusing on how each technique reduces potential faults in the program, clearly documenting their context of applicability (e.g., the small model hypothesis justifying partial unrolling of loops, properties not affected by approximations of complex program operations and datatypes often done by model-checkers, connections between the modeled and the actual environment, etc.) and ultimately connecting them to reducing uncertainties about whether the system satisfies the essential property are keys to making tangible progress in this area.

Finally, in Sect. 6, we showed how the assurance case view could apply to new development approaches such as ML. Although such new approaches provide benefits over traditional software development, they also create challenges for assurance. One challenge is that analysis techniques used for verification may be immature. For example, while neural networks have been studied since the

1950's, pragmatic approaches to their verification have been investigated only recently [53]. Another issue is that prerequisites for assurance may not be met by the development approach. For example, although they are expressive, neural networks suffer from uninterpretability [41] – that is, it is not feasible for a human to examine a trained network and understand what it is doing. This is a serious obstacle to assurance because formal and automated methods account for only part of the verification process, augmented by reviews. As a result, increasing the interpretability of ML models is an active area of current research.

While all these challenges are significant, the benefit of addressing them is worth the effort. As our world moves towards increasing automation, we must develop approaches for assuring the dependability of the complex systems we build. Without this, we either stall progress or run the risk of endangering ourselves – neither alternative seems desirable.

References

1. Bandur, V., McDermid, J.: Informing assurance case review through a formal interpretation of GSN core logic. In: Koornneef, F., van Gulijk, C. (eds.) SAFECOMP 2015. LNCS, vol. 9338, pp. 3–14. Springer, Cham (2015). https://doi.org/10.1007/978-3-319-24249-1_1
2. Bell, T.E., Thayer, T.A.: Software requirements: are they really a problem? In: Proceedings of the 2nd International Conference on Software Engineering, pp. 61–68. IEEE Computer Society Press (1976)
3. Bennion, M., Habli, I.: A candid industrial evaluation of formal software verification using model checking. In: Companion Proceedings of ICSE 2014, pp. 175–184 (2014)
4. Bloomfield, R., Bishop, P.: Safety and assurance cases: past, present and possible future - an Adelard perspective. In: Dale, C., Anderson, T. (eds.) Safety-Critical Systems: Problems, Process and Practice, pp. 51–67. Springer, London (2010). https://doi.org/10.1007/978-1-84996-086-1_4
5. Brunel, J., Cazin, J.: Formal verification of a safety argumentation and application to a complex UAV system. In: Ortmeier, F., Daniel, P. (eds.) SAFECOMP 2012. LNCS, vol. 7613, pp. 307–318. Springer, Heidelberg (2012). https://doi.org/10.1007/978-3-642-33675-1_27
6. Carlan, C., Beyene, T.A., Ruess, H.: Integrated formal methods for constructing assurance cases. In: Proceedings of ISSRE 2016 Workshops (2016)
7. Cârlan, C., Gallina, B., Kacianka, S., Breu, R.: Arguing on software-level verification techniques appropriateness. In: Tonetta, S., Schoitsch, E., Bitsch, F. (eds.) SAFECOMP 2017. LNCS, vol. 10488, pp. 39–54. Springer, Cham (2017). https://doi.org/10.1007/978-3-319-66266-4_3
8. Cârlan, C., Ratiu, D., Schätz, B.: On using results of code-level bounded model checking in assurance cases. In: Skavhaug, A., Guiochet, J., Schoitsch, E., Bitsch, F. (eds.) SAFECOMP 2016. LNCS, vol. 9923, pp. 30–42. Springer, Cham (2016). https://doi.org/10.1007/978-3-319-45480-1_3
9. Castaameda, V., Ballejos, L., Caliusco, M.L., Galli, M.R.: The use of ontologies in requirements engineering. Glob. J. Res. Eng. **10**(6) (2010)
10. Cooray, D., Malek, S., Roshandel, R., Kilgore, D.: RESISTing reliability degradation through proactive reconfiguration. In: Proceedings of ASE 2010, pp. 83–92. ACM (2010)

11. Cyra, L., Gorski, J.: Support for argument structures review and assessment. J. Reliab. Eng. Syst. Saf. **96**, 26–37 (2011)
12. Czarnecki, K., Salay, R.: Towards a framework to manage perceptual uncertainty for safe automated driving. In: Gallina, B., Skavhaug, A., Schoitsch, E., Bitsch, F. (eds.) SAFECOMP 2018. LNCS, vol. 11094, pp. 439–445. Springer, Cham (2018). https://doi.org/10.1007/978-3-319-99229-7_37
13. Davis, A., et al.: Identifying and measuring quality in a software requirements specification. In: 1993 Proceedings First International Software Metrics Symposium, pp. 141–152. IEEE (1993)
14. de la Vara, J.L.: Current and necessary insights into SACM: an analysis based on past publications. In: Proceedings of RELAW 2014, pp. 10–13. IEEE (2014)
15. Denney, E., Pai, G.: Evidence arguments for using formal methods in software vertification. In: Proceedings of ISSRE 2013 Workshops (2013)
16. Denney, E., Pai, G., Habli, I.: Towards measurement of confidence in safety cases. In: Proceedings of ESEM 2011 (2011)
17. Duan, L., Rayadurgam, S., Heimdahl, M.P.E., Sokolsky, O., Lee, I.: Representing confidence in assurance case evidence. In: Koornneef, F., van Gulijk, C. (eds.) SAFECOMP 2015. LNCS, vol. 9338, pp. 15–26. Springer, Cham (2015). https://doi.org/10.1007/978-3-319-24249-1_2
18. Elkhodary, A., Esfahani, N., Malek, S.: FUSION: a framework for engineering self-tuning self-adaptive software systems. In: Proceedings of FSE 2010, pp. 7–16. ACM (2010)
19. Esfahani, N., Malek, S.: Uncertainty in self-adaptive software systems. In: de Lemos, R., Giese, H., Müller, H.A., Shaw, M. (eds.) Software Engineering for Self-Adaptive Systems II. LNCS, vol. 7475, pp. 214–238. Springer, Heidelberg (2013). https://doi.org/10.1007/978-3-642-35813-5_9
20. Famelis, M., Chechik, M.: Managing design-time uncertainty. J. Softw. Syst. Model. (2017)
21. Fanmuy, G., Fraga, A., Llorens, J.: Requirements verification in the industry. In: Hammami, O., Krob, D., Voirin, J.L. (eds.) Complex Systems Design & Management, pp. 145–160. Springer, Heidelberg (2012). https://doi.org/10.1007/978-3-642-25203-7_10
22. Gal, Y., Ghahramani, Z.: Dropout as a Bayesian approximation: representing model uncertainty in deep learning. In: Proceedings of ICML 2016, pp. 1050–1059 (2016)
23. Gallina, B., Andrews, A.: Deriving verification-related means of compliance for a model-based testing process. In: Proceedings of DASC 2016 (2016)
24. Gehr, T., Milman, M., Drachsler-Cohen, D., Tsankov, P., Chaudhuri, S., Vechev, M.: AI2: safety and robustness certification of neural networks with abstract interpretation. In: Proceedings of IEEE S&P 2018 (2018)
25. Goodenough, J., Weinstock, C., Klein, A.: Eliminative induction: a basis for arguing system confidence. In: Proceedings of ICSE 2013 (2013)
26. Gopinath, D., Wang, K., Zhang, M., Pasareanu, C., Khunshid, S.: Symbolic execution for deep neural networks. arXiv:1807.10439v1 (2018)
27. Graydon, P.J., Holloway, C.M.: An investigation of proposed techniques for quantifying confidence in assurance arguments. J. Saf. Sci. **92**, 53–65 (2017)
28. Greenwell, W.S., Knight, J.C., Holloway, C.M., Pease, J.J.: A taxonomy of fallacies in system safety arguments. In: Proceedings of ISSC 2006 (2006)
29. Grigorova, S., Maibaum, T.: Argument evaluation in the context of assurance case confidence modeling. In: Proceedings of ISSRE Workshops (2014)

30. GSN: Goal Structuring Notation Working Group, "GSN Community Standard Version 1", November 2011. http://www.goalstructuringnotation.info/
31. Guiochet, J., Hoang, Q.A.D., Kaaniche, M.: A model for safety case confidence assessment. In: Koornneef, F., van Gulijk, C. (eds.) SAFECOMP 2015. LNCS, vol. 9337, pp. 313–327. Springer, Cham (2015). https://doi.org/10.1007/978-3-319-24255-2_23
32. Habli, I., Kelly, T.: A generic goal-based certification argument for the justification of formal analysis. ENTCS **238**(4), 27–39 (2009)
33. Hawkins, R., Kelly, T.: A structured approach to selecting and justifying software safety evidence. In: Proceedings of SAFECOMP 2010 (2010)
34. Huang, X., Kwiatkowska, M., Wang, S., Wu, M.: Safety verification of deep neural networks. In: Majumdar, R., Kunčak, V. (eds.) CAV 2017. LNCS, vol. 10426, pp. 3–29. Springer, Cham (2017). https://doi.org/10.1007/978-3-319-63387-9_1
35. International Organization for Standardization: ISO 26262: Road Vehicles – Functional Safety, 1st version (2011)
36. International Organization for Standardization: ISO/AWI PAS 21448: Road Vehicles – Safety of the Intended Functionality (2019)
37. Katz, G., Barrett, C., Dill, D.L., Julian, K., Kochenderfer, M.J.: Reluplex: an efficient SMT solver for verifying deep neural networks. In: Majumdar, R., Kunčak, V. (eds.) CAV 2017. LNCS, vol. 10426, pp. 97–117. Springer, Cham (2017). https://doi.org/10.1007/978-3-319-63387-9_5
38. Kelly, T., Weaver, R.: The goal structuring notation – a safety argument notation. In: Proceedings of Dependable Systems and Networks Workshop on Assurance Cases (2004)
39. Kokaly, S., Salay, R., Cassano, V., Maibaum, T., Chechik, M.: A model management approach for assurance case reuse due to system evolution. In: Proceedings of MODELS 2016, pp. 196–206. ACM (2016)
40. Kokaly, S., Salay, R., Chechik, M., Lawford, M., Maibaum, T.: Safety case impact assessment in automotive software systems: an improved model-based approach. In: Tonetta, S., Schoitsch, E., Bitsch, F. (eds.) SAFECOMP 2017. LNCS, vol. 10488, pp. 69–85. Springer, Cham (2017). https://doi.org/10.1007/978-3-319-66266-4_5
41. Lipton, Z.C.: The mythos of model interpretability. Commun. ACM **61**(10), 36–43 (2018)
42. Lutz, R.R.: Analyzing software requirements errors in safety-critical, embedded systems. In: Proceedings of IEEE International Symposium on Requirements Engineering, pp. 126–133. IEEE (1993)
43. Maksimov, M., Fung, N.L.S., Kokaly, S., Chechik, M.: Two decades of assurance case tools: a survey. In: Gallina, B., Skavhaug, A., Schoitsch, E., Bitsch, F. (eds.) SAFECOMP 2018. LNCS, vol. 11094, pp. 49–59. Springer, Cham (2018). https://doi.org/10.1007/978-3-319-99229-7_6
44. Nair, S., de la Vara, J.L., Sabetzadeh, M., Falessic, D.: Evidence management for compliance of critical systems with safety standards: a survey on the state of practice. Inf. Softw. Technol. **60**, 1–15 (2015)
45. Nair, S., Walkinshaw, N., Kelly, T., de la Vara, J.L.: An evidential reasoning approach for assessing confidence in safety evidence. In: Proceedings of ISSRE 2015 (2015)
46. Nikora, A., Hayes, J., Holbrook, E.: Experiments in automated identification of ambiguous natural-language requirements. In: Proceedings 21st IEEE International Symposium on Software Reliability Engineering. IEEE Computer Society, San Jose (2010, to appear)

47. Pei, K., Cao, Y., Yang, J., Jana, S.: DeepXplore: automated whitebox testing of deep learning systems. In: Proceedings of SOSP 2017 (2017)
48. Ramirez, A.J., Jensen, A.C., Cheng, B.H.: A taxonomy of uncertainty for dynamically adaptive systems. In: Proceedings of SEAMS 2012 (2012)
49. Ras, G., van Gerven, M., Haselager, P.: Explanation methods in deep learning: users, values, concerns and challenges. In: Escalante, H.J., et al. (eds.) Explainable and Interpretable Models in Computer Vision and Machine Learning. TSSCML, pp. 19–36. Springer, Cham (2018). https://doi.org/10.1007/978-3-319-98131-4_2
50. Ren, S., He, K., Girshick, R., Sun, J.: Faster R-CNN: towards real-time object detection with region proposal networks. In: Advances in Neural Information Processing Systems, pp. 91–99 (2015)
51. Rushby, J., Xu, X., Rangarajan, M., Weaver, T.L.: Understanding and evaluating assurance cases. Technical report CR-2015-218802, NASA (2015)
52. Sadigh, D., Kapoor, A.: Safe control under uncertainty with probabilistic signal temporal logic. In: Proceedings of RSS 2016 (2016)
53. Seshia, S.A., Sadigh, D.: Towards verified artificial intelligence. CoRR, abs/1606.08514 (2016)
54. Tian, Y., Pei, K., Jana, S., Ray, B.: DeepTest: automated testing of deep-neural-network-driven autonomous cars. In: Proceedings of ICSE 2018 (2018)
55. Van Lamsweerde, A.: Goal-oriented requirements engineering: a guided tour. In: Proceedings of RE 2001, pp. 249–262. IEEE (2001)
56. Verheij, B.: Evaluating arguments based on Toulmin's scheme. Argumentation **19**(3), 347–371 (2005)
57. Ward, S., Chapman, C.: Transforming project risk management into project uncertainty management. Int. J. Proj. Manag. **21**(2), 97–105 (2003)
58. Wassyng, A.: Private Communication (2019)
59. Yamamoto, S.: Assuring security through attribute GSN. In: Proceedings of ICITCS 2015 (2015)
60. Zeng, F., Lu, M., Zhong, D.: Using DS evidence theory to evaluation of confidence in safety case. J. Theoret. Appl. Inf. Technol. **47**(1) (2013)
61. Zhao, X., Zhang, D., Lu, M., Zeng, F.: A new approach to assessment of confidence in assurance cases. In: Ortmeier, F., Daniel, P. (eds.) SAFECOMP 2012. LNCS, vol. 7613, pp. 79–91. Springer, Heidelberg (2012). https://doi.org/10.1007/978-3-642-33675-1_7

Software Verification I

Tool Support for Correctness-by-Construction

Tobias Runge[1(✉)], Ina Schaefer[1], Loek Cleophas[2,3], Thomas Thüm[1], Derrick Kourie[3,4], and Bruce W. Watson[3,4]

[1] Software Engineering, TU Braunschweig, Braunschweig, Germany
{tobias.runge,i.schaefer,t.thuem}@tu-bs.de
[2] Software Engineering Technology, TU Eindhoven, Eindhoven, The Netherlands
[3] Information Science, Stellenbosch University, Stellenbosch, South Africa
{loek,derrick,bruce}@fastar.org
[4] Centre for Artificial Intelligence Research, CSIR, Pretoria, South Africa

Abstract. Correctness-by-Construction (CbC) is an approach to incrementally create formally correct programs guided by pre- and postcondition specifications. A program is created using refinement rules that guarantee the resulting implementation is correct with respect to the specification. Although CbC is supposed to lead to code with a low defect rate, it is not prevalent, especially because appropriate tool support is missing. To promote CbC, we provide tool support for CbC-based program development. We present CorC, a graphical and textual IDE to create programs in a simple while-language following the CbC approach. Starting with a specification, our open source tool supports CbC developers in refining a program by a sequence of refinement steps and in verifying the correctness of these refinement steps using the theorem prover KeY. We evaluated the tool with a set of standard examples on CbC where we reveal errors in the provided specification. The evaluation shows that our tool reduces the verification time in comparison to post-hoc verification.

1 Introduction

Correctness-by-Construction (CbC) [12,13,19,23] is a methodology to construct formally correct programs guided by a specification. CbC can improve program development because every part of the program is designed to meet the corresponding specification. With the CbC approach, source code is incrementally constructed with a low defect rate [19] mainly based on three reasons. First, introducing defects is hard because of the structured reasoning discipline that is enforced by the refinement rules. Second, if defects occur, they can be tracked through the refinement structure of specifications. Third, the trust in the program is increased because the program is developed following a formal process [14].

Despite these benefits, CbC is still not prevalent and not applied for large-scale program development. We argue that one reason for this is missing tool

R. Hähnle and W. van der Aalst (Eds.): FASE 2019, LNCS 11424, pp. 25–42, 2019.
https://doi.org/10.1007/978-3-030-16722-6_2

support for a CbC-style development process. Another issue is that the programmer mindset is often tailored to the prevalent post-hoc verification approach. CbC has been shown to be beneficial even in domains where post-hoc verification is required [29]. In post-hoc verification, a method is verified against pre- and postconditions. In the CbC approach, we refine the method stepwise, and we can check the method partially after each step since every statement is surrounded by a pair of pre- and postconditions. The verification of refinement steps and Hoare triples reduces the proof complexity since the proof task is split into smaller problems. The specifications and code developed using the CbC approach can be used to bootstrap the post-hoc verification process and allow for an easier post-hoc verification as the method constructed using CbC generally is of a structure that is more amenable to verification [29].

In this paper, we present CorC,[1] a tool designed to develop programs following the CbC approach. We deliberately built our tool on the well-known post-hoc verifier KeY [4] to profit from the KeY ecosystem and future extensions of the verifier. We also add CbC as another application area to KeY, which opens the possibility for KeY users to adopt the CbC approach. This could spread the constructive CbC approach to areas where post-hoc verification is prevalent.

Our tool CorC offers a hybrid textual-graphical editor to develop programs using CbC. The textual editor resembles a normal programming editor, but is enriched with support for pre- and postcondition specifications. The graphical editor visualizes the code, its specification, and the program refinements in a tree-like structure. The developers can switch back and forth between both views. In order to support the correct application of the refinement rules, the tool is integrated with KeY [4] such that proof obligations can be immediately discharged during program development. In a preliminary evaluation, we found benefits of CorC compared to paper-and-pencil-based application of CbC and compared to post-hoc verification.

2 Foundations of Correctness-by-Construction

Classically, CbC [19] starts with the specification of a program as a Hoare triple comprising a precondition, an abstract statement, and a postcondition. Such a triple, say T, should be read as a total correctness assertion: if T is in a state where the precondition holds and its abstract statement is executed, then the execution will terminate and the postcondition will hold. T will be true for a certain set of concrete program instantiations of the abstract program and false for other instantiations. A refinement of T is a triple, say T', which is true for a subset of concrete programs that render T to be true.

In our work, pre-/post-condition specifications for programs are written in *first-order logic* (FOL). A formula in FOL consists of atomic formulas which are logically connected. An atomic formula is a predicate which evaluates to true or

[1] https://github.com/TUBS-ISF/CorC, CorC is an acronym for Correctness-by-Construction.

{P} S {Q}	*can be refined to*
1. Skip :	{P} *skip* {Q} *iff* P *implies* Q
2. Assignment :	{P} $x := E$ {Q} *iff* P *implies* Q[x := E]
3. Composition :	{P} S1 ; S2 {Q} *iff there is an intermediate condition* M *such that* {P} S1 {M} *and* {M} S2 {Q}
4. Selection :	{P} **if** $G_1 \rightarrow S_1$ **elseif** ... $G_n \rightarrow S_n$ **fi** {Q} *iff* (P *implies* $G_1 \vee G_2 \vee \ldots \vee G_n$) *and* $\{P \wedge G_i\}$ S_i {Q} *holds for all i.*
5. Repetition :	{P} **do** [I, V] G → S **od** {Q} *iff* (P *implies* I) *and* ($I \wedge \neg G$ *implies* Q) *and* $\{I \wedge G\}$ S {I} *and* $\{I \wedge G \wedge V{=}V_0\}$ S $\{I \wedge 0{\leq}V \wedge V{<}V_0\}$
6. Weaken pre :	{P′} *S* {Q} *iff* P *implies* P′
7. Strengthen post :	{P} *S* {Q′} *iff* Q′ *implies* Q
8. Subroutine :	{P} *Sub* {Q} *with subroutine* {P′} *Sub* {Q′} *iff* P *is equal to* P′ *and* Q′ *is equal to* Q

Fig. 1. Refinement rules in CbC [19]

false. Programs in this work are written in the CorC language, which is inspired by the *Guarded Command Language* (GCL) [11] and presented below.

For the concrete instantiation of conditions and assignments, our tool uses a host language. We decided for Java, but other languages are also possible.

To create programs using CbC, we use refinement rules. A Hoare triple is refined by applying rules, which introduce CorC language statements, so that a concrete program is created. The concrete program obtained by refinement is guaranteed to be correct by construction, provided that the correctness-preserving refinement steps have been accurately applied. In Fig. 1, we present the statements and refinement rules used in CbC and our tool.

Skip. A skip or empty statement is a statement that does not alter the state of the program (i.e., it does nothing) [11,19]. This means a Hoare triple with a skip statement evaluates to true if the precondition implies the postcondition.

Assignment. An assignment statement assigns an expression of type T to a variable, also of type T. In the tool, we use a Java-like assignment (x = y). To refine a Hoare triple {P} S {Q} with an assignment statement, the assignment rule is used. This rule replaces the abstract statement S by an assignment {P} x = E {Q} iff P implies Q[x := E].

Composition. A composition statement is a statement which splits one abstract statement into two. A Hoare triple {P} S {Q} is split to {P} S_1 {M} and {M} S_2 {Q} in which S is refined to S1 and S2. M is an intermediate condition which evaluates to true after S1 and before S2 is executed [11].

Selection. Selection in our CorC language works as a switch statement. It refines a Hoare triple {P} S {Q} to {P} **if** $G_1 \rightarrow S_1$ **elseif** ... $G_n \rightarrow S_n$ **fi** {Q}. The guards G_i are evaluated, and the sub-statement S_i of the *first* satisfied guard is executed.

We use a switch-like statement so that every sub-statement has an associated guard for further reasoning. The selection refinement rule can only be used if the precondition P implies the disjunction of all guards so that at least one sub-statement could be executed.

Repetition. The repetition statement $\{\mathtt{P}\}$ **do** $[\mathtt{I}, \mathtt{V}]$ $\mathtt{G} \rightarrow$ S **od** $\{\mathtt{Q}\}$ works like a while loop in other languages. If the loop guard G evaluates to true, the associated loop statement S is executed. The repetition statement is specified with an invariant I and a variant V. To refine a Hoare triple $\{\mathtt{P}\}$ S $\{\mathtt{Q}\}$ with a repetition statement, (1) the precondition P has to imply the invariant I of the repetition statement, (2) the conjunction of invariant and the negation of the loop guard G have to imply the postcondition Q, and (3) the loop body has to preserve the invariant by showing that $\{\mathtt{I} \land \mathtt{G}\}$ S $\{\mathtt{I}\}$ holds. To verify termination, we have to show that the variant V monotonically decreases in each loop iteration and has 0 as a lower bound.

Weaken precondition. The precondition of a Hoare triple can be weakened if necessary. The weaken precondition rule replaces the precondition P with a new one $\mathtt{P}'$ only if P implies $\mathtt{P}'$ [12].

Strengthen postcondition. To strengthen a postcondition, the strengthen postcondition rule can be used. A postcondition Q is replaced by a new one $\mathtt{Q}'$ only if $\mathtt{Q}'$ implies Q [12].

Subroutine. A subroutine can be used to split a program into smaller parts. We use a simple subroutine call where we prohibit side effects and parameters. A triple $\{\mathtt{P}\}$ S $\{\mathtt{Q}\}$ can be refined to a subroutine $\{\mathtt{P}'\}$ *Sub* $\{\mathtt{Q}'\}$, if the precondition $\mathtt{P}'$ of the subroutine is equal to the precondition P of the refined statement and the postcondition $\mathtt{Q}'$ of the subroutine is equal to the postcondition Q of the refined statement. The subroutine can be constructed as a separate CbC program to verify that it satisfies the specification. The Hoare triple $\{\mathtt{P}'\}$ *Sub* $\{\mathtt{Q}'\}$ is the starting point to construct a program using CbC.

3 Correctness-by-Construction by Example

To introduce the programming style of CbC, we demonstrate the construction of a linear search algorithm using CbC [19]. The linear search problem is defined as follows: We have an integer array a of some length, and an integer variable x. We try to find an element in the array a which has the same value as the variable x, and we return the index i where the (last) element x was found, or −1 if the element is not in the array.

To construct the algorithm, we start with concretizing the pre- and postcondition of the algorithm. Before the algorithm is executed, we know that we have an integer array. Therefore, we specify $\mathtt{a}{\neq}\mathtt{null} \land \mathtt{a.length}{\geq}0$ as precondition P. The postcondition forces that if the index i is greater than or equal to zero, the element is found on the returned index i ($\mathtt{Q} := (\mathtt{i}{\geq}0 \implies \mathtt{a[i]}{=}\mathtt{x})$).

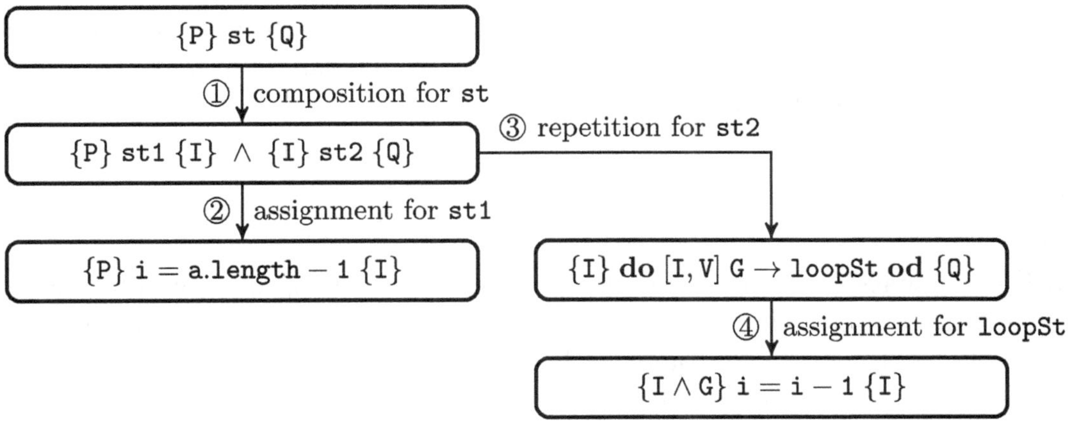

Fig. 2. Refinement steps for the linear search algorithm

Our algorithm traverses the array in reverse order and checks for each index whether the value is equal to x. In this case, the index is returned. To create this algorithm, we construct an invariant I for the loop:

$$\mathtt{I} := \neg\mathtt{appears}(\mathtt{a}, \mathtt{x}, \mathtt{i}+1, \mathtt{a.length}) \wedge \mathtt{i} \geq -1 \wedge \mathtt{i} < \mathtt{a.length}$$

The invariant is used to split the array into two parts. A part from $\mathtt{i}+1$ to a.length where x is not contained, and a part from zero to i which is not checked yet. In every iteration, the next index of the array is checked. The predicate $\mathtt{appears}(\mathtt{a}, \mathtt{x}, \mathtt{l}, \mathtt{h})$ asserts that x occurs in array a inside the range from l (included) to h (excluded). The predicate can be translated to FOL as $\exists \mathtt{i} : (\mathtt{i} \geq \mathtt{l} \wedge \mathtt{i} < \mathtt{h} \wedge \mathtt{a}[\mathtt{i}] = \mathtt{x})$.

We can use the CbC refinement rules to implement linear search. The refinement steps for the example are shown in Fig. 2 and numbered from ① to ④. To create a loop in the program, we need to initialize a loop counter variable to establish the invariant. Therefore, we split the program by introducing a composition statement (① in Fig. 2). The invariant I is used as intermediate condition (i.e., $\mathtt{M} := \mathtt{I}$), because it has to be true after the initialization, and before the first loop step. The statement st1 is refined to an assignment statement ②. We initialize i with $\mathtt{a.length} - 1$ to start at the end of the array. This assignment satisfies the intermediate condition I where i is replaced by $\mathtt{a.length} - 1$. The range of appears is empty, and therefore the predicate evaluates to true. To refine the second statement (st2), we use the repetition refinement rule ③. As long as x is not found, we iterate through the array. As guard of the repetition, we use $(\mathtt{i} \geq 0 \wedge \mathtt{a}[\mathtt{i}] \neq \mathtt{x})$. The invariant of the repetition is the invariant I introduced above. The variant V is $\mathtt{i} + 1$. To verify that this refinement is valid, we have to verify that the precondition of the repetition statement implies the invariant, and that the invariant and the negated guard imply the postcondition of the repetition (cf. Rule 5). Both are valid because the precondition is equal to the invariant and the postcondition of the repetition statement (in this case it is Q) is equal to the negated guard. The last step is to refine the abstract loop statement (loopSt) ④. We use an assignment to decrease i and get the final program. We can verify that the invariant holds after each loop iteration. The program terminates because the variant decreases in every step and it is always greater than or equal to zero.

4 Tool Support in CorC

CorC extends KeY's application area by enabling CbC to spread the constructive engineering to areas where post-hoc verification is prevalent. KeY programmers can use both approaches to construct formally correct programs. By using CorC, they develop specification and code that can bootstrap the post-hoc verification. The CorC tool[2] is realized as an Eclipse plug-in in Java. We use the Eclipse Modeling Framework (EMF)[3] to specify a CbC meta model. This meta model is used by two editor views, a textual and a graphical editor. The Hoare triple verification is implemented by the deductive program verification tool KeY [4]. In the following list, we summarize the features of CorC.

- Programs are written as Hoare triple specifications, including pre-/postcondition specifications and abstract statements or assignment/skip statements in concrete triples.
- CorC has eight rules to construct programs: skip, assignment, composition, selection, repetition, weakening precondition, strengthening postcondition, and subroutine (cf. Sect. 2).
- Pre-/postconditions and invariant specification are automatically propagated through the program.
- CorC comprises a graphical and a textual editor that can be used interchangeably.
- Up to now, CorC supports integers, chars, strings, arrays, and subroutine calls without side effects, I/O, and library calls.
- Hoare triples are typically verified by KeY automatically. If the proof cannot be closed automatically, the user can interact with KeY.
- Helper methods written in Java 1.5 can be used in a specification.
- CorC comprises content assist and an automatic generation of intermediate conditions.

4.1 Graphical Editor

The graphical editor represents CbC-based program refinement by a tree structure. A node represents the Hoare triple of a specific CorC language statement. Figure 3 presents the linear search algorithm of Sect. 3 in the graphical editor. The structure of the tree is the same as in Fig. 2. The additional nodes on the right specify used program variables including their type and global invariant

[2] https://github.com/TUBS-ISF/CorC.
[3] https://eclipse.org/emf/.

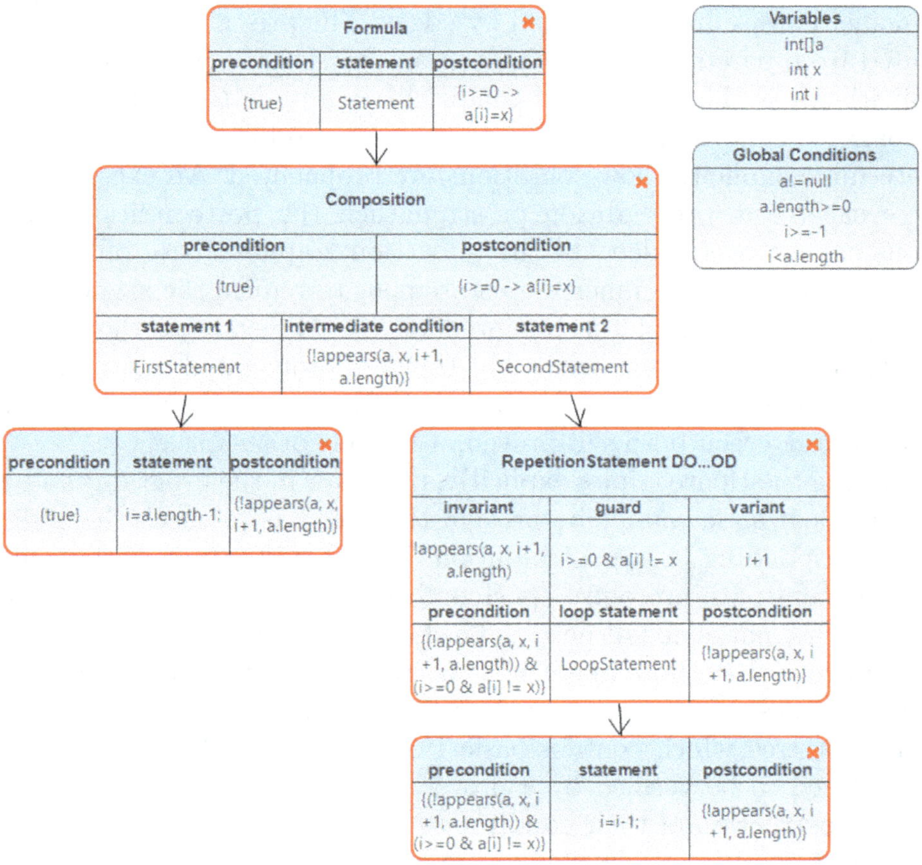

Fig. 3. Linear search example in the graphical editor

conditions. The global invariant conditions are added to every pre- and postcondition of Hoare triples to simplify the construction of the program. In the example, we specify the array `a` and the range of variable `i` to support the verification, as KeY requires this range to be explicit for verification.

The root node of the tree shows the abstract Hoare triple for the overall program with a symbolic name for the abstract statement. In every node, the pre- and postcondition are specified on the left and right of the node under the corresponding header. A composition statement node, the second statement of the tree, contains the pre- and postcondition and additionally defines an intermediate condition. The intermediate condition is the middle term in the bottom line. Both abstract sub-statements of the composition have a symbolic name and can be further refined by adding a connection to another node (i.e., creating a parent-child relation). The repetition node contains fields to specify the invariant, the guard and the variant of the repetition. These fields are in the middle row. The pre- and postcondition are associated to the inner loop statement. An assignment node (cf. both leaf nodes of the figure) contains the precondition, the assignment, and the postcondition. The representations of the nodes for the refinements not illustrated in this example are similar.

Refinement steps are represented by edges. The pre- and postconditions are propagated from parents to their children on drawing the parent/child relation. We explicitly show the propagated conditions in a node to improve readability. The propagated conditions from the parent are unmodifiable because refinement rules determine explicitly how conditions are propagated. An exception are the rules to weaken the precondition or strengthen the postcondition. Here, the conditions can be overridden. At the repetition statement, we only depict the pre-/postconditions of the inner loop statement to reduce the size of this node. The pre-/postconditions of the parent node (in our example the composition statement) are not shown explicitly, but they are propagated internally to verify that the repetition refinement rule is satisfied. To visualize the verification status, the nodes have a green border if proven, a red one otherwise.

By showing the Hoare triples explicitly, problems in the program can be localized. If some leaf node cannot be proven, the user has to check the assignment and the corresponding pre-/postcondition. If an error occurred, the conditions on the refinement path up to pre-/postcondition of the starting Hoare triple can be altered. Other paths do not need to be checked. To prove the program correct, we have to prove that the refinement is correct. Aside from the side conditions of refinement rules (cf. iff conditions in refinement rules), only the leaf nodes of the refinement tree which contain basic Hoare triples with skip or assignment statements need to be verified by a prover, while all composite statements are correct by construction of their conditions.

To support the user in developing intermediate conditions for composition statements, our tool can compute the weakest precondition from a postcondition and a concrete assignment by using the KeY theorem prover. So, the user can create a specific assignment statement and generate the intermediate conditions afterwards. We also support modularization, to cover cases where algorithms become too large. Sub-algorithms can be created using CbC in other CorC programs. We introduce a simple subroutine rule which can be used as a leaf node in the editor. The subroutine has a name and it is connected to a second diagram with the same name as the subroutine. This subroutine call is similar to a classic method call. It can be used to decompose larger CbC developments to multiple smaller programs.

4.2 Textual Editor

The textual editor is an editor for the CorC programming language described above. The user writes code by using keywords for the specific statements and enriches the code with conditions, such as invariants or intermediate conditions, and assignments in our CorC syntax. The syntax of the composed statements in the textual editor is shown in Fig. 4. In the `GlobalConditions` declaration, we enumerate the needed global conditions separated with a comma. The used variables are enumerated after the `JavaVariables` keyword.

The linear search example program presented in Sect. 3 is shown in the syntax of CorC in Listing 1. The program starts with keyword `Formula`. The pre- and postcondition of the abstract Hoare triple are written after the `pre:` and `post:`

Selection statement

if ("guard") **then** {`statement`}
elseif ("guard") **then** {`statement`}
...
fi

Repetition statement

while ("guard")
inv: ["invariant"] **var**: ["variant"]
do {`statement`} **od**

Fig. 4. Syntax of statements in textual editor

```
1  Formula "linearSearch"
2  pre: {"true"}
3  {
4    {
5      i=a.length-1;
6    }
7    intm: ["!appears(a, x, i+1, a.length)"]
8    {
9      while ("i>=0 & a[i]!=x")
10     inv: ["!appears(a, x, i+1, a.length)"]
11     var: ["i+1"] do
12     {
13       i=i-1;
14     } od
15   }
16 }
17 post: {"i>=0 -> a[i]=x"}
18
19 GlobalConditions
20   conditions {"a!=null", "a.length>=0",
21     "i>=-1", "i<a.length"}
22
23 JavaVariables
24   variables {"int[] a", "int x", "int i"}
```

Listing 1. Linear search example in the textual editor

keywords. The abstract statement of the Hoare triple is refined to a composition statement in lines 3–16. The statements are surrounded by curly brackets to establish the refinement structure. We have the first statement in lines 4–6, the intermediate condition in line 7 and the second statement in lines 8–15. The first statement is refined to an assignment (Line 5). The refinement is done by introducing an assignment in Java syntax (`i` = `a.length` − 1;). The second statement is refined to a repetition statement (cf. the syntax of a repetition statement in Fig. 4). We specify the guard, the invariant, and the variant. Finally, the single statement of the loop body is refined to an assignment in Line 13.

As in the graphical editor, pre-/postconditions are propagated top-down from a parent to a child statement. For example, the intermediate condition of a

```
\javaSource "src";
\include "helper.key";
\programVariables {int x;}
\problem {
  (x = 0) -> \<{x=x+1;}\> (x = 1)
}
```

Listing 2. KeY problem file

composition statement which is the postcondition of the first sub-statement and the precondition of the second, appears only once in the editor (e.g., Line 7). To support the user, we implemented syntax highlighting and a content assist. When starting to write a statement, a user may employ auto-completion where the statements are inserted following the syntax in Fig. 4. The user can specify the conditions, then the next statement can be refined. The editor also automatically checks the syntax and highlights syntax errors. Information markers are used to indicate statements which are not proven yet. For example, the Hoare triple of the assignment statement ($\mathtt{i} = \mathtt{a.length} - 1$) in Listing 1 has to be verified, and CorC marks the statement according to the proof completion results.

4.3 Verification of CorC Programs

To prove the refined program is correct, we have to prove side conditions of refinements correct (e.g., prove that an assignment satiesfies the pre-/postcondition specification). This reduces the proof complexity because the challenge to prove a complete program is decomposed into smaller verification tasks. The intermediate Hoare triples are verified indirectly through the soundness of the refinement rules and the propagation of the specifications from parent nodes to child nodes [19]. Side conditions occur in all refinements (cf. iff conditions in refinement rules). These side conditions, such as the termination of repetition statements or that at least one guard in a selection has to evaluate to true, are proven in separate KeY files.

For the proof of concrete Hoare triples, we use the deductive program verifier KeY [4]. Hoare triples are transformed to KeY's dynamic logic syntax. The syntax of KeY problem files is shown in Listing 2. Using the keyword `javaSource`, we specify the path to Java helper methods which are called in the specifications. These methods have to be verified independently with KeY. A KeY helper file, where the users can define their own FOL predicates for the specification, is included with the keyword `include`. For example, in CorC a predicate $appears(a, x, l, h)$ (cf. the linear search example) can be used which is specified in the helper file as a FOL formula. The variables used in the program are listed after the keyword `programVariables`. After `problem`, we define the Hoare triple to be proven, which is translated to dynamic logic as used by KeY. KeY problem files are verified by KeY. As we are only verifying simple Hoare triples with skip or assignment statements, KeY is usually able to close the proofs automatically if the Hoare triple is valid.

To verify total correctness of the program, we have to prove that all repetition statements terminate. The termination of repetition statements is shown by proving that the variants in the program monotonically decrease and are bounded. Without loss of generality, we assume this bound to equal 0, as this is what KeY requires. This is done by specifying the problem in the KeY file in the following way: `(invariant & guard) -> {var0:=var} \<{std}\> (invariant & var<var0 & var>=0)`. The code of the loop body is specified at `std` to verify that after one iteration of the loop body the variant `var` is smaller than before but greater than or equal to zero.

To verify Hoare triples in the graphical editor, we implemented a menu entry. The user can right-click on a statement and start the automatic proof. If the proof is not closed, the user can interact with the opened KeY interface. To prove Hoare triples in the textual editor, we automatically generate all needed problem files for KeY whenever the user saves the editor file. The proof of the files is started using a menu button. The user gets feedback which triples are not proven by means of markers in the editor.

4.4 Implementation as Eclipse Plugin

We extended the Eclipse modeling framework with plugins to implement the two editors. We have created a meta model of the CbC language to represent the required constructs (i.e., statements with specification). The statements can be nested to create the CbC refinement hierarchy. The graphical and the textual editor are projections on the same meta model. The graphical editor is implemented using the framework Graphiti.[4] It provides functionality to create nodes and to associate them to domain elements, such as statements and specifications. The nodes can be added from a palette at the side of the editor, so no incorrect statement with its associated specification can be created. We implemented editing functionality to change the text in the node; the background model is changed simultaneously. Graphiti also provides the possibility to update nodes (e.g., to propagate pre- and postconditions), if we connect those nodes by refinement edges. The refinement is checked for compliance with the CbC rules.

The textual editor is implemented using XText.[5] We created a grammar covering every statement and the associated specification. If the user writes a program, the text is parsed and translated to an instance of the meta model. If a program is created in one editor, a model (an instance of our meta model) of the program is created in the background. We can easily transform one view into the other. The transformation is a generation step and not a live synchronization between both views, but it is carried out invisibly for the user when changing the views.

[4] https://eclipse.org/graphiti/.
[5] https://eclipse.org/Xtext/.

Table 1. Evaluation of the example programs

Algorithm	#Nodes in GE	#Lines in TE	#Lines with JML	#Verified CorC triples	CbC Total Proof-Nodes	CbC Total Proof-Time	PhV Total Proof-Nodes	PhV Total Proof-Time
Linear Search	5	12	10	5/5	285	0.4 s	589	1.2 s
Max. Element	9	21	15	9/9	1023	1.2 s	993	1.8 s
Pattern Matching	14	23	20	13/13	21131	54.9 s	201619	1479.3 s
Exponentiation	7	21	17	7/7	6588	15.2 s	7303	20.4 s
Log. Approx.	5	16	12	5/5	13756	42.7 s	18835	68.5 s
Dutch Flag	8	26	24	8/8	4107	5.7 s	4993	13.4 s
Factorial	5	15	13	4/4	1554	3.6 s	1598	4.4 s

(GE) Grahical Editor, (TE) Textual Editor, (PhV) Post-hoc Verification

In implementing CorC, we considered the exchangeability of the host language. The specifications and assignments are saved as strings in the meta model. They are checked by a parser to comply with Java. This parser could be exchanged to support a different language. The verification is done by generating KeY files which are then evaluated by KeY. Here, we have to exchange the generation of the files if another theorem prover should be integrated. The information of the meta model may have to be adopted to fit the needs of the other prover. We also have to implement a programmatic call to the other prover.

5 Evaluation

The tool support offers new chances to evaluate CbC versus post-hoc verification. We quantitatively compare the development and verification of programs with CorC and with post-hoc verification. This is to check the hypothesis that the verification of algorithms is faster with CorC than with post-hoc verification. We created the first eight algorithms from the book by Kourie and Watson [19] in our graphical editor. For comparison purposes, we also wrote each example as a plain Java program with JML specifications in order to directly verify it with KeY. The specifications are the same as in CorC. We measured the verification time and the proof nodes that KeY needed to close the proofs for both approaches. The results of the evaluation are presented in Table 1 (verification time rounded).

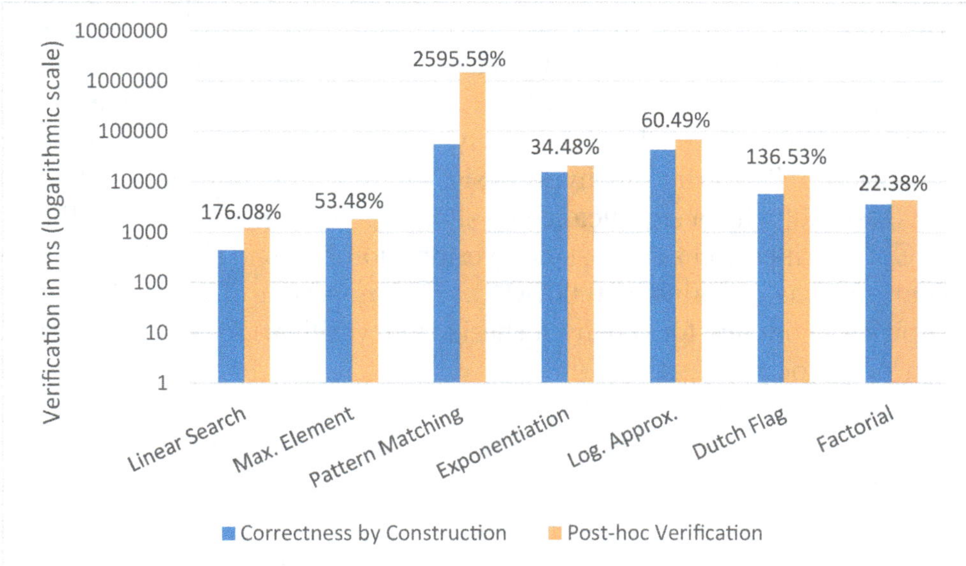

Fig. 5. Proof time of CbC and post-hoc verification in logarithmic scale

The algorithms have 5 to 14 nodes in the graphical editor and 12 to 26 lines of code in the textual editor. The Java version with a JML specification always has fewer lines (between 8% and 29% smaller). The additional specifications, such as the intermediate conditions of composition statements, and the global invariant conditions and variables cause more lines of code in the CbC program.

The verification of the eight algorithms worked nearly without problems. We verified 7 out of 8 examples within CorC. In the cases without problems, every Hoare triple and the termination of the loops could be proven. We had to prove fewer Hoare triples than nodes in the editor, as not every node has to be proven separately. Composition nodes are proven indirectly through the refinement structure. For *exponentiation*, *logarithm*, and *factorial*, we had to implement recursive helper methods which are used in the specification. Therefore, the programs impose upper bounds for integers to shorten the proof. The *binary search* algorithm could not be verified automatically in KeY using post-hoc verification or CorC. In each step, when the element is not found, the algorithm halves the array. KeY could not prove that the searched element is in the new boundaries because verification problems with arithmetic division are hard to prove for KeY automatically.

In the case of measured proof nodes, *maximum element* needs slightly fewer nodes proved with post-hoc verification than with CbC. In the other cases, the proofs for the algorithms constructed with CbC are 3% to 854% smaller. The largest difference was measured for the *pattern matching* algorithm. The proof is reduced to a ninth of the nodes.

The verification time is visualized in Fig. 5. The time is measured in milliseconds and scaled logarithmically. The proofs for the CbC approach are always faster showing lower proof complexity. For *maximum element*, *exponentiation*, *logarithm* and *factorial*, the post-hoc verification time requires between 22% and 60% more time. The difference increases for *Dutch flag* and *linear search* to 137% and 176%, respectively. Algorithm *pattern matching* has the biggest difference. Here, the CbC approach needs nearly a minute, but the post-hoc approach needs over 24 min. To verify our hypothesis, we apply the non-parametric paired Wilcoxon-Test [30] with a significance level of 5%. We can reject the null hypothesis that CbC verification and post-hoc verification have no significant difference in verification time (p-value = 0.007813). This rejection of the null hypothesis in an empirical evidence for our hypothesis that verification is faster with CorC than with post-hoc verification.

With our tool support, we were able to compare the CbC approach with post-hoc verification. For our examples, we evaluated that the verification effort is reduced significantly which indicates a reduced proof complexity. It is worthwhile to further investigate the CbC approach, also to profit from synergistic effects in combination with post-hoc verification. As we built CorC on top of KeY, the post-hoc verification of programs constructed with CorC is feasible.

An advantage of CorC is the overview on all Hoare triples during development. In this way, we found some specifications where descriptions in the book by Kourie and Watson [19] were not precise enough to verify the problem in KeY. For example, in the *pattern matching* algorithm, we had to verify two nested loops. At one point, we had to verify that the invariant of the inner loop implies the invariant of the outer loop. This was not possible, so we extended the invariant of the inner loop to be the conjunction of both invariants. In the book of Kourie and Watson [19], this conjunction of both invariants was not explicitly used.

6 Related Work

We compare CorC to other programming languages and tools using specification or refinements. The programming language Eiffel is an object-oriented programming language with a focus on design-by-contract [21,22]. Classes and methods are annotated with pre-/postconditions and invariants. Programs written in Eiffel can be verified using AutoProof [18,28]. The verification tool translates the program with assertions to a logic formula. An SMT-solver proves the correctness and returns the result. Spec# is a similar tool for specifying C# programs with pre-/postcondition contracts. These programs can be verified using Boogie. The code and specification is translated to an intermediate language (BoogiePL) and verified [5,6]. VCC [8] is a tool to annotate and verify C code. For this purpose, it reuses the Spec# tool chain. VeriFast [16] is another tool to verify C and Java programs with the help of contracts. The contracts are written in separation logic (a variant of Hoare logic). As in Eiffel, the focus of Spec#, VCC, and VeriFast is on post-hoc verification and debugging failed proof attempts.

The Event-B framework [2] is a related CbC approach. Automata-based systems including a specification are refined to a concrete implementation.

Atelier B [1] implements the B method by providing an automatic and interactive prover. Rodin [3] is another tool implementing the Event-B method. The main difference to CorC is that CorC works on code and specifications rather than on automata-based systems.

ArcAngel [25] is a tool supporting Morgan's refinement calculus. Rules are applied to an initial specification to produce a correct implementation. The tool implements a tactic language for refinements to apply a sequence of rules. In comparison to our tool, ArcAngel does not offer a graphical editor to visualize the refinement steps. Another difference is that ArcAngel creates a list of proof obligations which have to be proven separately. CRefine [26] is a related tool for the Circus refinement calculus, a calculus for state-rich reactive systems. Like our tool, CRefine provides a GUI for the refinement process. The difference is that we specify and implement source code, but they use a state-based language. ArcAngelC [10] is an extension to CRefine which adds refinement tactics.

The tools iContract [20] and OpenJML [9] apply design-by-contract. They use a special comment tag to insert conditions into Java code. These conditions are translated to assertions and checked at runtime which is a difference to our tool because no formal verification is done. DBC-Python is a similar approach for the Python language which also checks assertions at runtime [27].

To verify the CbC program, we need a theorem prover for Hoare triples, such as KeY [4]. There are other theorem provers which could be used (e.g., Coq [7] or Isabelle/HOL [24]). The Tecton Proof System [17] is a related tool to structure and interactively prove Hoare logic specification. The proofs are represented graphically as a set of linked trees. These interactive provers do not fit our needs because we want to automate the verification process. KeY provides a symbolic execution debugger (SED) that represents all execution paths with specifications of the code to the verification [15]. This visualization is similar to our tree representation of the graphical editor. The SED can be used to debug a program if an error occur during the post-hoc verification process.

7 Conclusion and Future Work

We implemented CorC to support the Correctness-by-Construction process of program development. We created a textual and a graphical editor that can be used interchangeably to enable different styles of CbC-based program development. The program and its specification are written in one of the editors and can be verified using KeY. This reduces the proof complexity with respect to post-hoc verification. We extended the KeY ecosystem with CorC. CorC opens the possibility to utilize CbC in areas where post-hoc verification is used as programmers could benefit from synergistic effects of both approaches. With tool support, CbC can be studied in experiments to determine the value of using CbC in industry.

For future work, we want to extend the tool support, and we want to evaluate empirically the benefits and drawbacks of CorC. To extend the expressiveness, we implement a rule for methods to use method calls in CorC. These methods have to be verified independently by CorC/KeY. We could investigate whether the method call rules of KeY can be used for our CbC approach. Another future work is the inference of conditions to reduce the manual effort. Postconditions can be generated automatically for known statements by using the strongest postcondition calculus. Invariants could be generated by incorporating external tools. As mentioned earlier, other host languages and other theorem provers can be integrated in our IDE.

The second work package for future work comprise the evaluation with a user study. We could compare the effort of creating and verifying algorithms with post-hoc verification and with our tool support. The feedback can be used to improve the usability of the tool.

References

1. Abrial, J.R.: The B-Book: Assigning Programs to Meanings. Cambridge University Press, Cambridge (2005)
2. Abrial, J.R.: Modeling in Event-B: System and Software Engineering. Cambridge University Press, Cambridge (2010)
3. Abrial, J.R., Butler, M., Hallerstede, S., Hoang, T.S., Mehta, F., Voisin, L.: Rodin: an open toolset for modelling and reasoning in Event-B. Int. J. Softw. Tools Technol. Transfer **12**(6), 447–466 (2010)
4. Ahrendt, W., Beckert, B., Bubel, R., Hähnle, R., Schmitt, P.H., Ulbrich, M.: Deductive Software Verification - The KeY Book: From Theory to Practice, vol. 10001. Springer, Heidelberg (2016). https://doi.org/10.1007/978-3-319-49812-6
5. Barnett, M., Fähndrich, M., Leino, K.R.M., Müller, P., Schulte, W., Venter, H.: Specification and verification: the Spec# experience. Commun. ACM **54**(6), 81–91 (2011)
6. Barnett, M., Leino, K.R.M., Schulte, W.: The Spec# programming system: an overview. In: Barthe, G., Burdy, L., Huisman, M., Lanet, J.-L., Muntean, T. (eds.) CASSIS 2004. LNCS, vol. 3362, pp. 49–69. Springer, Heidelberg (2005). https://doi.org/10.1007/978-3-540-30569-9_3
7. Bertot, Y., Castéran, P.: Interactive Theorem Proving and Program Development: Coq'Art: The Calculus of Inductive Constructions. Springer, Heidelberg (2013). https://doi.org/10.1007/978-3-662-07964-5
8. Cohen, E., et al.: VCC: a practical system for verifying concurrent C. In: Berghofer, S., Nipkow, T., Urban, C., Wenzel, M. (eds.) TPHOLs 2009. LNCS, vol. 5674, pp. 23–42. Springer, Heidelberg (2009). https://doi.org/10.1007/978-3-642-03359-9_2
9. Cok, D.R.: OpenJML: JML for Java 7 by extending OpenJDK. In: Bobaru, M., Havelund, K., Holzmann, G.J., Joshi, R. (eds.) NFM 2011. LNCS, vol. 6617, pp. 472–479. Springer, Heidelberg (2011). https://doi.org/10.1007/978-3-642-20398-5_35

10. Conserva Filho, M., Oliveira, M.V.M.: Implementing tactics of refinement in CRefine. In: Eleftherakis, G., Hinchey, M., Holcombe, M. (eds.) SEFM 2012. LNCS, vol. 7504, pp. 342–351. Springer, Heidelberg (2012). https://doi.org/10.1007/978-3-642-33826-7_24
11. Dijkstra, E.W.: Guarded commands, nondeterminacy and formal derivation of programs. Commun. ACM **18**(8), 453–457 (1975)
12. Dijkstra, E.W.: A Discipline of Programming. Prentice Hall, Upper Saddle River (1976)
13. Gries, D.: The Science of Programming. Springer, Heidelberg (1987). https://doi.org/10.1007/978-1-4612-5983-1
14. Hall, A., Chapman, R.: Correctness by construction: developing a commercial secure system. IEEE Softw. **19**(1), 18–25 (2002)
15. Hentschel, M.: Integrating symbolic execution, debugging and verification. Ph.D. thesis, Technische Universität Darmstadt (2016)
16. Jacobs, B., Smans, J., Piessens, F.: A quick tour of the verifast program verifier. In: Ueda, K. (ed.) APLAS 2010. LNCS, vol. 6461, pp. 304–311. Springer, Heidelberg (2010). https://doi.org/10.1007/978-3-642-17164-2_21
17. Kapur, D., Nie, X., Musser, D.R.: An overview of the Tecton proof system. Theoret. Comput. Sci. **133**(2), 307–339 (1994)
18. Khazeev, M., Rivera, V., Mazzara, M., Johard, L.: Initial steps towards assessing the usability of a verification tool. In: Ciancarini, P., Litvinov, S., Messina, A., Sillitti, A., Succi, G. (eds.) SEDA 2016. AISC, vol. 717, pp. 31–40. Springer, Cham (2018). https://doi.org/10.1007/978-3-319-70578-1_4
19. Kourie, D.G., Watson, B.W.: The Correctness-by-Construction Approach to Programming. Springer, Heidelberg (2012). https://doi.org/10.1007/978-3-642-27919-5
20. Kramer, R.: iContract - the Java design by contract tool. In: Proceedings, Technology of Object-Oriented Languages. TOOLS 26 (Cat. No. 98EX176), pp. 295–307. IEEE, August 1998
21. Meyer, B.: Eiffel: a language and environment for software engineering. J. Syst. Softw. **8**(3), 199–246 (1988)
22. Meyer, B.: Applying "design by contract". Computer **25**(10), 40–51 (1992)
23. Morgan, C.: Programming from Specifications, 2nd edn. Prentice Hall, Upper Saddle River (1994)
24. Nipkow, T., Paulson, L.C., Wenzel, M. (eds.): Isabelle/HOL. LNCS, vol. 2283. Springer, Heidelberg (2002). https://doi.org/10.1007/3-540-45949-9
25. Oliveira, M.V.M., Cavalcanti, A., Woodcock, J.: ArcAngel: a tactic language for refinement. Formal Aspects Comput. **15**(1), 28–47 (2003)
26. Oliveira, M.V.M., Gurgel, A.C., Castro, C.G.: CRefine: support for the circus refinement calculus. In: 2008 Sixth IEEE International Conference on Software Engineering and Formal Methods, pp. 281–290. IEEE, November 2008
27. Plosch, R.: Tool support for design by contract. In: Proceedings, Technology of Object-Oriented Languages. TOOLS 26 (Cat. No. 98EX176), pp. 282–294. IEEE, August 1998
28. Tschannen, J., Furia, C.A., Nordio, M., Polikarpova, N.: AutoProof: auto-active functional verification of object-oriented programs. In: Baier, C., Tinelli, C. (eds.) TACAS 2015. LNCS, vol. 9035, pp. 566–580. Springer, Heidelberg (2015). https://doi.org/10.1007/978-3-662-46681-0_53

29. Watson, B.W., Kourie, D.G., Schaefer, I., Cleophas, L.: Correctness-by-construction and post-hoc verification: a marriage of convenience? In: Margaria, T., Steffen, B. (eds.) ISoLA 2016. LNCS, vol. 9952, pp. 730–748. Springer, Cham (2016). https://doi.org/10.1007/978-3-319-47166-2_52
30. Wohlin, C., Runeson, P., Höst, M., Ohlsson, M.C., Regnell, B., Wesslén, A.: Experimentation in Software Engineering. Springer, Heidelberg (2012). https://doi.org/10.1007/978-3-642-29044-2

Automatic Modeling of Opaque Code for JavaScript Static Analysis

Joonyoung Park[1,2](✉), Alexander Jordan[1](✉), and Sukyoung Ryu[2](✉)

[1] Oracle Labs Australia, Brisbane, Australia
{joonyoung.p.park,alexander.jordan}@oracle.com
[2] KAIST, Daejeon, Republic of Korea
{sryu.cs,gmb55}@kaist.ac.kr

Abstract. Static program analysis often encounters problems in analyzing library code. Most real-world programs use library functions intensively, and library functions are usually written in different languages. For example, static analysis of JavaScript programs requires analysis of the standard built-in library implemented in host environments. A common approach to analyze such *opaque code* is for analysis developers to build models that provide the semantics of the code. Models can be built either manually, which is time consuming and error prone, or automatically, which may limit application to different languages or analyzers. In this paper, we present a novel mechanism to support automatic modeling of opaque code, which is applicable to various languages and analyzers. For a given static analysis, our approach automatically computes analysis results of opaque code via dynamic testing during static analysis. By using testing techniques, the mechanism does not guarantee *sound* over-approximation of program behaviors in general. However, it is fully automatic, is scalable in terms of the size of opaque code, and provides more precise results than conventional over-approximation approaches. Our evaluation shows that although not all functionalities in opaque code can (or should) be modeled automatically using our technique, a large number of JavaScript built-in functions are approximated soundly yet more precisely than existing manual models.

Keywords: Automatic modeling · Static analysis · Opaque code · JavaScript

1 Introduction

Static analysis is widely used to optimize programs and to find bugs in them, but it often faces difficulties in analyzing library code. Since most real-world programs use various libraries usually written in different programming languages, analysis developers should provide analysis results for libraries as well. For example, static analysis of JavaScript apps involves analysis of the builtin functions implemented in host environments like the V8 runtime system written in C++.

R. Hähnle and W. van der Aalst (Eds.): FASE 2019, LNCS 11424, pp. 43–60, 2019.
https://doi.org/10.1007/978-3-030-16722-6_3

A conventional approach to analyze such *opaque code* is for analysis developers to create models that provide the analysis results of the opaque code. Models approximate the behaviors of opaque code, they are often tightly integrated with specific static analyzers to support precise abstract semantics that are compatible with the analyzers' internals.

Developers can create models either manually or automatically. Manual modeling is complex, time consuming, and error prone because developers need to consider all the possible behaviors of the code they model. In the case of JavaScript, the number of APIs to be modeled is large and ever-growing as the language evolves. Thus, various approaches have been proposed to model opaque code automatically. They create models either from specifications of the code's behaviors [2,26] or using dynamic information during execution of the code [8,9,22]. The former approach heavily depends on the quality and format of available specifications, and the latter approach is limited to the capability of instrumentation or specific analyzers.

In this paper, we propose a novel mechanism to model the behaviors of opaque code to be used by static analysis. While existing approaches aim to create general models for the opaque code's behaviors, which can produce analysis results for all possible inputs, our approach computes specific results of opaque code during static analysis. This on-demand modeling is specific to the abstract states of a program being analyzed, and it consists of three steps: sampling, run, and abstraction. When static analysis encounters opaque code with some abstract state, our approach generates samples that are a subset of all possible inputs of the opaque code by concretizing the abstract state. After evaluating the code using the concretized values, it abstracts the results and uses it during analysis. Since the sampling generally covers only a small subset of infinitely many possible inputs to opaque code, our approach does not guarantee the soundness of the modeling results just like other automatic modeling techniques.

The sampling strategy should select well-distributed samples to explore the opaque code's behaviors as much as possible and to avoid redundant ones. Generating too few samples may miss too much behaviors, while redundant samples can cause the performance overhead. As a simple yet effective way to control the number of samples, we propose to use *combinatorial testing* [11].

We implemented the proposed automatic modeling as an extension of SAFE, a JavaScript static analyzer [13,17]. For opaque code encountered during analysis, the extension generates concrete inputs from abstract states, and executes the code dynamically using the concrete inputs via a JavaScript engine (Node.js in our implementation). Then, it abstracts the execution results using the operations provided by SAFE such as lattice-*join* and our over-approximation, and resumes the analysis.

Our paper makes the following contributions:

- We present a novel way to handle opaque code during static analysis by computing a precise on-demand model of the code using (1) input samples that represent analysis states, (2) dynamic execution, and (3) abstraction.

- We propose a combinatorial sampling strategy to efficiently generate well-distributed input samples.
- We evaluate our tool against hand-written models for large parts of JavaScript's builtin functions in terms of precision, soundness, and performance.
- Our tool revealed implementation errors in existing hand-written models, demonstrating that it can be used for automatic testing of static analyzers.

In the remainder of this paper, we present our Sample-Run-Abstract approach to model opaque code for static analysis (Sect. 2) and describe the sampling strategy (Sect. 3) we use. We then discuss our implementation and experiences of applying it to JavaScript analysis (Sect. 4), evaluate the implementation using ECMAScript 5.1 builtin functions as benchmarks (Sect. 5), discuss related work (Sect. 6), and conclude (Sect. 7).

2 Modeling via Sample-Run-Abstract

Our approach models opaque code by designing a universal model, which is able to handle arbitrary opaque code. Rather than generating a specific model for each opaque code statically, it produces a single general model, which produces results for given states using concrete semantics via dynamic execution. We call this universal model the *SRA model.*

In order to create the SRA model for a given static analyzer $\mathcal{A}$ and a dynamic executor $\mathcal{E}$, we assume the following:

- The static analyzer $\mathcal{A}$ is based on abstract interpretation [6]. It provides the abstraction function $\alpha : \wp(S) \rightarrow \widehat{S}$ and the concretization function $\gamma : \widehat{S} \rightarrow \wp(S)$ for a set of concrete states S and a set of abstract states $\widehat{S}$.
- An abstract domain forms a complete lattice, which has a partial order among its values from $\bot$(bottom) to $\top$(top).
- For a given program point $c \in C$, either $\mathcal{A}$ or $\mathcal{E}$ can identify the code corresponding to the point.

Then, the SRA model consists of the following three steps:

- *Sample* : $\widehat{S} \rightarrow \wp(S)$
  For a given abstract state $\widehat{s} \in \widehat{S}$, *Sample* chooses a finite set of elements from $\gamma(\widehat{s})$, a possible set of values for $\widehat{s}$. Because it is, in the general case, impossible to execute opaque code dynamically with all possible inputs, *Sample* should select representative elements efficiently as we discuss in the next section.
- *Run* : $C \times S \rightarrow S$
  For a given program point and a concrete state at this point, *Run* generates executable code corresponding to the point and state, executes the code, and returns the result state of the execution.
- *Abstract* : $\wp(S) \rightarrow \widehat{S}$
  For a given set of concrete states, *Abstract* produces an abstract state that encompasses the concrete states. One can apply α to each concrete state, join

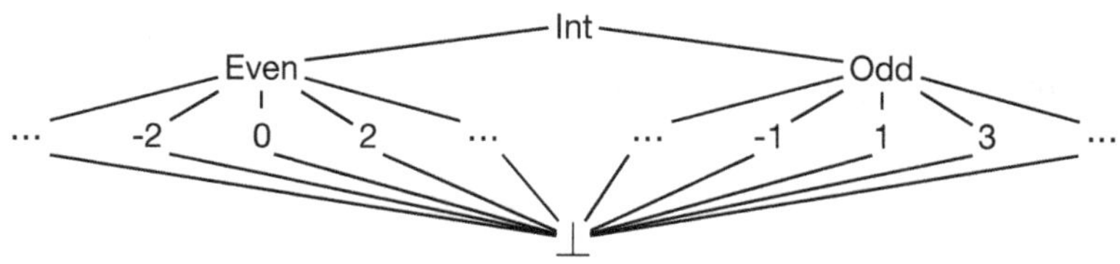

Fig. 1. An abstract domain for even and odd integers

all the resulting abstract states, and optionally apply an over-approximation heuristic, comparable to widening *Broaden* : $\widehat{S} \to \widehat{S}$ to mitigate missing behaviors of the opaque code due to the under-approximate sampling.

We write the SRA model as $\Downarrow_{SRA}: C \times \widehat{S} \to \widehat{S}$ and define it as follows:

$$\begin{aligned} \Downarrow_{SRA}(c, \widehat{s}) &= \quad Abstract(\{Run(c, s) \quad \mid s \in Sample(\widehat{s})\}) \\ &= Broaden(\bigsqcup\{\alpha(\{Run(c, s)\}) \mid s \in Sample(\widehat{s})\}) \end{aligned}$$

We now describe how $\Downarrow_{SRA}$ works using an example abstract domain for even and odd integers as shown in Fig. 1. Let us consider the code snippet `x := abs(x)` at a program point c where the library function `abs` is opaque. We use maps from variables to their concrete values for concrete states, maps from variables to their abstract values for abstract states, and the identity function for *Broaden* in this example.

Case $\widehat{s}_1 \equiv [\mathtt{x} : n]$ *where* n *is a constant integer:*

$$\begin{aligned} \Downarrow_{SRA}(c, \widehat{s}_1) &= \bigsqcup\{\alpha(\{Run(c, s)\}) \mid s \in Sample(\widehat{s}_1)\} \\ &= \bigsqcup\{\alpha(\{Run(c, s)\}) \mid s \in \{[\mathtt{x} : n]\}\} \\ &= \bigsqcup\{\alpha(\{Run(c, [\mathtt{x} : n])\})\} \\ &= \bigsqcup\{\alpha(\{[\mathtt{x} : |n|]\})\} \\ &= [\mathtt{x} : |n|] \end{aligned}$$

Because the given abstract state $\widehat{s}_1$ contains a single abstract value corresponding to a single concrete value, *Sample* produces the set of all possible states, which makes $\Downarrow_{SRA}$ provide a sound and also the most precise result.

Case $\widehat{s}_2 \equiv [\mathtt{x} : \mathtt{Even}]$*:*

$$\begin{aligned} \Downarrow_{SRA}(c, \widehat{s}_2) &= \bigsqcup\{\alpha(\{Run(c, s)\}) \mid s \in Sample(\widehat{s}_2)\} \\ &= \bigsqcup\{\alpha(\{Run(c, s)\}) \mid s \in \{[\mathtt{x} : -2], [\mathtt{x} : 0], [\mathtt{x} : 2]\}\} \\ &= \bigsqcup\{\alpha(\{[\mathtt{x} : 0], [\mathtt{x} : 2]\})\} \\ &= [\mathtt{x} : \mathtt{Even}] \end{aligned}$$

When *Sample* selects three elements from the set of all possible states represented by $\widehat{s}_2$, executing `abs` results in $\{[\mathtt{x} : 0], [\mathtt{x} : 2]\}$. Since joining these two abstract states produces `Even`, $\Downarrow_{SRA}$ models the correct behavior of `abs` by taking advantage of the abstract domain.

Case $\widehat{s}_3 \equiv [\mathtt{x} : \mathtt{Int}]$ *:*

$$\begin{aligned}
&\Downarrow_{SRA} (c, \widehat{s}_3) \\
&= \bigsqcup\{\alpha(\{Run(c, s)\}) \mid s \in Sample(\widehat{s}_3)\} \\
&= \bigsqcup\{\alpha(\{Run(c, s)\}) \mid s \in Sample(\widehat{s}_2) \cup Sample([\mathtt{x} : \mathtt{Odd}])\} \\
&= \bigsqcup\{\alpha(\{Run(c, s)\}) \mid s \in \{[\mathtt{x} : -2], [\mathtt{x} : -1], [\mathtt{x} : 0], [\mathtt{x} : 1], [\mathtt{x} : 2], [\mathtt{x} : 3]\}\} \\
&= \bigsqcup\{\alpha(\{[\mathtt{x} : 0], [\mathtt{x} : 1], [\mathtt{x} : 2], [\mathtt{x} : 3]\})\} \\
&= [\mathtt{x} : \mathtt{Int}]
\end{aligned}$$

When an abstract value has a finite number of elements that are immediately below it in the abstract domain lattice, our sampling strategy selects samples from them recursively. Thus, in this example, *Sample*$([\mathtt{x} : \mathtt{Int}])$ becomes the union of *Sample*$([\mathtt{x} : \mathtt{Even}])$ and *Sample*$([\mathtt{x} : \mathtt{Odd}])$. We explain this recursive sampling strategy in Sect. 3.

Case $\widehat{s}_4 \equiv [\mathtt{x} : \mathtt{Odd}]$*:*

$$\begin{aligned}
\Downarrow_{SRA} (c, \widehat{s}_4) &= \bigsqcup\{\alpha(\{Run(c, s)\}) \mid s \in Sample(\widehat{s}_4)\} \\
&= \bigsqcup\{\alpha(\{Run(c, s)\}) \mid s \in \{[\mathtt{x} : -1], [\mathtt{x} : 1]\}\} \\
&= \bigsqcup\{\alpha(\{[\mathtt{x} : 1]\})\} \\
&= [\mathtt{x} : 1]
\end{aligned}$$

While $\Downarrow_{SRA}$ produces sound and precise results for the above three cases, it does not guarantee soundness; it may miss some behaviors of opaque code due to the limitations of the sampling strategy. Let us assume that *Sample*$([\mathtt{x} : \mathtt{Odd}])$ selects $\{[\mathtt{x} : -1], [\mathtt{x} : 1]\}$ this time. Then, the model produces an unsound result $[\mathtt{x} : 1]$, which does not cover odd integers, because the selected values explore only partial behaviors of `abs`. When the number of possible states at a call site of opaque code is infinite, the sampling strategy can lead to unsound results. A well-designed sampling strategy is crucial for our modeling approach; it affects the analysis performance and soundness significantly. The approach is precise thanks to under-approximated results from sampling, but entails a tradeoff between the analysis performance and soundness depending on the number of samples. In the next section, we propose a strategy to generate samples for various abstract domains and to control sample sizes effectively.

3 Combinatorial Sampling Strategy

We propose to use a combinatorial sampling strategy (inspired by combinatorial testing) by the types of values that an abstract domain represents. The domains represent either *primitive* values like number and string, or *object* values like tuple, set, and map. Based on combinatorial testing, our strategy is recursively defined on the hierarchy of abstract domains used to represent program states. Assume that $\widehat{a}, \widehat{b} \in \widehat{A}$ are abstract values that we want to concretize using *Sample*.

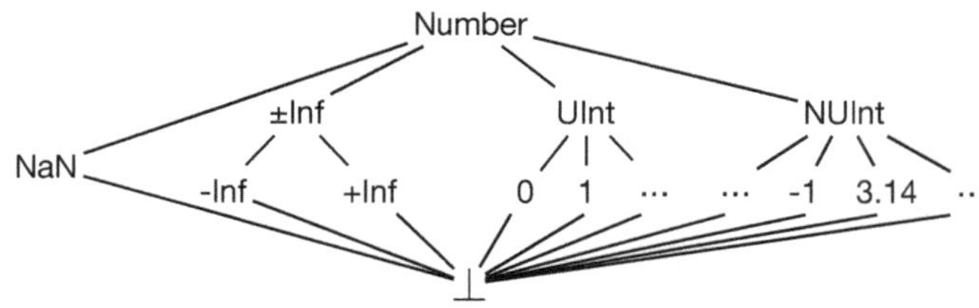

Fig. 2. The SAFE number domain for JavaScript

3.1 Abstract Domains for Primitive Values

To explain our sampling strategy for primitive abstract domains, we use the `DefaultNumber` domain from SAFE as an example. `DefaultNumber` represents JavaScript numbers with subcategories as shown in Fig. 2. The subcategories are `NaN` (not a number), ±`Inf` (positive/negative infinity), `UInt` (unsigned integer), and `NUInt` (not an unsigned integer, which is a negative integer or a floating point number).

Case $|\gamma(\widehat{a})| = constant$*:*

$$Sample(\widehat{a}) = \gamma(\widehat{a})$$

When $\widehat{a}$ represents a finite number of concrete values, *Sample* simply takes all the values. For example, ±`Inf` has two possible values, `+Inf` and `-Inf`. Therefore, *Sample*(±`Inf`) = {`+Inf`, `-Inf`}.

Case $|\gamma(\widehat{a})| = \infty$ *and* $|\{\widehat{b} \in \widehat{A} \mid \forall \widehat{x} \sqsubset \widehat{a}.\ \widehat{b} \not\sqsubseteq \widehat{x}\}| = constant$*:*

$$Sample(\widehat{a}) = \bigcup_{\widehat{b}} Sample(\widehat{b})$$

When $\widehat{a}$ represents an infinite number of concrete values, but it *covers* (that is, is immediately preceded by) a finite number of abstract values in the lattice, *Sample* applies to each predecessor recursively and merges the concrete results by set union. Note that, "y covers x" holds whenever $x \sqsubset y$ and there is no z such that $x \sqsubset z \sqsubset y$. The number of samples increases linearly in this step. `Number` falls into this case. It represents infinitely many numbers, but it covers four abstract values in the lattice: `NaN`, ±`Inf`, `UInt`, and `NUInt`.

Case $|\gamma(\widehat{a})| = \infty$ *and* $|\{\widehat{b} \in A \mid \forall \widehat{x} \sqsubset \widehat{a}.\ \widehat{b} \not\sqsubseteq \widehat{x}\}| = \infty$*:*

$$Sample(\widehat{a}) = H(\gamma(\widehat{a}))$$

When $\widehat{a}$ represents infinitely many concrete values and also covers infinitely many abstract values, we make the number of samples finite by applying a heuristic injection H of seed samples. For seed samples, we propose the following guidelines to manually select them:

- Use a small number of commonly used values. Our conjecture is that common values will trigger the same behavior in opaque code repeatedly.
- Choose values that have special properties for known operators. For example, for each operator, select the minimum, maximum, identity, and inverse elements, if any.

In the `DefaultNumber` domain example, `UInt` and `NUInt` fall into this case. For the evaluation of our modeling approach in Sect. 5, we selected seed samples based on the guidelines as follows:

$$\begin{aligned} \mathit{Sample}(\texttt{UInt}) &= \{0, 1, 3, 10, 9999\} \\ \mathit{Sample}(\texttt{NUInt}) &= \{-10, -3, -1, -0.5, -0, 0.5, 3.14\} \end{aligned}$$

We experimentally show that this simple heuristic works well for automatic modeling of JavaScript builtin functions.

3.2 Abstract Domains for Object Values

Our sampling strategy for object abstract domains consists of four steps. To sample from a given abstract object $\widehat{a} \in \widehat{A}$, we assume the following:

- A concrete object $a \in \gamma(\widehat{a})$ is a map from fields to their values: $\mathit{Map}[F, V]$.
- Abstract domains for fields and values are $\widehat{F}$ and $\widehat{V}$, respectively.
- The abstract domain $\widehat{A}$ provides two helper functions: $\mathit{mustF} : \widehat{A} \to \wp(F)$ and $\mathit{mayF} : \widehat{A} \to \widehat{F}$. The $\mathit{mustF}(\widehat{a})$ function returns a set of fields that $\forall a \in \gamma(\widehat{a})$ must have, and $\mathit{mayF}(\widehat{a})$ returns an abstract value $\widehat{f} \in \widehat{F}$ representing a set of fields that $\exists a \in \gamma(\widehat{a})$ may have.

Then, the sampling strategy follows the next four steps:

1. Sampling fields
In order to construct sampled objects, it first samples a finite number of fields. JavaScript provides open objects, where fields can be added and removed dynamically, and fields can be referenced not only by string literals but also by arbitrary expressions of string values. Thus, this step collects fields from a finite set of fields that all possible objects should contain (F_{must}) and samples from a possibly infinite set of fields that some possible objects may (but not must) contain (F_{may}):
$$\begin{aligned} F_{must} &= \mathit{mustF}(\widehat{a}) \\ F_{may} &= \mathit{Sample}(\mathit{mayF}(\widehat{a})) \setminus F_{must} \end{aligned}$$
2. Abstracting values for the sampled fields
For the fields in F_{must} and F_{may} sampled from the given abstract object $\widehat{a}$, it constructs two maps from fields to their abstract values, M_{must} and M_{may}, respectively, of type $\mathit{Map}[F, \widehat{V}]$:
$$\begin{aligned} M_{must} &= \lambda f \in F_{must}.\ \alpha(\{a(f) \mid a \in \gamma(\widehat{a})\}) \\ M_{may} &= \lambda f \in F_{may}\ .\ \alpha(\{a(f) \mid a \in \gamma(\widehat{a})\}) \end{aligned}$$
3. Sampling values
From M_{must} and M_{may}, it constructs another map $M_s : F \to \wp(V_{\nexists})$, where $V_{\nexists} = V \cup \{\nexists\}$ denotes a set of values and the absence of a field $\nexists$, by applying *Sample* to the value of each field in F_{must} and F_{may}. The value of each field in F_{may} contains $\nexists$ to denote that the field may not exist in M_s:

$$M_s = \lambda f \in F_{must} \cup F_{may}. \begin{cases} Sample(M_{must}(f)) & \text{if } f \in F_{must} \\ Sample(M_{may}(f)) \cup \{\nexists\} & \text{if } f \in F_{may} \end{cases}$$

4. Choosing samples by combinatorial testing
   Finally, since a number of all combinations from M_s, $\prod_{f \in Domain(M_s)} |M_s(f)|$, grows exponentially, the last step limits the number selections. We solve this selection problem by reducing it to a traditional testing problem with combinatorial testing [3]. Combinatorial testing is a well-studied problem and efficient algorithms for generating test cases exist. It addresses a similar problem to ours, increasing dynamic coverage of code under test, but in the context of finding bugs:

   > "The most common bugs in a program are generally triggered by either a single input parameter or an interaction between pairs of parameters."

   Thus, we apply each-used or pair-wise testing (1 or 2-wise) as the last step.

Now, we demonstrate each step using an abstract array object $\widehat{a}$, whose length is greater than or equal to 2 and the elements of which are `true` or `false`. We write $\top_b$ to denote an abstract value such that $\gamma(\top_b) = \{\texttt{true}, \texttt{false}\}$.

- Assumptions
  - A concrete array object a is a map from indices to boolean values: $Map[\texttt{UInt}, \texttt{Boolean}]$.
  - For given abstract object $\widehat{a}$, $mustF(\widehat{a}) = \{0, 1\}$ and $mayF(\widehat{a}) = \texttt{UInt}$.
  - From Sect. 3.1, we sample $\{0, 1, 3, 10, 9999\}$ for `UInt`.
  - $k\text{-}wise(M)$ generates a set of minimum number of test cases satisfying all the requirements of $k\text{-}wise$ testing for a map M. It constructs a test case by choosing one element from a set on each field.
- Step 1: Sampling fields

$$\begin{aligned} F_{must} &= \{0, 1\} \\ F_{may} &= Sample(\texttt{UInt}) \setminus \{0, 1\} = \{3, 10, 9999\} \end{aligned}$$

- Step 2: Abstracting values for the sampled fields

$$\begin{aligned} M_{must} &= [0 \mapsto \top_b, 1 \mapsto \top_b] \\ M_{may} &= [3 \mapsto \top_b, 10 \mapsto \top_b, 9999 \mapsto \top_b] \end{aligned}$$

- Step 3: Sampling values

$$M_s = [\begin{array}{rlrl} 0 \mapsto & \{\texttt{true}, \texttt{false}\}, & 1 \mapsto & \{\texttt{true}, \texttt{false}\}, \\ 3 \mapsto & \{\texttt{true}, \texttt{false}, \nexists\}, & 10 \mapsto & \{\texttt{true}, \texttt{false}, \nexists\}, \\ 9999 \mapsto & \{\texttt{true}, \texttt{false}, \nexists\} & & \end{array}]$$

- Step 4: Choosing samples by combinatorial testing
  The number of all combinations $\prod_{f \in Domain(M_s)} |M_s(f)|$ is 108 even after sampling fields and values in an under-approximate manner. We can avoid such

explosion of samples and manage well-distributed samples by using combinatorial testing. With each-used testing, three combinations can cover every element in a set on each field at least once:

$$1\text{-}wise(M_s) = \{\ [0 \mapsto \texttt{true},\ 1 \mapsto \texttt{false}, 3 \mapsto \texttt{true},\ 10 \mapsto \nexists,\ 9999 \mapsto \nexists], [0 \mapsto \texttt{false}, 1 \mapsto \texttt{true},\ 3 \mapsto \texttt{false}, 10 \mapsto \texttt{false}, 9999 \mapsto \texttt{true}], [0 \mapsto \texttt{false}, 1 \mapsto \texttt{true},\ 3 \mapsto \nexists,\ 10 \mapsto \texttt{true},\ 9999 \mapsto \texttt{false}]\ \}$$

With pair-wise testing, 12 samples can cover every pair of elements from different sets at least once.

4 Implementation

We implemented our automatic modeling approach for JavaScript because of its large number of builtin APIs and complex libraries, which are all opaque code for static analysis. They include the functions in the ECMAScript language standard [1] and web standards such as DOM and browser APIs. We implemented the modeling as an extension of SAFE [13,17], a JavaScript static analyzer. When the analyzer encounters calls of opaque code during analysis, it uses the SRA model of the code.

Sample. We applied the combinatorial sampling strategy for the SAFE abstract domains. Of the abstract domains for primitive JavaScript values, `UInt`, `NUInt`, and `OtherStr` represent an infinite number of concrete values (c.f. third case in Sect. 3.1) and thus require the use of heuristics. We describe the details of our heuristics and sample sets in Sect. 5.1.

We implemented the *Sample* step to use "each-used sample generation" for object abstract domains by default. In order to generate more samples, we added three options to apply pair-wise generation:

- `ThisPair` generates pairs between the values of `this` and heap,
- `HeapPair` among objects in the heap, and
- `ArgPair` among property values in an `arguments` object.

As an exception, we use the all-combination strategy for the `DefaultDataProp` domain representing a JavaScript property, consisting of a value and three booleans: `writable`, `enumerable`, and `configurable`. Note that *field* is used for language-independent objects and *property* is for JavaScript objects. The number of their combinations is limited to 2^3. We consider a linear increase of samples as acceptable. The *Sample* step returns a finite set of concrete states, and each element in the set, which in turn contains concrete values only, is passed to the *Run* step.

Run. For each concrete input state, the *Run* step obtains a result state by executing the corresponding opaque code in four steps:

1. Generation of executable code
   First, *Run* populates object values from the concrete state. We currently omit the JavaScript scope-chain information, because the library functions that we analyze as opaque code are independent from the scope of user code. It derives executable code to invoke the opaque code and adds argument values from the static analysis context.
2. Execution of the code using a JavaScript engine
   Run executes the generated code using the JavaScript `eval` function on Node.js. Populating objects and their properties from sample values before invoking the opaque function may throws an exception. In such cases, *Run* executes the code once again with a different sample value. If the second sample value also throws an exception during population of the objects and their properties, it dismisses the code.
3. Serialization of the result state
   After execution, the result state contains the objects from the input state, the return value of the opaque code, and all the values that it might refer to. Also, any mutation of objects of the input state as well as newly created objects are captured in this way. We use a snapshot module of SAFE to serialize the result state into a JSON-like format.
4. Transfer of the state to the analyzer
   The serialized snapshot is then passed to SAFE, where it is parsed, loaded, and combined with other results as a set of concrete result states.

Abstract. To abstract result states, we mostly used existing operations in SAFE, like lattice-*join*, and also implemented an over-approximation heuristic function, *Broaden*, comparable to widening. We use *Broaden* for property name sets in JavaScript objects, because *mayF* of a JavaScript abstract object can produce an abstract value that denotes an infinite set of concrete strings, and because $\Downarrow_{SRA}$ cannot produce such an abstract value from simple sampling and *join*. Thus, we regard all possibly absent properties as sampled properties. Then, we implemented the *Broaden* function merging all possibly absent properties into one abstract property representing any property, when the number of absent properties is greater than a certain threshold proportional to a number of sampled properties.

5 Evaluation

We evaluated the $\Downarrow_{SRA}$ model in two regards, (1) the feasibility of replacing existing manual models (RQ1 and RQ2) and (2) the effects of our heuristic H on the analysis soundness (RQ3). The research questions are as follow:

- **RQ1: Analysis performance of $\Downarrow_{SRA}$**
  Can $\Downarrow_{SRA}$ replace existing manual models for program analysis with decent performance in terms of soundness, precision, and runtime overhead?

- **RQ2: Applicability of $\Downarrow_{SRA}$**
  Is $\Downarrow_{SRA}$ broadly applicable to various builtin functions of JavaScript?
- **RQ3: Dependence on heuristic H**
  How much is the performance of $\Downarrow_{SRA}$ affected by the heuristics?

After describing the experimental setup for evaluation, we present our answers to the research questions with quantitative results, and discuss the limitations of our evaluation.

5.1 Experimental Setup

In order to evaluate the $\Downarrow_{SRA}$ model, we compared the analysis performance and applicability of $\Downarrow_{SRA}$ with those of the existing manual models in SAFE. We used two kinds of subjects: browser benchmark programs and builtin functions. From 34 browser benchmarks included in the test suite of SAFE, a subset of V8 Octane[1], we collected 13 of them that invoke opaque code. Since browser benchmark programs use a small number of opaque functions, we also generated test cases for 134 functions in the ECMAScript 5.1 specification.

Each test case contains abstract values that represent two or more possible values. Because SAFE uses a finite number of abstract domains for primitive values, we used all of them in the test cases. We also generated 10 abstract objects. Five of them are manually created to represent arbitrary objects:

`OBJ1` has an arbitrary property whose value is an arbitrary primitive.
`OBJ2` is a property descriptor whose `"value"` is an arbitrary primitive, and the others are arbitrary booleans.
`OBJ3` has an arbitrary property whose value is `OBJ2`.
`OBJ4` is an empty array whose `"length"` is arbitrary.
`OBJ5` is an arbitrary-length array with an arbitrary property

The other five objects were collected from SunSpider benchmark programs by using Jalangi2 [20] to represent frequently used abstract objects. We counted the number of function calls with object arguments and joined the most used object arguments in each program. Out of 10 programs that have function calls with object arguments, we discarded four programs that use the same objects for every function call, and one program that uses an argument with 2500 properties, which makes manual inspection impossible. We joined the first 10 concrete objects for each argument of the following benchmark to obtain abstract objects: 3d-cube.js, 3d-raytrace.js, access-binary-trees.js, regexp-dna.js, and string-fasta.js. For 134 test functions, when a test function consumes two or more arguments, we restricted each argument to have only an expected type to manage the number of test cases. Also, we used one or minimum number of arguments for functions with variable number of arguments.

In summary, we used 13 programs for RQ1, and 134 functions with 1565 test cases for RQ2 and RQ3. All experiments were on a 2.9 GHz quad-core Intel Core i7 with 16 GB memory machine.

[1] https://github.com/chromium/octane.

5.2 Answers to Research Questions

Answer to RQ1. We compared the precision, soundness, and analysis time of the SAFE manual models and the $\Downarrow_{SRA}$ model. Table 1 shows the precision and soundness for each opaque function call, and Table 2 presents the analysis time and number of samples for each program.

As for the precision, Table 1 shows that $\Downarrow_{SRA}$ produced more precise results than manual models for 9 (19.6%) cases. We manually checked whether each result of a model is sound or not by using the partial order function ($\sqsubseteq$) implemented in SAFE. We found that all the results of the SAFE manual models for the benchmarks were sound. The $\Downarrow_{SRA}$ model produced an unsound result for only one function: `Math.random`. While it returns a floating-point value in the range $[0, 1)$, $\Downarrow_{SRA}$ modeled it as `NUInt`, instead of the expected `Number`, because it missed 0.

As shown in Table 2, on average $\Downarrow_{SRA}$ took 1.35 times more analysis time than the SAFE models. The table also shows the number of context-sensitive opaque function calls during analysis (#Call), the maximum number of samples (#Max), and the total number of samples (#Total). To understand the runtime overhead better, we measured the proportion of elapsed time for each step. On average, *Sample* took 59%, *Run* 7%, *Abstract* 17%, and the rest 17%. The experimental results show that $\Downarrow_{SRA}$ provides high precision while slightly sacrificing soundness with modest runtime overhead.

Answer to RQ2. Because the benchmark programs use only 15 opaque functions as shown in Table 1, we generated abstracted arguments for 134 functions out of 169 functions in the ECMAScript 5.1 builtin library, for which SAFE has manual models. We semi-automatically checked the soundness and precision of the $\Downarrow_{SRA}$ model by comparing the analysis results with their expected results. Table 3 shows the results in terms of test cases (left half) and functions (right half). The **Equal** column shows the number of test cases or functions, for which both models provide equal results that are sound. The **SRA Pre.** column shows the number of such cases where the $\Downarrow_{SRA}$ model provides sound and more precise results than the manual model. The **Man. Uns.** column presents the number of such cases where $\Downarrow_{SRA}$ provides sound results but the manual one provides unsound results, and **SRA Uns.** shows the opposite case of **Man. Uns.** Finally, **Not Comp.** shows the number of cases where the results of $\Downarrow_{SRA}$ and the manual model are incomparable.

The $\Downarrow_{SRA}$ model produced sound results for 99.4% of test cases and 94.0% of functions. Moreover, $\Downarrow_{SRA}$ produced more precise results than the manual models for 33.7% of test cases and 50.0% of functions. Although $\Downarrow_{SRA}$ produced unsound results for 0.6% of test cases and 6.0% of functions, we found soundness bugs in the manual models using 1.3% of test cases and 7.5% of functions. Our experiments showed that the automatic $\Downarrow_{SRA}$ model produced less unsound results than the manual models. We reported the manual models producing unsound results to SAFE developers with the concrete examples that were generated in the *Run* step, which revealed the bugs.

Table 1. Precision and soundness by functions in the benchmarks

Function	Precision and Soundness		
	Equal Precise	More Precise	Unsound
`Array`, `Array.prototype.join`, `Array.prototype.push`	15	5	0
`Date`, `Date.prototype.getTime`	0	4	0
`Error`	5	0	0
`Math.cos`, `Math.max`, `Math.pow`, `Math.sin`, `Math.sqrt`	11	0	0
`Math.random`	0	0	1
`Number.prototype.toString`	1	0	0
`String`, `String.prototype.substring`	4	0	0
Total	36	9	1
Proportion	78.3%	19.6%	2.2%

Table 2. Analysis time overhead by programs in the benchmarks

Program	Manual		$\Downarrow_{SRA}$				Increased
	Time(ms)	#Call	Time(ms)	#Call	#Max	#Total	Time Ratio
3d-morph.js	1,423	50	2,641	50	16	408	1.86
access-binary-trees.js	1,926,132	10	1,784,866	10	16	95	0.93
access-fannkuch.js	1,615	31	2,627	31	15	413	1.63
access-nbody.js	10,125	132	25,564	324	16	4,274	2.52
access-nsieve.js	1,019	6	1,126	6	16	54	1.10
bitops-nsieve-bits.js	282	1	343	1	2	2	1.22
math-cordic.js	574	2	662	2	2	4	1.15
math-partial-sums.js	1,613	99	4,703	99	16	916	2.92
math-spectral-norm.js	10,702	6	10,986	6	16	96	1.03
string-fasta.js	22,170	78	6,147	30	226	2,555	0.28
navier-stokes.js	4,662	20	5,104	20	2	40	1.09
richards.js	86,013	85	88,902	85	54	4,018	1.03
splay.js	259,073	423	217,863	422	56	11,492	0.84
Total	2,325,404	943	2,151,533	1,086	453	24,367	1.35

Answer to RQ3. The sampling strategy plays an important role in the performance of $\Downarrow_{SRA}$ especially for soundness. Our sampling strategy depends on two factors: (1) manually sampled sets via the heuristic H and (2) each-used or pair-wise selection for object samples. We used manually sampled sets for three abstract values: `UInt`, `NUInt`, and `OtherStr`. To sample concrete values from them, we used three methods: Base simply follows the guidelines described in Sect. 3.1, Random generates samples randomly, and Final denotes the heuristics determined by our trials and errors to reach the highest ratio of sound results. For object samples, we used three pair-wise options: HeapPair, ThisPair, and ArgPair. For various sampling configurations, Table 4 summarizes the ratio of sound

Table 3. Precision and soundness for the builtin functions

Object	#Test Case							#Function						
	Equal	SRA Pre.	Man. Uns.	Man. Pre.	SRA Uns.	Not Comp.	Total	Equal	SRA Pre.	Man. Uns.	Man. Pre.	SRA Uns.	Not Comp.	Total
`Array`	59	144	1	0	0	0	174	8	7	1	0	0	0	16
`Boolean`	37	2	3	0	0	0	42	1	0	3	0	0	0	4
`Date`	74	241	0	2	1	1	319	8	35	0	2	1	1	47
`Global`	7	1	0	0	0	0	8	1	1	0	0	0	0	2
`Math`	106	5	0	0	6	0	117	11	2	0	0	5	1	18
`Number`	41	71	0	3	0	1	116	1	6	0	0	0	0	8
`Object`	370	24	7	1	3	5	410	12	2	5	0	2	0	21
`String`	300	70	9	0	0	0	379	3	14	1	0	0	0	18
Total	994	528	20	6	10	7	1565	45	67	10	2	8	2	134
Proportion	63.5%	33.7%	1.3%	0.4%	0.6%	0.4%	100%	33.6%	50.0%	7.5%	1.5%	6.0%	1.5%	100%

Table 4. Soundness and sampling cost for the builtin functions

Sampling Configuration						Builtin Function		
Set Heuristic			Pair Option			Sound Result Ratio	#Ave.	#Max
`UInt`	`NUInt`	`Other`	HeapPair	ThisPair	ArgPair			
Base	Base	Base	F	F	F	85.0%	17.4	41
Random	Random	Random	F	F	F	84.9%	17.4	41
Final	Final	Final	F	F	F	92.1%	32.6	98
			F	F	T	93.5%	38.1	226
			F	T	F	95.0%	181.9	4312
			F	T	T	95.5%	276.8	11752
			T	F	F	96.2%	323.0	7220
			T	F	T	97.4%	397.5	16498
			T	T	F	99.2%	513.7	11988
			T	T	T	99.4%	677.6	16498

results, the average and maximum numbers of samples for the test cases used in RQ2.

The table shows that Base and Random produced sound results for 85.0% and 84.9% (the worst case among 10 repetitions) of the test cases, respectively. Even without any sophisticated heuristics or pair-wise options, $\Downarrow_{SRA}$ achieved a decent amount of sound results. Using more samples collected by trials and errors with Final and all three pair-wise options, $\Downarrow_{SRA}$ generated sound results for 99.4% of the test cases by observing more behaviors of opaque code.

5.3 Limitations

A fundamental limitation of our approach is that the $\Downarrow_{SRA}$ model may produce unsound results when the behavior of opaque code depends on values that $\Downarrow_{SRA}$ does not support via sampling. For example, if a sampling strategy calls the `Date` function without enough time intervals, it may not be able to sample different results. Similarly, if a sampling strategy does not use 4-wise combinations for property descriptor objects that have four components, it cannot produce all the possible combinations. However, at the same time, simply applying more complex strategies like 4-wise combinations may lead to an explosion of samples, which is not scalable.

Our experimental evaluation is inherently limited to a specific use case, which poses a threat to validity. While our approach itself is not dependent on a particular programming language or static analysis, the implementation of our approach depends on the abstract domains of SAFE. Although the experiments used well-known benchmark programs as analysis subjects, they may not be representative of all common uses of opaque functions in JavaScript applications.

6 Related Work

When a textual specification or documentation is available for opaque code, one can generate semantic models by mining them. Zhai *et al.* [26] showed that natural language processing can successfully generate models for Java library functions and used them in the context of taint analysis for Android applications. Researchers also created models automatically from types written in WebIDL or TypeScript declarations to detect Web API misuses [2,16].

Given an executable (e.g. binary) version of opaque code, researchers also synthesized code by sampling the inputs and outputs of the code [7,10,12,19]. Heule *et al.* [8] collected partial execution traces, which capture the effects of opaque code on user objects, followed by code synthesis to generate models from these traces. This approach works in the absence of any specification and has been demonstrated on array-manipulating builtins.

While all of these techniques are a-priori attempts to generate general-purpose models of opaque code, to be usable for other analyses, researchers also proposed to construct models during analysis. Madsen *et al.*'s approach [14] infers models of opaque functions by combining pointer analysis and use analysis, which collects expected properties and their types from given application code. Hirzel *et al.* [9] proposed an online pointer analysis for Java, which handles native code and reflection via dynamic execution that ours also utilizes. While both approaches use only a finite set of pointers as their abstract values, ignoring primitive values, our technique generalizes such online approaches to be usable for all kinds of values in a given language.

Opaque code does matter in other program analyses as well such as model checking and symbolic execution. Shafiei and Breugel [22] proposed *jpf-nhandler*, an extension of Java PathFinder (JPF), which transfers execution between JPF and the host JVM by on-the-fly code generation. It does not need concretization and abstraction since a JPF object represents a concrete value. In the context of symbolic execution, concolic testing [21] and other hybrid techniques that combine path solving with random testing [18] have been used to overcome the problems posed by opaque code, albeit sacrificing completeness [4].

Even when source code of external libraries is available, substituting external code with models rather than analyzing themselves is useful to reduce time and memory that an analysis takes. Palepu *et al.* [15] generated summaries by abstracting concrete data dependencies of library functions observed on a training execution to avoid heavy execution of instrumented code. In model checking, Tkachuk *et al.* [24,25] generated over-approximated summaries of environments by points-to and side-effect analyses and presented a static analysis tool OCSEGen [23]. Another tool Modgen [5] applies a program slicing technique to reduce complexities of library classes.

7 Conclusion

Creating semantic models for static analysis by hand is complex, time-consuming and error-prone. We present a Sample-Run-Abstract approach ($\Downarrow_{SRA}$) as a promising way to perform static analysis in the presence of opaque code using automated on-demand modeling. We show how $\Downarrow_{SRA}$ can be applied to the abstract domains of an existing JavaScript static analyzer, SAFE. For benchmark programs and 134 builtin functions with 1565 abstracted inputs, a tuned $\Downarrow_{SRA}$ produced more sound results than the manual models and concrete examples revealing bugs in the manual models. Although not all opaque code may be suitable for modeling with $\Downarrow_{SRA}$, it reduces the amount of hand-written models a static analyzer should provide. Future work on $\Downarrow_{SRA}$ could focus on orthogonal testing techniques that can be used for sampling complex objects, and practical optimizations, such as caching of computed model results.

Acknowledgment. This work has received funding from National Research Foundation of Korea (NRF) (Grants NRF-2017R1A2B3012020 and 2017M3C4A7068177).

References

1. ECMAScript Language Specification. Edition 5.1. http://www.ecma-international.org/publications/standards/Ecma-262.htm
2. Bae, S., Cho, H., Lim, I., Ryu, S.: SAFEWAPI: web API misuse detector for web applications. In: Proceedings of the 22nd ACM SIGSOFT International Symposium on Foundations of Software Engineering, pp. 507–517. ACM (2014)
3. Black, R.: Pragmatic Software Testing: Becoming an Effective and Efficient Test Professional. Wiley, Hoboken (2007)
4. Cadar, C., Sen, K.: Symbolic execution for software testing: three decades later. Commun. ACM **56**(2), 82–90 (2013)
5. Ceccarello, M., Tkachuk, O.: Automated generation of model classes for Java PathFinder. ACM SIGSOFT Softw. Eng. Notes **39**(1), 1–5 (2014)
6. Cousot, P., Cousot, R.: Abstract interpretation: a unified lattice model for static analysis of programs by construction or approximation of fixpoints. In: Proceedings of the 4th ACM SIGACT-SIGPLAN Symposium on Principles of Programming Languages, pp. 238–252. ACM (1977)
7. Gulwani, S., Harris, W.R., Singh, R.: Spreadsheet data manipulation using examples. Commun. ACM **55**(8), 97–105 (2012)

8. Heule, S., Sridharan, M., Chandra, S.: Mimic: computing models for opaque code. In: Proceedings of the 2015 10th Joint Meeting on Foundations of Software Engineering, pp. 710–720. ACM (2015)
9. Hirzel, M., Dincklage, D.V., Diwan, A., Hind, M.: Fast online pointer analysis. ACM Trans. Program. Lang. Syst. (TOPLAS) **29**(2), 11 (2007)
10. Jha, S., Gulwani, S., Seshia, S.A., Tiwari, A.: Oracle-guided component-based program synthesis. In: Proceedings of the 32nd ACM/IEEE International Conference on Software Engineering, vol. 1, pp. 215–224. ACM (2010)
11. Kuhn, D.R., Wallace, D.R., Gallo, A.M.: Software fault interactions and implications for software testing. IEEE Trans. Softw. Eng. **30**(6), 418–421 (2004)
12. Lau, T., Domingos, P., Weld, D.S.: Learning programs from traces using version space algebra. In: Proceedings of the 2nd International Conference on Knowledge Capture, pp. 36–43. ACM (2003)
13. Lee, H., Won, S., Jin, J., Cho, J., Ryu, S.: SAFE: formal specification and implementation of a scalable analysis framework for ECMAScript. In: FOOL 2012: 19th International Workshop on Foundations of Object-Oriented Languages, p. 96. Citeseer (2012)
14. Madsen, M., Livshits, B., Fanning, M.: Practical static analysis of JavaScript applications in the presence of frameworks and libraries. In: Proceedings of the 2013 9th Joint Meeting on Foundations of Software Engineering, pp. 499–509. ACM (2013)
15. Palepu, V.K., Xu, G., Jones, J.A.: Improving efficiency of dynamic analysis with dynamic dependence summaries. In: Proceedings of the 28th IEEE/ACM International Conference on Automated Software Engineering, pp. 59–69. IEEE Press (2013)
16. Park, J.: JavaScript API misuse detection by using TypeScript. In: Proceedings of the Companion Publication of the 13th International Conference on Modularity, pp. 11–12. ACM (2014)
17. Park, J., Ryou, Y., Park, J., Ryu, S.: Analysis of JavaScript web applications using SAFE 2.0. In: 2017 IEEE/ACM 39th International Conference on Software Engineering Companion (ICSE-C), pp. 59–62. IEEE (2017)
18. Păsăreanu, C.S., Rungta, N., Visser, W.: Symbolic execution with mixed concrete-symbolic solving. In: Proceedings of the 2011 International Symposium on Software Testing and Analysis, pp. 34–44. ACM (2011)
19. Qi, D., Sumner, W.N., Qin, F., Zheng, M., Zhang, X., Roychoudhury, A.: Modeling software execution environment. In: 2012 19th Working Conference on Reverse Engineering (WCRE), pp. 415–424. IEEE (2012)
20. Sen, K., Kalasapur, S., Brutch, T., Gibbs, S.: Jalangi: a selective record-replay and dynamic analysis framework for JavaScript. In: Proceedings of the 2013 9th Joint Meeting on Foundations of Software Engineering, pp. 488–498. ACM (2013)
21. Sen, K., Marinov, D., Agha, G.: CUTE: a concolic unit testing engine for C. In: ACM SIGSOFT Software Engineering Notes, vol. 30, pp. 263–272. ACM (2005)
22. Shafiei, N., Breugel, F.V.: Automatic handling of native methods in Java PathFinder. In: Proceedings of the 2014 International SPIN Symposium on Model Checking of Software, pp. 97–100. ACM (2014)
23. Tkachuk, O.: OCSEGen: open components and systems environment generator. In: Proceedings of the 2nd ACM SIGPLAN International Workshop on State Of the Art in Java Program Analysis, pp. 9–12. ACM (2013)
24. Tkachuk, O., Dwyer, M.B.: Adapting side effects analysis for modular program model checking, vol. 28. ACM (2003)

25. Tkachuk, O., Dwyer, M.B., Pasareanu, C.S.: Automated environment generation for software model checking. In: Proceedings of the 18th IEEE International Conference on Automated Software Engineering, pp. 116–127. IEEE (2003)
26. Zhai, J., Huang, J., Ma, S., Zhang, X., Tan, L., Zhao, J., Qin, F.: Automatic model generation from documentation for Java API functions. In: 2016 IEEE/ACM 38th International Conference on Software Engineering (ICSE), pp. 380–391. IEEE (2016)

SMT-Based Bounded Schedulability Analysis of the Clock Constraint Specification Language

Min Zhang[1], Fu Song[2(✉)], Frédéric Mallet[3], and Xiaohong Chen[1]

[1] Shanghai Key Laboratory of Trustworthy Computing, ECNU, Shanghai, China
[2] ShanghaiTech University, Shanghai, China
songfu@shanghaitech.edu.cn
[3] Université Cote d'Azur, CNRS, Inria, I3S, Nice, France

Abstract. The Clock Constraint Specification Language (CCSL) is a formalism for specifying logical-time constraints on events for the design of real-time embedded systems. A central verification problem of CCSL is to check whether events are schedulable under logical constraints. Although many efforts have been made addressing this problem, the problem is still open. In this paper, we show that the bounded scheduling problem is NP-complete and then propose an efficient SMT-based decision procedure which is sound and complete. Based on this decision procedure, we present a sound algorithm for the general scheduling problem. We implement our algorithm in a prototype tool and illustrate its utility in schedulability analysis in designing real-world systems and automatic proving of algebraic properties of CCSL constraints. Experimental results demonstrate its effectiveness and efficiency.

Keywords: SMT · CCSL · Schedulability · Logical time · Real-time system

1 Introduction

Model-based design has been widely used, particularly in the design of safety-critical real-time embedded systems. It has achieved industrial successes through languages such as SCADE [12], AADL [15] and UML MARTE [26]. For example, UML MARTE provides syntactic annotations to implement, when the context allows, classical real-time scheduling algorithms such as EDF (Earliest Deadline First). It also provides a domain-specific language–Clock Constraint Specification Language (CCSL) [3], to express the real-time behaviors of a system under development as logical constraints on system events, but independently of any physical time and classical real-time scheduling algorithms. CCSL has been used on several industrial scenarios such as vehicle systems [16] and cyber-physical systems [10, 22].

This work is supported by NSFC grants 61872146, 61532019 and 61761136011.

R. Hähnle and W. van der Aalst (Eds.): FASE 2019, LNCS 11424, pp. 61–78, 2019.
https://doi.org/10.1007/978-3-030-16722-6_4

Model-based design usually starts with coarse-grained logical models that are progressively refined into more concrete ones until the final code deployment. It is well-known that the earlier one can detect and fix bugs in the refinement process, the better [7]. Therefore, it is critical to provide efficient methods and tools to check safety, liveness and schedulability on the logical models and not only on the definite deployed system. This has motivated a large body of works on verifying whether events are schedulable under a set of constraints expressed in CCSL [11,21,28,33,35,36,38], though its decidability is still open. These works first transform CCSL constraints into other formal representations such as transition systems [21], Promela [35], Büchi automata [36], timed automata [33], rewriting logics [38], instant relations [28], or timed-interval logics [11], and then apply existing tools. However, their approaches usually suffer from the state explosion problem. Moreover, most of these works only deal with the so-called safe subset of CCSL and the other ones only provide semi-algorithms. In our earlier work [39], we proposed an SMT-based verification approach to CCSL and demonstrated several applications of the approach to finding schedules, verifying temporal properties, proving constraint entailment, and analyzing the validity of system traces. Based on the approach, we implemented an efficient tool for verifying LTL properties of CCSL [40].

In this work we are focused on the scheduling problem of CCSL, a fundamental problem to which the aforementioned verification problems of CCSL can be reduced. We first prove that the *bounded* scheduling problem of CCSL with fixed bounds is NP-complete. To our knowledge, this is the first result regarding the complexity of the scheduling problem with CCSL. Then, we propose a decision procedure for the bounded scheduling problem with a given bound. The decision procedure is based on the transformation of CCSL into SMT formulas [39]. Our decision procedure is sound, complete, and efficient in practice. Based on this decision procedure, we turn to the general (i.e. unbounded) scheduling problem and present a binary-search based algorithm. Our algorithm is sound, i.e., if it proves either schedulable or unschedulable, then the result is conclusive. We implemented our algorithms in a prototype tool. The tool was used to analyze a real-world interlocking system in a rail transit system. Using the proposed approach, we also prove some algebraic properties of CCSL. The experimental results demonstrate the effectiveness and efficiency of the SMT-based approach.

The rest of this paper is organised as follows: Section 2 introduces CCSL. Section 3 defines the (bounded) scheduling problem of CCSL and shows that the bounded case is NP-complete. Section 4 presents an SMT-based decision procedure for the bounded scheduling problem and a sound algorithm for the general scheduling problem. Section 5 shows a case study and experimental results. Section 6 discusses related work, and Section 7 concludes the paper.

2 The Clock Constraint Specification Language

2.1 Logical Clock, History and Schedule

In CCSL, clocks are used to model occurrences of events, where a clock ticks when the corresponding event occurs. For instance, a clock may represent an event that is dispatch of a task, communications between tasks or acquisition of a shared resource by a task. Constraints over clocks are used to specify causal and temporal relations between system events. No global physical time is presumed for the clocks and their constraints. This feature allows CCSL to define a polychronous specification of a system at a logical level.

Definition 1 (Logical clock). *A* (logical) clock *c is an infinite sequence of ticks $(c^i)_{i\in\mathbb{N}^+}$ with each c^i being* tick *or* idle*, where $\mathbb{N}^+$ denotes the set of all the non-zero natural numbers.*

The value of c^i denotes whether an event associated with c occurs or not at step i. If c^i is *tick*, then the event occurs, otherwise not. In particular, we denote by $\mathbb{1}$ a global reference logical clock that always ticks at each step.

Definition 2 (Schedule). *Given a set C of clocks, a* schedule *of C is a total function $\delta : \mathbb{N}^+ \to 2^C$ such that $\forall i \in \mathbb{N}^+$, $\delta(i) = \{c \in C \mid c^i = tick\}$ and $\delta(i) \neq \emptyset$.*

Intuitively, a schedule δ defines a partial order between the ticks of the clocks. $\delta(i)$ is a subset of C such that $c \in \delta(i)$ iff c ticks at step i. The condition $\delta(i) \neq \emptyset$ expresses that step i cannot be empty. This forbids stuttering steps in schedules. As one can add or remove finite number of empty steps without effect on schedulability, we exclude them from schedules for succinctness.

A clock can memorize the number of ticks that it has made. We use *history* to represent the memorization.

Definition 3 (History). *Given a schedule δ for a set C of clocks, a* history *of δ is a function $\chi_\delta : C \times \mathbb{N}^+ \to \mathbb{N}$ such that for each $c \in C$ and $i \in \mathbb{N}^+$:*

$$\chi_\delta(c,i) = \begin{cases} 0, & \text{if } i = 1; \\ \chi_\delta(c, i-1), & \text{if } i > 1 \wedge c \notin \delta(i-1); \\ \chi_\delta(c, i-1) + 1, & \text{if } i > 1 \wedge c \in \delta(i-1). \end{cases}$$

$\chi_\delta(c,i)$ represents the number of the ticks that the clock c has made immediately before step i. (Note that the tick of c at step i is excluded in $\chi_\delta(c,i)$.) For simplicity, we may write χ for χ_δ if it is clear from the context.

2.2 Syntax and Semantics of CCSL

CCSL consists of 11 kinds of constraints, 4 of them are binary relations for specifying the *precedence*, *causality*, *subclocking*, and *exclusion* relations between clocks, and the others are used to define clocks from existing ones. Clocks defined by constraints may correspond to system events or are just introduced as auxiliary clocks without corresponding to any events.

Table 1. Semantics of CCSL with respect to schedules

	ϕ	$\delta \models \phi$
Precedence	$c_1\ [b]\!\prec c_2$	$\forall n \in \mathbb{N}^+ . \chi(c_2, n) - \chi(c_1, n) = b \Rightarrow c_2 \notin \delta(n)$
Causality	$c_1 \preccurlyeq c_2$	$\forall n \in \mathbb{N}^+ . \chi(c_1, n) \geq \chi(c_2, n)$
Subclock	$c_1 \subseteq c_2$	$\forall n \in \mathbb{N}^+ . c_1 \in \delta(n) \Rightarrow c_2 \in \delta(n)$
Exclusion	$c_1 \# c_2$	$\forall n \in \mathbb{N}^+ . c_1 \not\in \delta(n) \vee c_2 \not\in \delta(n)$
Union	$c_1 \triangleq c_2 + c_3$	$\forall n \in \mathbb{N}^+ . c_1 \in \delta(n) \Leftrightarrow c_2 \in \delta(n) \vee c_3 \in \delta(n)$
Intersection	$c_1 \triangleq c_2 * c_3$	$\forall n \in \mathbb{N}^+ . c_1 \in \delta(n) \Leftrightarrow c_2 \in \delta(n) \wedge c_3 \in \delta(n)$
Infimum	$c_1 \triangleq c_2 \wedge c_3$	$\forall n \in \mathbb{N}^+ . \chi(c_1, n) = \max(\chi(c_2, n), \chi(c_3, n))$
Supremum	$c_1 \triangleq c_2 \vee c_3$	$\forall n \in \mathbb{N}^+ . \chi(c_1, n) = \min(\chi(c_2, n), \chi(c_3, n))$
Periodicity	$c_1 \triangleq c_2 \propto p$	$\forall n \in \mathbb{N}^+ . c_1 \in \delta(n) \Leftrightarrow (c_2 \in \delta(n) \wedge \exists m \in \mathbb{N}^+ . \chi(c_2, n) = m \times p - 1)$
Filtering	$c_1 \triangleq c_2 \blacktriangledown w$	$\forall n \in \mathbb{N}^+ . c_1 \in \delta(n) \Leftrightarrow (c_2 \in \delta(n) \wedge w[n])$
DelayFor	$c_1 \triangleq c_2\ \$\ d\ on\ c_3$	$\forall n \in \mathbb{N}^+ . c_1 \in \delta(n) \Leftrightarrow (c_3 \in \delta(n) \wedge \exists m \in \mathbb{N}^+ . (c_2 \in \delta(m) \wedge \chi(c_3, n) - \chi(c_3, m) = d))$

Definition 4 (Syntax). *A* CCSL *constraint ϕ is defined by the following form:*

Precedence:	$c_1\ [b]\!\prec c_2$	| *Causality:*	$c_1 \preccurlyeq c_2$
Subclock:	$c_1 \subseteq c_2$	| *Exclusion:*	$c_1 \# c_2$
Union:	$c_1 \triangleq c_2 + c_3$	| *Intersection:*	$c_1 \triangleq c_2 * c_3$
Infimum:	$c_1 \triangleq c_2 \wedge c_3$	| *Supremum:*	$c_1 \triangleq c_2 \vee c_3$
Periodicity:	$c_1 \triangleq c_2 \propto p$	| *Filtering:*	$c_1 \triangleq c_2 \blacktriangledown w$
DelayFor:	$c_1 \triangleq c_2\ \$\ d\ on\ c_3$		

where $b \geq 0$, $d \geq 0$ and $p > 0$ are natural numbers, c_1, c_2, c_3 are logical clocks and w is a (possibly infinite) word over $\{0, 1\}$ expressed as a (ω-)regular expression.

For simplifying presentation, we denote by $c_1 \prec c_2$ the constraint $c_1\ [0]\!\prec c_2$, and $c_1 \triangleq c_2\ \$\ d$ the constraint $c_1 \triangleq c_2\ \$\ d\ on\ c_3$ such that $c_2 = c_3$.

The semantics of CCSL constraints is defined over schedules. Given a CCSL constraint ϕ and a schedule δ, the satisfiability relation $\delta \models \phi$ (i.e., δ satisfies constraint ϕ) is defined in Table 1.

The precedence constraint $c_1 \prec c_2$ (i.e., $c_1\ [0]\!\prec c_2$) expresses that the clock c_1 precedes the clock c_2. Suppose there is an unbounded buffer with two operations *fetch* and *store*, which respectively fetch data from and store data into the buffer. Fetch is only allowed when the buffer is nonempty. If the buffer is initially empty, store operation must strictly precede fetch operation. This behavior can be expressed by the constraint: *store* $\prec$ *fetch*. Likewise, the precedence constraint can be used to represent reentrant tasks by replacing *store* with *start* and *fetch* with *finish*.

The general precedence constraint $c_1\ [b]\!\prec c_2$ that can specify the differences b between the number of occurrences of two clocks before the precedence takes effect. Hence, it is able to express more complicated relations. For instance, if the buffer initially is nonempty, fetch operations can be performed prior to any store operation. Figure 1 shows such a scenario where 4 elements are initially presented in the buffer. This behavior can be represented as: *store* $[4] \prec$ *fetch*.

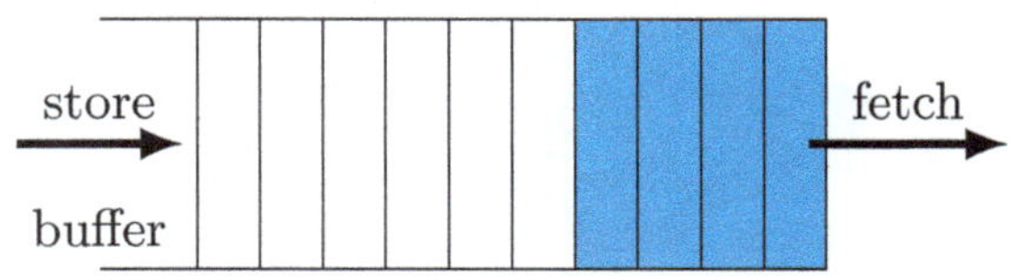

Fig. 1. Example for *store* $[4] \prec$ *fetch*

The causality, subclock and exclusion constraints are straightforward. The causality constraint $c_1 \preccurlyeq c_2$ specifies that the occurrence of c_2 must be caused by the occurrence of c_1, namely at any moment c_1 must have ticked at least as many times as c_2 has. The subclock constraint $c_1 \subseteq c_2$ expresses that c_1 occurs at some step only if c_2 occur at this step as well. The exclusion constraint $c_1 \# c_2$ specifies that two clocks c_1 and c_2 are exclusive, i.e., they cannot occur simultaneously at the same step.

The union and intersection constraints are used to define clocks. $c_1 \triangleq c_2 + c_3$ defines a clock c_1 such that c_1 ticks iff c_2 or c_3 ticks. Similarly, $c_1 \triangleq c_2 * c_3$ defines a clock c_1 such that c_1 ticks iff both c_2 and c_3 tick. The infimum (resp. supremum) constraint $c_1 \triangleq c_2 \wedge c_3$ (resp. $c_1 \triangleq c_2 \vee c_3$) is used to define a clock c_1 that is the slowest (resp. fastest) clock that is faster (resp. slower) than both c_2 and c_3. These two constraints are useful for expressing delay requirements between two events. Remark that clocks c_1 defined by constraints may correspond to system events, otherwise are auxiliary clocks. In the former case, these constraints can be seen as constraints specifying relations between clocks c_1, c_2 and c_3.

The periodicity constraint $c_1 \triangleq c_2 \propto p$ defines a clock c_1 such that c_1 has to be performed once every p occurrences of clock c_2. It is worth mentioning that the periodicity constraint defined in such a way is relative because of the logical nature of CCSL clocks. That is, clock c_1 is relatively periodic with respect to clock c_2. CCSL does not assume the existence of a global reference clock, most relations are defined relative to other clocks. These notions extend the equivalent behaviors which are usually defined relative to physical time. If c_2 represents a sensor that measures physical time, then c_1 becomes physically periodic.

The filtering constraint $c_1 \triangleq c_2 \blacktriangledown w$ is used to define a clock c_1 which can be seen as snapshots of the clock c_2 at some steps according to the (ω-)regular expression w. For instance, $c_1 \triangleq c_2 \blacktriangledown (01)^\omega$ expresses that c_1 simulates c_2 at every even step. It defines a logically periodic behavior of c_1 with respect to c_2.

The delayFor constraint $c_1 \triangleq c_2 \$ d$ (i.e., $c_1 \triangleq c_2 \$ d \text{ on } c_2$) defines a new clock c_1 that is delayed by the clock c_2 with d steps. The general form $c_1 \triangleq c_2 \$ d \text{ on } c_3$ defines a new clock c_1 that is delayed by c_2 with d times of the ticks of c_3. c_1 can be seen as a *sampled* clock of c_2 on the basis of c_3. For instance, $c_1 \triangleq c_2 \$ 1 \text{ on } c_3$, denotes that whenever c_2 ticks at least once between two successive ticks of c_3 at steps m and n, c_1 must tick at step n.

3 Scheduling Problem of CCSL

3.1 Schedulability

Given a set Φ of CCSL constraints, a schedule δ satisfies Φ, denoted by $\delta \models \Phi$, iff $\delta \models \phi$ for all constraints $\phi \in \Phi$.

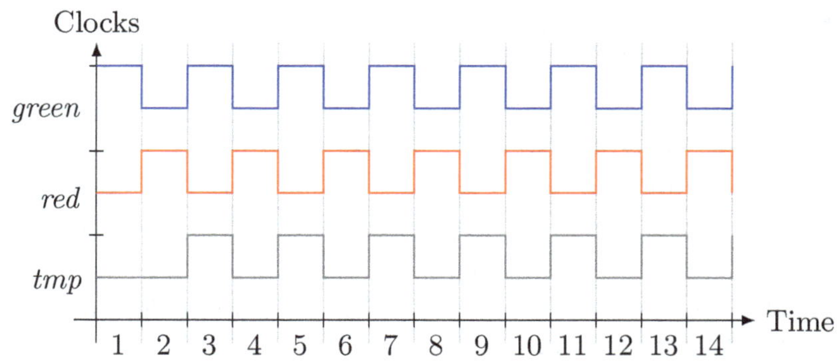

Fig. 2. The unique schedule that satisfies the three constraints in the example

Definition 5 (Logical time scheduling problem). *Given a set Φ of* CCSL *constraints,* the (logical time) scheduling problem *of* CCSL *is to determine whether there exists a schedule δ such that $\delta \models \Phi$.*

We illustrate the scheduling problem by a simple example. Consider alternative flickering between the green and red light using CCSL. We assume that green light starts first. The timing requirements can be formalized by the following three constraints:

$$green \prec red, \qquad tmp \triangleq green \,\$\, 1, \qquad red \prec tmp,$$

where *green* and *red* are clocks respectively representing whether the green (resp. red) light is turned on, the clock *tmp* is an auxiliary clock used to help specify the constraints on clocks.

There exists exactly one schedule satisfying the three constraints, as shown in Fig. 2. In this schedule, the clock *tmp* has the same behavior as *green* from step 2, while the clock *red* has the opposite behavior to *green*. Namely, *red* and *green* operates in an alternative manner. For simplicity, we also write $green \sim red$ to denote the *alternation* relation of the two clocks.

Although one may be able to find one or more schedules for some simple constraints, to our knowledge, there is no generally applicable decision procedure solving the scheduling problem of full CCSL. There are two main challenges. First, schedules are essentially *infinite*, i.e., defined on all the natural numbers. Second, the *precedence* is *stateful*, i.e., it depends on the history, and there is no upper bound on how far in the history one must go back. It may then require an infinite memory to store the history. As a first step to tackle this challenging problem, in this work, we first consider the *bounded* scheduling problem.

3.2 Bounded Scheduling Problem

Given a bound $k \in \mathbb{N}^+$, let $\sigma : \mathbb{N}^+_{\leq k} \to 2^C$ be a function. σ is an *k-bounded schedule* of a set Φ of CCSL constraints, denoted by $\sigma \models_k \Phi$, iff there exists a schedule δ such that $\delta(i) = \sigma(i)$ for every $i \in \mathbb{N}^+_{\leq k}$ and $\delta \models \Phi$ from step 1 up to k, where $\mathbb{N}^+_{\leq k} := \{1, \cdots, k\}$.

Definition 6 (Bounded scheduling problem). *The* bounded scheduling problem *is to determine, for a given set Φ of* CCSL *constraints and a bound k, whether there is an k-bounded schedule σ for Φ, i.e., $\sigma \models_k \Phi$.*

Theorem 1 (Sufficient condition of unschedulability). *If a set Φ of constraints has no k-bounded schedule for some $k \in \mathbb{N}^+$, then Φ is unschedulable.*

The proof is straightforward by contradiction.

It is easy to see that the bounded scheduling problem is decidable, as there are finitely many potential k-bounded schedules, i.e., $(2^{|C|}-1)^k$, where $|C|$ denotes the number of clocks. Furthermore, the satisfiability problem of Boolean formulas can be reduced to the bounded scheduling problem in polynomial time.

Theorem 2. *The k-bounded scheduling problem of* CCSL *is* NP*-complete, even if $k = 1$.*

Proof. The NP upper bound can be proved easily based on the facts that the number of possible k-bounded schedules is finite and the universal quantification $\forall n \in \mathbb{N}^+_{\leq k}$ can be eliminated by enumerating all the possible values in $\mathbb{N}^+_{\leq k}$.

We prove the NP-hardness by a reduction from the satisfiability problem of Boolean formulas which is known NP-complete. Consider the Boolean formula $\phi = \bigwedge_{i=1}^m (l_i^1 \vee l_i^2 \vee l_i^3)$, where $m \in \mathbb{N}^+$ and l_i^j for $j \in \{1,2,3\}$ is either a Boolean variable x or its negation $\neg x$. Let $\mathsf{Var}(\phi)$ denote the set of Boolean variables appearing in ϕ. We construct a set of CCSL constraints Φ as follows.

For each $x \in \mathsf{Var}(\phi)$, we have two clocks x^+ and x^-. Let $\mathsf{enc}(x) = x^+$ and $\mathsf{enc}(\neg x) = x^-$. Each clause $l_i^1 \vee l_i^2 \vee l_i^3$ in ϕ is encoded as the CCSL constraint $c_i \triangleq \mathsf{enc}(l_i^1)+\mathsf{enc}(l_i^2)+\mathsf{enc}(l_i^3)$, denoted by ψ_i. Note that $c_i \triangleq \mathsf{enc}(l_i^1)+\mathsf{enc}(l_i^2)+\mathsf{enc}(l_i^3)$ can be transformed into CCSL constraints by introducing one auxiliary clock c, i.e., $\{c_i \triangleq \mathsf{enc}(l_i^1) + \mathsf{enc}(l_i^2) + \mathsf{enc}(l_i^3)\} \equiv \{c_i \triangleq \mathsf{enc}(l_i^1) + c, c \triangleq \mathsf{enc}(l_i^2) + \mathsf{enc}(l_i^3)\}$.

Let $\mathsf{enc}(\phi)$ denote the following set of CCSL constraints

$$\{\mathbf{1} \triangleq *_{i=1}^m c_i, \psi_1, ..., \psi_m, x^+ \# x^-, \mathbf{1} \triangleq x^+ + x^- \mid x \in \mathsf{Var}(\phi)\}$$

where $x^+ \# x^-$ and $\mathbf{1} \triangleq x^+ + x^-$ enforce that either x^+ or x^- ticks at each step, but not both. This encodes that either x is true or $\neg x$ is true. Note that $\tau \triangleq *_{i=1}^m c_i$ is a shorthand of $\tau \triangleq c_1 * \cdots * c_m$, and can also be expressed in CCSL constraints by introducing polynomial number of auxiliary clocks. For instance, $\{c \triangleq c_1 * c_2 * c_3\} \equiv \{c \triangleq c_1 * c', c' \triangleq c_2 * c_3\}$. We can show that ϕ is satisfiable iff $\mathsf{enc}(\phi)$ is 1-bounded schedulable. The satisfiability problem of Boolean formulas is NP-complete, we get that the 1-bounded scheduling problem of CCSL is NP-hard. The k-bounded scheduling problem for $k > 1$ immediately follows by repeating the ticks of clocks at the first step. □

Theorem 2 indicates the time complexity of the bounded scheduling problem. Thus, we need to find practical solutions that are algorithmically efficient for it. In the next section, we propose an SMT-based decision procedure for the bounded scheduling problem and a sound algorithm for the scheduling problem. Thanks to advances in state-of-the-art SMT solvers such as Z3 [25], our approach is usually efficient in practice.

4 Decision Procedure for the Scheduling Problem

4.1 Transformation from CCSL into SMT

Let us fix a set of CCSL constraints Φ defined over a set C of clocks. Each clock $c \in C$ is interpreted as a predicate $t_c : \mathbb{N}^+ \rightarrow \mathsf{Bool}$ such that for all $i \in \mathbb{N}^+$, $t_c(i)$ is true iff the clock c ticks at i, where Bool denotes Boolean sort. A schedule δ of Φ is encoded as a set of predicates $\mathcal{T}_C = \{t_c | c \in C\}$ such that the following condition holds: for all $t_c \in \mathcal{T}_C$,

$$\forall i \in \mathbb{N}^+ . t_c(i) \Leftrightarrow c \in \delta(i).$$

Recalling that schedules forbid stuttering steps, this condition is enforced by restricting the predicates t_c in $\mathcal{T}_C$ to satisfy the following condition:

$$\forall i \in \mathbb{N}^+ . \vee_{c \in C} \, t_c(i) \tag{F1}$$

Formula F1 specifies that at each step i at least one clock c ticks, i.e., $t_c(i)$ holds.

For each clock $c \in C$, we introduce an auxiliary function $h_c : \mathbb{N}^+ \rightarrow \mathbb{N}$ to encode its history. For each $i \in \mathbb{N}^+$,

$$h_c(i) := \begin{cases} 0, & \text{if } i = 1; \\ h_c(i-1), & \text{if } i > 1 \wedge \neg t_c(i-1); \\ h_c(i-1)+1, & \text{if } i > 1 \wedge t_c(i-1). \end{cases} \tag{F2}$$

Intuitively, $h_c(i)$ is equivalent to $\chi(c, i)$ for each $i \in \mathbb{N}^+$. The set of all the auxiliary functions is denoted by $\mathcal{H}_C$.

By replacing each occurrence of clock c in $\delta(n)$ (resp. $c \notin \delta(n)$) with $t_c(n)$ (resp. $\neg t_c(n)$) and $\chi(c, n)$ with $h_c(n)$ in the definition of each CCSL constraint, each CCSL constraint ϕ can be encoded as an SMT formula $[\![\phi]\!]$.

We use $[\![\Phi]\!]$ to denote the conjunction of Formulas F1, F2 and the SMT encodings of CCSL constraints in Φ. Formally,

$$[\![\Phi]\!] := \text{F1} \wedge \text{F2} \wedge (\wedge_{\phi \in \Phi} [\![\phi]\!]).$$

Finding a schedule for Φ amounts to finding a solution, i.e., definitions of predicates in $\mathcal{T}_C$, which satisfies $[\![\Phi]\!]$.

Proposition 1. *Φ has a schedule iff $[\![\Phi]\!]$ is satisfiable.*

The scheduling problem of Φ is transformed into the satisfiability problem of the formula $[\![\Phi]\!]$. However, according to the SMT-LIB standard [4], $[\![\Phi]\!]$ belongs to the logic of UFLIA (formulas with Uninterpreted Functions and Linear Integer Arithmetic), whose satisfiability problem is undecidable in general. Nevertheless, the SMT encoding is still useful to solve the bounded scheduling problem, which we will present in the next subsection.

4.2 Decision Procedure for the Bounded Scheduling Problem

For k-bounded scheduling problem, it suffices to consider schedules $\delta : \mathbb{N}^{+}_{\leq k} \rightarrow 2^{C}$. Moreover, the quantifiers in $[\![\Phi]\!]$ can be eliminated once the bound k is fixed. Hence, we can resort to state-of-the-art SMT solvers. Formally, let $[\![\Phi]\!]_k$ be the formula obtained from $[\![\Phi]\!] = F1 \wedge F2 \wedge (\bigwedge_{\phi \in \Phi} [\![\phi]\!])$ by

- restricting the domain of predicates $t_c \in \mathcal{T}_C$ and functions $h_c \in \mathcal{H}_C$ to $\mathbb{N}^{+}_{\leq k}$;
- replacing quantifications $\forall n \in \mathbb{N}^{+}$ and $\exists m \in \mathbb{N}^{+}$ with $\forall n \in \mathbb{N}^{+}_{\leq k}$ and $\exists m \in \mathbb{N}^{+}_{\leq k}$ in $(\bigwedge_{\phi \in \Phi} [\![\phi]\!])$.

Proposition 2. *Φ is k-bounded schedulable iff $[\![\Phi]\!]_k$ is satisfiable. Moreover, if $[\![\Phi]\!]_k$ is satisfiable, then $[\![\Phi]\!]_{k'}$ is satisfiable for all $k' \leq k$.*

4.3 A Sound Algorithm for the Scheduling Problem

According to Theorem 1, Propositions 1 and 2, (1) if $[\![\Phi]\!]$ is satisfiable, then Φ is schedulable, and (2) if $[\![\Phi]\!]_k$ for some $k \in \mathbb{N}^{+}$ is unsatisfiable, then Φ is unschedulable. We can deduce a sound algorithm for checking the general scheduling problem. However, randomly choosing a bound k and checking whether or not $[\![\Phi]\!]_k$ is unsatisfiable may be inefficient, as the k-bounded scheduling problem is NP-hard (cf. Theorem 2), and larger bound k may result in time out, but smaller bound k may result in that $[\![\Phi]\!]_k$ is satisfiable. Indeed, if we consider the maximal bound B, then the random approach may have to call SMT solving $\mathbf{O}(B)$ times. Alternatively, we propose a binary-search based approach as shown in Algorithm 1 for a given maximal bound B, which invokes SMT solving at most $\mathbf{O}(|\log_2 B|)$ times.

Algorithm 1: A sound algorithm for the scheduling problem

```
Input  : a set of constraints Φ, a timeout threshold T, a maximal bound B
Output: {SAT, UNSAT, Timeout} × ℕ+
result1 ← SMTSolver([[Φ]], T);
if result1 = SAT then                                   /* Schedulable */
    return (SAT, 0)
l ← 0; u ← B;
while l ≤ u do                                          /* Binary search */
    k ← ⌊(l+u)/2⌋;
    result2 ← SMTSolver([[Φ]]_k, T);
    if result2 = SAT then l ← k + 1;                    /* Upper half */
    else                                                /* Lower half */
        u ← k − 1;
        if result1 = UNSAT ∨ result2 = UNSAT then
            result1 ← UNSAT;
if result2 ≠ SAT then k ← k − 1;
return (result1, k);
```

Given a set Φ of constraints in CCSL, a timeout threshold T and a maximal bound B, Algorithm 1 first invokes an `SMTSolver` to decide whether $[\![\Phi]\!]$ is satisfiable or not within T time. If $[\![\Phi]\!]$ is satisfiable, then Algorithm 1 returns (`SAT,0`), meaning that Φ is schedulable. Otherwise, it binary searches a bound $k \leq B$ such that $[\![\Phi]\!]_k$ is satisfiable while $[\![\Phi]\!]_{k+1}$ (if $k+1 \leq B$) is unsatisfiable or cannot be verified in time T.

Theorem 3. *Algorithm 1 has the following three properties:*

1. *If it returns* (`SAT,0`)*, then Φ is schedulable.*
2. *If it returns* (`UNSAT,k`)*, then Φ is unschedulable. If $k \neq 0$, then Φ has k-bounded schedulable, otherwise does not have any bounded schedulable.*
3. *If it returns* (`Timeout,k`)*, then Φ is k-bounded schedulable if $k \neq 0$, otherwise no bounded schedule is found for Φ.*

5 Case Study and Performance Evaluation

We implemented our approach in a prototype tool with Z3 [25] as its underlying SMT solver. We conduct a case study on expressing requirements of an interlocking system in CCSL constraints and analyzing its schedulability. Then, we prove 12 algebraic properties of CCSL constraints using the tool. Finally, we evaluate the performance of the tool using 9 sets of CCSL constraints.

5.1 Schedulability of an Interlocking System

The interlocking system is a subsystem of a rail transit system. It is used to prevent trains from collisions and derailments when they are moving under the control of signal lights. As shown in Fig. 3, the interlocking system monitors the occupancy status of the individual track section, and sends signals to inform drivers whether they are allowed to enter the route or not. The railway tracks are divided into sections. Each section is associated with a track circuit for detecting whether it is occupied by a train or not. Signal lights are placed between track sections. They can be red and green to indicate proceeding and stopping, respectively.

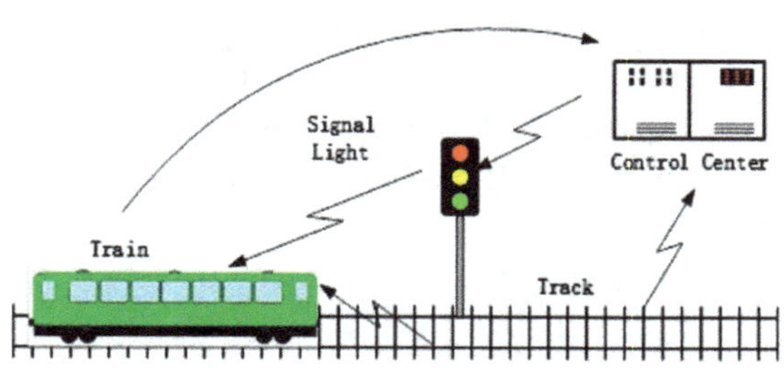

Fig. 3. Interlocking system

The mechanism and operation procedure of the interlocking system are summarized as follows.

1. To enter a track, a train first sends a request to the control center.
2. On receiving the request, the control center sends an inquiry to the track circuit to detect the status of the track.

Table 2. CCSL constraints of the interlocking system

$\texttt{request} \prec \texttt{inquiry}$	$\texttt{responseOfTrack} \triangleq \texttt{checkSucc} + \texttt{checkFail}$
$\texttt{checkFail} \prec \texttt{redPulse}$	$\texttt{responseOfTrain} \triangleq \texttt{enter} + \texttt{wait}$
$\texttt{redPulse} \preccurlyeq \texttt{showRed}$	$\texttt{inquiry} \prec \texttt{responseOfTrack}$
$\texttt{showRed} \prec \texttt{wait}$	$\texttt{getOccupied} \sim \texttt{getUnoccupied}$
$\texttt{checkSucc} \prec \texttt{greenPulse}$	$\texttt{getOccupied} \# \texttt{getUnoccupied}$
$\texttt{greenPulse} \preccurlyeq \texttt{showGreen}$	$\texttt{request} \sim \texttt{responseOfTrain}$
$\texttt{showGreen} \prec \texttt{enter}$	$\texttt{inquiry} - \texttt{responseOfTrack} \leq 40$
$\texttt{enter} \prec \texttt{leave}$	$\texttt{greenPulse} - \texttt{showGreen} \leq 30$
$\texttt{enter} \subseteq \texttt{getOccupied}$	$\texttt{redPulse} - \texttt{showRed} \leq 30$
$\texttt{leave} \subseteq \texttt{getUnoccupied}$	$\texttt{request} - \texttt{responseOfTrain} \leq 50$
$\texttt{getOccupied} \sim \texttt{tmp}_1$	$\texttt{checkFail} - \texttt{showRed} \leq 40$
$\texttt{getUnoccupied} \sim \texttt{tmp}_1$	$\texttt{checkSucc} - \texttt{showGreen} \leq 40$
$\texttt{checkFail} \subseteq \texttt{tmp}_1$	$\texttt{getUnoccupied} \prec \texttt{tmp}_2$
$\texttt{tmp}_2 \prec \texttt{getOccupied}$	$\texttt{checkSucc} \subseteq \texttt{tmp}_2$

3. If the track is occupied, it sends *checkFail* to the control center, and otherwise *checkSucc*.
4. On receiving the message *checkFail* (*resp. checkSucc*), the control center sends a red (*resp.* green) signal pulse to the signal light.
5. The signal light turns red (*resp.* green) on receiving the red (*resp.* green) signal pulse.
6. The train will enter after seeing the light is green, and the track becomes occupied. In case of the red light, the train must stop and wait.
7. The track becomes unoccupied after the train leaves. If the train is waiting, it must send a request again after some time.

There are time constraints on the above operations. For instance, the control center needs to get a response from the track circuit within 30 ms after sending an inquiry to it. The train must make decision within 50 ms after it sends a request to the control center. The light should turn to the corresponding color within 30 ms after it receives a pulse. After the track becomes occupied (*resp.* unoccupied), the light must turn red (*resp.* green) within 40 ms.

Table 2 shows the main logical constraints on the operations in the system and their timing constraints. We use some non-standard constraint expressions for the sake of compactness. Constraint $a - b \leq n$ denotes that b must tick within n steps after a ticks. It equals the set of the following three constraints:

$$a \prec b, \quad t \triangleq a \,\$\, n \ \mathit{on}\ \mathbf{1}, \quad b \preccurlyeq t.$$

Note that in this example the unit of time is millisecond (ms). Thus, there is an implicit assumption in the constraints that every tick of a logic clock means the elapse of one millisecond.

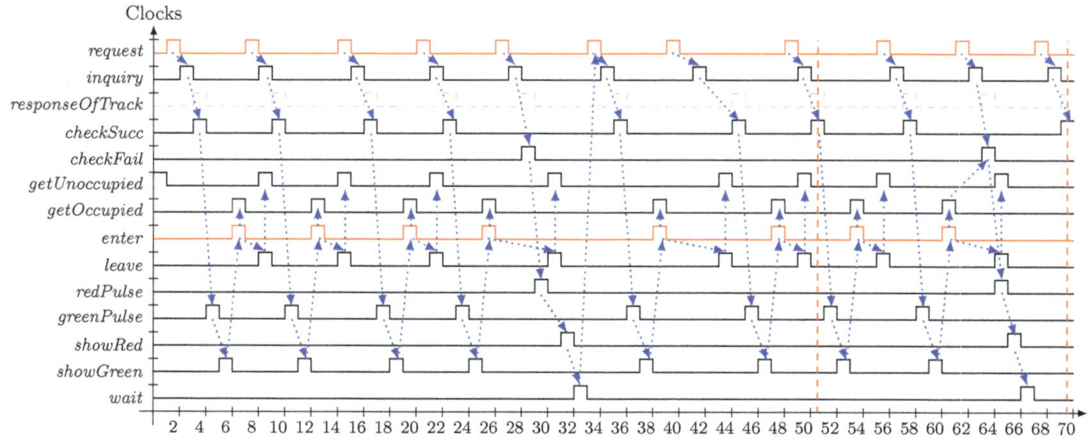

Fig. 4. A bounded schedule for the CCSL constraints in the case study

Most constraints in Table 2 are straightforward, except the six constraints marked with waved underlines. The first three constraints specify that `checkFail` only can occur between the occurrences of `getUnoccupied` and `getOccupied`. The others specify the following two requirements:

1. `checkSucc` only can occur after `getUnoccupied` and before `getOccupied`;
2. `getUnoccupied` precedes `getOccupied`.

Given these constraints, our tool found a bounded schedule as depicted in Fig. 4. From step 1 to step 7, one complete process is finished. Initially, the track gets unoccupied. At step 2, a request is made, which causes subsequent operations to occur from step 3 to step 7. At step 29, a fail case occurs because another train enters (step 26) but has not left (step 31). The train that made the request has to wait (step 33).

If we extend the bounded schedule by infinitely repeating the behaviors of all the clocks between step 51 and 69 from step 70, we obtain an infinite schedule. The extended schedule satisfies all the constraints, and thus it is a witness of the schedulability of designed mechanism for the interlocking system.

In this paper, we are only concerned with the schedulability of the constraints in the example. Some other kinds of temporal properties also need to verify. For instance, we must guarantee that whenever a train requests to enter the station, it must eventually enter. We also need to verify the system is deadlock-free. Such temporal properties can be verified by LTL model checking of CCSL constraints using SMT technique [40]. We omit it because it is beyond the scope of this paper.

5.2 Automatic Proof of CCSL Algebraic Properties

Using the proposed approach, we can also prove automatically algebraic properties of CCSL constraints such as the commutativity of exclusion and transitivity of causality. Algebraic properties of CCSL constraints can be represented as $\Phi \Rightarrow \phi$, where Φ is a set of CCSL constraints and ϕ is a constraint derived from Φ. Proving $\Phi \Rightarrow \phi$ is valid equals proving the unsatisfiability of $[\![\Phi]\!] \wedge \neg[\![\phi]\!]$, which can be solved by Algorithm 1.

Table 3. Proved algebraic properties of CCSL constraints

Algebraic property	Definition
Commutativity of exclusion	$c1 \# c2 \Rightarrow c2 \# c1$
Transitivity of causality	$c_1 \preccurlyeq c_2\ ,\ c_2 \preccurlyeq c_3 \Rightarrow c_1 \preccurlyeq c_3$
Antisymmetry of causality	$c_1 \preccurlyeq c_2\ ,\ c_2 \preccurlyeq c_1 \Rightarrow c_1 = c_2$
Fastness of infimum	$c_1 \triangleq c_2 \wedge c_3 \Rightarrow c_1 \preccurlyeq c_2, c_1 \preccurlyeq c_3$
Slowestness of infimum	$c_1 \triangleq c_2 \wedge c_3, c_4 \preccurlyeq c_2, c_4 \preccurlyeq c_3 \Rightarrow c_4 \preccurlyeq c_1$
Slowness of supremum	$c_1 \triangleq c_2 \vee c_3 \Rightarrow c_2 \preccurlyeq c_1, c_3 \preccurlyeq c_1$
Fastestness of supremum	$c_1 \triangleq c_2 \vee c_3, c_2 \preccurlyeq c_4, c_3 \preccurlyeq c_4 \Rightarrow c_1 \preccurlyeq c_4$
Causality of subclock	$c_1 \subseteq c_2 \Rightarrow c_2 \preccurlyeq c_1$
Causality of union	$c_1 \triangleq c_2 + c_3 \Rightarrow c_1 \preccurlyeq c_2, c_1 \preccurlyeq c_3$
Causality of intersection	$c_1 \triangleq c_2 * c_3 \Rightarrow c_2 \preccurlyeq c_1, c_3 \preccurlyeq c_1$
Subclocking of sampling	$c_1 \triangleq c_2 \lightning c_3 \Rightarrow c_1 \subseteq c_3$
Subclocking of union	$c_1 \triangleq c_2 + c_3 \Rightarrow c_2 \subseteq c_1, c_3 \subseteq c_1$
Subclocking of intersection	$c_1 \triangleq c_2 * c_3 \Rightarrow c_1 \subseteq c_2, c_1 \subseteq c_3$

Let us consider the proof of the slowestness of infimum as an example. The slowestness of infimum means that an infimum constraint $c_1 \triangleq c_2 \wedge c_3$ defines the slowest clock c_1 among those that are faster than both c_2 and c_3.

Proposition 3 (Slowestness of infimum). *Given two clocks c_2, c_3, let $c_1 \triangleq c_2 \wedge c_3$ and c_4 be an arbitrary clock such that $c_4 \preccurlyeq c_2$ and $c_4 \preccurlyeq c_3$, then $c_4 \preccurlyeq c_1$.*

This is proved by transforming CCSL constraints into the following SMT formula according the SMT encoding method:

$$[\![c_1 \triangleq c_2 \wedge c_3]\!] \wedge [\![c_4 \preccurlyeq c_2]\!] \wedge [\![c_4 \preccurlyeq c_3]\!] \wedge \neg[\![c_4 \preccurlyeq c_1]\!].$$

Algorithm 1 returns (`UNSAT`, 0), which means that the formula is proved unsatisfiable. The proposition is proved.

Table 3 lists the algebraic properties that have been successfully proved in our approach. Algebraic properties are useful to help understand the relation among CCSL constraints. Using them we can also verify whether some CCSL constraints are redundant or inconsistent for a given set of CCSL constraints.

5.3 Performance Evaluation

To evaluate the performance our tool, we collected 9 sets of CCSL constraints from the literature and real-world applications, and analyzed their schedulability using our tool. Under different time thresholds, we calculate the maximal bounds under which the constraints are schedulable.

Table 4 shows all the experimental results including the corresponding execution time. All the experiments were conducted on a Win 10 running on an i7 CPU with 2.70 GHz and 16 GB memory. The numbers followed by asterisks

Table 4. Experimental results of bounded schedulability analysis

CS	Clks.	Cons.	THD: 10 s		THD: 20 s		THD: 30 s		THD: 40 s	
			BD	TM	BD	TM	BD	TM	BD	TM
CS1	3	3	8	0.06	8	0.06	8	0.06	8	0.06
CS2	3	4	2*	0.06	2*	0.06	2*	0.06	2*	0.06
CS3	8	9	48	6.20	59	15.88	70	28.72	75	39.82
CS4	8	7	70	7.12	70	7.12	70	7.12	70	7.12
CS5	9	9	80	8.29	90	19.95	110	26.81	111	39.84
CS6	10	6	95	9.40	113	14.26	113	14.26	113	14.26
CS7	12	9	69	8.80	76	19.42	89	27.69	95	40.00
CS8	17	20	16	0.81	16	0.81	16*	27.36	16*	27.36
CS9	27	51	30	9.94	41	17.19	45	29.78	45	29.78

Remarks: CS: constraint set, Cons: the number of constraints, Clks: the number of clocks, THD: timeout threshold, TM: Time (second), BD: upper bound.

are the maximal bounds such that the corresponding constraints are bounded schedulable, but unschedulable in the next step. It is interesting to observe from Table 4 that time cost is loosely related to size (the number of clocks and constraints), thanks to efficient search strategies of SMT solvers. This is in striking contrasts to automata-based [29,35] and the rewriting-based approaches [38], whose scalability suffers from both the numbers of clocks and constraints.

6 Related Work

CCSL is directly derived from the family of synchronous languages, such as Lustre [9], Esterel [6] and Signal [5], and its the scheduling problem of CCSL is akin to what synchronous languages call clock calculus. The main differences are: CCSL is a specification language, while others are programming languages; and CCSL partially describes what is expected to happen in a declarative way and does not give a direct operational deterministic description of what must happen. Furthermore, CCSL only deals with pure clocks while the others deal with signals and extract the clocks when needed.

The Esterel compiler [31] applies a constructive approach to decide when a signal must occur (compute its clock) and what its value should be. This requires a detection of *causality cycles*, or intra-cycle data dependencies, which are also naturally addressed by our approach. However, the Esterel compiler compiles an imperative program into a Boolean circuit, or equivalently a finite state machine. Consequently, it cannot deal with CCSL unbounded schedules.

The clock calculus in Signal attempts to detect whether the specification is endochronous [30], in which case it can generate some efficient code. This analysis is mainly based on the subclock relationship that also exists in CCSL. In CCSL, we consider the problem whether there is at least one possible schedule or not.

In Lustre and its extensions, clocks are regarded as abstract types [13] and the clock calculus computes the relative rates of clocks while rejecting the program when computing the rates is not possible. In most cases, the compiler attempts to build bounded buffers and to ensure that the functional determinism can be preserved with a finite memory. In our case, we do not seek to reach a finite representation, as in the first specification steps this is not a primary goal for the designers. Indeed, this might lead to an over-specification of the problem.

Classical real-time scheduling problem [32] usually relies on task models, arrival patterns and constraints (e.g., precedence, resources) to propose algorithms for the scheduling problem with analytical results [19] or heuristics depending on the specific model (e.g., priorities, preemptive). Other solutions, based on timed automata [1,2,17] or timed Petri nets [8,18], propose a general framework for describing all the relevant aspects without assuming a specific task model. CCSL offers an alternative method based on logical time. It is believed that logical time and multiform time bases offer some flexibility to unify functional requirements and performance constraints. We rely on CCSL and we claim that after encoding a task model in CCSL, finding a schedule for the CCSL model also gives a schedule for the encoded task model [24].

There have been many efforts made towards the scheduling problem of CCSL, though no conclusion is drawn on its decidability. TimeSquare [14] is a simulation tool for CCSL which can produce a possible schedule for a given set of CCSL, up to a given user-defined bound. It also supports different simulation strategies for producing desired execution traces. Some earlier work [20] define the notion of *safe* CCSL specifications that can be encoded with a finite-state machine. The scheduling problem is decidable for safe specifications, as one can merely enumerate all the (finite) solutions. A semi-algorithm can build the finite representation when the specification is safe [21]. In [37], Zhang et al. proposed a state-based approach and a sufficient condition to decide whether safe and unsafe specifications accept a so-called *periodic schedule* [39]. This allows to build a finite solution for unsafe specifications, while there may also exist infinite solutions. Xu et al. proposed a notion of *divergence* of CCSL to study the schedulability of CCSL, and proved that a set of CCSL constraints is schedulable if all the constraints are divergent [34]. They resorted to the theorem prover PVS [27] to assist the divergence proof.

The scheduling problem of CCSL constraints in this work resorts to SMT solving to deal with the bounded and unbounded schedules. Using SMT solving has two advantages: (1) it is usually efficient in practice, and (2) it can deal with unsafe CCSL constraints such as infimum and supremum [21].

Some basic algebraic properties on CCSL relations have been established manually before [23] but we provide here an automatic framework to do so.

7 Conclusion and Future Work

In this work, we proved that the bounded scheduling problem of CCSL is NP-complete, and proposed an SMT-based decision procedure for the bounded scheduling problem. The procedure is sound and complete. The experimental results also show its efficiency in practice. Based on this decision procedure, we devised a sound algorithm for the general scheduling problem. We evaluated the effectiveness of the proposed approach on an interlocking system. We also showed our approach can be used to prove algebraic properties of CCSL constraints.

Our approach to the bounded scheduling problem of CCSL makes us one step closer to tackling the general (i.e. unbounded) scheduling problem. As the case study demonstrates, one may find an infinite schedule by extending a bounded one such that the extended infinite schedule still satisfies the constraints. This observation inspires future work to investigate mechanisms of finding such bounded schedules, hopefully with SMT solvers by extending our algorithm. In our earlier work [37], we proposed a similar approach to search for periodical schedules in bounded steps. In that approach, CCSL constraints are transformed into finite state machine and consequently suffers from the state explosion problem. We believe our SMT-based approach can be extended to their work while still avoiding state explosion. We leave it to future work.

References

1. Abdeddaïm, Y., Asarin, E., Maler, O.: Scheduling with timed automata. Theor. Comput. Sci. **354**(2), 272–300 (2006)
2. Amnell, T., Fersman, E., Mokrushin, L., Pettersson, P., Yi, W.: TIMES: a tool for schedulability analysis and code generation of real-time systems. In: Larsen, K.G., Niebert, P. (eds.) FORMATS 2003. LNCS, vol. 2791, pp. 60–72. Springer, Heidelberg (2004). https://doi.org/10.1007/978-3-540-40903-8_6
3. André, C., Mallet, F., de Simone, R.: Modeling time(s). In: Engels, G., Opdyke, B., Schmidt, D.C., Weil, F. (eds.) MODELS 2007. LNCS, vol. 4735, pp. 559–573. Springer, Heidelberg (2007). https://doi.org/10.1007/978-3-540-75209-7_38
4. Barrett, C., Fontaine, P., Tinelli, C.: The SMT-LIB standard (2016)
5. Benveniste, A., Guernic, P.L., Jacquemot, C.: Synchronous programming with events and relations: the SIGNAL language and its semantics. Sci. Comput. Program. **16**(2), 103–149 (1991)
6. Berry, G., Gonthier, G.: The esterel synchronous programming language: design, semantics, implementation. Sci. Comput. Program. **19**(2), 87–152 (1992)
7. Boehm, B., Basili, V.R.: Software defect reduction top 10 list. Computer **34**(1), 135–137 (2001)
8. Bucci, G., Fedeli, A., Sassoli, L., Vicario, E.: Modeling flexible real time systems with preemptive time petri nets. In: Proceedings of the 15th ECRTS, Porto, Portugal, pp. 279–286. IEEE (2003)
9. Caspi, P., Pilaud, D., Halbwachs, N., Plaice, J.: LUSTRE: a declarative language for programming synchronous systems. In: Proceedings of 14th POPL, Tucson, USA, pp. 178–188. ACM Press (1987)
10. Chen, X., Yin, L., Yu, Y., Jin, Z.: Transforming timing requirements into CCSL constraints to verify cyber-physical systems. In: Duan, Z., Ong, L. (eds.) ICFEM 2017. LNCS, vol. 10610, pp. 54–70. Springer, Cham (2017). https://doi.org/10.1007/978-3-319-68690-5_4
11. Chen, Y., Chen, Y., Madelaine, E.: Timed-pNets: a communication behavioural semantic model for distributed systems. Front. Comput. Sci. **9**(1), 87–110 (2015)

12. Colaço, J., Pagano, B., Pouzet, M.: SCADE 6: a formal language for embedded critical software development. In: Proceedings of the 11th TASE, Sophia Antipolis, France, pp. 1–11. IEEE (2017)
13. Colaço, J.-L., Pouzet, M.: Clocks as first class abstract types. In: Alur, R., Lee, I. (eds.) EMSOFT 2003. LNCS, vol. 2855, pp. 134–155. Springer, Heidelberg (2003). https://doi.org/10.1007/978-3-540-45212-6_10
14. Deantoni, J., Mallet, F.: TimeSquare: treat your models with logical time. In: Proceedings of the 50th TOOLS, Prague, Czech Republic, pp. 34–41. IEEE (2012)
15. Feiler, P.H., Gluch, D.P.: Model-based engineering with AADL - an introduction to the SAE architecture analysis and design language. SEI, Addison-Wesley (2012)
16. Kang, E., Schobbens, P.: Schedulability analysis support for automotive systems: from requirement to implementation. In: Proceedings of the 29th SAC, Gyeongju, Korea, pp. 1080–1085. ACM (2014)
17. Krčál, P., Yi, W.: Decidable and undecidable problems in schedulability analysis using timed automata. In: Jensen, K., Podelski, A. (eds.) TACAS 2004. LNCS, vol. 2988, pp. 236–250. Springer, Heidelberg (2004). https://doi.org/10.1007/978-3-540-24730-2_20
18. Lime, D., Roux, O.: A translation based method for the timed analysis of scheduling extended time petri nets. In: Proceedings of the 25th RTSS, pp. 187–196. IEEE (2004)
19. Liu, C.L., Layland, J.W.: Scheduling algorithms for multiprogramming in a hard-real-time environment. J. ACM **20**(1), 46–61 (1973)
20. Mallet, F., Millo, J.-V.: Boundness issues in CCSL specifications. In: Groves, L., Sun, J. (eds.) ICFEM 2013. LNCS, vol. 8144, pp. 20–35. Springer, Heidelberg (2013). https://doi.org/10.1007/978-3-642-41202-8_3
21. Mallet, F., de Simone, R.: Correctness issues on MARTE/CCSL constraints. Sci. Comput. Program. **106**, 78–92 (2015)
22. Mallet, F., Villar, E., Herrera, F.: MARTE for CPS and CPSoS. In: Nakajima, S., Talpin, J.-P., Toyoshima, M., Yu, H. (eds.) Cyber-Physical System Design from an Architecture Analysis Viewpoint, pp. 81–108. Springer, Singapore (2017). https://doi.org/10.1007/978-981-10-4436-6_4
23. Mallet, F., Millo, J., de Simone, R.: Safe CCSL specifications and marked graphs. In: Proceedings of the 11th MEMOCODE, Portland, OR, USA, pp. 157–166. IEEE (2013)
24. Mallet, F., Zhang, M.: Work-in-progress: from logical time scheduling to real-time scheduling. In: Proceedings of the 39th RTSS, Nashville, USA, pp. 143–146. IEEE (2018)
25. de Moura, L., Bjørner, N.: Z3: an efficient SMT solver. In: Ramakrishnan, C.R., Rehof, J. (eds.) TACAS 2008. LNCS, vol. 4963, pp. 337–340. Springer, Heidelberg (2008). https://doi.org/10.1007/978-3-540-78800-3_24
26. OMG: UML profile for MARTE: modeling and analysis of real-time embedded systems (2015)
27. Owre, S., Rushby, J.M., Shankar, N.: PVS: a prototype verification system. In: Kapur, D. (ed.) CADE 1992. LNCS, vol. 607, pp. 748–752. Springer, Heidelberg (1992). https://doi.org/10.1007/3-540-55602-8_217
28. Peters, J., Przigoda, N., Wille, R., Drechsler, R.: Clocks vs. instants relations: verifying CCSL time constraints in UML/MARTE models. In: Proceedings of the 14th MEMOCODE, Kanpur, India, pp. 78–84. IEEE (2016)
29. Peters, J., Wille, R., Przigoda, N., Kühne, U., Drechsler, R.: A generic representation of CCSL time constraints for UML/MARTE models. In: Proceedings of the 52nd DAC, pp. 122:1–122:6. ACM (2015)

30. Potop-Butucaru, D., Caillaud, B., Benveniste, A.: Concurrency in synchronous systems. Formal Methods Syst. Des. **28**(2), 111–130 (2006)
31. Potop-Butucaru, D., Edwards, S.A., Berry, G.: Compiling Esterel. Springer, Boston (2007). https://doi.org/10.1007/978-0-387-70628-3
32. Sha, L., et al.: Real time scheduling theory: a historical perspective. Real-Time Syst. **28**(2–3), 101–155 (2004)
33. Suryadevara, J., Seceleanu, C., Mallet, F., Pettersson, P.: Verifying MARTE/CCSL mode behaviors using UPPAAL. In: Hierons, R.M., Merayo, M.G., Bravetti, M. (eds.) SEFM 2013. LNCS, vol. 8137, pp. 1–15. Springer, Heidelberg (2013). https://doi.org/10.1007/978-3-642-40561-7_1
34. Xu, Q., de Simone, R., DeAntoni, J.: Divergence detection for CCSL specification via clock causality chain. In: Fränzle, M., Kapur, D., Zhan, N. (eds.) SETTA 2016. LNCS, vol. 9984, pp. 18–37. Springer, Cham (2016). https://doi.org/10.1007/978-3-319-47677-3_2
35. Yin, L., Mallet, F., Liu, J.: Verification of MARTE/CCSL time requirements in Promela/SPIN. In: Proceedings of the 16th ICECCS, USA, pp. 65–74. IEEE (2011)
36. Yu, H., Talpin, J., Besnard, L., et al.: Polychronous controller synthesis from MARTE/CCSL timing specifications. In: Proceedings of the 9th MEMOCODE, Cambridge, UK, pp. 21–30. IEEE (2011)
37. Zhang, M., Dai, F., Mallet, F.: Periodic scheduling for MARTE/CCSL: theory and practice. Sci. Comput. Program. **154**, 42–60 (2018)
38. Zhang, M., Mallet, F.: An executable semantics of clock constraint specification language and its applications. In: Artho, C., Ölveczky, P.C. (eds.) FTSCS 2015. CCIS, vol. 596, pp. 37–51. Springer, Cham (2016). https://doi.org/10.1007/978-3-319-29510-7_2
39. Zhang, M., Mallet, F., Zhu, H.: An SMT-based approach to the formal analysis of MARTE/CCSL. In: Ogata, K., Lawford, M., Liu, S. (eds.) ICFEM 2016. LNCS, vol. 10009, pp. 433–449. Springer, Cham (2016). https://doi.org/10.1007/978-3-319-47846-3_27
40. Zhang, M., Ying, Y.: Towards SMT-based LTL model checking of clock constraint specification language for real-time and embedded systems. In: Proceedings of the 18th LCTES, Barcelona, Spain, pp. 61–70. ACM (2017)

A Hybrid Dynamic Logic for Event/Data-Based Systems

Rolf Hennicker[1], Alexandre Madeira[2,3(✉)], and Alexander Knapp[4]

[1] Ludwig-Maximilians-Universität München, Munich, Germany
hennicke@pst.ifi.lmu.de
[2] CIDMA, University of Aveiro, Aveiro, Portugal
madeira@ua.pt
[3] QuantaLab, University of Minho, Braga, Portugal
[4] Universität Augsburg, Augsburg, Germany
knapp@informatik.uni-augsburg.de

Abstract. We propose $\mathcal{E}^{\downarrow}$-logic as a formal foundation for the specification and development of event-based systems with local data states. The logic is intended to cover a broad range of abstraction levels from abstract requirements specifications up to constructive specifications. Our logic uses diamond and box modalities over structured actions adopted from dynamic logic. Atomic actions are pairs $e /\!\!/ \psi$ where e is an event and ψ a state transition predicate capturing the allowed reactions to the event. To write concrete specifications of recursive process structures we integrate (control) state variables and binders of hybrid logic. The semantic interpretation relies on event/data transition systems; specification refinement is defined by model class inclusion. For the presentation of constructive specifications we propose operational event/data specifications allowing for familiar, diagrammatic representations by state transition graphs. We show that $\mathcal{E}^{\downarrow}$-logic is powerful enough to characterise the semantics of an operational specification by a single $\mathcal{E}^{\downarrow}$-sentence. Thus the whole development process can rely on $\mathcal{E}^{\downarrow}$-logic and its semantics as a common basis. This includes also a variety of implementation constructors to support, among others, event refinement and parallel composition.

1 Introduction

Event-based systems are an important kind of software systems which are open to the environment to react to certain events. A crucial characteristics of such systems is that not any event can (or should) be expected at any time. Hence the control flow of the system is significant and should be modelled by appropriate means. On the other hand components administrate data which may change upon the occurrence of an event. Thus also the specification of admissible data changes caused by events plays a major role.

A. Madeira—Supported by ERDF through COMPETE 2020 and by National Funds through FCT with POCI-01-0145-FEDER-016692 and UID/MAT/04106/2019, in a contract foreseen in nos. 4–6 of art. 23 of the DL 57/2016, changed by DL 57/2017.

R. Hähnle and W. van der Aalst (Eds.): FASE 2019, LNCS 11424, pp. 79–97, 2019.
https://doi.org/10.1007/978-3-030-16722-6_5

There is quite a lot of literature on modelling and specification of event-based systems. Many approaches, often underpinned by graphical notations, provide formalisms aiming at being constructive enough to suggest particular designs or implementations, like e.g., Event-B [1,7], symbolic transition systems [17], and UML behavioural and protocol state machines [12,16]. On the other hand, there are logical formalisms to express desired properties of event-based systems. Among them are temporal logics integrating state and event-based styles [4], and various kinds of modal logics involving data, like first-order dynamic logic [10] or the modal μ-calculus with data and time [9]. The gap between logics and constructive specification is usually filled by checking whether *the* model of a constructive specification satisfies certain logical formulae.

In this paper we are interested in investigating a logic which is capable to express properties of event/data-based systems on various abstraction levels in a common formalism. For this purpose we follow ideas of [15], but there data states, effects of events on them and constructive operational specifications (see below) were not considered. The advantage of an expressive logic is that we can split the transition from system requirements to system implementation into a series of gradual refinement steps which are more easy to understand, to verify, and to adjust when certain aspects of the system are to be changed or when a product line of similar products has to be developed.

To that end we propose $\mathcal{E}^{\downarrow}$-logic, a dynamic logic enriched with features of hybrid logic. The dynamic part uses diamond and box modalities over structured actions. Atomic actions are of the form $e/\!\!/\psi$ with e an event and ψ a state transition predicate specifying the admissible effects of e on the data. Using sequential composition, union, and iteration we obtain complex actions that, in connection with the modalities, can be used to specify required and forbidden behaviour. In particular, if E is a finite set of events, though data is infinite we are able to capture all reachable states of the system and to express safety and liveness properties. But $\mathcal{E}^{\downarrow}$-logic is also powerful enough to specify concrete, recursive process structures by integrating state variables and binders from hybrid logic [6] with the subtle difference that our state variables are used to denote control states only. We show that the dynamic part of the logic is bisimulation invariant while the hybrid part, due to the ability to bind names to states, is not.

An axiomatic specification $Sp = (\Sigma, Ax)$ in $\mathcal{E}^{\downarrow}$ is given by an event/data signature $\Sigma = (E, A)$, with a set E of events and a set A of attributes to model local data states, and a set of $\mathcal{E}^{\downarrow}$-sentences Ax, called axioms, expressing requirements. For the semantic interpretation we use event/data transition systems (edts). Their states are reachable configurations $\gamma = (c, \omega)$ where c is a control state, recording the current state of execution, and ω is a local data state, i.e., a valuation of the attributes. Transitions between configurations are labelled by events. The semantics of a specification Sp is "loose" in the sense that it consists of *all* edts satisfying the axioms of the specification. Such structures are called models of Sp. Loose semantics allows us to define a simple refinement notion: Sp_1 refines to Sp_2 if the model class of Sp_2 is included in the model class of Sp_1. We may also say that Sp_2 is an implementation of Sp_1.

Our refinement process starts typically with axiomatic specifications whose axioms involve only the dynamic part of the logic. Hybrid features will successively be added in refinements when specifying more concrete behaviours, like loops. Aiming at a concrete design, the use of an axiomatic specification style may, however, become cumbersome since we have to state explicitly also all negative cases, what the system should not do. For a convenient presentation of constructive specifications we propose operational event/data specifications, which are a kind of symbolic transition systems equipped again with a model class semantics in terms of edts. We will show that $\mathcal{E}^{\downarrow}$-logic, by use of the hybrid binder, is powerful enough to characterise the semantics of an operational specification. Therefore we have not really left $\mathcal{E}^{\downarrow}$-logic when refining axiomatic by operational specifications. Moreover, since several constructive notations in the literature, including (essential parts of) Event-B, symbolic transition systems, and UML protocol state machines, can be expressed as operational specifications, $\mathcal{E}^{\downarrow}$-logic provides a logical umbrella under which event/data-based systems can be developed.

In order to consider more complex refinements we take up an idea of Sannella and Tarlecki [18,19] who have proposed the notion of constructor implementation. This is a generic notion applicable to specification formalisms based on signatures and semantic structures for signatures. As both are available in the context of $\mathcal{E}^{\downarrow}$-logic, we complement our approach by introducing a couple of constructors, among them event refinement and parallel composition. For the latter we provide a useful refinement criterion relying on a relationship between syntactic and semantic parallel composition. The logic and the use of the implementation constructors will be illustrated by a running example.

Hereafter, in Sect. 2, we introduce syntax and semantics of $\mathcal{E}^{\downarrow}$-logic. In Sect. 3, we consider axiomatic as well as operational specifications and demonstrate the expressiveness of $\mathcal{E}^{\downarrow}$-logic. Refinement of both types of specifications using several implementation constructors is considered in Sect. 4. Section 5 provides some concluding remarks. Proofs of theorems and facts can be found in [11].

2 A Hybrid Dynamic Logic for Event/Data Systems

We propose the logic $\mathcal{E}^{\downarrow}$ to specify and reason about event/data-based systems. $\mathcal{E}^{\downarrow}$-logic is an extension of the hybrid dynamic logic considered in [15] by taking into account changing data. Therefore, we first summarise our underlying notions used for the treatment of data. We then introduce the syntax and semantics of $\mathcal{E}^{\downarrow}$ with its hybrid and dynamic logic features applied to events and data.

2.1 Data States

We assume given a universe $\mathcal{D}$ of *data values*. A *data signature* is given by a set A of *attributes*. An A-*data state* ω is a function $\omega : A \to \mathcal{D}$. We denote by $\Omega(A)$ the set of all A-data states. For any data signature A, we assume given a set $\Phi(A)$ of *state predicates* to be interpreted over single A-data states, and a set

$\Psi(A)$ of *transition predicates* to be interpreted over pairs of pre- and post-A-data states. The concrete syntax of state and transition predicates is of no particular importance for the following. For an attribute $a \in A$, a state predicate may be $a > 0$; and a transition predicate e.g. $a' = a + 1$, where a refers to the value of attribute a in the pre-data state and a' to its value in the post-data state. Still, both types of predicates are assumed to contain true and to be closed under negation (written $\neg$) and disjunction (written $\vee$); as usual, we will then also use false, $\wedge$, etc. Furthermore, we assume for each $A_0 \subseteq A$ a transition predicate $\mathrm{id}_{A_0} \in \Psi(A)$ expressing that the values of attributes in A_0 are the same in pre- and post-A-data states.

We write $\omega \models^{\mathcal{D}}_{A} \varphi$ if $\varphi \in \Phi(A)$ is satisfied in data state ω; and $(\omega_1, \omega_2) \models^{\mathcal{D}}_{A} \psi$ if $\psi \in \Psi(A)$ is satisfied in the pre-data state ω_1 and post-data state ω_2. In particular, $(\omega_1, \omega_2) \models^{\mathcal{D}}_{A} \mathrm{id}_{A_0}$ if, and only if, $\omega_1(a_0) = \omega_2(a_0)$ for all $a_0 \in A_0$.

2.2 $\mathcal{E}^{\downarrow}$-Logic

Definition 1. *An* event/data signature *(*ed signature*, for short)* $\Sigma = (E, A)$ *consists of a finite set of* events E *and a data signature* A*. We write* $E(\Sigma)$ *for* E *and* $A(\Sigma)$ *for* A*. We also write* $\Omega(\Sigma)$ *for* $\Omega(A(\Sigma))$*,* $\Phi(\Sigma)$ *for* $\Phi(A(\Sigma))$*, and* $\Psi(\Sigma)$ *for* $\Psi(A(\Sigma))$*. The class of ed signatures is denoted by* $Sig^{\mathcal{E}^{\downarrow}}$*.*

Any ed signature Σ determines a class of semantic structures, the *event/data transition systems* which are reachable transition systems with sets of initial states and events as labels on transitions. The states are pairs $\gamma = (c, \omega)$, called *configurations*, where c is a *control state* recording the current execution state and ω is an $A(\Sigma)$-data state; we write $c(\gamma)$ for c and $\omega(\gamma)$ for ω.

Definition 2. *A* Σ-event/data transition system *(*Σ-edts*, for short)* $M = (\Gamma, R, \Gamma_0)$ *over an ed signature* Σ *consists of a set of* configurations $\Gamma \subseteq C \times \Omega(\Sigma)$ *for a set of* control states C*; a family of* transition relations $R = (R_e \subseteq \Gamma \times \Gamma)_{e \in E(\Sigma)}$*; and a non-empty set of* initial configurations $\Gamma_0 \subseteq \{c_0\} \times \Omega_0$ *for an* initial control state $c_0 \in C$ *and a set of* initial data states $\Omega_0 \subseteq \Omega(\Sigma)$ *such that* Γ *is* reachable *via* R*, i.e., for all* $\gamma \in \Gamma$ *there are* $\gamma_0 \in \Gamma_0$*,* $n \geq 0$*,* $e_1, \ldots, e_n \in E(\Sigma)$*, and* $(\gamma_i, \gamma_{i+1}) \in R_{e_{i+1}}$ *for all* $0 \leq i < n$ *with* $\gamma_n = \gamma$*. We write* $\Gamma(M)$ *for* Γ*,* $C(M)$ *for* C*,* $R(M)$ *for* R*,* $c_0(M)$ *for* c_0*,* $\Omega_0(M)$ *for* Ω_0*, and* $\Gamma_0(M)$ *for* Γ_0*. The class of* Σ*-edts is denoted by* $Edts^{\mathcal{E}^{\downarrow}}(\Sigma)$*.*

Atomic actions are given by expressions of the form $e/\!\!/\psi$ with e an event and ψ a state transition predicate. The intuition is that the occurrence of the event e causes a state transition in accordance with ψ, i.e., the pre- and post-data states satisfy ψ, and ψ specifies the possible effects of e. Following the ideas of dynamic logic we also use complex, structured actions formed over atomic actions by union, sequential composition and iteration. All kinds of actions over an ed signature Σ are called Σ-*event/data actions* (Σ-*ed actions*, for short). The set $\Lambda(\Sigma)$ of Σ-ed actions is defined by the grammar

$$\lambda ::= e/\!\!/\psi \mid \lambda_1 + \lambda_2 \mid \lambda_1 ; \lambda_2 \mid \lambda^*$$

where $e \in E(\Sigma)$ and $\psi \in \Psi(\Sigma)$. We use the following shorthand notations for actions: For a subset $F = \{e_1, \dots, e_k\} \subseteq E(\Sigma)$, we use the notation F to denote the complex action $e_1 /\!\!/ \text{true} + \dots + e_k /\!\!/ \text{true}$ and $-F$ to denote the action $E(\Sigma) \setminus F$. For the action $E(\Sigma)$ we will write $\boldsymbol{E}$. For $e \in E(\Sigma)$, we use the notation e to denote the action $e /\!\!/ \text{true}$ and $-e$ to denote the action $\boldsymbol{E} \setminus \{e\}$. Hence, if $E(\Sigma) = \{e_1, \dots, e_n\}$ and $e_i \in E(\Sigma)$, the action $-e_i$ stands for $e_1 /\!\!/ \text{true} + \dots + e_{i-1} /\!\!/ \text{true} + e_{i+1} /\!\!/ \text{true} + \dots + e_n /\!\!/ \text{true}$.

The actions $\Lambda(\Sigma)$ are *interpreted* over a Σ-edts M as the family of relations $(R(M)_\lambda \subseteq \Gamma(M) \times \Gamma(M))_{\lambda \in \Lambda(\Sigma)}$ defined by

- $R(M)_{e/\!\!/\psi} = \{(\gamma, \gamma') \in R(M)_e \mid (\omega(\gamma), \omega(\gamma')) \models^{\mathcal{D}}_{A(\Sigma)} \psi\}$,
- $R(M)_{\lambda_1 + \lambda_2} = R(M)_{\lambda_1} \cup R(M)_{\lambda_2}$, i.e., union of relations,
- $R(M)_{\lambda_1 ; \lambda_2} = R(M)_{\lambda_1} ; R(M)_{\lambda_2}$, i.e., sequential composition of relations,
- $R(M)_{\lambda^*} = (R(M)_\lambda)^*$, i.e., reflexive-transitive closure of relations.

To define the event/data formulae of $\mathcal{E}^\downarrow$ we assume given a countably infinite set X of control state variables which are used in formulae to denote the control part of a configuration. They can be bound by the binder operator $\downarrow x$ and accessed by the jump operator $@x$ of hybrid logic. The dynamic part of our logic is due to the modalities which can be formed over any ed action over a given ed signature. $\mathcal{E}^\downarrow$ thus retains from hybrid logic the use of binders, but omits free nominals. Thus sentences of the logic become restricted to express properties of configurations reachable from the initial ones.

Definition 3. *The set* $\text{Frm}^{\mathcal{E}^\downarrow}(\Sigma)$ *of* Σ-ed formulae *over an ed signature* Σ *is given by*

$$\varrho ::= \varphi \mid x \mid \downarrow x \,.\, \varrho \mid @x \,.\, \varrho \mid \langle\lambda\rangle\varrho \mid \text{true} \mid \neg\varrho \mid \varrho_1 \vee \varrho_2$$

where $\varphi \in \Phi(\Sigma)$, $x \in X$, *and* $\lambda \in \Lambda(\Sigma)$. *We write* $[\lambda]\varrho$ *for* $\neg\langle\lambda\rangle\neg\varrho$ *and we use the usual boolean connectives as well as the constant* false *to denote* $\neg$true.[1] *The set* $\text{Sen}^{\mathcal{E}^\downarrow}(\Sigma)$ *of* Σ-ed sentences *consists of all* Σ*-ed formulae without free variables, where the free variables are defined as usual with* $\downarrow x$ *being the unique operator binding variables.*

Given an ed signature Σ and a Σ-edts M, the satisfaction of a Σ-ed formula ϱ is inductively defined w.r.t. valuations $v : X \to C(M)$, mapping variables to control states, and configurations $\gamma \in \Gamma(M)$:

- $M, v, \gamma \models^{\mathcal{E}^\downarrow}_\Sigma \varphi$ iff $\omega(\gamma) \models^{\mathcal{D}}_{A(\Sigma)} \varphi$;
- $M, v, \gamma \models^{\mathcal{E}^\downarrow}_\Sigma x$ iff $c(\gamma) = v(x)$;
- $M, v, \gamma \models^{\mathcal{E}^\downarrow}_\Sigma \downarrow x \,.\, \varrho$ iff $M, v\{x \mapsto c(\gamma)\}, \gamma \models^{\mathcal{E}^\downarrow}_\Sigma \varrho$;
- $M, v, \gamma \models^{\mathcal{E}^\downarrow}_\Sigma @x \,.\, \varrho$ iff $M, v, \gamma' \models^{\mathcal{E}^\downarrow}_\Sigma \varrho$ for all $\gamma' \in \Gamma(M)$ with $c(\gamma') = v(x)$;
- $M, v, \gamma \models^{\mathcal{E}^\downarrow}_\Sigma \langle\lambda\rangle\varrho$ iff $M, v, \gamma' \models^{\mathcal{E}^\downarrow}_\Sigma \varrho$ for some $\gamma' \in \Gamma(M)$ with $(\gamma, \gamma') \in R(M)_\lambda$;

[1] We use true and false for predicates and formulae; their meaning will always be clear from the context. For boolean values we will use instead the notations *tt* and *ff*.

- $M, v, \gamma \models^{\mathcal{E}^\downarrow}_{\Sigma}$ true always holds;
- $M, v, \gamma \models^{\mathcal{E}^\downarrow}_{\Sigma} \neg\varrho$ iff $M, v, \gamma \not\models^{\mathcal{E}^\downarrow}_{\Sigma} \varrho$;
- $M, v, \gamma \models^{\mathcal{E}^\downarrow}_{\Sigma} \varrho_1 \vee \varrho_2$ iff $M, v, \gamma \models^{\mathcal{E}^\downarrow}_{\Sigma} \varrho_1$ or $M, v, \gamma \models^{\mathcal{E}^\downarrow}_{\Sigma} \varrho_2$.

If ϱ is a sentence then the valuation is irrelevant. M *satisfies* a sentence $\varrho \in \mathrm{Sen}^{\mathcal{E}^\downarrow}(\Sigma)$, denoted by $M \models^{\mathcal{E}^\downarrow}_{\Sigma} \varrho$, if $M, \gamma_0 \models^{\mathcal{E}^\downarrow}_{\Sigma} \varrho$ for all $\gamma_0 \in \Gamma_0(M)$.

By borrowing the modalities from dynamic logic [9,10], $\mathcal{E}^\downarrow$ is able to express liveness and safety requirements as illustrated in our running ATM example below. There we use the fact that we can state properties over all reachable states by sentences of the form $[\boldsymbol{E}^*]\varphi$. In particular, deadlock-freedom can be expressed by $[\boldsymbol{E}^*]\langle\boldsymbol{E}\rangle$true. The logic $\mathcal{E}^\downarrow$, however, is also suited to directly express process structures and, thus, the implementation of abstract requirements. The binder operator is essential for this. For example, we can specify a process which switches a boolean value, denoted by the attribute val, from *tt* to *ff* and back by the following sentence:

$$\downarrow x_0 \,.\, \mathsf{val} = tt \wedge \langle \mathsf{switch} /\!\!/ \mathsf{val}' = ff\rangle\langle \mathsf{switch} /\!\!/ \mathsf{val}' = tt\rangle x_0.$$

2.3 Bisimulation and Invariance

Bisimulation is a crucial notion in both behavioural systems specification and in modal logics. On the specification side, it provides a standard way to identify systems with the same behaviour by abstracting the internal specifics of the systems; this is also reflected at the logic side, where bisimulation frequently relates states that satisfy the same formulae. We explore some properties of $\mathcal{E}^\downarrow$ w.r.t. bisimilarity. Let us first introduce the notion of bisimilarity in the context of $\mathcal{E}^\downarrow$:

Definition 4. *Let M_1, M_2 be Σ-edts. A relation $B \subseteq \Gamma(M_1) \times \Gamma(M_2)$ is a* bisimulation relation *between M_1 and M_2 if for all $(\gamma_1, \gamma_2) \in B$ the following conditions hold:*

(atom) for all $\varphi \in \Phi(\Sigma)$, $\omega(\gamma_1) \models^{\mathcal{D}}_{A(\Sigma)} \varphi$ iff $\omega(\gamma_2) \models^{\mathcal{D}}_{A(\Sigma)} \varphi$;
(zig) for all $e /\!\!/ \psi \in \Lambda(\Sigma)$ and for all $\gamma_1' \in \Gamma(M_1)$ with $(\gamma_1, \gamma_1') \in R(M_1)_{e/\!\!/\psi}$, there is a $\gamma_2' \in \Gamma(M_2)$ such that $(\gamma_2, \gamma_2') \in R(M_2)_{e/\!\!/\psi}$ and $(\gamma_1', \gamma_2') \in B$;
(zag) for all $e /\!\!/ \psi \in \Lambda(\Sigma)$ and for all $\gamma_2' \in \Gamma(M_2)$ with $(\gamma_2, \gamma_2') \in R(M_2)_{e/\!\!/\psi}$, there is a $\gamma_1' \in \Gamma(M_1)$ such that $(\gamma_1, \gamma_1') \in R(M_1)_{e/\!\!/\psi}$ and $(\gamma_1', \gamma_2') \in B$.

M_1 and M_2 are bisimilar*, in symbols $M_1 \sim M_2$, if there exists a bisimulation relation $B \subseteq \Gamma(M_1) \times \Gamma(M_2)$ between M_1 and M_2 such that*

(init) for any $\gamma_1 \in \Gamma_0(M_1)$, there is a $\gamma_2 \in \Gamma_0(M_2)$ such that $(\gamma_1, \gamma_2) \in B$ and for any $\gamma_2 \in \Gamma_0(M_2)$, there is a $\gamma_1 \in \Gamma_0(M_1)$ such that $(\gamma_1, \gamma_2) \in B$.

Now we are able to establish a Hennessy-Milner like correspondence for a fragment of $\mathcal{E}^\downarrow$. Let us call *hybrid-free sentences of* $\mathcal{E}^\downarrow$ the formulae obtained by the grammar

$$\varrho ::= \varphi \mid \langle\lambda\rangle\varrho \mid \text{true} \mid \neg\varrho \mid \varrho_1 \vee \varrho_2.$$

Theorem 1. *Let M_1, M_2 be bisimilar Σ-edts. Then $M_1 \models^{\mathcal{E}^{\downarrow}}_{\Sigma} \varrho$ iff $M_2 \models^{\mathcal{E}^{\downarrow}}_{\Sigma} \varrho$ for all hybrid-free sentences ϱ.*

The converse of Theorem 1 does not hold, in general, and the usual image-finiteness assumption has to be imposed: A Σ-edts M is *image-finite* if, for all $\gamma \in \Gamma(M)$ and all $e \in E(\Sigma)$, the set $\{\gamma' \mid (\gamma, \gamma') \in R(M)_e\}$ is finite. Then:

Theorem 2. *Let M_1, M_2 be image-finite Σ-edts and $\gamma_1 \in \Gamma(M_1)$, $\gamma_2 \in \Gamma(M_2)$ such that $M_1, \gamma_1 \models^{\mathcal{E}^{\downarrow}}_{\Sigma} \varrho$ iff $M_2, \gamma_2 \models^{\mathcal{E}^{\downarrow}}_{\Sigma} \varrho$ for all hybrid-free sentences ϱ. Then there exists a bisimulation B between M_1 and M_2 such that $(\gamma_1, \gamma_2) \in B$.*

3 Specifications of Event/Data Systems

3.1 Axiomatic Specifications

Sentences of $\mathcal{E}^{\downarrow}$-logic can be used to specify properties of event/data systems and thus to write system specifications in an axiomatic way.

Definition 5. *An* axiomatic ed specification $Sp = (\Sigma(Sp), Ax(Sp))$ *in* $\mathcal{E}^{\downarrow}$ *consists of an ed signature* $\Sigma(Sp) \in Sig^{\mathcal{E}^{\downarrow}}$ *and a set of* axioms $Ax(Sp) \subseteq \mathrm{Sen}^{\mathcal{E}^{\downarrow}}(\Sigma(Sp))$.

The semantics of Sp *is given by the pair* $(\Sigma(Sp), \mathrm{Mod}(Sp))$ *where* $\mathrm{Mod}(Sp) = \{M \in Edts^{\mathcal{E}^{\downarrow}}(\Sigma(Sp)) \mid M \models^{\mathcal{E}^{\downarrow}}_{\Sigma(Sp)} Ax(Sp)\}$. *The edts in* $\mathrm{Mod}(Sp)$ *are called* models *of* Sp *and* $\mathrm{Mod}(Sp)$ *is the* model class *of* Sp.

As a direct consequence of Theorem 1 we have:

Corollary 1. *The model class of an axiomatic ed specification exclusively expressed by hybrid-free sentences is closed under bisimulation.*

This result does not hold for sentences with hybrid features. For instance, consider the specification $Sp = ((\{e\}, \{a\}), \{\downarrow x \,.\, \langle e /\!\!/ a' = a \rangle x\})$: An edts with a single control state c_0 and a loop transition $R_e = \{(\gamma_0, \gamma_0)\}$ for $c(\gamma_0) = c_0$ is a model of Sp. However, this is obviously not the case for its bisimilar edts with two control states c_0 and c and the relation $R'_e = \{(\gamma_0, \gamma), (\gamma, \gamma_0)\}$ with $c(\gamma_0) = c_0$, $c(\gamma) = c$ and $\omega(\gamma_0) = \omega(\gamma)$.

Example 1. As a running example we consider an ATM. We start with an abstract specification Sp_0 of fundamental requirements for its interaction behaviour based on the set of events $E_0 = \{\mathsf{insertCard}, \mathsf{enterPIN}, \mathsf{ejectCard}, \mathsf{cancel}\}$[2] and on the singleton set of attributes $A_0 = \{\mathsf{chk}\}$ where chk is boolean valued and records the correctness of an entered PIN. Hence our first ed signature is $\Sigma_0 = (E_0, A_0)$ and $Sp_0 = (\Sigma_0, Ax_0)$ where Ax_0 requires the following properties expressed by corresponding axioms (0.1–0.3):

[2] For shortening the presentation we omit further events like withdrawing money, etc.

- "Whenever a card has been inserted, a correct PIN can eventually be entered and also the transaction can eventually be cancelled."

$$[\boldsymbol{E}^*; \mathsf{insertCard}](\langle \boldsymbol{E}^*; \mathsf{enterPIN} /\!\!/ \mathsf{chk}' = \mathit{tt}\rangle \mathrm{true} \wedge \langle \boldsymbol{E}^*; \mathsf{cancel}\rangle \mathrm{true}) \qquad (0.1)$$

- "Whenever either a correct PIN has been entered or the transaction has been cancelled, the card can eventually be ejected."

$$[\boldsymbol{E}^*; (\mathsf{enterPIN} /\!\!/ \mathsf{chk}' = \mathit{tt}) + \mathsf{cancel}]\langle \boldsymbol{E}^*; \mathsf{ejectCard}\rangle \mathrm{true} \qquad (0.2)$$

- "Whenever an incorrect PIN has been entered three times in a row, the current card is not returned." This means that the card is kept by the ATM which is not modelled by an extra event. It may, however, still be possible that another card is inserted afterwards. So an ejectCard can only be forbidden as long as no next card is inserted.

$$[\boldsymbol{E}^*; (\mathsf{enterPIN} /\!\!/ \mathsf{chk}' = \mathit{ff})^3; (-\mathsf{insertCard})^*; \mathsf{ejectCard}]\mathrm{false} \qquad (0.3)$$

where λ^n abbreviates the n-fold sequential composition $\lambda; \ldots; \lambda$.

The semantics of an axiomatic ed specification is loose allowing usually for many different realisations. A refinement step is therefore understood as a restriction of the model class of an abstract specification. Following the terminology of Sannella and Tarlecki [18,19], we call a specification refining another one an *implementation*. Formally, a specification Sp' is a *simple implementation* of a specification Sp over the same signature, in symbols $Sp \rightsquigarrow Sp'$, whenever $\mathrm{Mod}(Sp) \supseteq \mathrm{Mod}(Sp')$. Transitivity of the inclusion relation ensures gradual step-by-step development by a series of refinements.

Example 2. We provide a refinement $Sp_0 \rightsquigarrow Sp_1$ where $Sp_1 = (\Sigma_0, Ax_1)$ has the same signature as Sp_0 and Ax_1 are the sentences (1.1–1.4) below; the last two use binders to specify a loop. As is easily seen, all models of Sp_1 must satisfy the axioms of Sp_0.

- "At the beginning a card can be inserted with the effect that chk is set to *ff*; nothing else is possible at the beginning."

$$\begin{aligned}&\langle \mathsf{insertCard} /\!\!/ \mathsf{chk}' = \mathit{ff}\rangle \mathrm{true} \wedge \\ &[\mathsf{insertCard} /\!\!/ \neg(\mathsf{chk}' = \mathit{ff})]\mathrm{false} \wedge [-\mathsf{insertCard}]\mathrm{false}\end{aligned} \qquad (1.1)$$

- "Whenever a card has been inserted, a PIN can be entered (directly afterwards) and also the transaction can be cancelled; but nothing else."

$$\begin{aligned}[\boldsymbol{E}^*; \mathsf{insertCard}](&\langle \mathsf{enterPIN}\rangle \mathrm{true} \wedge \langle \mathsf{cancel}\rangle \mathrm{true} \wedge \\ &[-\{\mathsf{enterPIN}, \mathsf{cancel}\}]\mathrm{false})\end{aligned} \qquad (1.2)$$

– "Whenever either a correct PIN has been entered or the transaction has been cancelled, the card can eventually be ejected and the ATM starts from the beginning."

$$\downarrow x_0 \,.\, [\boldsymbol{E}^*; (\mathsf{enterPIN} /\!\!/ \mathsf{chk}' = tt) + \mathsf{cancel}]\langle \boldsymbol{E}^*; \mathsf{ejectCard}\rangle x_0 \tag{1.3}$$

– "Whenever an incorrect PIN has been entered three times in a row the ATM starts from the beginning." Hence the current card is kept.

$$\downarrow x_0 \,.\, [\boldsymbol{E}^*; (\mathsf{enterPIN} /\!\!/ \mathsf{chk}' = f\!f)^3] x_0 \tag{1.4}$$

3.2 Operational Specifications

Operational event/data specifications are introduced as a means to specify in a more constructive style the properties of event/data systems. They are not appropriate for writing abstract requirements for which axiomatic specifications are recommended. Though $\mathcal{E}^{\downarrow}$-logic is able to specify concrete models, as discussed in Sect. 2, the use of operational specifications allows a graphic representation close to familiar formalisms in the literature, like UML protocol state machines, cf. [12,16]. As will be shown in Sect. 3.3, finite operational specifications can be characterised by a sentence in $\mathcal{E}^{\downarrow}$-logic. Therefore, $\mathcal{E}^{\downarrow}$-logic is still the common basis of our development approach. Transitions in an operational specification are tuples $(c, \varphi, e, \psi, c')$ with c a source control state, φ a precondition, e an event, ψ a state transition predicate specifying the possible effects of the event e, and c' a target control state. In the semantic models an event must be enabled whenever the respective source data state satisfies the precondition. Thus isolating preconditions has a semantic consequence that is not expressible by transition predicates only. The effect of the event must respect ψ; no other transitions are allowed.

Definition 6. *An* operational ed specification $O = (\Sigma, C, T, (c_0, \varphi_0))$ *is given by an ed signature* Σ*, a set of* control states C*, a* transition relation specification $T \subseteq C \times \Phi(\Sigma) \times E(\Sigma) \times \Psi(\Sigma) \times C$*, an* initial control state $c_0 \in C$*, and an* initial state predicate $\varphi_0 \in \Phi(\Sigma)$*, such that* C *is* syntactically reachable*, i.e., for every* $c \in C \setminus \{c_0\}$ *there are* $(c_0, \varphi_1, e_1, \psi_1, c_1), \ldots, (c_{n-1}, \varphi_n, e_n, \psi_n, c_n) \in T$ *with* $n > 0$ *such that* $c_n = c$*. We write* $\Sigma(O)$ *for* Σ*, etc.*

A Σ*-edts* M *is a* model *of* O *if* $C(M) = C$ *up to a bijective renaming,* $c_0(M) = c_0$*,* $\Omega_0(M) \subseteq \{\omega \mid \omega \models^{\mathcal{D}}_{A(\Sigma)} \varphi_0\}$*, and if the following conditions hold:*

- *for all* $(c, \varphi, e, \psi, c') \in T$ *and* $\omega \in \Omega(A(\Sigma))$ *with* $\omega \models^{\mathcal{D}}_{A(\Sigma)} \varphi$*, there is a* $((c, \omega), (c', \omega')) \in R(M)_e$ *with* $(\omega, \omega') \models^{\mathcal{D}}_{A(\Sigma)} \psi$*;*

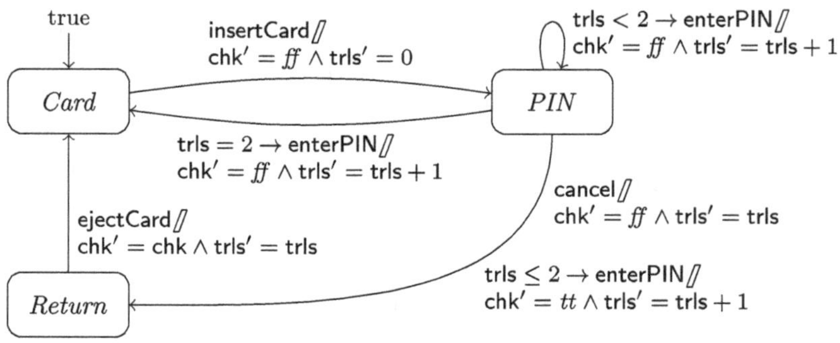

Fig. 1. Operational ed specification *ATM*

- *for all* $((c,\omega),(c',\omega')) \in R(M)_e$ *there is a* $(c,\varphi,e,\psi,c') \in T$ *with* $\omega \models^{\mathcal{D}}_{A(\Sigma)} \varphi$ *and* $(\omega,\omega') \models^{\mathcal{D}}_{A(\Sigma)} \psi$.

The class of all models of O is denoted by $\mathrm{Mod}(O)$. *The* semantics *of O is given by the pair* $(\Sigma(O), \mathrm{Mod}(O))$ *where* $\Sigma(O) = \Sigma$.

Example 3. We construct an operational ed specification, called ATM, for the ATM example. The signature of ATM extends the one of Sp_1 (and Sp_0) by an additional integer-valued attribute trls which counts the number of attempts to enter a correct PIN (with the same card). ATM is graphically presented in Fig. 1. The initial control state is *Card*, and the initial state predicate is true. Preconditions are written before the symbol $\rightarrow$. If no precondition is explicitly indicated it is assumed to be true. Due to the extended signature, ATM is not a simple implementation of Sp_1, and we will only formally justify the implementation relationship in Example 5.

Operational specifications can be composed by a syntactic parallel composition operator which synchronises shared events. Two ed signatures Σ_1 and Σ_2 are *composable* if $A(\Sigma_1) \cap A(\Sigma_2) = \emptyset$. Their parallel composition is given by $\Sigma_1 \otimes \Sigma_2 = (E(\Sigma_1) \cup E(\Sigma_2), A(\Sigma_1) \cup A(\Sigma_2))$.

Definition 7. *Let Σ_1 and Σ_2 be composable ed signatures and let O_1 and O_2 be operational ed specifications with $\Sigma(O_1) = \Sigma_1$ and $\Sigma(O_2) = \Sigma_2$. The* parallel composition *of O_1 and O_2 is given by the operational ed specification* $O_1 \parallel O_2 = (\Sigma_1 \otimes \Sigma_2, C, T, (c_0, \varphi_0))$ *with* $c_0 = (c_0(O_1), c_0(O_2))$, $\varphi_0 = \varphi_0(O_1) \wedge \varphi_0(O_2)$, *and C and T are inductively defined by $c_0 \in C$ and*

- *for* $e_1 \in E(\Sigma_1) \setminus E(\Sigma_2)$, $c_1, c_1' \in C(O_1)$, *and* $c_2 \in C(O_2)$, *if* $(c_1, c_2) \in C$ *and* $(c_1, \varphi_1, e_1, \psi_1, c_1') \in T(O_1)$, *then* $(c_1', c_2) \in C$ *and* $((c_1, c_2), \varphi_1, e_1, \psi_1 \wedge \mathrm{id}_{A(\Sigma_2)}, (c_1', c_2)) \in T$;
- *for* $e_2 \in E(\Sigma_2) \setminus E(\Sigma_1)$, $c_2, c_2' \in C(O_2)$, *and* $c_1 \in C(O_1)$, *if* $(c_1, c_2) \in C$ *and* $(c_2, \varphi_2, e_2, \psi_2, c_2') \in T(O_2)$, *then* $(c_1, c_2') \in C$ *and* $((c_1, c_2), \varphi_2, e_2, \psi_2 \wedge \mathrm{id}_{A(\Sigma_1)}, (c_1, c_2')) \in T$;

– *for* $e \in E(\Sigma_1) \cap E(\Sigma_2)$, $c_1, c_1' \in C(O_1)$, *and* $c_2, c_2' \in C(O_2)$, *if* $(c_1, c_2) \in C$, $(c_1, \varphi_1, e, \psi_1, c_1') \in T(O_1)$, *and* $(c_2, \varphi_2, e, \psi_2, c_2') \in T(O_2)$, *then* $(c_1', c_2') \in C$ *and* $((c_1, c_2), \varphi_1 \wedge \varphi_2, e, \psi_1 \wedge \psi_2, (c_1', c_2')) \in T$.[3]

3.3 Expressiveness of $\mathcal{E}^{\downarrow}$-Logic

We show that the semantics of an operational ed specification O with finitely many control states can be characterised by a single $\mathcal{E}^{\downarrow}$-sentence ϱ_O, i.e., an edts M is a model of O iff $M \models^{\mathcal{E}^{\downarrow}}_{\Sigma(O)} \varrho_O$. Using Algorithm 1, such a characterising sentence is

$$\varrho_O = \downarrow c_0 \,.\, \varphi_0 \wedge \mathrm{sen}(c_0, \mathit{Im}_O(c_0), C(O), \{c_0\}) \ ,$$

where $c_0 = c_0(O)$ and $\varphi_0 = \varphi_0(O)$. Algorithm 1 closely follows the procedure in [15] for characterising a finite structure by a sentence of $\mathcal{D}^{\downarrow}$-logic. A call $\mathrm{sen}(c, I, V, B)$ performs a recursive breadth-first traversal through O starting from c, where I holds the unprocessed quadruples (φ, e, ψ, c') of transitions outgoing from c, V the remaining states to visit, and B the set of already bound states. The function first requires the existence of each outgoing transition of I, provided its precondition holds, in the resulting formula, binding any newly reached state. Then it requires that no other transitions with source state c exist using calls to fin. Having visited all states in V, it finally requires all states in $C(O)$ to be pairwise different.

Algorithm 1. Constructing a sentence from an operational ed specification

Require: $O \equiv$ finite operational ed specification
$\quad \mathit{Im}_O(c) = \{(\varphi, e, \psi, c') \mid (c, \varphi, e, \psi, c') \in T(O)\}$ for $c \in C(O)$
$\quad \mathit{Im}_O(c, e) = \{(\varphi, \psi, c') \mid (c, \varphi, e, \psi, c') \in T(O)\}$ for $c \in C(O)$, $e \in E(\Sigma(O))$

function $\mathrm{sen}(c, I, V, B)$ ▷ c: state, I: image to visit, V: states to visit, B: bound states
 if $I \neq \emptyset$ **then**
  $(\varphi, e, \psi, c') \leftarrow$ **choose** I
  if $c' \in B$ **then**
   return $@c\,.\,\varphi \rightarrow \langle e /\!\!/ \psi \rangle (c' \wedge \mathrm{sen}(c, I \setminus \{(\varphi, e, \psi, c')\}, V, B))$
  else
   return $@c\,.\,\varphi \rightarrow \langle e /\!\!/ \psi \rangle (\downarrow c'\,.\,\mathrm{sen}(c, I \setminus \{(\varphi, e, \psi, c')\}, V, B \cup \{c'\}))$
 $V \leftarrow V \setminus \{c\}$
 if $V \neq \emptyset$ **then**
  $c' \leftarrow$ **choose** $B \cap V$
  return $\mathrm{fin}(c) \wedge \mathrm{sen}(c', \mathit{Im}_O(c'), V, B)$
 return $\mathrm{fin}(c) \wedge \bigwedge_{c_1 \in C(O), c_2 \in C(O) \setminus \{c_1\}} \neg @c_1 \,.\, c_2$

function $\mathrm{fin}(c)$
 return $@c\,.\,\bigwedge_{e \in E(\Sigma(O))} \bigwedge_{P \subseteq \mathit{Im}_O(c,e)}$
   $[e /\!\!/ (\bigwedge_{(\varphi,\psi,c') \in P} (\varphi \wedge \psi)) \wedge$
    $\neg(\bigvee_{(\varphi,\psi,c') \in \mathit{Im}_O(c,e) \setminus P} (\varphi \wedge \psi))](\bigvee_{(\varphi,\psi,c') \in P} c')$

[3] Note that joint moves with e cannot become inconsistent due to composability of ed signatures.

It is fin(c) where this algorithm mainly deviates from [15]: To ensure that no other transitions from c exist than those specified in O, fin(c) produces the requirement that at state c, for every event e and for every subset P of the transitions outgoing from c, whenever an e-transition can be done with the combined effect of P but not adhering to any of the effects of the currently not selected transitions, the e-transition must have one of the states as its target that are target states of P. The rather complicated formulation is due to possibly overlapping preconditions where for a single event e the preconditions of two different transitions may be satisfied simultaneously. For a state c, where all outgoing transitions for the same event have disjoint preconditions, the $\mathcal{E}^{\downarrow}$-formula returned by fin(c) is equivalent to

$$@c\,.\;\bigwedge_{e\in E(\Sigma(O))}\bigwedge_{(\varphi,\psi,c')\in Im_O(c,e)}[e/\!\!/\varphi\wedge\psi]c'\wedge\\ [e/\!\!/\neg(\bigvee_{(\varphi,\psi,c')\in Im_O(c,e)}(\varphi\wedge\psi))]\mathrm{false}.$$

Example 4. We show the first few steps of representing the operational ed specification ATM of Fig. 1 as an $\mathcal{E}^{\downarrow}$-sentence ϱ_{ATM}. This top-level sentence is

$$\downarrow Card\,.\,\mathrm{true}\wedge\mathrm{sen}(Card,\{(\mathrm{true},\mathsf{insertCard},\mathsf{chk}'=f\!f\wedge\mathsf{trls}'=0,PIN)\},\\ \{Card,PIN,Return\},\{Card\}).$$

The first call of sen($Card,\ldots$) explores the single outgoing transition from $Card$ to PIN, adds PIN to the bound states, and hence expands to

$$@Card\,.\,\mathrm{true}\rightarrow\langle\mathsf{insertCard}/\!\!/\mathsf{chk}'=f\!f\wedge\mathsf{trls}'=0\rangle{\downarrow}PIN.\\ \mathrm{sen}(Card,\emptyset,\{Card,PIN,Return\},\{Card,PIN\}).$$

Now all outgoing transitions from $Card$ have been explored and the next call of sen($Card,\emptyset,\ldots$) removes $Card$ from the set of states to be visited, resulting in

$$\mathrm{fin}(Card)\wedge\mathrm{sen}(PIN,\{(\mathsf{trls}<2,\mathsf{enterPIN},\ldots),(\mathsf{trls}=2,\mathsf{enterPIN},\ldots),\\ (\mathsf{trls}\leq 2,\mathsf{enterPIN},\ldots),(\mathrm{true},\mathsf{cancel},\ldots)\},\\ \{PIN,Return\},\{Card,PIN\}).$$

As there is only a single outgoing transition from $Card$, the special case of disjoint preconditions applies for the finalisation call, and fin($Card$) results in

$$@Card\,.\,[\mathsf{insertCard}/\!\!/\mathsf{chk}'=f\!f\wedge\mathsf{trls}'=0]PIN\wedge\\ [\mathsf{insertCard}/\!\!/\mathsf{chk}'=tt\vee\mathsf{trls}'\neq 0]\mathrm{false}\wedge\\ [\mathsf{enterPIN}/\!\!/\mathrm{true}]\mathrm{false}\wedge[\mathsf{cancel}/\!\!/\mathrm{true}]\mathrm{false}\wedge[\mathsf{ejectCard}/\!\!/\mathrm{true}]\mathrm{false}.$$

4 Constructor Implementations

The implementation notion defined in Sect. 3.1 is too simple for many practical applications. It requires the same signature for specification and implementation and does not support the process of constructing an implementation. Therefore,

Sannella and Tarlecki [18,19] have proposed the notion of constructor implementation which is a generic notion applicable to specification formalisms which are based on signatures and semantic structures for signatures. We will reuse the ideas in the context of $\mathcal{E}^{\downarrow}$-logic.

The notion of *constructor* is the basis: for signatures $\Sigma_1, \ldots, \Sigma_n, \Sigma \in \mathit{Sig}^{\mathcal{E}^{\downarrow}}$, a *constructor* κ from $(\Sigma_1, \ldots, \Sigma_n)$ to Σ is a (total) function $\kappa : \mathit{Edts}^{\mathcal{E}^{\downarrow}}(\Sigma_1) \times \ldots \times \mathit{Edts}^{\mathcal{E}^{\downarrow}}(\Sigma_n) \to \mathit{Edts}^{\mathcal{E}^{\downarrow}}(\Sigma)$. Given a constructor κ from $(\Sigma_1, \ldots, \Sigma_n)$ to Σ and a set of constructors κ_i from $(\Sigma_i^1, \ldots, \Sigma_i^{k_i})$ to Σ_i, $1 \leq i \leq n$, the constructor $(\kappa_1, \ldots, \kappa_n); \kappa$ from $(\Sigma_1^1, \ldots, \Sigma_1^{k_1}, \ldots, \Sigma_n^1, \ldots, \Sigma_n^{k_n})$ to Σ is obtained by the usual composition of functions. The following definitions apply to both axiomatic and operational ed specifications since the semantics of both is given in terms of ed signatures and model classes of edts. In particular, the implementation notion allows to implement axiomatic specifications by operational specifications.

Definition 8. *Given specifications $Sp, Sp_1, \ldots, Sp_n$ and a constructor κ from $(\Sigma(Sp_1), \ldots, \Sigma(Sp_n))$ to $\Sigma(Sp)$, the tuple $\langle Sp_1, \ldots, Sp_n \rangle$ is a* constructor implementation *via κ of Sp, in symbols $Sp \rightsquigarrow_\kappa \langle Sp_1, \ldots, Sp_n \rangle$, if for all $M_i \in \mathrm{Mod}(Sp_i)$ we have $\kappa(M_1, \ldots, M_n) \in \mathrm{Mod}(Sp)$. The implementation involves a* decomposition *if $n > 1$.*

The notion of simple implementation in Sect. 3.1 is captured by choosing the identity. We now introduce a set of more advanced constructors in the context of ed signatures and edts. Let us first consider two central notions for constructors: signature morphisms and reducts. For data signatures A, A' a *data signature morphism* $\sigma : A \to A'$ is a function from A to A'. The *σ-reduct* of an A'-data state $\omega' : A' \to \mathcal{D}$ is given by the A-data state $\omega'|\sigma : A \to \mathcal{D}$ defined by $(\omega'|\sigma)(a) = \omega'(\sigma(a))$ for every $a \in A$. If $A \subseteq A'$, the injection of A into A' is a particular data signature morphism and we denote the reduct of an A'-data state ω' to A by $\omega' \upharpoonright A$. If $A = A_1 \cup A_2$ is the disjoint union of A_1 and A_2 and ω_i are A_i-data states for $i \in \{1, 2\}$ then $\omega_1 + \omega_2$ denotes the unique A-data state ω with $\omega \upharpoonright A_i = \omega_i$ for $i \in \{1, 2\}$. The σ-reduct $\gamma|\sigma$ of a configuration $\gamma = (c, \omega')$ is given by $(c, \omega'|\sigma)$, and is lifted to a set of configurations Γ' by $\Gamma'|\sigma = \{\gamma'|\sigma \mid \gamma' \in \Gamma'\}$.

Definition 9. *An* ed signature morphism *$\sigma = (\sigma_E, \sigma_A) : \Sigma \to \Sigma'$ is given by a function $\sigma_E : E(\Sigma) \to E(\Sigma')$ and a data signature morphism $\sigma_A : A(\Sigma) \to A(\Sigma')$. We abbreviate both σ_E and σ_A by σ.*

Definition 10. *Let $\sigma : \Sigma \to \Sigma'$ be an ed signature morphism and M' a Σ'-edts. The* σ-reduct *of M' is the Σ-edts $M'|\sigma = (\Gamma, R, \Gamma_0)$ such that $\Gamma_0 = \Gamma_0(M')|\sigma$, and Γ and $R = (R_e)_{e \in E(\Sigma)}$ are inductively defined by $\Gamma_0 \subseteq \Gamma$ and for all $e \in E(\Sigma)$, $\gamma', \gamma'' \in \Gamma(M')$: if $\gamma'|\sigma \in \Gamma$ and $(\gamma', \gamma'') \in R(M')_{\sigma(e)}$, then $\gamma''|\sigma \in \Gamma$ and $(\gamma'|\sigma, \gamma''|\sigma) \in R_e$.*

Definition 11. *Let $\sigma : \Sigma \to \Sigma'$ be an ed signature morphism. The* reduct constructor *κ_σ from Σ' to Σ maps any $M' \in \mathit{Edts}^{\mathcal{E}^{\downarrow}}(\Sigma')$ to its reduct $\kappa_\sigma(M') = M'|\sigma$. Whenever σ_A and σ_E are bijective functions, κ_σ is a* relabelling constructor. *If σ_E and σ_A are injective, κ_σ is a* restriction constructor.

Example 5. The operational specification ATM is a constructor implementation of Sp_1 via the restriction constructor κ_ι determined by the inclusion signature morphism $\iota : \Sigma(Sp_1) \to \Sigma(ATM)$, i.e., $Sp_1 \rightsquigarrow_{\kappa_\iota} ATM$.

A further refinement technique for reactive systems (see, e.g., [8]), is the implementation of simple events by complex events, like their sequential composition. To formalise this as a constructor we use *composite events* $\Theta(E)$ over a given set of events E, given by the grammar $\theta ::= e \mid \theta + \theta \mid \theta ; \theta \mid \theta^*$ with $e \in E$. They are *interpreted* over an (E, A)-edts M by $R(M)_{\theta_1 + \theta_2} = R(M)_{\theta_1} \cup R(M)_{\theta_2}$, $R(M)_{\theta_1;\theta_2} = R(M)_{\theta_1} ; R(M)_{\theta_2}$, and $R(M)_{\theta^*} = (R(M)_\theta)^*$. Then we can introduce the intended constructor by means of reducts over signature morphisms mapping atomic to composite events:

Definition 12. *Let Σ, Σ' be ed signatures, D' a finite subset of $\Theta(E(\Sigma'))$, $\Delta' = (D', A(\Sigma'))$, and $\alpha : \Sigma \to \Delta'$ an ed signature morphism. The* event refinement *constructor κ_α from Δ' to Σ maps any $M' \in Edts^{\mathcal{E}^\downarrow}(\Delta')$ to its reduct $M'|\alpha \in Edts^{\mathcal{E}^\downarrow}(\Sigma)$.*

Finally, we consider a semantic, synchronous parallel composition constructor that allows for decomposition of implementations into components which synchronise on shared events. Given two composable signatures Σ_1 and Σ_2, the *parallel composition* $\gamma_1 \otimes \gamma_2$ of two configurations $\gamma_1 = (c_1, \omega_1)$, $\gamma_2 = (c_2, \omega_2)$ with $\omega_1 \in \Omega(A(\Sigma_1))$, $\omega_2 \in \Omega(A(\Sigma_2))$ is given by $((c_1, c_2), \omega_1 + \omega_2)$, and lifted to two sets of configurations Γ_1 and Γ_2 by $\Gamma_1 \otimes \Gamma_2 = \{\gamma_1 \otimes \gamma_2 \mid \gamma_1 \in \Gamma_1,\ \gamma_2 \in \Gamma_2\}$.

Definition 13. *Let Σ_1, Σ_2 be composable ed signatures. The* parallel composition constructor *$\kappa_\otimes$ from (Σ_1, Σ_2) to $\Sigma_1 \otimes \Sigma_2$ maps any $M_1 \in Edts^{\mathcal{E}^\downarrow}(\Sigma_1)$, $M_2 \in Edts^{\mathcal{E}^\downarrow}(\Sigma_2)$ to $M_1 \otimes M_2 = (\Gamma, R, \Gamma_0) \in Edts^{\mathcal{E}^\downarrow}(\Sigma_1 \otimes \Sigma_2)$, where $\Gamma_0 = \Gamma_0(M_1) \otimes \Gamma_0(M_2)$, and Γ and $R = (R_e)_{E(\Sigma_1) \cup E(\Sigma_2)}$ are inductively defined by $\Gamma_0 \subseteq \Gamma$ and*

- *for all $e_1 \in E(\Sigma_1) \setminus E(\Sigma_2)$, $\gamma_1, \gamma_1' \in \Gamma(M_1)$, and $\gamma_2 \in \Gamma(M_2)$, if $\gamma_1 \otimes \gamma_2 \in \Gamma$ and $(\gamma_1, \gamma_1') \in R(M_1)_{e_1}$, then $\gamma_1' \otimes \gamma_2 \in \Gamma$ and $(\gamma_1 \otimes \gamma_2, \gamma_1' \otimes \gamma_2) \in R_{e_1}$;*
- *for all $e_2 \in E(\Sigma_2) \setminus E(\Sigma_1)$, $\gamma_2, \gamma_2' \in \Gamma(M_2)$, and $\gamma_1 \in \Gamma(M_1)$, if $\gamma_1 \otimes \gamma_2 \in \Gamma$ and $(\gamma_2, \gamma_2') \in R(M_2)_{e_2}$, then $\gamma_1 \otimes \gamma_2' \in \Gamma$ and $(\gamma_1 \otimes \gamma_2, \gamma_1 \otimes \gamma_2') \in R_{e_2}$;*
- *for all $e \in E(\Sigma_1) \cap E(\Sigma_2)$, $\gamma_1, \gamma_1' \in \Gamma(M_1)$, and $\gamma_2, \gamma_2' \in \Gamma(M_2)$, if $\gamma_1 \otimes \gamma_2 \in \Gamma$, $(\gamma_1, \gamma_1') \in R(M_1)_{e_1}$, and $(\gamma_2, \gamma_2') \in R(M_2)_{e_2}$, then $\gamma_1' \otimes \gamma_2' \in \Gamma$ and $(\gamma_1 \otimes \gamma_2, \gamma_1' \otimes \gamma_2') \in R_e$.*

An obvious question is how the semantic parallel composition constructor is related to the syntactic parallel composition of operational ed specifications.

Proposition 1. *Let O_1, O_2 be operational ed specifications with composable signatures. Then $\mathrm{Mod}(O_1) \otimes \mathrm{Mod}(O_2) \subseteq \mathrm{Mod}(O_1 \parallel O_2)$, where $\mathrm{Mod}(O_1) \otimes \mathrm{Mod}(O_2)$ denotes $\kappa_\otimes(\mathrm{Mod}(O_1), \mathrm{Mod}(O_2))$.*

The converse $\mathrm{Mod}(O_1 \parallel O_2) \subseteq \mathrm{Mod}(O_1) \otimes \mathrm{Mod}(O_2)$ does not hold: Consider the ed signature $\Sigma = (E, A)$ with $E = \{e\}$, $A = \emptyset$, and the operational ed specifications $O_i = (\Sigma, C_i, T_i, (c_{i,0}, \varphi_{i,0}))$ for $i \in \{1, 2\}$ with $C_1 = \{c_{1,0}\}$, $T_1 = \{(c_{1,0}, \mathrm{true}, e, \mathrm{false}, c_{1,0})\}$, $\varphi_{1,0} = \mathrm{true}$; and $C_2 = \{c_{2,0}\}$, $T_2 = \emptyset$, $\varphi_{2,0} = \mathrm{true}$. Then $\mathrm{Mod}(O_1) = \emptyset$, but $\mathrm{Mod}(O_1 \parallel O_2) = \{M\}$ with M showing just the initial configuration.

The next theorem shows the usefulness of the syntactic parallel composition operator for proving implementation correctness when a (semantic) parallel composition constructor is involved. The theorem is a direct consequence of Proposition 1 and Definition 8.

Theorem 3. *Let Sp be an (axiomatic or operational) ed specification, O_1, O_2 operational ed specifications with composable signatures, and κ an implementation constructor from $\Sigma(O_1) \otimes \Sigma(O_2)$ to $\Sigma(Sp)$: If $Sp \rightsquigarrow_\kappa O_1 \parallel O_2$, then $Sp \rightsquigarrow_{\kappa_\otimes ; \kappa} \langle O_1, O_2 \rangle$.*

Example 6. We finish the refinement chain for the ATM specifications by applying a decomposition into two parallel components. The operational specification *ATM* of Example 3 (and Example 5) describes the interface behaviour of an ATM interacting with a user. For a concrete realisation, however, an ATM will also interact internally with other components, like, e.g., a clearing company which supports the ATM for verifying PINs. Our last refinement step hence realises the *ATM* specification by two parallel components, represented by the operational specification ATM' in Fig. 2a and the operational specification *CC* of a clearing company in Fig. 2b. Both communicate (via shared events) when an ATM sends a verification request, modelled by the event $\mathsf{verifyPIN}$, to the clearing company. The clearing company may answer with $\mathsf{correctPIN}$ or $\mathsf{wrongPIN}$ and then the ATM continues following its specification. For the implementation construction we use the parallel composition constructor $\kappa_\otimes$ from $(\Sigma(ATM'), \Sigma(CC))$ to $\Sigma(ATM') \otimes \Sigma(CC)$. The signature of *CC* consists of the events shown on the transitions in Fig. 2b. Moreover, there is one integer-valued attribute cnt counting the number of verification tasks performed. The signature of ATM' extends $\Sigma(ATM)$ by the events $\mathsf{verifyPIN}$, $\mathsf{correctPIN}$ and $\mathsf{wrongPIN}$. To fit the signature and the behaviour of the parallel composition of ATM' and *CC* to the specification *ATM* we must therefore compose $\kappa_\otimes$ with an event refinement constructor κ_α such that $\alpha(\mathsf{enterPIN}) = (\mathsf{enterPIN}; \mathsf{verifyPIN}; (\mathsf{correctPIN}{+}\mathsf{wrongPIN}))$; for the other events α is the identity and for the attributes the inclusion. The idea is therefore that the refinement looks like $ATM \rightsquigarrow_{\kappa_\otimes ; \kappa_\alpha} \langle ATM', CC \rangle$. To prove this refinement relation we rely on the syntactic parallel composition $ATM' \parallel CC$ shown in Fig. 2c, and on Theorem 3. It is easy to see that $ATM \rightsquigarrow_{\kappa_\alpha} ATM' \parallel CC$. In fact, all transitions for event $\mathsf{enterPIN}$ in Fig. 1 are split into several transitions in Fig. 2c according to the event refinement defined by α. For instance, the loop transition from *PIN* to *PIN* with precondition $\mathsf{trls} < 2$ in Fig. 1 is split into

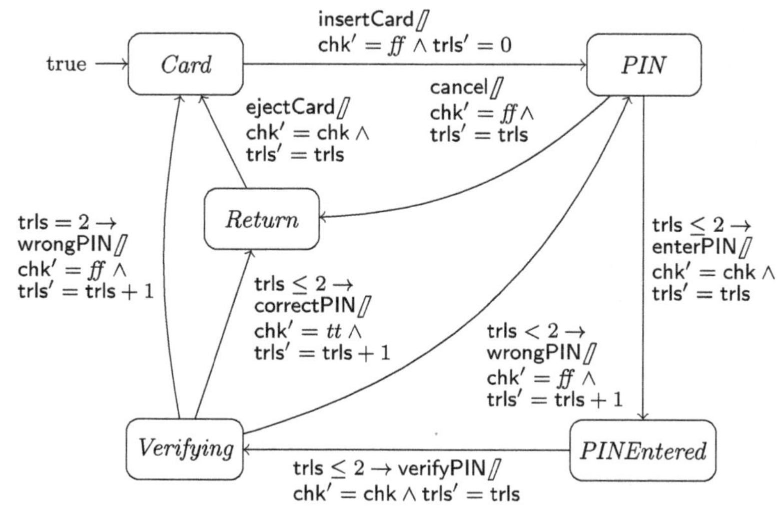

(a) Operational ed specification ATM'

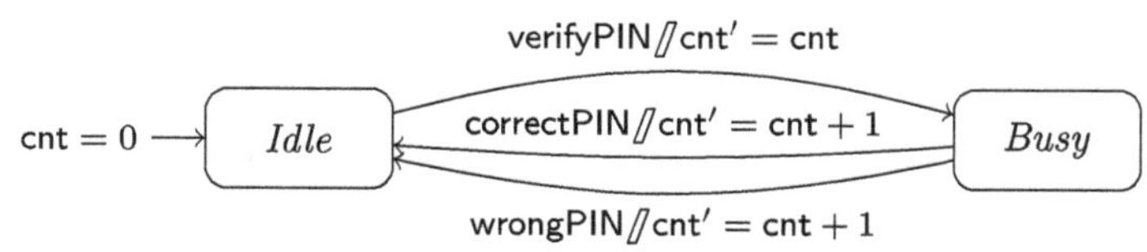

(b) Operational specification CC of a clearing company

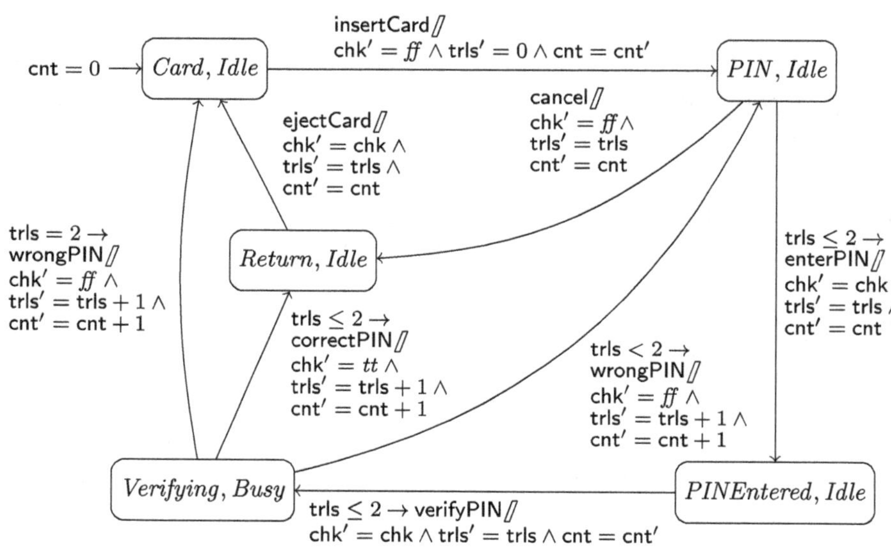

(c) Syntactic parallel composition $ATM' \parallel CC$

Fig. 2. Operational ed specifications ATM', CC and their parallel composition

the cycle from $(PIN, Idle)$ via $(PINEntered, Idle)$ and $(Verifying, Busy)$ back to $(PIN, Idle)$ in Fig. 2c. Thus, we have $ATM \rightsquigarrow_{\kappa_\alpha} ATM' \parallel CC$ and can apply Theorem 3 such that we get $ATM \rightsquigarrow_{\kappa_\otimes ; \kappa_\alpha} \langle ATM', CC \rangle$.

5 Conclusions

We have presented a novel logic, called $\mathcal{E}^{\downarrow}$-logic, for the rigorous formal development of event-based systems incorporating changing data states. To the best of our knowledge, no other logic supports the full development process for this kind of systems ranging from abstract requirements specifications, expressible by the dynamic logic features, to the concrete specification of implementations, expressible by the hybrid part of the logic.

The temporal logic of actions (TLA [13]) supports also stepwise refinement where state transition predicates are considered as actions. In contrast to TLA we model also the events which cause data state transitions. For writing concrete specifications we have proposed an operational specification format capturing (at least parts of) similar formalisms, like Event-B [1], symbolic transition systems [17], and UML protocol state machines [16]. A significant difference to Event-B machines is that we distinguish between control and data states, the former being encoded as data in Event-B. On the other hand, Event-B supports parameters of events which could be integrated in our logic as well. An institution-based semantics of Event-B has been proposed in [7] which coincides with our semantics of operational specifications for the special case of deterministic state transition predicates. Similarly, our semantics of operational specifications coincides with the unfolding of symbolic transition systems in [17] if we instantiate our generic data domain with algebraic specifications of data types (and consider again only deterministic state transition predicates). The syntax of UML protocol state machines is about the same as the one of operational event/data specifications. As a consequence, all of the aforementioned concrete specification formalisms (and several others) would be appropriate candidates for integration into a development process based on $\mathcal{E}^{\downarrow}$-logic.

There remain several interesting tasks for future research. First, our logic is not yet equipped with a proof system for deriving consequences of specifications. This would also support the proof of refinement steps which is currently achieved by purely semantic reasoning. A proof system for $\mathcal{E}^{\downarrow}$-logic must cover dynamic and hybrid logic parts at the same time, like the proof system in [15], which, however, does not consider data states, and the recent calculus of [5], which extends differential dynamic logic but does not deal with events and reactions to events. Both proof systems could be appropriate candidates for incorporating the features of $\mathcal{E}^{\downarrow}$-logic. Another issue concerns the separation of events into input and output as in I/O-automata [14]. Then also communication compatibility (see [2] for interface automata without data and [3] for interface theories with data) would become relevant when applying a parallel composition constructor.

References

1. Abrial, J.R.: Modeling in Event-B: System and Software Engineering. Cambridge University Press, Cambridge (2013)
2. de Alfaro, L., Henzinger, T.A.: Interface automata. In: Tjoa, A.M., Gruhn, V. (eds.) Proceedings 8th European Software Engineering Conference & 9th ACM SIGSOFT International Symposium Foundations of Software Engineering, pp. 109–120. ACM (2001)
3. Bauer, S.S., Hennicker, R., Wirsing, M.: Interface theories for concurrency and data. Theoret. Comput. Sci. **412**(28), 3101–3121 (2011)
4. ter Beek, M.H., Fantechi, A., Gnesi, S., Mazzanti, F.: An action/state-based model-checking approach for the analysis of communication protocols for service-oriented applications. In: Leue, S., Merino, P. (eds.) FMICS 2007. LNCS, vol. 4916, pp. 133–148. Springer, Heidelberg (2008). https://doi.org/10.1007/978-3-540-79707-4_11
5. Bohrer, B., Platzer, A.: A hybrid, dynamic logic for hybrid-dynamic information flow. In: Dawar, A., Grädel, E. (eds.) Proceedings of 33rd Annual ACM/IEEE Symposium on Logic in Computer Science, pp. 115–124. ACM (2018)
6. Braüner, T.: Hybrid Logic and its Proof-Theory. Applied Logic Series. Springer, Heidelberg (2010). https://doi.org/10.1007/978-94-007-0002-4
7. Farrell, M., Monahan, R., Power, J.F.: An institution for Event-B. In: James, P., Roggenbach, M. (eds.) WADT 2016. LNCS, vol. 10644, pp. 104–119. Springer, Cham (2017). https://doi.org/10.1007/978-3-319-72044-9_8
8. Gorrieri, R., Rensink, A.: Action refinement. In: Bergstra, J.A., Ponse, A., Smolka, S.A. (eds.) Handbook of Process Algebra, pp. 1047–1147. Elsevier, Amsterdam (2000)
9. Groote, J.F., Mousavi, M.R.: Modeling and Analysis of Communicating Systems. MIT Press, Cambridge (2014)
10. Harel, D., Kozen, D., Tiuryn, J.: Dynamic Logic. MIT Press, Cambridge (2000)
11. Hennicker, R., Madeira, A., Knapp, A.: A hybrid dynamic logic for event/data-based systems (2019). https://arxiv.org/abs/1902.03074
12. Knapp, A., Mossakowski, T., Roggenbach, M., Glauer, M.: An institution for simple UML state machines. In: Egyed, A., Schaefer, I. (eds.) FASE 2015. LNCS, vol. 9033, pp. 3–18. Springer, Heidelberg (2015). https://doi.org/10.1007/978-3-662-46675-9_1
13. Lamport, L.: Specifying Systems: The TLA+ Language and Tools for Hardware and Software Engineers. Addison-Wesley, Boston (2003)
14. Lynch, N.A.: Input/output automata: basic, timed, hybrid, probabilistic, dynamic, ... In: Amadio, R.M., Lugiez, D. (eds.) CONCUR 2003. LNCS, vol. 2761, pp. 191–192. Springer, Heidelberg (2003). https://doi.org/10.1007/978-3-540-45187-7_12
15. Madeira, A., Barbosa, L.S., Hennicker, R., Martins, M.A.: A logic for the stepwise development of reactive systems. Theoret. Comput. Sci. **744**, 78–96 (2018)
16. Object Management Group: Unified Modeling Language 2.5. Standard formal/2015-03-01, OMG (2015)
17. Poizat, P., Royer, J.C.: A formal architectural description language based on symbolic transition systems and modal logic. J. Univ. Comp. Sci. **12**(12), 1741–1782 (2006)

18. Sannella, D., Tarlecki, A.: Toward formal development of programs from algebraic specifications: implementations revisited. Acta Inf. **25**(3), 233–281 (1988)
19. Sannella, D., Tarlecki, A.: Foundations of Algebraic Specification and Formal Software Development. EATCS Monographs in Theoretical Computer Science. Springer, Heidelberg (2012). https://doi.org/10.1007/978-3-642-17336-3

Model-Driven Development and Model Transformation

Pyro: Generating Domain-Specific Collaborative Online Modeling Environments

Philip Zweihoff(✉), Stefan Naujokat, and Bernhard Steffen

Chair for Programming Systems, TU Dortmund University, Dortmund, Germany
{philip.zweihoff,stefan.naujokat,bernhard.steffen}@tu-dortmund.de

Abstract. We present Pyro, a framework for enabling domain-specific modeling via the internet. Provided with an adequate metamodel specification, Pyro turns your browser into a collaborative, domain-specific, graphical development environment with features reminiscent of desktop IDEs for textual programming languages. The required metamodeling is supported in a high-level, simplicity-driven fashion, and the entire ready-to-run browser-based domain-specific development environment is generated fully automatically. We will illustrate the steps of this development along the realization of a graphical IDE for the Architecture Analysis and Design Language (AADL).

1 Introduction

Domain-specific languages (DSLs) aim at closing the gap between domain knowledge and software development by explicitly supporting the required domain concepts. Graphical domain-specific languages have turned out to be particularly suitable for domain experts without any programming background. The bottleneck in practice is the enormous effort to develop the required domain-specific graphical modeling tools. The CINCO *SCCE Meta Tooling Suite* [26] has been designed to overcome this bottleneck by providing a holistic, simplicity-driven [22] approach for the creation of such domain-specific graphical modeling tools. A key feature of CINCO is that it generates the entire graphical modeling environment (referred to as 'CINCO Products' in the remainder of the paper) from high-level specifications of the defined model structures and functionalities. The (translational) semantics of the specified modeling language is defined in terms of code generation, model transformation, evaluation, and/or interpretation [20]. CINCO Products are Eclipse-based, graphical modeling tools that are realized via a number of Eclipse plug-ins [13]. Thus, setting up a CINCO Product involves some technical aspects that are beyond the competence of typical domain experts, and it becomes even more tedious when one wants to enable a cooperative development.

In this paper, we present *Pyro*, a tool that enables one to generate CINCO Products for collaborative modeling that run in a web browser. Conceptually, Pyro borrows from modern online editors for collaborative work, like Google

R. Hähnle and W. van der Aalst (Eds.): FASE 2019, LNCS 11424, pp. 101–115, 2019.
https://doi.org/10.1007/978-3-030-16722-6_6

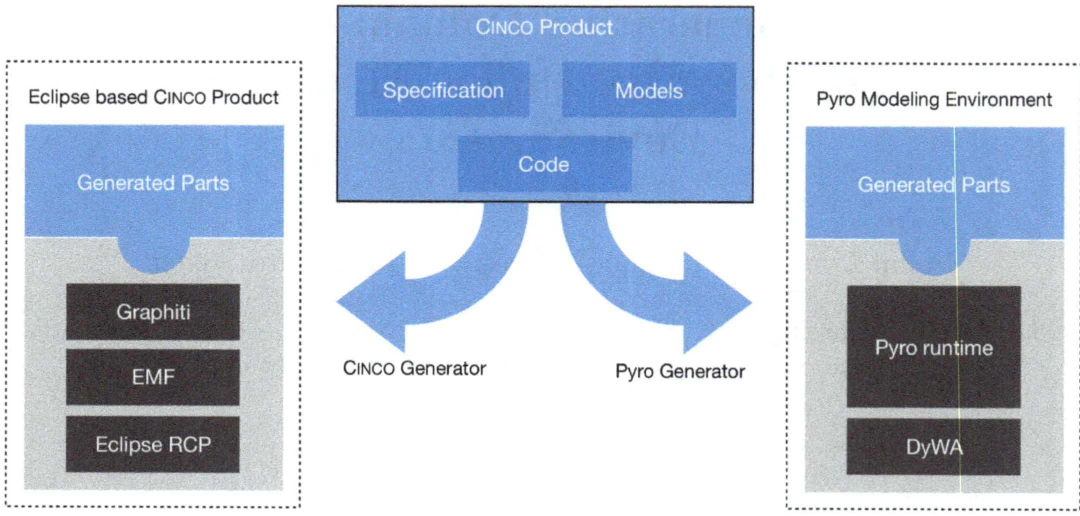

Fig. 1. Cinco generation architecture.

Docs, Microsoft Office 365, or solutions like ShareLaTeX/Overleaf that even free one from maintaining a corresponding build and runtime environment.

Key to the realization of Pyro is that Cinco follows a fully generative approach on the meta level, which allows one to modularly 'retarget' the Cinco Product Generation for the web (cf. Fig. 1). Technically, Pyro web modeling environments utilize *DyWA* [27] (Dynamic Web Application) for data modeling, empowering prototype-driven application development.

In order to achieve this retargeting and to enable collaborative work, Pyro needs to, in particular, compensate for all the required functionality provided by the Eclipse platform, like the EMF framework with GMF or Graphiti for graphical editors. Altogether, this poses the following three key challenges:

- Developing an adequate web solution for the metamodel-based model handling (API, persistence, event system, etc.) that in the Eclipse world is provided by the EMF framework [33] (see *Architecture Backend*, Sect. 3.1).
- Developing a frontend on top of these model structures that feels like a modern integrated development environment with a graphical editor for the models, which in the Eclipse world is provided by the Rich Client Platform (RCP) [24] and the Graphiti editor framework [2] (see *Architecture Frontend*, Sect. 3.2).
- Enabling real-time live collaborative working on models, which is not foreseen in an offline client like Eclipse (see *Collaborative Editing*, Sect. 4).

In the course of this tool paper, Pyro is illustrated along the development of a graphical modeling environment for the *Architecture Analysis and Design Language* (AADL), an SAE standard for modeling the architecture of embedded real-time systems [29]. Cinco was used to develop a graphical AADL modeling tool supporting a subset of AADL's features tailored to be used in teaching [28],

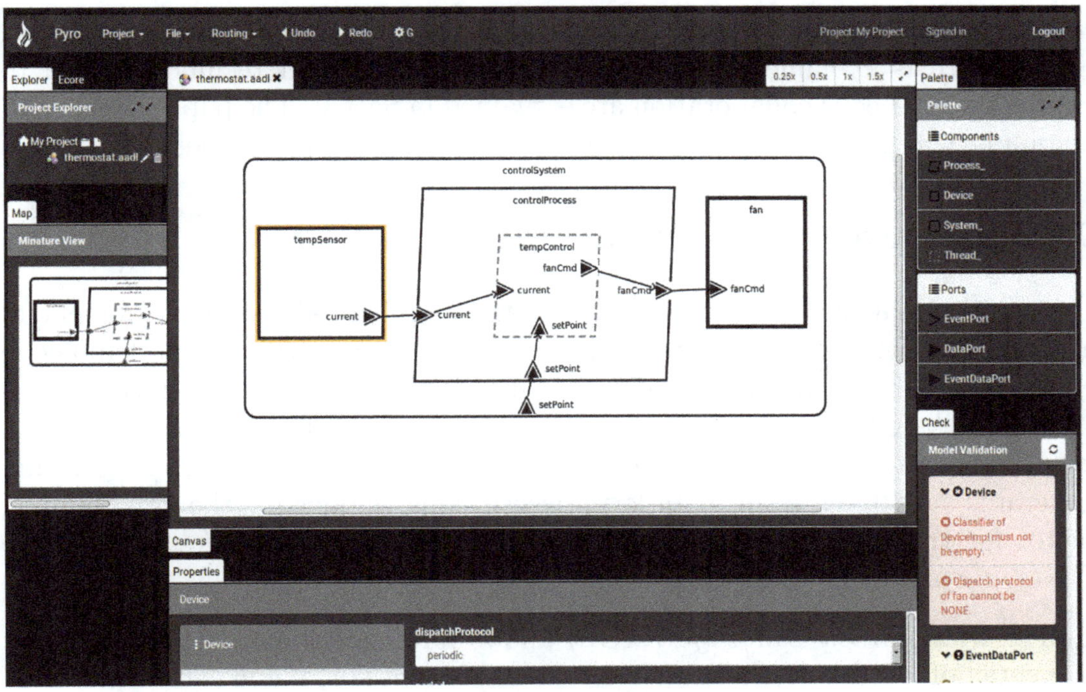

Fig. 2. Pyro web-based modeling environment for the AADL language.

where it replaces the graphical editor of the OSATE tool [8] (AADL's reference implementation). Furthermore, a dedicated code generator was developed to support verification with behavior specified with the BLESS language [17]. Another example for Pyro realizing a DSL for point and click adventures can be found in [21].

Figure 2 shows the web-based graphical AADL editor in Pyro[1]. We will use this editor in the remainder of this paper to illustrate CINCO's and Pyro's core ideas and concepts. The user interface is designed after commonly known concepts from integrated development environments, like Eclipse or IntelliJ. The main area in the center is covered by the *modeling canvas* showing the currently edited model. On the right, there is the *palette* showing the available types of modeling elements. They can be placed onto the canvas just by drag&drop. The attributes of the currently selected element in the editor can be set via the *properties* view at the bottom. The *validation* view (bottom right corner) constantly checks for the syntax and static semantics of the model in the canvas and provides appropriate error or warning messages. Finally, a *project explorer* and a *menu bar* complete the IDE-like appearance.

The remainder of the paper is organized as follows: While Sect. 2 briefly describes the use of CINCO's specification languages to define a sophisticated graphical

[1] The editor is available for experimentation on the Pyro website: https://pyro.scce.info.

modeling language, the generation to a web-based environment and the resulting architecture is explained in Sect. 3. The mechanisms and techniques used to enable simultaneous collaboration are explained in Sect. 4. The paper closes with a summary, related work, and an outlook of the future development in Sect. 5.

2 DSL Development with Cinco

CINCO is a language workbench [11] for the simplicity-driven development of graphical modeling environments that are domain-specific [12], support full code generation [10,15], and easily integrate existing solutions in the form of services [23]. As CINCO is itself a meta-level application of these principles [25], it is specialized to the domain of 'graph-based graphical modeling tools' and fully generates such tools from meta-level descriptions (models) – the key enabling factor for the whole Pyro approach. Primarily relevant in this regard are two CINCO metamodeling languages:[2]

1. The *Meta Graph Language* (MGL) allows for the definition of the abstract syntax of the developed language, i.e., which types of language elements exist and how they can be related. In the context of AADL, this means, for instance, that a *system* model consists of *devices*, *processes* and *threads*, and that all of them have *ports* (of different types) that can be connected with *data/information flow* edges.
2. The *Meta Style Language* (MSL) is used to specify the concrete graphical syntax of those MGL-defined concepts by means of simple hierarchical shapes and their appearance (such as color, line type/width, etc.). As can be seen in Fig. 2, for instance, *devices* are depicted by a black thick line rectangle, while *threads* appear as a grey dashed line parallelogram.

With these meta-level specification files, the CINCO Product Generator (which is part of CINCO) generates plug-ins for the Eclipse Rich Client Platform (RCP) that realize the editor based on the Eclipse Modeling Framework (EMF) and the Graphiti graphical editor framework. Further additions to the editor, which are not covered by these two specification files, can be injected in an aspect-oriented fashion [16]: CINCO provides a so-called mechanism of *hooks* that are triggered on the occurrence of certain events, for instance, when a node is created, moved, or deleted. Hooks are inserted into the MGL file with *annotations* on the model elements defined therein. The effect of a hook can either be modeled in a transformation language [20] or directly be written as Java code using the generated model API. In the context of the AADL editor, e.g., a `postMoveHook` is used to move a port to the nearest border within its container after it has been moved by the user. This results in a very natural 'snapping to the border' effect during modeling.

As CINCO follows a fully generative approach, the very same specification files are utilized by Pyro to generate a web-based modeling editor that runs in

[2] For a more elaborate introduction on how to define a graphical editor with CINCO, as well as other case studies and exemplary modeling languages, please refer to [26].

the browser (cf. Fig. 1). Of course, in this context, the running platform won't be based on Eclipse anymore, but based on common web frameworks like Angular for the frontend and Java EE for the backend. The aspects of a CINCO Product included in a service-oriented fashion via native components written in Java (for instance a code generator or editor-assisting features like the hooks discussed above) can thus directly be run also in the backend of the Pyro editor.

In the following, we will focus on two particularly important aspects of Pyro: After discussing the frontend/backend architecture of the generated Pyro modeling environments in Sect. 3, we will take a deeper look at the communication pattern between the involved components that facilitates synchronous collaborative modeling (cf. Sect. 4).

3 Architecture

In contrast to developing an Eclipse-based modeling environment, for the realization of a web-based solution one nearly has to start from scratch. Eclipse itself is built on a huge amount of plug-ins, developed over the past seventeen years. In particular, the Eclipse Modeling Project provides many frameworks for developing modeling languages based on metamodels and bundling them into a rich IDE. In the context of the web, development of integrated environments has just started, so that only a few best practices, plug-ins, and frameworks are available. This means, even fundamental features often have to be implemented to enable basic functionalities. The main difference between local desktop IDEs and a web-based environment like Pyro is the opportunity to provide distributed access to a centralized instance by multiple users at the same time. This results in new challenges and requirements regarding the synchronization between multiple users and conflict resolution for oppositional modifications.

Thus, the Pyro architecture must be built in a way that adequately substitutes what Eclipse already provides in the desktop application context, but also be prepared for the distributed setting with multiple users – in particular for supporting live collaborative editing on the same models. In this section, the generation of Pyro web-based modeling environments is described in a way that shows how the needed information is collected from CINCO's high-level specification metamodels and where the generated code is placed and distributed in the overall context to build the Pyro architecture.

The previously introduced specification of the AADL modeling language constitutes the source for the tool generation step. After the Pyro generator is triggered, all MGL and MSL files for a CINCO-based modeling tool are collected to gather the required information. At this point, all modeling languages, including their available node and edge types, are visible for the generator.

In the next step, a template of the modeling environment web application is created. The gray parts with dotted borders in Fig. 3 show the static elements independent of the given language specification, whereas the blue parts with solid borders are specifically generated from this specification. The template consists of a *DyWA*-based backend, extended by a specific *Domain Layer*

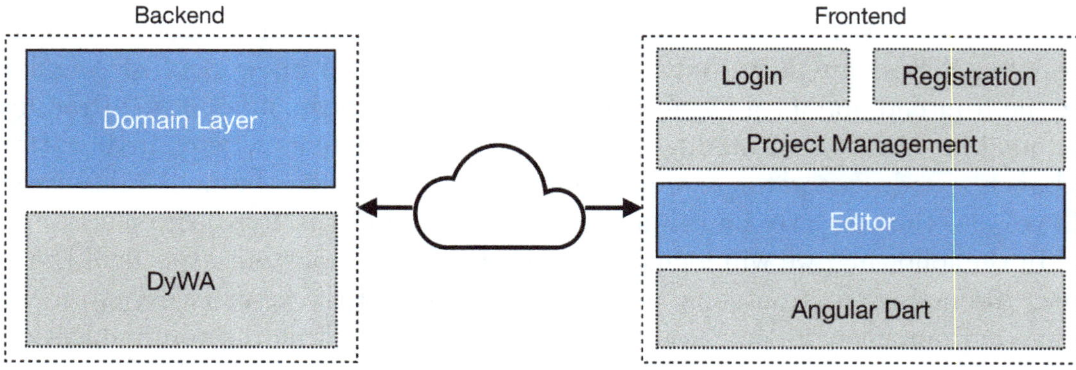

Fig. 3. Overall architecture of the generated web-based modeling environment.

for communication. On the client side, some general parts provide *Registration*, *Login*, and *Project Management*, but the main component is the specific *Editor* generated to handle instances of the graphical modeling language. The underlying single-page web application framework *Angular Dart* [1] is utilized to enable the required features of a rich internet application, like versatile user interaction and asynchronous communication.

Essentially, in the backend, the challenge of providing the metamodel-based model handling (persistence, API, event handling, etc.) is solved, which in the CINCO desktop client world is provided by the EMF framework. The frontend, on the other hand, realizes the rich IDE-like frame application with the graphical editor for the models. In the following, these two parts are explained in more detail to show how the different layers are connected and which parts are generated to establish the entire integrated environment.

3.1 Backend

The backend of a modeling environment generated using Pyro consists of two main layers: One is responsible for the centralized persistence of model instances, the other for receiving and distributing modifications. The lowest level of the web application is the database to store information in a centralized fashion. This layer handles the representation of predefined metamodels for the given domain-specific languages. Pyro modeling environments utilize the *DyWA* as an abstraction layer of a database to store types and objects in a dynamic and loosely coupled fashion [27]. Based on the specified languages' node and edge types, a *Domain Data Plug-in* (see Fig. 4) is generated by Pyro which declares types, associations, attributes, and inheritance. The main reason for using the *DyWA* as model layer is its *Domain Generator*, which generates a specific *DyWA API* providing entities and controllers for the previously given types to handle their instances on a simplified layer above the database. This closely resembles the APIs generated by EMF in the Eclipse world, so that the effort of generating the required *CINCO API* adapters is greatly reduced, which provides functionalities with identical signatures as EMF, so that already

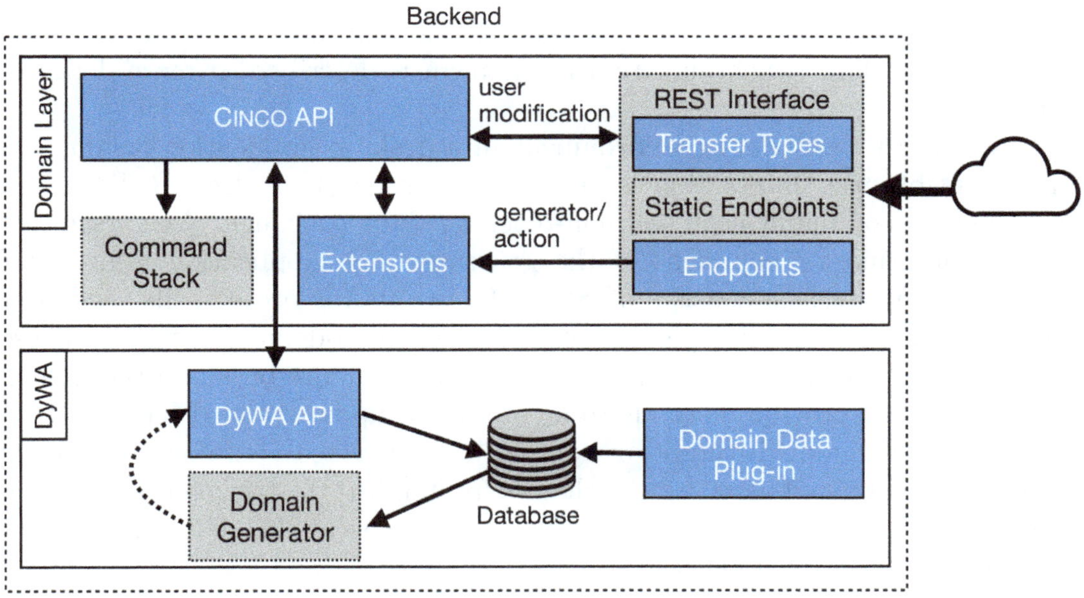

Fig. 4. Backend component architecture and interaction.

existing code can directly be applied (see below). Beyond that, DyWA is prepared for dynamic change of the metamodel, which becomes necessary during modeling language evolution (see [19]).

Since CINCO supports to extend the definition of graphical modeling languages by user-written Java code for hooks, actions, validation checks, and code generators, a holistic reuse mechanism has to be provided in the context of Pyro. To meet this goal, the same CINCO interfaces are rebuilt in the generated web-based modeling environment, providing the same structure and identical signatures. As a result of this, the domain-specific interfaces (see Fig. 4, *CINCO API*) generated by Pyro are compatible to the one CINCO generates for Eclipse and EMF to be used identically by these extensions. In contrast to the desktop-based CINCO Product, a Pyro graph model instance is not persisted in a file on the local system. The Pyro web modeling environment as a distributed system utilizes the DyWA database for storage and centralized access as a server. Thus, the *CINCO API* is internally connected to the corresponding generated *DyWA API* to persist changes in the database, which is hidden from the extensions.

Multi-user collaborative editing with the generated domain-specific modeling languages is one of the main challenges for Pyro. All changes to a centrally held instance of a graph model have to be shared with all participants. For the distribution of the changes performed on a graph model by calling the *CINCO API*) methods, a *Command Stack* is used, to store each individual modification. Since CINCO provides hooks for aspect-oriented extensions, a single action like the movement of a node on the canvas can result in multiple successive commands. As a result, all modifications on a model or any of their elements at runtime are encoded in commands and sequentially stored in the stack. The recorded commands during the *CINCO API* usage are used to synchronize between different clients looking at the same model as well as the realization of redo and undo functionalities. This synchronization mechanism is described in more detail in Sect. 4.

To use the web modeling environment in a desktop application fashion, an uninterruptible user interaction is necessary. Thus, Pyro utilizes REST-based asynchronous communication for non-blocking data exchange. As a result of this, the outermost component of the generated web application is a *REST Interface*. The interface consists of *Static Endpoints* for project, file, and user management, which are independent from the given modeling languages. These parts are supplemented by generated *Endpoints*, which are based on the CINCO specification and provide methods to create, read, update, and delete (CRUD) a single graph model. In addition to this, the interface contains the central endpoint for commands sent from a client's frontend to the backend. Depending on the used *Extensions*, additional *Endpoints* are generated to fetch and trigger user-written actions or a generator.

3.2 Frontend

To mimic the look and feel of a local desktop modeling environment, the web-based variant generated by Pyro has to provide versatile user interactions. As a result of this, the *Frontend* of the generated web application (see Fig. 5), which realizes the interface for the user, is focused on quick responses and familiar input behavior. To achieve this goal, the frontend part of a web modeling environment is built upon the *Angular Dart* [1] framework, which is used to realize single-page web applications with built-in cross-platform support and comprises an architecture focused on reusable components. In addition to this, it is tailored to asynchronous user interaction and client-side routing, so that it can be used to build rich internet applications, like, for instance, ones resembling integrated development environments (IDEs).

In contrast to a local desktop application, a web application requires additional multi-user focused interfaces. Therefore, the template for the frontend, which is initially created, consists of static user interfaces for *Registration* and *Login* as well as a *Project Management* area to create, edit, and share projects. The specifically generated parts are used by the *Editor*, which comprises domain-specific components. Its user interface is similar to the known Eclipse IDE used by regular CINCO Products (see Fig. 2).

The challenge of preventing delays in the system's response on a user input to enable fluent interaction can be met by avoiding synchronized communication with the backend. The *editor* facilitates this frontend-side computation by two layers used to interact with instances of the graph models. The *Mirror Layer* stores a snapshot of the model present in the database, whereas the *Interaction Layer* is a direct representation of a visible graph which can be modified by the user. This separation enables a delta between the last valid graph, stored in the *Mirror Layer* and the currently visible graph. Thanks to this, generated syntactical validators (e.g., for ensuring lower bounds of given cardinalities) can

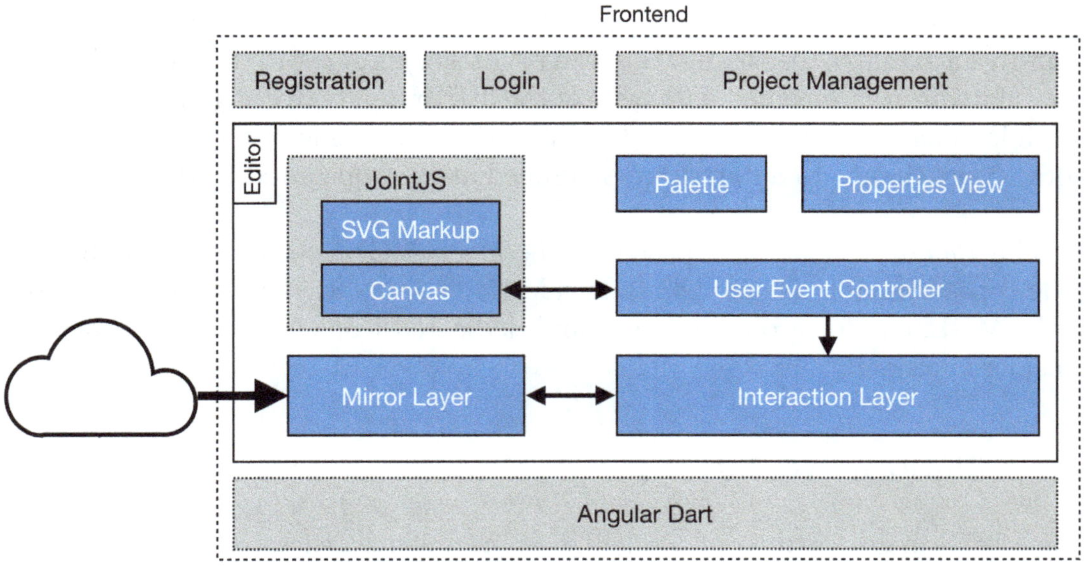

Fig. 5. Front end architecture.

raise errors and the appropriate rollback operation works immediately on the client side without additional communication with the backend.

Pyro specifically aims at supporting users switching from already existing CINCO Products to the web-based modeling environment. Thus, the *Editor*, which is the main part of the frontend, provides multiple components similar to the Eclipse IDE. To not confuse users, functions, behavior and arrangement are recreated. Besides common user interface parts like a project explorer and a menu, specific components for the modeling environment are generated, like the *Canvas*, a *Properties View*, and the *Palette*.

The *Canvas* is based on the *JointJS* framework [9], which in general renders SVGs and adds versatile user interaction for manipulation of nodes and edges via drag&drop functionalities. Using this, it was possible that the web modeling environment running in a browser provides very similar handling to the Eclipse-based desktop application with its Graphiti editor. The exact replication of the node and edge appearance is a central goal of the generated *Canvas*. Ideally, a user cannot distinguish between a Pyro and CINCO visualization of a graph model. This requires the same hierarchical shape structure for the web as in the Graphiti editor, which can be realized by scalable vector graphics (SVGs). The *SVG Markup*, which defines the shapes and styling information of the nodes and edges, is generated based on the concrete syntax specified in the MSL files of CINCO. The *JointJS* framework and *SVG Markup* files are observed by a domain-specific *User Event Controller*, which realizes the listeners and stream handling mechanisms for a single graph model to modify the underlying layers.

Besides the distinct and visible modifications available directly in the *Canvas*, attributes of an edge, node or the graph model (as defined in the MGL metamodel) can be modified using the *Properties View*. It has a generic frame based on a tree view to recursively walk through associated types of the currently selected element. For every type present in an MGL file, a form for editing the primitive attributes (e.g string, Boolean or integer) is generated. The single fields are tailored to the specified data type of the attribute, to give as much support as possible. Thanks to the two-way data binding of the underlying Angular framework, every change to an attribute is immediately propagated to the underlying layer.

The *Palette* is generated based on the given MGL specifications. It lists all node types available for modeling. In addition to this, the optional annotations of the MGL, e.g. for grouping nodes and dedicated icons for visual support, are considered as well.

4 Collaborative Editing

One of the main features of modeling environments generated by Pyro is the simultaneous editing of graph models by multiple clients at the same time. The continuous synchronization between clients avoids classical revision control repositories for distributed access and instead enables immediate collaboration. To reach the goal of simultaneous synchronization, different aspects have been considered to maintain consistency, scalability and achieve a real-time effect.

In this section, the mechanism used for Pyro web-based modeling environments to communicate is presented and explained. The first part discusses the different challenges of a distributed system with respect to the domain of graphical modeling environments, whereas the second part describes the realization of the command pattern used to exchange modifications on a graph model.

4.1 Simultaneous Synchronization Mechanism

The main communication concept of a generated modeling environment by Pyro as a distributed system is the *optimistic replication strategy* [30]. This concept replicates data and allows the single replicas to diverge, which in the context of Pyro is realized by the separated graph model replicas held in each client. The optimistic replication belongs to the *eventually consistent* consistency model and is furthermore classified as *basically available, soft state and eventually consistent* (BASE) [36]. It benefits from high availability, since it only exchanges updates on given items. In the context of a web-based modeling environment, the updates are based on the modifications a client can do to a node or edge. To enable conflict resolution and maintain consistency regarding commutativity and idempotency, *conflict-free replicated data types* (CRDTs) are represented by commands. CRDT was originally used for text-based synchronization as a simplification of *operational transformation* [34]. It utilizes an additional data structure, based on an identifier of the client, the changed value and the position to create a unique identifier for each changed character of the text. Regarding the graph models handled by Pyro, CRDTs are realized by commands for each type of possible model element modification, which store a unique identifier and the changed properties of the relevant element. In addition to this, the previous values of the updated properties are stored as well, to enable rollback, undo, and redo functionalities. Thus, Pyro uses operation-based and state-based CRDTs. Thanks to the CRDTs, conflicts of simultaneously editing the same model element at the same time can be detected. In the context of graphical DSLs, conflicts can arise by violating the given static semantics defined in the metamodel. If a conflict is detected, the corresponding command is flagged for rollback and returned to its sender. The client then inverts the modification encoded by the command and applies it to revert the conflicting change.

4.2 Distributed Command Pattern

The distribution of modifications made to a graph model in the Pyro web modeling environment is realized by a *command pattern* [14]. It belongs to the behavioral design pattern, which is used to encapsulate all information needed to perform an update on an object. The commands are sent as HTTP POST requests, combining the graph model and client identifier. An exemplified collaboration of two clients (red and green) modifying the same graph model simultaneously is presented in Fig. 6.

After the initial read from the database, a client only calculates, exchanges and receives commands when a modification is done (see Fig. 6(1)). For every possible change on nodes and edges (e.g., moving a node or bending an edge), a dedicated command encoding the modification is created and sent to the server, extended with a unique identifier of the sender. Thanks to this assignment, all commands can be differentiated (see red commands by client A and green commands by client B in Fig. 6). As an example, the command for the creation of a node consists of the node type, the position and an identifier of the container where it should be instantiated. Other commands, e.g., the move node commands, contain information of the previous as well as the new position, so that they store the delta of the modification.

The *Serializer* (see Fig. 6(2)) is used to parse the received payload and assign the commands to the associated *Command Applier*. Thanks to additional reflective *type* annotations, the received payload can be parsed to recreate the correct command type. The assignment depends on the given graph model type the command belongs to.

The *Command Applier* (see Fig. 6(3)) is the main component of the web server, since it receives, validates and executes the commands. Every modification encoded by a command is initially validated against the syntactical constraints defined by the graph model type. In the case of a constraint violation, the command is inverted based on the given delta, and returned to undo the invalid operation sent from a client. After a successful validation, the modification encoded by the command is applied to the generated domain-specific API, which also triggers the annotated hooks and finally modify the node or edge instances in the central database. Modifications performed on the API itself (e.g., performed by a hook implementation) are again internally encoded as commands for further distribution to other clients. The updates resulting from the hook execution inside the API are combined with the initial command to be

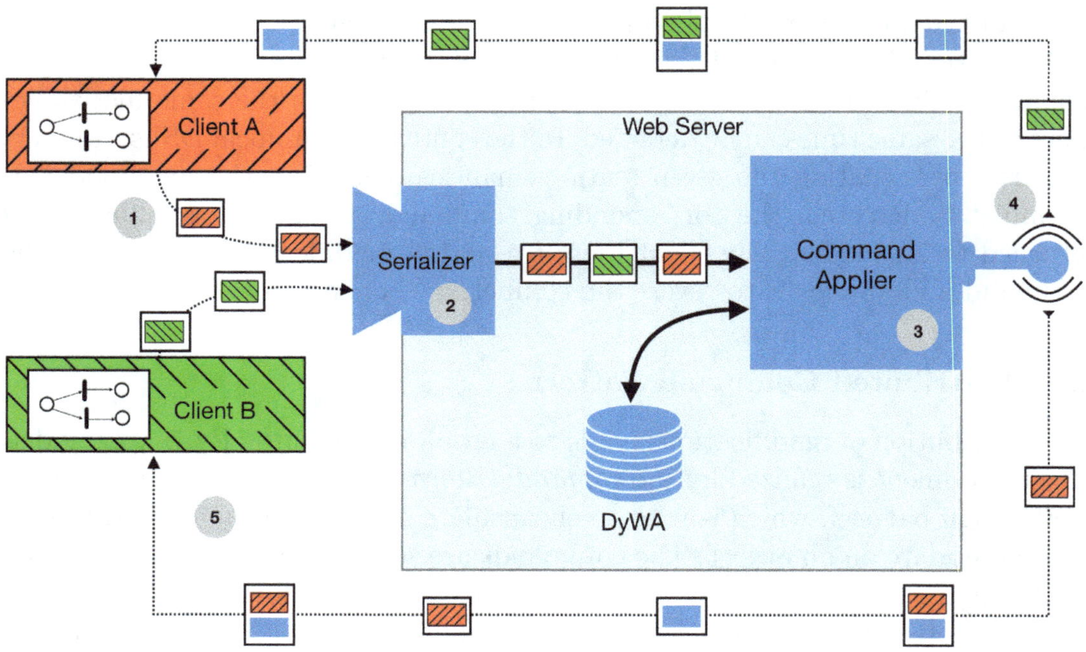

Fig. 6. Concept of the distributed command pattern. (Color figure online)

interpreted as a single transaction shown by the packages of Fig. 6. To ensure the consistency between the sender of a command and the other clients, the initiator is also informed about internally arisen modification based on hook execution. All commands, collected during the execution of the initial modification, are broadcast to other listening clients (see Fig. 6(4)). This mechanism uses bidirectional ongoing connections, so that clients can request to listen on changes made to their currently open graph model.

The commands received by a client (see Fig. 6(5)) are parsed and inspected, to ensure that commands initiated by the client itself are neglected. New changes from other clients are applied to all layers and displayed on the canvas. In addition to this, the client is notified about received changes. Updates caused as a result of self-sent commands (e.g., a modification performed during a hook execution), are only partially applied to guarantee that nodes and edges will not be modified twice.

The command pattern applied to the generated modeling environments is tailored to enable real-time collaborative editing. The main design decisions are focused on scalability and high availability by BASE and CRDT. The operational approach realized with this command pattern is more suitable than a textual language protocol like the *Language Server Protocol* (LSP) [3]. The main difference between the command pattern and the LSP is the way of distributing modifications on the model. In contrast to the presented communication protocol of Pyro, the LSP uses changed regions of a text document for propagation. The intention of the modification has to be evaluated afterwards, whereas in graphical DSLs the commands are used for a direct representation of the occurred change.

5 Conclusion and Perspectives

We have presented Pyro, a framework for enabling domain-specific modeling via the internet. Provided with an adequate metamodel specification, Pyro turns a browser into a collaborative, domain-specific, graphical development environment with features reminiscent of desktop IDEs for programming textual languages. The required metamodeling is supported in a high-level, simplicity-driven fashion: The MGL describes the available node types, edge types, and syntactical constraints, whereas the MSL defines the visual appearance of the modeling artifacts defined in the MGL. Based on these specifications, the entire ready-to-run browser-based domain-specific development environment is generated fully automatically, as has been illustrated along the construction of a graphical development environment for the Architecture Analysis and Design Language (AADL).

The field of web-based development environments is still quite young, so that not many related solutions exist yet. There are the aforementioned collaborative online text editors like Google Docs, Microsoft Office 365 and ShareLaTeX/Overleaf, but in the area of DSLs and modeling, so far we only encountered WebGME [5], an (early stage) online adaption of Vanderbilt University's Generic Modeling Environment [18] and Theia [4], a cross-platform web and desktop IDE for textual DSLs. In addition, itemis (the German company who significantly contributed to the well-known Xtext [6] DSL framework) is currently working on a platform called 'Convecton', which aims at bringing modeling with and execution of domain-specific languages online into the cloud [35]. However, none of these solutions provide a Pyro-like, graphical, collaborative modeling support.

Pyro is still in an early stage of development, and there is a lot of room for improvement, like further enhancing and easing the graphical modeling features, or improving the performance of collaborative modeling by taking advantage of peer-to-peer communication. Pyro is envisioned to enable cross-competence collaboration on a single project in a domain/purpose-specific fashion according to the Language-Driven Engineering (LDE) paradigm [31]. LDE aims at allowing the different stakeholders to formulate their intents in they way they are used to, i.e., in their domain language, and restricted in a fashion that the efforts of the other involved stakeholders are maintained, or as we say, constitute Archimedean points [32] of the considered domain-specific language. Currently, we are starting to explore the impact of the Pyro technology on a larger scale for DIME [7], our framework for developing Web applications.

References

1. About AngularDart. https://webdev.dartlang.org/angular. Accessed 13 Feb 2019
2. Graphiti - A Graphical Tooling Infrastructure. http://www.eclipse.org/graphiti/. Accessed 13 Feb 2019
3. Official page for Language Server Protocol. https://microsoft.github.io/language-server-protocol/. Accessed 12 Feb 2019
4. Theia - Cloud and Desktop IDE. https://www.theia-ide.org. Accessed 12 Feb 2019

5. WebGME. https://webgme.org/. Accessed 13 Feb 2019
6. Xtext - Language Engineering Made Easy! http://www.eclipse.org/Xtext/. Accessed 13 Feb 2019
7. Boßelmann, S., et al.: DIME: a programming-less modeling environment for web applications. In: Margaria, T., Steffen, B. (eds.) ISoLA 2016. LNCS, vol. 9953, pp. 809–832. Springer, Cham (2016). https://doi.org/10.1007/978-3-319-47169-3_60
8. Carnegie Mellon University: Welcome to OSATE. http://osate.org/. Accessed 13 Feb 2019
9. client IO: Joint API. http://www.jointjs.com/api. Accessed 13 Feb 2019
10. Czarnecki, K., Eisenecker, U.W.: Generative Programming: Methods, Tools, and Applications. ACM Press/Addison-Wesley Publishing Co., New York (2000)
11. Fowler, M.: Language Workbenches: The Killer-App for Domain Specific Languages? June 2005. http://martinfowler.com/articles/languageWorkbench.html. Accessed 13 Feb 2019
12. Fowler, M., Parsons, R.: Domain-Specific Languages. Addison-Wesley/ACM Press (2011). http://books.google.de/books?id=ri1muolw_YwC
13. Gronback, R.C.: Eclipse Modeling Project: A Domain-Specific Language (DSL) Toolkit. Addison-Wesley, Boston (2008)
14. Hannemann, J., Kiczales, G.: Design pattern implementation in Java and AspectJ. In: Proceedings of the 17th ACM SIGPLAN Conference on Object-Oriented Programming, Systems, Languages, and Applications (OOPSLA 2002). ACM SIGPLAN Notices, vol. 37, pp. 161–173. ACM (2002)
15. Kelly, S., Tolvanen, J.P.: Domain-Specific Modeling: Enabling Full Code Generation. Wiley/IEEE Computer Society Press, Hoboken (2008)
16. Kiczales, G., et al.: Aspect-oriented programming. In: Akşit, M., Matsuoka, S. (eds.) ECOOP 1997. LNCS, vol. 1241, pp. 220–242. Springer, Heidelberg (1997). https://doi.org/10.1007/BFb0053381
17. Larson, B.R., Chalin, P., Hatcliff, J.: BLESS: formal specification and verification of behaviors for embedded systems with software. In: Brat, G., Rungta, N., Venet, A. (eds.) NFM 2013. LNCS, vol. 7871, pp. 276–290. Springer, Heidelberg (2013). https://doi.org/10.1007/978-3-642-38088-4_19
18. Ledeczi, A., et al.: The generic modeling environment. In: Workshop on Intelligent Signal Processing (WISP 2001) (2001)
19. Lybecait, M., Kopetzki, D., Naujokat, S., Steffen, B.: Towards Language-to-Language Transformation (2019, to appear)
20. Lybecait, M., Kopetzki, D., Steffen, B.: Design for 'X' through model transformation. In: Margaria, T., Steffen, B. (eds.) ISoLA 2018. LNCS, vol. 11244, pp. 381–398. Springer, Cham (2018). https://doi.org/10.1007/978-3-030-03418-4_23
21. Lybecait, M., Kopetzki, D., Zweihoff, P., Fuhge, A., Naujokat, S., Steffen, B.: A tutorial introduction to graphical modeling and metamodeling with CINCO. In: Margaria, T., Steffen, B. (eds.) ISoLA 2018. LNCS, vol. 11244, pp. 519–538. Springer, Cham (2018). https://doi.org/10.1007/978-3-030-03418-4_31
22. Margaria, T., Steffen, B.: Simplicity as a driver for agile innovation. Computer **43**(6), 90–92 (2010)
23. Margaria, T., Steffen, B.: Service-orientation: conquering complexity with XMDD. In: Hinchey, M., Coyle, L. (eds.) Conquering Complexity, pp. 217–236. Springer, London (2012). https://doi.org/10.1007/978-1-4471-2297-5_10
24. McAffer, J., Lemieux, J.M., Aniszczyk, C.: Eclipse Rich Client Platform, 2nd edn. Addison-Wesley Professional (2010)

25. Naujokat, S.: Heavy Meta. Model-Driven Domain-Specific Generation of Generative Domain-Specific Modeling Tools. Dissertation, TU Dortmund, Dortmund, Germany, August 2017. http://hdl.handle.net/2003/36060
26. Naujokat, S., Lybecait, M., Kopetzki, D., Steffen, B.: CINCO: a simplicity-driven approach to full generation of domain-specific graphical modeling tools. Softw. Tools Technol. Transf. **20**(3), 327–354 (2017)
27. Neubauer, J., Frohme, M., Steffen, B., Margaria, T.: Prototype-driven development of web applications with DyWA. In: Margaria, T., Steffen, B. (eds.) ISoLA 2014. LNCS, vol. 8802, pp. 56–72. Springer, Heidelberg (2014). https://doi.org/10.1007/978-3-662-45234-9_5
28. Robby, Hatcliff, J., Belt, J.: Model-based development for high-assurance embedded systems. In: Margaria, T., Steffen, B. (eds.) ISoLA 2018. LNCS, vol. 11244, pp. 539–545. Springer, Cham (2018). https://doi.org/10.1007/978-3-030-03418-4_32
29. SAE International: Architecture Analysis & Design Language (AADL), January 2017. https://www.sae.org/standards/content/as5506c/. SAE Standard AS5506C
30. Saito, Y., Shapiro, M.: Optimistic replication. ACM Comput. Surv. (CSUR) **37**(1), 42–81 (2005)
31. Steffen, B., Gossen, F., Naujokat, S., Margaria, T.: Language-driven engineering: from general-purpose to purpose-specific languages. In: Steffen, B., Woeginger, G. (eds.) Computing and Software Science: State of the Art and Perspectives. LNCS, vol. 10000. Springer, Heidelberg (2019, to appear)
32. Steffen, B., Naujokat, S.: Archimedean points: the essence for mastering change. LNCS Trans. Found. Mastering Change (FoMaC) **1**(1), 22–46 (2016)
33. Steinberg, D., Budinsky, F., Paternostro, M., Merks, E.: EMF: Eclipse Modeling Framework, 2nd edn. Addison-Wesley, Boston (2008)
34. Sun, C., Ellis, C.: Operational transformation in real-time group editors: issues, algorithms, and achievements. In: Proceedings of the 1998 ACM Conference on Computer Supported Cooperative Work (CSCW 1998), pp. 59–68. ACM (1998)
35. Voelter, M.: Convecton Presentation at LangDev Meetup at CWI 8–9 March 2018. https://github.com/cwi-swat/langdev/blob/gh-pages/slides/Convecton@LangDev.pdf. Accessed 13 Feb 2019
36. Vogels, W.: Eventually consistent. Commun. ACM **52**(1), 40–44 (2009)

Efficient Model Synchronization by Automatically Constructed Repair Processes

Lars Fritsche[1(✉)], Jens Kosiol[2], Andy Schürr[1], and Gabriele Taentzer[2]

[1] TU Darmstadt, Darmstadt, Germany
{lars.fritsche,andy.schuerr}@es.tu-darmstadt.de
[2] Philipps-Universität Marburg, Marburg, Germany
{kosiolje,taentzer}@mathematik.uni-marburg.de

Abstract. Model synchronization, i.e., the task of restoring consistency between two interrelated models after a model change, is a challenging task. Triple Graph Grammars (TGGs) specify model consistency by means of rules. They can be used to automatically derive specifications of edit operations for single models and repair rules that propagate model changes to related models. model (re-)synchronization activities more effectively, a construction mechanism for *short-cut* rules has been recently developed. They describe consistency-preserving complex edit operations across model boundaries. We show that edit and repair rules can be derived from *short-cut* rules. As proof of concept, we implemented the construction and application of *short-cut* edit and repair rules in eMoflon. Our evaluation shows that *short-cut*-rule-based repair processes have considerably decreased data loss and improved runtime compared to former model synchronization processes in eMoflon.

Keywords: Model synchronization · Triple Graph Grammars · Short-cut rule

1 Introduction

Model-driven engineering has become an important technique to cope with the increasing complexity of modern software systems. In the field of Concurrent Engineering [7], for example, products are no longer realized in series but allow parallel tasks. Each of these tasks has its view onto the product and, as a view evolves, it may become inconsistent with the other ones. Keeping views synchronized by checking and preserving their consistency can be a challenging problem which is not only subject to ongoing research but also of practical interest for industrial applications such as stated above.

Triple Graph Grammars (TGGs) [24] are a declarative, rule-based bidirectional transformation approach that aims to synchronize models stemming from different views (usually called *domains* in the TGG literature). Their purpose

R. Hähnle and W. van der Aalst (Eds.): FASE 2019, LNCS 11424, pp. 116–133, 2019.
https://doi.org/10.1007/978-3-030-16722-6_7

is to define a consistency relationship between pairs of models in a rule-based manner by defining traces between their elements. Given a finite set of rules that define how both models co-evolve, a TGG can be automatically *operationalized* into *source* and *forward rules*. The source rules of an operationalized TGG can be used to build up models of one domain while forward rules translate them to models of the other domain, thereby establishing traces between their elements. From a synchronization point of view, source rules specify edit operations to change one model while forward rules specify repair operations to synchronize model changes with one another [16,19,24]. Even though both, the translation and the synchronization process, are formally defined and sound, there are in fact several practical issues that arise for model synchronization from (potentially transitive) dependencies between rule applications: To synchronize changed models, popular TGG approaches do not always fix inconsistencies locally but revert all dependent rule applications and start a retranslation process. However, this kind of synchronization often deletes and recreates a lot of model elements to reestablish model consistency, potentially losing information that is local to just one model and wasting processing time. Existing solutions for this problem are rather ad hoc and come without any guarantee to reestablish the consistency of modified models [12,14].

As a new solution to this synchronization problem, we derive *repair rules* from *short-cut* rules [8] that we recently introduced to handle complex consistency-preserving model updates more effectively and efficiently. The construction of *short-cut* rules is a kind of sequential rule composition that allows to replace a rule application with another one while preserving involved model elements (instead of deleting and re-creating them). We used *short-cut* rules to describe model changes exchanging one edit step by another one. Since in this paper we want to use *short-cut* rules for model synchronization as well, they have to be operationalized into *source* and *forward* rules.

Our formal contributions (in Sect. 4) are two-fold: As *short-cut* rules may be non-monotonic, i.e., may be deleting, we formalize the operationalization of non-monotonic TGG rules which decomposes short-cut rules into (semantically equivalent sequences of) source (edit) and forward (repair) rules. Moreover, we obtain sufficient conditions under which an application of a *short-cut* rule preserves the consistency of related pairs of models. This was left to future work in [8]. Together, this constitutes the correctness of our approach using operationalized *short-cut* rules for model synchronization.

Practically, we implement our synchronization approach in eMoflon [21], a state-of-the-art bidirectional graph transformation tool, and evaluate it (Sect. 5). The results show that the construction of *short-cut* repair rules enables us to react to model changes in a less invasive way by preserving information and increasing the performance. We thus contribute to a more comprehensive research trend in the bx-community towards *Least Change* synchronization [5]. Before presenting these results in detail, we illustrate our approach using an example in (Sect. 2) and recall some preliminaries in (Sect. 3). Finally, we discuss related work in (Sect. 6) and conclude with pointers to future work in (Sect. 7). A technical report that includes additional preliminaries, all proofs, and the rule set used for our evaluation (including more complex examples) is available online [9].

2 Introductory Example

We motivate the use of *short-cut* repair processes by synchronizing a Java AST (abstract syntax tree) model and a custom documentation model. For model synchronization, we consider a Java AST model as *source* model and its documentation model as *target* model, i.e., changes in a Java AST model have to be transferred to its documentation model. There are correspondence links in between such that both models become correlated.

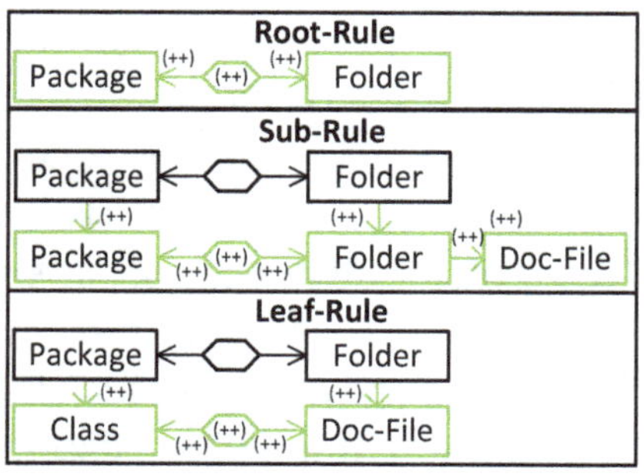

Fig. 1. Example: TGG rules (Color figure online)

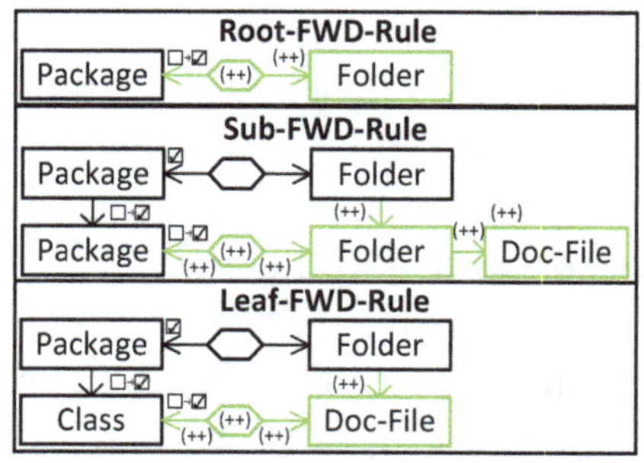

Fig. 2. Example: TGG forward rules

TGG rules. Figure 1 shows the rule set of our running example consisting of three TGG rules: *Root-Rule* creates a root *Package* together with a root *Folder* and a correspondence link in between. This rule has an empty precondition and only creates elements which are depicted in green and with the annotation (++). *Sub-Rule* creates a *Package* and *Folder* hierarchy given that an already correlated *Package* and *Folder* pair exists. Finally, *Leaf-Rule* creates a *Class* and a *Doc-File* under the same precondition as *Sub-Rule*.

These rules can be used to generate consistent triple graphs in a synchronized way consisting of source, correspondence, and target graph. A more general scenario of model synchronization is, however, to restore the consistency of a triple graph that has been altered on just one side. For this purpose, each TGG rule has to be operationalized to two kinds of rules: *source* rules enable changes of source models which is followed by translating this model to the target domain with *forward* rules. As *source* rules for single models are just projections of TGG rules to one domain, we do not show them explicitly.

Forward translation rules. Figure 2 depicts the *forward* rules. Using these rules, we can translate the Java AST model depicted on the source side of the triple graph in Fig. 3(a) to a documentation model such that the result is the complete graph in Fig. 3(a). To obtain this result we apply *Root-FWD-Rule* at the root

Package, *Sub-FWD-Rule* at *Packages* `p` and `subP`, and finally *Leaf-FWD-Rule* at *Class* `c`. To guide the translation process, context elements that have already been translated are annotated with ☑ in *forward* rules. A formerly created source element gets the marking ☐ → ☑ to indicate that applying the rule will mark this element as translated; a formalization of this marking is given in [20]. Note that *Root-FWD-Rule* can always be applied when *Sub-FWD-Rule* is applicable which can lead to untranslated edges. For simplicity, we assume that the correct rule is applied which in praxis can be achieved through negative application conditions [15].

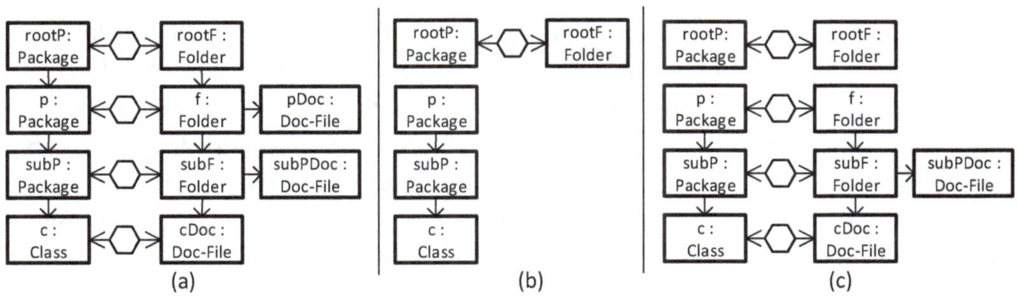

Fig. 3. Exemplary synchronization scenario

Model synchronization. Given the triple graph in Fig. 3(a), a user might want to change a sub *Package* such as `p` to be a root *Package*, e.g., as could be the case when the project is split up into multiple projects. Since `p` was created and translated as a sub *Package* rather than a root element, this change introduces an inconsistency. To resolve this issue, one approach is to revert the translation of `p` into `f` and re-translate `p` with an appropriate translation rule such as *Root-FWD-Rule*. Reverting the former translation step may lead to further inconsistencies as we remove elements that were needed as context elements by other rule applications. The result is a reversion of all translation steps except for the first one which translated the original root element. The result is shown in Fig. 3(b). Now, we can re-translate the unmarked elements yielding the result graph in (c). This example shows that this synchronization approach may delete and re-create a lot of similar structures which appears to be inefficient. Second, it may lose information that exists on the target side only, e.g., a use case may be assigned to a document which does not have a representation in the corresponding Java project.

Model synchronization with short-cut repair. In [8] we introduced short-cut rules as a kind of rule composition mechanism that allows to replace a rule application by another one while preserving elements (instead of deleting and re-creating them). In our example, *Root-Rule* and *Sub-Rule* overlap in elements as the first rule can be completely embedded into the latter one. Figure 4 depicts two possible short-cut rules based on *Root-Rule* and *Sub-Rule*. While the upper short-cut

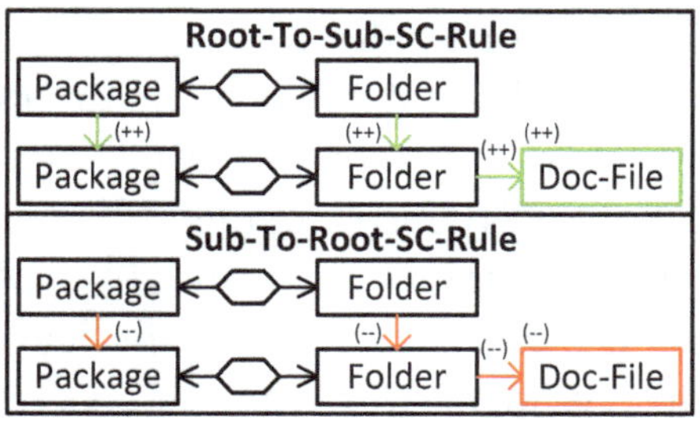

Fig. 4. Short-cut rules (Color figure online)

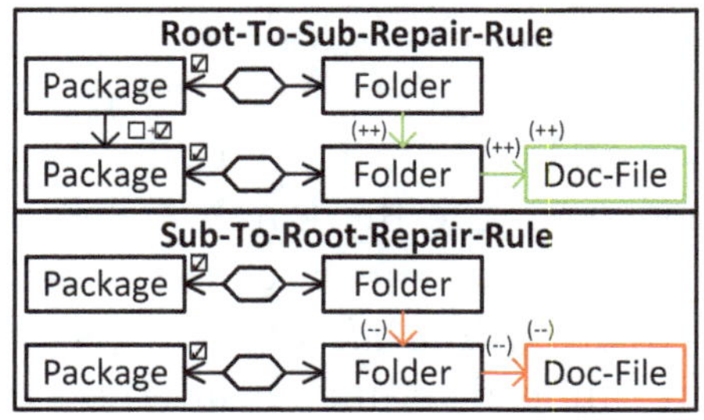

Fig. 5. Repair rules

rule replaces *Root-Rule* with *Sub-Rule*, the lower short-cut rule replaces *Sub-Rule* with *Root-Rule*. Both short-cut rules preserve the model elements on both sides and solely create elements that do not yet exist (++), or delete those depicted in red and annotated with (−−). They are constructed by overlapping both original rules such that each created element that can be mapped to the other rule becomes context and as such, is not touched. When a created element cannot be mapped because it only appears in the replacing rule, it is created. Consequently, an element is deleted if the created element only appears in the replaced rule. Finally, context elements occurring in both rules appear also in the short-cut rule while overlapped context elements appear only once. Using *Sub-To-Root-SC-Rule* enables the user to transform the triple graph in Fig. 3(a) directly to the one in (c).

Yet, these rules can still not cope with the change of a single model since short-cut rules transform both models at once as TGG rules usually do. Hence, in order to be able to handle the deleted edge between `rootP` and `p`, we have to forward operationalize short-cut rules, thereby obtaining *short-cut repair* rules. Figure 5 depicts the resulting *short-cut repair* rules derived from *short-cut* rules in Fig. 4. A non-monotonic TGG-rule is forward operationalized by removing deleted elements from the rule's source graphs as they should not be present after a source rule application. *Short-cut repair* rules allow to propagate source graph changes directly to target graphs to restore consistency. In our example, after having transformed Package `p` into a root element, the rule of choice is *Sub-To-Root-Repair-Rule* which transforms Folder `f` in Fig. 3(a) into a root element and deletes the superfluous *Doc-File*. The result is again the consistent triple graph depicted in Fig. 3(c). This repair allows to skip the costly reversion process with the intermediate result in Fig. 3(b). Note that applying *Sub-To-Root-Repair-Rule* at arbitrary matches may have undesired consequences: One could, e.g., delete the edge between two *Folders* even if the matched *Packages* are still connected. Our Theorem 8 characterizes matches where such violations of the language of the grammar cannot happen. In our implementation, we exploit an incremental pattern matcher to identify valid matches. Using suitable *negative application conditions* [6] would be an alternative approach.

3 Preliminaries

To understand our formal contributions, we assume familiarity with the basics of double-pushout rewriting in graph transformation and, more generally in adhesive categories [6,18] as well as the definition of TGGs and in particular, their operationalizations [24]. Here, we recall non-basic preliminaries for our work which are the construction of short-cut rules, the notion of sequential independence, and a (simple) categorical definition of partial maps.

In [8], we introduced short-cut rules as a new way of sequential composition for monotonic rules. Given an inverse rule of a monotonic rule (i.e., a rule that only deletes) and a monotonic rule, a short-cut rule combines their respective actions into a single rule. Its construction allows to identify elements that are deleted by the first rule as re-created by the second one. These elements are preserved in the resulting short-cut rule. A *common kernel*, i.e., a common subrule of both, serves to identify how the two rules overlap and which elements are preserved instead of being deleted and re-created. We recall their construction since our construction of repair rules is based on it. Examples are depicted in Fig. 4.

Definition 1 (Short-cut rule). *In an adhesive category* $\mathbf{C}$*, given two monotonic rules* $r_i : L_i \hookrightarrow R_i$*,* $i = 1, 2$*, and a common kernel rule* $k : L_\cap \hookrightarrow R_\cap$ *for them, the* Short-cut rule $r_1^{-1} \ltimes_k r_2 := (L \overset{l}{\hookleftarrow} K \overset{r}{\hookrightarrow} R)$ *is computed by executing the following steps depicted in Figs. 6 and 7:*

1. *The union* $L_\cup$ *of* L_1 *and* L_2 *along* $L_\cap$ *is computed as pushout* (2).
2. *The LHS* L *of the short-cut rule* $r_1^{-1} \ltimes_k r_2$ *is computed as pushout* (3a).
3. *The RHS* R *of the short-cut rule* $r_1^{-1} \ltimes_k r_2$ *is computed as pushout* (3b).
4. *The interface* K *of the short-cut rule* $r_1^{-1} \ltimes_k r_2$ *is computed as pushout* (4).
5. *Morphisms* $l : K \to L$ *and* $r : K \to R$ *are obtained by the universal property of* K.

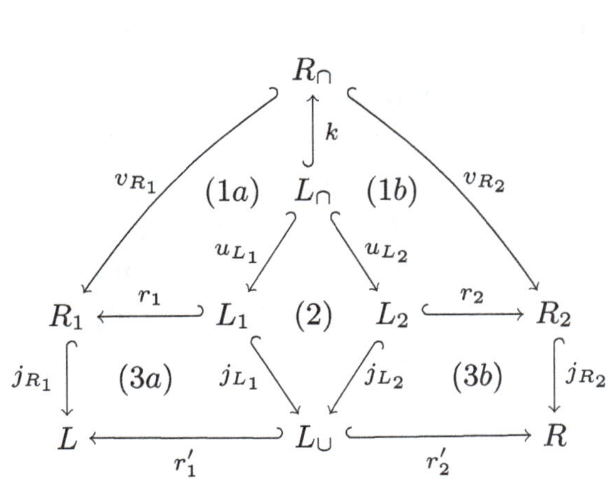

Fig. 6. Construction of LHS and RHS of short-cut rule $r_1^{-1} \ltimes_k r_2$

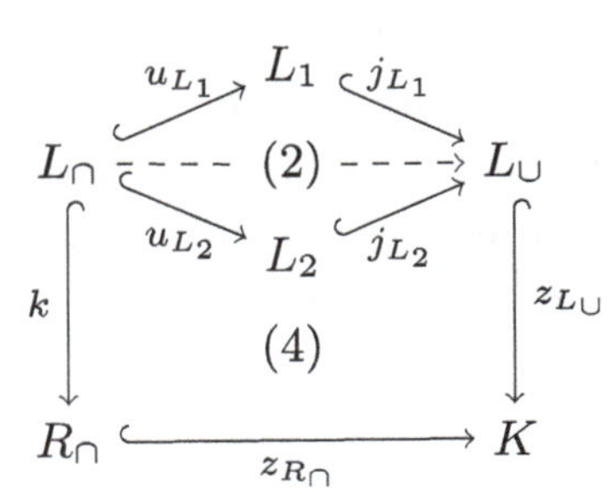

Fig. 7. Construction of interface K of $r_1^{-1} \ltimes_k r_2$

Sequential independence of two rule applications intuitively means that none of these applications enables the other one. This implies that the order of their application may be switched. The definition of sequential independence can be extended to a sequence of rule applications longer than 2. In Theorem 8, we will use this to identify language-preserving applications of short-cut rules.

Definition 2 (Sequential independence). *Given two rules* $p_i = (L_i \overset{l_i}{\hookleftarrow} K_i \overset{r_i}{\hookrightarrow} R_i)$ *with* $i = 1, 2$, *two direct transformations* $G \Rightarrow_{p_1,m_1} H_1$ *and* $H_1 \Rightarrow_{p_2,m_2} H_2$ *via the rules* r_1 *and* r_2 *are* sequentially independent *if there exist two morphisms* $d_1 : R_1 \rightarrow D_2$ *and* $d_2 : L_2 \rightarrow D_1$ *as depicted below such that* $n_1 = f_2 \circ d_1$ *and* $m_2 = f_1 \circ d_2$.

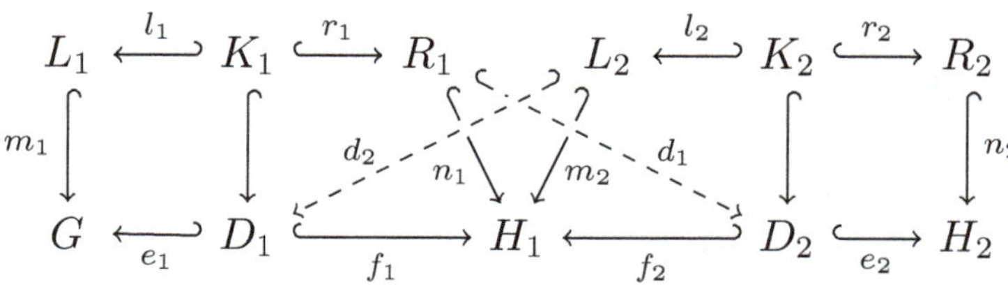

Given rules $p = (L \hookleftarrow K \hookrightarrow R)$ *and* $p_i = (L_i \hookleftarrow K_i \hookrightarrow R_i)$ *with* $1 \leq i \leq t$, *a transformation* $G_t \Rightarrow_{p,m} H$ *is* sequentially independent from a sequence of transformations $G_0 \Rightarrow_{p_1,m_1} G_1 \Rightarrow_{p_2,m_2} \cdots \Rightarrow_{p_t,m_t} G_t, t \geq 2$ *if first,* $G_t \Rightarrow_{p,m} H$ *and* $G_{t-1} \Rightarrow_{p_t,m_t} G_t$ *are sequentially independent and then, the arising transformations* $G_{t-1} \Rightarrow_{p,e_t \circ d_2^t} G'_t$ *and* $G_{t-2} \Rightarrow_{p_{t-1},m_{t-1}} G_{t-1}$ *are sequentially independent and so forth back to the transformations* $G_0 \Rightarrow_{p_1,m_1} G_1$ *and* $G_1 \Rightarrow_{p,e_2 \circ d_2^2} G'_2$ *(where* $e_i : D_i \hookrightarrow G_{i-1}$ *is given by the transformation and* $d_2^i : L \hookrightarrow D_i$ *exists by sequential independence as in the figure above).*

To formalize the application of non-monotonic TGG rules, we need to consider triple graphs with partial morphisms from correspondence to source (or target) graphs. For expressing such triple graphs categorically, we recall a simple definition of partial morphisms [23] to be used in Sect. 4.1. An elaborated theory of triple graphs with partial morphisms is out of scope of this paper.

Definition 3 (Partial morphism. Commuting square with partial morphisms). *A* partial morphism *a from an object A to an object B is a(n equivalence class of) span(s)* $A \overset{\iota_A}{\hookleftarrow} A' \overset{a}{\rightarrow} B$ *where* ι_A *is a monomorphism (denoted by* $\hookrightarrow$*). A partial morphism is denoted as* $a : A \dashrightarrow B$; A' *is called the* domain *of* a. *A diagram with two partial morphisms* a *and* c *as depicted as square* (1) *in Fig. 8 is said to be* commuting *if there exists a (necessarily unique) morphism* $x : A' \rightarrow C'$ *such that both arising squares* (2) *and* (3) *in Fig. 9 commute.*

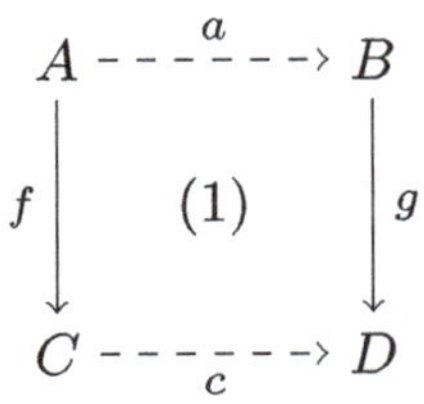

Fig. 8. Square of partial morphisms

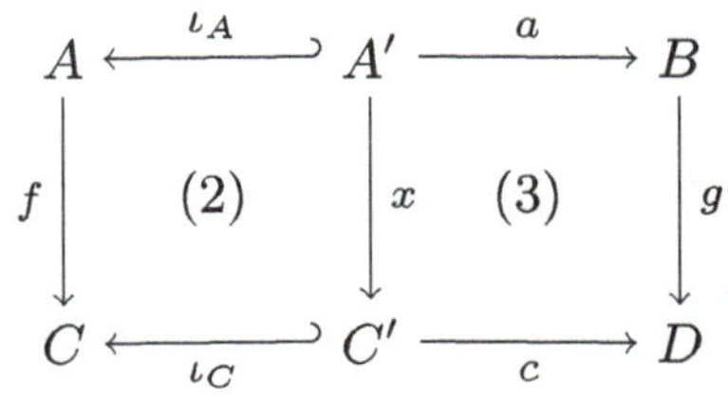

Fig. 9. Commuting square of partial morphisms

4 Constructing Language-Preserving Repair Rules

The general idea of this paper is to use *short-cut repair* rules allowing an optimized model synchronization process based on TGGs. To this end, we operationalize short-cut rules being constructed from the rules of a given TGG. Since those rules are not necessarily monotonic, we generalize the well-known operationalization of TGG rules to the non-monotonic case and show that the basic property is still valid: An application of a source rule followed by an application of the corresponding forward rule is equivalent to applying the original rule instead. This is the content of Sect. 4.1. Constructing *shortspscut* rules in [8], we identified the following problem: Applying a short-cut rule derived from rules of a given grammar might lead to an instance that is not part of the language defined by that grammar. Therefore, in Sect. 4.2, we provide sufficient conditions for applications of short-cut rules leading to instances of the grammar-defined language only. Combining both results ensures the correctness of our approach, i.e., a *shortspscut* repair rule actually propagates a model change from the source to the target model if it is correctly matched.

4.1 Operationalization of Generalized TGG Rules

Since the operationalization of TGG rules has been introduced for monotonic rules only, we extend the theory to general triple rules and, moreover, allow for partial morphisms from correspondence to source and target graph in triple graphs. We split a rule on triple graphs into a *source rule* that only affects the source part and a *forward rule* that affects correspondence and target part.

Definition 4 (TGG rule). *Let the category of triple graphs and graph morphisms be given. A triple rule p is a span of triple graph morphisms*

$$p = ((L_S \xleftarrow{\sigma_L} L_C \xrightarrow{\tau_L} L_T) \xhookleftarrow{(l_S, l_C, l_T)} (K_S \xleftarrow{\sigma_K} K_C \xrightarrow{\tau_K} K_T) \xhookrightarrow{(r_S, r_C, r_T)} (R_S \xleftarrow{\sigma_R} R_C \xrightarrow{\tau_R} R_T))$$

which, wherever possible, are abbreviated by

$$p = (L_{SCT} \xhookleftarrow{(l_S, l_C, l_T)} K_{SCT} \xhookrightarrow{(r_S, r_C, r_T)} R_{SCT}).$$

Rules p_S and p_F are called source rule *and* forward rule *of p.*

$$p_S = ((L_S \leftarrow \emptyset \rightarrow \emptyset) \xhookleftarrow{(l_S, id_\emptyset, id_\emptyset)} (K_S \leftarrow \emptyset \rightarrow \emptyset) \xhookrightarrow{(r_S, id_\emptyset, id_\emptyset)} (R_S \leftarrow \emptyset \rightarrow \emptyset)),$$

$$p_F = (R_S L_{CT} \xleftarrow{(id_{R_S}, l_C, l_T)} R_S K_{CT} \xrightarrow{(id_{R_S}, r_C, r_T)} R_{SCT})$$

with $\emptyset$ *being the empty graph. In* $R_S L_{CT} = (R_S \dashleftarrow L_C \xhookrightarrow{\tau_L} L_T)$*, the morphism from* L_C *to* R_S *may be partial and is defined by the span* $(L_C \xhookleftarrow{l_C} K_C \xhookrightarrow{r_S \circ \sigma_K} R_S)$ *with* $\sigma_K : K_C \hookrightarrow R_C$. Target *and* backward rules p_T *and* p_B *are defined symmetrically in the other direction.*

Given a TGG, a short-cut repair rule *is a forward rule* p_F *of a short-cut rule* $p = r_1^{-1} \ltimes_k r_2$ *where* r_1, r_2 *are (monotonic) rules of the TGG, i.e., a repair rule is an operationalized short-cut rule.*

The above definition is motivated by our application scenario, i.e., the case where a user edits the source (or target) model independently of the other parts. The partial morphism in the forward rule reflects that a model change may introduce a situation where the result is no longer a triple graph. A deleted source element may have a preimage in the correspondence graph that is not deleted as well. In the example *short-cut* rules in Fig. 4, this problem does not occur since edges are deleted only. But in general, this definition of p_S has the disadvantage that often, p_S is not applicable to any triple graph since the result would not be one.

In practical applications, however, the source rule specifies a user edit action that is performed on the source part only, ignoring correspondence and target graphs. The fact that the result is not a triple graph any longer is not a technical problem. A missing source element that should be referenced by a correspondence element gives information about a location that needs some repair. Therefore, we define the application of a source rule such that the resulting triple graph is allowed to be partial. Furthermore, forward rules may be applied to partial triple graphs allowing for dangling correspondence relations.

Definition 5 (Constructing an operationalized rule application). *Let a triple graph rule* $p = (L_{SCT} \xleftarrow{(l_S, l_C, l_T)} K_{SCT} \xrightarrow{(r_S, r_C, r_T)} R_{SCT})$ *with source rule* p_S *and forward rule* p_F *be given. An operationalized rule application* $G \Rightarrow_{p_S, m_S} G' \Rightarrow_{p_F, m_F} H$ *is constructed as follows:*

1. *The rule* $p_S^{\mathrm{pr}} = L_S \xleftarrow{l_S} K_S \xrightarrow{r_S} R_S$ *is the* projection *of* p_S *to its source part.*
2. *Given a match* m_S^{pr} *for* p_S^{pr}*, construct the transformation* $t_S^{\mathrm{pr}} : G_S \Rightarrow_{p_S^{\mathrm{pr}}, m_S^{\mathrm{pr}}} H_S$*, called* source application *and inducing the span* $G_S \xhookleftarrow{f_S} D_S \xhookrightarrow{g_S} H_S$.
3. *The transformation* t_S^{pr} *can be extended to the transformation* $t_S : G = (G_S \xleftarrow{\sigma_G} G_C \xrightarrow{\tau_G} G_T) \Rightarrow_{p_S, m_S} G' = (H_S \dashleftarrow G_C \xrightarrow{\tau_G} G_T)$ *via* p_S *at match* m_S*. The partial morphism* $G_C \dashrightarrow H_S$ *is given as the span* $G_C \hookleftarrow G'_C \rightarrow H_S$ *that arises as pullback of the co-span* $G_C \rightarrow G_S \hookleftarrow D_S$ *as depicted in Fig. 10, i.e., as morphism* $g_S \circ p_D : G_C \dashrightarrow H_S$ *with domain* G'_C.
4. *Given co-match* $n_S : R_S \hookrightarrow H_S$ *and matches* $m_X : L_X \hookrightarrow G_X$ *with* $X \in \{C, T\}$ *such that both arising squares are commuting, i.e.,* $m_F = (n_S, m_C, m_T)$ *is a morphism of partial triple graphs, construct transformation* $t_F : G' \Rightarrow_{p_F, m_F} H = (H_S \xleftarrow{\sigma_H} H_C \xrightarrow{\tau_H} H_T)$*, called* forward application, *using transformations* $G_X \Rightarrow_{p_X, m_X} H_X$ *for* $X \in \{C, T\}$ *if they exist*

and if there are morphisms $\sigma'_D : D_C \to H_S$ *and* $\tau_D : D_C \to D_T$ *such that* $H_S D_C D_T \hookrightarrow H_S G_C G_T$ *and* $R_S K_C K_T \hookrightarrow H_S D_C D_T$ *are triple morphisms.*

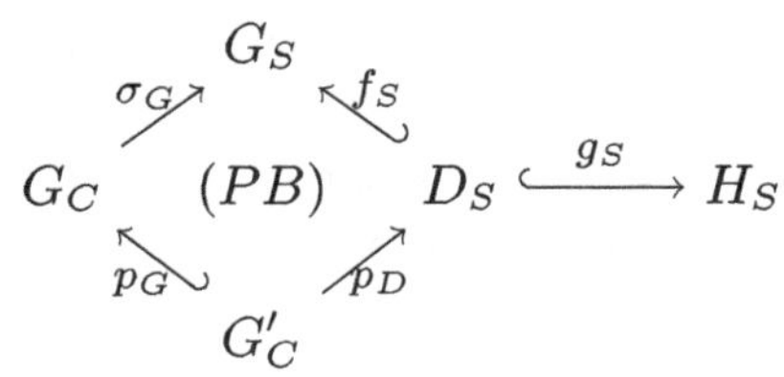

Fig. 10. Retrieval of partial morphism $G_C \dashrightarrow H_S$

In the setting of this paper, it is enough to allow for partial morphisms only in the input graph and not in the output graph of a forward rule application. Intuitively this means that such an application deletes those elements from the correspondence graph that could not be mapped to elements in the source graph any longer and additionally deletes the preimages in the correspondence graph of all deleted elements from the target graph as well (if there are any). The next lemma states that the application of a source rule is well-defined, i.e., that the mentioned partial morphism actually exists.

Lemma 6 (Correctness of application of source rules). *Let a (non-monotonic) triple graph rule*

$$p = (L_{SCT} \xleftarrow{(l_S, l_C, l_T)} K_{SCT} \xrightarrow{(r_S, r_C, r_T)} R_{SCT})$$

with source rule p_S *and projection* p_S^{pr} *to the source part be given. Given a match* m_S *for* p_S *to a triple graph* $G = (G_S \xleftarrow{\sigma_G} G_C \xrightarrow{\tau_G} G_T)$ *such that* $G_S \Rightarrow_{p_S^{\mathrm{pr}}, m_S} H_S$, *the partial morphism* $D_C \dashrightarrow H_S$ *as described in Definition 5 exists.*

The next theorem states that a sequential application of a source and a forward rule indeed coincides with an application of the original rule as long as the matches are consistent. This means that the forward rule has to match the RHS R_S of the source rule again and the LHS L_C of the correspondence rule needs to be matched in such a way that all elements not belonging to the domain of the partial morphism from correspondence to source part in the input model are deleted. The forward rule application defined in Definition 5 fulfills this condition by construction.

Theorem 7 (Synthesis of rule applications). *Let a triple graph rule* p *with source and forward rules* p_S *and* p_F *be given. If there are applications* $G \Rightarrow_{p_S, m_S} G'$ *with co-match* n_S *and* $G' \Rightarrow_{p_F, m_F} H$ *with* $m_F = (n_S, m_C, m_T)$ *as constructed above, then there is an application* $G \Rightarrow_{p,m} H$ *with* $m = (m_S, m_C, m_T)$.

4.2 Language-Preserving Short-Cut Rules

In this section we identify sufficient conditions for an application of a short-cut rule that guarantee the result to be an element of the language of the original grammar. Since our conditions apply to arbitrary adhesive categories and are not specific for TGGs, we present the result in its general form.

Theorem 8 (Characterization of valid applications). *In an adhesive category $\mathcal{C}$, given a sequence of transformations*

$$G \Rightarrow_{r,m} G_0 \Rightarrow_{p_1,m_1} G_1 \Rightarrow_{p_2,m_2} \cdots \Rightarrow_{p_t,m_t} G_t \Rightarrow_{r^{-1} \ltimes_k r',m_{sc}} H$$

with rules $p_1, \ldots, p_t$ and $r^{-1} \ltimes_k r'$ being the short-cut rule of monotonic rules $r : L \hookrightarrow R$ and $r' : L' \hookrightarrow R'$ along a common kernel k, there is a match m' for r' in G and a transformation sequence

$$G \Rightarrow_{r',m'} G'_1 \Rightarrow_{p_1,m'_1} \ldots G'_{t-1} \Rightarrow_{p_t,m'_t} H,$$

provided that

1. *the application of $r^{-1} \ltimes_k r'$ with match m_{sc} is sequentially independent of the sequence of transformations $G_0 \Rightarrow_{p_1,m_1} G_1 \Rightarrow_{p_2,m_2} \cdots \Rightarrow_{p_t,m_t} G_t$ and*
2. *the thereby implied match m'_{sc} for $r^{-1} \ltimes_k r'$ in G_0, restricted to the RHS R of r, equals the co-match $n : R \hookrightarrow G_0$ of the transformation $G \Rightarrow_{r,m} G_0$ (i.e., $m'_{sc} \circ j_R = n$ where j_R embeds R into the LHS of $r^{-1} \ltimes_k r'$ as in Fig. 6).*

In particular, given a grammar $GG = (\mathcal{R}, S)$ such that $r, r', p_1, \ldots, p_t \in \mathcal{R}$ and $G \in \mathcal{L}(GG)$, then $H \in \mathcal{L}(GG)$.

Independence of the short-cut rule application $t_{sc} : G_t \Rightarrow_{r^{-1} \ltimes_k r',m_{sc}} H$ from the preceding transformation sequence $t : G \Rightarrow G_t$ requires the existence of morphisms in two directions: morphisms d_2^i from the LHS of the short-cut rule to the context objects D_i arising in t and morphisms d_1^i from the right-hand sides R_i of the rules p_i to the context object of t_{sc} (shifted further and further to the beginning of the sequence). In the case of (typed triple) graphs, the existence of morphisms d_2^i ensures that none of the rule applications in t enabled the transformation t_{sc}. The existence of morphisms d_1^i ensures that the transformation t_{sc} does not delete structure needed to perform the transformation sequence t.

Application to model synchronization. The results in Theorems 7 and 8 are the formal basis for an automatic construction of repair rules. Theorem 7 ensures that a suitable edit action followed by application of a repair rule at the right match is equivalent to the application of a short-cut rule. Thus, whenever an edit action on the source model (or symmetrically the target model) corresponds to the source-action (target-action) of a short-cut rule, application of the corresponding forward (backward) rule synchronizes the model again. Since the language of a TGG is defined by its rules, every valid model can be reached from every other valid model by inverse application of some of the rules of the grammar followed by normal application of some rules. Often, edit actions are rather small steps (or at least consist of those). Thus, it is not unreasonable to expect that many typical edit actions can be realized as short-cut rules as these formalize the inverse application of a rule followed by application of a normal one. Theorem 8 characterizes the matches for short-cut rules at which application stays in the language of the TGG. For operational short-cut rules, this can either be used for detecting invalid edit actions or determining valid matches for synchronizing forward rules.

5 Implementation and Evaluation

Implementation. Our implementation[1] of an optimized model synchronizer is based on the existing EMF-based general purpose graph and model transformation tool eMoflon [21]. It offers support for rule-based unidirectional and bidirectional graph transformations where the latter is based on TGGs. To support an effective model synchronizer, we automatically calculate a small but useful subset of all possible short-cut rules. This is done by overlapping as many created elements as possible and only varying in the way that context elements are mapped onto each other. These selected short-cut rules are operationalized to get repair rules that allow us to repair broken links similar to our example in Sect. 2. The model synchronization process is based on an *incremental graph pattern matcher* that tracks all matches that dis-/appear due to model changes. Thus, it offers the ability to react to model changes without the need to recompute matches from scratch. Our implementation uses this technique by processing all those matches marked as broken by the pattern matcher after a model change. A broken match is the starting point to find a repair match as it is defined by the co-match of the performed model change and has to be extended. If the pattern matcher can extend a broken match to a repair match, the corresponding *short-cut* repair rule can be applied. Otherwise, we fall back to the old synchronization strategy of revoking the current step. This completely automatized synchronization process ensures that we are able to restore consistency as long as the edited domain model still resides in the language of our TGG.

Evaluation. Our experimental setup consists of 23 TGG rules (shown in our technical report [9]) that specify consistency between Java AST and custom documentation models and 37 short-cut rules derived from our TGG rule set. A small modified excerpt of this rule set was given in Sect. 2. For this evaluation, however, we define consistency not only between *Package* and *Folder* hierarchies but also between type definitions, e.g., *Classes* and *Interfaces*, and *Methods* with their corresponding documentation entries. We extracted five models from Java projects hosted on Github using the tool MoDisco [4] and translated them into our own documentation structure. Also, we generated five synthetic models consisting of n-level *Package* hierarchies with each non-leaf*Package* containing five sub-*Packages* and each leaf *Package* containing five *Classes*. Given such Java

[1] Both the implementation and evaluation workspace can be accessed via https://github.com/Arikae00/FASE19_eMoflon-evaluation.

models, we refactored each model in three different scenarios such as by moving a *Class* from one *Package* to another or completely relocating a *Package*. Then we used eMoflon to synchronize these changes in order to restore consistency to the documentation model, with and without *repair rules*.

These synchronization steps are subject to our evaluation and we pose the following research questions: **(RQ1)** *For different kinds of changes, how many elements can be preserved that would otherwise be deleted and recreated?* **(RQ2)** *How does our new approach affect the runtime performance?* **(RQ3)** *Are there specific scenarios in which our approach performs especially good or bad?*

Repair rules were developed to avoid unnecessary deletions of elements by reverting too many rule applications in order to restore consistency as shown exemplary in Sect. 2. This means that model changes where our approach should perform especially good, have to target rule applications close to the beginning of a rule sequence as this possibly renders many rule applications invalid. This means that altering a root *Package* by creating a new *Package* as root would imply that many rule applications have to be reverted to synchronize the changes correctly (Scenario 1). In contrast, our approach might perform poorly when a model change does not inflict a large cascade of invalid rule applications. Hence, we move *Classes* between *Packages* to measure if the effort of applying *repair rules* does infer a performance loss when both the new and old algorithm do not have to repair many broken rule applications (Scenario 2). Finally, we simulate a scenario between the first two by relocating leaf *Packages* (Scenario 3).

Table 1. Legacy vs. new synchronizer – Time in sec. and number of created elements

	Both		Legacy Synchronization						Synchro. by Repair Rules					
	Trans.		Scen. 1		Scen. 2		Scen. 3		Scen. 1		Scen. 2		Scen. 3	
Models	Sec	Elts	Sec	Elts	Sec	Elts	Sec	Elts	Sec	Elts	Sec	Elts	Sec	Elts
lang.List	0.3	25	0.2	20	–	–	0.06	5	0.2	0	–	–	0.03	0
tgg.core	6.4	1.6k	39	1.6k	3.8	99	0.64	17	0.8	0	0.11	0	0.05	0
modisco.java	9.9	3.2k	228	3.3k	18.6	192	3.6	33	2.5	0	0.2	0	0.09	0
eclipse.graphiti	20.7	6.5k	704	6.5k	63.9	490	5.65	25	6.1	0	0.21	0	0.09	0
eclipse.compare	10.74	3.8k	83	3.7k	3.1	76	2.36	47	0.7	0	0.08	0	0.04	0
synthetic $n = 1$	0.3	35	0.32	30	0.2	30	0.03	1	0.1	0	0.05	0	0.03	0
synthetic $n = 2$	0.9	160	1.03	155	0.3	30	0.03	1	0.1	0	0.05	0	0.02	0
synthetic $n = 3$	2.8	785	6	780	0.4	30	0.04	1	0.1	0	0.07	0	0.02	0
synthetic $n = 4$	13.5	3.9k	86.3	3.9k	1.2	30	0.08	1	0.4	0	0.14	0	0.04	0
synthetic $n = 5$	91.5	20k	2731	20k	17.4	30	0.14	1	1.5	0	0.37	0	0.09	0

Table 1 depicts the measured times (Sec) and the number of created elements (Elts) in each scenario. Each created element also represents a deleted element, e.g., through revoking and reapplying a rule or applying a repair rule that creates and deletes elements. In more detail, the table shows measurements for the initial translation of the MoDisco model into the documentation structure and synchronization steps for each scenario using the legacy synchronizer without *repair rules* and the new synchronizer with *repair rules*.

W.r.t. our research questions stated above, we interpret this table as follows: The right columns of the table show clearly that using repair rules preserves all those elements in our scenarios that would otherwise be deleted and recreated by the legacy algorithm[2] **(RQ1)**. The runtime shows a significant performance gain for Scenario 1 including a worst-case model change **(RQ2)**. *Repair rules* do not introduce an overhead compared to the legacy algorithm as can be seen for the synthetic time measurements in Scenario 3 where only one rule application has to be repaired or reapplied. **(RQ2)**. Our new approach excels when the cascade of invalidated rule applications is long. Even if this is not the case, it does not introduce any measurable overhead compared to the legacy algorithm as shown in Scenarios 2 and 3 (**RQ3**).

Threats to validity. Our evaluation is based on five real world and five synthetic models. Of course, there exists a wide range of projects that differ significantly from each other due to their size, purpose, and developer styles. Thus, the results may probably differ for other projects. Nonetheless, we argue that the four larger projects extracted from Github are representative since they are part of established tools from the Eclipse community. In this evaluation, we selected three edit operations that are representative w.r.t. their dependency on other edit operations. They may not be representative w.r.t. other aspects such as size or kind of change, which seems to be of minor importance in this context. Also we limited our evaluation to one TGG rule set due to space issues. However, in our experience the approach shows similar results for a broader range of TGGs which can be accessed through eMoflon.

6 Related Work

Reuse in existing work on TGGs. Several approaches to model synchronization based on TGGs suffer from the fact that the revocation of a certain rule application triggers the revocation of all dependent rule applications as well [12,16,19]. Especially from a practical point of view such cascades of deletions shall be avoided: In [10], Giese and Hildebrandt propose rules that save nodes instead of deleting and then re-creating them. Their examples can be realized by our construction of *repair rules*. But they do not present a general construction or proof of correctness. This is left as future work in [11] again, where other aspects of [10] are formalized and proven to be correct.

In [3], Blouin et al. added a specially designed repair rule to the rules of their case study to avoid information loss. Greenyer et al. [14] also propose to not directly delete elements but to mark them for deletion and allow for reuse of these marked elements in other rule applications. But this approach comes without any formalization or proof of correctness as well. Again, the given example can be realized as short-cut repair. These uncontrolled and informal approaches are

[2] Scenario 1: We expect the new root element to already be translated.

potentially harmful. Re-using elements wrongly may lead to, e.g., containment cycles or unconnected data. Hence, providing precise and sufficient conditions for correct re-use of data is highly desirable as re-use may improve scalability and decrease data-loss. Our short-cut rules formalize when data can be correctly reused. In summary, we do not only offer a unifying principle behind different practically used improvements of TGGs but also give a precise formalization that allows for automatic construction of the rules needed. Thereby, we present conditions under which rule applications lead to valid outputs.

Comparison to other bx approaches. Anjorin et al. [2] compared three state-of-the-art bx tools, namely eMoflon [21] (rule-based), mediniQVT [1] (constraint-based) and BiGUL [17] (bx programming language) w.r.t. model synchronization. They point out that synchronization with eMoflon is faster than with both other tools as the runtime of these tools correlates with the overall model size while the runtime of eMoflon correlates with the size of the changes done by edit operations. Furthermore, eMoflon was the only tool able to solve all but one synchronization scenario. One scenario was not solved because it deleted more model elements than absolutely necessary in that case. Using short-cut repair rules, we can solve the remaining scenario and moreover, can further increase eMoflons model synchronization performance.

Change-preserving model repair. Change-preserving model repair as presented in [22,25] is closely related to our approach. Assuming a set of consistency-preserving rules and a set of edit rules to be given, each edit rule is accompanied by one or more repair rules completing the edit step, if possible. Such a complement rule is considered as repair rule of an edit rule w.r.t. an overarching consistency-preserving rule. Operationalized TGG rules fit into that approach but provide more structure: As graphs and rules are structured in triples, a source rule is also an edit rule being complemented by a forward rule. In contrast to that approach, source and forward rules can be automatically deduced from a given TGG rule. By our use of short-cut rules we introduce a pre-processing step to first enlarge the sets of consistency-preserving rules and edit rules.

Generalization of correspondence relation. Golas et al. provide a formalization of TGGs in [13] which allows to generalize correspondence relations between source and target graphs as well. They use special typings for the source, target, and correspondence parts of a TGG and for edges between a correspondence part and source and target part instead of using graph morphisms. That approach also allows for partial correspondence relations. But it makes the deletion of elements more complex as it becomes important how many incident edges a node has (at least in the double-pushout approach). We therefore opted for introducing triple graphs with partial morphisms. They allow us to just delete a node without caring if it is needed within an existing correspondence relation.

7 Conclusion

Model synchronization, i.e., the task of restoring consistency between two models after a model change, poses challenges to modern bx approaches and tools: We expect them to synchronize changes without losing data in the process, thus, preserving information and furthermore, we expect them to show a reasonable performance. While Triple Graph Grammars (TGGs) provide the means to perform model synchronization tasks in general, both requirements cannot always be fulfilled since basic TGG rules do not define the adequate means to support intermediate model editing. Therefore, we propose additional edit operations being short-cut rules, a special form of generalized TGG rules that allow to take back one edit action and to perform an alternative one. In our evaluation, we show that operationalized short-cut rules allow for a model synchronization with considerably decreased data loss and improved runtime.

To better cope with practical application scenarios, we like to extend our approach by formally incorporating type inheritance, application conditions and attributes in the model synchronization process. Since all of these have been formalized in the setting of ($\mathcal{M}$-)adhesive categories and our present work uses that framework as well, these extensions are prepared but up to future work. Propagating changes from one domain to another is basically done here by operationalizing short-cut rules. A more challenging task is what we call model integration where related pairs of models are edited concurrently and have to be synchronized. These model edits may be in conflict across model boundaries. It is up to future work to allow short-cut rules in model integration. Our hope is to decrease data loss and to improve runtime of model integration tasks as well.

References

1. Ikv++: Medini QVT. http://projects.ikv.de/qvt
2. Anjorin, A., Diskin, Z., Jouault, F., Ko, H., Leblebici, E., Westfechtel, B.: Benchmarx reloaded: a practical benchmark framework for bidirectional transformations. In: Proceedings of the 6th International Workshop on Bidirectional Transformations co-located with The European Joint Conferences on Theory and Practice of Software, BX@ETAPS 2017, Uppsala, Sweden, 29 April 2017, pp. 15–30 (2017). http://ceur-ws.org/Vol-1827/paper6.pdf
3. Blouin, D., Plantec, A., Dissaux, P., Singhoff, F., Diguet, J.-P.: Synchronization of models of rich languages with triple graph grammars: an experience report. In: Di Ruscio, D., Varró, D. (eds.) ICMT 2014. LNCS, vol. 8568, pp. 106–121. Springer, Cham (2014). https://doi.org/10.1007/978-3-319-08789-4_8
4. Bruneliàre, H., Cabot, J., Dupé, G., Madiot, F.: MoDisco: a model driven reverse engineering framework. Inf. Softw. Technol. **56**(8), 1012–1032 (2014). https://doi.org/10.1016/j.infsof.2014.04.007
5. Cheney, J., Gibbons, J., McKinna, J., Stevens, P.: On principles of least change and least surprise for bidirectional transformations. J. Object Technol. **16**(1), 3:1–3:31 (2017). https://doi.org/10.5381/jot.2017.16.1.a3
6. Ehrig, H., Ehrig, K., Prange, U., Taentzer, G.: Fundamentals of Algebraic Graph Transformation. Monographs in Theoretical Computer Science. Springer, Heidelberg (2006). https://doi.org/10.1007/3-540-31188-2

7. Eppinger, S.D.: Model-based approaches to managing concurrent engineering. J. Eng. Des. **2**(4), 283–290 (1991). https://doi.org/10.1080/09544829108901686
8. Fritsche, L., Kosiol, J., Schürr, A., Taentzer, G.: Short-cut rules. Sequential composition of rules avoiding unnecessary deletions. In: Mazzara, M., Ober, I., Salaün, G. (eds.) STAF 2018. LNCS, vol. 11176, pp. 415–430. Springer, Cham (2018). https://doi.org/10.1007/978-3-030-04771-9_30
9. Fritsche, L., Kosiol, J., Schürr, A., Taentzer, G.: Optimizing TGG-based model synchronization by automatic short-cut repair processes: extended version. Technical report, Philipps-Universität Marburg (2019). https://www.uni-marburg.de/fb12/arbeitsgruppen/swt/forschung/publikationen/2019/FKST19-TR.pdf
10. Giese, H., Hildebrandt, S.: Efficient model synchronization of large-scale models. Technical report 28, Hasso-Plattner-Institut (2009)
11. Giese, H., Hildebrandt, S., Lambers, L.: Bridging the gap between formal semantics and implementation of triple graph grammars. Softw. Syst. Model. **13**(1), 273–299 (2014). https://doi.org/10.1007/s10270-012-0247-y
12. Giese, H., Wagner, R.: From model transformation to incremental bidirectional model synchronization. Softw. Syst. Model. **8**(1), 21–43 (2009). https://doi.org/10.1007/s10270-008-0089-9
13. Golas, U., Lambers, L., Ehrig, H., Giese, H.: Toward bridging the gap between formal foundations and current practice for triple graph grammars. In: Ehrig, H., Engels, G., Kreowski, H.J., Rozenberg, G. (eds.) ICGT 2012. LNCS, vol. 7562, pp. 141–155. Springer, Heidelberg (2012). https://doi.org/10.1007/978-3-642-33654-6_10
14. Greenyer, J., Pook, S., Rieke, J.: Preventing information loss in incremental model synchronization by reusing elements. In: France, R.B., Kuester, J.M., Bordbar, B., Paige, R.F. (eds.) ECMFA 2011. LNCS, vol. 6698, pp. 144–159. Springer, Heidelberg (2011). https://doi.org/10.1007/978-3-642-21470-7_11
15. Hermann, F., Ehrig, H., Golas, U., Orejas, F.: Efficient analysis and execution of correct and complete model transformations based on triple graph grammars. In: Proceedings of the First International Workshop on Model-Driven Interoperability. pp. 22–31. MDI 2010. ACM, New York (2010). https://doi.org/10.1145/1866272.1866277
16. Hermann, F., et al.: Model synchronization based on triple graph grammars: correctness, completeness and invertibility. Softw. Syst. Model. **14**(1), 241–269 (2015). https://doi.org/10.1007/s10270-012-0309-1
17. Ko, H., Zan, T., Hu, Z.: BiGUL: a formally verified core language for putback-based bidirectional programming. In: Proceedings of the 2016 ACM SIGPLAN Workshop on Partial Evaluation and Program Manipulation, PEPM 2016, St. Petersburg, FL, USA, 20–22 January 2016, pp. 61–72 (2016). https://doi.org/10.1145/2847538.2847544
18. Lack, S., Sobociński, P.: Adhesive and quasiadhesive categories. Theor. Inform. Appl. **39**(3), 511–545 (2005). https://doi.org/10.1051/ita:2005028
19. Lauder, M., Anjorin, A., Varró, G., Schürr, A.: Efficient model synchronization with precedence triple graph grammars. In: Ehrig, H., Engels, G., Kreowski, H.J., Rozenberg, G. (eds.) ICGT 2012. LNCS, vol. 7562, pp. 401–415. Springer, Heidelberg (2012). https://doi.org/10.1007/978-3-642-33654-6_27
20. Leblebici, E., Anjorin, A., Fritsche, L., Varró, G., Schürr, A.: Leveraging incremental pattern matching techniques for model synchronisation. In: de Lara, J., Plump, D. (eds.) ICGT 2017. LNCS, vol. 10373, pp. 179–195. Springer, Cham (2017). https://doi.org/10.1007/978-3-319-61470-0_11

21. Leblebici, E., Anjorin, A., Schürr, A.: Developing eMoflon with eMoflon. In: Di Ruscio, D., Varró, D. (eds.) ICMT 2014. LNCS, vol. 8568, pp. 138–145. Springer, Cham (2014). https://doi.org/10.1007/978-3-319-08789-4_10
22. Ohrndorf, M., Pietsch, C., Kelter, U., Kehrer, T.: Revision: a tool for history-based model repair recommendations. In: Proceedings of the 40th International Conference on Software Engineering: Companion Proceeedings, ICSE 2018, Gothenburg, Sweden, 27 May–03 June 2018, pp. 105–108. ACM (2018). https://doi.org/10.1145/3183440.3183498
23. Robinson, E., Rosolini, G.: Categories of partial maps. Inf. Comput. **79**(2), 95–130 (1988). https://doi.org/10.1016/0890-5401(88)90034-X
24. Schürr, A.: Specification of graph translators with triple graph grammars. In: Mayr, E.W., Schmidt, G., Tinhofer, G. (eds.) WG 1994. LNCS, vol. 903, pp. 151–163. Springer, Heidelberg (1995). https://doi.org/10.1007/3-540-59071-4_45
25. Taentzer, G., Ohrndorf, M., Lamo, Y., Rutle, A.: Change-preserving model repair. In: Huisman, M., Rubin, J. (eds.) FASE 2017. LNCS, vol. 10202, pp. 283–299. Springer, Heidelberg (2017). https://doi.org/10.1007/978-3-662-54494-5_16

Offline Delta-Driven Model Transformation with Dependency Injection

Artur Boronat[✉]

Department of Informatics,
University of Leicester, Leicester, UK
aboronat@le.ac.uk

Abstract. When model transformations are used to implement consistency relations between very large models (VLMs), incrementality plays a cornerstone role in the realization of practical consistency maintainers. State-of-the-art model transformation engines with support for incrementality normally rely on a publish-subscribe model for linking model updates – deltas – to the application of model transformation rules, in so called dependencies, at run time. These deltas can then be propagated along an already executed model transformation. A small number of such engines use domain-specific languages (DSLs) for representing model deltas offline in order to enable their use in asynchronous, event-based execution environments.

The principal contribution of this work is the design of a forward delta propagation mechanism for incremental execution of model transformations, which decouples dependency tracking from delta propagation using two innovations. First, the publish-subscribe model is replaced with dependency injection, physically decoupling domain models from consistency maintainers. Second, a standardized representation of model deltas is reused, facilitating interoperability with EMF-compliant tools, both for defining deltas and for processing them asynchronously. This procedure has been implemented in a model transformation engine, whose performance has been evaluated empirically using the VIATRA CPS benchmark. In the experiments performed, the new transformation engine shows gains in the form of several orders of magnitude in the initial phase of the incremental execution of the benchmark model transformation and delta propagation is performed in real time, independently of the size of the models involved, whereas the up-to-now best-performant approach is dependent.

Keywords: Mappings between languages · Traceability · Incremental model transformation · Performance benchmark

1 Introduction

Significant issues in the application of Model-Driven Engineering (MDE) in large-scale industrial problems stem from interoperability and scalability of

R. Hähnle and W. van der Aalst (Eds.): FASE 2019, LNCS 11424, pp. 134–150, 2019.
https://doi.org/10.1007/978-3-030-16722-6_8

current MDE tools [1,16,17]. Model transformation, widely accepted as the *heart and soul* of MDE [23], deals with model manipulation either by translating models or by synchronizing them. Current tool support for model transformation is a key root cause for many of the bottlenecks hampering scalability in MDE [2,8]. This is particularly crucial when transformations are used to implement consistency maintainers between very large models (VLMs), consisting of milions of elements. In this context, incrementality ensures that only those parts of the model that are inconsistent or that have been modified – a model delta – are transformed or, more precisely, propagated along an already executed transformation [11,12].

Current state-of-the-art approaches that support incremental execution of model transformations share common features: the delta propagation mechanism is usually decoupled from the delta detection mechanism in order to facilitate maintainability of the consistency maintainer; and deltas are represented either in memory for synchronous notification or offline, with dedicated domain-specific languages, for asynchronous notification. The most mature tools rely on a publish/subscribe mechanism, where model deltas are notified at run time whenever a model is updated. This notification mechanism is synchronous and loosely couples model updates with the delta propagation mechanism, facilitating maintainability of the underlying transformation engine after fixing the type of notification. However, it usually requires an observer for each object that can be modified, with a consequent impact on performance, and the model transformation must be live, in memory, in order to listen for changes. These problems can be avoided by using offline deltas. The publish/subscribe mechanism can be extended to enable asynchronous delta notification but this is normally achieved by using dedicated domain-specific languages to represent deltas offline, which do not involve standardized formats, hindering the interoperability of those transformation engines in existing modeling tool ecosystems.

In this paper, the design of a forward delta propagation procedure is presented for executing model transformations in incremental mode that can handle documented change scenarios [4], i.e. documents representing a change to a given source model. Such documents are defined with the EMF change model [24], both conceptually and implementation-wise, guaranteeing interoperability with EMF-compliant tools. This design decision replaces a publish/subscribe notification with dependency injection: each notification is directly performed by the implementation of the domain model at run time by injecting the dependency corresponding to the model update that has been performed. Aspect-oriented programming is used to weave code into an already existing implementation of a domain model totally decoupling domain models from the consistency maintainer at design time. The proposed forward delta propagation procedure has been implemented in YAMTL [6], a model transformation engine for VLMs, enabling the execution of model transformations both in batch mode and in incremental mode without additional user specification overhead. This new extension dramatically improves the performance of the batch execution mode when dealing with sparse model deltas, which can be propagated in real time (i.e. in μs.).

This work is structured as follows: Sect. 2 provides a self-contained description of the class of model transformations supported using a class diagram to relational schema model transformation; Sect. 3 presents the forward propagation procedure implemented in the model transformation engine together with the main innovations; Sect. 4 discusses the performance of the transformation engine with an adaptation of the VIATRA CPS benchmark; Sect. 5 discusses related work from reactive and bidirectional model transformation.

2 Model Transformation: A Running Example

The type of model transformations that are considered in this work are classified as unidirectional and out-place. For example, when considering the well-known example that maps class diagrams to relational schemas, a class diagram is used by queries to extract information and a relational schema is built from scratch. If we consider a graph transformation perspective, both models are considered to form part of the same graph in order to enable transformation by rewriting. In that case, we are only considering transformations where the two models are two clearly disjoint subgraphs and where rewriting is performed deterministically.

In this work, model transformations are represented using an implementation-agnostic graphical syntax, quite close to that used in the graph transformation literature. In this representation, metamodels are given as class diagrams, the abstract syntax of models is given as object diagrams and model transformations are represented as a collection of rules, where each rule is defined as a pair of model patterns, called left-hand side (LHS) and right-hand side (RHS). The notion of metamodel, model and model pattern correspond to those of type graph, attributed graph with containments and node inheritance, and graph pattern in the graph transformation literature [5,10]. For example, the rules `A->C` and `R->FK` of Fig. 1 map attributes to columns. The $ before a variable denotes string interpolation.

Graph patterns in rules can be augmented with universally quantified variables (represented by an overlaid box). Moreover, rules are augmented with a `when` clause to express conditions that must be satisfied by the variables in LHS, and with a `where` clause to indicate how variables from LHS and from RHS are related via the application of other rules, expressed as two graph patterns. Formulas in a `when` clause may be expressed in conjunctive form, as all filter conditions must be satisfied in order for the rule to be applied, whereas formulas in a `where` clause may be expressed in disjunctive form (assuming mutually exclusive conditions), as all the side effects expressed in a `where` clause must be evaluated. The variables of RHS of the main rule must appear either in the LHS of the main rule or in the RHS of a `where` transformation step. The rule `C->T` of Fig. 1 illustrates how to map a class to a table with a primary key column `PK_COL` and for each attribute `A` whose type is a `DataType`, the corresponding column is obtained by applying a rule, with the rule `A->C`, and for each attribute `OTHER` whose type is the class `C`, matched in LHS of the main rule, a new foreign key column is added to the table `T`, with the rule `R->FK`.

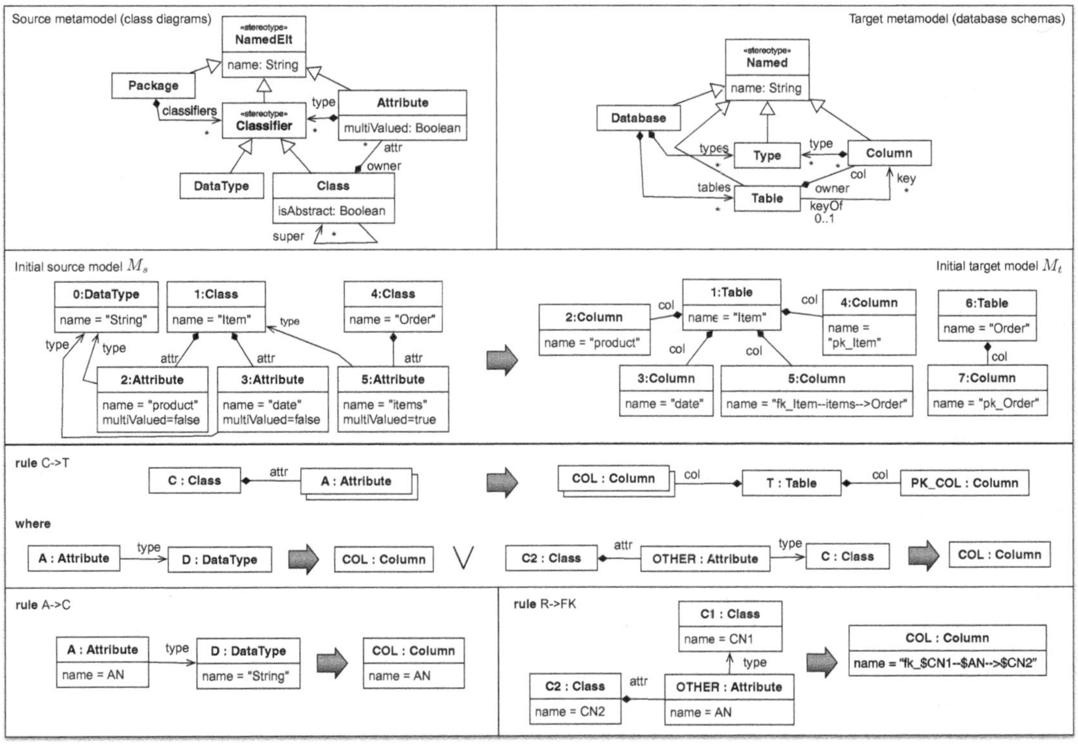

Fig. 1. Metamodels, example and transformation rules.

From an operational point of view, transformation rules are applied unidirectionally from LHS to RHS performing an out-place transformation following two steps. First, during the *matching phase*, matches for the rules in the model transformation are found as long as they are not shared by different rules and these are included in a set *matchPool*. A match is formally defined as a graph morphism from LHS to the source graph, which satisfies the `when` conditions, but it is represented as a map from variables to object identifiers for the sake of presentation in this paper.

Second, during the *execution phase*, each match is processed by triggering the application of a transformation rule, which is represented as a transformation step, denoted by $r : \overrightarrow{in \mapsto \varsigma} \rightarrow \overrightarrow{out \mapsto \varsigma}$, which consists of a labelled pair of two matches, the match for the input pattern of the rule, which enables its application, and the match for the output pattern of the rule, with the objects that result from applying the rule. When a rule is applied, the source model is only used for query purposes but the target model is constructed by adding the pattern of the RHS instantiated with values from the variables both in the LHS and in the RHS of `where` transformation steps. In addition, `where` transformation steps may further expand the structure of the target model. This execution model resembles the application of forward rules used in triple graph grammars (TGGs) [22], where the source graph is annotated as rules are applied and only the target graph is constructed together with a link in a correspondence graph, where each link denotes a transformation step.

3 Delta-Driven Model Transformations

This section presents the mechanism to propagate documented deltas δ_t from a source model M_s to a target model M_t in an incremental way, when the (unidirectional) synchronization correspondence between these two models is represented with a model transformation t as described in the previous section. This has been implemented in the YAMTL transformation engine [6], which has been extended with two modes of execution: *initialization*, the transformation is executed in batch mode but, additionally, tracks those parts of the source model involved in transformation steps as *dependencies*; *propagation*, the transformation is executed incrementally for a given source delta.

In order for a model transformation to be executed in propagation mode, it first needs to be executed in initialization mode in order both to create transformation steps and to inject the dependencies that facilitate the analysis of the impact of changes in the already executed model transformation. Therefore, the transformation t is applied to M_s using the original batch semantics [6] while injecting dependencies in the transformation engine. Once the initialization is done, any number of source forward deltas δ_s can be propagated.

Given a source documented delta δ_s between a source model M_s, already synchronized with a target model M_t via a model transformation $t : M_s \xrightarrow{*} M_t$ (where $\xrightarrow{*}$ denotes a sequence of transformation steps), and an updated source model M'_s, the transformation engine propagates the model update δ_s along t. The effect of this forward propagation is the application of an update δ_t on the target model M_t.

In the following subsections, we explain the different phases of the new execution modes, initialization and propagation, in more detail. As the initialization mode faithfully corresponds to the batch execution of a model transformation, the discussion of this mode focuses on the type of dependencies that are injected in the transformation engine in Sect. 3.1. The discussion on the propagation mode focuses on how deltas are represented in Sect. 3.2. Then, the two main phases of the propagation execution mode, namely impact analysis and delta propagation, are explained in Sects. 3.3 and 3.4, respectively.

3.1 Dependency Injection

When running a model transformation in initialization mode, the engine monitors the source model and whenever an object ς is matched or a feature call, represented as a pair (ς, f) of an EMF object ς and a feature name f, is performed, a dependency is injected into the dependency registry. A dependency thereby links either an object ς or a feature call (ς, f) to transformation steps $r : \overrightarrow{in \mapsto \varsigma} \to \overrightarrow{out \mapsto \varsigma}$ in which it is used. Such dependencies are detected both during the matching phase and during the execution phase.

In the matching phase, while finding a match for a rule, the engine keeps track of all of the feature calls used in both element and rule `when` conditions. When a match is found to be valid, the collection of dependencies is injected into the dependency registry for the transformation step that uses that match. Otherwise,

Table 1. Analysis of dependencies for the initial MT $t : M_s \xrightarrow{*} M_t$ of Fig. 2.

Rule	Source Match	Target Match	Dependencies from M_s
C->T	c $\mapsto$ 1	t $\mapsto$ 1,	(1,name), (1,att),
		pk_col $\mapsto$ 4	(5, type), (5, multiValued)
C->T	c $\mapsto$ 4	t $\mapsto$ 6, pk_col $\mapsto$ 7	(4, name), (4, attr)
A->C	att $\mapsto$ 2	col $\mapsto$ 2	(2, name)
A->C	att $\mapsto$ 3	col $\mapsto$ 3	(3, name)
R->FK	ref $\mapsto$ 5	fk_col $\mapsto$ 5	(5,name), (5,type),
		fk_col $\mapsto$ 5	(1, name), (4,name)

when the match is not valid, the collected dependencies are discarded. Additionally, when inserting a match in the *matchPool*, the transformation engine also records reverse matches as injected dependencies between matched objects ς and the transformation step in which they are matched.

Dependencies may also be found when executing a transformation step, e.g., while executing initialization expressions associated with attributes in model patterns in RHS and in `where` clauses. In such cases, the transformation engine injects a dependency for the transformation step every time a feature call in the source model is detected. As a result, note that several transformation steps may depend on the same object ς, when rules have more than one single input element, or on the same feature call (ς, f).

Table 1 shows the dependencies that are found when executing the transformation of Fig. 1 in initialization mode from model M_s. Each row in the table represents a transformation step, where: the source match indicates where the rule has been applied, the target match indicates what objects were created, and dependencies refers to the set of feature calls associated with a transformation step. Reverse matches are extracted from source matches, by reading them in the opposite direction.

Dependency injection is configured with an aspect whose pointcut matches feature calls under a user-defined namespace. Hence, the model transformation engine is entirely decoupled from the domain model at design time. They become tightly coupled at compilation time and, hence, at run time.

3.2 Representable Deltas

The EMF change model [24] is used to represent deltas to an instance of any other EMF model. It is built-in in EMF and, therefore, available for any EMF-compliant tool. In this section, we describe how a documented delta is represented with the EMF change model and how it can be automatically defined given any potentially *live* atomic update.

A delta consists of a `ChangeDescription` which contains a map of `objectChanges`, which refer to those objects that are updated and, for each such object, it contains a list of `FeatureChanges`. A `FeatureChange` (`FC`) refers to the structural feature that needs to be updated and provides the new value. For single-valued attributes, a `FeatureChange` contains the new `dataValue` if the feature is an attribute. For references and multi-valued attributes, a `FeatureChange` includes a containment reference `listChanges` pointing to `ListChange`. `ListChanges` are used to represent addition to, removal from, or movement *within* the given feature values. In particular, movement only captures when an object changes to a different index within the collection. However, it does not capture structural changes, e.g. change of container, which are represented as a removal from and an addition to the corresponding containment references. When a `FeatureChange` refers to a containment reference, objects to be added are pointed by `objectsToAttach` and objects to be removed are pointed by `objectsToDetach`.

`FeatureChanges` capture when a feature value is updated for an object but EMF also permits adding and removing root objects to a resource, representing the model in memory, which need not be contained by any other object. Such changes are considered to be performed on the resource itself and are represented with `ResourceChanges`, one for each changed resource. A `ResourceChange` (`RC`) contains the `ListChanges` for the root objects of the corresponding resource, similarly to multi-valued features. For a more detailed explanation of the EMF change model, we refer the reader to [24].

Table 2 shows a classification of atomic model updates that are representable with the EMF change model as explained above. Note that moving and object structurally, case 12 – *move (inter.)*, – is represented in a composite delta by two opposite actions, removing the object either from the root contents of the resource – if it is a root object (case 2) – or from a containment reference – if it is a contained object (case 10) – and adding it either to the root contents of the resource – if it is to become a root object (case 1) – or to another containment reference in another container object (case 9). This case is not captured by the EMF change model explicitly but the transformation engine is able to infer it, as explained in the following section.

Table 2. Summary of model update types, with their representation in EMF.

Cases	Granularity	Level	Feature	Delta action	Delta representation	*DO*	*DFC*
1,2	atomic	root		add/remove	`RC::listChanges`	✓	
3	atomic	root		move (intra.)	`RC::listChanges`		
4,5	atomic	any	single-valued att	add/remove	`FC`		✓
6,7	atomic	any	multi-valued att	add/remove	`FC::listChanges`	✓	✓
8	atomic	any	multi-valued att	move (intra.)	`FC::listChanges`		✓
9,10	atomic	any	ref	add/remove	`FC::listChanges`		✓
11	atomic	any	ref	move (intra.)	`FC::listChanges`		✓
12	composite	any	containment ref	move (inter.)	opposite remove and add actions in cases $\{2,10\}/\{1,9\}$		✓

A delta, which may represent atomic and composite changes, is defined as an instance of the EMF change model and can be serialized. EMF also provides facilities for applying them and reversing them. Furthermore, EMF provides a change recorder, which enables recording *live updates* as a `ChangeDescription` for either a root object, a collection of root objects, a resource or a resource set. The resulting `ChangeDescription` is the representation of a *history scenario* [4], from the updated model to the original one, which is optimized. That is, atomic changes for the same feature of the same object may be discarded or merged, as long as the optimization process preserves reversibility. Hence, reversing the recorded delta may yield less changes than were originally made. Reversed deltas represent *documented scenarios* and can be propagated along a model transformation, as discussed in subsequent sections.

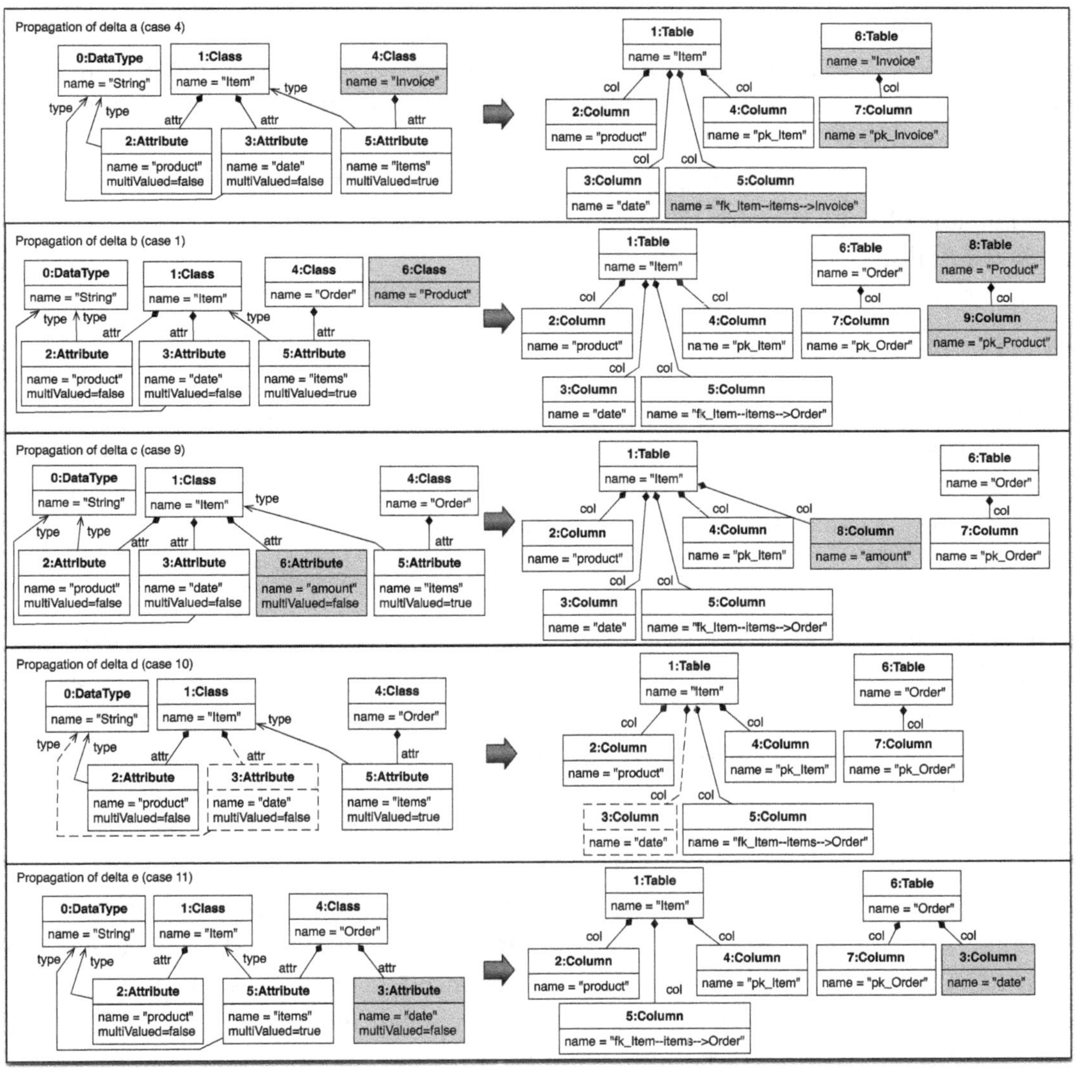

Fig. 2. Source/target metamodels, initial synchronized models and forward delta propagation (a–e).

The EMF change recorder enables the possibility of deferring the observation of updates to the point in which they occur, saving memory resources, and interoperability. Furthermore, recorded (history) deltas can be regarded as a rollback mechanism for implementing transactional model updates, which may be performed live.

Figure 2 shows examples of documented deltas, defined over the source model M_s of the running example. Such deltas are representable as EMF model changes, i.e. operationally, but are graphically depicted using the abstract syntax of M_s, using their state-based representation for the sake of presentation. Additions and updates, including moves, are highlighted in grey colour. Objects that are added, and thus created, have a new identifier. Objects that are updated and/or moved preserve their identifier. Removals are highlighted by using dashed lines for the contour lines of the corresponding shapes. The given deltas are instantiations of case 4 (delta `a`), changing the name of the class `Order` to `Invoice`; case 1 (delta `b`), adding a root class `Product`; case 9 (delta `c`), adding a single-valued attribute `amount` to class `Item`; case 10 (delta `d`), removing the attribute `date` from class `Item`; and case 11 (delta `e`), structurally moving the attribute `date` from class `Item` to class `Order`.

In the following subsections, the different phases of the procedure for forward propagation of source deltas is discussed and the aforementioned examples will be used for illustrating them.

3.3 Impact Analysis

In this subsection, we discuss how source documented deltas are analyzed in order to determine which transformation steps are affected by source changes. This analysis is comprised of three main steps: identification of atomic model updates from a documented delta, initialization of locations for newly enabled rules, and marking of transformation steps impacted by changes.

Identification of atomic model updates. In the first step, the transformation engine infers which objects and which feature calls have been impacted by changes. For objects, it also infers whether an object has been added or removed, ignoring if the object is moved, either within the same collection or structurally.

For affected objects, such information is recorded in the set *DO* of *dirty objects* of the form (ς, *ctype*), where ς is the affected object and *ctype* is the type of change from the set { `ADD`, `DEL`}. To obtain a dirty object from the delta, `FeatureChanges` and `ResourceChanges` are traversed considering two cases: when an object ς is added either to a containment feature (for a `FeatureChange`) or to the root contents of the resource (for a `ResourceChange`) and such object is not removed elsewhere in the delta, either from a containment reference or from the root contents of the resource; and, similarly, when an object is deleted and it is not added elsewhere in the delta. *DO* is augmented with (ς, `ADD`) in the first case and with (ς, `DEL`) in the second case.

For affected feature calls, such information is recorded in the set *DFC* of *dirty feature calls* of the form (ς, f), where ς is an object and f is a feature

Table 3. Impact analysis of source deltas a–e.

	Case	*DO*	*DFC*	Rule	Source Match	Target Match	$matchPool_{\Delta}$	dirty?
a	4	–	(4, `name`)	`C->T`	$\texttt{c} \mapsto 4$	$\texttt{t} \mapsto 6, \texttt{pk\_col} \mapsto 7$	✓	✓
b	1	(6, *ADD*)	–	`C->T`	$\texttt{c} \mapsto 6$		✓	
c	9		(1, `attr`)	`C->T`	$\texttt{c} \mapsto 1$	$\texttt{t} \mapsto 1, \texttt{pk\_col} \mapsto 4$	✓	✓
		(6, *ADD*)		`A->C`	$\texttt{att} \mapsto 6$		✓	
d	10		(1, `attr`)	`C->T`	$\texttt{c} \mapsto 1$	$\texttt{t} \mapsto 1, \texttt{pk\_col} \mapsto 4$	✓	✓
		(3, *DEL*)		`A->C`	$\texttt{att} \mapsto 3$	$\texttt{col} \rightarrow 3$		✓
e	11	–	(1, `attr`),	`C->T`	$\texttt{c} \mapsto 1$	$\texttt{t} \mapsto 1, \texttt{pk\_col} \mapsto 4$	✓	✓
			(4, `attr`)	`C->T`	$\texttt{c} \mapsto 4$	$\texttt{t} \mapsto 6, \texttt{pk\_col} \mapsto 7$	✓	✓

name. For each `FeatureChange` of an `ObjectChange`, the dirty feature call (ς, f) with the object ς referred by the `ObjectChange` and the feature name f referred to by the `FeatureChange` is added to *DFC*.

Table 2 shows how atomic model update types are represented using the EMF change model (column *delta representation*), internally, using the sets *DO* and *DFC*. Table 3 shows the sets *DO* of dirty objects and *DFC* of dirty feature calls for the source deltas of Fig. 2. Note that the sets *DO* and *DFC* decouple the transformation engine from the EMF change model and provide another entry point for defining deltas programmatically, which can be used for capturing atomic *live changes* received via EMF adapters.

Initialization of delta locations. For each dirty object (ς, `ADD`), the object ς is added to the extent associated with *type*(o) in the location map used for delta propagation. This potentially enables new matches when rules are matched during the delta propagation phase.

Marking of impacted transformation steps. In this step, transformation steps that are affected by the atomic changes in the source delta are marked as dirty. For each dirty object (ς, `ADD`) $\in DO$, the extent of type `type`(ς) is augmented with ς. This will potentially enable new matches for some rule during the change propagation phase. For each dirty object (ς, `DEL`) $\in DO$, we obtain the list of transformation steps that are affected from the map of reverse matches. Such transformation steps will then remain transient and the objects in their target match will not be linked to other objects in the target models. In particular, note that when processing root objects or a containment reference, an object that is removed in the delta is not present in the updated source model and, therefore, it does not trigger the transformation step that had been executed in the initial transformation.

For each dirty feature call $(\varsigma, f) \in DFC$ we obtain the list of transformation steps that are affected from the registry of dependencies. For each such transformation step, the satisfaction of its source match is checked. If such source match is still valid, then it is inserted into $matchPool_{\Delta}$, the pool of matches that are used to schedule rule applications during the change propagation phase.

For each atomic change in Fig. 2, Table 3 shows the marking of transformation steps that are (re-)scheduled according to the dependencies of Table 1. In particular, if a transformation step is re-scheduled, its current source and target matches are included, it is marked as dirty and included in $matchPool_\Delta$. If a transformation step is not to be re-executed, it is simply marked as dirty. New transformation steps, with fresh matches due to new objects, are scheduled in $matchPool_\Delta$. This last step is actually achieved by augmenting the corresponding type extent with the new objects and the matches are scheduled during the change propagation phase, explained in the next subsection.

3.4 Change Propagation

After the impact analysis phase, delta propagation proceeds by executing a model transformation using the matching and execution phases, as outlined in Sect. 2. Figure 2 illustrates the propagation of source deltas according to the model transformation of Fig. 1. We highlight how incrementality has been considered in these two phases below.

Matching Phase. During the matching phase (in batch/initialization execution mode), matches for a given rule are found by traversing objects from the extent of the types associated with the elements of the source pattern of the rule, with the constraints specified in the form of graphical patterns and `when` conditions. In propagation mode, the transformation engine employs the same pattern matching algorithm but it fetches objects from the location map used for delta propagation, initialized during the change impact analysis phase. Therefore, new matches may be found for objects that have been created by the source delta. Those matches are inserted both into *matchPool* and $matchPool_\Delta$, scheduling new transformation steps. Table 3 shows that two new transformation steps are scheduled, one for rule `C->T` in delta `b`, and one for rule `A->C` in delta `c`.

Execution Phase. During the execution phase, transformation steps determined by the matches in $matchPool_\Delta$ are executed. Such matches originate from the impact analysis phase, corresponding to transformation steps that are *dirty* and need to be re-executed, and from the matching phase above, corresponding to new transformation steps.

The re-execution of a transformation step is performed as in the batch/initialization mode but for the creation of transformation steps. Whereas a newly scheduled transformation step needs to get its output objects initialized (instantiated for output elements), a dirty transformation step *reuses* the objects of the target match and unsets their features. This avoids loss of contextual information, which is not affected by changes, when re-executing a transformation step. In particular, those references to output objects that emerge from the external context are preserved. On the other hand, references from those output objects are re-calculated by re-executing the transformation step. It is worth noting that the transformation engine uses `where` clauses to define references to objects that are created by other rules, which in turn uses a cache mechanism to avoid re-executing the transformation step that produced it. Therefore, when a dirty transformation rule is re-executed, the initialization of output element bindings are performed again. However, those bindings that are initialized in a `where` clause are also initialized incrementally. That is, only those objects that belong to a match of a new scheduled transformation step will be transformed from scratch. References to already initialized objects will be simply fetched. Hence, the granularity of the target delta is as fine grained (at binding level) as the source delta for the underlying graph structure of the model.

4 Performance Analysis

For the empirical analysis of the incremental execution of model transformations in YAMTL using the propagation procedure presented above, we have used the VIATRA CPS benchmark [27]. The transformation *YAMTL-incr* implemented for our model transformation engine passes the sanity checks of the benchmark. The software artifacts used in this section and the results obtained are publicly available in a GitHub repository [7] and YAMTL is available at https://yamtl.github.io/.

This evaluation is an extension of the one performed for the batch component of the VIATRA CPS benchmark in [6]. From the original VIATRA CPS benchmark, two incremental variants of the transformation implemented with *EMF-IncQuery* have been selected: *ExplicitTraceability* (EXPL) [25] and *QueryResultTraceability* (QRT) [26], out of which the first one is the best performing solution up to now. These transformations have been extracted as independent Java projects. Classes implementing them have been kept intact in the new projects, including their namespaces, so that errors are not introduced due to lack of expertise. Although these two transformations produce results that are different from the other transformations, the main differences are due to reordering of multi-valued references and we have considered them valid for this evaluation. On the other hand, a benchmark measurement harness considering the best practices recommended by the VIATRA team [13] was developed in order both to fine-tune measurements and to crosscheck results. This harness removes dependencies to other components of the VIATRA CPS benchmark so that experiments can be run locally.

In the present work, we aimed at answering the following research questions: *(RQ1)* Does *YAMTL-incr* show any performance penalty w.r.t. its execution in batch mode (*YAMTL-batch*)? *(RQ2)* Does *YAMTL-incr* show any improvement in performance w.r.t *EXPL* or *QRT* during initialization phase? *(RQ3)* And during propagation phase?

From the scenarios provided in the original benchmark, the scenarios *client-server* and *statistic based* [29] were considered. The CPS model generator [28] was used to obtain the input models to be used for the analysis so that their size depends on a logarithmic factor. The biggest models considered, in the client server scenario, consist of millions of nodes (10.16M) and edges (27.53M) and are, hence, VLMs.

For each tool and scenario, the experiments are run in isolation, i.e. in a separate Java process. For each of the input models, an initial experiment is performed to warm up the JVM and, then, twelve more experiments to measure performance. Each experiment consists of four phases: model load and engine initialization, initial transformation, delta propagation and model storage. In between each execution phase, the harness sends hints to the JVM to run garbage collection and waits for one second before proceeding on to the next phase. The first phase includes the instantiation of a fresh engine instance, avoiding interference between experiments as caches are not reused. The delta propagation phase includes the application of the delta to the source model and its propagation. Only initial transformation and delta propagation times have been considered in the quantitative analysis. For the results the median obtained for each of these two phases out of ten experiments is used, after removing the minimum and the maximum results.

In both solutions *EXPL* [25] and *QRT* [26], the delta is applied to the source model by directly modifying the resource containing the model. In the solution with YAMTL such delta was recorded and persisted using the EMF change model as described in Sect. 3.2. To analyze whether this feature could become a threat to validity, a separate experiment was run by excluding the query part of the model update (searching for the objects to be updated) in the solution *EXPL* but this change did not affect performance results perceptibly and the original solutions provided by the authors of the VIATRA CPS benchmark were considered. Therefore, the actions performed during the propagation phase are equivalent in all of the evaluated solutions.

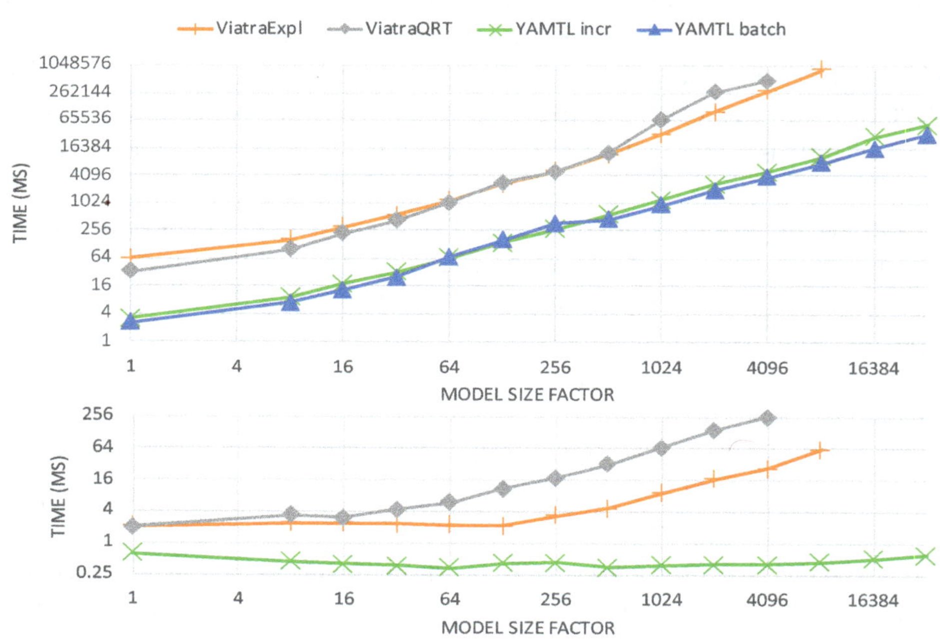

Fig. 3. Performance of initialization (top) and delta propagation (bottom).

Figure 3 shows the performance results obtained both for the initial model transformation and for forward delta propagation for the models generated for the client-server scenario. Scales both for time (ms.) along Y axis and for model size factors along X axis are logarithmic allowing us to compare the scalability of the different approaches. In the initialization phase, we have included the execution of YAMTL in batch mode (*YAMTL-batch*) over the source model, and it can be seen that tracking dependencies incurs a small penalty. However, the other two solutions (*EXPL* and *QRT*) operate several orders of magnitude slower. In the propagation phase, it can be observed that while *YAMTL-incr* exhibits a constant propagation time (in μs.) for the source delta, the cost of the other solutions depends on the size of the input model. Furthermore, for the other incremental approaches, when both initial and propagation time are combined their performance worsens due to their costly initialization phase.

5 Related Work

In this section, we discuss techniques used in related work for achieving incrementality in both reactive and bidirectional model transformation.

Reactive model transformation [3,21] enable the propagation of model updates from source models to target models on demand. State-of-the-art tool support relies on notification mechanisms, enabling live detection of source model updates either for immediate processing, as in VIATRA [3], or for deferred processing, as in ReactiveATL [21]. In these approaches, source model update notifications are usually fine-grained and kept in memory. Such notifications can only be detected when the transformation engine is in memory (live) as well. The use of a notification mechanism means that models are *loosely coupled* to the transformation engine. Working with offline model updates, as in the proposed delta propagation procedure, completely decouples detection of deltas from the transformation engine, freeing model update developers from the overhead of having the transformation infrastructure in memory. The latter is only needed for propagating changes but not for defining them. In reactive approaches, when an observer receives an update notification, information about the intent of the overall model delta, i.e. the contextual information relating different atomic updates, is lost. This problem is avoided using documented deltas, which may be serialized, enabling their processing – e.g. aggregating composite changes like the *move operation* – and optimization – reduction of atomic operations that are cancelled when composed. We refer the reader to [9] for an additional discussion of delta-based model updates against state-based model updates.

Among bidirectional model transformation approaches, Triple Graph Grammars (TGG), introduced in [22], are a declarative approach for specifying bidirectional consistency relations between models. Although our approach is not bidirectional, it is worth comparing how incrementality is supported in operational TGG rules. Incrementality was first introduced in TGG synchronization in [11,12]. Efficient approaches for TGG synchronization [18–20] avoid analyzing the whole model by relying on dependencies which hint at the impact of a model update directly. Precedence-based approaches [18,20] keep a binary precedence relation over the set of model elements in order to determine when creation or deletion of a model element affects another one. While [18] overestimates the actual dependencies by defining them at the type level, others underestimate them relying on user feedback [20] or on special correspondences [12]. [19] decouples impact analysis of model updates from consistency restoration by delegating the former to VIATRA's incremental pattern matcher, which has a built-in dependency tracker, and by defining operational rules using a reactive model transformation approach. However, these two phases are still tightly coupled using a synchronous communication mechanism between the incremental pattern matcher and the synchronization procedure since the pattern matcher may trigger revocations/applications of forward marking rules after revoking/applying one of them. That is, the model synchronization procedure uses the pattern matcher to know when synchronization terminates. In the delta propagation mechanism proposed in the present work, either the revocation of applied transformation steps or the creation of new transformation steps cannot trigger further applications because rule matches are computed against the source model and they are unique, that is the same match cannot enable two different rules. A new transformation step may be found when new elements are inserted in the source model. On the other hand, when a transformation step is revoked, no other rule can be applied or a conflict would have been detected when the rule was applied the first time.

Some transformation engines with support for bidirectional transformations, like NMF [14,15], support the offline representation of model deltas. However, to the best of our knowledge, none of the aforementioned approaches uses a standardized notation for them, such as the EMF model change, which can be regarded as the de-facto standard for representing model deltas in the EMF modeling tool ecosystem.

6 Concluding Remarks

The main contribution of this work is the design of a delta propagation procedure for executing delta-driven model transformations, which has been implemented in YAMTL. The novelty of the approach consists in the use of a standardized representation of model deltas, which facilitates interoperability with EMF-compliant tools, and in the use of dependency injection mechanism, which allows the transformation engine to be aware of model updates without having to rely on a publish-subscribe infrastructure. The VIATRA CPS benchmark has been used to justify that *(1)* the initialization transformation in YAMTL is several orders of magnitude faster than the up-to-now fastest incremental solutions and that *(2)* propagation of sparse deltas can be performed in real time for VLMs, independently of their size, whereas other solutions show a clear dependence on their size. Hence, YAMTL shows satisfactory scalability in incremental execution of model transformations on VLMs. Additional studies with larger classes of models will be considered in future work.

References

1. Baker, P., Loh, S., Weil, F.: Model-driven engineering in a large industrial context — Motorola case study. In: Briand, L., Williams, C. (eds.) MODELS 2005. LNCS, vol. 3713, pp. 476–491. Springer, Heidelberg (2005). https://doi.org/10.1007/11557432_36
2. Benelallam, A., Gómez, A., Tisi, M., Cabot, J.: Distributing relational model transformation on mapreduce. J. Syst. Softw. **142**, 1–20 (2018)
3. Bergmann, G., et al.: VIATRA 3: a reactive model transformation platform. In: Kolovos, D., Wimmer, M. (eds.) ICMT 2015. LNCS, vol. 9152, pp. 101–110. Springer, Cham (2015). https://doi.org/10.1007/978-3-319-21155-8_8
4. Bergmann, G., Ráth, I., Varró, G., Varró, D.: Change-driven model transformations - change (in) the rule to rule the change. Softw. Syst. Model. **11**(3), 431–461 (2012)
5. Biermann, E., Ermel, C., Taentzer, G.: Formal foundation of consistent EMF model transformations by algebraic graph transformation. Softw. Syst. Model. **11**(2), 227–250 (2012)
6. Boronat, A.: Expressive and efficient model transformation with an internal DSL of Xtend. In: MODELS 2018, pp. 78–88. ACM (2018)
7. Boronat, A.: YAMTL evaluation repository with the incremental component of the VIATRA CPS benchmark (2018). https://github.com/yamtl/viatra-cps-incr-benchmark
8. Daniel, G., Jouault, F., Sunyé, G., Cabot, J.: Gremlin-ATL: a scalable model transformation framework. In: ASE, pp. 462–472. IEEE Computer Society (2017)
9. Diskin, Z., Xiong, Y., Czarnecki, K., Ehrig, H., Hermann, F., Orejas, F.: From state- to delta-based bidirectional model transformations: the symmetric case. In: Whittle, J., Clark, T., Kühne, T. (eds.) MODELS 2011. LNCS, vol. 6981, pp. 304–318. Springer, Heidelberg (2011). https://doi.org/10.1007/978-3-642-24485-8_22
10. Ehrig, H., Ehrig, K., Prange, U., Taentzer, G.: Fundamentals of Algebraic Graph Transformation. Springer, Heidelberg (2006). https://doi.org/10.1007/3-540-31188-2
11. Giese, H., Wagner, R.: Incremental model synchronization with triple graph grammars. In: Nierstrasz, O., Whittle, J., Harel, D., Reggio, G. (eds.) MODELS 2006. LNCS, vol. 4199, pp. 543–557. Springer, Heidelberg (2006). https://doi.org/10.1007/11880240_38
12. Giese, H., Wagner, R.: From model transformation to incremental bidirectional model synchronization. Softw. Syst. Model. **8**(1), 21–43 (2009)
13. Harmath, D., Ráth, I.: VIATRA/query/FAQ: performance optimization guidelines (2016). https://wiki.eclipse.org/VIATRA/Query/FAQ#Performance_optimization_guidelines
14. Hinkel, G.: Change propagation in an internal model transformation language. In: Kolovos, D., Wimmer, M. (eds.) ICMT 2015. LNCS, vol. 9152, pp. 3–17. Springer, Cham (2015). https://doi.org/10.1007/978-3-319-21155-8_1
15. Hinkel, G., Burger, E.: Change propagation and bidirectionality in internal transformation DSLs. Softw. Syst. Model. **18**(1), 249–278 (2017)
16. Hutchinson, J., Whittle, J., Rouncefield, M., Kristoffersen, S.: Empirical assessment of MDE in industry. In: ICSE, pp. 471–480. ACM (2011)
17. Kolovos, D.S., Paige, R.F., Polack, F.A.C.: The grand challenge of scalability for model driven engineering. In: Chaudron, M.R.V. (ed.) MODELS 2008. LNCS, vol. 5421, pp. 48–53. Springer, Heidelberg (2009). https://doi.org/10.1007/978-3-642-01648-6_5

18. Lauder, M., Anjorin, A., Varró, G., Schürr, A.: Efficient model synchronization with precedence triple graph grammars. In: Ehrig, H., Engels, G., Kreowski, H.-J., Rozenberg, G. (eds.) ICGT 2012. LNCS, vol. 7562, pp. 401–415. Springer, Heidelberg (2012). https://doi.org/10.1007/978-3-642-33654-6_27
19. Leblebici, E., Anjorin, A., Fritsche, L., Varró, G., Schürr, A.: Leveraging incremental pattern matching techniques for model synchronisation. In: de Lara, J., Plump, D. (eds.) ICGT 2017. LNCS, vol. 10373, pp. 179–195. Springer, Cham (2017). https://doi.org/10.1007/978-3-319-61470-0_11
20. Orejas, F., Pino, E.: Correctness of incremental model synchronization with triple graph grammars. In: Di Ruscio, D., Varró, D. (eds.) ICMT 2014. LNCS, vol. 8568, pp. 74–90. Springer, Cham (2014). https://doi.org/10.1007/978-3-319-08789-4_6
21. Perez, S.M., Tisi, M., Douence, R.: Reactive model transformation with ATL. Sci. Comput. Program. **136**, 1–16 (2017)
22. Schürr, A.: Specification of graph translators with triple graph grammars. In: Mayr, E.W., Schmidt, G., Tinhofer, G. (eds.) WG 1994. LNCS, vol. 903, pp. 151–163. Springer, Heidelberg (1995). https://doi.org/10.1007/3-540-59071-4_45
23. Sendall, S., Kozaczynski, W.: Model transformation: the heart and soul of model-driven software development. IEEE Softw. **20**(5), 42–45 (2003)
24. Steinberg, D., Budinsky, F., Paternostro, M., Merks, E.: EMF: Eclipse Modeling Framework 2.0., 2nd edn. Addison-Wesley Professional (2009)
25. VIATRA Team: Explicit traceability M2M transformation (2016). https://github.com/viatra/viatra-docs/blob/master/cps/Explicit-traceability-M2M-transformation.adoc
26. VIATRA Team: Query result traceability M2M transformation (2016). https://github.com/viatra/viatra-docs/blob/master/cps/Query-result-traceability-M2M-transformation.adoc
27. VIATRA Team: VIATRA CPS benchmark (cps to deployment transformation) (2016). https://github.com/viatra/viatra-docs/blob/master/cps/CPS-to-Deployment-Transformation.adoc
28. VIATRA Team: VIATRA CPS benchmark (model generator) (2016). https://github.com/viatra/viatra-docs/blob/master/cps/Model-Generator.adoc
29. VIATRA Team: VIATRA CPS benchmark (scenario specification) (2016). https://github.com/viatra/viatra-cps-benchmark/wiki/Benchmark-specification#cases

A Logic-Based Incremental Approach to Graph Repair

Sven Schneider[1(✉)], Leen Lambers[1], and Fernando Orejas[2]

[1] Hasso Plattner Institut, University of Potsdam, Potsdam, Germany
Sven.Schneider@HPI.de

[2] Universitat Politècnica de Catalunya, Barcelona, Spain

Abstract. Graph repair, restoring consistency of a graph, plays a prominent role in several areas of computer science and beyond: For example, in model-driven engineering, the abstract syntax of models is usually encoded using graphs. Flexible edit operations temporarily create inconsistent graphs not representing a valid model, thus requiring graph repair. Similarly, in graph databases—managing the storage and manipulation of graph data—updates may cause that a given database does not satisfy some integrity constraints, requiring also graph repair.

We present a logic-based incremental approach to graph repair, generating a sound and complete (upon termination) overview of least-changing repairs. In our context, we formalize consistency by so-called graph conditions being equivalent to first-order logic on graphs. We present two kind of repair algorithms: State-based repair restores consistency independent of the graph update history, whereas delta-based (or incremental) repair takes this history explicitly into account. Technically, our algorithms rely on an existing model generation algorithm for graph conditions implemented in AutoGraph. Moreover, the delta-based approach uses the new concept of satisfaction (ST) trees for encoding if and how a graph satisfies a graph condition. We then demonstrate how to manipulate these STs incrementally with respect to a graph update.

1 Introduction

Graph repair, restoring consistency of a graph, plays a prominent role in several areas of computer science and beyond. For example, in model-driven engineering, models are typically represented using graphs and the use of flexible edit operations may temporarily create inconsistent graphs not representing a valid model, thus requiring graph repair. This includes the situation where different views of an artifact are represented by a different model, i.e., the artifact is described by a multi-model, see, e.g. [6], and updates in some models may cause a global inconsistency in the multimodel. Similarly, in graph databases—managing the storage

F. Orejas has been supported by the Salvador de Madariaga grant PRX18/00308 and by funds from the Spanish Research Agency (AEI) and the European Union (FEDER funds) under grant GRAMM (ref. TIN2017-86727-C2-1-R).

R. Hähnle and W. van der Aalst (Eds.): FASE 2019, LNCS 11424, pp. 151–167, 2019.
https://doi.org/10.1007/978-3-030-16722-6_9

and manipulation of graph data—updates may cause that a given database does not satisfy some integrity constraints [1], requiring also graph repair.

Numerous approaches on model inconsistency and repair (see [12] for an excellent recent survey) operate in varying frameworks with diverse assumptions. In our framework, we consider a typed directed graph (cf. [7]) to be inconsistent if it does not satisfy a given finite set of constraints, which are expressed by graph conditions [8], a formalism with the expressive power of first-order logic on graphs. A graph repair is, then, a description of an update that, if applied to the given graph, makes it consistent. Our algorithms do not just provide one repair, but a set of them from which the user must select the right repair to be applied. Moreover, we derive only least changing repairs, which do not include other smaller viable repairs. Our approach uses techniques (and the tool AutoGraph) [17] designed for model generation of graph conditions.

We consider two scenarios: In the first one, the aim is to repair a given graph (state-based repair). In the second one, a consistent graph is given together with an update that may make it inconsistent. In this case, the aim is to repair the graph in an incremental way (delta-based repair).

The main contributions of the paper are the following ones:

- A precise definition of what an update is, together with the definition of some properties, like e.g. least changing, that a repair update may satisfy.
- Two kind of graph repair algorithms: state-based and incremental (for the delta-based case). Moreover, we demonstrate for all algorithms *soundness* (the repair result provided by the algorithms is consistent) and *completeness* (upon termination, our algorithms will find all possible desired repairs)[1].

Summarizing, most repair techniques do not provide guarantees for the functional semantics of the repair and suffer from lack of information for the deployment of the techniques (see conclusion of the survey [12]). With our logic-based graph repair approach we aim at alleviating this weakness by presenting formally its functional semantics and describing the details of the underlying algorithms.

The paper is organized as follows: After introducing preliminaries in Sect. 2, we proceed in Sect. 3 with defining graph updates and repairs. In Sect. 4, we present the state-based scenario. We continue with introducing satisfaction trees in Sect. 5 that are needed for the delta-based scenario in Sect. 6. We close with a comparison with related work in Sect. 7 and conclusion with outlook in Sect. 8. For proofs of theorems and example details we refer to our technical report [18].

2 Preliminaries on Graph Conditions

We recall graph conditions (GCs), defined here over typed directed graphs, used for representing properties on such graphs. In our running example[2], we employ

[1] Note that completeness implies totality (if the given set of constraints is satisfiable by a finite graph, then the algorithms will find a repair for any inconsistent graph).

[2] We refer to Sect. 1 with pointers to related work including diverse use cases in Software Engineering for graph repair with more complex and motivating examples.

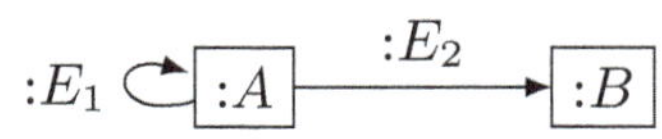

$$\neg\exists(a, \neg(\exists(a \xrightarrow{e} b, \mathit{true}) \wedge \neg\exists(a \circlearrowleft e, \mathit{true})))$$

Fig. 1. The type graph TG (left) and the GC ψ (right) for our running example

the type graph TG from Fig. 1 and we use nodes with names a_i and b_i to indicate that they are of type $:A$ and $:B$, respectively.

GCs state facts about the existence of graph patterns in a given graph, called a host graph. For example, in the syntax used in our running example, the GC $\exists(a, \mathit{true})$ means that the host graph must include a node of type $:A$. Also, $\exists(a \longrightarrow b, \mathit{true})$ means that the host graph must include a node of type $:A$, another node of type $:B$, and an edge from the $:A$-node to the $:B$-node.

In general, in the syntax that we use in our running example, an atomic GC is of the form $\exists(H, \phi)$ (or $\neg\exists(H, \phi)$) where H is a graph that must be (or must not be) included in the host graph and where ϕ is a condition expressing more restrictions on how this graph is found (or not found) in the host graph. For instance, $\exists(a, \neg\exists(a \xrightarrow{e} b, \mathit{true}))$ states that the host graph must include an $:A$-node such that it has no outgoing edge e to a $:B$-node. Moreover, we use the standard boolean operators to combine atomic GCs to form more complex ones. For instance, $\exists(a, \neg(\exists(a \xrightarrow{e} b, \mathit{true}) \wedge \neg\exists(a \circlearrowleft e, \mathit{true})))$ states that the host graph must include an $:A$-node, such that it does not hold that there is an outgoing edge e to a $:B$-node and node a has no loop. In addition, as an abbreviation for readability, we may use the universal quantifier with the meaning $\forall(H, \phi) = \neg\exists(H, \neg\phi)$. In this sense, the condition ϕ from Fig. 1, used in our running example, states that every node of type $:A$ must have an outgoing edge to a node of type $:B$ and that such an $:A$-node must have no loop.

Formally, the syntax of GCs [8], expressively equivalent to first-order logic on graphs [5], is given subsequently. This logic encodes properties of graph extensions, which must be explicitly mentioned as graph inclusions. For instance, the GC $\exists(a, \neg\exists(a \xrightarrow{e} b, \mathit{true}))$ in simplified notation is formally given in the syntax of GCs as $\exists(\mathrm{i}_H, \neg\exists(a \hookrightarrow (a \xrightarrow{e} b), \mathit{true}))$, where i_H denotes the inclusion $\emptyset \hookrightarrow H$ with H the graph consisting of node a. This is because it expresses a property of the extension i_H. Moreover, therein the GC $\neg\exists(a \hookrightarrow (a \xrightarrow{e} b), \mathit{true})$ is actually a property of the extension $a \hookrightarrow (a \xrightarrow{e} b)$.

Definition 1 (Graph Conditions (GCs) [8]). *The class of* graph conditions Φ_H^{GC} *for the graph H is defined inductively:*

- $\wedge S \in \Phi_H^{\mathrm{GC}}$ *if* $S \subseteq_{\mathrm{fin}} \Phi_H^{\mathrm{GC}}$.
- $\neg\phi \in \Phi_H^{\mathrm{GC}}$ *if* $\phi \in \Phi_H^{\mathrm{GC}}$.
- $\exists(a : H \hookrightarrow H', \phi) \in \Phi_H^{\mathrm{GC}}$ *if* $\phi \in \Phi_{H'}^{\mathrm{GC}}$.

In addition true, false, $\vee S$, $\phi_1 \Rightarrow \phi_2$, and $\forall(a, \phi)$ can be used as abbreviations, with their obvious replacement.

A mono $m : H \hookrightarrow G$ satisfies *a GC $\psi \in \Phi_H^{\mathrm{GC}}$, written $m \models_{\mathrm{GC}} \psi$, if one of the following cases applies.*

– $\psi = \wedge S$ *and* $m \models_{\mathrm{GC}} \phi$ *for each* $\phi \in S$.
– $\psi = \neg\phi$ *and not* $m \models_{\mathrm{GC}} \phi$.
– $\psi = \exists(a : H \hookrightarrow H', \phi)$ *and* $\exists q : H' \hookrightarrow G.\ q \circ a = m \wedge q \models_{\mathrm{GC}} \phi$.

A graph G *satisfies a* GC $\psi \in \Phi_{\emptyset}^{\mathrm{GC}}$, *written* $G \models_{\mathrm{GC}} \psi$ *or* $G \in [\![\psi]\!]$, *if* $\mathrm{i}_G \models_{\mathrm{GC}} \psi$.

3 Graph Updates and Repairs

In this section, we define graph updates to formalize arbitrary modifications of graphs, graph repairs as the desired graph updates resulting in repaired graphs, as well as further desireable properties of graph updates.

In particular, it is well known that a modification or update of G_1 resulting in a graph G_2 can be represented by two inclusions or, in general two monos, which we denote by $(l : I \hookrightarrow G_1, r : I \hookrightarrow G_2)$, where I represents the part of G_1 that is preserved by this update. Intuitively, $l : I \hookrightarrow G_1$ describes the deletion of elements from G_1 (i.e., all elements in $G_1 \setminus l(I)$ are deleted) and $r : I \hookrightarrow G_2$ describes the addition of elements to I to obtain G_2 (i.e., all elements in $G_2 \setminus r(I)$ are added).

Definition 2 (Graph Update). *A* (graph) update u *is a pair* $(l : I \hookrightarrow G_1, r : I \hookrightarrow G_2)$ *of monos. The class of all updates is denoted by* $\mathcal{U}$.

Graph updates such as $(\mathrm{i}_G : \emptyset \hookrightarrow G, \mathrm{i}_G : \emptyset \hookrightarrow G)$ where G is not the empty graph delete all the elements in G that are added by r afterwards. To rule out such updates, we define an update $(l : I \hookrightarrow G_1, r : I \hookrightarrow G_2)$ to be *canonical* when the graph I is as large as possible, i.e. intuitively $I = G_1 \cap G_2$. Formally:

Definition 3 (Canonical Graph Update). *If* $(l : I \hookrightarrow G_1, r : I \hookrightarrow G_2) \in \mathcal{U}$ *and every* $(l' : I' \hookrightarrow G_1, r' : I' \hookrightarrow G_2) \in \mathcal{U}$ *and mono* $i : I \hookrightarrow I'$ *with* $l' \circ i = l$ *and* $r' \circ i = r$ *satisfies that* i *is an isomorphism then* (l, r) *is* canonical, *written* $(l, r) \in \mathcal{U}_{\mathrm{can}}$.

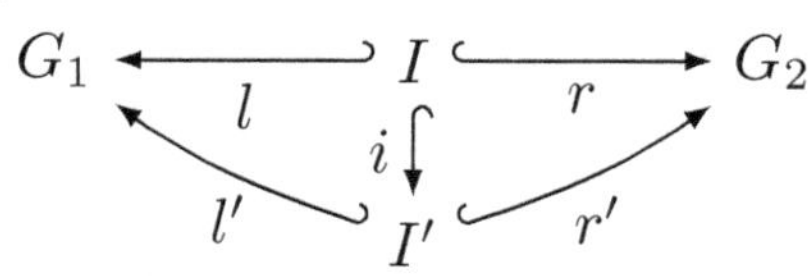

An update u_1 is a sub-update (see [14]) of u whenever the modifications defined by u_1 are fully contained in the modifications defined by u. Intuitively, this is the case when u_1 can be composed with another update u_2 such that (a) the resulting update has the same effect as u and (b) u_2 does not delete any element that was added before by u_1. This is stated, informally speaking, by requiring that I is the intersection (pullback) of I_1 and I_2 and that G_2 is its union (pushout).

Definition 4 (Sub-update [14]). *If* $u = (l : I \hookrightarrow G_1, r : I \hookrightarrow G_2) \in \mathcal{U}$, $u_1 = (l_1 : I_1 \hookrightarrow G_1, r_1 : I_1 \hookrightarrow G_3) \in \mathcal{U}$, $u_2 = (l_2 : I_2 \hookrightarrow G_3, r_2 : I_2 \hookrightarrow G_2) \in \mathcal{U}$,

$(r_1' : I \hookrightarrow I_1, l_2' : I \hookrightarrow I_2)$ is the pullback of (r_1, l_2), and (r_1, l_2) is the pushout of (r_1', l_2') then u_1 is a sub-update *of u, written $u_1 \leq^{u_2} u$ or simply $u_1 \leq u$.*

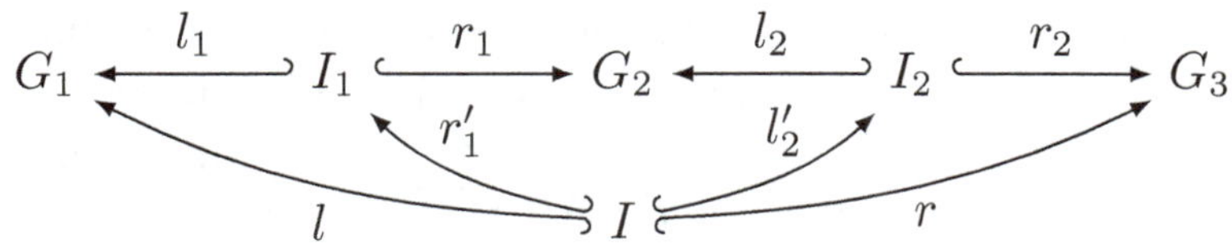

Moreover, we write $u_1 <^{u_2} u$ or $u_1 < u$ when $u_1 \leq^{u_2} u$ and not $u \leq u_1$.

We now define graph repairs as graph updates where the result graph satisfies the given consistency constraint ψ.

Definition 5 (Graph Repair). *If $u = (l : I \hookrightarrow G_1, r : I \hookrightarrow G_2) \in \mathcal{U}$, $\psi \in \Phi_{\emptyset}^{\mathrm{GC}}$, and $G_2 \models_{\mathrm{GC}} \psi$ then u is a* graph repair *or simply* repair *of G_1 with respect to ψ, written $u \in \mathcal{U}(G_1, \psi)$.*

To define a finite set of desirable repairs, we introduce the notion of least changing repairs that are repairs for which no sub-updates exist that are also repairs.

Definition 6 (Least Changing Graph Repair). *If $\psi \in \Phi_{\emptyset}^{\mathrm{GC}}$, $u = (l : I \hookrightarrow G_1, r : I \hookrightarrow G_2) \in \mathcal{U}(G_1, \psi)$, and there is no $u' \in \mathcal{U}(G_1, \psi)$ such that $u' < u$ then u is a* least changing graph repair *of G_1 with respect to ψ, written $u \in \mathcal{U}_{\mathrm{lc}}(G_1, \psi)$.*

Note that every least changing repair is canonical according to this definition. Moreover, the notion of least changing repairs is unrelated to other notions of repairs such as the set of all repairs that require a smallest amount of atomic modifications of the graph at hand to result in a graph satisfying the consistency constraint. For instance, a repair u_1 adding two nodes of type $:A$ may be a least changing repair even if there is a repair u_2 adding only one node of type $:B$.

A graph repair algorithm is *stable* [12], if the repair procedure returns the identity update $(\mathrm{id}_G : G \hookrightarrow G, \mathrm{id}_G : G \hookrightarrow G)$ when graph G is already consistent. Obviously, a graph repair algorithm that only returns least changing repairs is stable, since the identity update is a sub-update of any other repair.

4 State-Based Repair

In this section, we introduce two state-based graph repair algorithms (see [18] for additional technical detail), which compute a set of graph repairs restoring consistency for a given graph.

Definition 7 (State-Based Graph Repair Algorithm). *A state-based graph repair algorithm takes a graph G and a* GC *$\psi \in \Phi_{\emptyset}^{\mathrm{GC}}$ as inputs and returns a set of graph repairs in $\mathcal{U}(G, \psi)$.*

Note that the tool AutoGraph [17] can be used to verify this condition as follows: It determines the operation $\mathcal{A}$ that constructs a finite set of all minimal graphs satisfying a given GC ψ. Formally, $\mathcal{A}(\psi) = \cap\{S \subseteq [\![\psi]\!] \mid \forall G' \in [\![\psi]\!]. \exists G \in$

$S. \exists m : G \hookrightarrow G'.true\}$. While AutoGraph may not terminate when computing this operation due to the inherent expressiveness of GCs, it is known that AutoGraph terminates whenever ψ is not satisfied by any graph.

The state-based algorithm $\mathcal{R}\mathrm{epair}_{\mathrm{sb},1}$ uses $\mathcal{A}$ to obtain repairs. $\mathcal{R}\mathrm{epair}_{\mathrm{sb},1}$ computes the set $\mathcal{A}(\psi \wedge \exists(\mathrm{i}_G, \mathit{true}))$ that contains all minimal graphs that (a) satisfy ψ and (b) include a copy of G. All these extensions of G correspond to a graph repair. For our running example, we do not obtain any repair for graph $\mathbf{G'_u}$ from Fig. 2 and GC ψ from Fig. 1 because the loop on node a_2 would invalidate any graph including $\mathbf{G'_u}$. We state that $\mathcal{R}\mathrm{epair}_{\mathrm{sb},1}$ indeed computes the non-deleting least changing graph repairs.

Theorem 1 (Functional Semantics of $\mathcal{R}\mathrm{epair}_{\mathrm{sb},1}$). *$\mathcal{R}\mathrm{epair}_{\mathrm{sb},1}$ is* sound, *i.e., $\mathcal{R}\mathrm{epair}_{\mathrm{sb},1}(G, \psi) \subseteq \mathcal{U}_{\mathrm{lc}}(G, \psi)$, and* complete (upon termination) *with respect to non-deleting repairs in $\mathcal{U}_{\mathrm{lc}}(G, \psi)$.*

The second state-based algorithm $\mathcal{R}\mathrm{epair}_{\mathrm{sb},2}$ computes *all* least changing graph repairs. In this algorithm we use the approach of $\mathcal{R}\mathrm{epair}_{\mathrm{sb},1}$ but compute $\mathcal{A}(\psi \wedge \exists(\mathrm{i}_{G_c}, \mathit{true}))$ whenever an inclusion $l : G_c \hookrightarrow G$ describes how G can be restricted to one of its subgraphs G_c. Every graph G' obtained from the application of $\mathcal{A}$ for one of these graphs G_c then results in one graph repair returned by $\mathcal{R}\mathrm{epair}_{\mathrm{sb},2}$ except for those that are not least changing.

To this extent we introduce the notion of a restriction tree (see example in Fig. 2) having all subgraphs G_c of a given graph G as nodes as long as they include the graph G_{min}, which is the empty graph in the state-based algorithm $\mathcal{R}\mathrm{epair}_{\mathrm{sb},2}$ but not in the algorithm $\mathcal{R}\mathrm{epair}_{\mathrm{db}}$ in Sect. 6, and where edges are given in this tree by inclusions that add precisely one node or edge.

Definition 8 (Restriction Tree RT). *If G and G_{min} are graphs and $S = \{l : G_c \hookrightarrow G_p \mid G_{min} \subseteq G_c \subset G_p \subseteq G, l \text{ is an inclusion}\}$, S' is the least subset of S such that the closure of S' under $\circ$ equals S then a* restriction tree $\mathrm{RT}(G, G_{min})$ *is a least subset of S' such that for all two inclusions $l_1 : G \hookrightarrow G_1 \in S'$ and $l_2 : G \hookrightarrow G_2 \in S'$ one of them is in $\mathrm{RT}(G, G_{min})$.*

Considering our running example, the restriction tree in Fig. 2 is traversed entirely except for the four graphs without a border, which are not traversed as they have the supergraph marked 9 satisfying ψ and therefore traversing those would generate repairs that are not least changing. The resulting graph repairs for the condition ψ are given by the graphs marked by 3–6.

Our second state-based graph repair algorithm is indeed sound and complete whenever the calls to AutoGraph using $\mathcal{A}$ terminate.

Theorem 2 (Functional Semantics of $\mathcal{R}\mathrm{epair}_{\mathrm{sb},2}$). *$\mathcal{R}\mathrm{epair}_{\mathrm{sb},2}$ is* sound, *i.e., $\mathcal{R}\mathrm{epair}_{\mathrm{sb},2}(G, \psi) \subseteq \mathcal{U}_{\mathrm{lc}}(G, \psi)$, and* complete, *i.e., $\mathcal{U}_{\mathrm{lc}}(G, \psi) \subseteq \mathcal{R}\mathrm{epair}_{\mathrm{sb},2}(G, \psi)$, upon termination.*

5 Satisfaction Trees

The state-based algorithms introduced in the previous section are inefficient when used in a scenario where a graph needs repair after a sequence of updates

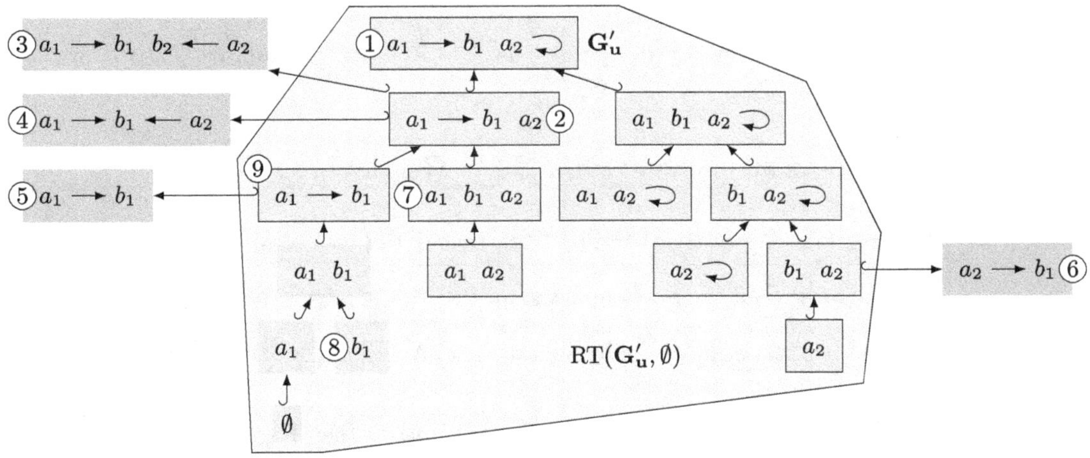

Fig. 2. The restriction tree $\mathrm{RT}(\mathbf{G}'_{\mathbf{u}}, \emptyset)$ (enclosed by the polygon) and four graph repairs (marked 3–6) generated using $\mathcal{R}\mathrm{epair}_{\mathrm{sb},2}$

that all need repair. We thus present in Sect. 6 an incremental algorithm reducing the computational cost for a repair when an update is provided. This algorithm uses an additional data structure, called *satisfaction tree* or ST, which stores information on if and how a graph G satisfies a GC ψ (according to Definition 1). In this section, given ψ and G, we define how such an ST γ is constructed and how it is updated once the graph G is updated.

If ψ is a conjunction of conditions, its associated ST γ is a conjunction of STs and if ψ is a negation of a conditions, its associated γ is a negation of an ST. In the case when ψ is a $\exists(a : H \hookrightarrow H', \phi)$, recall that a match $m : H \hookrightarrow G$ satisfies ψ if there exists a $q : H' \hookrightarrow G$ such that $m = q \circ a$ and $q \models_{\mathrm{GC}} \phi$. For this case, we keep in ST each q satisfying these two conditions and also each q that satisfies the first condition, but not the second. More precisely, for the case of existential quantification, the corresponding ST is of the form $\exists(a : H \hookrightarrow H', \phi, m_t, m_f)$, where m_t and m_f are partial mappings (we use $\sup(f)$ to denoted the elements actually mapped by a partial map f) that map matches $q : H' \hookrightarrow G$ that satisfy $m = q \circ a$ (for a previously known $m : H \hookrightarrow G$) to an ST for the subcondition ϕ. The difference between both partial functions is that m_t maps matches q to STs for which $q \models_{\mathrm{GC}} \phi$ while m_f maps matches q to STs for which $q \not\models_{\mathrm{GC}} \phi$. Consider Fig. 3b for an example of an ST $\gamma_{\mathbf{u}}$.

The following definition describes the syntax of STs. The STs are defined over matches into a graph G to allow for the basic well-formedness condition that every mapped match q satisfies $q \circ a = m$.

Definition 9 (Satisfaction Trees (STs)). *The class of all* Satisfaction Trees Γ^{ST}_m *for a mono* $m : H \hookrightarrow G$ *contains* γ *if one of the following cases applies.*

- $\gamma = \wedge S$ *and* $S \subseteq_{\mathrm{fin}} \Gamma^{\mathrm{ST}}_m$.
- $\gamma = \neg\chi$ *and* $\chi \in \Gamma^{\mathrm{ST}}_m$.
- $\gamma = \exists(a, \phi, m_t, m_f)$, $a : H \hookrightarrow H'$, $\phi \in \Phi^{\mathrm{GC}}_{H'}$, $m_t, m_f \subseteq_{\mathrm{fin}} \{(q : H' \hookrightarrow G, \bar{\gamma}) \mid q \circ a = m, \bar{\gamma} \in \Gamma^{\mathrm{ST}}_q\}$, *and* m_t, m_f *are partial maps.*

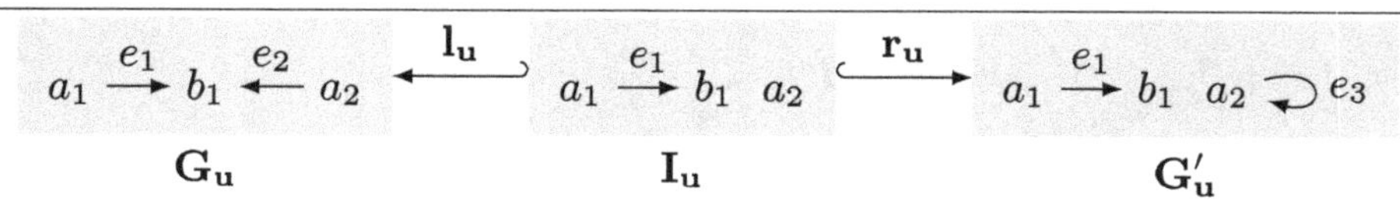

(a) A graph update $\mathbf{u} = (\mathbf{l_u} : \mathbf{I_u} \hookrightarrow \mathbf{G_u}, \mathbf{r_u} : \mathbf{I_u} \hookrightarrow \mathbf{G'_u})$

$$\gamma_{\mathbf{u}} = \neg\exists(a, \underline{\neg(\exists(a \xrightarrow{e} b, \mathit{true}) \wedge \neg\exists(a \circlearrowleft e, \mathit{true}))}, \emptyset, \{a_2 \mapsto \gamma_{\mathbf{u},\mathbf{1}}, a_1 \mapsto \gamma_{\mathbf{u},\mathbf{2}}\})$$

$$\gamma_{\mathbf{u},\mathbf{1}} = \neg(\exists(a \xrightarrow{e} b, \underline{\mathit{true}}, \{a_2 \xrightarrow{e_2} b_1 \mapsto \mathit{true}\}, \emptyset) \wedge \neg\exists(a \circlearrowleft e, \underline{\mathit{true}}, \emptyset, \emptyset))$$

$$\gamma_{\mathbf{u},\mathbf{2}} = \neg(\exists(a \xrightarrow{e} b, \underline{\mathit{true}}, \{a_1 \xrightarrow{e_1} b_1 \mapsto \mathit{true}\}, \emptyset) \wedge \neg\exists(a \circlearrowleft e, \underline{\mathit{true}}, \emptyset, \emptyset))$$

(b) The ST $\gamma_{\mathbf{u}}$ for $\mathbf{G_u}$ (see Fig. 3a) and ψ (see Fig. 1).

$$\gamma^{\mathbf{I}}_{\mathbf{u}} = \neg\exists(a, \underline{\neg(\exists(a \xrightarrow{e} b, \mathit{true}) \wedge \neg\exists(a \circlearrowleft e, \mathit{true}))}, \{a_2 \mapsto \gamma^{\mathbf{I}}_{\mathbf{u},\mathbf{1}}\}, \{a_1 \mapsto \gamma^{\mathbf{I}}_{\mathbf{u},\mathbf{2}}\})$$

$$\gamma^{\mathbf{I}}_{\mathbf{u},\mathbf{1}} = \neg(\exists(a \xrightarrow{e} b, \underline{\mathit{true}}, \emptyset, \emptyset) \wedge \neg\exists(a \circlearrowleft e, \underline{\mathit{true}}, \{a_2 \circlearrowleft e_3 \mapsto \mathit{true}\}, \emptyset))$$

$$\gamma^{\mathbf{I}}_{\mathbf{u},\mathbf{2}} = \neg(\exists(a \xrightarrow{e} b, \underline{\mathit{true}}, \{a_1 \xrightarrow{e_1} b_1 \mapsto \mathit{true}\}, \emptyset) \wedge \neg\exists(a \circlearrowleft e, \underline{\mathit{true}}, \emptyset, \emptyset))$$

(c) The ST $\gamma^{\mathbf{I}}_{\mathbf{u}}$ for $\mathbf{I_u}$ (see Fig. 3a) and ψ (see Fig. 1) that is obtained as the backward propagation $\mathrm{ppgB}(\gamma_{\mathbf{u}}, \mathbf{l_u})$ from $\gamma_{\mathbf{u}}$ (see Fig. 3b) and $\mathbf{l_u}$ (see Fig. 3a)

$$\gamma'_{\mathbf{u}} = \neg\exists(a, \underline{\neg(\exists(a \xrightarrow{e} b, \mathit{true}) \wedge \neg\exists(a \circlearrowleft e, \mathit{true}))}, \{a_2 \overset{(\mathsf{R1})}{\mapsto} \gamma'_{\mathbf{u},\mathbf{1}}\}, \{a_1 \mapsto \gamma'_{\mathbf{u},\mathbf{2}}\})$$

$$\gamma'_{\mathbf{u},\mathbf{1}} = \neg(\exists(a \xrightarrow{e} b, \underline{\mathit{true}}, \emptyset_{(\mathsf{R2})}, \emptyset) \wedge \neg\exists(a \circlearrowleft e, \underline{\mathit{true}}, \{a_2 \circlearrowleft e_3 \overset{(\mathsf{R3})}{\mapsto} \mathit{true}\}, \emptyset))$$

$$\gamma'_{\mathbf{u},\mathbf{2}} = \neg(\exists(a \xrightarrow{e} b, \underline{\mathit{true}}, \{a_1 \xrightarrow{e_1} b_1 \mapsto \mathit{true}\}, \emptyset) \wedge \neg\exists(a \circlearrowleft e, \underline{\mathit{true}}, \emptyset, \emptyset))$$

(d) The ST $\gamma'_{\mathbf{u}}$ for $\mathbf{G'_u}$ (see Fig. 3a) and ψ (see Fig. 1) that is obtained as the forward propagation $\mathrm{ppgF}(\gamma^{\mathbf{I}}_{\mathbf{u}}, \mathbf{r_u})$ from $\gamma^{\mathbf{I}}_{\mathbf{u}}$ (see Fig. 3b) and $\mathbf{r_u}$ (see Fig. 3a). Also $\gamma'_{\mathbf{u}}$ is the result of $\mathrm{ppgU}(\gamma_{\mathbf{u}}, \mathbf{u})$ that applies backward and forward propagation. The viable points for the delta-based repair discussed in Sec. 6 are indicated by (R1)–(R3).

Fig. 3. A graph update and an ST with its propagation over the graph update where GCs are underlined in STs for readability

The following satisfaction predicate $\models_{\mathrm{GC}}$ for STs defines when an ST γ for a mono m states that the contained GC ψ is satisfied by the morphism m.

Definition 10 (ST Satisfaction). *An* ST $\gamma \in \Gamma^{\mathrm{ST}}_{m:H \hookrightarrow G}$ *is* satisfied, *written* $\models_{\mathrm{ST}} \gamma$, *if one of the following cases applies.*

- $\gamma = \wedge S$ *and* $\models_{\mathrm{ST}} \chi$ *(for each* $\chi \in S$*)*
- $\gamma = \neg\chi$ *and* $\not\models_{\mathrm{ST}} \chi$*.*
- $\gamma = \exists(a, \phi, m_t, m_f)$ *and* $m_t \neq \emptyset$*.*

The following recursive operation constructs an ST γ for a graph G and a condition ψ so that γ represents how G satisfies (or not satisfies) ψ. Note that the match m in the definition of STs above and the construction of an ST below corresponds to the match $m : H \hookrightarrow G$ from Definition 1 that we operationalize in the following definition. For conjunction and negation, we construct the STs from the STs for the subconditions. For the case of existential quantification, we consider all morphisms $q : H' \hookrightarrow G$ for which the triangle $q \circ a = m$ commutes and construct the STs for the subcondition ϕ under this extended match q. The resulting STs are inserted into m_t and m_f according to whether they are satisfied.

Definition 11 (Construct ST (cst)**).** *Given $m : H \hookrightarrow G$ and $\psi \in \Phi_H^{\mathrm{GC}}$, we define* $\mathrm{cst}(\psi, m) = \gamma$, *with $\gamma \in \Gamma_m^{\mathrm{ST}}$ as follows.*

- *If $\psi = \wedge S$ then $\gamma = \wedge\{\mathrm{cst}(\phi, m) \mid \phi \in S\}$.*
- *If $\psi = \neg\phi$ then $\gamma = \neg\,\mathrm{cst}(\phi, m)$.*
- *If $\psi = \exists(a : H \hookrightarrow H', \phi)$, $m_{all} = \{(q : H' \hookrightarrow G, \chi) \mid q \circ a = m, \mathrm{cst}(\phi, q) = \chi\}$, $m_t = \{(q, \chi) \in m_{all} \mid \models_{\mathrm{ST}} \chi\}$, $m_f = m_{all} \setminus m_t$, then $\gamma = \exists(a, \phi, m_t, m_f)$.*

If G is a graph and $\psi \in \Phi_\emptyset^{\mathrm{GC}}$, then $\mathrm{cst}(\psi, G) = \mathrm{cst}(\psi, \mathrm{i}_G)$.

This construction of STs then ensures that $\models_{\mathrm{ST}} \gamma$ if and only if $G \models_{\mathrm{GC}} \psi$. Note that $\models_{\mathrm{ST}} \gamma_{\mathbf{u}}$ holds for the ST $\gamma_{\mathbf{u}}$ from Fig. 3b, the GC $\boldsymbol{\psi}$ from Fig. 1, and the graph $\mathbf{G_u}$ from Fig. 3.

Theorem 3 (Sound Construction of STs). *Given $m : H \hookrightarrow G$, $\psi \in \Phi_H^{\mathrm{GC}}$, and $\mathrm{cst}(\psi, m) = \gamma$ then $\models_{\mathrm{ST}} \gamma$ iff $m \models_{\mathrm{GC}} \psi$.*

Subsequently, we define a propagation operation ppgU of an ST γ for a graph update $u = (l : I \hookrightarrow G, r : I \hookrightarrow G')$ to obtain an ST γ' such that $\gamma' = \mathrm{cst}(\psi, G')$ whenever $\gamma = \mathrm{cst}(\psi, G)$. This overall propagation is performed by a backward propagation of γ for l using the operation ppgB followed by a forward propagation of the resulting ST for r using the operation ppgF.

For backward propagation, we describe how the deletion of elements in G by $l : I \hookrightarrow G$ affect its associated ST γ. To this end, we preserve those matches $q : H \hookrightarrow G$ for which no matched elements are deleted. This is formalized by requiring a mono $q' : H \hookrightarrow I$ such that $l \circ q' = q$. The matches q with deleted matched elements can not be preserved and are therefore removed.

Definition 12 (Propagate Match (ppgMatch)**).** *If $q : H \hookrightarrow G$ and $l : I \hookrightarrow G$ are monos, then* $\mathrm{ppgMatch}(q, l)$ *is the unique $q' : H \hookrightarrow I$ such that $l \circ q' = q$ if it exists and $\perp$ otherwise.*

The following recursive backward propagation defines how deletions affect the maps m_t and m_f of the given ST. That is, when $\gamma = \exists(a, \phi, m_t, m_f)$, we (a) entirely remove a mapping (m, χ) from m_t or m_f if $\mathrm{ppgMatch}(q, l) = \perp$ and (b) construct for a mapping (m, χ) from m_t or m_f the pair $(\mathrm{ppgMatch}(q, l), \chi')$ where χ' is obtained from recursively applying the backward propagation on χ when $\mathrm{ppgMatch}(q, l) \neq \perp$. The updated pair $(\mathrm{ppgMatch}(q, l), \chi')$ must be rechecked to decide to which partial map this pair must be added to ensure that the resulting ST corresponds to the ST that would be constructed for G' directly.

Definition 13 (Backward Propagation (ppgB)**).** *If* $m : H \hookrightarrow G$, $\gamma \in \Gamma^{\mathrm{ST}}_{m}$, $l : I \hookrightarrow G$, $\mathrm{ppgMatch}(m, l) = m' : H \hookrightarrow I$, *and* $\gamma' \in \Gamma^{\mathrm{ST}}_{m'}$ *then* $\mathrm{ppgB}(\gamma, l) = \gamma'$ *if one of the following cases applies.*

- $\gamma = \wedge S$ *and* $\gamma' = \wedge\{\mathrm{ppgB}(\chi, l) \mid \chi \in S\}$.
- $\gamma = \neg\chi$ *and* $\gamma' = \neg\,\mathrm{ppgB}(\chi, l)$.
- $\gamma = \exists(a, \phi, m_t, m_f)$, $m_{all} = \{(q', \chi') \mid (q, \chi) \in m_t \cup m_f \wedge \mathrm{ppgMatch}(q, l) = q' \neq \bot \wedge \mathrm{ppgB}(\chi, l) = \chi'\}$, $m'_t = \{(q, \chi) \in m_{all} \mid\models_{\mathrm{ST}} \chi\}$, $m'_f = m_{all} \setminus m'_t$, *and* $\gamma' = \exists(a, \phi, m'_t, m'_f)$.

Note that $\mathrm{ppgMatch}(\mathrm{i}_G, l) = \mathrm{i}_G$ and, hence, the operation ppgB is applicable for all ST $\gamma \in \Gamma^{\mathrm{ST}}_{\mathrm{i}_G}$, which is sufficient as we define consistency constraints using GCs over the empty graph as well.

In the case of forward propagation where additions are given by $r : I \hookrightarrow G'$ we can preserve all matches using an adaptation. But the addition of further elements may result in additional matches as well that may satisfy the conditions to be included in the corresponding m_t and m_f from the ST at hand.

Definition 14 (Forward Propagation (ppgF)**).** *If* $\gamma \in \Gamma^{\mathrm{ST}}_{m:H\hookrightarrow I}$, $r : I \hookrightarrow G'$, *and* $\gamma' \in \Gamma^{\mathrm{ST}}_{r \circ m}$ *then* $\mathrm{ppgF}(\gamma, r) = \gamma'$ *if one of the following cases applies.*

- $\gamma = \wedge S$ *and* $\gamma' = \wedge\{\mathrm{ppgF}(\chi, r) \mid \chi \in S\}$.
- $\gamma = \neg\chi$ *and* $\gamma' = \neg\,\mathrm{ppgF}(\chi, r)$.
- $\gamma = \exists(a, \phi, m_t, m_f)$, $m_{all} = \{(r \circ q, \gamma') \mid (q, \chi) \in m_t \cup m_f \wedge \mathrm{ppgF}(\chi, r) = \gamma'\} \cup \{(q, \gamma_q) \mid q \circ a = r \circ m, (\nexists q' \in \mathrm{sup}(m_t) \cup \mathrm{sup}(m_f).\ r \circ q' = q), \mathrm{cst}(\phi, q) = \gamma_q\}$, $m'_t = \{(q, \chi) \in m_{all} \mid\models_{\mathrm{ST}} \chi\}$, $m'_f = m_{all} \setminus m'_t$, *and* $\gamma' = \exists(a, \phi, m'_t, m'_f)$.

We now define the composition of both propagations to obtain the operation ppgU that updates an ST for an entire graph update.

Definition 15 (Update Propagation (ppgU)**).** *If* $m : H \hookrightarrow G$, $\gamma \in \Gamma^{\mathrm{ST}}_{m}$, $l : I \hookrightarrow G$, $\mathrm{ppgMatch}(m, l) = m' : H \hookrightarrow G'$, *and* $r : I \hookrightarrow G'$ *then* $\mathrm{ppgU}(\gamma, (l, r)) = \mathrm{ppgF}(\mathrm{ppgB}(\gamma, l), r) \in \Gamma^{\mathrm{ST}}_{m'}$.

The overall propagation given by this operation is *incremental*, in the sense that the operation cst is only used in the forward propagation on parts of the graph G', where the addition of graph elements by r from the graph update results in additional matches q according to the satisfaction relation for GCs. Finally, we state that ppgU incrementally computes the ST obtained using cst. The proof of this theorem relies on the fact that this property also holds for ppgB and ppgF.

Theorem 4 (ppgU **is Compatible with** cst)**.** *If* G *is a graph,* $\psi \in \Phi^{\mathrm{GC}}_{\emptyset}$, $l : I \hookrightarrow G$, *and* $r : I \hookrightarrow G'$ *then* $\mathrm{ppgU}(\mathrm{cst}(\psi, G), (l, r)) = \mathrm{cst}(\psi, G')$.

6 Delta-Based Repair

The local states of delta-based graph repair algorithms may contain, besides the current graph as in state-based graph repair algorithms, an additional value. In our delta-based graph repair algorithm this will be an ST.

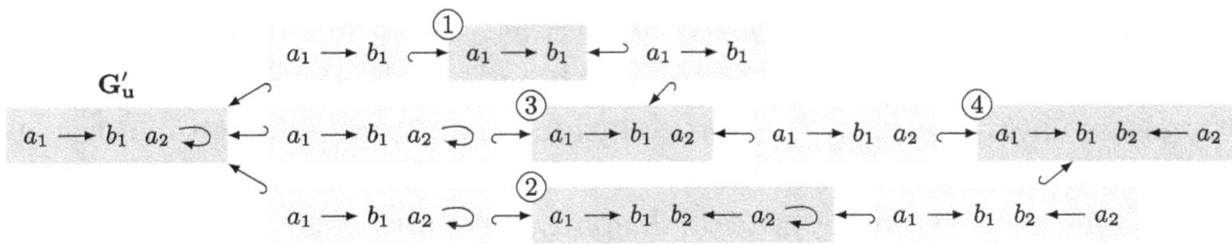

Fig. 4. An example for delta-based graph repair using $\mathcal{R}\mathrm{epair}_{\mathrm{db}}$

Definition 16 (Delta-Based Graph Repair Algorithm). *Delta-based graph repair algorithms take a graph G, a GC $\psi \in \Phi_{\emptyset}^{\mathrm{GC}}$, and a value q as inputs and return a set of pairs (u, q') where $u \in \mathcal{U}(G, \psi)$ is a graph repair and q' is a value.*

Our delta-based graph repair algorithm $\mathcal{R}\mathrm{epair}_{\mathrm{db}}$ will be based on the single step operation $\mathcal{R}\mathrm{epair}_{\mathrm{db1}}$. Given a graph G, a GC $\psi \in \Phi_{\emptyset}^{\mathrm{GC}}$, the ST γ that equals $\mathrm{cst}(\psi, G)$, and a graph update $u = (l : I \hookrightarrow G, r : I \hookrightarrow G')$, the single step operation $\mathcal{R}\mathrm{epair}_{\mathrm{db}}$ first updates γ using ppgU for the graph update u and then determines using $\mathcal{R}\mathrm{epair}_{\mathrm{db1}}$, if necessary, graph repairs for the resulting ST γ' according to the repair rules described in the following. The algorithm $\mathcal{R}\mathrm{epair}_{\mathrm{db}}$ then uses $\mathcal{R}\mathrm{epair}_{\mathrm{db1}}$ in a breadth first manner to obtain multi-step repairs.

For our example from Fig. 3a, such a multi-step repair of $\mathbf{G'_u}$ is given in Fig. 4 where the graph updates are obtained resulting in the graphs marked 1–3, of which only the graph marked 1 satisfies ψ. The algorithm $\mathcal{R}\mathrm{epair}_{\mathrm{db}}$ then computes further graph updates resulting in the graph marked 4 also satisfying ψ.

The operation $\mathcal{R}\mathrm{epair}_{\mathrm{db1}}$ for deriving single-step repairs depends on two local modifications. Firstly, a GC $\exists(a : H \hookrightarrow H', \phi)$ occurring as a subcondition in the consistency constraint ψ may be violated because, for the match $m : H \hookrightarrow G$ that locates a copy of H in the graph G under repair, no suitable match $q : H' \hookrightarrow G$ can be found for which $q \circ a = m$ and $q \models_{\mathrm{GC}} \phi$ are satisfied. The operation $\mathcal{R}\mathrm{epair}_{\mathrm{add}}$ resolves this violation by (a) using AutoGraph to construct a suitable graph H_s and by (b) integrating this graph H_s into G resulting in G' such that a suitable match $q : H' \hookrightarrow G'$ can be found.

Definition 17 (Local Addition Operation $\mathcal{R}\mathrm{epair}_{\mathrm{add}}$). *If $a : H \hookrightarrow H'$, $\phi \in \Phi_{H'}^{\mathrm{GC}}$, $m : H \hookrightarrow G$, $H_s \in \mathcal{A}(\exists(\mathrm{i}_H, \exists(a, \phi)))$, $k : H \hookrightarrow H_s$, and $(\bar{m} : H_s \hookrightarrow G', r : G \hookrightarrow G')$ is the pushout of (m, k) then $r \in \mathcal{R}\mathrm{epair}_{\mathrm{add}}(a, \phi, m)$.*

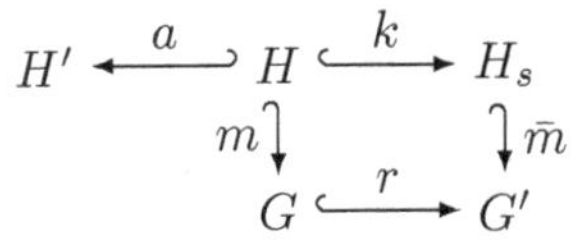

In our running example, $\mathcal{R}\mathrm{epair}_{\mathrm{add}}$ determines a graph repair resulting in the graph marked 2 in Fig. 4. For this repair, we considered the sub-ST marked by (R2) in Fig. 3d, where the morphism m matches the node a from ψ to the node a_2 in $\mathbf{G'_u}$, but where no extension of m can also match a node $:B$ and an edge between these two nodes. The repair performed then uses $a \xrightarrow{e} b$ for the graph H_s, resulting in the addition of the node b_2 and the edge from a_2 to b_2.

Secondly, a GC $\exists(a : H \hookrightarrow H', \phi)$ occurring as a subcondition in the consistency constraint ψ may be satisfied even though it should not when occurring underneath some negation. Such a violation is determined, again for a given match $m : H \hookrightarrow G$, by some match $q : H' \hookrightarrow G$ satisfying $q \circ a = m$ and $q \models_{\mathrm{GC}} \phi$. The local repair operation $\mathcal{R}\mathrm{epair}_{\mathrm{del}}$ repairs such an undesired satisfaction by selecting a graph H_p such that $H \subseteq H_p \subset H'$ using a restriction tree (see Definition 8) and deleting $G_{del} = q(H') \setminus q(H_p)$ from G. Technically, we can not use the pushout complement of a' and q as it does not exists when edges from $G \setminus G_{del}$ are attached to nodes in G_{del}. Hence, we determine the pushout complement of a'' and k', which must be constructed for this purpose suitably.

Definition 18 (Local Deletion Operation $\mathcal{R}\mathrm{epair}_{\mathrm{del}}$). *If $a : H \hookrightarrow H'$, $q : H' \hookrightarrow G$, $a' : H_p \hookrightarrow H' \in \mathrm{RT}(H', H)$, $m_1 : H' \hookrightarrow X_2$ where X_2 is obtained from $q(H')$ by adding all edges (with their nodes) that are connected to nodes in $q(H') \setminus q(a'(H_p))$, $k' : X_2 \hookrightarrow G$ is obtained such that $k' \circ m_1 = q$, $m_2 : H_p \hookrightarrow X_1$ where X_1 is obtained from H_p by adding all nodes in $X_2 \setminus q(H')$, $a'' : X_1 \hookrightarrow X_2$ is obtained such that $a'' \circ m_2 = m_1 \circ a'$, and $(l : G' \hookrightarrow G, m' : X_1 \hookrightarrow G')$ is the pushout complement of (a'', k') then $l \in \mathcal{R}\mathrm{epair}_{\mathrm{del}}(a, q)$.*

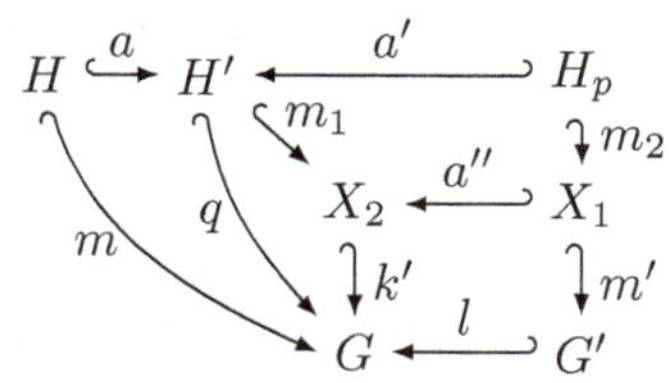

In our example, $\mathcal{R}\mathrm{epair}_{\mathrm{del}}$ determines a repair resulting in the graph marked 1 in Fig. 4. For this repair, we considered the sub-ST marked by (R1) in Fig. 3d where the mono m matches the node a from ψ to the node a_2 in $\mathbf{G'_u}$. The repair performed then uses $H_p = \emptyset$ for the removal of the node a_2 along with its adjacent loop (for which the technical handling in $\mathcal{R}\mathrm{epair}_{\mathrm{del}}$ is required).

The recursive operation $\mathcal{R}\mathrm{epair}_{\mathrm{db1}}$ below derives updates from an ST γ that corresponds to the current graph G (for our running example, these are $\gamma'_{\mathbf{u}}$ and $\mathbf{G'_u}$ from Fig. 3d). In the algorithm $\mathcal{R}\mathrm{epair}_{\mathrm{db}}$, we apply $\mathcal{R}\mathrm{epair}_{\mathrm{db1}}$ for the initial match i_G, γ, and *true* where this boolean indicates that we want γ to be satisfied. This boolean is changed in Rule 3 whenever the recursion is applied to an ST $\neg\gamma'$ because we expect that γ' is not to be satisfied iff we expect that $\neg\gamma'$ is to be satisfied. For conjunction, we either attempt to repair a sub-ST for $b = \mathit{true}$ in Rule 1 or we attempt to break one sub-ST for $b = \mathit{false}$. For existential quantification and $b = \mathit{true}$, we use $\mathcal{R}\mathrm{epair}_{\mathrm{add}}$ as discussed before in Rule 4 or we attempt to repair one existing match contained in m_f in Rule 5. Also, for existential quantification and $b = \mathit{false}$, we use $\mathcal{R}\mathrm{epair}_{\mathrm{del}}$ as discussed before in Rule 6 or we attempt to break one existing match contained in m_t in Rule 7.

Definition 19 (Single-Step Delta-Based Repair Algorithm $\mathcal{R}\mathrm{epair}_{\mathrm{db1}}$). *If $m : H \hookrightarrow G$, $\gamma \in \Gamma^{\mathrm{ST}}_m$, and $b \in \mathbf{B}$ then $(l : I \hookrightarrow G, r : I \hookrightarrow G') \in \mathcal{R}\mathrm{epair}_{\mathrm{db1}}(m, \gamma, b)$ if one of the following cases applies.*

- Rule 1 (repair one subcondition of a conjunction):
  $b = \mathit{true}, \gamma = \wedge S,\ \chi \in S,\ \not\models_{\mathrm{ST}} \chi,\ (l, r) \in \mathcal{R}\mathrm{epair}_{\mathrm{db1}}(m, \chi, b)$.
- Rule 2 (break one subcondition of a conjunction):
  $b = \mathit{false}, \gamma = \wedge S,\ \chi \in S,\ \models_{\mathrm{ST}} \chi,\ (l, r) \in \mathcal{R}\mathrm{epair}_{\mathrm{db1}}(m, \chi, b)$.
- Rule 3 (repair/break the subcondition of a negation):
  $\gamma = \neg\chi,\ (l, r) \in \mathcal{R}\mathrm{epair}_{\mathrm{db1}}(m, \chi, \neg b)$.
- Rule 4 (repair an existential quantification by local extension):
  $b = \mathit{true}, \gamma = \exists(a, \phi, m_t, m_f),\ m_t = \emptyset,\ r \in \mathcal{R}\mathrm{epair}_{\mathrm{add}}(a, \phi, m),\ l = \mathrm{id}_G$.
- Rule 5 (repair an existential quantification recursively):
  $b = \mathit{true}, \gamma = \exists(a, \phi, m_t, m_f),\ m_t = \emptyset,\ m_f(k) = \chi,\ (l, r) \in \mathcal{R}\mathrm{epair}_{\mathrm{db1}}(k, \chi, b)$.
- Rule 6 (break an existential quantification by local removal):
  $b = \mathit{false}, \gamma = \exists(a, \phi, m_t, m_f),\ m_t(k) \neq \bot,\ l \in \mathcal{R}\mathrm{epair}_{\mathrm{del}}(a, k),\ r = \mathrm{id}_{G'}$.
- Rule 7 (break an existential quantification recursively):
  $b = \mathit{false}, \gamma = \exists(a, \phi, m_t, m_f),\ m_t(k) = \chi,\ (l, r) \in \mathcal{R}\mathrm{epair}_{\mathrm{db1}}(k, \chi, b)$.

We define the recursive algorithm $\mathcal{R}\mathrm{epair}_{\mathrm{db}}$ to apply $\mathcal{R}\mathrm{epair}_{\mathrm{db1}}$ to obtain repairs as iterated applications of single-step repairs computed by $\mathcal{R}\mathrm{epair}_{\mathrm{db1}}$.

Definition 20 (Delta-Based Repair Algorithm $\mathcal{R}\mathrm{epair}_{\mathrm{db}}$). *If $u = (l : I \hookrightarrow G, r : I \hookrightarrow G') \in \mathcal{U}$, $\gamma \in \Gamma^{\mathrm{ST}}_{\mathrm{i}_G}$, and $\gamma' = \mathrm{ppgU}(\gamma, u)$ then $\mathcal{R}\mathrm{epair}_{\mathrm{db}}(u, \gamma) = S$ if one of the following cases applies.*

- $\models_{\mathrm{ST}} \gamma'$ *and* $S = \{((\mathrm{id}_{G'}, \mathrm{id}_{G'}), \gamma')\}$.
- $\not\models_{\mathrm{ST}} \gamma'$, $S' = \{(u', \mathrm{ppgU}(\gamma', u')) \mid u' \in \mathcal{R}\mathrm{epair}_{\mathrm{db1}}(\mathrm{i}_G, \gamma', \mathit{true})\}$, *and*
  $S = \{(u', \gamma') \in S' \mid \models_{\mathrm{ST}} \gamma'\} \cup \bigcup\{(u'' \circ u', \gamma'') \mid (u', \gamma') \in S', \not\models_{\mathrm{ST}} \gamma', (u'', \gamma'') \in \mathcal{R}\mathrm{epair}_{\mathrm{db}}(u', \gamma'), u'' \circ u' \neq \bot\}$.[3]

This computation does not terminate when repairs trigger each other ad infinitum. However, a breadth-first-computation of $\mathcal{R}\mathrm{epair}_{\mathrm{db}}$ gradually computes a set of sound repairs. Obviously, GCs that trigger such nonterminating computations should be avoided but machinery for detecting such GCs is called for.

Note that the algorithm $\mathcal{R}\mathrm{epair}_{\mathrm{db}}$ computes fewer graph repairs compared to $\mathcal{R}\mathrm{epair}_{\mathrm{sb},2}$ because repairs are applied locally in the scope defined by the GC ψ. For example, no repair would be constructed resulting in the graph marked 4 in Fig. 2. In general, explicitly also using bigger contexts in ψ results in the additional computation of less–local graph repairs. For example, the condition ψ may be rephrased into $\psi' = \psi \wedge \neg\exists(a\ \ b, \neg\exists(a \xrightarrow{e} b, \mathit{true}))$ to also obtain the graph repair marked 4 in Fig. 2. We now define the updates, which we expect to be computed by $\mathcal{R}\mathrm{epair}_{\mathrm{db1}}$, as those that repair a single violation of the GC ψ by defining a local update to be embeddable into the resulting update via a double pushout diagram as in the DPO approach to graph transformation [16].

Definition 21 (Locally Least Changing Graph Update). *If G_1 is a graph, $\psi \in \Phi^{\mathrm{GC}}_{\emptyset}$, $G_1 \not\models_{\mathrm{GC}} \psi$, $(l : I \hookrightarrow G_1, r : I \hookrightarrow G_2) \in \mathcal{U}_{\mathrm{lc}}(G_1, \psi)$, $G_2 \models_{\mathrm{GC}} \psi$, X_1 is a minimal subgraph of G_1 with a violation of ψ that is also a violation of ψ in*

[3] If u_1 and u_2 are updates then $u_1 \circ u_2 = u$ if $u_1 \leq^{u_2} u$ or $u = \bot$ otherwise (see Definition 4).

G, and the diagram below exists and the right part of it is a DPO diagram then (l, r) *is a* locally least changing graph update.

$$\begin{array}{ccccc} X_1 & \hookleftarrow & I' & \hookrightarrow & X_2 \\ \downarrow & & \downarrow & & \downarrow \\ G_1 & \overset{l}{\hookleftarrow} & I & \overset{r}{\hookrightarrow} & G_2 \end{array}$$

$\mathcal{R}\text{epair}_{\text{db1}}$ indeed generates such locally least changing graph updates because the graph X_1 in this definition corresponds to the H_1 and the H_2 from an ST $\exists(a : H_1 \hookrightarrow H_2, \phi, m_t, m_f)$ that is subject to $\mathcal{R}\text{epair}_{\text{add}}$ and $\mathcal{R}\text{epair}_{\text{del}}$, respectively. For example, for $\mathcal{R}\text{epair}_{\text{add}}$, the graph H_1 in the ST determines a subgraph in G_1 that is a violation of the overall consistency condition given by a GC ψ as its match can not be extended to the graph H_2.

We now define the locally least changing graph repairs (which are to be computed by $\mathcal{R}\text{epair}_{\text{db}}$ such as for example the graphs marked 1 and 4 in Fig. 4) as the composition of a sequence of locally least changing updates where precisely the last graph update results in a graph satisfying the GC ψ.

Definition 22 (Locally Least Changing Graph Repair). *If* G_1 *is a graph,* $\psi \in \Phi_{\emptyset}^{\text{GC}}$, $\pi = (l_1 : I_1 \hookrightarrow G_1, r_1 : I_1 \hookrightarrow G_2) \ldots (l_n : I_n \hookrightarrow G_n, r_n : I_n \hookrightarrow G_{n+1})$ *is a sequence of locally least changing graph updates,* $G_1 \in [\![\psi]\!]$ *implies* $n = 0$ *and* $l_1 = r_1 = \text{id}_{G_1}$, $G_i \notin [\![\psi]\!]$ *(for each* $2 \leq i \leq n$*),* $G_{n+1} \in [\![\psi]\!]$, (l, r) *is the iterated composition of the updates in* π*, and* $(l, r) \in \mathcal{U}(G_1, \psi)$ *is a least changing graph repair then* (l, r) *is a* locally least changing graph repair.

We now state that our delta-based graph repair algorithm $\mathcal{R}\text{epair}_{\text{db}}$ returns all desired locally least changing graph repairs upon termination.

Theorem 5 (Functional Semantics of $\mathcal{R}\text{epair}_{\text{db}}$). $\mathcal{R}\text{epair}_{\text{db}}$ *is sound (i.e., it generates only locally least changing graph repairs) and complete (upon termination) with respect to locally least changing graph repairs.*

The state-based algorithms $\mathcal{R}\text{epair}_{\text{sb,1}}$ and $\mathcal{R}\text{epair}_{\text{sb,2}}$ are inappropriate in environments where numerous updates that may invalidate consistency are applied to a large graph because the procedure of AutoGraph has exponential cost. The incremental delta-based algorithm $\mathcal{R}\text{epair}_{\text{db}}$ is a viable alternative when additional memory requirements for storing the ST are acceptable. The AutoGraph applications for this algorithm have negligible costs because they may be performed a priori and must only be performed for subconditions of the consistency constraint, which can be assumed to feature reasonably small graphs only.

Finally, a classification of locally least changing repairs is useful for user-based repair selection. Delta preserving repairs defined below represent such a basic class, containing only those repairs that preserve the update resulting in a graph not satisfying GC ψ, i.e., it may be desirable to avoid repairs that revert additions or deletions of this update. In our example, the repair related to the graph marked 4 in Fig. 4 is not delta preserving w.r.t. $\mathbf{u}$ from Fig. 3a.

Definition 23 (Delta Preserving Graph Repair). *If* $\psi \in \Phi_{\emptyset}^{\text{GC}}$, $u_2 = (l_2 : I_2 \hookrightarrow G_2, r_2 : I_2 \hookrightarrow G_3) \in \mathcal{U}(G_2, \psi)$ *is a graph repair,* $u_1 = (l_1 : I_1 \hookrightarrow G_1, r_1 :$

$I_1 \hookrightarrow G_2$) *is a graph update, and there exists a graph update* u *such that* $u_1 <^{u_2} u$ *then* u_2 *is a* delta preserving graph repair *with respect to* u_1.

7 Related Work

According to the recent survey on *model repair* [12], and the corresponding exhaustive classification of primary studies selected in the literature review, published online [11], we can see that the amount and wide variety of existing approaches makes a detailed comparison with all of them infeasible.

We consider our approach to be innovative, not only because of the proposed solutions, but because it addresses the issues of *completeness* and *least changing* for incremental graph repair in a precise and formal way. From the survey [11,12] we can see that only two other approaches [10,19] address completeness and least changing, relying also on constraint-solving technology. The main difference with our approach is that they are not incremental. In particular, the work of Schoenboeck et al. [19] proposes a logic programming approach allowing the exploration of model repair solutions ranked according to some quality criteria, re-establishing conformance of a model with its metamodel. Soundness and completeness of these repair actions is not formally proven. Moreover, the least changing bidirectional model transformation approach of Macedo et al. [10] has only a bounded search for repairs, relying on a bounded constraint solver.

Some *recent work* on rule-based *graph repair* [9] (not covered by the survey) addresses the least-changing principle by developing so-called maximally preserving (items are preserved whenever possible) repair programs. This state-based approach considers a subset of consistency constraints (up to nesting depth 2) handled by our approach, and is not complete, since it produces repairs including only a minimal amount of deletions. Some other recent rule-based graph repair approach [13,20] (also not covered by the survey) proposes so-called change preserving repairs (similar to what we define as delta-preserving). The main difference with our work is that we do not require the user to specify consistency-preserving operations from which repairs are generated, since we derive repairs using constraint solving techniques directly from the consistency constraints.

Finally, there is a variety of work on *incremental evaluation of graph queries* (see e.g. [2,4]), developed with the aim of efficiently re-evaluating a graph query after an update has been performed. Although not employed with the specific aim of complete and least changing graph repair, this work is related to our newly introduced concept of satisfaction trees, also using specific data structures to record with some detail the set of answers to a given query (as described for graph conditions, for example, also in [3]). It is part of ongoing work to evaluate how STs can be employed similarly in this field of incremental query evaluation.

8 Conclusion and Future Work

We presented a logic-based incremental approach to graph repair. It is the first approach to graph repair returning a sound and complete overview of least changing repairs with respect to graph conditions equivalent to first-order logic on graphs. Technically, it relies on an existing model generation procedure for graph conditions together with the newly introduced concept of satisfaction trees, encoding if and how a graph satisfies a graph condition.

As future work, we aim at supporting partial consistency and gradually improving it. We are confident that we can extend our work to support attributes, since our underlying model generation procedure supports it. Ongoing work is the support of more expressive consistency constraints, allowing path-related properties. Moreover, we are in the process of implementing the algorithms presented here and evaluating them on a variety of case studies. The evaluation also pertains to the overall efficiency (for which we employ techniques for localized pattern matching) and includes a comparison with other approaches for graph repair. Finally, we aim at presenting new and refined properties distinguishing between all possible repairs supporting the implementation of interactive repair selection procedures.

References

1. Angles, R., Gutiérrez, C.: Survey of graph database models. ACM Comput. Surv. **40**(1), 1:1–1:39 (2008). https://doi.org/10.1145/1322432.1322433
2. Bergmann, G., Ökrös, A., Ráth, I., Varró, D., Varró, G.: Incremental pattern matching in the viatra model transformation system. In: GRaMoT, pp. 25–32. ACM (2008). https://doi.org/10.1145/1402947.1402953
3. Beyhl, T., Blouin, D., Giese, H., Lambers, L.: On the operationalization of graph queries with generalized discrimination networks. In: Echahed, R., Minas, M. (eds.) ICGT 2016. LNCS, vol. 9761, pp. 170–186. Springer, Cham (2016). https://doi.org/10.1007/978-3-319-40530-8_11
4. Beyhl, T., Giese, H.: Incremental view maintenance for deductive graph databases using generalized discrimination networks. In: GaM@ETAPS, EPTCS, vol. 231, pp. 57–71 (2016). https://doi.org/10.4204/EPTCS.231.5
5. Courcelle, B.: The expression of graph properties and graph transformations in monadic second-order logic. In: Rozenberg [16], pp. 313–400
6. Diskin, Z., König, H., Lawford, M.: Multiple model synchronization with multiary delta lenses. In: Russo, A., Schürr, A. (eds.) FASE 2018. LNCS, vol. 10802, pp. 21–37. Springer, Cham (2018). https://doi.org/10.1007/978-3-319-89363-1_2
7. Ehrig, H., Ehrig, K., Prange, U., Taentzer, G.: Fundamentals of Algebraic Graph Transformation. Springer, Heidelberg (2006). https://doi.org/10.1007/3-540-31188-2
8. Habel, A., Pennemann, K.: Correctness of high-level transformation systems relative to nested conditions. MSCS **19**(2), 245–296 (2009). https://doi.org/10.1017/S0960129508007202
9. Habel, A., Sandmann, C.: Graph repair by graph programs. In: Mazzara, M., Ober, I., Salaün, G. (eds.) STAF 2018. LNCS, vol. 11176, pp. 431–446. Springer, Cham (2018). https://doi.org/10.1007/978-3-030-04771-9_31
10. Macedo, N., Cunha, A.: Least-change bidirectional model transformation with QVT-R and ATL. Softw. Syst. Model. **15**(3), 783–810 (2016). https://doi.org/10.1007/s10270-014-0437-x

11. Macedo, N., Tiago, J., Cunha, A.: Systematic literature review of model repair approaches. http://tinyurl.com/hv7eh6h. Accessed 14 Nov 2018
12. Macedo, N., Tiago, J., Cunha, A.: A feature-based classification of model repair approaches. IEEE Trans. Softw. Eng. **43**(7), 615–640 (2017). https://doi.org/10.1109/TSE.2016.2620145
13. Ohrndorf, M., Pietsch, C., Kelter, U., Kehrer, T.: Revision: a tool for history-based model repair recommendations. In: ICSE, pp. 105–108. ACM (2018). https://doi.org/10.1145/3183440.3183498
14. Orejas, F., Boronat, A., Ehrig, H., Hermann, F., Schölzel, H.: On propagation-based concurrent model synchronization. ECEASST **57** (2013). http://journal.ub.tu-berlin.de/eceasst/article/view/871
15. Rensink, A.: Representing first-order logic using graphs. In: Ehrig, H., Engels, G., Parisi-Presicce, F., Rozenberg, G. (eds.) ICGT 2004. LNCS, vol. 3256, pp. 319–335. Springer, Heidelberg (2004). https://doi.org/10.1007/978-3-540-30203-2_23
16. Rozenberg, G. (ed.): Handbook of Graph Grammars and Computing by Graph Transformations, Volume 1: Foundations. World Scientific (1997)
17. Schneider, S., Lambers, L., Orejas, F.: Automated reasoning for attributed graph properties. STTT **20**(6), 705–737 (2018). https://doi.org/10.1007/s10009-018-0496-3
18. Schneider, S., Lambers, L., Orejas, F.: A logic-based incremental approach to graph repair. Technical report, 126, Hasso Plattner Institute at the University of Potsdam, Potsdam, Germany (2019)
19. Schoenboeck, J., et al.: CARE - A constraint-based approach for re-establishing conformance-relationships. In: APCCM 2014, vol. 154, pp. 19–28. Australian Computer Society (2014). http://crpit.com/abstracts/CRPITV154Schoenboeck.html
20. Taentzer, G., Ohrndorf, M., Lamo, Y., Rutle, A.: Change-preserving model repair. In: Huisman, M., Rubin, J. (eds.) FASE 2017. LNCS, vol. 10202, pp. 283–299. Springer, Heidelberg (2017). https://doi.org/10.1007/978-3-662-54494-5_16

Software Verification II

DeepFault: Fault Localization for Deep Neural Networks

Hasan Ferit Eniser[1(✉)], Simos Gerasimou[2], and Alper Sen[1]

[1] Bogazici University, Istanbul, Turkey
{hasan.eniser,alper.sen}@boun.edu.tr
[2] University of York, York, UK
simos.gerasimou@york.ac.uk

Abstract. Deep Neural Networks (DNNs) are increasingly deployed in safety-critical applications including autonomous vehicles and medical diagnostics. To reduce the residual risk for unexpected DNN behaviour and provide evidence for their trustworthy operation, DNNs should be thoroughly tested. The DeepFault whitebox DNN testing approach presented in our paper addresses this challenge by employing suspiciousness measures inspired by fault localization to establish the hit spectrum of neurons and identify suspicious neurons whose weights have not been calibrated correctly and thus are considered responsible for inadequate DNN performance. DeepFault also uses a suspiciousness-guided algorithm to synthesize new inputs, from correctly classified inputs, that increase the activation values of suspicious neurons. Our empirical evaluation on several DNN instances trained on MNIST and CIFAR-10 datasets shows that DeepFault is effective in identifying suspicious neurons. Also, the inputs synthesized by DeepFault closely resemble the original inputs, exercise the identified suspicious neurons and are highly adversarial.

Keywords: Deep Neural Networks · Fault localization · Test input generation

1 Introduction

Deep Neural Networks (DNNs) [33] have demonstrated human-level capabilities in several intractable machine learning tasks including image classification [10], natural language processing [56] and speech recognition [19]. These impressive achievements raised the expectations for deploying DNNs in real-world applications, especially in safety-critical domains. Early-stage applications include air traffic control [25], medical diagnostics [34] and autonomous vehicles [5]. The responsibilities of DNNs in these applications vary from carrying out well-defined tasks (e.g., detecting abnormal network activity [11]) to controlling the entire behaviour system (e.g., end-to-end learning in autonomous vehicles [5]).

This research was supported in part by Bogazici University; Research Fund 13662.

R. Hähnle and W. van der Aalst (Eds.): FASE 2019, LNCS 11424, pp. 171–191, 2019.
https://doi.org/10.1007/978-3-030-16722-6_10

Despite the anticipated benefits from a widespread adoption of DNNs, their deployment in safety-critical systems must be characterized by a high degree of dependability. Deviations from the expected behaviour or correct operation, as expected in safety-critical domains, can endanger human lives or cause significant financial loss. Arguably, DNN-based systems should be granted permission for use in the public domain only after exhibiting high levels of trustworthiness [6].

Software testing is the de facto instrument for analysing and evaluating the quality of a software system [24]. Testing enables at one hand to reduce the risk by proactively finding and eliminating problems (*bugs*), and on the other hand to evidence, through using the testing results, that the system actually achieves the required levels of safety. Research contributions and advice on best practices for testing conventional software systems are plentiful; [63], for instance, provides a comprehensive review of the state-of-the-art testing approaches.

Nevertheless, there are significant challenges in applying traditional software testing techniques for assessing the quality of DNN-based software [54]. Most importantly, the little correlation between the behaviour of a DNN and the software used for its implementation means that the behaviour of the DNN cannot be explicitly encoded in the control flow structures of the software [51]. Furthermore, DNNs have very complex architectures, typically comprising thousand or millions of parameters, making it difficult, if not impossible, to determine a parameter's contribution to achieving a task. Likewise, since the behaviour of a DNN is heavily influenced by the data used during training, collecting enough data that enables exercising all potential DNN behaviour under all possible scenarios becomes a very challenging task. Hence, there is a need for systematic and effective testing frameworks for evaluating the quality of DNN-based software [6].

Recent research in the DNN testing area introduces novel white-box and black-box techniques for testing DNNs [20,28,36,37,48,54,55]. Some techniques transform valid training data into adversarial through mutation-based heuristics [65], apply symbolic execution [15], combinatorial [37] or concolic testing [55], while others propose new DNN-specific coverage criteria, e.g., neuron coverage [48] and its variants [35] or MC/DC-inspired criteria [52]. We review related work in Section 6. These recent advances provide evidence that, while traditional software testing techniques are not directly applicable to testing DNNs, the sophisticated concepts and principles behind these techniques, if adapted appropriately, could be useful to the machine learning domain. Nevertheless, none of the proposed techniques uses *fault localization* [4,47,63], which can identify parts of a system that are most responsible for incorrect behaviour.

In this paper, we introduce *DeepFault*, the first fault localization-based white-box testing approach for DNNs. The objectives of DeepFault are twofold: (i) *identification* of *suspicious* neurons, i.e., neurons likely to be more responsible for incorrect DNN behaviour; and (ii) *synthesis* of new inputs, using correctly classified inputs, that exercise the identified suspicious neurons. Similar to conventional fault localization, which receives as input a faulty software and outputs a ranked list of suspicious code locations where the software may be defective [63], DeepFault *analyzes* the behaviour of neurons of a DNN after training to establish their hit spectrum and *identifies* suspicious neurons by employing suspiciousness measures. DeepFault employs a suspiciousness-guided algorithm to *synthesize* new inputs, that achieve high activation values for suspicious neurons, by modifying correctly classified inputs. Our empirical evaluation on the popular publicly available datasets MNIST [32] and CIFAR-10 [1] provides evidence that DeepFault can identify neurons which can be held responsible for insufficient network performance. DeepFault can also synthesize new inputs, which closely resemble the original inputs, are highly adversarial and increase the activation values of the identified suspicious neurons. To the best of our knowledge, DeepFault is the first research attempt that introduces *fault localization* for DNNs to identify suspicious neurons and synthesize new, likely adversarial, inputs.

Overall, the main contributions of this paper are:

- The DeepFault approach for whitebox testing of DNNs driven by fault localization;
- An algorithm for identifying suspicious neurons that adapts suspiciousness measures from the domain of spectrum-based fault localization;
- A suspiciousness-guided algorithm to synthesize inputs that achieve high activation values of potentially suspicious neurons;
- A comprehensive evaluation of DeepFault on two public datasets (MNIST and CIFAR-10) demonstrating its feasibility and effectiveness;

The reminder of the paper is structured as follows. Section 2 presents briefly DNNs and fault localization in traditional software testing. Section 3 introduces *DeepFault* and Section 4 presents its open-source implementation. Section 5 describes the experimental setup, research questions and evaluation carried out. Sections 6 and 7 discuss related work and conclude the paper, respectively.

2 Background

2.1 Deep Neural Networks

We consider Deep Learning software systems in which one or more system modules is controlled by DNNs [13]. A typical feed-forward DNN comprises multiple interconnected neurons organised into several layers: the *input* layer, the *output* layer and at least one *hidden* layer (Fig. 1). Each DNN layer comprises a sequence of neurons. A *neuron* denotes a computing unit that applies a *nonlinear activation function* to its inputs and transmits the result to neurons in the successive layer. Commonly used

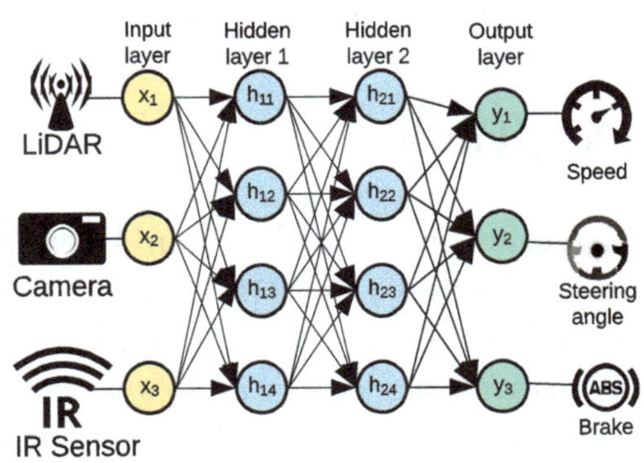

Fig. 1. A four layer fully-connected DNN that receives inputs from vehicle sensors (camera, LiDAR, infrared) and outputs a decision for speed, steering angle and brake.

activation functions are sigmoid, hyperbolic tangent, ReLU (Rectified Linear Unit) and leaky ReLU [13]. Except from the input layer, every neuron is connected to neurons in the successive layer with *weights*, i.e., edges, whose values signify the strength of a connection between neuron pairs. Once the DNN architecture is defined, i.e., the number of layers, neurons per layer and activation functions, the DNN undergoes a *training process* using a large amount of labelled training data to find weight values that minimise a *cost function*.

In general, a DNN could be considered as a parametric multidimensional function that consumes input data (e.g, raw image pixels) in its input layer, extracts *features*, i.e., semantic concepts, by performing a series of nonlinear transformations in its *hidden layers*, and, finally, produces a decision that matches the effect of these computations in its *output layer*.

2.2 Software Fault Localization

Fault localization (FL) is a white box testing technique that focuses on identifying source code elements (e.g., statements, declarations) that are more likely to contain faults. The general FL process [63] for traditional software uses as inputs a program P, corresponding to the system under test, and a test suite T, and employs an FL technique to test P against T and establish subsets that represent the passed and failed tests. Using these sets and information regarding program elements $p \in P$, the FL technique extracts fault localization data which is then employed by an FL measure to establish the "suspiciousness" of each program element p. Spectrum-based FL, the most studied class of FL techniques, uses program traces (called program spectra) of successful and failed test executions to establish for program element p the tuple (e_s, e_f, n_s, n_f). Members e_s and e_f (n_s and n_f) represent the number of times the corresponding program element has been (has not been) executed by tests, with success and fail, respectively. A spectrum-based FL measure consumes this list of tuples and ranks the program elements in decreasing order of suspiciousness enabling software engineers to inspect program elements and find faults effectively. For a comprehensive survey of state-of-the-art FL techniques, see [63].

3 DeepFault

In this section, we introduce our DeepFault whitebox approach that enables to systematically test DNNs by identifying and localizing highly erroneous neurons across a DNN. Given a pre-trained DNN, DeepFault, whose workflow is shown in Fig. 2, performs a series of *analysis*, *identification* and *synthesis* steps to identify highly erroneous DNN neurons and synthesize new inputs that exercise erroneous neurons. We describe the DeepFault steps in Sections 3.1, 3.2 and 3.3.

We use the following notations to describe DeepFault. Let $\mathcal{N}$ be a DNN with l layers. Each layer $L_i, 1 \leq i \leq l$, consists of s_i neurons and the total number of neurons in $\mathcal{N}$ is given by $s = \sum_{i=1}^{l} s_i$. Let also $n_{i,j}$ be the j-th neuron in the i-th layer. When the context is clear, we use $n \in \mathcal{N}$ to denote any neuron which is part of the DNN $\mathcal{N}$ irrespective of its layer. Likewise, we use N_H to denote the neurons which belong to the hidden layers of N, i.e., $N_H = \{n_{ij} | 1 < i < l, 1 \leq j \leq s_j\}$. We use $\mathcal{T}$ to denote the set of test inputs from the input domain of $\mathcal{N}$, $t \in \mathcal{T}$ to denote a concrete input, and $u \in t$ for an element of t. Finally, we use the function $\phi(t, n)$ to signify the output of the activation function of neuron $n \in \mathcal{N}$.

3.1 Neuron Spectrum Analysis

The first step of DeepFault involves the analysis of neurons within a DNN to establish suitable neuron-based attributes that will drive the detection and localization of faulty neurons. As highlighted in recent research [18,48], the adoption of whitebox testing techniques provides additional useful insights regarding internal neuron activity and network behaviour. These insights cannot be easily extracted through black-box DNN testing, i.e., assessing the performance of a DNN considering only the decisions made given a set of test inputs $\mathcal{T}$.

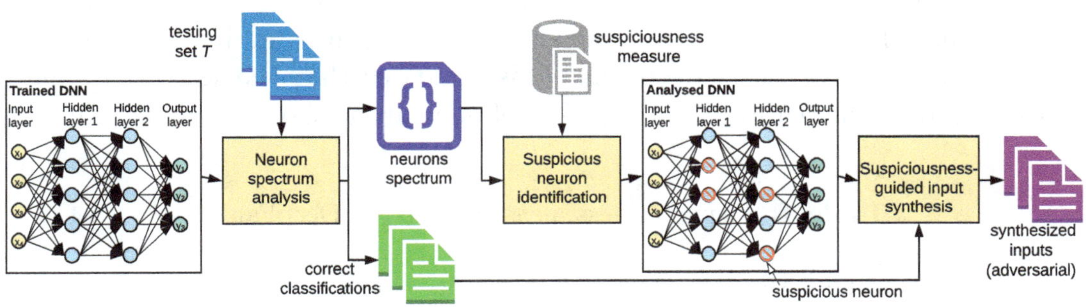

Fig. 2. DeepFault workflow.

DeepFault initiates the identification of suspicious neurons by establishing attributes that capture a neuron's execution pattern. These attributes are defined as follows. Attributes $attr_n^{\text{as}}$ and $attr_n^{\text{af}}$ signify the number of times neuron n was active (i.e., the result of the activation function $\phi(t, n)$ was above the predefined threshold) and the network made a successful or failed decision, respectively. Similarly, attributes $attr_n^{\text{ns}}$ and $attr_n^{\text{nf}}$ cover the case in which neuron n is not active. DeepFault analyses the behaviour of neurons in the DNN hidden layers, under a specific test set $\mathcal{T}$, to assemble a *Hit Spectrum (HS)* for each neuron, i.e., a tuple describing its dynamic behaviour. We define formally the HS as follows.

Definition 1. Given a DNN $\mathcal{N}$ and a test set $\mathcal{T}$, we say that for any neuron $n \in \mathcal{N}_H$ its hit spectrum is given by the tuple $HS_n = (attr_n^{\text{as}}, attr_n^{\text{af}}, attr_n^{\text{ns}}, attr_n^{\text{nf}})$.

Note that the sum of each neuron's HS should be equal to the size of $\mathcal{T}$.

Clearly, the interpretation of a hit spectrum (cf. Definition 1) is meaningful only for neurons in the hidden layers of a DNN. Since neurons within the input layer L_1 correspond to elements from the input domain (e.g., pixels from an image captured by a camera in Fig. 1), we consider them to be "correct-by-construction". Hence, these neurons cannot be credited or held responsible for a successful or failed decision made by the network. Furthermore, input neurons are always active and thus propagate one way or another their values to neurons in the following layer. Likewise, neurons within the output layer L_l simply aggregate values from neurons in the penultimate layer L_{l-1}, multiplied by the corresponding weights, and thus have limited influence in the overall network behaviour and, accordingly, to decision making.

3.2 Suspicious Neurons Identification

During this step, DeepFault consumes the set of hit spectrums, derived from DNN analysis, and identifies *suspicious* neurons which are likely to have made significant contributions in achieving inadequate DNN performance (low accuracy/high loss). To achieve this identification, DeepFault employs a spectrum-based suspiciousness measure which computes a suspiciousness score per neuron using spectrum-related information. Neurons with the highest suspiciousness score are more likely to have been trained unsatisfactorily and, hence, contributing more to incorrect DNN decisions. This indicates that the weights of these neurons need further calibration [13]. We define neuron suspiciousness as follows.

Table 1. Suspiciousness measures used in DeepFault

Suspiciousness Measure	Algebraic Formula
Tarantula [23]:	$\frac{attr_n^{af}/(attr_n^{af}+attr_n^{nf})}{attr_n^{af}/(attr_n^{af}+attr_n^{nf})+attr_n^{as}/(attr_n^{as}+attr_n^{ns})}$
Ochiai [42]:	$\frac{attr_n^{af}}{\sqrt{(attr_n^{af}+attr_n^{nf})\cdot(attr_n^{af}+attr_n^{as})}}$
D* [62]:	$\frac{attr_n^{af^*}}{attr_n^{as}+attr_n^{nf}}$

$* > 0$ is a variable. We used $* = 3$, among the most widely explore values [47,63].

Algorithm 1. Identification of suspicious neurons

function SuspiciousNeuronsIdentification($\mathcal{N}, \mathcal{T}, k$)
  $S \leftarrow \emptyset$ ▷ suspiciousness vector
  for all $n \in N$ **do**
    $HS_n \leftarrow \emptyset$ ▷ n-th neuron hit spectrum vector
    for all $p \in \{as, af, ns, nf\}$ **do**
      $a_n^p = \text{ATTR}(\mathcal{T}, p)$ ▷ establish attribute for property p
      $HS_n = HS_n \cup \{a_n^p\}$ ▷ construct hit spectrum (cf. Def. 1)
    $S = S \cup \{\text{Susp}(HS_n)\}$ ▷ determine neuron suspiciousness (cf. Def. 2)
  SN $= \{n \mid \text{Susp}(HS_n) \in \text{Select}(S, k)\}$ ▷ select the k most suspicious neurons
  return SN

Definition 2. Given a neuron $n \in \mathcal{N}_H$ with HS_n being its hit spectrum, a neuron's spectrum-based suspiciousness is given by the function $\textsc{Susp}_n : HS_n \rightarrow \mathbb{R}$.

Intuitively, a suspiciousness measure facilitates the derivation of correlations between a neuron's behaviour given a test set $\mathcal{T}$ and the failure pattern of $\mathcal{T}$ as determined by the overall network behaviour. Neurons whose behaviour pattern is *close* to the failure pattern of $\mathcal{T}$ are more likely to operate unreliably, and consequently, they should be assigned higher suspiciousness. Likewise, neurons whose behaviour pattern is *dissimilar* to the failure pattern of $\mathcal{T}$ are considered more trustworthy and their suspiciousness values should be low.

In this paper, we instantiate DeepFault with three different suspiciousness measures, i.e., Tarantula [23], Ochiai [42] and D* [62] whose algebraic formulae are shown in Table 1. The general principle underlying these suspiciousness measures is that the more often a neuron is activated by test inputs for which the DNN made an incorrect decision, and the less often the neuron is activated by test inputs for which the DNN made a correct decision, the more suspicious the neuron is. These suspiciousness measures have been adapted from the domain of fault localization in software engineering [63] in which they have achieved competitive results in automated software debugging by isolating the root causes of software failures while reducing human input. To the best of our knowledge, DeepFault is the first approach that proposes to incorporate these suspiciousness measures into the DNN domain for the identification of defective neurons.

The use of suspiciousness measures in DNNs targets the identification of a set of defective neurons rather than diagnosing an isolated defective neuron. Since the output of a DNN decision task is typically based on the aggregated effects of its neurons (computation units), with each neuron making its own contribution

Algorithm 2. New input synthesis guided by the identified suspicious neurons

Input: $SN \leftarrow$ suspicious neurons (Algorithm 1), $step \leftarrow$ step size in gradient ascent
$T_s \leftarrow$ test inputs correctly classified by $\mathcal{N}$, $d \leftarrow$ new inputs maximum allowed distance

function $\textsc{SuspiciousnessGuidedInputSynthesis}(SN, \mathcal{T}_s, d, step)$
  $NT \leftarrow \emptyset$ ▷ set of synthesized inputs
  for all $t \in T_s$ **do**
    $G_t \leftarrow \emptyset$ ▷ gradient collection of suspicious neurons
    for all $n \in SN$ **do**
      $n^v = \phi(t, n)$ ▷ determine output of neuron
      $G = \partial n^v / \partial t$ ▷ establish gradient of neuron for t
      $G_t = G_t \cup \{G\}$ ▷ collect gradients of suspicious neurons for t
    $t' \leftarrow \emptyset$ ▷ initialisation of input to be synthesised
    for all $u \in t$ **do**
      $u_{gradient} = \sum_{G \in G_t} G/|G_t|$ ▷ determine average gradient of u
      $u_{gradient} = \textsc{GradientConstraint}(u_{gradient}, d, step)$
      $t' = t' \frown \{\textsc{DomainConstraints}(u + u_{gradient})\}$
    $NT = NT \cup \{t'\}$
  return NT

to the whole computation procedure [13], identifying a single point of failure (i.e., a single defective neuron) has limited value. Thus, after establishing the suspiciousness of neurons in the hidden layers of a DNN, the neurons are ordered in decreasing order of suspiciousness and the $k, 1 \leq l \leq s$, most probably defective (i.e., "undertrained") neurons are selected. Algorithm 1 presents the high-level steps for identifying and selecting the k most suspicious neurons. When multiple neurons achieve the same suspiciousness score, DeepFault resolves ties by prioritising neurons that belong to deeper hidden layers (i.e., they are closer to the output layer). The rationale for this decision lies in fact that neurons in deeper layers are able to learn more meaningful representations of the input space [69].

3.3 Suspiciousness-Guided Input Synthesis

DeepFault uses the selected k most suspicious neurons (cf. Section 3.2) to synthesize inputs that exercise these neurons and could be adversarial (see Section 5). The premise underlying the synthesis is that increasing the activation values of suspicious neurons will cause the propagation of degenerate information, computed by these neurons, across the network, thus, shifting the decision boundaries in the output layer. To achieve this, DeepFault applies targeted modification of test inputs from the test set $\mathcal{T}$ for which the DNN made correct decisions (e.g., for a classification task, the DNN determined correctly their ground truth classes) aiming to steer the DNN decision to a different region (see Fig. 2).

Algorithm 2 shows the high-level process for synthesising new inputs based on the identified suspicious neurons. The synthesis task is underpinned by a gradient ascent algorithm that aims at determining the extent to which a correctly classified input should be modified to increase the activation values of suspicious neurons. For any test input $t \in T_s$ correctly classified by the DNN, we extract the value of each suspicious neuron and its gradient in lines 6 and 7, respectively. Then, by iterating over each input dimension $u \in t$, we determine the gradient value $u_{gradient}$ by which u will be perturbed (lines 11–12). The value of $u_{gradient}$ is based on the mean gradient of u across the suspicious neurons controlled by the function GradientConstraints. This function uses a test set specific *step* parameter and a distance d parameter to facilitate the synthesis of realistic test inputs that are sufficiently *close*, according to L_∞-norm, to the original inputs. We demonstrate later in the evaluation of DeepFault (cf. Table 4) that these parameters enable the synthesis of inputs similar to the original. The function DomainConstraints applies domain-specific constraints thus ensuring that u changes due to gradient ascent result in realistic and physically reproducible test inputs as in [48]. For instance, a domain-specific constraint for an image classification dataset involves bounding the pixel values of synthesized images to be within a certain range (e.g., 0–1 for the MNIST dataset [32]). Finally, we append the updated u to construct a new test input t' (line 13).

As we experimentally show in Section 5, the suspiciousness measures used by DeepFault can synthesize adversarial inputs that cause the DNN to misclassify previously correctly classified inputs. Thus, the identified suspicious neurons can be attributed a degree of responsibility for the inadequate network performance meaning that their weights have not been optimised. This reduces the DNN's ability for high generalisability and correct operation in untrained data.

4 Implementation

To ease the evaluation and adoption of the DeepFault approach (cf. Fig. 2), we have implemented a prototype tool on top of the open-source machine learning framework Keras (v2.2.2) [9] with Tensorflow (v1.10.1) backend [2]. The full experimental results summarised in the following section are available on DeepFault project page at https://DeepFault.github.io.

5 Evaluation

5.1 Experimental Setup

We evaluate DeepFault on two popular publicly available datasets. MNIST [32] is a handwritten digit dataset with 60,000 training samples and 10,000 testing samples; each input is a 28×28 pixel image with a class label from 0 to 9. CIFAR-10 [1] is an image dataset with 50,000 training samples and 10,000 testing samples; each input is a 32×32 image in ten different classes (e.g., dog, bird, car).

For each dataset, we study three DNNs that have been used in previous research [1,60] (Table 2). All DNNs have different architecture and number of trainable parameters. For MNIST, we use fully connected neural networks (dense) and for CIFAR-10 we use convolutional neural networks with max-pooling and dropout layers that have been trained to achieve at least 95% and 70% accuracy on the provided test sets, respectively. The column 'Architecture' shows the number of fully connected hidden layers and the number of neurons per layer. Each DNN uses a leaky ReLU [38] as its activation function ($\alpha = 0.01$), which has been shown to achieve competitive accuracy results [67].

We instantiate DeepFault using the suspiciousness measures Tarantula [23], Ochiai [42] and D* [62] (Table 1). We analyse the effectiveness of DeepFault instances using different number of suspicious neurons, i.e., $k \in \{1, 2, 3, 5, 10\}$ and $k \in \{10, 20, 30, 40, 50\}$ for MNIST and CIFAR models, respectively. We also ran preliminary experiments for each model from Table 2 to tune the hyper-parameters of Algorithm 2 and facilitate replication of our findings. Since gradient values are model and input specific, the perturbation magnitude should reflect these values and reinforce their impact. We determined empirically that $step = 1$ and $step = 10$ are good values, for MNIST and CIFAR models, respectively, that enable our algorithm to perturb inputs. We also set the maximum allowed distance d to be at most 10% (L_∞) with regards to the range of each input dimension (maximum pixel value). As shown in Table 4, the synthesized inputs are very similar to the original inputs and are rarely constrained by d. Studying other *step* and d values is part of our future work. All experiments were run on an Ubuntu server with 16 GB memory and Intel Xeon E5-2698 2.20 GHz.

Table 2. Details of MNIST and CIFAR-10 DNNs used in the evaluation.

Dataset	Model Name	# Trainable Params	Architecture	Accuracy
MNIST	MNIST_1	27,420	$<5 \times 30>$	96.6%
	MNIST_2	22,975	$<6 \times 25>$	95.8%
	MNIST_3	18,680	$<8 \times 20>$	95%
CIFAR-10	CIFAR_1	411,434	$<4 \times 128>$	70.1%
	CIFAR_2	724,010	$<2 \times 256>$	72.6%
	CIFAR_3	1,250,858	$<1 \times 512>$	76.1%

5.2 Research Questions

Our experimental evaluation aims to answer the following research questions.

RQ1 (Validation): Can DeepFault find suspicious neurons effectively? If suspicious neurons do exist, suspiciousness measures used by DeepFault should comfortably outperform a random suspiciousness selection strategy.

RQ2 (Comparison): How do DeepFault instances using different suspiciousness measures compare against each other? Since DeepFault can work with multiple suspiciousness measures, we examined the results produced by DeepFault instances using Tarantula [23], Ochiai [42] and D* [62].

RQ3 (Suspiciousness Distribution): How are suspicious neurons found by DeepFault distributed across a DNN? With this research question, we analyse the distribution of suspicious neurons in hidden DNN layers using different suspiciousness measures.

RQ4 (Similarity): How realistic are inputs synthesized by DeepFault? We analysed the distance between synthesized and original inputs to examine the extent to which DeepFault synthesizes realistic inputs.

RQ5 (Increased Activations): Do synthesized inputs increase activation values of suspicious neurons? We assess whether the suspiciousness-guided input synthesis algorithm produces inputs that reinforce the influence of suspicious neurons across a DNN.

RQ6 (Performance): How efficiently can DeepFault synthesize new inputs? We analysed the time consumed by DeepFault to synthesize new inputs and the effect of suspiciousness measures used in DeepFault instances.

5.3 Results and Discussion

RQ1 (Validation). We apply the DeepFault workflow to the DNNs from Table 2. To this end, we instantiate DeepFault with a suspiciousness measure, *analyse* a pre-trained DNN given the dataset's test set $\mathcal{T}$, *identify* k neurons with the highest suspiciousness scores and *synthesize* new inputs, from *correctly classified* inputs, that exercise these suspicious neurons. Then, we measure the prediction performance of the DNN on the synthesized inputs using the standard performance metrics: cross-entropy *loss*, i.e., the divergence between output and target distribution, and *accuracy*, i.e., the percentage of correctly classified inputs over all given inputs. Note that DNN analysis is done per class, since the activation pattern of inputs from the same class is similar to each other [69].

Table 3 shows the average loss and accuracy for inputs synthesized by DeepFault instances using Tarantula (T), Ochiai (O), D* (D) and a random selection strategy (R) for different number of suspicious neurons k on the MNIST (top) and CIFAR-10 (bottom) models from Table 2. Each cell value in Table 3, except from random R, is averaged over 100 synthesized inputs (10 per class). For R, we collected 500 synthesized inputs (50 per class) over five independent runs, thus, reducing the risk that our findings may have been obtained by chance.

As expected (see Table 3), DeepFault using any suspiciousness measure (T, O, D) obtained considerably lower prediction performance than R on MNIST models. The suspiciousness measures T and O are also effective on CIFAR-10 model, whereas the performance between D and R is similar. These results show that the identified k neurons are actually *suspicious* and, hence, their weights are insufficiently trained. Also, we have sufficient evidence that increasing the activation value of suspicious neurons by slightly perturbing inputs that have been classified correctly by the DNN could transform them into adversarial.

We applied the non-parametric statistical test Mann-Whitney with 95% confidence level [61] to check for statistically significant performance difference between the various DeepFault instances and random. We confirmed the significant difference among T-R and O-R (p-value < 0.05) for all MNIST and CIFAR-10 models and for all k values. We also confirmed the interesting observation that significant difference between D-R exists only for MNIST models (all k values). We plan to investigate this observation further in our future work.

Another interesting observation from Table 3 is the small performance difference of DeepFault instances for different k values. We investigated this further by analyzing the activation values of the next k' most suspicious neurons according to the suspiciousness order given by Algorithm 1. For instance, if $k = 2$ we analysed the activation values of the next $k' \in \{3, , 5, 10\}$ most suspicious neurons. We observed that the synthesized inputs frequently increase the activation values of the k' neurons whose suspiciousness scores are also high, in addition to increasing the values of the top k suspicious neurons.

Considering these results, we have empirical evidence about the existence of *suspicious* neurons which can be responsible for inadequate DNN performance. Also, we confirmed that DeepFault instances using sophisticated suspiciousness measures significantly outperform a random strategy for most of the studied DNN models (except from the D-R case on CIFAR models; see RQ3).

RQ2 (Comparison). We compare DeepFault instances using different suspiciousness measures and carried out pairwise comparisons using the Mann-Whitney test to check for significant difference between T, O, and D*. We show the results of these comparisons on the project's webpage. Ochiai achieves better results on MNIST_1 and MNIST_3 models for various k values. This result suggests that the suspicious neurons reported by Ochiai are more responsible

Table 3. Accuracy and loss of inputs synthesized by DeepFault on MNIST (top) and CIFAR-10 (bottom) datasets. The best results per suspiciousness measure are shown in bold. (k:#suspicious neurons, T:Tarantula, O:Ochiai, D:D*, R:Random)

k	Measure	MNIST_1				MNIST_2				MNIST_3			
		T	O	D	R	T	O	D	R	T	O	D	R
1	Loss	3.55	**6.19**	4.03	2.42	3.48	3.53	**3.97**	2.78	7.35	**8.23**	6.36	3.66
	Accuracy	0.26	**0.16**	0.2	0.59	0.3	**0.2**	0.5	0.49	0.16	**0.1**	0.13	0.39
2	Loss	3.73	**6.08**	3.18	2.67	3.12	3.76	**4.08**	0.9	4.27	**6.81**	6.5	3.06
	Accuracy	**0.16**	0.23	0.4	0.58	0.23	0.23	**0.13**	0.77	0.29	**0.13**	0.26	0.56
3	Loss	4.1	6.19	**6.25**	1.14	2.39	**3.94**	3.04	1.61	3.33	**7.59**	6.98	2.91
	Accuracy	**0.23**	**0.23**	0.33	0.77	0.46	0.26	**0.23**	0.67	0.26	**0.06**	0.16	0.61
5	Loss	4.63	6.68	**6.97**	1.1	2.49	**3.64**	3.48	0.94	4.15	**7.22**	6.47	1.22
	Accuracy	0.23	0.23	**0.13**	0.79	0.26	0.26	**0.2**	0.73	0.16	**0.1**	0.26	0.77
10	Loss	4.97	6.95	**7.4**	1.3	2.08	3.06	**3.82**	0.49	4.45	**7.16**	5.9	0.57
	Accuracy	0.23	**0.2**	0.23	0.75	0.4	**0.23**	0.26	0.86	**0.13**	**0.13**	**0.13**	0.87

k	Measure	CIFAR_1				CIFAR_2				CIFAR_3			
		T	O	D	R	T	O	D	R	T	O	D	R
10	Loss	12.75	**13.49**	1.33	3.25	**8.42**	8.41	0	2.49	**6.12**	1.77	1.12	1.21
	Accuracy	0.2	**0.16**	0.9	0.79	**0.47**	**0.47**	1.0	0.84	**0.62**	0.88	0.92	0.91
20	Loss	**12.79**	12.43	0.45	1.8	**8.81**	6.92	0.32	1.67	**6.12**	1.12	0.96	0.64
	Accuracy	**0.2**	0.22	0.96	0.88	**0.44**	0.55	0.97	0.89	**0.62**	0.92	0.93	0.95
30	Loss	**13.19**	13.13	0.38	1.43	**8.35**	6.32	0.55	0.86	**5.64**	0.76	0.42	0.41
	Accuracy	**0.18**	**0.18**	0.95	0.9	**0.48**	0.6	0.95	0.94	**0.64**	0.93	0.96	0.97
40	Loss	**13.69**	11.92	0.8	1.29	**9.4**	5.01	0.32	0.61	**4.51**	1.12	0.22	0.54
	Accuracy	**0.14**	0.26	0.92	0.91	**0.41**	0.68	0.97	0.95	**0.72**	0.92	0.97	0.96
50	Loss	12.1	**13.37**	0.36	0.9	**9.59**	3.38	0	0.56	**4.67**	0.04	0.64	0.48
	Accuracy	0.24	**0.17**	0.96	0.94	**0.4**	0.78	1.0	0.96	**0.71**	0.98	0.96	0.96

for insufficient DNN performance. D* performs competitively on MNIST_1 and MNIST_3 for $k \in \{3, 5, 10\}$, but its performance on CIFAR-10 models is significantly inferior to Tarantula and Ochiai. The best performing suspiciousness measure in CIFAR models for most k values is, by a great amount, Tarantula.

These findings show that multiple suspiciousness measures could be used for instantiating DeepFault with competitive performance. We also have evidence that DeepFault using D* is ineffective for some complex networks (e.g., CIFAR-10), but there is insufficient evidence for the best performing DeepFault instance. Our findings conform to the latest research on software fault localization which claims that there is no single best spectrum-based suspiciousness measure [47].

RQ3 (Suspiciousness Distribution). We analysed the distribution of suspicious neurons identified by DeepFault instances across the hidden DNN layers.

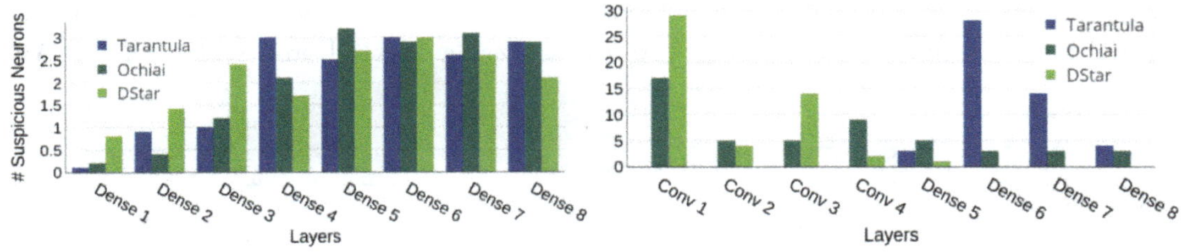

Fig. 3. Suspicious neurons distribution on MNIST_3 (left) and CIFAR_3 (right) models.

Figure 3 shows the distribution of suspicious neurons on MNIST_3 and CIFAR_3 models with $k = 10$ and $k = 50$, respectively. Considering MNIST_3, the majority of suspicious neurons are located at the deeper hidden layers (Dense 4-Dense 8) irrespective of the suspiciousness measure used by DeepFault. This observation holds for the other MNIST models and k values. On CIFAR_3, however, we can clearly see variation in the distributions across the suspiciousness measures. In fact, D* suggests that most of the suspicious neurons belong to initial hidden layers which is in contrast with Tarantula's recommendations. As reported in RQ2, the inputs synthesized by DeepFault using Tarantula achieved the best results on CIFAR models, thus showing that the identified neurons are actually suspicious. This difference in the distribution of suspicious neurons explains the inferior inputs synthesized by D* on CIFAR models (Table 3).

Another interesting finding concerns the relation between the suspicious neurons distribution and the "adversarialness" of synthesized inputs. When suspicious neurons belong to deeper hidden layers, the likelihood of the synthesized input being adversarial increases (cf. Table 3 and Fig. 3). This finding is explained by the fact that initial hidden layers transform input features (e.g., pixel values) into abstract features, while deeper hidden layers extract more semantically meaningful features and, thus, have higher influence in the final decision [13].

RQ4 (Similarity). We examined the distance between original, correctly classified, inputs and those synthesized by DeepFault, to establish DeepFault's ability to synthesize realistic inputs. Table 4 (left) shows the distance between original and synthesized inputs for various distance metrics (L_1 Manhattan, L_2 Euclidean, $L\infty$ Chebyshev) for different k values (# suspicious neurons). The distance values, averaged over inputs synthesized using the DeepFault suspiciousness measures (T, O and D*), demonstrate that the degree of perturbation is similar irrespective of k for MNIST models, whereas for CIFAR models the distance decreases as k increases. Given that a MNIST input consists of 784 pixels, with each pixel taking values in $[0, 1]$, the average perturbation per input is less than 5.28% of the total possible perturbation (L_1 distance). Similarly, for a CIFAR input that comprises 3072 pixels, with each pixel taking values in $\{0, 1, ..., 255\}$, the average perturbation per input is less that 0.03% of the total possible perturbation (L_1 distance). Thus, for both datasets, the difference of synthesized inputs to their original versions is very small. We qualitatively

Table 4. Distance between synthesized and original inputs. The values shown represent minimal perturbation to the original inputs (< 5% for MNIST and < 1% for CIFAR-10).

k	MNIST			CIFAR		
MNIST(CIFAR)	L_1	L_2	L_∞	L_1	L_2	L_∞
1(10)	41.4	2.0	0.1	179.07	7216.6	15.46
2(20)	41.2	1.99	0.1	144.95	5897.4	12.45
3(30)	40.9	1.98	0.1	124.61	5073.9	10.67
5(40)	40.7	1.97	0.1	113.45	4579.2	9.89
10(50)	40.3	1.96	0.1	104.72	4273	9.24

Susp.	MNIST			CIFAR		
measure	L_1	L_2	L_∞	L_1	L_2	L_∞
Tarantula	40.3	1.97	0.1	180.23	6575.6	19.41
Ochiai	41.0	1.98	0.1	110.45	4825.3	7.84
D*	41.5	1.99	0.1	109.4	4823.2	7.39
Random	39.2	1.92	0.1	121.73	4988.1	11.63

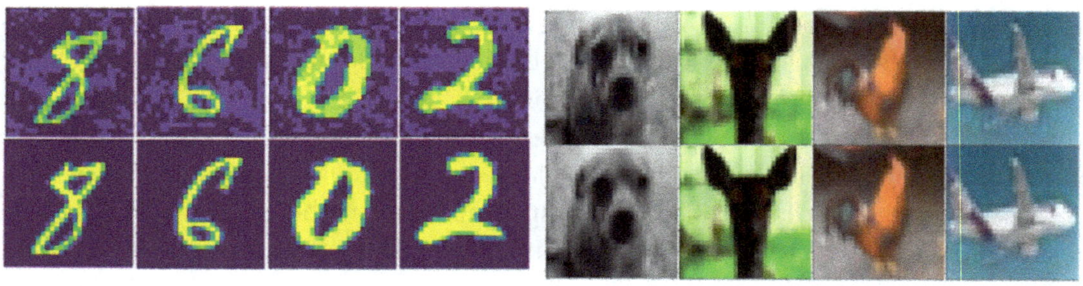

Fig. 4. Synthesized images (top) and their originals (bottom). For each dataset, suspicious neurons are found using (from left to right) Tarantula, Ochiai, D* and Random.

support our findings by showing in Fig. 4 the synthesized images and their originals for an example set of inputs from the MNIST and CIFAR-10 datasets.

We also compare the distances between original and synthesized inputs based on the suspiciousness measures (Table 4 right). The inputs synthesized by DeepFault instances using T, O or D* are very close to the inputs of the random selection strategy (L_1 distance). Considering these results, we can conclude that DeepFault is effective in synthesizing highly adversarial inputs (cf. Table 3) that closely resemble their original counterparts.

RQ5 (Increasing Activations). We studied the activation values of suspicious neurons identified by DeepFault to examine whether the synthesized inputs increase the values of these neurons. The gradients of suspicious neurons used in our suspiciousness-guided input synthesis algorithm might be conflicting and a global increase in all suspicious neurons' values might not be feasible. This can occur if some neurons' gradients are negative, indicating a decrease in an input feature's value, whereas other gradients are positive and require to increase the value of the same feature. Table 5 shows the percentage of suspicious neurons k, averaged over all

Table 5. Effectiveness of *suspiciousness-guided input synthesis* algorithm to increase activations values of suspicious neurons.

	k: MNIST(CIFAR)				
Datasets	1(10)	2(20)	3(30)	5(40)	10(50)
MNIST	98%	99%	97%	97%	91%
CIFAR	91%	92%	90%	89%	88%

suspiciousness measures for all considered MNIST and CIFAR-10 models from Table 2, whose values were increased by the inputs synthesized by DeepFault. For MNIST models, DeepFault synthesized inputs that increase the suspicious neurons' values with success at least 97% for $k \in \{1, 2, 3, 5\}$, while the average effectiveness for CIFAR models is 90%. These results show the effectiveness of our suspiciousness-guided input synthesis algorithm in generating inputs that increase the activation values of suspicious neurons (see https://DeepFault.github.io).

RQ6 (Performance). We measured the performance of Algorithm 2 to synthesize new inputs (https://DeepFault.github.io). The average time required to synthesize a single input for MNIST and CIFAR models is 1 s and 24.3 s, respectively. The performance of the algorithm depends on the number of suspicious neurons (k), the distribution of those neurons over the DNN and its architecture. For CIFAR models, for instance, the execution time per input ranges between 3 s ($k = 10$) and 48 s ($k = 50$). We also confirmed empirically that more time is taken to synthesize an input if the suspicious neurons are in deeper hidden layers.

5.4 Threats to Validity

Construct validity threats might be due to the adopted experimental methodology including the selected datasets and DNN models. To mitigate this threat, we used widely studied public datasets (MNIST [32] and CIFAR-10 [1]), and applied DeepFault to multiple DNN models of different architectures with competitive prediction accuracies (cf. Table 2). Also, we mitigate threats related to the identification of suspicious neurons (Algorithm 1) by adapting suspiciousness measures from the fault localization domain in software engineering [63].

Internal validity threats might occur when establishing the ability of DeepFault to synthesize new inputs that exercise the identified suspicious neurons. To mitigate this threat, we used various distance metrics to confirm that the synthesized inputs are close to the original inputs and similar to the inputs synthesized by a random strategy. Another threat could be that the suspiciousness measures employed by DeepFault accidentally outperform the random strategy. To mitigate this threat, we reported the results of the random strategy over five independent runs per experiment. Also, we ensured that the distribution of the randomly selected suspicious neurons resembles the distribution of neurons identified by DeepFault suspiciousness measures. We also used the non-parametric statistical test Mann-Whitney to check for significant difference in the performance of DeepFault instances and random with a 95% confidence level.

External validity threats might exist if DeepFault cannot access the internal DNN structure to assemble the hit spectrums of neurons and establish their suspiciousness. We limit this threat by developing DeepFault using the open-source frameworks Keras and Tensorflow which enable whitebox DNN analysis. We also examined various spectrum-based suspiciousness measures, but other measures can be investigated [63]. We further reduce the risk that DeepFault might be difficult to use in practice by validating it against several DNN instances trained on two widely-used datasets. However, more experiments are needed to assess the applicability of DeepFault in domains and networks with characteristics different from those used in our evaluation (e.g., LSTM and Capsule networks [50]).

6 Related Work

DNN Testing and Verification. The inability of blackbox DNN testing to provide insights about the internal neuron activity and enable identification of corner-case inputs that expose unexpected network behaviour [14], urged researchers to leverage whitebox testing techniques from software engineering [28,35,43,48,54]. DeepXplore [48] uses a differential algorithm to generate inputs that increase neuron coverage. DeepGauge [35] introduces multi-granularity coverage criteria for effective test synthesis. Other research proposes testing criteria and techniques inspired by metamorphic testing [58], combinatorial testing [37], mutation testing [36], MC/DC [54], symbolic execution [15] and concolic testing [55].

Formal DNN verification aims at providing guarantees for trustworthy DNN operation [20]. Abstraction refinement is used in [49] to verify safety properties of small neural networks with sigmoid activation functions, while AI^2 [12] employs abstract interpretation to verify similar properties. Reluplex [26] is an SMT-based approach that verifies safety and robustness of DNNs with ReLUs, and DeepSafe [16] uses Reluplex to identify safe regions in the input space. DLV [60] can verify local DNN robustness given a set of user-defined manipulations.

DeepFault adopts spectrum-based fault localization techniques to systematically identify suspicious neurons and uses these neurons to synthesize new inputs, which is mostly orthogonal to existing research on DNN testing and verification.

Adversarial Deep Learning. Recent studies have shown that DNNs are vulnerable to adversarial examples [57] and proposed search algorithms [8,40,41,44], based on gradient descent or optimisation techniques, for generating adversarial inputs that have a minimal difference to their original versions and force the DNN to exhibit erroneous behaviour. These types of adversarial examples have been shown to exist in the physical world too [29]. The identification of and protection against these adversarial attacks, is another active area of research [45,59]. DeepFault is similar to these approaches since it uses the identified suspicious neurons to synthesize perturbed inputs which as we have demonstrated in Section 5 are adversarial. Extending DeepFault to support the synthesis of adversarial inputs using these adversarial search algorithms is part of our future work.

Fault Localization in Traditional Software. Fault localization is widely studied in many software engineering areas including including software debugging [46], program repair [17] and failure reproduction [21,22]. The research focus in fault localization is the development of identification methods and suspiciousness measures that isolate the root causes of software failures with reduced engineering effort [47]. The most notable fault localization methods are spectrum-based [3,23,30,31,62], slice-based [64] and model-based [39]. Threats to the value of empirical evaluations of spectrum-based fault localization are studied in [53], while the theoretical analyses in [66,68] set a formal foundation about desirable formal properties that suspiciousness measures should have. We refer interested readers to a recent comprehensive survey on fault localization [63].

7 Conclusion

The potential deployment of DNNs in safety-critical applications introduces unacceptable risks. To reduce these risks to acceptable levels, DNNs should be tested thoroughly. We contribute in this effort, by introducing DeepFault, the first fault localization-based whitebox testing approach for DNNs. DeepFault *analyzes* pre-trained DNNs, given a specific test set, to establish the hit spectrum of each neuron, *identifies suspicious neurons* by employing suspiciousness measures and *synthesizes* new inputs that increase the activation values of the suspicious neurons. Our empirical evaluation on the widely-used MNIST and CIFAR-10 datasets shows that DeepFault can identify neurons which can be held responsible for inadequate performance. DeepFault can also synthesize new inputs, which closely resemble the original inputs, are highly adversarial and exercise the identified suspicious neurons. In future work, we plan to evaluate DeepFault on other DNNs and datasets, to improve the suspiciousness-guided synthesis algorithm and to extend the synthesis of adversarial inputs [44]. We will also explore techniques to repair the identified suspicious neurons, thus enabling to reason about the safety of DNNs and support safety case generation [7,27].

References

1. Cifar10 model in keras. https://github.com/keras-team/keras/blob/master/examples/cifar10_cnn.py. Accessed 08 Oct 2018
2. Abadi, M., Barham, P., Chen, J., et al.: TensorFlow: a system for large-scale machine learning. In: 12th USENIX Symposium on Operating Systems Design and Implementation, pp. 265–283 (2016)
3. Abreu, R., Zoeteweij, P., Golsteijn, R., Van Gemund, A.J.: A practical evaluation of spectrum-based fault localization. J. Syst. Softw. **82**(11), 1780–1792 (2009)
4. Artzi, S., Dolby, J., Tip, F., Pistoia, M.: Directed test generation for effective fault localization. In: International Symposium on Software Testing and Analysis (ISSTA), pp. 49–60 (2010)
5. Bojarski, M., Del Testa, D., Dworakowski, D., Firner, B., et al.: End to end learning for self-driving cars (2016)
6. Burton, S., Gauerhof, L., Heinzemann, C.: Making the case for safety of machine learning in highly automated driving. In: Tonetta, S., Schoitsch, E., Bitsch, F. (eds.) SAFECOMP 2017. LNCS, vol. 10489, pp. 5–16. Springer, Cham (2017). https://doi.org/10.1007/978-3-319-66284-8_1
7. Calinescu, R., Weyns, D., Gerasimou, S., Iftikhar, M.U., Habli, I., Kelly, T.: Engineering trustworthy self-adaptive software with dynamic assurance cases. IEEE Trans. Softw. Eng. **44**(11), 1039–1069 (2018)
8. Carlini, N., Wagner, D.: Towards evaluating the robustness of neural networks. In: IEEE Symposium on Security and Privacy (S&P), pp. 39–57 (2017)

9. Chollet, F., et al.: Keras (2015). https://keras.io
10. Cireşan, D., Meier, U., Schmidhuber, J.: Multi-column deep neural networks for image classification. In: Conference on Computer Vision and Pattern Recognition (CVPR), pp. 3642–3649 (2012)
11. Cui, Z., Xue, F., Cai, X., Cao, Y., et al.: Detection of malicious code variants based on deep learning. IEEE Trans. Ind. Inform. **14**(7), 3187–3196 (2018)
12. Gehr, T., Mirman, M., Drachsler-Cohen, D., Tsankov, P., et al.: AI2: safety and robustness certification of neural networks with abstract interpretation. In: IEEE Symposium on Security and Privacy (S&P), pp. 1–16 (2018)
13. Goodfellow, I., Bengio, Y., Courville, A.: Deep Learning. MIT Press (2016). http://www.deeplearningbook.org
14. Goodfellow, I., Papernot, N.: The challenge of verification and testing of machine learning (2017)
15. Gopinath, D., Wang, K., Zhang, M., Pasareanu, C.S., Khurshid, S.: Symbolic execution for deep neural networks. In: arXiv preprint arXiv:1807.10439 (2018)
16. Gopinath, D., Katz, G., Pasareanu, C.S., Barrett, C.: DeepSafe: a data-driven approach for checking adversarial robustness in neural networks. arXiv preprint arXiv:1710.00486 (2017)
17. Goues, C.L., Nguyen, T., Forrest, S., Weimer, W.: GenProg: a generic method for automatic software repair. IEEE Trans. Softw. Eng. **38**(1), 54–72 (2012)
18. Guo, J., Jiang, Y., Zhao, Y., Chen, Q., Sun, J.: DLFuzz: differential fuzzing testing of deep learning systems. In: ACM Joint European Software Engineering Conference and Symposium on the Foundations of Software Engineering (ESEC/FSE), pp. 739–743 (2018)
19. Hinton, G., Deng, L., Yu, D., Dahl, G.E., et al.: Deep neural networks for acoustic modeling in speech recognition: the shared views of four research groups. IEEE Signal Process. Mag. **29**(6), 82–97 (2012)
20. Huang, X., Kwiatkowska, M., Wang, S., Wu, M.: Safety verification of deep neural networks. In: Majumdar, R., Kunčak, V. (eds.) CAV 2017. LNCS, vol. 10426, pp. 3–29. Springer, Cham (2017). https://doi.org/10.1007/978-3-319-63387-9_1
21. Jin, W., Orso, A.: BugRedux: reproducing field failures for in-house debugging. In: International Conference on Software Engineering (ICSE), pp. 474–484 (2012)
22. Jin, W., Orso, A.: F3: fault localization for field failures. In: ACM International Symposium on Software Testing and Analysis (ISSTA), pp. 213–223 (2013)
23. Jones, J.A., Harrold, M.J.: Empirical evaluation of the tarantula automatic fault-localization technique. In: IEEE/ACM International Conference on Automated Software Engineering (ASE), pp. 273–282 (2005)
24. Jorgensen, P.C.: Software Testing: A Craftsman's Approach. Auerbach Publications (2013)
25. Julian, K.D., Lopez, J., Brush, J.S., Owen, M.P., Kochenderfer, M.J.: Policy compression for aircraft collision avoidance systems. In: IEEE Digital Avionics Systems Conference (DASC), pp. 1–10 (2016)
26. Katz, G., Barrett, C., Dill, D.L., Julian, K., Kochenderfer, M.J.: Reluplex: an efficient SMT solver for verifying deep neural networks. In: Majumdar, R., Kunčak, V. (eds.) CAV 2017. LNCS, vol. 10426, pp. 97–117. Springer, Cham (2017). https://doi.org/10.1007/978-3-319-63387-9_5
27. Kelly, T.P.: Arguing safety: a systematic approach to managing safety cases. Ph.D. thesis, University of York, York (1999)
28. Kim, J., Feldt, R., Yoo, S.: Guiding deep learning system testing using surprise adequacy. In: arXiv preprint arXiv:1808.08444 (2018)

29. Kurakin, A., Goodfellow, I., Bengio, S.: Adversarial examples in the physical world. arXiv preprint arXiv:1607.02533 (2016)
30. Landsberg, D., Chockler, H., Kroening, D., Lewis, M.: Evaluation of measures for statistical fault localisation and an optimising scheme. In: Egyed, A., Schaefer, I. (eds.) FASE 2015. LNCS, vol. 9033, pp. 115–129. Springer, Heidelberg (2015). https://doi.org/10.1007/978-3-662-46675-9_8
31. Landsberg, D., Sun, Y., Kroening, D.: Optimising spectrum based fault localisation for single fault programs using specifications. In: International Conference on Fundamental Approaches to Software Engineering (FASE), pp. 246–263 (2018)
32. LeCun, Y.: The MNIST database of handwritten digits (1998). http://yann.lecun.com/exdb/mnist
33. Lecun, Y., Bengio, Y., Hinton, G.: Deep learning. Nature **521**(7553), 436–444 (2015)
34. Litjens, G., Kooi, T., Bejnordi, B.E., et al.: A survey on deep learning in medical image analysis. Med. Image Anal. **42**, 60–88 (2017)
35. Ma, L., Juefei-Xu, F., Zhang, F., Sun, J., et al.: DeepGauge: multi-granularity testing criteria for deep learning systems. In: IEEE/ACM International Conference on Automated Software Engineering (ASE) (2018)
36. Ma, L., Zhang, F., Sun, J., Xue, M., et al.: DeepMutation: mutation testing of deep learning systems. In: IEEE International Symposium on Software Reliability Engineering (ISSRE) (2018)
37. Ma, L., Zhang, F., Xue, M., Li, B., et al.: Combinatorial testing for deep learning systems. In: arXiv preprint arXiv:1806.07723 (2018)
38. Maas, A.L., Hannun, A.Y., Ng, A.Y.: Rectifier nonlinearities improve neural network acoustic models. In: International Conference on Machine Learning (ICML), vol. 30, p. 3 (2013)
39. Mayer, W., Stumptner, M.: Evaluating models for model-based debugging. In: IEEE/ACM International Conference on Automated Software Engineering (ASE), pp. 128–137 (2008)
40. Moosavi-Dezfooli, S.M., Fawzi, A., Frossard, P.: DeepFool: a simple and accurate method to fool deep neural networks. In: IEEE Conference on Computer Vision and Pattern Recognition (CVPR), pp. 2574–2582 (2016)
41. Nguyen, A., Yosinski, J., Clune, J.: Deep neural networks are easily fooled: high confidence predictions for unrecognizable images. In: Conference on Computer Vision and Pattern Recognition (CVPR), pp. 427–436 (2015)
42. Ochiai, A.: Zoogeographic studies on the soleoid fishes found in Japan and its neighbouring regions. Bull. Jpn. Soc. Sci. Fish. **22**, 526–530 (1957)
43. Odena, A., Goodfellow, I.: TensorFuzz: debugging neural networks with coverage-guided fuzzing. arXiv preprint arXiv:1807.10875 (2018)
44. Papernot, N., McDaniel, P., Jha, S., Fredrikson, M., et al.: The limitations of deep learning in adversarial settings. In: International Symposium on Security and Privacy (S&P), pp. 372–387 (2016)
45. Papernot, N., McDaniel, P., Wu, X., Jha, S., Swami, A.: Distillation as a defense to adversarial perturbations against deep neural networks. In: International Symposium on Security and Privacy (S&P), pp. 582–597 (2016)
46. Parnin, C., Orso, A.: Are automated debugging techniques actually helping programmers? In: International Symposium on Software Testing and Analysis (ISSTA), pp. 199–209 (2011)
47. Pearson, S., Campos, J., Just, R., Fraser, G., et al.: Evaluating and improving fault localization. In: International Conference on Software Engineering (ICSE), pp. 609–620 (2017)

48. Pei, K., Cao, Y., Yang, J., Jana, S.: DeepXplore: automated whitebox testing of deep learning systems. In: Symposium on Operating Systems Principles (SOSP), pp. 1–18 (2017)
49. Pulina, L., Tacchella, A.: An abstraction-refinement approach to verification of artificial neural networks. In: Touili, T., Cook, B., Jackson, P. (eds.) CAV 2010. LNCS, vol. 6174, pp. 243–257. Springer, Heidelberg (2010). https://doi.org/10.1007/978-3-642-14295-6_24
50. Sabour, S., Frosst, N., Hinton, G.E.: Dynamic routing between capsules. In: Advances in Neural Information Processing Systems, pp. 3856–3866 (2017)
51. Salay, R., Queiroz, R., Czarnecki, K.: An analysis of ISO26262: using machine learning safely in automotive software. arXiv preprint arXiv:1709.02435 (2017)
52. Seshia, S.A., et al.: Formal specification for deep neural networks. Technical report, University of California at Berkeley (2018)
53. Steimann, F., Frenkel, M., Abreu, R.: Threats to the validity and value of empirical assessments of the accuracy of coverage-based fault locators. In: International Symposium on Software Testing and Analysis (ISSTA), pp. 314–324 (2013)
54. Sun, Y., Huang, X., Kroening, D.: Testing deep neural networks. arXiv preprint arXiv:1803.04792 (2018)
55. Sun, Y., Wu, M., Ruan, W., Huang, X., et al.: Concolic testing for deep neural networks. In: Proceedings of the 33rd ACM/IEEE International Conference on Automated Software Engineering (ASE), pp. 109–119 (2018)
56. Sutskever, I., Vinyals, O., Le, Q.V.: Sequence to sequence learning with neural networks. In: International Conference on Neural Information Processing Systems, pp. 3104–3112 (2014)
57. Szegedy, C., Zaremba, W., Sutskever, I., Bruna, J., et al.: Intriguing properties of neural networks. arXiv preprint arXiv:1312.6199 (2013)
58. Tian, Y., Pei, K., Jana, S., Ray, B.: DeepTest: automated testing of deep-neural-network-driven autonomous cars. In: International Conference on Software Engineering (ICSE), pp. 303–314 (2018)
59. Tramèr, F., Kurakin, A., Papernot, N., Goodfellow, I., et al.: Ensemble adversarial training: attacks and defenses. arXiv preprint arXiv:1705.07204 (2017)
60. Wicker, M., Huang, X., Kwiatkowska, M.: Feature-guided black-box safety testing of deep neural networks. In: International Conference on Tools and Algorithms for the Construction and Analysis of Systems (TACAS), pp. 408–426 (2018)
61. Wohlin, C., Runeson, P., Höst, M., Ohlsson, M.C., et al.: Experimentation in Software Engineering. Springer, Heidelberg (2012). https://doi.org/10.1007/978-3-642-29044-2
62. Wong, W.E., Debroy, V., Gao, R., Li, Y.: The DStar method for effective software fault localization. IEEE Trans. Reliab. **63**(1), 290–308 (2014)
63. Wong, W.E., Gao, R., Li, Y., Abreu, R., Wotawa, F.: A survey on software fault localization. IEEE Trans. Softw. Eng. **42**(8), 707–740 (2016)
64. Wong, W.E., Qi, Y.: Effective program debugging based on execution slices and inter-block data dependency. J. Syst. Softw. **79**(7), 891–903 (2006)
65. Wu, M., Wicker, M., Ruan, W., Huang, X., Kwiatkowska, M.: A game-based approximate verification of deep neural networks with provable guarantees. arXiv preprint arXiv:1807.03571 (2018)
66. Xie, X., Chen, T.Y., Kuo, F.C., Xu, B.: A theoretical analysis of the risk evaluation formulas for spectrum-based fault localization. ACM Trans. Softw. Eng. Methodol. **22**(4), 31–40 (2013)
67. Xu, B., Wang, N., Chen, T., Li, M.: Empirical evaluation of rectified activations in convolutional network. arXiv preprint arXiv:1505.00853 (2015)

68. Yoo, S., Xie, X., Kuo, F.C., Chen, T.Y., Harman, M.: Human competitiveness of genetic programming in spectrum-based fault localisation: theoretical and empirical analysis. ACM Trans. Softw. Eng. Methodol. **26**(1), 4–30 (2017)
69. Zeiler, M.D., Fergus, R.: Visualizing and understanding convolutional networks. In: Fleet, D., Pajdla, T., Schiele, B., Tuytelaars, T. (eds.) ECCV 2014. LNCS, vol. 8689, pp. 818–833. Springer, Cham (2014). https://doi.org/10.1007/978-3-319-10590-1_53

Variability Abstraction and Refinement for Game-Based Lifted Model Checking of Full CTL

Aleksandar S. Dimovski[1(✉)], Axel Legay[2], and Andrzej Wasowski[3]

[1] Mother Teresa University, 12 Udarna Brigada 2a, 1000 Skopje, Macedonia
aleksandar.dimovski@unt.edu.mk
[2] UCLouvain, Belgium and IRISA/Inria Rennes, Rennes, France
[3] IT University of Copenhagen, Rued Langgaards Vej 7, 2300 Copenhagen, Denmark

Abstract. Variability models allow effective building of many custom model variants for various configurations. Lifted model checking for a variability model is capable of verifying all its variants simultaneously in a single run by exploiting the similarities between the variants. The computational cost of lifted model checking still greatly depends on the number of variants (the size of configuration space), which is often huge. One of the most promising approaches to fighting the configuration space explosion problem in lifted model checking are *variability abstractions*. In this work, we define a novel game-based approach for variability-specific abstraction and refinement for lifted model checking of the full CTL, interpreted over 3-valued semantics. We propose a direct algorithm for solving a 3-valued (abstract) lifted model checking game. In case the result of model checking an abstract variability model is indefinite, we suggest a new notion of refinement, which eliminates indefinite results. This provides an iterative incremental variability-specific abstraction and refinement framework, where refinement is applied only where indefinite results exist and definite results from previous iterations are reused.

1 Introduction

Software Product Line (SPL) [6] is an efficient method for systematic development of a family of related models, known as *variants* (*valid products*), from a common code base. Each variant is specified in terms of *features* (static configuration options) selected for that particular variant. SPLs are particularly popular in the embedded and critical system domains (e.g. cars, phones, avionics, healthcare).

Lifted model checking [4,5] is a useful approach for verifying properties of variability models (SPLs). Given a variability model and a specification, the lifted model checking algorithm, unlike the standard non-lifted one, returns precise conclusive results for all individual variants, that is, for each variant it reports whether it satisfies or violates the specification. The main disadvantage of lifted model checking is the *configuration space explosion problem*, which refers

R. Hähnle and W. van der Aalst (Eds.): FASE 2019, LNCS 11424, pp. 192–209, 2019.
https://doi.org/10.1007/978-3-030-16722-6_11

to the high number of variants in the variability model. In fact, exponentially many variants can be derived from only few configuration options (features). One of the most successful approaches to fighting the configuration space explosion are so-called *variability abstractions* [12,14,15,17]. They hide some of the configuration details, so that many of the concrete configurations become indistinguishable and can be collapsed into a single abstract configuration (variant). This results in smaller abstract variability models with a smaller number of abstract configurations. In order to be conservative w.r.t. the full CTL temporal logic, abstract variability models have two types of transitions: *may-transitions* which represent possible transitions in the concrete model, and *must-transitions* which represent the definite transitions in the concrete model. May and must transitions correspond to over and under approximations, and are needed in order to preserve universal and existential CTL properties, respectively.

Here we consider the 3-valued semantics for interpreting CTL formulae over abstract variability models. This semantics evaluates a formula on an abstract model to either *true*, *false*, or *indefinite*. Abstract variability models are designed to be conservative for both *true* and *false*. However, the *indefinite* answer gives no information on the value of the formula on the concrete model. In this case, a refinement is needed in order to make the abstract models more precise.

The technique proposed here significantly extends the scope of existing automatic variability-specific abstraction refinement procedures [8,18], which currently support the verification of universal LTL properties only. They use conservative variability abstractions to construct over-approximated abstract variability models, which preserve LTL properties. If a spurious counterexample (introduced due to the abstraction) is found in the abstract model, the procedures [8,18] use Craig interpolation to extract relevant information from it in order to define the refinement of abstract models. Variability abstractions that preserve all (universal and existential) CTL properties have been previously introduced [12], but without an automatic mechanism for constructing them and no notion of refinement. The abstractions [12] has to be constructed manually by an engineer before verification. In order to make the entire verification procedure automatic, we need to develop an abstraction and refinement framework for CTL properties.

In this work, we propose the first variability-specific abstraction refinement procedure for automatically verifying arbitrary formulae of CTL. To achieve this aim, model checking *games* [24–26] represent the most suitable framework for defining the refinement. In this way, we establish a brand new connection between games and family-based (SPL) model checking. The refinement is defined by finding the reason for the indefinite result of an algorithm that solves the corresponding model checking game, which is played by two players: Player $\forall$ (trying to refute the formula Φ on an abstract model $\mathcal{M}$) and Player $\exists$ (trying to verify Φ on $\mathcal{M}$). The game is played on a *game board*, which consists of configurations of the form (s, Φ') where s is a state of the abstract model $\mathcal{M}$ and Φ' is a subformula of Φ, such that the value of Φ' in s is relevant for determining the final model checking result. The players make moves between configurations in which they try to verify or refute Φ' in s. All possible plays of a game are captured in the game-graph, whose nodes are the elements of the game board and whose edges are the possible moves of the players. The model checking game is solved via a coloring algorithm which colors each node (s, Φ') in the game-graph by T, F, or ? iff the value of Φ' in s is *true*, *false*, or indefinite, respectively. Player $\forall$ has a winning strategy at the node (s, Φ') iff the node is colored by F iff Φ' does not hold in s, and Player $\exists$ has a winning strategy at (s, Φ') iff the node is colored by T iff Φ' holds in s. In addition, it is also possible that neither of players has a winning strategy, in which case the node is colored by ? and the value of Φ' in s is indefinite. In this case, we want to refine the abstract model. We can find the reason for the tie by examining the game-graph. We choose a refinement criterion, which splits abstract configurations so that the new, refined abstract configurations represent smaller subsets of concrete configurations.

2 Background

Variability Models. Let $\mathbb{F} = \{A_1, \ldots, A_n\}$ be a finite set of Boolean variables representing the features available in a variability model. A specific subset of features, $k \subseteq \mathbb{F}$, known as *configuration*, specifies a *variant* (valid product) of a variability model. We assume that only a subset $\mathbb{K} \subseteq 2^{\mathbb{F}}$ of configurations are *valid*. An alternative representation of configurations is based upon propositional formulae. Each configuration $k \in \mathbb{K}$ can be represented by a formula: $k(A_1) \wedge \ldots \wedge k(A_n)$, where $k(A_i) = A_i$ if $A_i \in k$, and $k(A_i) = \neg A_i$ if $A_i \notin k$ for $1 \leq i \leq n$.

We use *transition systems* (TS) to describe behaviors of single-systems.

Definition 1. *A transition system (TS) is a tuple $\mathcal{T} = (S, Act, trans, I, AP, L)$, where S is a set of states; Act is a set of actions; $trans \subseteq S \times Act \times S$ is a transition relation which is* total, *so that for each state there is an outgoing transition; $I \subseteq S$ is a set of initial states; AP is a set of atomic propositions; and $L : S \to 2^{AP}$ is a labelling function specifying which propositions hold in a state. We write $s_1 \xrightarrow{\lambda} s_2$ whenever $(s_1, \lambda, s_2) \in trans$.*

An *execution* (behaviour) of a TS $\mathcal{T}$ is an *infinite* sequence $\rho = s_0\lambda_1 s_1 \lambda_2 \ldots$ with $s_0 \in I$ such that $s_i \xrightarrow{\lambda_{i+1}} s_{i+1}$ for all $i \geq 0$. The *semantics* of the TS $\mathcal{T}$, denoted as $[\![\mathcal{T}]\!]_{TS}$, is the set of its executions.

A *featured transition system* (FTS) is a particular instance of a variability model, which describes the behavior of a whole family of systems in a single monolithic description, where the transitions are guarded by a *presence condition* that identifies the variants they belong to. The presence conditions ψ are drawn from the set of feature expressions, *FeatExp*($\mathbb{F}$), which are propositional logic formulae over $\mathbb{F}$: $\psi ::= true \mid A \in \mathbb{F} \mid \neg\psi \mid \psi_1 \wedge \psi_2$. We write $[\![\psi]\!]$ to denote the set of configurations from $\mathbb{K}$ that satisfy ψ, i.e. $k \in [\![\psi]\!]$ iff $k \models \psi$.

Definition 2. *A featured transition system (FTS) represents a tuple $\mathcal{F} = (S, Act, trans, I, AP, L, \mathbb{F}, \mathbb{K}, \delta)$, where $S, Act, trans, I, AP$, and L form a TS; $\mathbb{F}$ is the set of available features; $\mathbb{K}$ is a set of valid configurations; and $\delta : trans \to FeatExp(\mathbb{F})$ is a total function decorating transitions with presence conditions.*

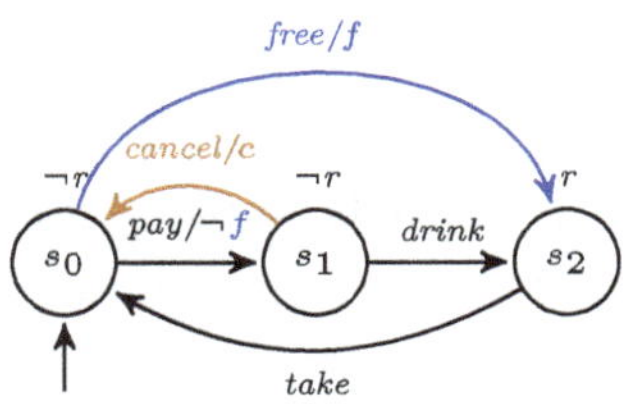

Fig. 1. VENDMACH

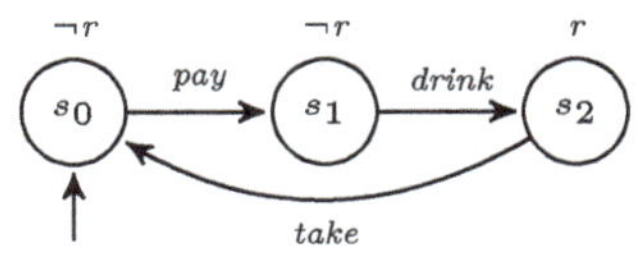

Fig. 2. $\pi_\emptyset$(VENDMACH)

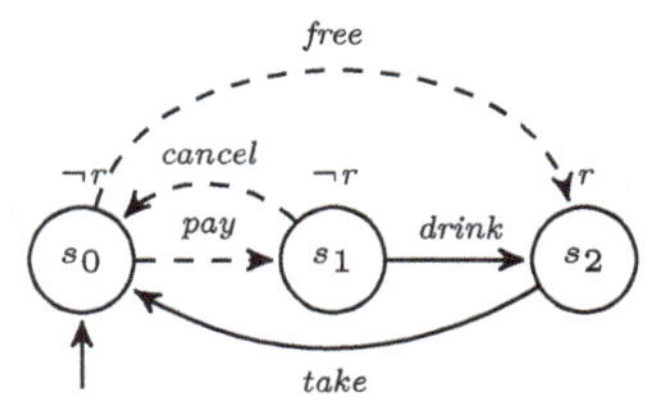

Fig. 3. α^{join}(VENDMACH)

The *projection* of an FTS $\mathcal{F}$ to a configuration $k \in \mathbb{K}$, denoted as $\pi_k(\mathcal{F})$, is the TS $(S, Act, trans', I, AP, L)$, where $trans' = \{t \in trans \mid k \models \delta(t)\}$. We lift the definition of *projection* to sets of configurations $\mathbb{K}' \subseteq \mathbb{K}$, denoted as $\pi_{\mathbb{K}'}(\mathcal{F})$, by keeping the transitions admitted by at least one of the configurations in $\mathbb{K}'$. That is, $\pi_{\mathbb{K}'}(\mathcal{F})$, is the FTS $(S, Act, trans', I, AP, L, \mathbb{F}, \mathbb{K}', \delta')$, where $trans' = \{t \in trans \mid \exists k \in \mathbb{K}'.k \models \delta(t)\}$ and $\delta' = \delta|_{trans'}$ is the restriction of δ to $trans'$. The *semantics* of an FTS $\mathcal{F}$, denoted as $[\![\mathcal{F}]\!]_{FTS}$, is the union of behaviours of the projections on all valid variants $k \in \mathbb{K}$, i.e. $[\![\mathcal{F}]\!]_{FTS} = \cup_{k \in \mathbb{K}} [\![\pi_k(\mathcal{F})]\!]_{TS}$.

Modal transition systems (MTSs) [22] are a generalization of transition systems equipped with two transition relations: *must* and *may*. The former (must) is used to specify the required behavior, while the latter (may) to specify the allowed behavior of a system. We will use MTSs for representing abstractions of FTSs.

Definition 3. *A modal transition system (MTS) is represented by a tuple* $\mathcal{M} = (S, Act, trans^{may}, trans^{must}, I, AP, L)$, *where* $trans^{may} \subseteq S \times Act \times S$ *describe may transitions of* $\mathcal{M}$; $trans^{must} \subseteq S \times Act \times S$ *describe must transitions of* $\mathcal{M}$, *such that* $trans^{may}$ *is total and* $trans^{must} \subseteq trans^{may}$.

A *may-execution* in $\mathcal{M}$ is an execution (infinite sequence) with all its transitions in $trans^{\text{may}}$; whereas a *must-execution* in $\mathcal{M}$ is a maximal sequence with all its transitions in $trans^{\text{must}}$, which cannot be extended with any other transition from $trans^{\text{must}}$. Note that since $trans^{\text{must}}$ is not necessarily total, must-executions can be finite. We use $[\![\mathcal{M}]\!]^{\text{may}}_{MTS}$ (resp., $[\![\mathcal{M}]\!]^{\text{must}}_{MTS}$) to denote the set of all may-executions (resp., must-executions) in $\mathcal{M}$ starting in an initial state.

Example 1. Throughout this paper, we will use a beverage vending machine as a running example [4]. Figure 1 shows the FTS of a VENDMACH family. It has two features, and each of them is assigned an identifying letter and a color. The features are: `CancelPurchase` (c, in brown), for canceling a purchase after a coin is entered; and `FreeDrinks` (f, in blue) for offering free drinks. Each transition is labeled by an *action* followed by a *feature expression*. For instance, the transition $s_0 \xrightarrow{free/f} s_2$ is included in variants where the feature f is enabled. For clarity, we omit to write the presence condition *true* in transitions. There is only one atomic proposition `served` $\in AP$, which is abbreviated as r. Note that $r \in L(s_2)$, whereas $r \notin L(s_0)$ and $r \notin L(s_1)$.

By combining various features, a number of variants of this VENDMACH can be obtained. The set of valid configurations is: $\mathbb{K}^{\text{VM}} = \{\emptyset, \{c\}, \{f\}, \{c, f\}\}$ (or, equivalently $\mathbb{K}^{\mathrm{VM}} = \{\neg c \wedge \neg f, c \wedge \neg f, \neg c \wedge f, c \wedge f\}$). Figure 2 shows a basic version of VENDMACH that only serves a drink, described by the configuration: $\emptyset$ (or, as formula $\neg c \wedge \neg f$). It takes a coin, serves a drink, opens a compartment so the customer can take the drink. Figure 3 shows an MTS, where must transitions are denoted by solid lines, while may transitions by dashed lines. □

CTL Properties. We present Computation Tree Logic (CTL) [1] for specifying system properties. CTL state formulae Φ are given by:

$$\Phi ::= true \mid false \mid l \mid \Phi_1 \wedge \Phi_2 \mid \Phi_1 \vee \Phi_2 \mid A\phi \mid E\phi, \qquad \phi ::= \bigcirc\Phi \mid \Phi_1 \mathsf{U} \Phi_2 \mid \Phi_1 \mathsf{V} \Phi_2$$

where $l \in Lit = AP \cup \{\neg a \mid a \in AP\}$ and ϕ represent CTL path formulae. Note that the CTL state formulae Φ are given in negation normal form ($\neg$ is applied only to atomic propositions). The path formula $\bigcirc\Phi$ can be read as "in the next state Φ", $\Phi_1 \mathsf{U} \Phi_2$ can be read as "Φ_1 until Φ_2", and its dual $\Phi_1 \mathsf{V} \Phi_2$ can be read as "Φ_2 while not Φ_1" (where Φ_1 may never hold).

We assume the standard CTL semantics over TSs is given [1] (see also [16, Appendix A]). We write $[\mathcal{T} \models \Phi] = tt$ to denote that $\mathcal{T}$ satisfies the formula Φ, whereas $[\mathcal{T} \models \Phi] = f\!f$ to denote that $\mathcal{T}$ does not satisfy Φ.

We say that an FTS $\mathcal{F}$ satisfies a CTL formula Φ, written $[\mathcal{F} \models \Phi] = tt$, iff all its valid variants satisfy the formula, i.e. $\forall k \in \mathbb{K}.\, [\pi_k(\mathcal{F}) \models \Phi] = tt$. Otherwise, we say $\mathcal{F}$ does not satisfy Φ, written $[\mathcal{F} \models \Phi] = f\!f$. In this case, we also want to determine a non-empty set of violating variants $\mathbb{K}' \subseteq \mathbb{K}$, such that $\forall k' \in \mathbb{K}'.\, [\pi_{k'}(\mathcal{F}) \models \Phi] = f\!f$ and $\forall k \in \mathbb{K} \backslash \mathbb{K}'.\, [\pi_k(\mathcal{F}) \models \Phi] = tt$.

We define the 3-valued semantics of CTL over an MTS $\mathcal{M}$ slightly differently from the semantics for TSs. A CTL state formula Φ is satisfied in a state s of an MTS $\mathcal{M}$, denoted $[\mathcal{M}, s \models^3 \Phi]$, iff ($\mathcal{M}$ is omitted when clear from context):[1]

$$(1)\ [s \models^3 a] = \begin{cases} tt, & \text{if } a \in L(s) \\ f\!f, & \text{if } a \notin L(s) \end{cases}, \quad [s \models^3 \neg a] = \begin{cases} tt, & \text{if } a \notin L(s) \\ f\!f, & \text{if } a \in L(s) \end{cases}$$

$$(2)\ [s \models^3 \Phi_1 \wedge \Phi_2] = \begin{cases} tt, & \text{if } [s \models^3 \Phi_1] = tt \text{ and } [s \models^3 \Phi_2] = tt \\ f\!f, & \text{if } [s \models^3 \Phi_1] = f\!f \text{ or } [s \models^3 \Phi_2] = f\!f \\ \bot, & \text{otherwise} \end{cases}$$

$$(3)\ [s \models^3 A\phi] = \begin{cases} tt, & \text{if } \forall \rho \in [\![\mathcal{M}]\!]^{\mathrm{may},s}_{MTS}.\, [\rho \models^3 \phi] = tt \\ f\!f, & \text{if } \exists \rho \in [\![\mathcal{M}]\!]^{\mathrm{must},s}_{MTS}.\, [\rho \models^3 \phi] = f\!f \\ \bot, & \text{otherwise} \end{cases}$$

$$[s \models^3 E\phi] = \begin{cases} tt, & \text{if } \exists \rho \in [\![\mathcal{M}]\!]^{\mathrm{must},s}_{MTS}.\, [\rho \models^3 \phi] = tt \\ f\!f, & \text{if } \forall \rho \in [\![\mathcal{M}]\!]^{\mathrm{may},s}_{MTS}.\, [\rho \models^3 \phi] = f\!f \\ \bot, & \text{otherwise} \end{cases}$$

where $[\![\mathcal{M}]\!]^{\mathrm{may},s}_{MTS}$ (resp., $[\![\mathcal{M}]\!]^{\mathrm{must},s}_{MTS}$) denotes the set of all may-executions (must-executions) starting in the state s of $\mathcal{M}$. Satisfaction of a path formula ϕ for a may- or must-execution $\rho = s_0\lambda_1 s_1 \lambda_2 \ldots$ of an MTS $\mathcal{M}$ (we write $\rho_i = s_i$ to

[1] See [16, Appendix A] for definitions of $[s \models^3 \Phi_1 \vee \Phi_2]$, $[\rho \models^3 \bigcirc\Phi]$, and $[\rho \models^3 (\Phi_1 \mathsf{V} \Phi_2)]$.

denote the i-th state of ρ, and $|\rho|$ to denote the number of states in ρ), denoted $[\mathcal{M}, \rho \models^3 \phi]$, is defined as ($\mathcal{M}$ is omitted when clear from context):

$$(4)\ \ [\rho \models^3 (\Phi_1 \mathsf{U} \Phi_2)] = \begin{cases} tt, & \text{if } \exists 0 \leq i \leq |\rho|.([\rho_i \models^3 \Phi_2] = tt \wedge (\forall j < i.[\rho_j \models^3 \Phi_1] = tt)) \\ ff, & \text{if } \begin{array}{l} \forall 0 \leq i \leq |\rho|.(\forall j < i.[\rho_j \models^3 \Phi_1] \neq ff \Longrightarrow [\rho_i \models^3 \Phi_2] = ff) \\ \wedge\ \forall i \geq 0.[\rho_i \models^3 \Phi_1] \neq ff \Longrightarrow |\rho| = \infty \end{array} \\ \bot, & \text{otherwise} \end{cases}$$

A MTS $\mathcal{M}$ satisfies a formula Φ, written $[\mathcal{M} \models^3 \Phi] = tt$, iff $\forall s_0 \in I. [s_0 \models^3 \Phi] = tt$. We say that $[\mathcal{M} \models^3 \Phi] = ff$ if $\exists s_0 \in I. [s_0 \models^3 \Phi] = ff$. Otherwise, $[\mathcal{M} \models^3 \Phi] = \bot$.

Example 2. Consider the FTS VENDMACH and MTS $\boldsymbol{\alpha}^{\text{join}}$(VENDMACH) in Figs. 1 and 3. The property $\Phi_1 = A(\neg r \mathsf{U} r)$ states that in the initial state along every execution will eventually reach the state where r holds. Note that [VENDMACH $\models \Phi_1$] = ff. E.g., if the feature c is enabled, a counter-example where the state s_2 that satisfies r is never reached is: $s_0 \to s_1 \to s_0 \to \ldots$. The set of violating products is $[\![c]\!] = \{\{c\}, \{f, c\}\} \subseteq \mathbb{K}^{VM}$.However, $[\pi_{[\![\neg c]\!]}(\text{VENDMACH}) \models \Phi_1] = tt$. We also have that $[\boldsymbol{\alpha}^{\text{join}}(\text{VENDMACH}) \models^3 \Phi_1] = \bot$, since (1) there is a may-execution in $\boldsymbol{\alpha}^{\text{join}}$(VENDMACH) where s_2 is never reached: $s_0 \to s_1 \to s_0 \to \ldots$, and (2) there is no must-execution that violates Φ_1.

Consider the property $\Phi_2 = E(\neg r \mathsf{U} r)$, which describes a situation where in the initial state there exists an execution that will eventually reach s_2 that satisfies r. Note that [VENDMACH $\models \Phi_2$] = tt, since even for variants with the feature c there is a continuation from the state s_1 to s_2. But, $[\boldsymbol{\alpha}^{\text{join}}(\text{VENDMACH}) \models \Phi_2] = \bot$ since (1) there is no a must-execution in $\boldsymbol{\alpha}^{\text{join}}$(VENDMACH) that reaches s_2 from s_0, and (2) there is a may-execution that satisfies Φ_2. □

3 Abstraction of FTSs

We now introduce the variability abstractions [12] which preserve full CTL. We start working with Galois connections[2] between Boolean complete lattices of feature expressions, and then induce a notion of abstraction of FTSs.

The Boolean complete lattice of feature expressions (propositional formulae over $\mathbb{F}$) is: $(FeatExp(\mathbb{F})_{/\equiv}, \models, \vee, \wedge, true, false, \neg)$. The elements of the domain $FeatExp(\mathbb{F})_{/\equiv}$ are equivalence classes of propositional formulae $\psi \in FeatExp(\mathbb{F})$ obtained by quotienting by the semantic equivalence $\equiv$. The ordering $\models$ is the standard entailment between propositional logics formulae, whereas the least upper bound and the greatest lower bound are just logical disjunction and conjunction respectively. Finally, the constant *false* is the least, *true* is the greatest element, and negation is the complement operator.

[2] $\langle L, \leq_L \rangle \underset{\alpha}{\overset{\gamma}{\leftrightarrows}} \langle M, \leq_M \rangle$ is a *Galois connection* between complete lattices L (concrete domain) and M (abstract domain) iff $\alpha : L \to M$ and $\gamma : M \to L$ are total functions that satisfy: $\alpha(l) \leq_M m \iff l \leq_L \gamma(m)$, for all $l \in L, m \in M$.

Over-approximating abstractions. The *join abstraction*, $\boldsymbol{\alpha}^{\text{join}}$, replaces each feature expression ψ with *true* if there exists at least one configuration from $\mathbb{K}$ that satisfies ψ. The abstract set of features is empty: $\boldsymbol{\alpha}^{\text{join}}(\mathbb{F}) = \emptyset$, and abstract set of configurations is a singleton: $\boldsymbol{\alpha}^{\text{join}}(\mathbb{K}) = \{true\}$. The abstraction and concretization functions between *FeatExp*($\mathbb{F}$) and *FeatExp*($\emptyset$) are:

$$\boldsymbol{\alpha}^{\text{join}}(\psi) = \begin{cases} true & \text{if } \exists k \in \mathbb{K}. k \models \psi \\ false & \text{otherwise} \end{cases} \qquad \gamma^{\text{join}}(\psi) = \begin{cases} true & \text{if } \psi \text{ is } true \\ \bigvee_{k \in 2^{\mathbb{F}} \setminus \mathbb{K}} k & \text{if } \psi \text{ is } false \end{cases}$$

which form a Galois connection [15]. In this way, we obtain a single abstract variant that includes all transitions occurring in any variant.

Under-approximating abstractions. The *dual join abstraction*, $\widetilde{\boldsymbol{\alpha}^{\text{join}}}$, replaces each feature expression ψ with *true* if all configurations from $\mathbb{K}$ satisfy ψ. The abstraction and concretization functions between *FeatExp*($\mathbb{F}$) and *FeatExp*($\emptyset$), forming a Galois connection [12], are defined as [9]: $\widetilde{\boldsymbol{\alpha}^{\text{join}}} = \neg \circ \boldsymbol{\alpha}^{\text{join}} \circ \neg$ and $\widetilde{\gamma^{\text{join}}} = \neg \circ \gamma^{\text{join}} \circ \neg$, that is:

$$\widetilde{\boldsymbol{\alpha}^{\text{join}}}(\psi) = \begin{cases} true & \text{if } \forall k \in \mathbb{K}. k \models \psi \\ false & \text{otherwise} \end{cases} \qquad \widetilde{\gamma^{\text{join}}}(\psi) = \begin{cases} \bigwedge_{k \in 2^{\mathbb{F}} \setminus \mathbb{K}} (\neg k) & \text{if } \psi \text{ is } true \\ false & \text{if } \psi \text{ is } false \end{cases}$$

In this way, we obtain a single abstract variant that includes only those transitions that occur in all variants.

Abstract MTS and Preservation of CTL. Given a Galois connection $(\boldsymbol{\alpha}^{\text{join}}, \gamma^{\text{join}})$ defined on the level of feature expressions, we now define the abstraction of an FTS as an MTS with two transition relations: one (may) preserving universal properties, and the other (must) preserving existential properties. The may transitions describe the behaviour that is possible in some variant of the concrete FTS, but not need be realized in the other variants; whereas the must transitions describe behaviour that has to be present in all variants of the FTS.

Definition 4. *Given the FTS* $\mathcal{F} = (S, Act, trans, I, AP, L, \mathbb{F}, \mathbb{K}, \delta)$, *define MTS* $\boldsymbol{\alpha}^{\text{join}}(\mathcal{F}) = (S, Act, trans^{may}, trans^{must}, I, AP, L)$ *to be its* abstraction, *where* $trans^{may} = \{t \in trans \mid \boldsymbol{\alpha}^{\text{join}}(\delta(t)) = true\}$, *and* $trans^{must} = \{t \in trans \mid \widetilde{\boldsymbol{\alpha}^{\text{join}}}(\delta(t)) = true\}$.

Note that the abstract model $\boldsymbol{\alpha}^{\text{join}}(\mathcal{F})$ has no variability in it, i.e. it contains only one abstract configuration. We now show that the 3-valued semantics of the MTS $\boldsymbol{\alpha}^{\text{join}}(\mathcal{F})$ is designed to be *sound* in the sense that it preserves both satisfaction (*tt*) and refutation (*ff*) of a formula from the abstract model to the concrete one. However, if the truth value of a formula in the abstract model is $\bot$, then its value over the concrete model is not known. We prove [16, Appendix B]:

Theorem 1 (Preservation results). *For every $\Phi \in CTL$, we have:*

(1) $[\boldsymbol{\alpha}^{\text{join}}(\mathcal{F}) \models^3 \Phi] = tt \implies [\mathcal{F} \models \Phi] = tt.$
(2) $[\boldsymbol{\alpha}^{\text{join}}(\mathcal{F}) \models^3 \Phi] = ff \implies [\mathcal{F} \models \Phi] = ff$ *and* $[\pi_k(\mathcal{F}) \models \Phi] = ff$ *for all* $k \in \mathbb{K}$.

Divide-and-conquer strategy. The problem of evaluating $[\mathcal{F} \models \Phi]$ can be reduced to a number of smaller problems by partitioning the configuration space $\mathbb{K}$. Let the subsets $\mathbb{K}_1, \mathbb{K}_2, \ldots, \mathbb{K}_n$ form a *partition* of the set $\mathbb{K}$. Then, $[\mathcal{F} \models \Phi] = tt$ iff $[\pi_{\mathbb{K}_i}(\mathcal{F}) \models \Phi] = tt$ for all $i = 1, \ldots, n$. Also, $[\mathcal{F} \models \Phi] = ff$ iff $[\pi_{\mathbb{K}_j}(\mathcal{F}) \models \Phi] = ff$ for some $1 \leq j \leq n$. By using Theorem 1, we obtain the following result.

Corollary 1. *Let* $\mathbb{K}_1, \mathbb{K}_2, \ldots, \mathbb{K}_n$ *form a* partition *of* $\mathbb{K}$.

(1) *If* $[\boldsymbol{\alpha}^{\text{join}}(\pi_{\mathbb{K}_1}(\mathcal{F})) \models \Phi] = tt \wedge \ldots \wedge [\boldsymbol{\alpha}^{\text{join}}(\pi_{\mathbb{K}_n}(\mathcal{F})) \models \Phi] = tt$, *then* $[\mathcal{F} \models \Phi] = tt$.
(2) *If* $[\boldsymbol{\alpha}^{\text{join}}(\pi_{\mathbb{K}_j}(\mathcal{F})) \models \Phi] = ff$ *for some* $1 \leq j \leq n$, *then* $[\mathcal{F} \models \Phi] = ff$ *and* $[\pi_k(\mathcal{F}) \models \Phi] = ff$ *for all* $k \in \mathbb{K}_j$.

Example 3. Recall the FTS VENDMACH of Fig. 1. Figure 3 shows the MTS $\boldsymbol{\alpha}^{\text{join}}$(VENDMACH), where the allowed (may) part of the behavior includes the transitions that are associated with the optional features c and f in VENDMACH, and the required (must) part includes transitions with the presence condition *true*. Consider the properties introduced in Example 2. We have $[\boldsymbol{\alpha}^{\text{join}}(\text{VENDMACH}) \models^3 \Phi_1] = \bot$ and $[\boldsymbol{\alpha}^{\text{join}}(\text{VENDMACH}) \models^3 \Phi_2] = \bot$, so we cannot conclude whether Φ_1 and Φ_2 are satisfied by VENDMACH or not. □

4 Game-Based Abstract Lifted Model Checking

The 3-valued model checking game [24,25] on an MTS $\mathcal{M}$ with state set S, a state $s \in S$, and a CTL formula Φ is played by Player $\forall$ and Player $\exists$ in order to evaluate Φ in s of $\mathcal{M}$. The goal of Player $\forall$ is either to refute Φ on $\mathcal{M}$ or to prevent Player $\exists$ from verifying it. The goal of Player $\exists$ is either to verify Φ on $\mathcal{M}$ or to prevent Player $\forall$ from refuting it. The *game board* is the Cartesian product $S \times sub(\Phi)$, where $sub(\Phi)$ is defined as:

$$\text{if } \Phi = true, false, l, \text{ then } sub(\Phi) = \{\Phi\}; \text{ if } \Phi = Æ\bigcirc\Phi_1, \text{ then } sub(\Phi) = \{\Phi\} \cup sub(\Phi_1)$$
$$\text{if } \Phi = \Phi_1 \wedge \Phi_2, \Phi_1 \vee \Phi_2, \text{ then } sub(\Phi) = \{\Phi\} \cup sub(\Phi_1) \cup sub(\Phi_2)$$
$$\text{if } \Phi = Æ(\Phi_1 \mathsf{U} \Phi_2), Æ(\Phi_1 \mathsf{V} \Phi_2), \text{ then } sub(\Phi) = exp(\Phi) \cup sub(\Phi_1) \cup sub(\Phi_2)$$

where Æ ranges over both A and E. The expansion $exp(\Phi)$ is defined as:

$$\Phi = Æ(\Phi_1 \mathsf{U} \Phi_2) : exp(\Phi) = \{\Phi, \Phi_2 \vee (\Phi_1 \wedge Æ \bigcirc \Phi), \Phi_1 \wedge Æ \bigcirc \Phi, Æ \bigcirc \Phi\}$$
$$\Phi = Æ(\Phi_1 \mathsf{V} \Phi_2) : exp(\Phi) = \{\Phi, \Phi_2 \wedge (\Phi_1 \vee Æ \bigcirc \Phi), \Phi_1 \vee Æ \bigcirc \Phi, Æ \bigcirc \Phi\}$$

A *single play* from (s, Φ) is a possibly infinite sequence of configurations $C_0 \rightarrow_{p_0} C_1 \rightarrow_{p_1} C_2 \rightarrow_{p_2} \ldots$, where $C_0 = (s, \Phi)$, $C_i \in S \times sub(\Phi)$, and $p_i \in \{\text{Player } \forall, \text{Player } \exists\}$. The subformula in C_i determines which player p_i makes the next move. The possible moves at each configuration are:

(1) $C_i = (s, \mathit{false})$, $C_i = (s, \mathit{true})$, $C_i = (s, l)$: the play is finished. Such configurations are called *terminal.*
(2) if $C_i = (s, A \bigcirc \Phi)$, Player $\forall$ chooses a must-transition $s \longrightarrow s'$ (for refutation) or a may-transition $s \longrightarrow s'$ of $\mathcal{M}$ (to prevent satisfaction), and $C_{i+1} = (s', \Phi)$.
(3) if $C_i = (s, E \bigcirc \Phi)$, Player $\exists$ chooses a must-transition $s \longrightarrow s'$ (for satisfaction) or a may-transition $s \longrightarrow s'$ of $\mathcal{M}$ (to prevent refutation), and $C_{i+1} = (s', \Phi)$.
(4) if $C_i = (s, \Phi_1 \wedge \Phi_2)$, then Player $\forall$ chooses $j \in \{1, 2\}$ and $C_{i+1} = (s, \Phi_j)$.
(5) if $C_i = (s, \Phi_1 \vee \Phi_2)$, then Player $\exists$ chooses $j \in \{1, 2\}$ and $C_{i+1} = (s, \Phi_j)$.
(6), (7) if $C_i = (s, Æ(\Phi_1 \mathsf{U} \Phi_2))$, then $C_{i+1} = (s, \Phi_2 \vee (\Phi_1 \wedge Æ \bigcirc Æ(\Phi_1 \mathsf{U} \Phi_2)))$.
(8), (9) if $C_i = (s, Æ(\Phi_1 \mathsf{V} \Phi_2))$, then $C_{i+1} = (s, \Phi_2 \wedge (\Phi_1 \vee Æ \bigcirc Æ(\Phi_1 \mathsf{V} \Phi_2)))$.

The moves (6)–(9) are deterministic, thus any player can make them.

A play is a *maximal play* iff it is infinite or ends in a terminal configuration. A play is infinite [26] iff there is exactly one subformula of the form $A\mathsf{U}$, $A\mathsf{V}$, $E\mathsf{U}$, or $E\mathsf{V}$ that occurs infinitely often in the play. Such a subformula is called a *witness.* We have the following *winning criteria*:

- Player $\forall$ *wins* a (maximal) play iff in each configuration of the form $C_i = (s, A \bigcirc \Phi)$, Player $\forall$ chooses a move based on must-transitions and one of the following holds: (1) the play is finite and ends in a terminal configuration of the form $C_i = (s, \mathit{false})$ or $C_i = (s, a)$ where $a \notin L(s)$ or $C_i = (s, \neg a)$ where $a \in L(s)$; (2) the play is infinite and the witness is of the form $A\mathsf{U}$ or $E\mathsf{U}$.
- Player $\exists$ *wins* a (maximal) play iff in each configuration of the form $C_i = (s, E \bigcirc \Phi)$, Player $\exists$ chooses a move based on must-transitions and one of the following holds: (1) the play is finite and ends in a terminal configuration of the form $C_i = (s, \mathit{true})$ or $C_i = (s, a)$ where $a \in L(s)$ or $C_i = (s, \neg a)$ where $a \notin L(s)$; (2) the play is infinite and the witness is of the form $A\mathsf{V}$ or $E\mathsf{V}$.
- Otherwise, the play ends in a *tie.*

A *strategy* is a set of rules for a player, telling the player which move to choose in the current configuration. A *winning strategy* from (s, Φ) is a set of rules allowing the player to win every play that starts at (s, Φ) if he plays by the rules. It was shown in [24,25] that the model checking problem of evaluating $[\mathcal{M}, s \models^3 \Phi]$ can be reduced to the problem of finding which player has a winning strategy from (s, Φ) (i.e. to solving the given 3-valued model checking game).

The algorithm proposed in [24,25] for solving the given 3-valued model checking game consists of two parts. First, it constructs a *game-graph*, then it runs an *algorithm for coloring* the game-graph. The game-graph is $G_{\mathcal{M} \times \Phi} = (N, E)$ where $N \subseteq S \times sub(\Phi)$ is the set of nodes and $E \subseteq N \times N$ is the set of edges. N contains a node for each configuration that was reached during the construction of the game-graph that starts from initial configurations $I \times \{\Phi\}$ in a BFS manner, and E contains an edge for each possible move that was applied. The nodes of the game-graph can be classified as: terminal nodes, $\wedge$-nodes, $\vee$-nodes, $A\bigcirc$-nodes, and $E\bigcirc$-nodes. Similarly, the edges can be classified as: progress edges, which originate in $A\bigcirc$ or $E\bigcirc$ nodes and reflect real transitions of the MTS $\mathcal{M}$, and auxiliary nodes, which are all other edges. We distinguish two types of progress edges, two types of children, and two types of SCCs

(Strongly Connected Components). *Must-edges* (*may-edges*) are edges based on must-transitions (may-transitions) of MTSs. A node n' is a *must-child* (*may-child*) of the node n if there exists a must-edge (may-edge) (n, n'). A *must-SCC* (*may-SCC*) is an SCC in which all progress edges are must-edges (may-edges).

The game-graph is partitioned into its may-Maximal SCCs (may-MSCCs), denoted Q_i's. This partition induces a partial order $\leq$ on the Q_i's, such that edges go out of a set Q_i only to itself or to a smaller set Q_j. The partial order is extended to a total order $\leq$ arbitrarily. The *coloring algorithm* processes the Q_i's according to $\leq$, bottom-up. Let Q_i be the smallest set that is not fully colored. The nodes of Q_i are colored in two phases, as follows.
Phase 1. Apply these rules to all nodes in Q_i until none of them is applicable.

- A terminal node C is colored: by T if Player $\exists$ wins in it (when $C = (s, true)$ or $C = (s, a)$ with $a \in L(s)$ or $C = (s, \neg a)$ with $a \notin L(s)$); and by F if Player $\forall$ wins in it (when $C = (s, false)$ or $C = (s, a)$ with $a \notin L(s)$ or $C = (s, \neg a)$ with $a \in L(s)$).
- An $A\bigcirc$ node is colored: by T if all its may-children are colored by T; by F if it has a must-child colored by F; by ? if all its must-children are colored by T or ?, and it has a may-child colored by F or ?.
- An $E\bigcirc$ node is colored: by T if it has a must-child colored by T; by F if all its may-children are colored by F; by ? if it has a may-child colored by T or ?, and all its must-children are colored by F or ?.
- An $\wedge$-node ($\vee$-node) is colored: by T (F) if both its children are colored by T (F); by F (T) if it has a child that is colored by F (T); by ? if it has a child colored by ? and the other child is colored by ? or T (F).

Phase 2. If after propagation of the rules of Phase 1, there are still nodes in Q_i that remain uncolored, then Q_i must be a non-trivial may-MSCC that has exactly one witness. We consider two cases.

Case U. The witness is of the form $A(\Phi_1 \mathsf{U} \Phi_2)$ or $E(\Phi_1 \mathsf{U} \Phi_2)$.

Phase 2a. Repeatedly color by ? each node in Q_i that satisfies one of the following conditions, until there is no change:
(1) An $A\bigcirc$ node that all its must-children are colored by T or ?; (2) An $E\bigcirc$ node that has a may-child colored by T or ?; (3) An $\wedge$ node that both its children are colored T or ?; (4) An $\vee$ node that has a child colored by T or ?. In fact, each node for which the F option is no longer possible according to the rules of Phase 1 is colored by ?.

Phase 2b. Color the remaining nodes in Q_i by F.

Case V. The witness is of the form $A(\Phi_1 \mathsf{V} \Phi_2)$ or $E(\Phi_1 \mathsf{V} \Phi_2)$ (see [16, Appendix B]).

The result of the coloring is a *3-valued coloring function* $\chi : N \to \{T, F, ?\}$.

Theorem 2 ([24]). *For each* $n = (s, \Phi') \in G_{\mathcal{M} \times \Phi}$*:*

(1) $[(\mathcal{M}, s) \models^3 \Phi'] = tt$ *iff* $\chi(n) = T$ *iff Player* $\exists$ *has a winning strategy at* n.
(2) $[(\mathcal{M}, s) \models^3 \Phi'] = ff$ *iff* $\chi(n) = F$ *iff Player* $\forall$ *has a winning strategy at* n.

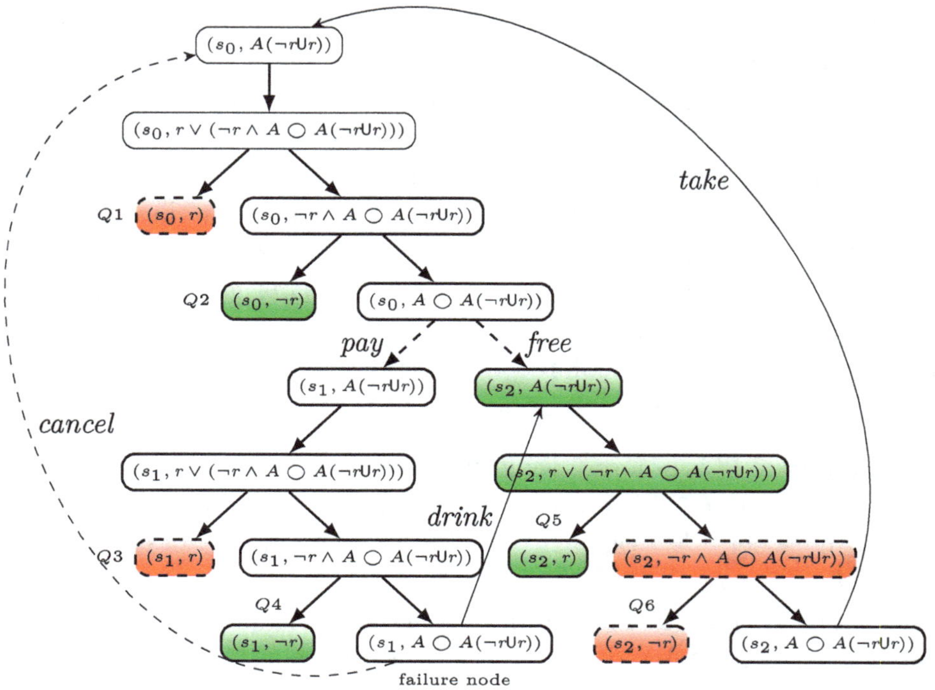

Fig. 4. The colored game-graph for $\boldsymbol{\alpha}^{\text{join}}(\text{VENDMACH})$ and $\Phi_1 = A(\neg r \mathsf{U} r)$. (Color figure online)

(3) $[(\mathcal{M}, s) \models^3 \Phi'] = \bot$ *iff* $\chi(n) = ?$ *iff none of players has a winning strategy at* n.

Using Theorems 1 and 2, given the colored game-graph of the MTS $\boldsymbol{\alpha}^{\text{join}}(\mathcal{F})$, if all its initial nodes are colored by T then $[\mathcal{F} \models \Phi] = tt$, if at least one of them is colored by F then $[\mathcal{F} \models \Phi] = ff$. Otherwise, we do not know.

Example 4. The colored game-graph for the MTS $\boldsymbol{\alpha}^{\text{join}}(\text{VENDMACH})$ and $\Phi_1 = A(\neg r \mathsf{U} r)$ is shown in Fig. 4. Green, red (with dashed borders), and white nodes denote nodes colored by T, F, and ?, respectively. The partitions from Q_1 to Q_6 consist of a single node shown in Fig. 4, while Q_7 contains all the other nodes. The initial node (s_0, Φ_1) is colored by ?, so we obtain an indefinite answer. □

5 Incremental Refinement Framework

Given an FTS $\pi_{\mathbb{K}'}(\mathcal{F})$ with a configuration set $\mathbb{K}' \subseteq \mathbb{K}$, we show how to exploit the game-graph of the abstract MTS $\mathcal{M} = \boldsymbol{\alpha}^{\text{join}}(\pi_{\mathbb{K}'}(\mathcal{F}))$ in order to do refinement in case that the model checking resulted in an indefinite answer. The refinement consists of two parts. First, we use the information gained by the coloring algorithm of $G_{\mathcal{M} \times \Phi}$ in order to split the single abstract configuration $\mathit{true} \in \boldsymbol{\alpha}^{\text{join}}(\mathbb{K}')$ that represents the whole concrete configuration set $\mathbb{K}'$. We then construct the refined abstract models, using the refined abstract configurations.

Algorithm. `Verify`$(\mathcal{F}, \mathbb{K}, \Phi)$

1 Check by game-based model checking algorithm $[\boldsymbol{\alpha}^{\text{join}}(\mathcal{F}) \models^3 \Phi]$?
2 If the result is *tt*, then return that Φ is satisfied for all variants in $\mathbb{K}$. If the result is *ff*, then return that Φ is violated for all variants in $\mathbb{K}$.
3 Otherwise, an indefinite result is returned. Let the may-edge from $n = (s, \Phi_1)$ to $n' = (s', \Phi_1')$ be the reason for failure, and let ψ be the feature expression guarding the transition from s to s' in $\mathcal{F}$. We generate $\mathcal{F}_1 = \pi_{[\![\psi]\!]}(\mathcal{F})$ and $\mathcal{F}_2 = \pi_{[\![\neg\psi]\!]}(\mathcal{F})$, and call `Verify`$(\mathcal{F}_1, \mathbb{K} \cap [\![\psi]\!], \Phi)$ and `Verify`$(\mathcal{F}_2, \mathbb{K} \cap [\![\neg\psi]\!], \Phi)$.

Fig. 5. The refinement procedure that checks $[\mathcal{F} \models \Phi]$.

There are a failure node and a failure reason associated with an indefinite answer. The goal in the refinement is to find and eliminate at least one of the failure reasons.

Definition 5. *A node n is a* failure node *if it is colored by ?, whereas none of its children was colored by ? at the time n got colored by the coloring algorithm.*

Such failure node can be seen as the point where the loss of information occurred, so we can use it in the refinement step to change the final model checking result.

Lemma 1 ([24])**.** *A failure node is one of the following.*

- *An $A\bigcirc$-node ($E\bigcirc$-node) that has a may-child colored by F (T).*
- *An $A\bigcirc$-node ($E\bigcirc$-node) that was colored during Phase 2a based on an AU (AV) witness, and has a may-child colored by ?.*

Given a failure node $n = (s, \Phi)$, suppose that its may-child is $n' = (s', \Phi_1')$ as identified in Lemma 1. Then the may-edge from n to n' is considered as *the failure reason.* Since the failure reason is a may-transition in the abstract MTS $\boldsymbol{\alpha}^{\text{join}}(\pi_{\mathbb{K}'}(\mathcal{F}))$, it needs to be refined in order to result either in a must transition or no transition at all. Let $s \xrightarrow{\alpha/\psi} s'$ be the transition in the concrete model $\pi_{\mathbb{K}'}(\mathcal{F})$ corresponding to the above (failure) may-transition. We split the configuration space $\mathbb{K}'$ into $[\![\psi]\!]$ and $[\![\neg\psi]\!]$ subsets, and we partition $\pi_{\mathbb{K}'}(\mathcal{F})$ in $\pi_{[\![\psi]\!]\cap\mathbb{K}'}(\mathcal{F})$ and $\pi_{[\![\neg\psi]\!]\cap\mathbb{K}'}(\mathcal{F})$. Then, we repeat the verification process based on abstract models $\boldsymbol{\alpha}^{\text{join}}(\pi_{[\![\psi]\!]\cap\mathbb{K}'}(\mathcal{F}))$ and $\boldsymbol{\alpha}^{\text{join}}(\pi_{[\![\neg\psi]\!]\cap\mathbb{K}'}(\mathcal{F}))$. Note that, in the former, $\boldsymbol{\alpha}^{\text{join}}(\pi_{[\![\psi]\!]\cap\mathbb{K}'}(\mathcal{F}))$, $s \xrightarrow{\alpha} s'$ becomes a must-transition, while in the latter, $\boldsymbol{\alpha}^{\text{join}}(\pi_{[\![\neg\psi]\!]\cap\mathbb{K}'}(\mathcal{F}))$, $s \xrightarrow{\alpha} s'$ is removed. The complete refinement procedure is shown in Fig. 5. We prove that (see [16, Appendix A]):

Theorem 3. *The procedure* `Verify`$(\mathcal{F}, \mathbb{K}, \Phi)$ *terminates and is correct.*

Example 5. We can do a failure analysis on the game-graph of $\boldsymbol{\alpha}^{\text{join}}$(VENDMACH) in Fig. 4. The failure node is $(s_1, A \bigcirc A(\neg r \mathsf{U} r))$ and the reason is the may-edge $(s_1, A \bigcirc A(\neg r \mathsf{U} r)) \xrightarrow{cancel} (s_0, A(\neg r \mathsf{U} r))$. The corresponding concrete transition in VENDMACH is $s_1 \xrightarrow{cancel/c} s_0$. So, we partition the configuration space $\mathbb{K}^{\text{VM}}$ into subsets $[\![c]\!]$ and $[\![\neg c]\!]$, and in the next second iteration we consider FTSs $\pi_{[\![c]\!]}$(VENDMACH) and $\pi_{[\![\neg c]\!]}$(VENDMACH). □

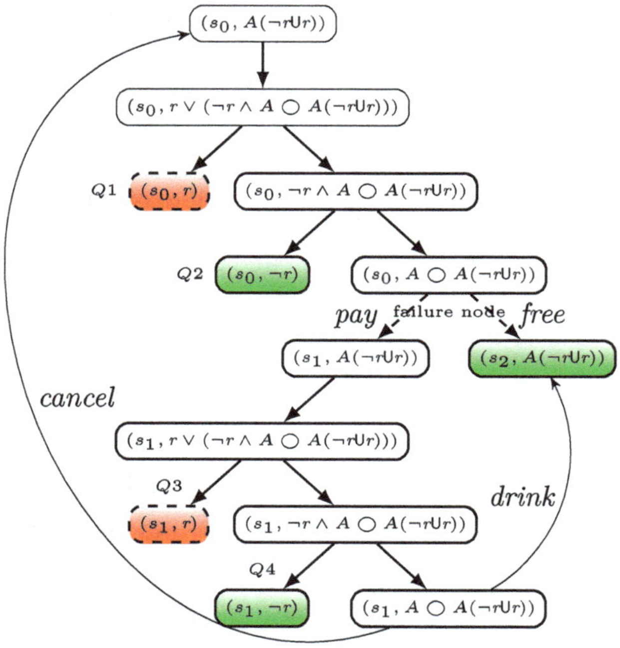

Fig. 6. $G_{\alpha^{\text{join}}(\pi_{[\![c]\!]}(\text{VENDMACH})) \times \Phi_1}$.

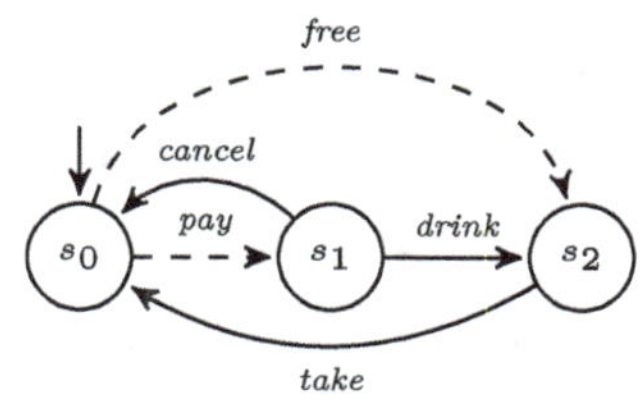

Fig. 7. $\alpha^{\text{join}}(\pi_{[\![c]\!]}(\text{VENDMACH}))$

The game-based model checking algorithm provides us with a convenient framework to use results from previous iterations and avoid unnecessary calculations. At the end of the i-th iteration of abstraction-refinement, we remember those nodes that were colored by definite colors. Let D denote the set of such nodes. Let $\chi_D : D \to \{T, F\}$ be the coloring function that maps each node in D to its definite color. The incremental approach uses this information both in the construction of the game-graph and its coloring. During the construction of a new refined game-graph performed in a BFS manner in the next $i+1$-th iteration, we prune the game-graph in nodes that are from D. When a node $n \in D$ is encountered, we add n to the game-graph and do not continue to construct the game-graph from n onwards. That is, $n \in D$ is considered as terminal node and colored by its previous color. As a result of this pruning, only the reachable sub-graph that was previously colored by ? is refined.

Example 6. The property Φ_1 holds for $\pi_{[\![\neg c]\!]}(\text{VENDMACH})$. The initial node of the game-graph $G_{\alpha^{\text{join}}(\pi_{[\![\neg c]\!]}(\text{VENDMACH})) \times \Phi_1}$ (see [16, Fig. 13, Appendix C]), is colored by T. On the other hand, we obtain an indefinite answer for $\pi_{[\![c]\!]}(\text{VENDMACH})$. The model $\alpha^{\text{join}}(\pi_{[\![c]\!]}(\text{VENDMACH}))$ is shown in Fig. 7, whereas the final colored game-graph $G_{\alpha^{\text{join}}(\pi_{[\![c]\!]}(\text{VENDMACH})) \times \Phi_1}$ is given in Fig. 6. The failure node is $(s_0, A \bigcirc A(\neg r \mathsf{U} r))$, and the reason is the may-edge $(s_0, A \bigcirc A(\neg r \mathsf{U} r)) \xrightarrow{pay} (s_1, A(\neg r \mathsf{U} r))$. The corresponding concrete transition in $\pi_{[\![c]\!]}(\text{VENDMACH})$ is $s_0 \xrightarrow{pay/\neg f} s_1$. So, in the next third iteration we consider FTSs $\pi_{[\![c \wedge \neg f]\!]}(\text{VENDMACH})$ and $\pi_{[\![c \wedge f]\!]}(\text{VENDMACH})$.

The initial node of the graph $G_{\alpha^{\text{join}}(\pi_{[\![c \wedge \neg f]\!]}(\text{VENDMACH})) \times \Phi_1}$ (see [16, Fig. 16, Appendix C]) is colored by F in Phase 2b. The initial node of $G_{\alpha^{\text{join}}(\pi_{[\![c \wedge f]\!]}(\text{VENDMACH})) \times \Phi_1}$ (see [16, Fig. 17, Appendix C]) is colored by T.

In the end, we conclude that Φ_1 is satisfied by the variants $\{\neg c \wedge \neg f, \neg c \wedge f, c \wedge f\}$, and Φ is violated by the variant $\{c \wedge \neg f\}$.

On the other hand, we need two iterations to conclude that $\Phi_2 = E(\neg r \mathsf{U} r)$ is satisfied by all variants in $\mathbb{K}^{\mathrm{VM}}$ (see [16, Appendix D] for details). □

6 Evaluation

To evaluate our approach, we use a synthetic example to demonstrate specific characteristics of our approach, and the ELEVATOR model which is often used as benchmark in SPL community [4,12,15,20,23]. We compare (1) our abstraction-refinement procedure `Verify` with the game-based model checking algorithm implemented in Java from scratch vs. (2) family-based version of the NUSMVmodel checker, denoted fNUSMV, which implements the standard lifted model checking algorithm [5]. For each experiment, we measure T(IME) to perform an analysis task, and CALL which is the number of times an approach calls the model checking engine. All experiments were executed on a 64-bit Intel®Core^{TM} i5-3337U CPU running at 1.80 GHz with 8 GB memory. All experimental data is available from: https://aleksdimovski.github.io/automatic-ctl.html.

Synthetic example. The FTS M_n (where $n > 0$) consists of n features $A_1, \ldots, A_n$ and an integer data variable x, such that the set AP consists of all evaluations of x which assign nonnegative integer values to x. The set of valid configurations is $\mathbb{K}_n = 2^{\{A_1,\ldots,A_n\}}$. M_n has a tree-like structure, where in the root is the initial state with $x = 0$. In each level k ($k \geq 1$), there are two states that can be reached with two transitions leading from a state from a previous level. One transition is allowable for variants with the feature A_k enabled, so that in the target state the variable's value is $x + 2^{k-1}$ where x is its value in the source state, whereas the other transition is allowable for variants with A_k disabled, so that the value of x does not change. For example, M_2 is shown in Fig. 8, where in each state we show the current value of x and all transitions have the silent action τ.

We consider two properties: $\Phi = A(\mathit{true}\,\mathsf{U}(x \geq 0))$ and $\Phi' = A(\mathit{true}\,\mathsf{U}(x \geq 1))$. The property Φ is satisfied by all variants in $\mathbb{K}$, whereas Φ' is violated only by one configuration $\neg A_1 \wedge \ldots \wedge \neg A_n$ (where all features are disabled). We have verified M_n against Φ and Φ' using fNUSMV (e.g. see fNUSMVmodels for M_1 and M_2 in [16, Fig. 23, Appendix E]). We have also checked M_n using our `Verify` procedure. For Φ, `Verify` terminates in one iteration since $\boldsymbol{\alpha}^{\mathrm{join}}(M_n)$ satisfies Φ (see $G_{\boldsymbol{\alpha}^{\mathrm{join}}(M_1)\times\Phi}$ in [16, Fig. 24, Appendix E]). For Φ', `Verify` needs $n+1$ iterations. First, an indefinite result is reported for $\boldsymbol{\alpha}^{\mathrm{join}}(M_n)$ (e.g. see $G_{\boldsymbol{\alpha}^{\mathrm{join}}(M_1)\times\Phi'}$ in [16, Fig. 27, Appendix E]), and the configuration space is split into $[\![\neg A_1]\!]$ and $[\![A_1]\!]$ subsets. The refinement procedure proceeds in this way until we obtain definite results for all variants. The performance results are shown in Fig. 9. Notice that, fNUSMV reports all results in only one iteration. As n grows, `Verify` becomes faster than fNUSMV. For $n = 11$ ($|\mathbb{K}| = 2^{11}$), fNUSMV timeouts after 2 h. In contrast, `Verify` is feasible even for large values of n.

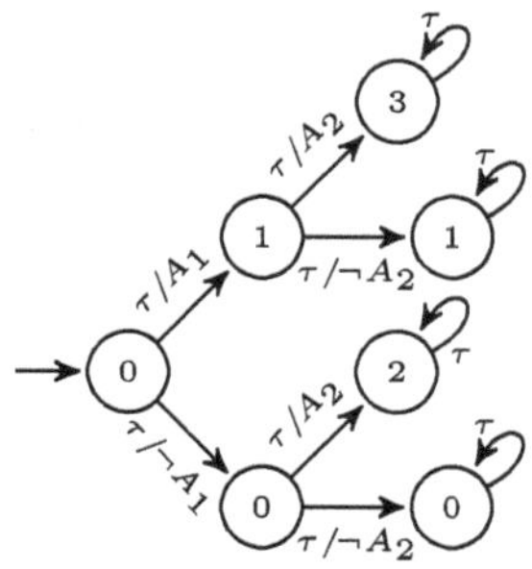

Fig. 8. The model M_2.

n	Φ				Φ'			
	fNuSMV		`Verify`		fNuSMV		`Verify`	
	Call	T	Call	T	Call	T	Call	T
2	1	0.08	1	0.07	1	0.08	5	0.83
7	1	1.64	1	0.16	1	1.68	15	2.68
10	1	992.80	1	0.68	1	1019.27	21	4.57
11	1	infeasible	1	1.42	1	infeasible	23	5.98
15	1	infeasible	1	26.55	1	infeasible	31	41.64

Fig. 9. Verification of M_n (T in seconds).

prop- *-erty*	fNuSMV		`Verify`		*Improvement*
	Call	T	Call	T	Time
Φ_1	1	15.22 s	1	0.55 s	28 ×
Φ_2	1	1.59 s	1	0.59 s	2.7 ×
Φ_3	1	1.76 s	1	0.67 s	2.6 ×

Fig. 10. Verification of Elevator properties (T in seconds).

Elevator. We have experimented with the Elevator model with four floors, designed by Plath and Ryan [23]. It contains about 300 LOC of fNuSMV code and 9 independent optional features that modify the basic behaviour of the elevator, thus yielding $2^9 = 512$ variants. To use our `Verify` procedure, we have manually translated the fNuSMV model into an FTS and then we have called `Verify` on it. The basic Elevator system consists of a single lift that travels between four floors. There are four platform buttons and a single lift, which declares variables *floor*, *door*, *direction*, and a further four cabin buttons. When serving a floor, the lift door opens and closes again. We consider three properties "$\Phi_1 = E(tt\,\mathsf{U}(floor{=}1 \land idle \land door{=}closed))$", "$\Phi_2 = A(tt\,\mathsf{U}(floor{=}1 \land idle \land door{=}closed))$", and "$\Phi_3 = E(tt\,\mathsf{U}((floor{=}3 \land \neg liftBut3.pressed \land direction{=}up) \implies door = closed))$". The performance results are shown in Fig. 10. The properties Φ_1 and Φ_2 are satisfied by all variants, so `Verify` achieves speed-ups of 28 times for Φ_1 and 2.7 times for Φ_2 compared to the fNuSMV approach. fNuSMV takes 1.76 sec to check Φ_3, whereas `Verify` ends in 0.67 sec thus giving 2.6 times performance speed-up.

7 Related Work and Conclusion

There are different formalisms for representing variability models [2,21]. Classen et al. [4] present Featured Transition Systems (FTSs). They show how specifically designed lifted model checking algorithms [5,7] can be used for verifying FTSs against LTL and CTL properties. The variability abstractions that preserve LTL are introduced in [14,15,17], and subsequently automatic abstraction refinement procedures [8,18] for lifted model checking of LTL are proposed, by using Craig interpolation to define the refinement. The variability abstractions that preserve the full CTL are introduced in [12], but they are constructed manually and no notion of refinement is defined there. In this paper, we define an automatic abstraction refinement procedure for lifted model checking of full CTL by using games to define the refinement. To the best of our knowledge, this is the first such procedure in lifted model checking.

One of the earliest attempts for using games for CTL model checking has been proposed by Stirling [26]. Shoham and Grumberg [3,19,24,25] have extended this game-based approach for CTL over 3-valued semantics. In this work, we exploit and apply the game-based approach in a completely new direction, for automatic CTL verification of variability models.

The works [11,13] present an approach for software lifted model checking of `#ifdef`-based program families using symbolic game semantics models [10].

To conclude, in this work we present a game-based lifted model checking for abstract variability models with respect to the full CTL. We also suggest an automatic refinement procedure, in case the model checking result is indefinite.

References

1. Baier, C., Katoen, J.: Principles of Model Checking. MIT Press, Cambridge (2008)
2. ter Beek, M.H., Fantechi, A., Gnesi, S., Mazzanti, F.: Modelling and analysing variability in product families: model checking of modal transition systems with variability constraints. J. Log. Algebr. Methods Program. **85**(2), 287–315 (2016). https://doi.org/10.1016/j.jlamp.2015.09.004
3. Campetelli, A., Gruler, A., Leucker, M., Thoma, D.: *Don't Know* for multi-valued systems. In: Liu, Z., Ravn, A.P. (eds.) ATVA 2009. LNCS, vol. 5799, pp. 289–305. Springer, Heidelberg (2009). https://doi.org/10.1007/978-3-642-04761-9_22
4. Classen, A., Cordy, M., Schobbens, P., Heymans, P., Legay, A., Raskin, J.: Featured transition systems: foundations for verifying variability-intensive systems and their application to LTL model checking. IEEE Trans. Softw. Eng. **39**(8), 1069–1089 (2013). http://doi.ieeecomputersociety.org/10.1109/TSE.2012.86
5. Classen, A., Heymans, P., Schobbens, P.Y., Legay, A.: Symbolic model checking of software product lines. In: Proceedings of the 33rd International Conference on Software Engineering, ICSE 2011, pp. 321–330. ACM (2011). http://doi.acm.org/10.1145/1985793.1985838
6. Clements, P., Northrop, L.: Software Product Lines: Practices and Patterns. Addison-Wesley, Boston (2001)
7. Cordy, M., Classen, A., Heymans, P., Schobbens, P., Legay, A.: Provelines: a product line of verifiers for software product lines. In: 17th International SPLC 2013 Workshops, pp. 141–146. ACM (2013). http://doi.acm.org/10.1145/2499777.2499781
8. Cordy, M., Heymans, P., Legay, A., Schobbens, P., Dawagne, B., Leucker, M.: Counterexample guided abstraction refinement of product-line behavioural models. In: Proceedings of the 22nd ACM SIGSOFT International Symposium on Foundations of Software Engineering, (FSE-22), pp. 190–201. ACM (2014). http://doi.acm.org/10.1145/2635868.2635919

9. Cousot, P.: Partial completeness of abstract fixpoint checking. In: Choueiry, B.Y., Walsh, T. (eds.) SARA 2000. LNCS (LNAI), vol. 1864, pp. 1–25. Springer, Heidelberg (2000). https://doi.org/10.1007/3-540-44914-0_1
10. Dimovski, A.S.: Program verification using symbolic game semantics. Theor. Comput. Sci. **560**, 364–379 (2014). https://doi.org/10.1016/j.tcs.2014.01.016
11. Dimovski, A.S.: Symbolic game semantics for model checking program families. In: Bošnački, D., Wijs, A. (eds.) SPIN 2016. LNCS, vol. 9641, pp. 19–37. Springer, Cham (2016). https://doi.org/10.1007/978-3-319-32582-8_2
12. Dimovski, A.S.: Abstract family-based model checking using modal featured transition systems: preservation of CTL*. In: Russo, A., Schürr, A. (eds.) FASE 2018. LNCS, vol. 10802, pp. 301–318. Springer, Cham (2018). https://doi.org/10.1007/978-3-319-89363-1_17
13. Dimovski, A.S.: Verifying annotated program families using symbolic game semantics. Theor. Comput. Sci. **706**, 35–53 (2018). https://doi.org/10.1016/j.tcs.2017.09.029
14. Dimovski, A.S., Al-Sibahi, A.S., Brabrand, C., Wąsowski, A.: Family-based model checking without a family-based model checker. In: Fischer, B., Geldenhuys, J. (eds.) SPIN 2015. LNCS, vol. 9232, pp. 282–299. Springer, Cham (2015). https://doi.org/10.1007/978-3-319-23404-5_18
15. Dimovski, A.S., Al-Sibahi, A.S., Brabrand, C., Wasowski, A.: Efficient family-based model checking via variability abstractions. STTT **19**(5), 585–603 (2017). https://doi.org/10.1007/s10009-016-0425-2
16. Dimovski, A.S., Legay, A., Wasowski, A.: Variability abstraction and refinement for game-based lifted model checking of full CTL (extended version). CoRR (2019). http://arxiv.org/
17. Dimovski, A.S., Wąsowski, A.: From transition systems to variability models and from lifted model checking back to UPPAAL. In: Aceto, L., Bacci, G., Bacci, G., Ingólfsdóttir, A., Legay, A., Mardare, R. (eds.) Models, Algorithms, Logics and Tools. LNCS, vol. 10460, pp. 249–268. Springer, Cham (2017). https://doi.org/10.1007/978-3-319-63121-9_13
18. Dimovski, A.S., Wąsowski, A.: Variability-specific abstraction refinement for family-based model checking. In: Huisman, M., Rubin, J. (eds.) FASE 2017. LNCS, vol. 10202, pp. 406–423. Springer, Heidelberg (2017). https://doi.org/10.1007/978-3-662-54494-5_24
19. Grumberg, O., Lange, M., Leucker, M., Shoham, S.: When not losing is better than winning: abstraction and refinement for the full mu-calculus. Inf. Comput. **205**(8), 1130–1148 (2007). https://doi.org/10.1016/j.ic.2006.10.009
20. Iosif-Lazar, A.F., Melo, J., Dimovski, A.S., Brabrand, C., Wasowski, A.: Effective analysis of c programs by rewriting variability. Program. J. **1**(1), 1 (2017). https://doi.org/10.22152/programming-journal.org/2017/1/1
21. Larsen, K.G., Nyman, U., Wąsowski, A.: Modal I/O automata for interface and product line theories. In: De Nicola, R. (ed.) ESOP 2007. LNCS, vol. 4421, pp. 64–79. Springer, Heidelberg (2007). https://doi.org/10.1007/978-3-540-71316-6_6
22. Larsen, K.G., Thomsen, B.: A modal process logic. In: Proceedings of the Third Annual Symposium on Logic in Computer Science (LICS 1988), pp. 203–210. IEEE Computer Society (1988). http://dx.doi.org/10.1109/LICS.1988.5119
23. Plath, M., Ryan, M.: Feature integration using a feature construct. Sci. Comput. Program. **41**(1), 53–84 (2001). https://doi.org/10.1016/S0167-6423(00)00018-6
24. Shoham, S., Grumberg, O.: A game-based framework for CTL counterexamples and 3-valued abstraction-refinement. ACM Trans. Comput. Log. **9**(1), 1 (2007). https://doi.org/10.1145/1297658.1297659

25. Shoham, S., Grumberg, O.: Compositional verification and 3-valued abstractions join forces. Inf. Comput. **208**(2), 178–202 (2010). https://doi.org/10.1016/j.ic.2009.10.002
26. Stirling, C.: Modal and Temporal Properties of Processes. Texts in Computer Science. Springer, New York (2001). https://doi.org/10.1007/978-1-4757-3550-5

Formal Verification of Safety & Security Related Timing Constraints for a Cooperative Automotive System

Li Huang[1] and Eun-Young Kang[2(✉)]

[1] School of Data and Computer Science, Sun Yat-Sen University, Guangzhou, China
huangl223@mail2.sysu.edu.cn
[2] The Maersk Mc-Kinney Moller Institute, University of Southern Denmark, Odense, Denmark
eyk@mmmi.sdu.dk

Abstract. Modeling and analysis of timing constraints is crucial in real-time automotive systems. Modern vehicles are interconnected through wireless networks which creates vulnerabilities to external malicious attacks. Violations of cyber-security can cause safety related accidents and serious damages. To identify the potential impacts of security related threats on safety properties of interconnected automotive systems, this paper presents analysis techniques that support verification and validation (V&V) of safety & security (S/S) related timing constraints on those systems: Probabilistic extension of S/S timing constraints are specified in PrCCSL (probabilistic extension of clock constraint specification language) and the semantics of the extended constraints are translated into verifiable UPPAAL models with stochastic semantics for formal verification. A set of mapping rules are proposed to facilitate the translation. An automatic translation tool, namely ProTL, is implemented based on the mapping rules. Formal verification are performed on the S/S timing constraints using UPPAAL-SMC under different attack scenarios. Our approach is demonstrated on a cooperative automotive system case study.

Keywords: Automotive system · Safety and security · PrCCSL · UPPAAL-SMC

1 Introduction

Model based development (MBD) is rigorously applied in automotive systems in which the software controllers interact with physical environments. The continuous time behaviors of those systems often rely on complex dynamics as well as on stochastic behaviors. Formal verification and validation (V&V) technologies are indispensable and highly recommended for development of safe and reliable automotive systems [11, 12]. Conventional V&V, i.e., testing and model checking have limitations in terms of assessing the reliability of hybrid systems due to both stochastic and non-linear dynamical features. To ensure the reliability of safety

R. Hähnle and W. van der Aalst (Eds.): FASE 2019, LNCS 11424, pp. 210–227, 2019.
https://doi.org/10.1007/978-3-030-16722-6_12

critical hybrid dynamic systems, *statistical model checking (SMC)* techniques have been proposed [7,8,19]. These techniques for fully stochastic models validate probabilistic performance properties of given deterministic (or stochastic) controllers in given stochastic environments.

Modern vehicles are being equipped with communication devices and interconnected with each other through wireless networks. Vehicular Ad Hoc Networks (VANET) [28] are the technologies of wireless networks that establish communication among vehicles and roadside units (RSU). Nevertheless vehicular communication contributes to the safety and efficiency of traffic, it introduces vulnerabilities to vehicles. Transmitted information can be corrupted or modified by attackers, resulting in serious safety consequences (e.g., rear-end collision). Analysis of the potential impacts of cyber-security violations on safety properties is crucial in automotive systems. However, traditional automotive system design often addresses the correctness of safety properties without consideration of security breaches. There is still a lack of techniques that enable an integrated analysis of safety & security (S/S) properties. Moreover, message transmission in VANET that pertains to S/S requires restrictions by time deadlines [10]. In this paper, we focus on S/S related timing constraints and propose analysis techniques that support formal verification on interconnected automotive systems.

EAST-ADL [9,22] is an architectural description language for modeling of automotive systems. The latest release of EAST-ADL has adopted the time model proposed in Timing Augmented Description Language (TADL2) [5], which expresses and composes basic timing constraints, i.e., repetition rates, end-to-end delays. TADL2 specializes the time model of MARTE, the UML profile for Modeling and Analysis of Real-Time and Embedded systems [30]. MARTE provides CCSL, a Clock Constraint Specification Language, that supports specification of both logical and dense timing constraints, as well as functional causality constraints [16,23]. A probabilistic extension of CCSL, called PrCCSL [14], has been proposed to formally specify timing constraints associated with stochastic properties in weakly-hard real-time systems [4], i.e., a bounded number of constraints violations would not lead to system failures when the results of the violations are negligible.

In this paper, we present a formal analysis of S/S related timing constraints for interconnected automotive systems at the design level: 1. To identify vulnerabilities of automotive systems under malicious attacks, we adopt and modify the behavioral model of a cooperative automotive system (CAS) [13] in UPPAAL-SMC by adding it with the models of an RSU-aided (RAISE) communication protocol in VANET and malicious attacks. The modification results in a refined behavioral model of the system, i.e., more details in terms of vehicular communication and security breaches are depicted; 2. Probabilistic extension of S/S timing constraints are specified in PrCCSL and the semantics of the extended constraints are translated into verifiable models with stochastic semantics for formal verification; 3. A set of mapping rules are proposed to facilitate the translation, based on which an automatic translation tool ProTL is implemented;

4. Formal verification is performed on the S/S timing constraints using UPPAAL-SMC under different attack scenarios.

The paper is organized as follows: Sect. 2 presents an overview of PrCCSL and UPPAAL-SMC. CAS is introduced as a running example in Sect. 3. Section 4.1 presents the UPPAAL-SMC model of CAS complemented with model of RAISE protocol and three types of attacks. S/S related timing constraints are specified in PrCCSL and translated into verifiable UPPAAL-SMC models in Sect. 5. The applicability of our approach is demonstrated by performing verification on CAS case study in Sect. 6. Sections 7 and 8 present related works and conclusion.

2 Preliminary

In our framework, S/S related timing constraints are specified in PrCCSL. UPPAAL-SMC is employed to perform formal verification on the timing constraints.

2.1 Probabilistic Extension of Clock Constraint Specification Language (PrCCSL)

PrCCSL [14] is a probabilistic extension of CCSL [3,23] for formal specification of timing constraints associated with stochastic behaviors. In PrCCSL, a clock represents a sequence of (possibly infinite) instants. An event is a clock and the occurrences of an event correspond to a set of ticks of the clock. PrCCSL provides two types of clock constraints, i.e., *expressions* and *relations*, to specify the progression/occurrences of clocks. An *expression* derives new clocks from the already defined clocks [3]. Let $c1, c2 \in C$, `ITE` (if-then-else) *expression*, denoted as $\beta \ ? \ c1 : c2$, defines a new clock that behaves either as $c1$ or as $c2$ according to the value of the boolean variable/formula β. `DelayFor` (denoted $ref \ (d) \rightsquigarrow base$) results in a new clock by delaying the reference clock ref for d ticks (or d time units) of a $base$ clock. `FilterBy` ($c \triangleq base \blacktriangledown u(v)$) builds a new clock c by filtering the instants of a *base* clock according to a binary word $w{=}u(v)$, where u is the *prefix* and v is the *period*. "*(v)*" denotes the infinite repetition of v. This expression results in a clock c that $\forall \ k \ \in N^{+}$, if the kth bit in w is 1, then at the kth tick of *base*, c ticks.

A *relation* limits the occurrences among different events, which are defined based on `run` and `history`. A `run` corresponds to an execution of the system model where the clocks tick/progress. The history of a clock c represents the number of times the clock c has ticked prior to the current step.

Definition 1 (Run). *A* `run` *R consists of a finite set of consecutive steps where a set of clocks tick at each step i. The set of clocks ticking at step i is denoted as $R(i)$, i.e., for all i, $0 \leqslant i \leqslant n$, $R(i) \in R$, where n is the number of steps of R.*

Definition 2 (History). *The* `history` *of clock c in a run R is a function: H_R^c: $\mathbb{N} \rightarrow \mathbb{N}$. $H_R^c(i)$ indicates the number of times the clock c has ticked prior to step i in run R, which is initialized as 0 at step 0. It is defined as: (1) $H_R^c(0) = 0$;*

(2) $\forall\ i \in \mathbb{N}^+,\ c \notin R(i) \implies H_R^c(i+1) = H_R^c(i)$; *(3)* $\forall\ i \in \mathbb{N}^+,\ c \in R(i) \implies H_R^c(i+1) = H_R^c(i)\ +\ 1$.

A probabilistic *relation* in PrCCSL is satisfied if and only if the probability of the *relation* constraint being satisfied is greater than or equal to the probability threshold $p \in [0,\ 1]$. Given k `runs` $= \{R_1, \ldots, R_k\}$, the probabilistic `subclock`, `coincidence`, `exclusion` and `precedence` in PrCCSL are defined as follows:

Probabilistic Subclock: $c1 \subseteq_p c2 \iff Pr[c1 \subseteq c2] \geqslant p$, where $Pr[c1 \subseteq c2] = \frac{1}{k}\sum_{j=1}^{k}\{R_j \models c1 \subseteq c2\}$, representing the ratio of `runs` that satisfies the relation out of k `runs`. A `run` R_j satisfies the `subclock` relation between $c1$ and $c2$ "if $c1$ ticks, $c2$ must tick" holds at every step i in R_j, s.t., $(R_j \models c1 \subseteq c2) \iff (\forall i\ 0 \leqslant i \leqslant n,\ c1 \in R(i) \implies c2 \in R(i))$. "$R_j \models c1 \subseteq c2$" returns 1 if R_j satisfies $c1 \subseteq c2$, otherwise it returns 0.

Probabilistic Coincidence: $c1 \equiv_p c2 \iff Pr[c1 \equiv c2] \geqslant p$, where $Pr[c1 \equiv c2] = \frac{1}{k}\sum_{j=1}^{k}\{R_j \models c1 \equiv c2\}$, which represents the ratio of `runs` that satisfies the `coincidence` relation out of k `runs`. A `run`, R_j satisfies the `coincidence` relation on $c1$ and $c2$ if the assertion holds: $\forall i,\ 0 \leqslant i \leqslant n,\ (c1 \in R(i) \implies c2 \in R(i)) \wedge (c2 \in R(i) \implies c1 \in R(i))$. In other words, the satisfaction of `coincidence` relation is established when the two conditions "if $c1$ ticks, $c2$ must tick" and "if $c2$ ticks, $c1$ must tick" hold at every step.

Probabilistic Exclusion: $c1 \#_p c2 \iff Pr[c1 \# c2] \geqslant p$, where $Pr[c1 \# c2] = \frac{1}{k}\sum_{j=1}^{k}\{R_j \models c1 \# c2\}$, indicating the ratio of `runs` that satisfies the `exclusion` relation out of k `runs`. A `run`, R_j, satisfies the `exclusion` relation on $c1$ and $c2$ if $\forall i,\ 0 \leqslant i \leqslant n,\ (c1 \in R(i) \implies c2 \notin R(i)) \wedge (c2 \in R(i) \implies c1 \notin R(i))$, i.e., for every step, if $c1$ ticks, $c2$ must not tick and vice versa.

Probabilistic Precedence: $c1 \prec_p c2 \iff Pr[c1 \prec c2] \geqslant p$, where $Pr[c1 \prec c2] = \frac{1}{k}\sum_{j=1}^{k}\{R_j \models c1 \prec c2\}$, which denotes the ratio of `runs` that satisfies the `precedence` relation out of k `runs`. A `run` R_j satisfies the `precedence` relation if the condition $\forall i,\ 0 \leqslant i \leqslant n,\ (H_R^{c1}(i) \geqslant H_R^{c2}(i))$ and $(H_R^{c2}(i) = H_R^{c1}(i)) \implies (c2 \notin R(i))$ hold, i.e., the history of $c1$ is greater than or equal to the history of $c2$, and $c2$ must not tick when the history of the two clocks are equal.

2.2 UPPAAL-SMC

UPPAAL-SMC [31] performs the probabilistic analysis of properties by monitoring simulations of the complex hybrid system in a given stochastic environment and using results from the statistics to determine whether the system satisfies the property with some degree of confidence. UPPAAL-SMC provides a number of queries related to the stochastic interpretation of Timed Automata (STA)

[8] and they are as follows, where N and *bound* indicate the number of simulations to be performed and the time bound on the simulations respectively: 1. *Probability Estimation* estimates the probability of a requirement property ϕ being satisfied for a given STA model within the time bound: $Pr[bound]\ \phi$; 2. *Hypothesis Testing* checks if the probability of ϕ is satisfied within a certain probability P_0: $Pr[bound]\ \phi \geq P_0$; 3. *Simulations*: UPPAAL-SMC runs multiple simulations on the STA model and the k (state-based) properties/expressions $\phi_1, ..., \phi_k$ are monitored and visualized along the simulations: *simulate* $N\ [\leq bound]\{\phi_1, ..., \phi_k\}$.

3 Running Example

A cooperative automotive system (CAS) [13] is adopted to illustrate our approaches. CAS includes distributed and coordinated sensing, control, and actuation over three vehicles (denoted as v_i, where $i \in \{0, 1, 2\}$) which are running in the same lane. As shown in Fig. 1, a lead vehicle (v_0) runs automatically by recognizing traffic signs on the road. The following vehicle must set its desired velocity identical to that of its immediate preceding vehicle. Vehicles should maintain sufficient braking distance to avoid rear-end collision while remaining close enough to guarantee communication quality. Vehicle movement relies on availability of environmental information, e.g., traffic signs, obstacles, etc. The position of v_i is represented by Cartesian coordinate (x_i, y_i), where x_i and y_i are distances measured from the vehicle to the two fixed perpendicular lines, i.e., x-axis and y-axis, respectively.

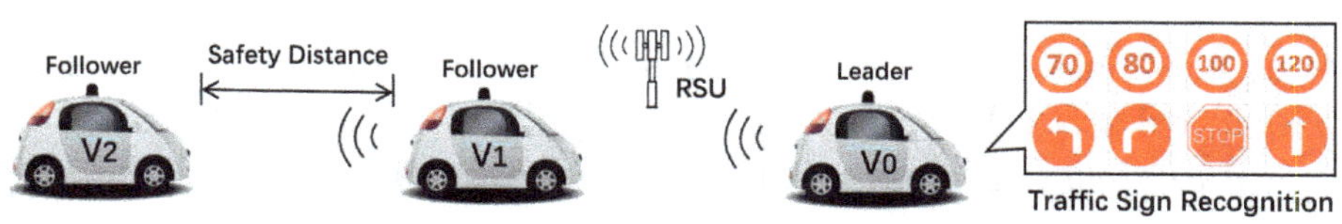

Fig. 1. Overview of Cooperative Automotive System

The cooperative driving of CAS requires prompt and secure information transmission among vehicles. We adopt a roadside unit aided (RAISE) [33] communication protocol in VANET to achieve the data transmission. Each vehicle periodically broadcasts its own position and velocity to its immediate following vehicle through wireless connection. The authentication of the identities of each vehicle and verification of messages sent by the vehicles is performed by RSU. For further details of RAISE, refer to Sect. 4.1. The following S/S properties on CAS are considered:

R1. The follower vehicle should not overtake its leading vehicle when the vehicles run at a positive direction of x-axis.

R2. When the lead vehicle detects a stop sign, all the three vehicles must stop within a given time, e.g., 2000 ms.

R3. If the distance between a vehicle and its preceding vehicle is less than minimum safety distance, the vehicle should decelerate within a certain time (200 ms).
R4. If the distance between a vehicle and its preceding vehicle is greater than the maximum safety distance (e.g., 100 m), the vehicle should accelerate within a certain time, e.g., 300 ms.
R5. When the lead vehicle starts to turn left (or turn right), the two follower vehicles should finish turning and run in the same lane within a given time.
R6. Authenticity: If a vehicle receives a message, its preceding vehicle must have sent a corresponding message before, i.e., the protocol should be resistant to message spoofing attack.
R7. Secrecy: Symmetric keys of vehicles should be kept confidential to attackers.
R8. Integrity: The content of messages must not be modified during transmission, i.e., the protocol should be resistant to message falsification attack.
R9. Freshness: The vehicles should not accept an "obsolete" message, namely, the difference between the current time and the *timestamp* of the accepted message should be less than the predefined time threshold.
R10. The symmetric key agreement (i.e., mutual authentication) process between RSU and three vehicles should be completed within a certain time, e.g., 600 ms.
R11. A vehicle should send messages to its subsequent vehicle periodically with a period 200 ms and a jitter 100 ms.

Among the above S/S requirements, R1–R5 are safety [20] properties, which specify that the system should not cause undesirable results on its environment and aim at protecting human lives, health and assets from being damaged. R6-R11 are security properties, which refer to the inability of the environment to affect the system in an undesirable way and aim to guarantee the confidentiality and integrity of transmitted information. The interdependencies among those S/S properties are conditional dependencies [17], i.e., violations of security properties can lead to the violations on safety properties. The events associated with those S/S properties can be interpreted as logical clocks in PrCCSL, which provides a way to express S/S properties in the logical time manner [16]. Therefore, S/S properties can be interpreted as logical timing constraints, i.e., the temporal and causality clock *relations* in PrCCSL.

The methodology for analysis of S/S related timing constraints in this paper can be generalized in Fig. 2. First, on the basis of the existing behavioral model of CAS described in [13], we enhance the CAS model by augmenting (parallelly composing) it with models of RAISE protocol and malicious attacks, resulting in a refined CAS model regarding vehicular communication characteristics and security-related adversary interference. Second, we specify S/S timing constraints (R1–R11) in PrCCSL and translate the PrCCSL specifications into corresponding STA and probabilistic queries. Finally, we combine the model of CAS and the STA of PrCCSL specifications, and perform formal verification based on the combined model using UPPAAL-SMC.

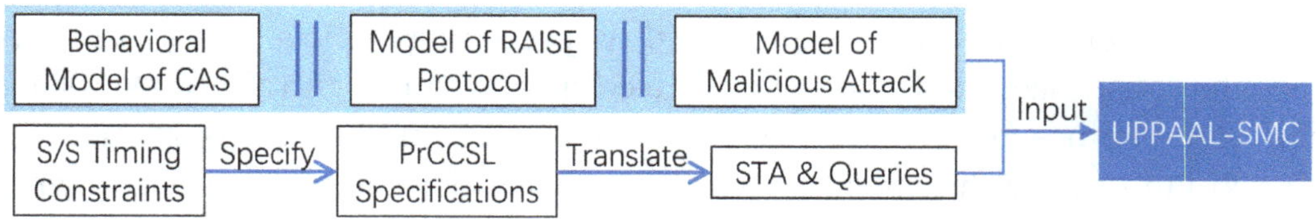

Fig. 2. Methodology for analysis of S/S timing constraints

4 Modeling and Refinement of CAS in UPPAAL-SMC

The behaviors of CAS are modeled as a network of stochastic timed automata (NSTA) in UPPAAL-SMC described in [13]. In this section, we refine the CAS model by adding it with the models of RAISE protocol and security attacks.

4.1 Modeling of RAISE Protocol in UPPAAL-SMC

We present a simplified version of RAISE protocol [33] and its UPPAAL-SMC model. The original RAISE protocol is modified to facilitate the communication mechanism of CAS, i.e., each follower vehicle receives messages from its immediate preceding vehicle and RSU. Furthermore, timing constraints are also appended to restrict the time duration of each step (e.g., encryption and decryption) during communication process. There are two phases in RAISE protocol, i.e., *symmetric key agreement* and *information transmission*.

1. **Symmetric key agreement (SKA)** is performed to obtain symmetric key k_i for guaranteeing security of communication and generates pseudo identities ID_i of vehicles for covering their real identities. The shared symmetric key between RSU and v_i is $k_i = g^{ab}$, where g, a, b are three positive random numbers. As shown in Fig. 3, $Encry(msg, k)$ ($Decry(msg, k)$) denotes the encryption (decryption) of message msg with key k, where k can be either a public key or symmetric key. $Sign(msg, k)$ generates signature of msg with a private key k. We use PK_i to denote the public key of v_i and SK_i to represent the corresponding private key. "$||$" is the concatenation operation on messages.

Initially, v_i randomly picks g and a (step 1), encrypts "$g||a$" and sends the encrypted result (m_i) to RSU (step 2). Upon receiving m_i, RSU decrypts the message (step 3). It then generates b and ID_i, signs and sends the signed message (rm_i) to v_i (step 4 and 5). v_i verifies the rm_i's signature (step 6) and sends back the signature of $g||a||b||ID_i$ (step 7). Finally, RSU verifies the signature s_i (step 8). If all the steps are completed correctly, the key agreement process succeeds.

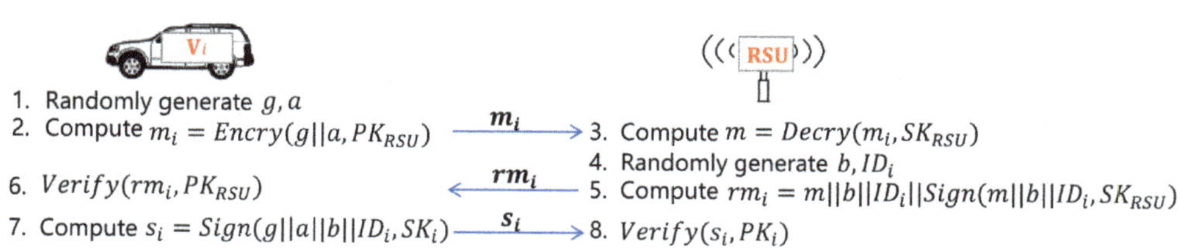

Fig. 3. Symmetric key agreement in RAISE

2. **Information transmission (IT)** initiates after the SKA is completed. The traffic information (i.e, brake, direction, position and speed) of v_i is integrated into a message $msg_i = brake_i||direction_i||x_i||y_i||speed_i$. As presented in Fig. 4, initially, v_i generates the message authentication code (MAC) of msg_i with the symmetric key k_i (generated in SKA). Then, v_i concatenates the MAC code with

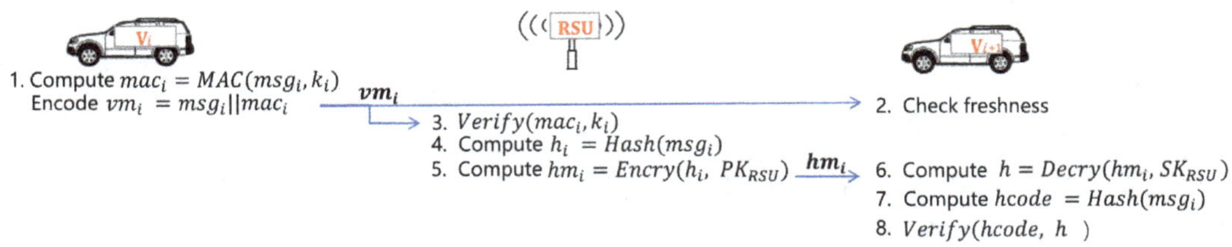

Fig. 4. Information transmission in RAISE

msg_i and sends it to *RSU* and v_{i+1} (step 1). Upon receiving vm_i, v_{i+1} checks the freshness of the message (step 2), i.e., if the time interval between the current time and the time when vm_i is sent is greater than the predefined threshold, v_{i+1} drops vm_i. At the same time, *RSU* checks the authenticity of vm_i (step 3). If mac_i is correct, *RSU* computes the hash code h_i of message msg_i (step 4). Afterwards, it encrypts h_i and sends the encrypted result hm_i to v_{i+1} (step 5). v_{i+1} decrypts hm_i and get the hash code h (step 6). Furthermore, to ensure the consistency of the message, v_{i+1} itself also computes the hash code of msg_i (step 7). It then verifies whether the hash code calculated by itself is the same as the decrypted hash code and decides to accept or reject msg_i (step 8).

To model RAISE in UPPAAL-SMC, interactions among vehicles and RSU (i.e., sending/receiving messages) are modeled by *synchronization channels* [31] and global variables. The cryptographic operations in RAISE refer to public and private key encryption and decryption, i.e., a message encrypted by public key can be decrypted using the corresponding private key, and vice versa. The automaton of `cryptographic device` [6] is adopted to model the encryption and decryption. Figure 5 presents the STA capturing behaviors of vehicle v_i and RSU in SKA. *startEn* (resp. *startDe*) and *finDe* (resp. *finEn*) are channels for indicating the starting and finishing of encryption (resp. decryption). The encryption/decryption result is denoted *en_res*/*de_res*. In the STA, names of locations indicate the corresponding steps pictured in Fig. 3.

IT phase from v_0 to v_1 is established with the help of RSU, modeled as the STA shown in Fig. 6 (the transmission from v_1 to v_2 can be modeled similarly). The behaviors of v_0 (sender), v_1 (receiver) and RSU in the IT phase are modeled in `IT_v0`, `IT_v1` and `IT_RSU` STA, respectively.

The SKA (or IT) succeeds if each step of the SKA (IT) is completed correctly within a given time interval, modeled by invariant "t $\leq$ d" (the value of d varies in different steps). If timeout occurs (i.e., "t $\geq$ d"), *fail* location will be activated and the procedure is restarted from the initial step.

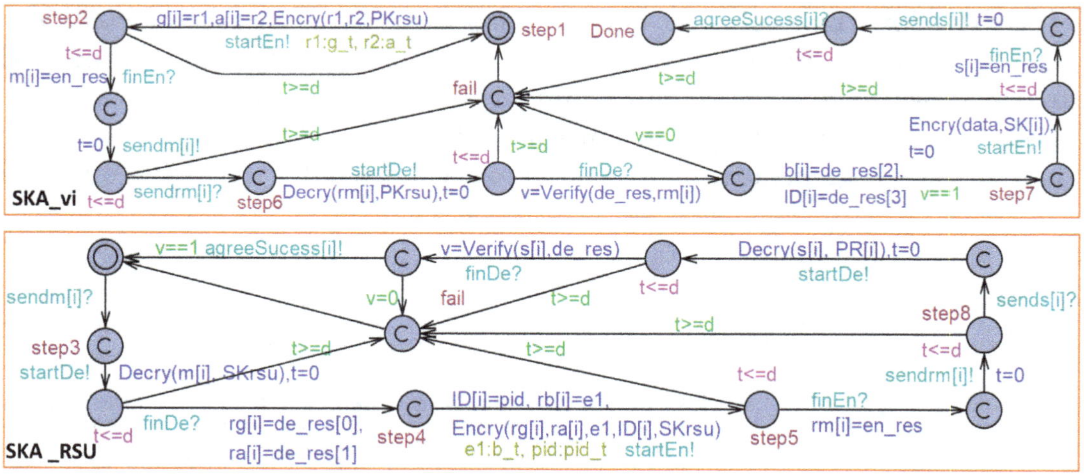

Fig. 5. UPPAAL-SMC model of SKA

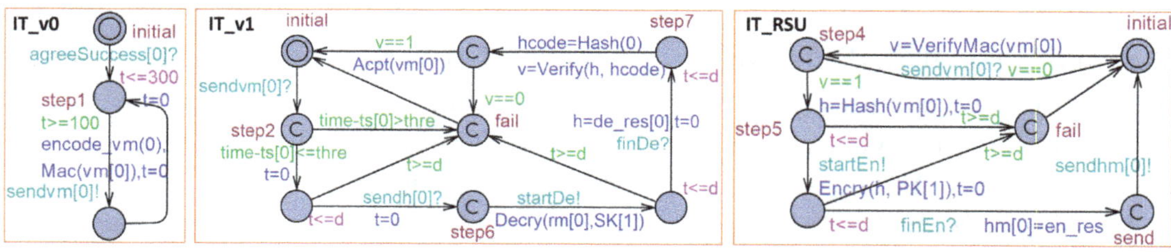

Fig. 6. UPPAAL-SMC model of IT

4.2 Modeling of Attacks in UPPAAL-SMC

We present the modeling of three types of attacks commonly used in the security analysis, i.e., message falsification, message replaying and message spoofing attacks [2]. The models of attacks are illustrated in Fig. 7, where the ls parameter ($ls \in [0, 100]$) serves as an indicator of level of adversarial strength while qc ($qc \in [0, 100]$) is an indicator of the adversarial channel quality.

Message Falsification Attack (MFA) aims to falsify messages transmitted from v_i to v_{i+1}, which is modeled as `MFA` STA in Fig. 7. As described earlier, in RAISE, RSU verifies the authenticity of messages by checking the correctness of the MAC code of messages. To deceive the RSU on the validity of the modified message and avoid exposing itself to RSU, MFA attempts to obtain the symmetric key and utilizes the key to compute the MAC code of the falsified message. At `s1` state, `MFA` eavesdrops on rm_i (generated at step 5 in Fig. 3), which contains the information for symmetric key generation (i.e., g, a, b). It tries to decrypt rm_i when receiving it via $sendrm[i]?$. The probability that the decryption can succeed is $ls\%$, modeled by probabilistic choices [31] (dashed edges) with probability weight as $\frac{ls}{100}$ and $\frac{100-ls}{100}$. If the decryption succeeds, MFA obtains the symmetric key of v_i based on the decrypted result ($getKey(de\_res)$). Finally, it modifies the content of message using the key, and tries to send the modified message to v_{i+1} ($sendvm[i]!$). The probability that the message can be sent successfully is

(100-qc)%. In our setting, MFA modifies the $speed_i$ field in the message into a random value in [100, 120], and changes the direction as $direction_i = 4$, which indicates that the v_i is running at the positive direction on y-axis.

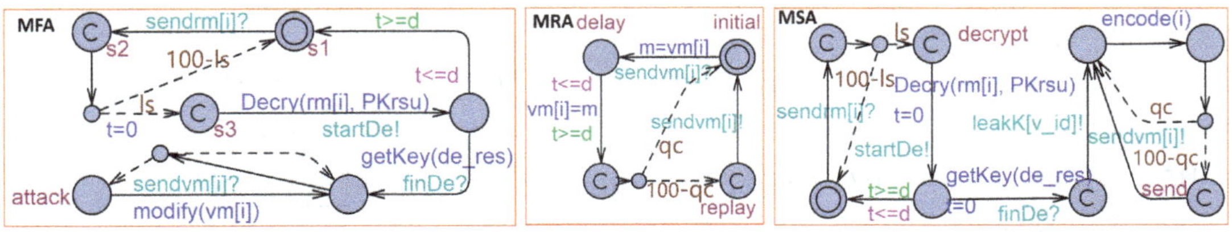

Fig. 7. STA of attacks

Message Replaying Attack (MRA) targets to replay obsolete messages that contain old information. The `MRA` STA represents an MRA that replays messages sent by v_i. Upon capturing a message (via $sendvm[i]?$), MRA stores the message ($m = vm[i]$) and tries to replay it at a later time (i.e., after *10* s). The probability that the attacker can replay the message successfully is (100-qc)%.

Message Spoofing Attack (MSA) impersonates a vehicle (v_i) in order to inject fraudulent information into its subsequent vehicle (v_{i+1}). Similar to `MFA`, `MSA` STA first obtains the symmetric key of v_i by detecting and decrypting rm_i. It then fabricates a new message whose content is "$brake_i = 0$, $speed_i = 0$, $direction_i = 4$, $x_i = 0$, $y_i = 10$" (denoted "*encode(i)*") and tries to send the message to v_{i+1} ($sendvm[i]!$), with the probability of the message being sent successfully as (100-qc)%.

5 Representation of S/S Related Timing Constraints in UPPAAL-SMC

To enable the formal verification of S/S related timing constraints (given in Sect. 3), we first investigate how to specify those constraints in PrCcsl. Then, translation from PrCcsl specifications of the constraints into verifiable STA is demonstrated. Furthermore, a tool ProTL that supports the automatic transformation based on the proposed translation rules is introduced.

5.1 Specifications of S/S Related Timing Constraints in PrCCSL

The specifications of R1–R11 are presented in Table 1, where ac is a clock that always ticks while nc represents a clock that never ticks. R1 is specified as an `exclusion` *relation* between $xdir$ (the event that the vehicles are running at the positive direction of x-axis) and $ovtake$ (the event that the position of follower v_1 on x-axis is greater than that of leader v_0). Similarly, R7 and R9 can be specified as `exclusion` *relations*.

In the specification of R2, $stopD$ is a clock generated by delaying $stopSign$ (the event that the leader vehicle detects a stop sign) for 2000 ms. $vstop$ refers

Table 1. PrCCSL specifications of R1–R11

Req	PrCCSL Specification
R1	$xdir \triangleq dir = 1 \,?\, ac : nc$, $ovtake \triangleq x_1 \geq x_0 \,?\, ac : nc$, $xdir \#_{0.95}\, ovtake$
R2	$stopSign \triangleq sign = 5 \,?\, signRec : nc$, $stopD \triangleq stopSign\ (2000) \rightsquigarrow ms$, $vstop \preceq_{0.95} stopD$
R3	$vUnsafeDe \triangleq vUnsafe\ (200) \rightsquigarrow ms$, $vDec \prec_{0.95} vUnsafeDe$
R4	$vFarDisDe \triangleq vFarDis\ (300) \rightsquigarrow ms$, $startAcc \prec_{0.95} vFarDisDe$
R5	$v0TurnDe \triangleq v0Turn\ (3000) \rightsquigarrow ms$, $finTurn \preceq_{0.95} v0TurnDe$
R6	$msgRec \subseteq_{0.95} msgSent$
R7	$leakK \#_{0.95}\, ac$
R8	$validMsg \triangleq rMsg = sMsg \,?\, msgRec : nc$, $msgRec \equiv_{0.95} validMsg$
R9	$oldMsg \triangleq time - ts > thre \,?\, msgAcpt : nc$, $msgAcpt \#_{0.95}\, oldMsg$
R10	$startSKADe \triangleq startSKA\ (600) \rightsquigarrow ms$, $finSKA \prec_{0.95} startSKADe$
R11	$fclk \triangleq msgSent \blacktriangledown 01(1)$, $sentDe1 \triangleq msgSent\ (100) \rightsquigarrow ms$, $sentDe2 \triangleq msgSent\ (300) \rightsquigarrow ms$, $sentDe1 \preceq_{0.95} fclk$, $fclk \preceq_{0.95} sentDe2$

to the event that three vehicles are completely stopped, which should occur no later than *stopD*. Hence, R2 is expressed as a `causality` *relation* between *vstop* and *stopD*. R3–R5 can be specified in a similar manner.

R6 (authenticity) is expressed as a `subclock` *relation* between *msgRec* and *msgSent*, where *msgRec* (*msgSent*) represents the event that a message is received (sent) by the follower (leader) vehicle. R8 is specified as a `coincidence` *relation* between *msgRec* and *validMsg*, where *validMsg* is a clock that ticks with *msgRec* when the received message *rMsg* is identical with the sent message *sMsg* (i.e., $rMsg == sMsg$). For R10, *startSKA* (*finSKA*) represents the starting (completion) of SKA. *startSKADe* is a clock constructed by delaying *startSKA* for 600 ms. R10 delimits that *finSKA* must occur before *startSKADe*. R11 states that two consecutive occurrences of *msgSent* must has a interval of $[period - jitter,\ period + jitter]$ms (i.e., [100, 300] ms). In the specification of R11, *fclk* is a clock generated by filtering out the 1st tick of *msgSent*. *sentDe1* and *sentDe2* are two clocks generated by delaying *msgSent* for 100 ms and 300 ms. R11 can be interpreted as: $\forall i \in \mathbb{N}^+$, the ith tick of *fclk* should occur later than the ith tick of *sentDe1* but prior to the ith tick of *sentDe2*.

5.2 Translation of PrCCSL into STA

We present how the S/S related timing constraints specified in PrCCSL can be transformed into STA and probabilistic queries in UPPAAL-SMC. We first describe how clock tick and history (introduced in Sect. 2) can be represented in UPPAAL-SMC. Using the mapping, we then demonstrate that *expressions* and *relations* in PrCCSL can be translated into STA and queries.

In the earlier work [14], the semantics of PrCcsl operators are translated into STA based on discrete time, i.e., the continuous physical time is discretized into a set of equalized steps. As a result, two clock instants are still considered coincident even if they are one time step apart. To alleviate this restriction and enable the representation of PrCcsl that pertains to continuous real-time semantics, the mapping patterns are refined: two clock instants are coinstantaneous only if the time difference between them is insignificant, i.e., the time difference between them is less than a positive infinitesimal value e, e.g., $e = 0.000001$.

In PrCcsl, a logical clock represents an event and the instants of the clock correspond to the occurrences of the event. A logical clock c is represented as a *synchronization channel* $c!$ in Uppaal-SMC. The history of c is modeled as the STA shown in Fig. 8: whenever c occurs ($c?$), the value of its history is increased by 1 (i.e., $h{+}{+}$).

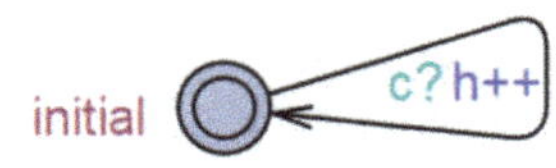

Fig. 8. `History`

Based on the mapping patterns of tick and history, the PrCcsl *expressions* (including `ITE`, `DelayFor` and `filterBy`), as well as *relations* (including `subclock`, `coincidence`, `exclusion` and `precedence`), can be represented as STA and queries shown in Fig. 9.

The STA of *expressions* trigger the ticks of the new clock (denoted $res!$) based on the occurrences of existed clocks. To represent *relations*, observer STA that capture the semantics of standard `subclock`, `coincidence`, `exclusion` and `precedence` *relations* are constructed. Each observer STA contains a "*fail*" location (see Fig. 9), which indicates the violation of the corresponding *relation*. Recall the definition of PrCcsl in Sect. 2, the probability of a *relation* being satisfied is interpreted as a ratio of runs that satisfies the *relation* among all runs. It is specified as *Hypothesis Testing* queries in Uppaal-SMC, H_0: $\frac{m}{k} \geqslant p$ against H_1: $\frac{m}{k} < p$, where m is the number of runs satisfying the given *relation* out of all k runs. As a result, the probabilistic *relations* are interpreted as the query (see Fig. 9): $Pr[bound]([\,]\ \neg STA.fail) \geq p$, which means that the probability of the "*fail*" location of the observer STA never being reached should be greater than or equal to p. The STA of *expressions* and *relations* are composed to the system NSTA in parallel. Then, the probabilistic analysis is performed over the composite NSTA that enables us to verify the S/S related timing constraints over the entire system using Uppaal-SMC.

Tool support: Manual translation of PrCcsl specifications into Uppaal models for verification can be time-consuming and error-prone. To improve the accuracy and efficiency of translation, we implement a tool ProTL (Probabilistic-Ccsl TransLator) [26] that provides a push-button transformation from PrCcsl specifications into corresponding STA & queries. Furthermore, verification and simulation support is provided in ProTL by employing the Uppaal-SMC as the backend analysis engine. ProTL encompasses the following features: (1) An editor for editing PrCcsl specification of requirements (stored as "*.txt*" files); (2) Automated transformation of PrCcsl specifications into Uppaal-SMC STA; (3) Integration of the STA and the system behavioral model (imported by users); (4) A configuration palette for setting parameters (e.g., time bound of simula-

STA of PrCCSL Operators	Remarks
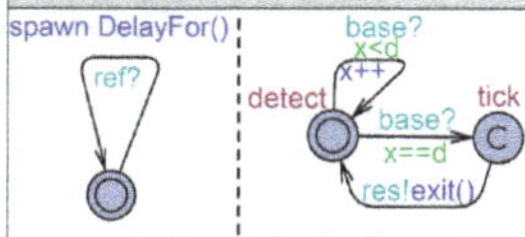 Detect(ref) DelayFor(base,d,res)	**DelayFor**: $res \triangleq ref\ (d) \rightsquigarrow base$ When *ref* occurs (ref?), its DelayFor STA is spawned by Detect STA. The spawned STA stays in the detect location until *base* ticks *d* times. When *base* ticks *d* times (x == d), it transits to the tick location and triggers *res* (res!). Then it becomes inactive (denoted "exit()"), i.e., calculation of the current tick of *res* is completed.
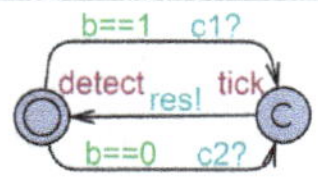 ITE(c1, c2, b, res)	**ITE (if-then-else)**: $res \triangleq b\ ?\ c1 : c2$ ITE generates a new clock *res* that behaves either as *c1* or as *c2* base on the value of boolean variable *b*. If *b* is true (b == 1), the tick of *res* will be triggered (denoted res!) whenever *c1* occurs (c1?). Otherwise, *res* ticks with *c2* when *b* is false (b == 0).
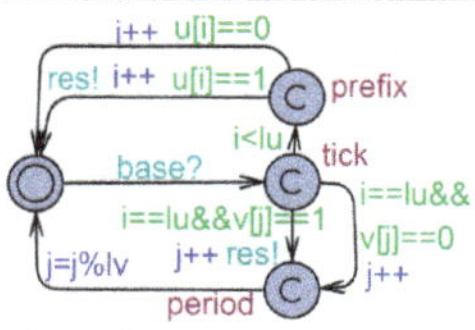 FilterBy(base, u, v, lu, lv, res)	**FilterBy**: $res \triangleq base \blacktriangledown u(v)$ FilterBy filters the instants of *base* based on a binary word *w=u(v)*, i.e., ∀ k ∈ N , if the *kth* bit in *w* is 1, then at the *kth* tick of *base*, *res* ticks. *u* and v are two boolean arrays. *lu* and *lv* represent the size of *u* and *v*. As *base* ticks (base?), the STA firstly traverses the bits in u (at prefix state) and then iterates the bits in v (at period state). If the present bit (indicated by the index) of the binary word is 1, the STA triggers *res* (res!). Otherwise, it moves to the initial state, updates the index to refer to the next bit of *w* (i++/j++) and repeats the process.
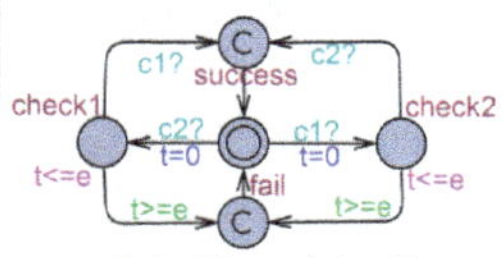 Coincidence(c1, c2)	**Probabilistic Coincidence:** $c1 \equiv_p c2$ When *c1* (*c2*) ticks via c1? (c2?), the STA checks if the other clock, *c2* (*c1*), ticks at the same time. If c2 (c1) occurs within a positive infinitesimal value (t<=e), the STA transits to success location. Otherwise, the coincidence relation is violated and STA transits to fail location. Probabilistic coincidence is expressed as: *Pr[bound]([ ] ¬ Coincidence.fail) ≥ p*.
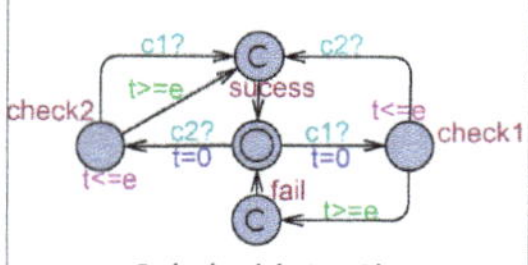 Subclock(c1, c2)	**Probabilistic Subclock:** $c1 \subseteq_p c2$ The relation limits that *c2* (superclock) must tick when *c1* (subclock) ticks, i.e., when *c1* ticks, c2 must coincide with c1. When c1 (c2) occurs, the STA checks whether the other clock also ticks at the same time. When c1 (subclock) ticks but c2 does not occur (within e time unit), the relation is violated and the STA transits to fail location. Probabilistic subclock is expressed as: *Pr[bound]([ ] ¬ Subclock.fail) ≥ p*.
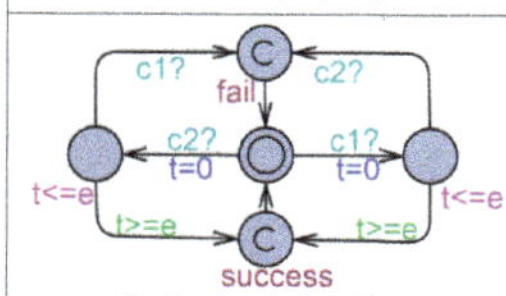 Exclusion(c1, c2)	**Probabilistic Exclusion:** $c1 \#_p c2$ When *c1* (*c2*) ticks via c1? (c2?), the STA checks if the other clock, *c2* (*c1*), ticks at the same tme, i.e., whether *c1* (*c2*) occurs or not when t ≤ e. If it occurs, the exclusion relation is violated and STA moves to fail location. Probabilistic exclusion is expressed as: *Pr[bound]([ ] ¬ Exclusion.fail) ≥ p*.
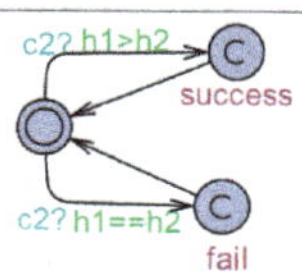 Precedence(c2, h1, h2)	**Probabilistic Precedence:** $c1 \prec_p c2$ The relation states that *c1* must run faster than *c2*, i.e., the history of *c1* (*h1*) must be greater than or equal to the history of *c2* (*h2*), and *c2* must not tick when the histories of the two clocks are equal. Therefore, if *c1* ticks via c1? and *c1* runs slower (i.e., h1<h2), or c2 ticks via c2? when their histories are equal (h1==h2), the precedence relation is violated and fail location is activated. Probabilistic precedence is expressed as: *Pr[bound]([ ] ¬ Precedence.fail) ≥ p*.

Fig. 9. STA of PrCCSL operators

tion, number of simulations) used for verification and simulation; (5) Automatic generation of probabilistic queries (introduced in Sect. 2) based on user-specified parameters; (6) Capability of performing verification and simulation on PrCCSL specifications against the integrated model and generated queries.

The GUI of ProTL is implemented by applying the Python package TKINTER [27]. The implementation of *Translator* is achieved by the ANother Tool for Language Recognition (ANTLR) [24], a parser generator that can constructs lexical parsers for a language by analyzing user-defined syntax of the language. We specified the syntax of PrCCSL in Backus-Naur Form (BNF) and apply ANTLR to generate a *parser* that can analyze and recognize encodings in the format of PrCCSL. The *parser* reads the PrCCSL specifications and generates abstract syntax trees (AST), i.e., an intermediate form that has tree structures.

By traversing AST, the information (i.e., operators and parameters) of PrCcsl can be extracted and utilized for generation of corresponding STA.

6 Experiment

To identify vulnerabilities of system to external malicious attackers, we combine the refined CAS system model (including the models of Raise protocol) with models of three different attackers. Formal verification on S/S related timing constraints (R1–R11) for the combined model is performed by Uppaal-SMC. The combined CAS model contains the stochastic behaviors in terms of the unpredictable environments (e.g., the traffic signs are randomly recognized by the leader vehicle of CAS and the probability of each sign type occurring is equally set as 16.7%), as well as the indeterministic behaviors modeled by weighted probability choices in the STA of attacks (see Fig. 7). In our setting, ls and qc are configured as 10 and 90, respectively. To estimate the probability of an attack being launched on CAS successfully, *Probability Estimation* query is applied to check the probability that the "*attack*" location in each attack STA is reachable from the system NSTA. The time bound of the verification is set as 10000. The probability of message falsification, message replaying and message spoofing attack being successfully completed by the corresponding attacker is within the range of [0.109, 0.209], [0.563, 0.663] and [0.143, 0.243], respectively.

In our experiments, S/S related timing constraints are specified in PrCcsl and transformed into STA using ProTL. Each constraint is specified as a PrCcsl *relation* (as described in Sect. 5.1) whose probability threshold is 95%. The verification results are demonstrated in Table 2, in which "√" denotes the corresponding requirement is satisfied while "×" indicates the violation of the requirement: Under the message replaying attack, all the S/S timing constraints are established as valid with 95% level of confidence. In the message falsification attack, the secrecy and integrity properties (R7 and R8), as well as three safety properties (R3–R5), are violated. The MSA damages the authenticity (R6) and secrecy (R7) of communication, and leads to the violations of four safety properties, i.e., R1 and R3–R5.

Table 2. Verification results of timing constraints under different attacks

Attacks	R1	R2	R3	R4	R5	R6	R7	R8	R9	R10	R11	Average Time	Mem (Mb)
Message Falsification	√	√	×	×	×	√	×	×	√	√	√	40.20	57.94
Message Replaying	√	√	√	√	√	√	√	√	√	√	√	68.33	61.49
Message Spoofing	×	√	×	×	×	×	×	√	√	√	√	58.11	40.23

The experiment results indicate the severity of impacts on safety and security caused by the demonstrated attacks on CAS: No requirement is violated under MRA scenario while the MSA causes the violations of most safety properties.

When CAS is attached with the STA of MSA or MFA, the secrecy of symmetric key is violated. With the obtained symmetric key, MSA can masquerade message as legitimate vehicles and MFA is able to tamper the content of messages without being detected, leading to the violations of authenticity (R6) and integrity (R7) respectively. To explore how the malicious attackers can influence the safety of system, we conduct simulation by using *Simulations* queries. The simulation results in Fig. 10 illustrate how an MSA drives the system to undesirable states.

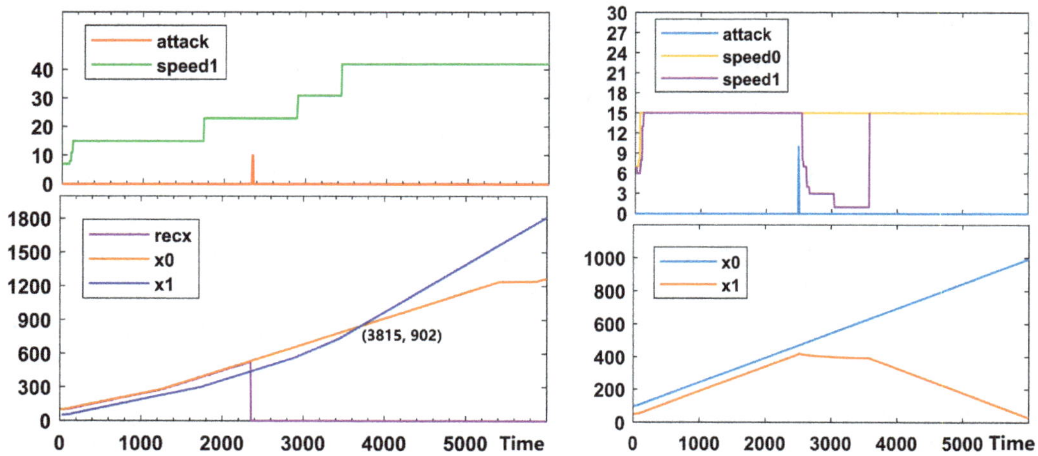

(a) R1 (b) R4

Fig. 10. Simulation results of R1 and R4: (a) At *Time* = 2345, the attack occurs (indicated by the rising edge of the red line). MSA sends the fabricated position information of V_0 to V_1 (the value of *recx* becomes 0), which tricks V_1 to think that the distance between V_0 and V_1 exceeds the maximum limit. V_1 keeps increasing its speed (*speed*1) and thus leading to the collision (indicated by $x_0 == x_1$) at *Time* = 3815, which violates R1. (b) When an attack takes place at *Time* = 2496 (indicated by the rising edge of the blue line), V_1 receives the message from the attacker and is deluded into believing that the speed of V_0 is 0. Therefore, V_1 keeps decreasing its speed even if the distance between V_0 and V_1 becomes greater than 100 m, which violates R4. (Color figure online)

7 Related Work

Formal verification of (non)-functional properties of automotive systems containing stochastic behaviors were investigated in several works [13–15]. In these works, systems are by default resilient to security threats and the safety properties are analyzed under no malicious attack scenarios, which is inadequate for design of automotive systems interconnected via wireless communications. Combined analysis of safety and security (S/S) properties for interconnected cyber physical systems have been addressed in earlier works [1,21,29], which are however, limited to theoretical frameworks and high-level descriptions of S/S properties without the support for formal verification. Pedroza et al. [25] proposed a SysML based environment called AVATAR for the formal verification of S/S properties, which enables assessment of the impacts of cyber-security threats on functional safety. Wardell et al. [32] proposed an approach for identifying security vulnerabilities of industrial control systems by modeling malicious attacks as PROMELA models amenable to formal verification. However, those approaches lack precise probabilistic annotations specifying stochastic properties regarding to S/S aspects. Kumar et al. [18] introduced the attack-fault trees formalism for descriptions of attack scenarios and conducted formal analysis by using UPPAAL-SMC to obtain quantitative estimation on impacts of system failures or security threats. On the other hand, our work is based on the probabilistic extension of S/S related timing constraints with the focus on probabilistic verification of the extended constraints.

8 Conclusion

This paper presents a model-based approach for probabilistic formal analysis of safety and security (S/S) related timing constraints for interconnected automotive system in EAST-ADL at the early design phase. The behavioral model of automotive system in UPPAAL-SMC is refined by adding the models of vehicular communication protocol and malicious attacks, which facilitates to exploit the impacts of adversary environment on S/S of the system. Timing constraints are specified in PrCCSL and translated into stochastic timed automata (STA) amenable to formal verification using UPPAAL-SMC. A set of translation rules from PrCCSL to STA, as well as the corresponding tool support for automating the translation are provided. We demonstrate our approach by performing formal verification on a cooperative automotive system (CAS) case study. Although, we have shown the one-to-one mapping patterns from a subset of PrCCSL operators to STA for conducting formal verification on timing constraints using UPPAAL-SMC, as ongoing work, systematic and formal translation techniques covering a full set of PrCCSL constraints are further studied. Furthermore, new features of ProTL with respect to analysis of UPPAAL-SMC models involving wider range of variable/query types (e.g., *urgent channels*, *bounded integers*) are further developed.

Acknowledgment. This work is supported by the EASY project funded by NSFC, a collaborative research between Sun Yat-Sen University and University of Southern Denmark.

References

1. Abdo, H., Kaouk, M., Flaus, J.M., Masse, F.: A safety/security risk analysis approach of industrial control systems: a cyber bowtie-combining new version of attack tree with bowtie analysis. Comput. Secur. **72**, 175–195 (2018)
2. Amoozadeh, M., et al.: Security vulnerabilities of connected vehicle streams and their impact on cooperative driving. IEEE Commun. Mag. **53**(6), 126–132 (2015)
3. André, C.: Syntax and semantics of the clock constraint specification language (CCSL). Ph.D. thesis, Inria (2009)

4. Bernat, G., Burns, A., Llamosi, A.: Weakly hard real-time systems. Trans. Comput. **50**(4), 308–321 (2001)
5. Blom, H., et al.: TIMMO-2-USE timing model, tools, algorithms, languages, methodology, use cases. Technical report, TIMMO-2-USE (2012)
6. Corin, R., Etalle, S., Hartel, P.H., Mader, A.: Timed model checking of security protocols. In: ACM Workshop on Formal Methods in Security Engineering (FMSE), pp. 23–32. ACM (2004)
7. David, A., et al.: Statistical model checking for stochastic hybrid systems. In: Hybrid Systems and Biology (HSB), pp. 122–136. EPTCS (2012)
8. David, A., Larsen, K.G., Legay, A., Mikučionis, M., Poulsen, D.B.: UPPAAL-SMC tutorial. Int. J. Softw. Tools Technol. Transf. **17**(4), 397–415 (2015)
9. EAST-ADL: EAST-ADL specification v2.1.9. Technical report, MAENAD (2011). https://www.maenad.eu/public/EAST-ADL-Specification_M2.1.9.1.pdf
10. Engoulou, R.G., Bellaïche, M., Pierre, S., Quintero, A.: VANET security surveys. Comput. Commun. **44**, 1–13 (2014)
11. IEC 61508: Functional safety of electrical electronic programmable electronic safety related systems (2010)
12. ISO 26262-6: Road vehicles functional safety part 6. Product development at the software level (2011)
13. Kang, E.Y., Huang, L., Mu, D.: Formal verification of energy and timed requirements for a cooperative automotive system. In: ACM/SIGAPP Symposium On Applied Computing (SAC), pp. 1492–1499. ACM (2018)
14. Kang, E.-Y., Mu, D., Huang, L.: Probabilistic verification of timing constraints in automotive systems using UPPAAL-SMC. In: Furia, C.A., Winter, K. (eds.) IFM 2018. LNCS, vol. 11023, pp. 236–254. Springer, Cham (2018). https://doi.org/10.1007/978-3-319-98938-9_14
15. Kang, E.Y., Mu, D., Huang, L., Lan, Q.: Verification and validation of a cyber-physical system in the automotive domain. In: IEEE International Conference on Software Quality, Reliability and Security Companion (QRS), pp. 326–333. IEEE (2017)
16. Khan, A.M., Mallet, F., Rashid, M.: Combining SysML and MARTE/CCSL to model complex electronic systems. In: Information Systems Engineering (ICISE), pp. 12–17. IEEE (2016)
17. Kriaa, S., Pietre-Cambacedes, L., Bouissou, M., Halgand, Y.: A survey of approaches combining safety and security for industrial control systems. Reliab. Eng. Syst. Saf. **139**, 156–178 (2015)
18. Kumar, R., Stoelinga, M.: Quantitative security and safety analysis with attack-fault trees. In: High Assurance Systems Engineering (HASE), pp. 25–32. IEEE (2017)
19. Legay, A., Viswanathan, M.: Statistical model checking: challenges and perspectives. Int. J. Softw. Tools Technol. Transf. **17**(4), 369–376 (2015)
20. Line, M.B., Nordland, O., Røstad, L., Tøndel, I.A.: Safety vs. Security. In: International Conference on Probabilistic Safety Assessment and Management (PSAM) (2006)
21. Macher, G., Höller, A., Sporer, H., Armengaud, E., Kreiner, C.: A combined safety-hazards and security-threat analysis method for automotive systems. In: Koornneef, F., van Gulijk, C. (eds.) SAFECOMP 2015. LNCS, vol. 9338, pp. 237–250. Springer, Cham (2015). https://doi.org/10.1007/978-3-319-24249-1_21
22. MAENAD (2011). http://www.maenad.eu/
23. Mallet, F., De Simone, R.: Correctness issues on MARTE/CCSL constraints. Sci. Comput. Program. **106**, 78–92 (2015)

24. Parr, T.: The definitive ANTLR 4 reference. Pragmatic Bookshelf (2013)
25. Pedroza, G., Apvrille, L., Knorreck, D.: Avatar: a SysML environment for the formal verification of safety and security properties. In: New Technologies of Distributed Systems (NOTERE), pp. 1–10. IEEE (2011)
26. ProTL. https://sites.google.com/view/protl
27. Tkinter: Python interface to Tcl/Tk. https://docs.python.org/3/library/tkinter.html
28. Raya, M., Hubaux, J.P.: Securing vehicular Ad Hoc networks. J. Comput. Secur. **15**(1), 39–68 (2007)
29. Sabaliauskaite, G., Mathur, A.P.: Aligning cyber-physical system safety and security. In: Cardin, M.A., Krob, D., Lui, P., Tan, Y., Wood, K. (eds.) Complex Systems Design & Management Asia, pp. 41–53. Springer, Cham (2015). https://doi.org/10.1007/978-3-319-12544-2_4
30. Specification, O.: UML profile for MARTE: modeling and analysis of real-time embedded systems. Technical report, Object Management Group (2011)
31. UPPAAL-SMC. http://people.cs.aau.dk/~adavid/smc/
32. Wardell, D.C., Mills, R.F., Peterson, G.L., Oxley, M.E.: A method for revealing and addressing security vulnerabilities in cyber-physical systems by modeling malicious agent interactions with formal verification. Proc. Comput. Sci. **95**, 24–31 (2016)
33. Zhang, C., Lin, X., Lu, R., Ho, P.H., Shen, X.: An efficient message authentication scheme for vehicular communications. IEEE Trans. Veh. Technol. **57**(6), 3357–3368 (2008)

Checking Observational Purity of Procedures

Himanshu Arora[1], Raghavan Komondoor[1], and G. Ramalingam[2](✉)

[1] Indian Institute of Science, Bangalore, India
{himanshua,raghavan}@iisc.ac.in
[2] Microsoft Research, Bellevue, WA, USA
grama@microsoft.com

Abstract. Verifying whether a procedure is *observationally pure* (that is, it always returns the same result for the same input argument) is challenging when the procedure uses mutable (private) global variables, e.g., for memoization, and when the procedure is recursive.

We present a deductive verification approach for this problem. Our approach encodes the procedure's code as a logical formula, with recursive calls being modeled using a mathematical function symbol *assuming that the procedure is observationally pure*. Then, a theorem prover is invoked to check whether this logical formula agrees with the function symbol referred to above in terms of input-output behavior for all arguments. We prove the soundness of this approach.

We then present a conservative approximation of the first approach that reduces the verification problem to one of checking whether a quantifier-free formula is satisfiable and prove the soundness of the second approach.

We evaluate our approach on a set of realistic examples, using the Boogie intermediate language and theorem prover. Our evaluation shows that the invariants are easy to construct manually, and that our approach is effective at verifying observationally pure procedures.

1 Introduction

A procedure in an imperative programming language is said to be *observationally pure* (OP) if for each specific argument value it has a specific return value, across all possible sequences of calls to the procedure, irrespective of what other code runs between these calls. In other words, the input-output behavior of an OP procedure mimics a mathematical function.

A deterministic procedure that does not read any pre-existing state other than its arguments is trivially OP. However, it is common for procedures to update and read global variables, typically for performance optimization, while still being OP. In this paper, we focus on the problem of checking observational purity of procedures that read and write global variables, especially in the presence of recursion, which makes the problem harder.

R. Hähnle and W. van der Aalst (Eds.): FASE 2019, LNCS 11424, pp. 228–243, 2019.
https://doi.org/10.1007/978-3-030-16722-6_13

```
1
2  int g := -1;
3  int lastN := 0;
4  int factCache( int n) {
5    if(n <= 1) {
6      result := 1;
7    } else if (g != -1 && n == lastN) {
8      result := g;
9    } else {
10     g = n * factCache( n - 1 );
11     lastN = n;
12     result := g;
13   }
14   return result;
15 }
```

Listing 1.1. Procedure factCache: returns n!, and memoizes most recent result.

Motivating Example. We use procedure 'factCache' in Listing 1.1 as our running example. It returns `n`! for a given argument `n`, and caches the return value of the most recent call. It uses two *private global* variables, `g` and `lastN`, to implement the caching. `g` is initialized to −1. After the first call to the procedure onwards, `g` stores the return value of the most recent call, and `lastN` stores the argument of the most recent call. Clearly this procedure is OP, and mimics the input-output behavior of a factorial procedure that does not cache any results.

Proposed Approach. Our approach is based on Floyd-Hoare logic, which typically requires a specification of the procedure to be provided. One candidate specification would be a full functional specification of the procedure. If the user specifies that `factCache` realizes `n`!, then the verifier could replace Line 10 in the code with '`g = n * (n−1)!`'. This, on paper, is sufficient to assert that Line 12 always assigns `n`! to `result`. However, to establish that Line 8 also does the same, an invariant would need to be provided that describes the possible values of `g` before an invocation to the procedure. In our example, a suitable invariant would be '$(\texttt{g} = -1) \vee (\texttt{g} = \texttt{lastN}!)$'. The verifier would also need to verify that at the procedure's exit the invariant is re-established. Lines 10–12, with the recursive call replaced by $(\texttt{n} - 1)!$, suffices on paper to re-establish the invariant.

The candidate approach described above, while plausible, suffers from two weaknesses. First, a mathematical specification of the function being computed may be complex and non-trivial to write. (Note, for example, that `factCache` is defined for negative integers while factorial is not. Thus, the previous candidate specification is actually incorrect for this edge case.) Second, the underlying theorem prover would need to prove complex arithmetic properties, e.g., that $\texttt{n} * (\texttt{n} - 1)!$ is equal to `n`!. Complex proofs such as this may be beyond the scope of many existing theorem provers.

Our key insight is to sidestep the challenges mentioned by introducing a function symbol, say *factCache*, and replacing the recursive call for the purposes of verification with this function symbol. (Note that we reuse the same symbol for two purposes, which may be slightly confusing here. One denotes the procedure name, while the other denotes a function symbol for use in a logical formula. The italicized name here denotes the function symbol.) Intuitively, *factCache* represents the mathematical function that the given procedure mimics *if* the procedure is OP. In our example, Line 10 would become 'g = n * *factCache*(n − 1)'. This step needs no human involvement. The approach needs an invariant; however, in a novel manner, we allow the invariant also to refer to *factCache*. In our example, a suitable invariant would be '$(\texttt{g} = -1) \vee (\texttt{g} = \texttt{lastN} * \mathit{factCache}(\texttt{lastN} - 1))$'. This sort of invariant is relatively easy to construct; e.g., a human could arrive at it just by looking at Line 2 and with a local reasoning on Lines 10 and 11. Given this invariant, (a) a theorem prover could infer that the condition in Line 7 implies that Line 8 necessarily copies the value of '$\texttt{n} * \mathit{factCache}(\texttt{n} - 1)$' into '`result`'. Due to the transformation to Line 10 mentioned above, (b) the theorem prover can infer that Line 12 also does the same. Note that since these two expressions are syntactically identical, a theorem prover can easily establish that they are equal in value. Finally, since Line 6 is reached under a different condition than Lines 8 and 12, the verifier has finished establishing that the procedure always returns the same expression in `n` for any given value of `n`.

Similarly, using the modified Line 10 mentioned above and from Line 11, the prover can re-establish that `g` is equal to '$\texttt{lastN} * \mathit{factCache}(\texttt{lastN} - 1)$' when control reaches Line 12. Hence, the necessary step of proving the given invariant to be a valid invariant is also complete.

Note, the effectiveness of the approach depends on the nature of the given invariant. For instance, if the given invariant was '$(\texttt{g} = -1) \vee (\texttt{g} = \text{lastN!})$', which is also technically correct, then the theorem prover may not be able to establish that in Lines 8 and 12 the variable '`g`' always stores the same expression in `n`. However, it is our claim that in fact it is the invariant '$(\texttt{g} = -1) \vee (\texttt{g} = \texttt{lastN} * \mathit{factCache}(\texttt{lastN} - 1))$' that is easier to infer by a human or by a potential tool, as justified by us two paragraphs above.

Salient Aspects of Our Approach. This paper makes two significant contributions. First, it tackles the circularity problem that arises due to the use of a presumed-to-be OP procedure in assertions and invariants and the use of these invariants in proving the procedure to be OP. This requires us to prove the soundness of an approach that *simultaneously* verifies observational purity as well the validity of invariants (as they cannot be decoupled).

Secondly, we show that a direct approach to this verification problem (which we call the existential approach) reduces it to a problem of verifying that a logical formula is a tautology. The structure of the generated formula, however, makes the resulting theorem prover instances hard. We show how a conservative approximation can be used to convert this hard problem into an easier problem of checking satisfiability of a quantifier-free formula, which is something within the scope of state-of-the-art theorem provers.

The most closely related previous approaches are by Barnett et al. [1,2], and by Naumann [3]. These approaches check observational purity of procedures that maintain mutable global state. However, none of these approaches use a function

$$
\begin{array}{rl}
\texttt{L} \in \texttt{Lib} & \texttt{::=}\ \overline{\texttt{g := c}}\ \overline{\texttt{P}} \\
\texttt{P} \in \texttt{Proc} & \texttt{::= p (x) \{ S; return y \}} \\
\texttt{S} \in \texttt{Stmt} & \texttt{::= x := e | x := p(y) | S ; S | if (e) then S else S} \\
\texttt{e} \in \texttt{Expr} & \texttt{::= c | x | e op e | unop e} \\
\texttt{op} \in \texttt{Ops} & \texttt{::= + | - | / | * | \% | > | < | == |}\ \wedge\ \texttt{|}\ \vee \\
\texttt{unop} \in \texttt{UnOps} & \texttt{::=}\ \neg \\
\multicolumn{2}{l}{\texttt{x, y} \in \texttt{LocalId} \cup \texttt{GlobalId},\ \texttt{g} \in \texttt{GlobalId},\ \texttt{c} \in \mathcal{V},\ \texttt{p} \in \texttt{ProcId}}
\end{array}
$$

Fig. 1. Programming language syntax and meta-variables

symbol in place of recursive calls or within invariants. Therefore, it is not clear that these approaches can verify recursive procedures. Barnett et al., in fact, state "there is a circularity - it would take a delicate argument, and additional conditions, to avoid unsoundness in this case". To the best of our knowledge ours is the first paper to show that it is feasible to check observational purity of procedures that maintain mutable global state for optimization purposes and that make use of recursion.

Being able to verify that a procedure is OP has many potential applications. The most obvious one is that OP procedures can be memoized. That is, input-output pairs can be recorded in a table, and calls to the procedure can be elided whenever an argument is seen more than once. This would not change the semantics of the overall program that calls the procedure, because the procedure always returns the same value for the same argument (and mutates only private global variables). Another application is that if a loop contains a call to an OP procedure, then the loop can be parallelized (provided the procedure is modified to access and update its private global variables in a single atomic operation).

The rest of this paper is structured as follows. Section 2 introduces the core programming language that we address. Section 3 provides formal semantics for our language, as well as definitions of invariants and observational purity. Section 4 describes our approach formally. Section 5 discusses an approach for generating an invariant automatically in certain cases. Section 6 describes evaluation of our approach on a few realistic examples. Section 7 describes related work. More details about the proofs and the examples can be found in [4].

2 Language Syntax

In this paper, we assume that the input to the purity checker is a library consisting of one or more procedures, with shared state consisting of one or more variables that are private to the library. We refer to these variables as "global" variables to indicate that they retain their values across multiple invocations of the library procedures, but they cannot be accessed or modified by procedures outside the library (that is, the clients of the library).

In Fig. 1, we present the syntax of a simple programming language that we address in this paper. Given the foundational focus of this work, we keep the programming language very simple, but the ideas we present can be generalized. A `return` statement is required in each procedure, and is permitted only as the last statement of the procedure. The language does not contain any looping construct. Loops can be modelled as recursive procedures. The formal parameters of a procedure are readonly and cannot be modified within the procedure. We omit types from the language. We permit only variables of primitive types. In particular, the language does not allow pointers or dynamic memory allocation. Note that expressions are pure (that is, they have no side effects) in this language, and a procedure call is not allowed in an expression. Each procedure call is modelled as a separate statement.

For simplicity of presentation, without loss of conceptual generality, we assume that the library consists of a single (possibly recursive) procedure, with a single formal parameter. In the sequel, we will use the symbol P (as a metavariable) to represent this library procedure, p (as a metavariable) to represent the *name* of this procedure, and will assume that the name of the formal parameter is `n`. If the procedure is of the form "p `(n) { S; return r }`", we refer to `r` as the *return* variable, and refer to "`S; return r`" as the *procedure body* and denote it as body(P). The library also contains, outside of the procedure's code, a sequence of initializing declarations of the global variables used in the procedure, of the form "`g1 := c1`; ...; `gN := cN`". These initializations are assumed to be performed once during any execution of the client application, just before the first call to the procedure P is placed by the client application.

Throughout this paper we use the word 'procedure' to refer to the library procedure P, and use the word 'function' to refer to a mathematical function.

3 A Semantic Definition of Purity

In this section, we formalize the input-output semantics of the procedure P as a relation $\rightsquigarrow_{\text{P}}$, where $n \rightsquigarrow_{\text{P}} r$ indicates that an invocation of P with input n may return a result of r. The procedure is defined to be observationally pure if the relation $\rightsquigarrow_{\text{P}}$ is a (partial) function: that is, if $n \rightsquigarrow_{\text{P}} r_1$ and $n \rightsquigarrow_{\text{P}} r_2$, then $r_1 = r_2$.

The object of our analysis is a single-procedure library, not the entire (client) application. (Our approach can be generalized to handle multi-procedure libraries.) The result of our analysis is valid for any client program that uses the procedure/library. The only assumptions we make are: (a) The shared state used by the library (the global variables) are private to the library and cannot be modified by the rest of the program, and (b) The client invokes the library procedures sequentially: no concurrent or overlapping invocations of the library procedures by a concurrent client are permitted.

The following semantic formalism is motivated by the above observations. It can be seen as the semantics of the so-called "most general sequential client" of procedure P, which is the program: `while (*) x =` p `(random());`. The executions (of P) produced by this program include all possible executions (of P) produced by all sequential clients.

Let G denote the set of global variables. Let L denote the set of local variables. Let $\mathcal{V}$ denote the set of numeric values (that the variables can take). An element

$$[\text{ASSIGN-LOCAL}]\ \frac{\texttt{x} \in L \qquad (\rho_\ell \uplus \rho_g, \texttt{e}) \Downarrow v}{((\texttt{x := e; S}, \rho_\ell)\gamma, \rho_g) \rightarrow_{\text{P}} ((\texttt{S}, \rho_\ell[\texttt{x} \mapsto v])\gamma, \rho_g)}$$

$$[\text{ASSIGN-GLOBAL}]\ \frac{\texttt{x} \in G \qquad (\rho_\ell \uplus \rho_g, \texttt{e}) \Downarrow v}{((\texttt{x := e; S}, \rho_\ell)\gamma, \rho_g) \rightarrow_{\text{P}} ((\texttt{S}, \rho_\ell)\gamma, \rho_g[\texttt{x} \mapsto v])}$$

$$[\text{SEQ}]\ (((\texttt{S}_1;\texttt{S}_2);\texttt{S}_3, \rho_\ell)\gamma, \rho_g) \rightarrow_{\text{P}} ((\texttt{S}_1;(\texttt{S}_2;\texttt{S}_3), \rho_\ell)\gamma, \rho_g)$$

$$[\text{IF-TRUE}]\ \frac{(\rho_\ell \uplus \rho_g, \texttt{e}) \Downarrow \texttt{true}}{(((\texttt{if (e) then S}_1\texttt{else S}_2\texttt{); S}_3, \rho_\ell)\gamma, \rho_g) \rightarrow_{\text{P}} ((\texttt{S}_1\texttt{; S}_3, \rho_\ell)\gamma, \rho_g)}$$

$$[\text{IF-FALSE}]\ \frac{(\rho_\ell \uplus \rho_g, \texttt{e}) \Downarrow \texttt{false}}{(((\texttt{if (e) then S}_1\texttt{ else S}_2\texttt{); S}_3, \rho_\ell)\gamma, \rho_g) \rightarrow_{\text{P}} ((\texttt{S}_2\texttt{; S}_3, \rho_\ell)\gamma, \rho_g)}$$

$$[\text{CALL}]\ \frac{(\rho_\ell \uplus \rho_g, \texttt{e}) \Downarrow v \qquad \text{P} = p(\texttt{n})\ \texttt{S}_1}{((\texttt{y := }p\texttt{(e); S}_2, \rho_\ell)\gamma, \rho_g) \rightarrow_{\text{P}} ((\texttt{S}_1, [n \mapsto v])(\texttt{y := }p\texttt{(e); S}_2, \rho_\ell)\gamma, \rho_g)}$$

$$[\text{RETURN}]\ \frac{(\rho_\ell \uplus \rho_g, \texttt{r}) \Downarrow v}{((\texttt{return r}, \rho_\ell)(\texttt{y := }p\texttt{(e); S}, \rho_\ell')\gamma, \rho_g) \rightarrow_{\text{P}} (\texttt{S}, \rho_\ell'[\texttt{y} \mapsto v])\gamma, \rho_g)}$$

$$[\text{TOP-LEVEL-CALL}]\ \frac{\texttt{B} = \text{body}(\text{P}) \qquad v \in \mathcal{V}}{([], \rho_g) \rightarrow_{\text{P}} ([(\texttt{B}, [n \mapsto v])], \rho_g)}$$

$$[\text{TOP-LEVEL-RETURN}]\ \frac{}{([(\texttt{return r}, \rho_\ell)], \rho_g) \rightarrow_{\text{P}} ([], \rho_g)}$$

Fig. 2. A small-step operational semantics for our language, represented as a relation $\sigma_1 \rightarrow_{\text{P}} \sigma_2$. A state σ_i is a configuration of the form $((\texttt{S}, \rho_\ell)\gamma, \rho_g)$ where S captures statements to be executed in current procedure, ρ_ℓ assigns values to local variables, γ is the call-stack (excluding current procedure), and ρ_g assigns values to global variables.

$\rho_g \in \Sigma_G = G \hookrightarrow \mathcal{V}$ maps global variables to their values. An element $\rho_\ell \in \Sigma_L = L \hookrightarrow \mathcal{V}$ maps local variables to their values. We define a *local continuation* to be a statement sequence ending with a `return` statement. We use a local continuation to represent the part of the procedure body that still remains to be executed. Let Σ_C represent the set of local continuations. The set of runtime states (or simply, *states*) is defined to be $(\Sigma_C \times \Sigma_L)^* \times \Sigma_G$, where the first component represents a runtime stack, and the second component the values of global variables. We denote individual states using symbols $\sigma, \sigma_1, \sigma_i$, etc. The runtime stack is a sequence, each element of which is a pair $(\texttt{S}, \rho_\ell)$ consisting of the remaining procedure fragment S to be executed and the values of local variables ρ_ℓ. We write $(\texttt{S}, \rho_\ell)\gamma$ to indicate a stack where the topmost entry is $(\texttt{S}, \rho_\ell)$ and γ represents the remaining part of the stack.

We say that a state $((\texttt{S}, \rho_\ell)\gamma, \rho_g)$ is an *entry-state* if its location is at the procedure entry point (*i.e.*, if S is the entire body of the procedure), and we say that it is an *exit-state* if its location is at the procedure exit point (*i.e.*, if S consists of just a `return` statement).

A procedure P determines a single-step execution relation $\rightarrow_{\text{P}}$, where $\sigma_1 \rightarrow_{\text{P}} \sigma_2$ indicates that execution proceeds from state σ_1 to state σ_2 in a single step. Figure 2 defines this semantics. The semantics of evaluation of a side-effect-free expression is captured by a relation $(\rho, \mathtt{e}) \Downarrow v$, indicating that the expression e evaluates to value v in an *environment* ρ (by *environment*, we mean an element of $(G \cup L) \hookrightarrow \mathcal{V}$). We omit the definition of this relation, which is straightforward. We use the notation $\rho_1 \uplus \rho_2$ to denote the union of two disjoint maps ρ_1 and ρ_2.

Note that most rules captures the usual semantics of the language constructs. The last two rules, however, capture the semantics of the most-general sequential client explained previously: when the call stack is empty, a new invocation of the procedure may be initiated (with an arbitrary parameter value).

Note that all the following definitions are parametric over a given procedure P. E.g., we will use the word "execution" as shorthand for "execution of P".

We define an *execution* (of P) to be a sequence of states $\sigma_0\sigma_1\cdots\sigma_n$ such that $\sigma_i \rightarrow_{\text{P}} \sigma_{i+1}$ for all $0 \leq i < n$. Let σ_{init} denote the *initial state* of the library; i.e., this is the element of Σ_G that is induced by the sequence of initializing declarations of the library, namely, "`g1 := c1`; ...; `gN := cN`". We say that an execution $\sigma_0\sigma_1\cdots\sigma_n$ is a *feasible* execution if $\sigma_0 = \sigma_{\text{init}}$. Note, intuitively, a feasible execution corresponds to the sequence of states visited within the library across all invocations of the library procedure over the course of a single execution of the most-general client mentioned above; also, since the most-general client supplies a random parameter value to each invocation of P, in general multiple feasible executions of the library may exist.

We define a *trace* (of P) to be a substring $\pi = \sigma_0\cdots\sigma_n$ of a feasible execution such that: (a) σ_0 is entry-state (b) σ_n is an exit-state, and (c) σ_n corresponds to the return from the invocation represented by σ_0. In other words, a trace is a state sequence corresponding to a single invocation of the procedure. A trace may contain within it nested sub-traces due to recursive calls, which are themselves traces. Given a trace $\pi = \sigma_0\cdots\sigma_n$, we define *initial*$(\pi)$ to be σ_0, *final*(π) to be σ_n, *input*(π) to be value of the input parameter in *initial*(π), and *output*(π) to be the value of the return variable in *final*(π).

We define the relation $\rightsquigarrow_{\text{P}}$ to be $\{(\mathit{input}(\pi), \mathit{output}(\pi)) \mid \pi \text{ is a trace of P}\}$.

Definition 1 (Observational Purity). *A procedure* P *is said to be* observationally pure *if the relation* $\rightsquigarrow_{\text{P}}$ *is a (partial) function: that is, if for all* n, r_1, r_2, *if* $n \rightsquigarrow_{\text{P}} r_1$ *and* $n \rightsquigarrow_{\text{P}} r_2$, *then* $r_1 = r_2$.

Logical Formula and Invariants. Our methodology makes use of *logical formulae* for different purposes, including to express a given *invariant*. Our logical formulae use the local and global variables in the library procedure as free variables, use the same operators as allowed in our language, and make use of universal as well as existential quantification. Given a formula φ, we write $\rho \models \varphi$ to denote that φ evaluates to true when its free variables are assigned values from the environment ρ.

As discussed in Sect. 1, one of our central ideas is to allow the names of the library procedures to be referred to in the invariant; *e.g.*, our running example becomes amenable to our analysis using an invariant such as '(g = −1) ∨ (g = lastN * *factCache*(lastN − 1))'. We therefore allow the use of library procedure names (in our simplified presentation, the name p) as free variables in logical formulae. Correspondingly, we let each environment ρ map each procedure name to a mathematical function in addition to mapping variables to numeric values, and extend the semantics of $\rho \models \varphi$ by substituting the values of both variables and procedure names in φ from the environment ρ.

Given an environment ρ, a procedure name p, and a mathematical function f, we will write $\rho[p \mapsto f]$ to indicate the updated environment that maps p to the value f and maps every other variable x to its original value $\rho[x]$. We will write $(\rho, f) \models \varphi$ to denote that $\rho[p \mapsto f] \models \varphi$.

Given a state $\sigma = ((\mathtt{S}, \rho_\ell)\gamma, \rho_g)$, we define env($\sigma$) to be $\rho_\ell \uplus \rho_g$, and given a state $\sigma = ([], \rho_g)$, we define env(σ) to be just ρ_g. We write $(\sigma, f) \models \varphi$ to denote that $(\text{env}(\sigma), f) \models \varphi$. For any execution or trace π, we write $(\pi, f) \models \varphi$ if for every entry-state and exit-state σ in π, $(\sigma, f) \models \varphi$. We now introduce another definition of observational purity.

Definition 2 (Observational Purity wrt an Invariant). *Given an invariant* φ^{inv}, *a library procedure* P *is said to satisfy* pure(φ^{inv}) *if there exists a function* f *such that for every trace* π *of* P, *output*(π) $=$ f(*input*(π)) *and* $(\pi, f) \models \varphi^{inv}$.

It is easy to see that if procedure P satisfies pure(φ^{inv}) wrt any given candidate invariant φ^{inv}, then P is observationally pure as per Definition 1.

4 Checking Purity Using a Theorem Prover

In this section we provide two different approaches that, given a procedure P and a candidate invariant φ^{inv}, use a theorem prover to check conservatively whether procedure P satisfies pure(φ^{inv}).

4.1 Verification Condition Generation

We first describe an adaptation of standard verification-condition generation techniques (*e.g.*, see [5]) that we use as a common first step in both our approaches. Given a procedure P, a candidate invariant φ^{inv}, our goal is to compute a pair $(\varphi^{post}, \varphi^{vc})$ where φ^{post} is a postcondition describing the state that exists after an execution of body(P) starting from a state that satisfies φ^{inv}, and φ^{vc} is a verification-condition that must hold true for the execution to satisfy its invariants and assertions.

We first transform the procedure body as below to create an internal representation that is input to the postcondition and verification condition generator. In the internal representation, we allow the following extra forms of statements (with their usual meaning): `havoc(x)`, `assume e`, and `assert e`.

1. For any assignment statement "x := e" where e contains x, we introduce a new temporary variable t and replace the assignment statement with "t := e; x := t".
2. For every procedure invocation "x := p(y)", we first ensure that y is a local variable (by introducing a temporary if needed). We then replace the statement by the code fragment "assert φ^{inv}; havoc(g1); ... havoc(gN); assume $\varphi^{inv} \wedge$ x = p(y)", where g1 to gN are the global variables.
   Note that the procedure call has been eliminated, and replaced with an "assume" expression that refers to the function symbol p. In other words, there are no procedure calls in the transformed procedure.
3. We replace the "return x" statement by "assert φ^{inv}". Note that we intentionally do *not* assert that the return value equals $p(n)$.

Let $\mathrm{TB}(\mathrm{P}, \varphi^{inv})$ denote the transformed body of procedure P obtained as above.

$$\begin{array}{ll}
\mathrm{POST}(\varphi^{pre}, \texttt{x := e}) & = (\exists \texttt{x}.\varphi^{pre}) \wedge (\texttt{x = e}) \text{ (if } \texttt{x} \notin \mathrm{vars}(\texttt{e})) \\
\mathrm{POST}(\varphi^{pre}, \texttt{havoc(x)}) & = \exists \texttt{x}.\varphi^{pre} \\
\mathrm{POST}(\varphi^{pre}, \texttt{assume e}) & = \varphi^{pre} \wedge \texttt{e} \\
\mathrm{POST}(\varphi^{pre}, \texttt{assert e}) & = \varphi^{pre} \\
\mathrm{POST}(\varphi^{pre}, \texttt{S}_1; \texttt{S}_2) & = \mathrm{POST}(\mathrm{POST}(\varphi^{pre}, \texttt{S}_1), \texttt{S}_2) \\
\mathrm{POST}(\varphi^{pre}, \texttt{if e then S}_1 \texttt{ else S}_2) & = \mathrm{POST}(\varphi^{pre} \wedge \texttt{e}, \texttt{S}_1) \vee \mathrm{POST}(\varphi^{pre} \wedge \neg\texttt{e}, \texttt{S}_2)
\end{array}$$

$$\begin{array}{ll}
\mathrm{VC}(\varphi^{pre}, \texttt{assert e}) & = (\varphi^{pre} \Rightarrow e) \\
\mathrm{VC}(\varphi^{pre}, \texttt{S}_1; \texttt{S}_2) & = \mathrm{VC}(\varphi^{pre}, \texttt{S}_1) \wedge \mathrm{VC}(\mathrm{POST}(\varphi^{pre}, \texttt{S}_1), \texttt{S}_2) \\
\mathrm{VC}(\varphi^{pre}, \texttt{if e then S}_1 \texttt{ else S}_2) & = \mathrm{VC}(\varphi^{pre} \wedge \texttt{e}, \texttt{S}_1) \wedge \mathrm{VC}(\varphi^{pre} \wedge \neg\texttt{e}, \texttt{S}_2) \\
\mathrm{VC}(\varphi^{pre}, \texttt{S}) & = \text{true(for all other } \texttt{S})
\end{array}$$

$$\mathrm{POSTVC}(\mathrm{P}, \varphi^{inv}) = (\mathrm{POST}(\varphi^{inv}, \mathrm{TB}(\mathrm{P}, \varphi^{inv})), \mathrm{VC}(\varphi^{inv}, \mathrm{TB}(\mathrm{P}, \varphi^{inv})) \wedge (\mathrm{INIT}(\mathrm{P}) \Rightarrow \varphi^{inv}))$$

Fig. 3. Generation of verification-condition and postcondition.

We then compute postconditions as formally described in Fig. 3. This lets us compute for each program point ℓ in the procedure, a condition φ_ℓ that describes what we expect to hold true when execution reaches ℓ if we start executing the procedure in a state satisfying φ^{inv} and if every recursive invocation of the procedure also terminates in a state satisfying φ^{inv}. We compute this using the standard rules for the postcondition of a statement. For an assignment statement "x := e", we use existential quantification over x to represent the value of x prior to the execution of the statement. If we rename these existentially quantified variables with unique new names, we can lift all the existential quantifiers to the outermost level. When transformed thus, the condition φ_ℓ takes the form $\exists x_1 \cdots x_n.\varphi$, where φ is quantifier-free and $x_1, \cdots, x_n$ denote intermediate values of variables along the execution path from procedure-entry to program point ℓ.

We compute a verification condition φ^{vc} that represents the conditions we must check to ensure that an execution through the procedure satisfies its obligations: namely, that the invariant holds true at every call-site and at procedure-exit. Let ℓ denote a call-site or the procedure-exit. We need to check that

```
g := -1;
lastN := 0;
factCache (n) {
  if(n <= 1) {
    result := 1;
  } else if (g != -1 && n == lastN) {
    result := g;
  } else {
    t1 := n-1;
    // t2 := factCache(t1);
    assert φ^inv;
    havoc (g); havoc (lastN);
    assume φ^inv∧ (t2 = factCache(t1));
    g := n * t2;
    lastN := n;
    result := g;
  }
  // return result;
  assert φ^inv;
}
```

Listing 1.2. Procedure factCache from Listing 1.1 transformed to incorporate a supplied candidate invariant φ^{inv}.

$\varphi_\ell \Rightarrow \varphi^{inv}$ holds. Thus, the generated verification condition essentially consists of the conjunction of this check over all call-sites and procedure-exit.

Finally, the function POSTVC computes the postcondition and verification condition for the entire procedure as shown in Fig. 3. (Thus, it returns a pair of formulae.) Note that this function also adds the check that the initial state must satisfy φ^{inv} to the verification condition (as the basis condition for induction). INIT(P) is basically the formula "`g1 = c1` $\wedge \ldots$ `gN = cN`" (see Sect. 2).

Example. We now illustrate the postcondition and verification condition generated from our factorial example presented in Listing 1.1. Listing 1.2 shows the example expressed in our language and transformed as described earlier (using function TB), using a supplied candidate invariant φ^{inv}.

Figure 4 illustrates the computation of postcondition and verification condition from this transformed example. In this figure, we use φ_{cs}^{pre} to denote the precondition computed to hold just before the recursive callsite, and φ_{cs}^{post} to denote the postcondition computed to hold just after the recursive callsite. The postcondition φ^{post} (at the end of the procedure body) is itself a disjunction of three path-conditions representing execution through the three different paths in the program. In this illustration, we have simplified the logical conditions by omitting useless existential quantifications (that is, any quantification of the form $\exists x.\psi$ where x does not occur in ψ). Note that the existentially quantified `g` and `lastN` in φ_{cs}^{post} denote the values of these globals before the recursive call. Similarly, the existentially quantified `g` and `lastN` in φ_3^{path} denote the values of these globals when the recursive call terminates, while the free variables `g` and `lastN` denote the final values of these globals.

$$\begin{aligned}
\text{INIT}(\text{P}) &= (\texttt{g = -1}) \land (\texttt{lastN = 0}) \\
\varphi_1^{path} &= \varphi^{inv} \land (\texttt{n <= 1}) \land (\texttt{result = 1}) \\
\varphi_2^{path} &= \varphi^{inv} \land \neg(\texttt{n <= 1}) \land (\texttt{g != 1}) \land (\texttt{n = lastN}) \land (\texttt{result = g}) \\
\varphi_{cs}^{pre} &= \varphi^{inv} \land \neg(\texttt{n <= 1}) \land \neg((\texttt{g != 1}) \land (\texttt{n = lastN})) \land (\texttt{t1 = n-1}) \\
\varphi_{cs}^{post} &= (\exists \texttt{g} \exists \texttt{lastN}\ \varphi_{cs}^{pre}) \land \varphi^{inv} \land (\texttt{t2 = } \mathit{factCache}\texttt{(t1)}) \\
\varphi_3^{path} &= (\exists \texttt{g} \exists \texttt{lastN}\ \varphi_{cs}^{post}) \land (\texttt{g = n * t2}) \land (\texttt{last N = n}) \land (\texttt{result = g}) \\
\varphi^{post} &= \varphi_1^{path} \lor \varphi_2^{path} \lor \varphi_3^{path} \\
\varphi^{vc} &= (\varphi_{cs}^{pre} \Rightarrow \varphi^{inv}) \land (\varphi^{post} \Rightarrow \varphi^{inv}) \land (\text{INIT}(\text{P}) \Rightarrow \varphi^{inv})
\end{aligned}$$

Fig. 4. The different formulae computed from the procedure in Listing 1.2 by our post-condition and verification-condition computation.

4.2 Approach 1: Existential Approach

Let P be a procedure with input parameter n and return variable r. Let $\text{POSTVC}(\text{P}, \varphi^{inv}) = (\varphi^{post}, \varphi^{vc})$. Let ψ^e denote the formula $\varphi^{vc} \land (\varphi^{post} \Rightarrow (r = p(n)))$. Let $\overline{x}$ denote the sequence of all free variables in ψ^e except for p. We define $\text{EA}(\text{P}, \varphi^{inv})$ to be the formula $\forall \overline{x}.\psi^e$.

In this approach, we use a theorem prover to check whether $\text{EA}(\text{P}, \varphi^{inv})$ is satisfiable. As shown by the following theorem, satisfiability of $\text{EA}(\text{P}, \varphi^{inv})$ establishes that P satisfies $\text{pure}(\varphi^{inv})$.

Theorem 1. *A procedure* P *satisfies* $\text{pure}(\varphi^{inv})$ *if* $\exists p.\text{EA}(\text{P}, \varphi^{inv})$ *is a tautology (which holds iff* $\text{EA}(\text{P}, \varphi^{inv})$ *is satisfiable).*

Proof. Note that p is the only free variable in $\text{EA}(\text{P}, \varphi^{inv})$. Assume that $[p \mapsto f]$ is a satisfying assignment for $\forall \overline{x}.\psi^e$. We show that for every feasible execution π: (P1) $(\pi, f) \vdash \varphi^{inv}$, and (P2) for every trace π' inside π, $\mathit{output}(\pi') = f(\mathit{input}(\pi'))$. This implies that P satisfies $\text{pure}(\varphi^{inv})$.

In particular, for any feasible execution π, we prove by induction over the execution steps in π that

1. For any entry state σ in π, $(\sigma, f) \vdash \varphi^{inv}$.
2. For any exit state σ in π, $(\sigma, f) \vdash \varphi^{inv}$.
3. For any exit state σ in π, if it is the exit state of a trace π', then $\mathit{output}(\pi') = f(\mathit{input}(\pi'))$.

If the above properties fail to hold, we can identify a trace π' corresponding to the first such failure. It can be shown that the sequence of states visited by this trace, when substituted for $\overline{x}$, are a witness that $[p \mapsto f]$ is not a satisfying assignment for $\forall \overline{x}.\psi^e$. This is a contradiction of our original assumption.

Please see [4] for more details of the proof. □

4.3 Approach 2: Impurity Witness Approach

The existential approach presented in the previous section has a drawback. Checking satisfiability of $\text{EA}(\text{P}, \varphi^{inv})$ is hard because it contains universal quantifiers and existing theorem provers do not work well enough for this approach. We now present an approximation of the existential approach that is easier to use with existing theorem provers. This new approach, which we will refer to as the impurity witness approach, reduces the problem to that of checking whether a quantifier-free formula is unsatisfiable, which is better suited to the capabilities of state-of-the-art theorem provers. This approach focuses on finding a counterexample to show that the procedure is impure or it violates the candidate invariant.

Let P be a procedure with input parameter n and return variable r. Let $\text{POSTVC}(\text{P}, \varphi^{inv}) = (\varphi^{post}, \varphi^{vc})$. Let φ^{post}_{α} denote the formula obtained by replacing every free variable x other than p in φ^{post} by a new free variable x_{α}. Define φ^{post}_{β} similarly. Define $\text{IW}(\text{P}, \varphi^{inv})$ to be the formula $(\neg\varphi^{vc}) \vee (\varphi^{post}_{\alpha} \wedge \varphi^{post}_{\beta} \wedge (n_{\alpha} = n_{\beta}) \wedge (r_{\alpha} \neq r_{\beta}))$.

The impurity witness approach checks whether $\text{IW}(\text{P}, \varphi^{inv})$ is satisfiable. This can be done by separately checking whether $\neg\varphi^{vc}$ is satisfiable and whether $(\varphi^{post}_{\alpha} \wedge \varphi^{post}_{\beta} \wedge (n_{\alpha} = n_{\beta}) \wedge (r_{\alpha} \neq r_{\beta}))$ is satisfiable. As formally defined, φ^{vc} and φ^{post} contain embedded existential quantifications. As explained earlier, these existential quantifiers can be moved to the outside after variable renaming and can be omitted for a satisfiability check. (A formula of the form $\exists\overline{x}.\psi$ is satisfiable iff ψ is satisfiable.) As usual, these existential quantifiers refer to intermediate values of variables along an execution path. Finding a satisfying assignment to these variables essentially identifies a possible execution path (that satisfies some other property).

Theorem 2. *A procedure* P *satisfies* $\text{pure}(\varphi^{inv})$ *if* $\text{IW}(\text{P}, \varphi^{inv})$ *is unsatisfiable.*

Proof. We say that two traces disagree if they receive the same argument value but return different values. We say that a pair of feasible executions (π_1, π_2) is an *impurity witness* if there is a trace π_a in π_1 and a trace π_b in π_2 such that π_a and π_b disagree.

A trace is said to be compatible with a function f (and vice versa) if the trace's input-output behavior matches that of the function. An execution is said to be compatible with a function (and vice versa) if every trace in the execution is compatible with the function. We say that a feasible execution π *strongly satisfies* φ^{inv} if for every function f that is compatible with π, $(\pi, f) \models \varphi^{inv}$.

We prove the theorem using the following lemmas: if $\text{IW}(\text{P}, \varphi^{inv})$ is unsatisfiable, then Lemmas 2 and 3 imply that the preconditions of Lemma 1 hold and, hence, P satisfies $\text{pure}(\varphi^{inv})$.

1. If there exists no impurity witness, and every feasible execution strongly satisfies φ^{inv}, then P satisfies $\text{pure}(\varphi^{inv})$.
2. If a feasible execution π that does not strongly satisfy φ^{inv} exists, $\text{IW}(\text{P}, \varphi^{inv})$ is satisfiable.

3. If an impurity witness exists, then $\text{IW}(\text{P}, \varphi^{inv})$ is satisfiable.

1 is straightforward.

For 2, we use a "minimal" feasible execution π that does not strongly satisfy φ^{inv} to construct a satisfying assignment to $\neg\varphi^{vc}$.

For 3, we use a "minimal" impurity witness to construct a satisfying assignment to $(\varphi_\alpha^{post} \wedge \varphi_\beta^{post} \wedge (n_\alpha = n_\beta) \wedge (r_\alpha \neq r_\beta))$.

Please see [4] for more details of the proof. □

5 Generating the Invariant

We now describe a simple but reasonably effective semi-algorithm for generating a candidate invariant automatically from the given procedure. Our approach of Sect. 4 can be used with a manually provided invariant or the candidate invariant generated by this semi-algorithm (whenever it terminates).

The invariant-generation approach is iterative and computes a sequence of progressively weaker candidate invariants $I_0, I_1, \cdots$ and terminates if and when $I_m \equiv I_{m+1}$, at which point I_m is returned as the candidate invariant. The initial candidate invariant I_0 captures the initial values of the global variable. In iteration k, we apply a procedure similar to the one described in Sect. 4 and compute the strongest conditions that hold true at every program point if the execution of the procedure starts in a state satisfying I_{k-1} and if every recursive invocation terminates in a state satisfying I_{k-1}. We then take the disjunction of the conditions computed at the points before the recursive call-sites and at the end of the procedure, and existentially quantify all local variables. We refer to the resulting formula as $\text{NEXT}(I_{k-1}, \text{TB}(\text{P}, I_{k-1}))$. We take the disjunction of this formula with I_{k-1} and simplify it to get I_k.

Figure 5 formalizes this semi-algorithm. Here, we exploit the fact that the `assert` statements are added precisely at every recursive callsite and end of procedure and these are the places where we take the conditions to be disjuncted.

In our running example, I_0 is '$\text{g} = -1 \wedge \text{lastN} = 0$'. Applying NEXT to I_0 yields I_0 itself as the pre-condition at the point just before the recursive call-site, and '$(\text{g} = -1 \wedge \text{lastN} = 0) \vee \text{g} = \text{lastN} * p(\text{lastN} - 1)$' (after certain simplifications) as the pre-condition at the end of the procedure. Therefore, I_1 is '$(\text{g} = -1 \wedge \text{lastN} = 0) \vee \text{g} = \text{lastN} * p(\text{lastN} - 1)$'. When we apply NEXT to I_1,

$$I_0 = \text{INIT}(\text{P})$$
$$I_k = \text{SIMPLIFY}(I_{k-1} \vee \text{NEXT}(I_{k-1}, \text{TB}(\text{P}, I_{k-1})))$$

$$\text{NEXT}(\varphi^{pre}, \texttt{assert e}) = \exists \ell_1 \cdots \ell_m \varphi^{pre} (\text{where } \ell_1, \cdots, \ell_m \text{ are local variables in } \varphi^{pre})$$
$$\text{NEXT}(\varphi^{pre}, \text{S}_1; \text{S}_2) = \text{NEXT}(\varphi^{pre}, \text{S}_1) \vee \text{NEXT}(\text{POST}(\varphi^{pre}, \text{S}_1), \text{S}_2)$$
$$\text{NEXT}(\varphi^{pre}, \texttt{if e then } \text{S}_1 \texttt{ else } \text{S}_2) = \text{NEXT}(\varphi^{pre} \wedge \text{e}, \text{S}_1) \vee \text{NEXT}(\varphi^{pre} \wedge \neg\text{e}, \text{S}_2)$$
$$\text{NEXT}(\varphi^{pre}, \text{S}) = \text{false}(\text{for all other S})$$

Fig. 5. Iterative computation of invariant.

the computed pre-conditions are I_1 itself at both the program points mentioned above. Therefore, the approach terminates with I_1 as the candidate invariant.

6 Evaluation

We have implemented our OP checking approach as a prototype using the Boogie framework [6], and have evaluated the approach using this implementation on several examples. The objective of this evaluation was primarily a sanity check, to test how our approach does on a set of OP as well as non-OP procedures.

We tried several simple non-OP programs, and our implementation terminated with a "no" answer on all of them. We also tried the approach on several OP procedures: (1) the 'factCache' running example, (2) a version of a factorial procedure that caches all arguments seen so far and their corresponding return values in an array, (3) a version of factorial that caches only the return value for argument value 19 in a scalar variable, (4) a recursive procedure that returns the nth Fibonacci number and caches all its arguments and corresponding return values seen so far in an array, and (5) a "matrix chain multiplication" (MCM) procedure. The last example is based on dynamic programming, and hence naturally uses a table to memoize results for sub-problems. Here, observational purity implies that the procedure always returns the same solution for a given sub-problem, whether a hit was found in the table or not. The appendix of a technical report associated with this paper depicts all the procedures mentioned above as created by us directly in Boogie's language, as well as the invariants that we supplied manually (in SMT2 format).

It is notable that the theorem prover was not able to handle the instances generated by the"existential approach" even for simple examples. The "impurity witness" approach, however, terminated on all the examples mentioned above with the correct answer, with the theorem prover taking less than 1 s on each example. Please see [4] for more information about the examples used in our evaluation.

7 Related Work

The previous work that is most closely related to our work is by Barnett et al. [1,2]. Their approach is based on the same notion of observational purity as our approach. Their approach is structurally similar to ours, in terms of needing an invariant, and using an inductive check for both the validity of the invariant as well as the uniqueness of return values for a given argument. However, their approach is based on a more complex notion of invariant than our approach, which relates pairs of global states, and does not use a function symbol to represent recursive calls within the procedure. Hence, their approach does not extend readily to recursive procedures; they in fact state that "there is a circularity - it would take a delicate argument, and additional conditions, to avoid unsoundness in this case". Our idea of allowing the function symbol in the invariant to represent the recursive call allows recursive procedures to be checked, and also simplifies the specification of the invariant in many cases.

Cok et al. [7] generalize the work of Barnett et al.'s work, and suggest classifying procedures into categories "pure", "secret", and "query". The "query" procedures are observationally pure. Again, recursive procedures are not addressed.

Naumann [3] proposes a notion of observational purity that is also the same as ours. Their paper gives a rigorous but manual methodology for proving the observational purity of a given procedure. Their methodology is not similar to ours; rather, it is based finding a *weakly pure* procedure that simulates the given procedure as far as externally visible state changes and the return value are concerned. They have no notion of an invariant that uses a function symbol that represents the procedure, and they don't explicitly address the checking of recursive procedures.

There exists a significant body of work on identifying differences between two similar procedures. For instance, differential assertion checking [8] is a representative from this body, and is for checking if two procedures can ever start from the same state but end in different states such that exactly one of the ending states fails a given assertion. Their approach is based on logical reasoning, and accommodates recursive procedures. Our impurity witness approach has some similarity with their approach, because it is based on comparing the given procedure with itself. However, our comparison is stricter, because in our setting, starting with a common argument value but from different global states that are both within the invariant should not cause a difference in the return value. Furthermore, technically our approach is different because we use an invariant that refers to a function symbol that represents the procedure being checked, which is not a feature of their invariants. Partush et al. [9] solve a similar problem as differential assertion checking, but using abstract interpretation instead of logical reasoning.

There is a substantial body of work on checking if a procedure is *pure*, in the sense that it does not modify any objects that existed before the procedure was invoked, and does not modify any global variables. Sălcianu et al. [10] describe a static analysis to check purity and Madhavan et al. [11] present an abstract-interpretation based generalization of this analysis. Various tools exist, such as JML [12] and Spec# [13], that use logical techniques based on annotations to prove procedures as pure. Purity is a more restrictive notion than observational purity; procedures such as our 'factCache' example are observationally pure, but not pure because they use as well as update state that persists between calls to the procedure.

References

1. Barnett, M., Naumann, D.A., Schulte, W., Sun, Q.: 99.44% pure: useful abstractions in specifications. In: ECOOP Workshop on Formal Techniques for Java-like Programs (FTfJP) (2004)
2. Barnett, M., Naumann, D.A., Schulte, W., Sun, Q.: Allowing state changes in specifications. In: Müller, G. (ed.) ETRICS 2006. LNCS, vol. 3995, pp. 321–336. Springer, Heidelberg (2006). https://doi.org/10.1007/11766155_23

3. Naumann, D.A.: Observational purity and encapsulation. Theor. Comput. Sci. **376**(3), 205–224 (2007)
4. Arora, H., Komondoor, R., Ramalingam, G.: Checking observational purity of procedures. CoRR https://arxiv.org/abs/1902.05436 (2019)
5. Flanagan, C., Saxe, J.B.: Avoiding exponential explosion: generating compact verification conditions. In: Conference Record of POPL 2001: The 28th ACM SIGPLAN-SIGACT Symposium on Principles of Programming Languages, London, UK, 17–19 January 2001, pp. 193–205 (2001)
6. Leino, K.R.M.: This is Boogie 2. Manuscript KRML 178(131) (2008)
7. Cok, D.R., Leavens, G.T.: Extensions of the theory of observational purity and a practical design for JML. In: Seventh International Workshop on Specification and Verification of Component-Based Systems (SAVCBS 2008). Number CS-TR-08-07 in Technical report, School of EECS, UCF, vol. 4000 (2008)
8. Lahiri, S.K., McMillan, K.L., Sharma, R., Hawblitzel, C.: Differential assertion checking. In: Proceedings of the 2013 9th Joint Meeting on Foundations of Software Engineering, pp. 345–355. ACM (2013)
9. Partush, N., Yahav, E.: Abstract semantic differencing for numerical programs. In: Logozzo, F., Fähndrich, M. (eds.) SAS 2013. LNCS, vol. 7935, pp. 238–258. Springer, Heidelberg (2013). https://doi.org/10.1007/978-3-642-38856-9_14
10. Sălcianu, A., Rinard, M.: Purity and side effect analysis for Java programs. In: Cousot, R. (ed.) VMCAI 2005. LNCS, vol. 3385, pp. 199–215. Springer, Heidelberg (2005). https://doi.org/10.1007/978-3-540-30579-8_14
11. Madhavan, R., Ramalingam, G., Vaswani, K.: Purity analysis: an abstract interpretation formulation. In: Yahav, E. (ed.) SAS 2011. LNCS, vol. 6887, pp. 7–24. Springer, Heidelberg (2011). https://doi.org/10.1007/978-3-642-23702-7_6
12. Leavens, G.T., et al.: JML reference manual (2008)
13. Barnett, M., Leino, K.R.M., Schulte, W.: The Spec# programming system: an overview. In: Barthe, G., Burdy, L., Huisman, M., Lanet, J.L., Muntean, T. (eds.) CASSIS 2004. LNCS, vol. 3362, pp. 49–69. Springer, Heidelberg (2005). https://doi.org/10.1007/978-3-540-30569-9_3

Software Evolution and Requirements Engineering

Structural and Nominal Cross-Language Clone Detection

Lawton Nichols(✉), Mehmet Emre, and Ben Hardekopf

University of California, Santa Barbara, USA
{lawtonnichols,emre,benh}@cs.ucsb.edu

Abstract. In this paper we address the challenge of cross-language clone detection. Due to the rise of cross-language libraries and applications (e.g., apps written for both Android and iPhone), it has become common for code fragments in one language to be ported over into another language in an extension of the usual "copy and paste" coding methodology. As with single-language clones, it is important to be able to detect these cross-language clones. However there are many real-world cross-language clones that existing techniques cannot detect.

We describe the first general, cross-language algorithm that combines both structural and nominal similarity to find syntactic clones, thereby enabling more complete clone detection than any existing technique. This algorithm also performs comparably to the state of the art in single-language clone detection when applied to single-language source code; thus it generalizes the state of the art in clone detection to detect both single- and cross-language clones using one technique.

1 Introduction

The clone detection problem has long been recognized by the community, with many existing papers exploring different techniques for finding clones amongst code written in a single language [5,13,14,21,22]. However, in recent years an interesting twist has arisen due to the rising popularity of cross-language libraries and applications: *cross-language clones*. Consider the parser generator ANTLR [3], which has runtimes that are written in C#, C++, Go, Java, JavaScript, Python (2 and 3), and Swift. Also consider multi-platform mobile applications, which are often ported between Java and Objective-C or Swift, the languages used by Android and iPhone applications. In these kinds of settings, clones can actually cross language boundaries: a fragment of code in one language can be copied and massaged to conform to the syntax and semantics of another language. Existing single-language clone detection techniques are unable to effectively detect these sorts of cross-language clones. In this paper we propose a method to detect cross-language clones and demonstrate that it (1) finds cross-language clones that no existing method can detect; and (2) performs comparably to existing single-language clone detectors for finding clones within a corpus of single-language code sources. Therefore, our technique generalizes

R. Hähnle and W. van der Aalst (Eds.): FASE 2019, LNCS 11424, pp. 247–263, 2019.
https://doi.org/10.1007/978-3-030-16722-6_14

```
Trees._findAllNodes = function(t, index, findTokens, nodes) {
        // check this node (the root) first
        if(findTokens && (t instanceof TerminalNode)) {
                if(t.symbol.type===index) {
                        nodes.push(t);
                }
        } else if(!findTokens && (t instanceof ParserRuleContext)) {
                if(t.ruleIndex===index) {
                        nodes.push(t);
                }
        }
        // check children
        for(var i=0;i<t.getChildCount();i++) {
                Trees._findAllNodes(t.getChild(i), index, findTokens, nodes);
        }
};
```

```
template<typename T>
static void _findAllNodes(ParseTree *t, size_t index, bool findTokens, std::vector<T> &nodes) {
  // check this node (the root) first
  if (findTokens && is<TerminalNode *>(t)) {
    TerminalNode *tnode = dynamic_cast<TerminalNode *>(t);
    if (tnode->getSymbol()->getType() == index) {
      nodes.push_back(t);
    }
  } else if (!findTokens && is<ParserRuleContext *>(t)) {
    ParserRuleContext *ctx = dynamic_cast<ParserRuleContext *>(t);
    if (ctx->getRuleIndex() == index) {
      nodes.push_back(t);
    }
  }
  // check children
  for (size_t i = 0; i < t->children.size(); i++) {
    _findAllNodes(t->children[i], index, findTokens, nodes);
  }
}
```

Fig. 1. A JavaScript (top) and C++ (bottom) clone pair doing a pre-order search.

```
VerletParticle2D.prototype.setWeight = function(w){
  this.weight = w;
  this.invWeight =
   (w !== 0) ? 1 / w : 0; //avoid divide by zero
};
```

```
public void setWeight(float w) {
  weight = w;
  invWeight = 1f / w;
}
```

Fig. 2. A JavaScript (left) and Java (right) clone pair setting the weight and inverse weight of a particle in a graphics application. A bug-fix has been applied to the JavaScript clone but not the Java clone.

the current state of the art in clone detection by extending it to allow for both single-language and cross-language clone detection using a single technique.

To make this problem more concrete, consider Fig. 1, which shows a real-life case (found during our evaluation described in Sect. 6) of code clones involving C++ and JavaScript source code from the ANTLR parser generator [3]. To demonstrate the importance of finding cross-language clones, consider Fig. 2, which shows another real-life case (also found during our evaluation) of code clones involving JavaScript and Java in which a bug-fix has been applied to one of the clones but not the other. In addition, a quick search of the CVE (Common Vulnerabilities and Exposures) database yields a vulnerability due to incorrect message authentication checking that exists in multiple different language implementations of the relevant code [9].

There are only four existing papers that we are aware of that introduce new techniques for cross-language clone detection (discussed in more detail in Sect. 2). That initial work has either focused on clones across languages that share a common intermediate representation such as .NET [1,15] or has deviated from classical clone detection and taken a more restricted, natural language-based approach, sometimes relying on assumptions that may not be met in real code [7,8]. None of that existing work would detect the clone examples given in Figs. 1 and 2 without extensive modification.

The main reason for these restrictions in previous work is that the *syntactic structure* (i.e., parse trees) of different languages can be extremely different even for code that, at the source level, seems similar. We demonstrate this phenomenon later in this paper. In order to overcome this problem, previous work has either restricted itself to languages with a common intermediate representation (thus enforcing that the syntactic structure is similar for similar code) or abandoned structural matching entirely and looked only at the names of variables and other user-defined abstractions (what we call *nominal* clone detection). We observe that using purely structural or purely nominal matching is sub-optimal in a cross-language setting, in that each can yield both false positives and false negatives.

Our technique consists of (1) a method for enabling structural matching for cross-language clones even in those cases where syntactic structure is different (Sect. 4); and (2) a method for composing both structural and nominal matching into a singular matcher, maintaining the strengths of each while mitigating their individual weaknesses (Sect. 5). We have implemented our technique in a tool called FETT[1] that works at the granularity of function pairs; we use FETT to empirically compare our proposed technique against existing techniques (Sect. 6). We begin by describing related work and background information in Sect. 2 and giving a high-level overview of our technique in Sect. 3.

2 Background and Related Work

The concept of clone detection is not new, and the different techniques involved have been surveyed extensively [5,21]. Most existing non-semantics-based techniques can be categorized into the classes of "structural," "nominal," or "hybrid," which we define below.

Before we begin, there is a bit of misleading terminology in the literature: there exist many clone detection tools that are considered language-generic or language-agnostic (e.g., [22]), but can only be configured to work for programs written in a single language at a time. CCFinder [14], for example, can detect clones for six different programming languages; however, the user cannot (outside of naive text-only modes) truly cross language boundaries during a "language-generic" clone detection phase.

2.1 What Exactly Is a Cross-Language Clone?

Intuitively, we consider a cross-language clone to be the same as any same-language clone—two pieces of code that implement similar functionality—the only difference is the setting. We highlight here what kinds of clones our tool is able to find, and what kinds of clones we include in our evaluation based on their classification (i.e., Type I, II, III or IV [24]).

[1] Our implementation is located at http://www.cs.ucsb.edu/~pllab under the "Downloads" link.

The usual code clone hierarchy does not translate well to a cross-language setting: type I and type II clones [24] may not exist across languages because of syntactic differences between languages (e.g., switch statements exist in C but not in Python). In this paper, we present methods that discover syntactic clones modulo the differences in language syntax, and we do this by creating a correspondence between related but different constructs. We do not consider semantic (type IV) clones that implement the same functionality in a different way (e.g., quicksort vs. selection sort). Readers familiar with the standard clone hierarchy can think of the clones that we find as type III clones generalized across languages.

2.2 Structural Program Similarity

Intuitively, two programs (or subprograms) can be considered similar if they look the same, disregarding identifier names—i.e., if their syntax trees have roughly the same shape. We refer to structural clone detection as the process of taking advantage of this similarity.

Same-language clone detection tools usually also consider identifier data, and we are not aware of any purely structural cross-language clone detector. A notable same-language tool that operates via structural similarity is Deckard, which converts syntax trees into vectors for fast comparison [13].

Structural similarity is useful in all settings, but it is a hard problem in a multi-language setting—all the hybrid structural/nominal methods we describe below make some restriction on the languages involved. A major part of the novelty of our technique is a method for purely structural matching across languages (though the final algorithm then combines structural with nominal (i.e., identifier-based) techniques for greater accuracy).

2.3 Nominal Program Similarity

Whereas structural similarity disregards identifiers and instead looks at code shape, nominal similarity does the exact opposite. Nominal similarity relies on the insight that similar code, especially copied and pasted snippets, will have the same identifier names throughout, regardless of code structure.

Notable same-language clone detection tools that operate via nominal similarity are CCFinder and SourcererCC, which compare program tokens [14,25].

Across Languages. Cheng et al. describe CLCMiner [8], the first cross-language clone detection tool that does not require the languages involved to translate to the same intermediate form. It compares revision histories (diffs) in repository logs for cross-platform C# and Java programs; the tokens inside commits are used to compute similarity scores. CLCMiner is the basis for the Nominal algorithm defined in Sect. 5.1.

Cheng et al. study a different notion of nominal similarity in [7], where they measure the effectiveness of token distributions in finding clones among cross-platform mobile applications; they obtain a negative result for identifier names alone. Flores et al. [10] use natural language processing techniques to discover cross language clones at the function level.

2.4 Hybrid Program Similarity

It is logical to combine structural and nominal similarity methods, as the results they provide are complementary. A notable same-language, hybrid clone detection tool is NiCad, which performs its comparisons at the parse tree level [23]. Syntax tree-based comparison is quite common [4,27].

Tree similarity is computationally expensive [6], and it is more efficient to linearize programs in some way; sequence similarity algorithms can then do the comparison. Existing same-language work compares the tokens in the order in which they appear in the parse tree [11], and we also take advantage of linearization of full parse trees in this work.

Across Languages. Kraft et al. present C2D2 [15], the first cross-language clone detection tool, for C# and Visual Basic programs. This work requires that the languages involved be compiled to the same intermediate representation (IR)—.NET IR in this case. From a graph derived from that IR, they create sequences of tokens for subgraphs and use a Levenshtein distance-based token similarity algorithm to compare them.

Al-Omari et al. build on Kraft et al.'s work and find clones by comparing CIL intermediate code text [1]. Again, they are restricted to .NET languages.

This work. Our method is a hybrid method, works on any language with a grammar definition, and relies on just the source code (in contrast to, e.g., CLCMiner which requires the existence of revision history). We linearize preprocessed parse trees at the function level and compare the linearized sequences in a novel way that generalizes Kraft et al.'s work and incorporates features of Cheng et al.'s work.

2.5 CLCMiner

Our main comparison is with the only tool designed for cross-language clone detection and capable of handling arbitrary languages: CLCMiner [8]. We provide further background on it here. CLCMiner is based on having the source code in a version control system, and requires a revision history by design. Section 5.1 gives a detailed explanation of our adaptation of CLCMiner. The original CLCMiner algorithm works on diffs and lexes them, whereas our version works on function parse trees.

We were not able to obtain access to the original CLCMiner source code from the authors. In order to compare against this method, we implement our own version which adapts CLCMiner to work with the entire text of a function and have it calculate the distance metric above when given a function pair. Our new implementation may perform better or worse than the original (which uses revision history rather than function pairs) in certain cases.

We incorporate CLCMiner's distance metric in a novel way in FETT, and show that our combination of structural and nominal information produces better results. As we have adapted CLCMiner's algorithm to work on functions instead of diffs, it relies on having a parser to extract the functions and does not rely on a version control system. We refer to our nominal-only adaptation of CLCMiner's algorithm as "Nominal" for the rest of the paper.

3 Overview

In this section we provide a high-level overview of FETT and provide justification for some of our steps. We give an end-to-end example of our clone detection process in our tech report [18]. FETT's pipeline is:

1. Take as input a corpus of source code (which may exist in multiple languages);
2. Using existing ANTLR grammars, parse and create a separate parse tree for each function (we currently handle C++, Java, and JavaScript);
3. Simplify parse trees that have an unnecessarily large depth;
4. Abstract the multilingual parse trees into a common representation to facilitate comparison;
5. Linearize the resulting trees using a preorder traversal;
6. Compare all linearized function pairs using a Smith-Waterman local sequence alignment algorithm; and finally
7. Present the pairwise similarity scores to the user.

The following sections fill in the details of the structural and nominal aspects of FETT's cross-language clone detection process.

4 Structural Clone Detection

One key insight of our structural algorithm is that *abstract* syntax trees (ASTs), which eliminate details in the concrete parse trees about how exactly the input was parsed or what language it came from, tend to look more similar for similar code even across languages. Unfortunately, ASTs are not part of a language's specification, and AST grammars and formats are implementation dependent. We are not aware of any single compiler that has frontends for the variety of languages that we compare. Our structural clone detection algorithm processes *reduced parse trees* (Sect. 4.1) to eliminate nonessential details about parsing and obtain a structure similar to ASTs.

Another source of disparity between trees generated by two grammars is that the nonterminals are different. The other key insight of our structural algorithm is that abstracting reduced parse trees by putting nonterminals in *equivalence classes* (Sect. 4.2) strikes a balance between preserving necessary information and smoothing out differences across languages.

Our structural algorithm proceeds by extracting functions from an abstracted parse tree and then computes similarity scores between functions using the Smith-Waterman local sequence alignment algorithm.

Flattening a tree using a preorder traversal helps smooth out most remaining inconsistencies between inter-language reduced parse trees. To demonstrate the dissimilarities due to grammatical differences that preorder traversal removes, see Fig. 3: a grammar that uses nested `if` statements will have a parse tree like Fig. 3b, while a grammar that uses unnested `if` statements will look more like Fig. 3c. As the `else if` cases become more numerous in the first grammar the nesting becomes more severe, emphasizing the differences in the resulting parse trees.

if (exp) block [*else block*] (G1)
if exp : block [*elif exp : block*]* [*else block*] (G2)

(a) Two different kinds of grammars for if statements.

(b) An example parse tree using the nested `if` grammar (G1).

(c) An example parse tree using the unnested `if` grammar (G2).

Fig. 3. Grammars and parse trees for nested vs. unnested `if` statements.

4.1 Precedence Woes

Some grammar definitions encode operator precedence into the grammar[2], whereas others use facilities provided by the parser generators to encode the precedence. Direct encoding of precedence causes spurious chains of nonterminals in the resulting parse tree, which would be removed when the parse tree is converted to an AST. We collapse the chains of nonterminals encountered in a parse tree for the direct encoding case to remove the chains and mitigate this disparity between different styles of grammars. Figure 4 demonstrates the kinds of issues that are apparent when a grammar hard-codes precedence—because precedence in this case appears in the form of nested productions, we always see "AdditiveExpression" even when there is only a multiplication expression present; this will throw off any clone detector that is working directly on plain parse trees.

If precedence is handled indirectly through the parser generator, then the resulting parse tree is much closer to an AST. This is an example of an issue that only arises in a cross-language setting, and which makes cross-language clone detection strictly more difficult than same-language clone detection. We condense any chains of nonterminals, and we refer to the parse trees after this stage as *reduced parse trees.*

[2] We encountered this only in the C++ grammar during our evaluation.

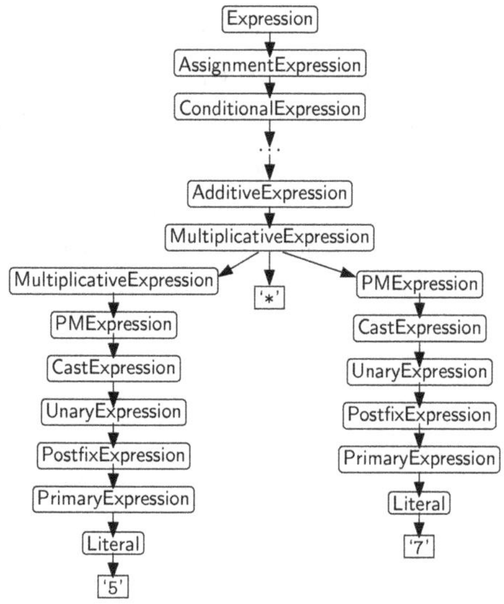

Fig. 4. A subtree of the original C++ parse tree for the text "`5*7`".

4.2 Abstracting Parse Tree Nonterminals

Consider the two reduced parse trees for the expression `binarySearch(array, mid+1, high, x)` in Figs. 5a and b. Although they look similar to the naked eye, because the node names are different, even a tree edit distance algorithm would say that the trees are not similar at all. We thus need to abstract the nonterminal names while preserving essential information about the tree structure. After performing this abstraction, we call the resulting parse trees *abstracted parse trees*.

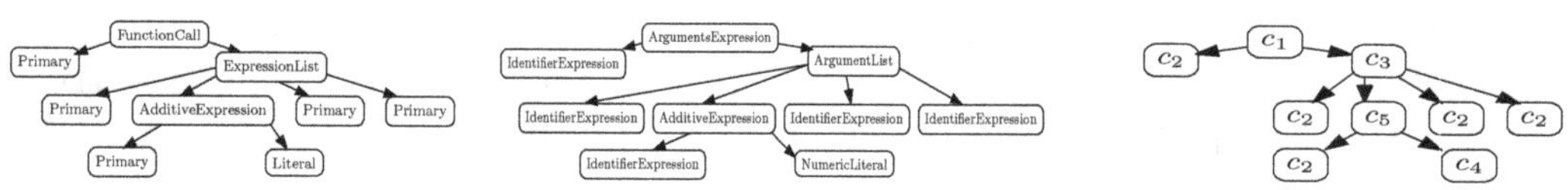

(a) Reduced parse tree from a Java parser . (b) Reduced parse tree from a JavaScript parser . (c) Abstraction of the trees in Figures 5a and 5b .

Fig. 5. Reduced parse trees for expression `binarySearch(array, mid+1, high, x)` in Java and JavaScript, and their abstraction. The terminals are omitted for simplicity.

Our method instead groups node types with similar meanings across languages, so that node types that "mean" similar things are in the same group. To do this, we *manually* categorize node types into equivalence classes *once per pair of languages*. For example, consider the equivalence classes $c_1 =$ {FunctionCall, ArgumentsExpression}, $c_2 =$ {Primary, IdentifierExpression}, $c_3 =$ {ArgumentList, ExpressionList}, $c_4 =$ {NumericLiteral, Literal}, $c_5 =$ {AdditiveExpression} and the set $C = \{c_1, c_2, c_3, c_4, c_5\}$. After replacing each node in Figs. 5a and b with its equivalence class in C, we end up with trees that are exactly the same (Fig. 5c). In this specific example the abstracted trees are the same, though this is not always the case in practice.

We define the abstraction algorithm in two parts: $\mathsf{EqClassMapOf}(C)$ produces a map from each node to a symbol corresponding to its equivalence class. $\mathsf{Abstract}(tree, map)$ does the abstraction by traversing the given tree bottom up and applying the map. It removes the *nonterminals* which do not belong to any equivalence class. When the abstraction algorithm removes a node, it connects any children of the removed node to the removed node's parent.

4.3 Sequence Alignment for Clone Detection

Linearizing the trees via a preorder traversal of the nodes will remove most traces of the structural differences demonstrated in Fig. 3. Moreover, the state of the art tree edit distance algorithms are not as scalable as sequence alignment algorithms[3]. These observations led us to explore sequence alignment algorithms as an alternative to tree-edit distance. Levenshtein distance is a popular choice in this category. Smith-Waterman is strictly more general than Levenshtein distance, and it supports assigning weights to different elements in the sequence. Hence, we use the Smith-Waterman algorithm on preordered trees to compute similarity scores. We evaluate the precision and recall of both Smith-Waterman and tree edit distance in Sect. 6 and observe that sequence alignment performs better in terms of precision and scalability.

We convert function subtrees to sequences by computing the preorder traversal. Finally, we execute Smith-Waterman using custom weights on each sequence pair and normalize the resulting score using the normalization factor Z described below. We chose the weights based on the hypothesis that certain nodes like conditionals indicate important program structure, and should generally appear in the same order in a cloned pair of functions; therefore, we assign higher weights to penalize the function pairs in which this alignment does not occur. In the algorithm, the function $\mathsf{SmithWaterman}(a, b, M, g)$ computes a similarity score between two sequences a and b using the Smith-Waterman algorithm with substitution matrix M and linear gap penalty coefficient g; a detailed explanation of these parameters can be found in [2].

Normalizing Smith-Waterman results. The result of the Smith-Waterman algorithm depends on the size of the input, and longer sequence pairs have higher scores. In order to find both short and long clones, we normalize the resulting similarity score from the Smith-Waterman algorithm to neutralize the bias towards longer clones.

We define the *self-similarity score* of a sequence a as the score assigned to the pair (a, a) by the *unnormalized* Smith-Waterman algorithm; denote this score $\mathsf{S}(a)$. We normalize score assigned to a pair (a, b) by $\frac{1}{Z}$ where $Z = \max\{\mathsf{S}(a), \mathsf{S}(b)\}$. Note that Z is an upper bound for the score obtained by Smith-Waterman, and the score is equal to Z if and only if $a = b$. Thus,

[3] APTED, the state of the art tree edit distance algorithm has a time complexity of $O(n^3)$ [20] whereas the variant of Smith-Waterman algorithm we use is $O(n^2)$ [2].

using the normalization factor $\frac{1}{Z}$ is useful if one is looking for similar whole functions rather than looking for a small snippet in a larger piece of code.

5 Hybrid Algorithm

Combining nominal and structural clone detection in a cross-language setting provides the best of both worlds, and mitigates any issues that running just one detection method might have.

Identifier names carry some meaning about the programmer intent and give a code snippet context. On the other hand, structure of code (conditionals, loops, function calls etc.) also carry information about programmer intent. Without this structural information, we might misidentify two pieces of code as clones. Our hybrid algorithm is guided by structural information while consulting the Nominal algorithm to use local context within structurally similar pieces of code.

5.1 Our Nominal Algorithm

We have adapted CLCMiner's algorithm to work on functions as our purely Nominal algorithm. For a given pair of functions (f_1, f_2), our nominal matching algorithm consists of two parts.

The first part takes a function f, removes the comments and splits the tokens on each non-letter character (such as underscores or dashes). It then splits the camel case tokens into words and converts them to lowercase—each function becomes a bag of words that is represented by a characteristic vector, which holds the number of occurrences of each word. We denote the resulting characteristic vector as $\mathsf{v}(f)$.

The second part of the algorithm computes a normalized distance between the two characteristic vectors v_1, v_2 according to the formula $\mathrm{d}(v_1, v_2) = \frac{\|v_1 - v_2\|_1}{\|v_1\|_1 + \|v_2\|_1}$ where $\|\cdot\|_1$ is the ℓ_1 norm (i.e., the sum of the absolute values of every entry in the vector). This algorithm computes a distance between two given functions; to make it comparable to the other algorithms, we use $1 - \mathrm{d}(v_1, v_2)$ as a similarity score.

5.2 Full Algorithm

Our full algorithm is provided in our tech report [18]. It is a combination of the structural and nominal algorithms: we linearize the parse trees, and consecutive terminal nodes become bags of words. Nonterminals are compared using our structural method, and bags of words are compared using our nominal method.

6 Evaluation

In this section we compare our work against existing work on both cross-language and same-language clone detection.

6.1 Implementation and Environment

We have implemented our tool FETT in Scala and used the ANTLR parser framework as its front end, so that any language with an ANTLR grammar can be easily connected.

To test whether FETT can handle same-language clone detection with similar accuracy as specialized, language-specific tools, we configured NiCad 4.0 [23] to work at the function-level granularity and experimented with configurations until we found the best-performing one for our tests[4].

Because we are comparing parse *trees*, we also want to determine how well we compete against the state-of-the-art tree edit distance algorithms, thus we compare one data set with APTED [19,20]. We normalize the similarities using the method described in [17], and, as this normalization method requires a metric distance, we could not introduce weights for matches. We can still weight mismatches, though. We found that the parameters *mismatch* = 1, *deletion* = *insertion* = 5, *match* = 0 gave us the best results overall.

We chose the threshold for ignored functions (defined in Sect. 4.3) to be $\theta = 35$ for every experiment, and the exact tolerance parameters are given below for each case. We used the same set of equivalence classes with the same weights for all cases: conditional, loop, return, and function call were all weighted 5; assignments were weighted 2; and all other considered nodes were weighted 1.

Our experiments were run on a computer with an Intel i7 4790 3.6 GHz processor. FETT, Structural, Tree Edit Distance, and Nominal were given 8 GB maximum heap size and were set to use 4 threads.

6.2 Methodology

We used the standard statistical metrics of precision, recall, and F-measure to quantitatively assess the effectiveness of our different techniques.

Due to the sheer amount of possible clone candidates in large projects, it is difficult to manually obtain complete ground truth for clones in real-world programs. Hence, we created two separate data sets for evaluation:

Manual programs set (handwritten set). We implemented a set of small programs in different languages to create a setting in which we have complete knowledge of whether a pair of functions are clones. Statistics about the code are in Table 1.

Randomly sampled program set (large set). We chose four libraries that have implementations in different languages and set the tolerance parameters[5] defined in our algorithm (see [18]) to give the best results on a per-language

[4] NiCad: threshold = 0.5, minsize = 4, maxsize = 2500, rename = blind, filter = none, abstract = none, normalize = none.

[5] For FETT: $\mu = 6$ (match coefficient) and $g = -4$ (gap penalty) for the case of comparing Java and JavaScript, and $(\mu, g) = (9, -1)$ for Java/C++ and JavaScript/C++, and $(8, -3)$ for Java/Java. The nominal multiplier was set to 2 for all but the Java/C++ and JavaScript/C++ cases, where it was set to 3. For the Structural algorithm: $(7, -1)$ for JavaScript/Java, $(8, -4)$ for Java/C++, $(0.5, -2)$ for Java/Java, and $(9, -4)$ for JavaScript/C++.

Table 1. Statistics of handwritten clones.

Language Pair	LoC	#Functions	#Pairs	#Clones
Java	201	12	132	11
JavaScript	177	11		
Java	201	12	144	12
C++	195	12		
JavaScript	177	11	132	11
C++	195	12		

pair basis. We randomly sampled functions from the files with the same names (ignoring extensions) and manually checked the pairs to create a sample with ground truth—this is essentially the sampling strategy used by Cheng et al. [8] applied to functions instead of diffs. We chose to reuse this sampling strategy due to the manual nature of our evaluation, and because we only possess finite human resources; it does not reflect the true distribution of clones, as function clone pairs are unlikely to be chosen in a standard uniform random sample—had we gone that route, our precision and recall scores would not have been meaningful. We are not aware of a better solution to this problem.

The first three libraries considered for this set are: the ANTLR parser framework, version 4 [3]; the toxiclibs computational design library [26]; and the ZXing barcode image processing library [28]. We also considered two ports of the LAME MP3 encoding library in different languages that were ported by different developers to assess the efficacy of clone detection tools in such a scenario: lamejs, a JavaScript port [16]; and java-lame, a Java port [12]. Statistics about the libraries are in Table 2.

Table 2. Statistics of libraries considered for evaluation. LoC: non-blank non-comment lines of code, Fun's: # of functions found in each project, Nont'l (Nontrivial) Fun's: # of functions whose reduced parse trees are $> \theta$ (the chosen threshold), Pairs: the # of possible fun. pairs, Same-File Pairs: # of pairs of functions coming from files with the same name (ignoring extensions), Sel'd: # of selected pairs, Runtime: total time (H:M:S) to run our method.

Data set	Library	Lang. Pair	LoC	Fun's	Nont'l Fun's	Pairs	Same-File Pairs	Sel'd	Runtime	Clones
antlrj	ANTLR	Java	13,770	1,393	694	240,471	4,942	505	0:56:18	14
		Java	13,770	1,393	694					
antlrjsj	ANTLR	Java	13,770	1,393	694	281,070	6,240	663	0:25:01	45
		JavaScript	7,323	728	405					
antlrcppjs	ANTLR	C++	15,766	1,222	480	194,400	3,762	752	0:17:11	17
		JavaScript	7,323	728	405					
toxic	toxiclibs	Java	36,178	3,734	2,156	5,004,076	11,637	1,060	3:01:12	63
		JavaScript	36,976	4,108	2,321					
zxing	ZXing	Java	38,968	2,659	1,689	684,045	1,388	254	2:10:51	45
		C++	22,784	866	405					
lame	java-lame	Java	20,950	575	436	101,152	4,645	873	0:27:37	34
	lamejs	JavaScript	11,112	285	232					

6.3 Results

For our main set of tests, we compare FETT against (1) our purely Structural algorithm (i.e., no token similarity), and (2) our Nominal algorithm. We also apply the APTED tree edit distance algorithm combined with our abstraction method on our handwritten data set; tree edit distance takes at least an order of magnitude longer than the other tools, and we did not evaluate the large data set using tree edit distance because of this and due to its poor performance on the handwritten tests. We use NiCad on the Java-Java same-language case of our large data set.

Cumulative clone ratios. We look at the graphs of cumulative clone distributions to choose a good cut-off point for each of the three techniques. These graphs were originally used in [8], and they are meant to give an intuition about where a clone detector separates clones from non-clones.

Similarity vs. cumulative clone ratio graphs track the ratio of clones to non-clones as the similarity score varies from 1.0 to 0. For example, at point 0.4 on the similarity axis, we plot the ratio of clones to non-clones of all samples with similarity scores > 0.4. A successful clone detector would have a similarity value at which there is a significant drop in this ratio, and that would create the optimal cutoff point. A clone detector may not assign very high scores to any pairs based on its similarity metric; in such cases, we start the plot from the first nonempty bin. Figure 7 shows the cumulative clone ratios for antlrj and toxic; graphs of other test cases are omitted because of space constraints, but they are of similar overall shape. We chose a cutoff point for each clone detector based on the drops from these graphs (e.g. we chose the cutoff point of 0.4 for FETT's Java/Java case). The relative shape of the graph is more important than absolute scores—squishing or stretching the similarity scores only affects the choice of the optimal cutoff point.

Handwritten test set. When evaluating the manually created (handwritten) data set, we used the same parameters $\mu = 7$, $g = -2$ overall for all pairs of functions in the data set and considered the combined results for both FETT and the Structural algorithm. FETT had its nominal multiplier set to 2. Figure 6 shows the clone distributions of different clone detection methods for the handwritten program set; and precision, recall, and F-measure (harmonic mean of precision and recall) for this set are given in Table 3. FETT and the Structural algorithm had a cutoff of 0.5, and the Nominal algorithm's cutoff was 0.6.

Handwritten test set discussion. The table and the figures paint a similar picture. Both FETT and the Structural algorithm seem to perform the best on this data set—the graphs for the higher similarity scores have a high clone ratio, and there is a sharp decline visible in both graphs as the similarity score is allowed to lower. The Nominal algorithm has a less sharp drop, and this indicates that it is assigning mid-range similarity scores with low precision. It is also notable that tree edit distance does so poorly; we believe that this is because we are not allowed to give weights to matches, as described above.

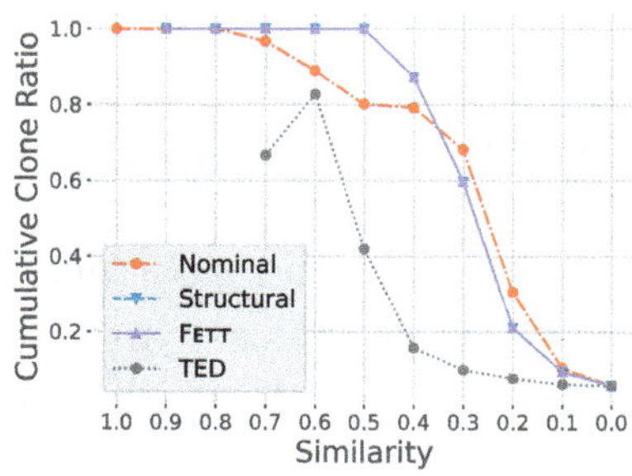

Fig. 6. Cumulative clone ratio distribution for handwritten programs. Results of FETT and structural coincide.

Table 3. Precision, recall, and F-measure for handwritten program set.

Data set	Method	Precision	Recall	F-measure
Handwritten	FETT	1.000	0.970	0.985
	Structural	1.000	0.970	0.985
	Nominal	0.886	0.939	0.912
	Tree Edit Dist.	0.821	0.697	0.754

Large test set. We now present and discuss all the cross-language results for our large test set. The same-language case is different from the cross-language cases, so the reader is asked to consult Fig. 7b, which is indicative of all the cross-language cases, and not Fig. 7a.

Cutoffs were chosen on a per-language pair basis that maximized a given tool's score. For FETT, for the three JavaScript/Java test cases and the Java/C++ test case, we used a cutoff of 0.4, and the rest used a cutoff of 0.5. For the Structural algorithm, we used a cutoff of 0.6 for JavaScript/Java, 0.5 for Java/C++ and JavaScript/C++, and 0.4 for Java/Java. For the Nominal algorithm, we used a cutoff of 0.5 for JavaScript/C++, and 0.6 for the rest.

Figure 8 shows precision, recall and F-measure of all the tools we compared for each data set and provides a visual and quantitative assessment of efficacy of all the techniques.

Large test set discussion. Clone ratios relate most closely to the precision scores for each data set, and from the results it appears that the Structural algorithm generally has the upper hand in this area—applying the intuition described above, we see that the Structural algorithm seems to cut off at the sharpest angle in most cases. It makes sense why this is the case, as pieces of code that look similar across languages are generally prime candidates for clones.

Precision is of course not the whole story. It is clear that FETT is able to take the best of both the nominal and structural worlds, and the F-measure is always the highest. When it comes to Structural's results, the toxiclibs case is an outlier, where we found that there were more cases of the structural differences; FETT's hybrid structural/nominal algorithm was able to make up for this, though.

Same-language test case. To assess performance on same-language clones, we compared our tool with NiCad on the Java version of ANTLR. Returning to the same figures, the antlrj case is quite similar to the other language pairs in terms of precision, recall, and F-measure, which demonstrates that our tool is capable of holding its ground in a same-language setting.

FETT performs slightly worse (by one percentage point in terms of F-measure) than NiCad. This result is not surprising because NiCad uses more

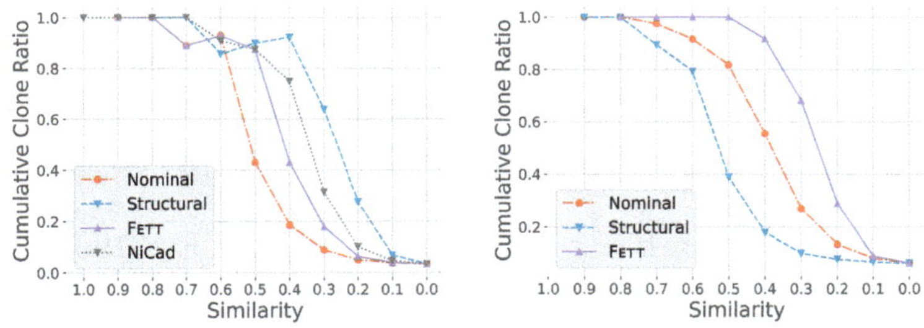

(a) antlrj (b) toxic

Fig. 7. Similarity vs. cumulative clone ratio for the samples from the large open-source program set.

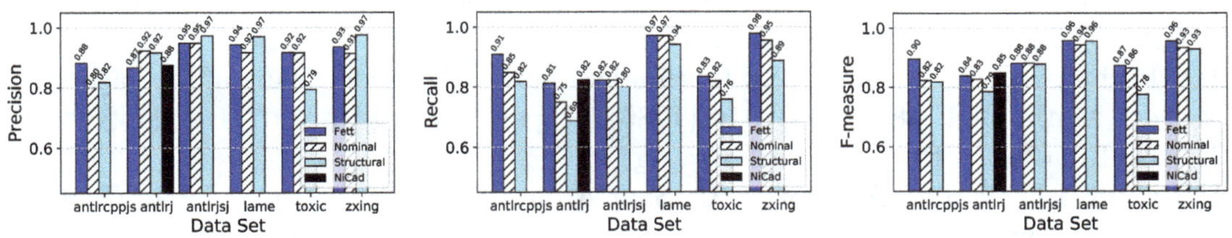

Fig. 8. Precision, recall and F-measure of clone detection tools on the large program set.

information about the code whereas we deliberately discard some information by abstracting parse trees to work in a cross-language setting. Even with our filtering of parse trees, FETT's F-measure score is very close, and this shows that our tool is capable of producing similar results to a dedicated same-language tool.

Overall results. We observe that the FETT's hybrid algorithm, in terms of F-measure, outperforms both the Nominal algorithm and the Structural algorithm consistently in our large test set experiments.

Limitations. FETT may have difficulty scaling to repositories with large numbers of large functions—a run of FETT on the entire toxiclibs library (comparing every function pair, not just same file pairs) takes 5.13 h—and so further improvements will be required to enable such a target. One possible future direction for improvements could be to develop semi-automated solutions where we have the user use her domain knowledge and pick out the files or functions to compare beforehand, or the user can prune the search space by telling the tool which modules are unrelated.

7 Conclusion

We have presented FETT, a hybrid structural/nominal clone detection method that is capable of operating across programming languages and that is generic in the sense that it does not require any languages involved to belong to the same language family. It is syntax-based, uses ready-made grammar specifications, and requires minimal manual effort—the keys to the process are syntax abstraction and sequence alignment. We have provided a two-part evaluation of FETT, and we empirically demonstrate on multiple test sets that FETT is accurate in terms of the standard metrics of precision and recall. We also confirm that our method is on a par with previous work when it comes to same-language clone detection, thus proving that it is strictly more general than single-language methods.

Acknowledgments. This work was supported by NSF CCF-1319060.

References

1. Al-Omari, F., Keivanloo, I., Roy, C.K., Rilling, J.: Detecting clones across Microsoft .NET programming languages. In: 19th Working Conference on Reverse Engineering, WCRE 2012, Kingston, ON, Canada, 15–18 October 2012, pp. 405–414 (2012). https://doi.org/10.1109/WCRE.2012.50
2. Altschul, S.F., Erickson, B.W.: Optimal sequence alignment using affine gap costs. Bull. Math. Biol. **48**(5), 603–616 (1986). https://doi.org/10.1007/BF02462326
3. ANTLR (2017). http://www.antlr.org/
4. Baxter, I.D., Yahin, A., Moura, L., Sant'Anna, M., Bier, L.: Clone detection using abstract syntax trees. In: 1998 Proceedings of the International Conference on Software Maintenance, pp. 368–377. IEEE (1998)
5. Bellon, S., Koschke, R., Antoniol, G., Krinke, J., Merlo, E.: Comparison and evaluation of clone detection tools. IEEE Trans. Softw. Eng. **33**(9), 577–591 (2007)
6. Bille, P.: A survey on tree edit distance and related problems. Theor. Comput. Sci. **337**(1–3), 217–239 (2005). https://doi.org/10.1016/j.tcs.2004.12.030
7. Cheng, X., Jiang, L., Zhong, H., Yu, H., Zhao, J.: On the feasibility of detecting cross-platform code clones via identifier similarity. In: Proceedings of the 5th International Workshop on Software Mining, pp. 39–42. ACM (2016)
8. Cheng, X., Peng, Z., Jiang, L., Zhong, H., Yu, H., Zhao, J.: Mining revision histories to detect cross-language clones without intermediates. In: 2016 31st IEEE/ACM International Conference on Automated Software Engineering (ASE), pp. 696–701. IEEE (2016)
9. CVE-2013-1624 : The TLS implementation in the Bouncy Castle Java library before 1.48 and C# library before 1.8 does not properly consider (2017). http://www.cvedetails.com/cve/CVE-2013-1624/
10. Flores, E., Barrón-Cedeno, A., Rosso, P., Moreno, L.: Desocore: detecting source code re-use across programming languages. In: Proceedings of the 2012 Conference of the North American Chapter of the Association for Computational Linguistics: Human Language Technologies: Demonstration Session, pp. 1–4. Association for Computational Linguistics (2012)
11. Gitchell, D., Tran, N.: Sim: a utility for detecting similarity in computer programs. In: ACM SIGCSE Bulletin, vol. 31, pp. 266–270. ACM (1999)
12. java-lame (2017). https://github.com/nwaldispuehl/java-lame
13. Jiang, L., Misherghi, G., Su, Z., Glondu, S.: Deckard: scalable and accurate tree-based detection of code clones. In: Proceedings of the 29th International Conference on Software Engineering, pp. 96–105. IEEE Computer Society (2007)
14. Kamiya, T., Kusumoto, S., Inoue, K.: CCFinder: a multilinguistic token-based code clone detection system for large scale source code. IEEE Trans. Softw. Eng. **28**(7), 654–670 (2002)
15. Kraft, N.A., Bonds, B.W., Smith, R.K.: Cross-language clone detection. In: SEKE, pp. 54–59 (2008)
16. lamejs (2017). https://github.com/zhuker/lamejs

17. Li, Y., Chenguang, Z.: A metric normalization of tree edit distance. Front. Comput. Sci. China **5**(1), 119–125 (2011). https://doi.org/10.1007/s11704-011-9336-2
18. Nichols, L., Emre, M., Hardekopf, B.: Structural and nominal cross-language clone detection. Technical report 2019-01, University of California, Santa Barbara, February 2019. https://cs.ucsb.edu/research/tech-reports/2019-01
19. Pawlik, M., Augsten, N.: Efficient computation of the tree edit distance. ACM Trans. Database Syst. **40**(1), 3:1–3:40 (2015). https://doi.org/10.1145/2699485
20. Pawlik, M., Augsten, N.: Tree edit distance: robust and memory-efficient. Inf. Syst. **56**, 157–173 (2016). https://doi.org/10.1016/j.is.2015.08.004
21. Rattan, D., Bhatia, R., Singh, M.: Software clone detection: a systematic review. Inf. Softw. Technol. **55**(7), 1165–1199 (2013)
22. Rieger, M.: Effective clone detection without language barriers. Ph.D. thesis, University of Bern (2005)
23. Roy, C.K., Cordy, J.R.: NICAD: accurate detection of near-miss intentional clones using flexible pretty-printing and code normalization. In: 2008 16th IEEE International Conference on Program Comprehension, pp. 172–181, June 2008. https://doi.org/10.1109/ICPC.2008.41
24. Roy, C.K., Cordy, J.R.: A survey on software clone detection research. Technical report 541, Queen's School of Computing (2007)
25. Sajnani, H., Saini, V., Svajlenko, J., Roy, C.K., Lopes, C.V.: SourcererCC: scaling code clone detection to big-code. In: Proceedings of the 38th International Conference on Software Engineering, ICSE 2016, pp. 1157–1168. ACM, New York (2016). https://doi.org/10.1145/2884781.2884877
26. toxiclibs (2017). http://toxiclibs.org/
27. Yang, W.: Identifying syntactic differences between two programs. Softw.: Pract. Exp. **21**(7), 739–755 (1991)
28. Zxing (2017). https://github.com/zxing/zxing

Check for updates

SL2SF: Refactoring Simulink to Stateflow

Stephen Wynn-Williams[1(✉)], Zinovy Diskin[1], Vera Pantelic[1], Mark Lawford[1], Gehan Selim[1], Curtis Milo[1], Moustapha Diab[2], and Feisel Weslati[2]

[1] McMaster Centre for Software Certification, McMaster University, Hamilton, ON, Canada
{wynnwisj,diskinz,pantelv,lawford,selimg,milocj}@mcmaster.ca
[2] FCA US LLC, Auburn Hills, MI, USA
moustapha.diab@external.fcagroup.com, faz.weslati@fcagroup.com

Abstract. In the Matlab Simulink environment, systems can be modelled using Simulink block diagrams and Stateflow state charts. While stateful logic is more naturally modelled using Stateflow, in practice complex block diagrams are often used instead, resulting in models that are hard to understand and maintain. In order to improve the maintainability and understandability of large industrial models, this paper presents a strategy for refactoring Simulink block diagrams implementing stateful logic into functionally equivalent Stateflow state charts that more naturally represent the intended behaviour. To bridge the gap between the syntax of block diagrams and state charts, Mealy machines represented by tabular expressions are used as an intermediate representation. The compositional language of block diagrams is used to combine tables modelling individual blocks into a table for the entire block diagram which describes the high level state machine encoded in the Simulink subsystem. A prototype tool that performs the translation from Simulink to Stateflow automatically is discussed.

Keywords: Simulink · Stateflow · Refactoring · Mealy machines · Tabular expressions · Monoidal categories

1 Introduction

The adoption of Model-Based Design in the development of embedded control systems across industries has led to the wide use of Matlab/Simulink/Stateflow as a supporting environment. The modelling capabilities provided by Simulink block diagrams and Stateflow state charts complement each other by providing languages for functional and stateful system specifications. Due to their individual strengths, one modelling formalism may be preferable for specifying certain classes of behaviours. For example, the MathWorks Automotive Advisory Board (MAAB) guidelines [25] advise the use of Stateflow over Simulink for modelling stateful logic. This is because Simulink block diagrams that are used to model mode switching logic are often cumbersome and difficult to understand. In this

R. Hähnle and W. van der Aalst (Eds.): FASE 2019, LNCS 11424, pp. 264–281, 2019.
https://doi.org/10.1007/978-3-030-16722-6_15

case, Stateflow state charts should be used to implement the same logic resulting in a structure which is easier to read, maintain, and verify.

For example, each model in Fig. 1 executes periodically to update its state and outputs. When the block diagram in Fig. 1a updates, each signal line is given a value and each block uses the values of the incoming signals to determine the values of the outgoing signals. When the state chart in Fig. 1b updates, it checks each condition on transitions leaving its current mode (i.e. state node). If a condition is satisfied, the state chart transitions to the associated target mode and executes the *exit* actions of the mode it is leaving, the actions on the transition it is taking, and the *entry* actions of the mode it is entering. If no transitions are valid, the state chart remains in its current mode and executes the *during* actions of that mode.

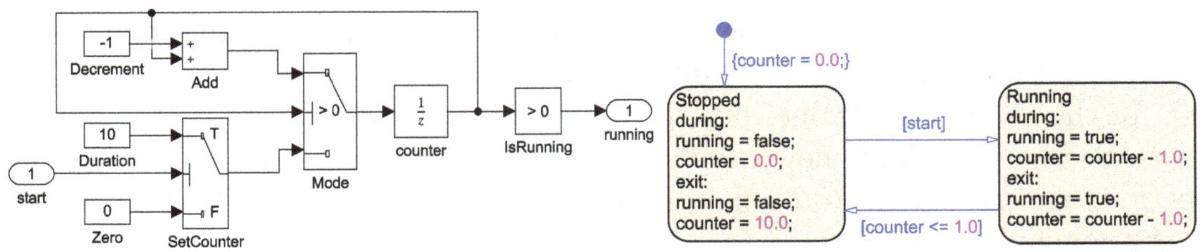

(a) Before: Simulink Block Diagram (b) After: Stateflow State Chart

Fig. 1. Model of a timer in Simulink and Stateflow.

The Simulink and Stateflow models shown in Fig. 1 are functionally equivalent. Both models capture a timer with one boolean input, *start*, and one boolean output, *running*. When *start* becomes true, the system starts counting down from ten to zero. While the system is counting down, *running* is true. Once the counter reaches zero, *running* is set to false and becomes true again if *start* is true. Although there are relatively few blocks in Fig. 1a, it is difficult to understand how this model achieves the behaviour while the state chart in Fig. 1b clearly captures the system's modes and the conditions triggering mode changes.

Our industrial experience has identified the need to refactor Simulink block diagrams to Stateflow state charts for easier comprehension and maintenance. More precisely, practice shows that Simulink is often used to specify stateful logic even though Stateflow would be a more appropriate implementation language. This might occur during model evolution when modes of operation are added to previously mode-free block diagrams, and developers find it easier to modify the existing Simulink logic to accommodate the change than to reproduce the behaviour from scratch in a state chart. Other times, a developer's preference dictates the choice of modelling formalism. Manual refactoring from Simulink to Stateflow, although feasible, is a time consuming and error prone process which requires that the behaviour of complex Simulink models is completely understood.

This paper presents an approach to translate block diagrams into behaviourally equivalent state charts. The approach converts individual blocks into tabular expressions [21] to expose their latent state variables and decision logic. The data flow between blocks is then used to combine tables into a single, larger table describing the entire block diagram. Then, the elements of state charts (states, transitions) are identified by reconfiguring the combined tables into a form similar to state charts. Behavioural equivalence is established by giving semantics to block diagrams, state charts, and the intermediate tables as Mealy machines. The paper's main contributions are: (i) A method for translating Simulink block diagrams to Stateflow state charts via tabular expressions. (ii) A categorical framework for composing Mealy machines by combining their update functions as the basis of the translation. (iii) A prototype tool implementing the translation from Simulink to Stateflow.

This paper is organized as follows. Section 2 describes how we model systems and our categorical framework for combining them. Section 3 illustrates the translation method with a simple example. Section 4 describes the application of the categorical framework to convert block diagrams to tabular expressions. Section 5 explains how tabular expressions are converted to state charts. Section 6 describes the prototype tool. Related work is covered in Sect. 7 and the paper concludes with Sect. 8.

2 Background: Modelling Systems and Their Combinations

This section describes the formalisms underlying the proposed translation approach: Mealy machines, tabular expressions, and monoidal categories.

2.1 Mealy Machines: Modelling Stateful Systems

To preserve behaviour, the semantics of both block diagrams and state charts are modeled using *Mealy machines*.

Definition 1. *A* Mealy Machine m *is a tuple* $(S, s_0, \Sigma, \Lambda, ud)$*, where* S *is a* set of states *(the* state space*),* $s_0 \in S$ *(the* initial state*),* Σ *is a set of input* values *(the* input alphabet*),* Λ *is a set of output values (the* output alphabet*),* and $ud : \Sigma \times S \to \Lambda \times S$ *is a function (the* update function*) which computes the* current output and next state from the current input and current state.

For example, the unit delay $\frac{1}{z}$ block labelled *counter* in Fig. 1a can be modelled as the Mealy machine $delay = (\mathbb{R}, 0, \mathbb{R}, \mathbb{R}, shift)$. The block has an input variable (port) i, an output variable (port) o, and an internal state variable *counter*, where $i, o, counter \in \mathbb{R}$. When the block updates, it outputs the current state value $o = counter$, and updates the state to store the current input value $counter' = i$, i.e. $(o, counter') = shift(i, counter)$, where $shift : \mathbb{R}^2 \to \mathbb{R}^2$ is defined as $shift(i, counter) = (counter, i)$.

While Simulink has no formal semantics, our use of Mealy machines to model their behaviours is consistent with the informal semantics described in Chap. 3 of the Simulink User Guide [26].

2.2 Tabular Expressions: Representing Conditional Behaviours

Both block diagrams and state charts can specify decision logic, but in rather distinct ways. We unify the presentation of decision logic in the two formalisms using two similar forms of tabular expressions: *horizontal condition tables* (HCTs) as presented in [28]; and *state transition tables* (STTs), which specialize HCTs to describe state charts similarly to the ones presented in [24].

		running	*counter′*
start	$counter > 0$	*true*	$counter - 1$
	$counter \leq 0$	*false*	10
$\neg start$	$counter > 0$	*true*	$counter - 1$
	$counter \leq 0$	*false*	0

(a) Horizontal Condition Table

Source	**Condition**	*running*	*counter′*	**Target**
Running	$counter - 1 > 0$	*true*	$counter - 1$	*Running*
	$counter - 1 \leq 0$	*true*	$counter - 1$	*Stopped*
Stopped	*start*	*false*	10	*Running*
	$\neg start$	*false*	0	*Stopped*

(b) State Transition Table

Fig. 2. Intermediate representations

An HCT is represented in Fig. 2a. It is a tabular representation of the update function of a Mealy machine which models the block diagram from Fig. 1a. Given the variable values $start = true$ and $counter = 0$, the table can be evaluated from left to right in the following way. Since the first condition *start* of the first column is satisfied, and the sub-condition $counter \leq 0$ in the second row of the second column is satisfied, we use the second row to determine that *running* is given the value of *false*, and $counter'$ is given a value of 10.

The second tabular representation, STTs, are also used to represent the update function of Mealy machines. Their special format closely matches the state charts they model. For example, the STT in Fig. 2b represents the state chart in Fig. 1b. Each mode is listed in the first column, and the condition of each transition is listed in the second column, adjacent to the mode they leave. The columns after the double bars describe how each output/state variable is updated by the actions of the associated transition. The final column of each row indicates which mode the associated transition leads to.

Tabular expressions were given a precise semantics in [10]. The structure of tables can be rearranged without changing the function they describe, e.g., conditions can be reordered as in [4]; conditions can be combined with sub-conditions (via conjunction) to flatten the hierarchy of conditions; and normal expressions in the table can be simplified by assuming the conditions to their left hold.

2.3 Categorical Framework: Combining Systems

The key idea of block diagrams is to combine simple, predefined blocks to describe a behaviour. The language of *monoidal categories* explains how to break down the complex data flow of block diagrams and describe it in terms of simpler data flow [5] (i.e. cascading blocks in sequence, placing blocks in parallel, and feeding outputs of blocks back to their inputs).

Monoidal categories describe data flow in an abstract setting where blocks are called *morphisms*. Simple data flow constructs are described as operations on morphisms, which can be visualized using block diagrams called *string diagrams* [5,22]. In this section, we discuss the wiring constructs in the concrete setting of the category **Set**, where morphisms are functions from an input set of tuples to an output set of tuples (called the *domain/codomain objects* of the morphism).

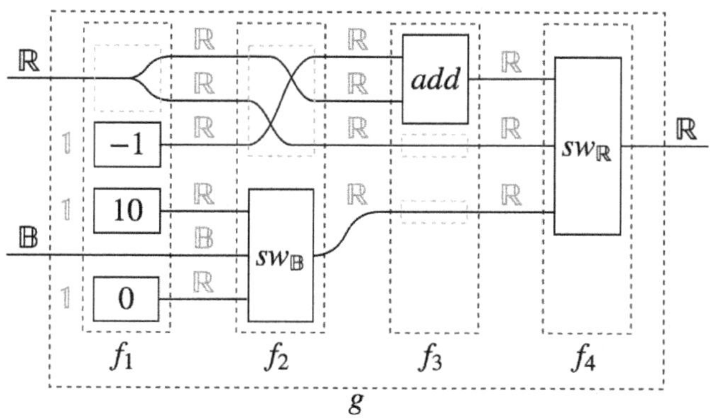

Fig. 3. Functional fragment of timer example

A fragment of the block diagram from Fig. 1a can be used to illustrate the idea behind the basic data flow operations. The string diagram in Fig. 3 describes a function that is broken down into sub-functions combined via two operations: sequential combination (denoted ";") and parallel combination (denoted "$\otimes$"). The fragment describes a function g from $\mathbb{R} \times \mathbb{B}$ to $\mathbb{R}$. Each wire extending from the left/right of the large compound function indicates an input/output value, respectively. The wire is labelled with the set from which the value comes. If there are multiple wires, the domain or codomain of the function is given as the Cartesian product of those sets. In monoidal categories, the Cartesian product is generalized as an operation called the *monoidal product on objects.*

The function g is composed of a sequence of sub-functions, $g = f_1; f_2; f_3; f_4$. The sub-functions (except for f_4) consist of functions composed in parallel with wires and other functions. The wiring "data routing functions" are then defined as follows: a normal wire is the *identity* function $\mathrm{id}_X = \{(x) \mapsto (x)\}$; wires crossing over each other define the *braiding* function $\mathrm{Br}_{A,B} = \{(a,b) \mapsto (b,a)\}$; and branching wires are called the *diagonal* function $\Delta_X = \{(x) \mapsto (x,x)\}$. The functions are indexed with the set(s) over which they are defined. Morphisms like these functions have special status in monoidal categories and must satisfy some axioms to verify that they "act like wiring" in the host category.

Sub-function f_3 can now be described as $f_3 = add \otimes \mathrm{id}_{\mathbb{R}} \otimes \mathrm{id}_{\mathbb{R}}$. Functions combined in parallel have domains/codomains which are the Cartesian products of the domain/codomain of the component functions. The parallel combination uses each component function independently to calculate each component of the output. For example, taking $add = \{(x_1, x_2) \mapsto (x_1 + x_2)\}$, the function $add \otimes \mathrm{id}_{\mathbb{R}} \otimes \mathrm{id}_{\mathbb{R}}$ is given by $\{(x_1, x_2, x_3, x_4) \mapsto (x_1 + x_2, x_3, x_4)\}$. In monoidal categories this operation is generalized as the *monoidal product on morphisms*, where the domain/codomain of a product morphism is given by the monoidal product of the domain/codomain objects of the component morphisms. It is notable that we can also describe sub-function f_3 as $f_3 = add \otimes \mathrm{id}_{\mathbb{R}^2}$, where the two wires are treated as one function. This is useful, for example, when describing the sub-function f_2 as $f_2 = \mathrm{Br}_{\mathbb{R}^2,\mathbb{R}} \otimes sw_{\mathbb{B}}$.

Describing f_1 requires modelling constant blocks as functions. Therefore, constants are described as functions with inputs from the singleton set $\mathbb{1} = \{()\}$, and we draw functions with domain/codomain $\mathbb{1}$ as blocks with no wires extending from the left/right side, respectively. Functions modelling constant blocks, $[k] = \{() \mapsto (k)\}$, always take the empty tuple as input, and always produce the same value k as output. The function f_1 can now be described as $f_1 = \Delta_{\mathbb{R}} \otimes [-1] \otimes [10] \otimes \mathrm{id}_{\mathbb{B}} \otimes [0]$. Objects like $\mathbb{1}$ have special status in monoidal categories and are called the *monoidal unit.* Taking their monoidal product with any other object X yields the same object X. Intuitively, this means that concatenating any tuple $(x_1, .., x_n)$ with the empty tuple $()$ does nothing. This explains why the product of the domains of the functions in f_1 is the set $\mathbb{R} \times \mathbb{1} \times \mathbb{1} \times \mathbb{B} \times \mathbb{1}$, but the domain of f_1 is described as $\mathbb{R} \times \mathbb{B}$—the former simplifies to the latter.

We now describe the entire function g in terms of simple data flow:

$$g = (\Delta_{\mathbb{R}} \otimes [-1] \otimes [10] \otimes \mathrm{id}_{\mathbb{B}} \otimes [0]); (\mathrm{Br}_{\mathbb{R}^2,\mathbb{R}} \otimes sw_{\mathbb{B}}); (add \otimes \mathrm{id}_{\mathbb{R}} \otimes \mathrm{id}_{\mathbb{R}}); sw_{\mathbb{R}}$$

However, this example does not contain feedback loops. Loops are obtained when inputs and outputs of a function are connected by some common wire(s), such as the wire connecting the first input and first output of the inner box in Fig. 4a. Adding looping wires to a function $f : X \times A \to X \times B$ yields a new function $f^* : A \to B$ (e.g., the outer box in Fig. 4a) where $f^*(a) = b$ if there exists a unique $x \in X$ such that $f(x, a) = (x, b)$. When such an x exists for each $a \in A$, the loop configuration is considered *well-formed.* Following [11], we encode the addition of such loops with a *trace* operation: $\mathrm{Tr}^X_{A,B}(f) = f^*$.

For example, consider the function $f = \{(x, y) \mapsto (x + x, x + y)\}$. In the function $\mathrm{Tr}^{\mathbb{R}}_{\mathbb{R},\mathbb{R}}(f)$ the trace applies the constraint that the first input is equal to the first output (i.e. $x = x + x$) to which there is a unique solution: $x = 0$. Given any $y \in \mathbb{R}$, $f(0, y) = (0, y)$, therefore $\mathrm{Tr}^{\mathbb{R}}_{\mathbb{R},\mathbb{R}}(f) = \{(y) \mapsto (y)\}$. This approach uses *fixed point equations* to specify traces, which is generalized by the approach from [8]. Since these fixed point equations are not guaranteed to have a unique solution, the trace operation is *partial*—it is only defined for loop configurations that are well-formed. Partial traces have been described in [15], and the guarded structure introduced in [7] compositionally describes which feedback configurations are valid. For the loops to "act like wiring", certain axioms must be satisfied, e.g., the *yanking* axiom (as shown in Fig. 4b) states that $\mathrm{Tr}^X_{X,X}(\mathrm{Br}_{X,X}) = \mathrm{id}_X$ for any set X.

(a) $\mathrm{Tr}^X_{A,B}(f)$ (b) Yanking: $\mathrm{Tr}^X_{X,X}(\mathrm{Br}_{X,X}) = \mathrm{id}_X$

Fig. 4. String diagrams for traced categories

3 Translation Strategy

The translation strategy is composed of three steps. This section illustrates these steps by considering the example from Fig. 1.

First, the decision logic implemented by the block diagram is encoded as the HCT in Fig. 8a. This step is described in Sect. 4. In the second step, the representation is simplified as, depending on the value of *counter*, only some rows of the table can be valid. By associating a certain range of state variable values with a mode of operation, we simplify the representation by considering only the conditions which are possible. This allows us to leverage the conditions from HCTs to determine the modes of operation by rearranging HCTs into equivalent STTs such as Fig. 2b. The final step trivially rearranges the information from STTs into a state chart by creating a transition for each row. The conversion from HCTs to STTs to state charts is described in Sect. 5, and possible simplifications to the resulting state chart are discussed.

Even with such a simple example, the importance of automated refactoring becomes apparent. If the model were to be refactored manually, a state chart that is not equivalent to the block diagram could be created unintentionally. For example, one can manually produce a state chart that transitions out of the *Running* mode when *counter* is zero, rather than one.

4 Block Diagrams to HCTs: Mealy Composition

The first step of the translation strategy is to model the entire block diagram as a Mealy machine whose update function is represented as a HCT. To achieve this, Simulink block diagrams are modelled in a category **Mealy**, where morphisms (i.e. blocks) are Mealy machines, not functions. We then show how the update functions of composite Mealy machines built from the operations described in Sect. 2.3 can be built from the update functions of the component

Mealy machines using the same operations on functions. Then, the predefined update functions of individual blocks can be represented using HCTs and combined according to the functional combinations derived from the block diagram.

4.1 Mealy Machines and Their Combinations via Functions

In this section, we consider a category **Mealy** whose objects are sets, and whose morphisms $m : \Sigma \to \Lambda$ are Mealy machines with input alphabet Σ, and output alphabet Λ. Composition of morphisms is given by the usual definition of cascade composition of Mealy machines [13]. We also introduce a monoidal product, giving the category a monoidal structure. It is defined on objects as the Cartesian product of sets, and on morphisms as the parallel composition of Mealy machines. The unit of the monoidal product is the same as for sets, the set containing one element: $\mathbb{1}$. Considering equality of morphisms up to bisimilarity results in a structure similar to the one used in [9] to describe symmetric lenses—according to [9], this structure forms a (symmetric) monoidal category.

While the cascade/parallel composition of Mealy machines is well understood (see, e.g. [13]), we introduce a definition for the update functions of the composed machines which wires together the update functions of the individual machines. Because string diagrams are used to represent both Mealy machines and their update functions, let us introduce some graphical notation to differentiate them. For Mealy machines, the string diagrams use black boxes to denote component Mealy machines (e.g. Fig. 5a). The update function ud of a Mealy machine m can be expressed using the projection mapping $[\![m]\!]_{ud} = ud$. For update functions, the string diagram is decorated with grey backing to group the inputs/outputs of the update function into two main components: the upper components describe the inputs/outputs to the Mealy machine, and the lower components describe the current/next state (e.g. Fig. 5d).

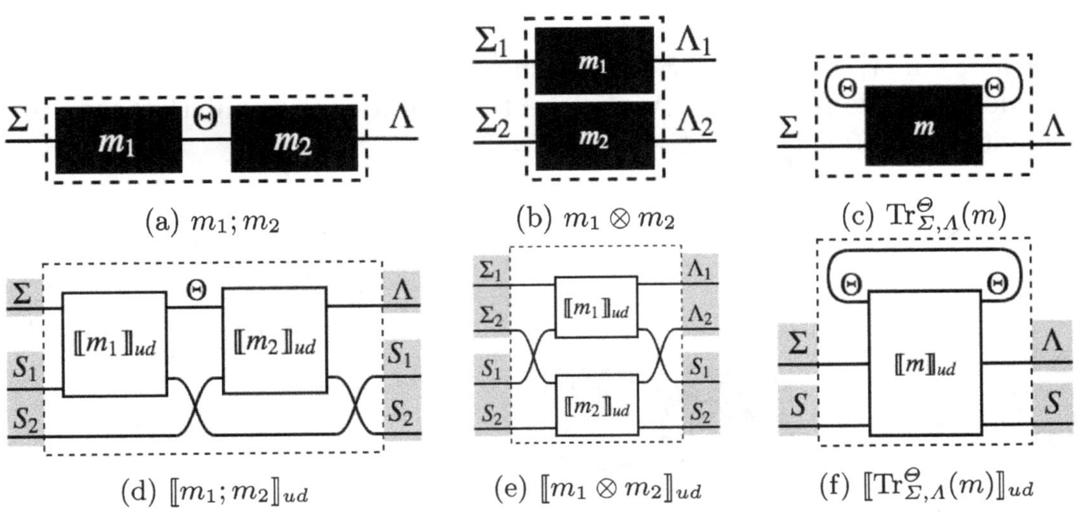

Fig. 5. Composite Mealy machines and their update functions

Two Mealy machines $m_1 = (S_1, s_0^1, \Sigma, \Theta, ud_1)$, and $m_2 = (S_2, s_0^2, \Theta, \Lambda, ud_2)$ can be composed in sequence as illustrated by Fig. 5a to form the composite Mealy machine $m_1; m_2 = (S_1 \times S_2, (s_0^1, s_0^2), \Sigma, \Lambda, ud')$. The update function ud' for $m_1; m_2$ with the string diagram in Fig. 5d, is defined as:

$$[\![m_1; m_2]\!]_{ud} = ([\![m_1]\!]_{ud} \otimes id_{S_2}); (id_\Theta \otimes \mathrm{Br}_{S_1,S_2}); ([\![m_2]\!]_{ud} \otimes id_{S_1}); (id_\Lambda \otimes \mathrm{Br}_{S_2,S_1})$$

The parallel composition of m_1 and m_2 is the Mealy machine $m_1 \otimes m_2 = (S_1 \times S_2, (s_0^1, s_0^2), \Sigma_1 \times \Sigma_2, \Lambda_1 \times \Lambda_2, ud')$ as illustrated by Fig. 5b. The update function ud' for $m_1 \otimes m_2$, with string diagram Fig. 5e, is defined as:

$$[\![m_1 \otimes m_2]\!]_{ud} = (\mathrm{id}_{\Sigma_1} \otimes \mathrm{Br}_{\Sigma_2,S_1} \otimes \mathrm{id}_{S_2}); ([\![m_1]\!]_{ud} \otimes [\![m_2]\!]_{ud}); (\mathrm{id}_{\Lambda_1} \otimes \mathrm{Br}_{S_1,\Lambda_2} \otimes \mathrm{id}_{S_2})$$

Feedback configurations of Mealy machines (e.g., Fig. 5c) can be defined with fixed-point equations, such as in [13]. We give an equivalent description in terms of the trace operation in **Set**. A Mealy machine $m = (S, s_0, \Theta \times \Sigma, \Theta \times \Lambda, ud)$ can be traced to form the machine $\mathrm{Tr}^{\Theta}_{\Sigma,\Lambda}(m) = (S, s_0, \Sigma, \Lambda, ud')$ where the update function ud' is defined as $[\![\mathrm{Tr}^{\Theta}_{\Sigma,\Lambda}(m)]\!]_{ud} = \mathrm{Tr}^{\Theta}_{\Sigma \times S, \Lambda \times S}([\![m]\!]_{ud})$ as illustrated by Fig. 5f. Since this operation is defined in terms of traces in **Set**, many of the properties of traces can be derived from traces in **Set**.

The above results mean that if we know the update functions of individual Simulink blocks, then we can model the update functions of block diagrams which configure those blocks in sequence, in parallel, and with feedback.

4.2 Functional Embedding and Wiring Morphisms

In this section, we address the fact that a large part of a Simulink block diagram *looks* very functional (i.e. stateless). For example, many of the blocks and wiring in Fig. 1a can be modelled as functions. For this reason, we consider a class of Mealy machines which produce outputs as a function of only their current inputs. Any function $f : X \to Y$ can be described as the Mealy machine $\mathcal{M}f = (\mathbb{1}, (), X, Y, f)$, with one state, and update function f (see Fig. 6a). The mapping $\mathcal{M}$ *embeds* morphisms from **Set** into the category **Mealy**, because any two embedded functions $\mathcal{M}f$ and $\mathcal{M}g$ interact in **Mealy** very similarly to the way they interact as functions in **Set**.

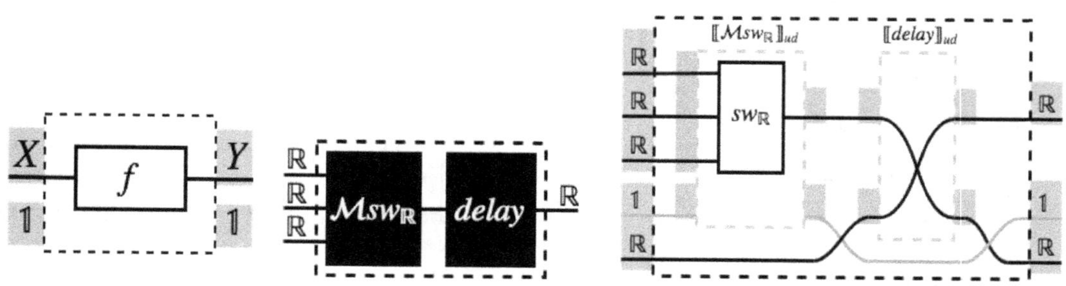

(a) $[\![\mathcal{M}f]\!]_{ud} = f$ (b) $\mathcal{M}sw_{\mathbb{R}}; delay$ (c) $[\![\mathcal{M}sw_{\mathbb{R}}; delay]\!]_{ud}$

Fig. 6. Embedded functions and their interactions

This explains how functional aspects of Simulink block diagrams can be modelled with Mealy machines. For example, the block labelled *Mode* in Fig. 1a can be modelled with the Mealy machine $\mathcal{M}sw_{\mathbb{R}}$. Perhaps more importantly, the morphisms introduced to describe wiring in functional diagrams (i.e. id_X, Δ_X, $\mathrm{Br}_{A,B}$) can again be used to describe the same (functional) wiring for Mealy machines. Therefore, in string diagrams representing Mealy machines, plain wires represent the morphism $\mathcal{M}\mathrm{id}_X$ which carries data without changing it, branching wires represent the morphism $\mathcal{M}\Delta_X$ which duplicates data, and crossing wires represent the morphism $\mathcal{M}\mathrm{Br}_{A,B}$ which reorders the components of data. The fact that $\mathcal{M}\mathrm{id}_X$ and $\mathcal{M}\mathrm{Br}_{A,B}$ "act like wiring" is established in [9].

This establishes how to model wiring and functional blocks in Simulink block diagrams as Mealy machines. We can now use the operations from Sect. 4.1 to describe block diagrams which use complex wiring and functional blocks in combinations with stateful blocks.

4.3 Block Diagrams to Horizontal Condition Tables

We have explained how the categorical structure from Sect. 2.3 applies to **Mealy**, and related it to the same structure in **Set**. This framework allows us to combine update functions of individual blocks into update functions of entire block diagrams using the above definitions. For example, the update function $[\![\mathcal{M}sw_{\mathbb{R}}; delay]\!]_{ud}$ of the machine from Fig. 6b is equal to

$$([\![\mathcal{M}sw_{\mathbb{R}}]\!]_{ud} \otimes \mathrm{id}_{\mathbb{R}}); (\mathrm{id}_{\mathbb{R}} \otimes \mathrm{Br}_{\mathbb{1},\mathbb{R}}); ([\![delay]\!]_{ud} \otimes \mathrm{id}_{\mathbb{1}}); (\mathrm{id}_{\mathbb{R}} \otimes \mathrm{Br}_{\mathbb{R},\mathbb{1}}),$$

as shown in Fig. 6c, where the "$\mathbb{1}$" wire is drawn in grey to illustrate how it achieves the data flow described by Fig. 5d (normally, this wire is not drawn). This can be simplified, e.g., the final sequential sub-function $\mathrm{id}_{\mathbb{R}} \otimes \mathrm{Br}_{\mathbb{R},\mathbb{1}}$ is given by $\{(x,(y,())) \mapsto (x,((),y))\}$ which simplifies to $\{(x,y) \mapsto (x,y)\}$ by flattening tuples. Our presentation of monoidal categories skips the formalities which describe this simplification, but it can be intuitively understood by considering the data flow described in Fig. 6c if the grey wire were absent (as usual). Taking $[\![delay]\!]_{ud} = shift$ (as defined in Sect. 2.1) which we now describe as $\mathrm{Br}_{\mathbb{R},\mathbb{R}}$ and using $[\![\mathcal{M}sw_{\mathbb{R}}]\!]_{ud} = sw_{\mathbb{R}}$ along with appropriate axioms over the wiring morphisms, $[\![\mathcal{M}sw_{\mathbb{R}}; delay]\!]_{ud}$ simplifies to $(sw_{\mathbb{R}} \otimes \mathrm{id}_{\mathbb{R}}); \mathrm{Br}_{\mathbb{R},\mathbb{R}}$. This simplification can be intuitively understood by considering only the black data flow in Fig. 6c. In the same way that we describe the functional data flow of Fig. 3, this approach can be repeated to describe the entire block diagram in Fig. 1a, not just the combination of blocks labelled *Mode* and *counter*.

This example illustrates how our categorical algebra for Mealy machines is structurally similar to the one used in [6] which describes the algorithm that represents block diagrams in terms of sequential/parallel/feedback configurations of components. The algorithm from [6] constructs descriptions which contain no feedback operations. A similar result can be shown in our framework, allowing us to produce trace-free descriptions of update functions in terms of the update functions of their components.

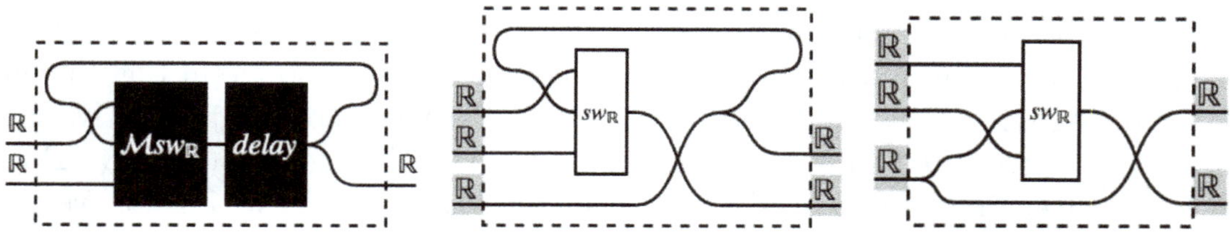

(a) Mealy Machine (b) Update Function (c) Function Rearranged

Fig. 7. The update function of a Mealy machine with feedback

As mentioned in Sect. 2.3, not all feedback configurations are valid. The validity of a feedback configuration describing a Mealy machine is decided by determining whether or not the trace on its update function is defined. In many settings, the trace is defined if the aforementioned fixed-point equations have a unique solution [13]. However, for Simulink models that are used to generate embedded software, the configuration must satisfy a more strict validity condition: there must be no *algebraic loops*. This means there can be no cyclic dependencies in the underlying update function, any feedback can be trivially removed by rearranging the components and wiring to "yank out" the loops while preserving the connections between blocks. For example, Fig. 7 illustrates how the update function of a simple feedback configuration can be rearranged to remove loops. This can be formalized by the notion of vacuous guardedness introduced in [7].

This means that the update functions of well-formed block diagrams can be modelled without traces. In this manner, the update function of the block diagram in Fig. 1a can be described as

$$\mathrm{Br}_{\mathbb{B},\mathbb{R}}; ([-1]\otimes\Delta_{\mathbb{R}}\otimes[10]\otimes\mathrm{id}_{\mathbb{B}}\otimes[0]); (add\otimes\Delta_{\mathbb{R}}\otimes sw_{\mathbb{B}}); (\mathrm{id}_{\mathbb{R}^2}\otimes\mathrm{Br}_{\mathbb{R},\mathbb{R}}); (sw_{\mathbb{R}}\otimes gtz); \mathrm{Br}_{\mathbb{R},\mathbb{B}}$$

where each individual function has a fixed definition, and can be represented as a predefined tabular expression. Here gtz denotes the > 0 block labelled *IsRunning*. Functions whose behaviours are not conditional are trivially represented by a table with a single condition: *true*.

HCTs—being representations of functions—can be composed like functions. We modify the composition operation in [20] to describe HCTs so that we can compose predefined tabular expressions as stated above. When composing two HCTs sequentially, the conditions of the first HCT appear first in the composed HCT and the conditions of the second HCT are included as sub-conditions. The conditions from the second HCT are evaluated using the output values from the first one. Consider, for example, the composition of Fig. 8a with Fig. 8b, where the output *counter'* of the first table is routed to the input *counter* of the second (ignore the *running* output for now). Their composition is shown in Fig. 8c (ignore the *running* and *counter'* outputs). The conditions $counter > 0$ and *start* (and their complements) appear in the same configuration as the first HCT. However, the sub-conditions (e.g. $counter - 1 \leq 0$) come

		running	*counter'*
$counter > 0$		*true*	$counter - 1$
$counter \leq 0$	*start*	*false*	10
	$\neg start$	*false*	0

(a) *ud*

	mode
$counter > 0$	*Running*
$counter \leq 0$	*Stopped*

(b) *md*

			running	*counter'*	*mode'*
$counter > 0$	$counter - 1 > 0$		*true*	$counter - 1$	*Running*
	$counter - 1 \leq 0$		*true*	$counter - 1$	*Stopped*
$counter \leq 0$	*start*	$10 > 0$	*false*	10	*Running*
		$10 \leq 0$	*false*	10	*Stopped*
	$\neg start$	$0 > 0$	*false*	0	*Running*
		$0 \leq 0$	*false*	0	*Stopped*

(c) ud^+

Fig. 8. Introducing modes

from the conditions ($counter \leq 0$) in the second HCT, evaluated with the values ($counter \mapsto counter - 1$) from the row in the first HCT associated with the parent condition ($counter > 0$). The conditions $10 > 0$ and $0 > 0$ (and their complements) are generated in a similar manner, but because they are trivially satisfied/impossible conditions, the sub-conditions/entire row can be removed (the removable conditions/rows are shaded in Fig. 8c).

Similarly to the conditions, the output expressions of the second HCT are evaluated with the corresponding values from the first HCT, and those are used as the output expressions of the combined HCT. In Fig. 8b, the output values for *mode* are constants, therefore they appear unchanged in Fig. 8c. For HCTs composed in parallel, the conditions from the second HCT are once again used as sub-conditions, but they are not modified. Similarly, the output expressions from both HCTs are placed in the combined table unchanged.

The predefined HCTs representing each function in the equation above can be combined using the operations described above to achieve a tabular expression for the entire block diagram. For example, the tabular expression in Fig. 2a can be obtained this way.

5 HCTs to STTs: Modes via Tables

The HCTs produced using the technique described in Sect. 4 are an intermediate representation in our translation strategy. They illustrate the decision logic of the system as a whole, but the logic is not related to state the way it is for state charts, i.e., through modes. This section explains how HCTs are augmented with modes to form STTs, and finally state charts.

5.1 Defining Modes

The STTs described in Sect. 2.2 have obvious similarities to state charts, but they are just syntactic sugar for HCTs. STTs and state charts are modelled as Mealy machines with a special state variable *mode* with values from an enumerated set M (see, e.g., extended state machines in [2]). The cells in the first column of STTs (see Fig. 2b) express conditions of the form $mode = Running$ which compare the value of *mode* to each element of M. The last column identifies the updated value of $mode'$. Therefore, the state spaces of Mealy machines modelling

STTs and state charts have the form $Q = S \times M$, where M is the set of modes, and S contains tuples of the other state variable values.

A HCT produced via the techniques in the previous section describes the update function ud of a Mealy machine $m = (S, s_0, \Sigma, \Lambda, ud)$. We will enhance m with a state variable $mode$ to produce a Mealy machine $m^+ = (S \times M, (s_0, mode_0), \Sigma, \Lambda, ud^+)$ whose update function is given by a HCT which matches the format of an STT. To achieve the goal of improving readability, we leverage the existing decision logic in HCTs.

When a state chart updates, it only considers the transitions leaving its current mode, i.e., depending on its *state*, only some behaviours are possible. The same dependence on state is expressed in HCTs by conditions which depend only on the values of state variables, which will be referred to as *state conditions*. For example, in Fig. 8a, if the condition $counter > 0$ is satisfied, the system can only do one thing: decrement $counter$ and set $running$ to true. Our strategy associates the condition $counter > 0$ with a mode of operation $Running \in M$, and replaces the original condition with $mode = Running$. We augment the HCTs into STTs in a way that preserves the behaviour of the Mealy machines.

As the modes are all listed in the first column of an STT, the first augmentation reorders conditions in HCTs so that the state conditions appear first. For example, the conditions in Fig. 2a can be rearranged via the methods in [4] to obtain Fig. 8a. While our example contains only one pair of state conditions, HCTs describing general block diagrams may contain multiple nested state conditions. The second augmentation uses conjunction to flatten nested state conditions into a single column with a condition for each branch of the stateful logic.

The augmented HCT now has a specific form (Fig. 8a) which superficially resembles an STT, but the behaviour is unchanged. We now introduce a set of modes M with each element associated with a distinct condition in the first column of the augmented HCT. This association is defined by a function $md : S \to M$ which maps tuples of state variable values to the mode whose associated state condition is satisfied. This function is represented by an HCT with the state conditions from the augmented HCT, and distinct values from M as outputs. The md function for the timer example is given by the HCT in Fig. 8b.

Next, the Mealy machine is enhanced by introducing a state variable $mode$ with values from M. We design the enhancement to maintain the invariant that the value of $mode$ always corresponds with the state condition which the other state variables satisfy. The invariant is satisfied by the initial state $(s_0, md(s_0))$. The enhanced update function trivially preserves the original behaviour by ignoring the value of $mode$, but updates $mode'$ to maintain the invariant by evaluating md with the updated state variable values. The update function is therefore defined as $ud^+ = (ud \otimes !_M); (id_\Lambda \otimes (\Delta_S; (id_S \otimes md)))$, where $!_M : M \to \mathbb{1} = \{(mode) \mapsto ()\}$ introduces an input whose value is discarded. Since ud and md are given as HCTs (e.g. Fig. 8a and b), the enhanced update function can be achieved through composition of tables (e.g. Fig. 8c).

This enhanced Mealy machine operates within a subset of the state space $S \times M$ where the aforementioned invariant holds. The validity of any state condition can now be deduced from the value of the mode variable (e.g. $(counter > 0) \Leftrightarrow (mode = Running)$). Thus, replacing those conditions with the corresponding modes in the HCT representation of ud^+ does not modify its behaviour. This is the final step in rearranging the HCT from Fig. 8c into the STT in Fig. 2b.

5.2 Converting to State Charts and Simplifying

The state chart in Fig. 9 implements the STT in Fig. 2b by creating a transition for each row and by creating assignment actions to update state and output variables. State charts produced in this manner can often be simplified by moving common actions from transitions to *entry*/*exit* actions of modes, or by removing transitions and performing the corresponding actions as *during* actions. For example, the state chart in Fig. 9 simplifies to the one in Fig. 1b.

In the example given above, it is crucial that the new state variable *mode* is tracked in addition to the existing variable *counter*. The *mode* variable tracks the high level system state, but the *counter* variable is still important for tracking the detailed system state. This additional information is not always important, i.e., sometimes the mode is sufficient and the old state variable may be removed from the description of the Mealy machine. This may happen if a Boolean state variable generates a state condition; knowing the value of *mode* can be sufficient to deduce the value of the original state variable. It is also possible that a state variable from the block diagram stores more detailed information than necessary, and knowing the mode is sufficient for the state chart to act. In these cases, the unnecessary state variables can be removed from the state chart.

6 Prototype, Evaluation, and Future Work

The methodologies presented here have been used to develop a prototype tool which automatically refactors Simulink model fragments to Stateflow [18]. The tool supports a large subset of discrete Simulink blocks typically used for implementation of embedded software. The refactoring tool is implemented in Matlab and integrates with Simulink allowing the user to select the blocks they would like to replace. When the tool is invoked, it generates a Stateflow chart and uses the Simulink Design Verifier [17] to verify that it is equivalent to the selected blocks.

The prototype tool improves the readability of small to medium sized block diagrams such as the one in Fig. 1a. However, we found that the stateful logic of complex industrial-scale models incorporates multiple state machines interacting with each other and with stateless conditional logic. To elegantly represent these complex block diagrams in Stateflow, the translation methodologies presented here can be enhanced to utilize the more sophisticated mechanisms of state charts such as hierarchical/parallel modes. We believe that many state chart mechanisms have analogies in tabular expressions, e.g., using hierarchies of state conditions can be leveraged to specify sub-modes. We found that block diagrams encoding more than 4 high-level modes can often become difficult to understand without these mechanisms.

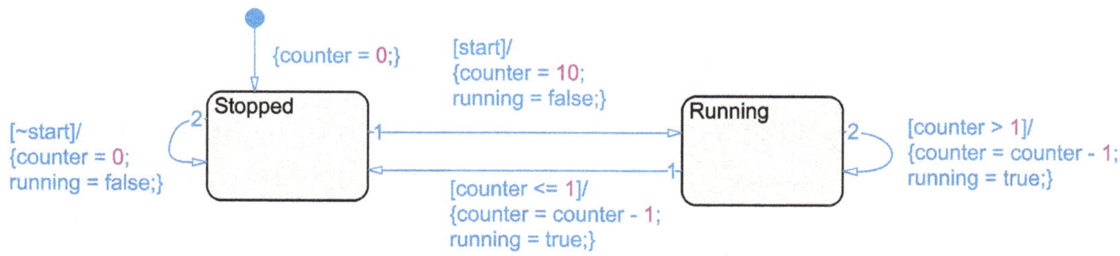

Fig. 9. State chart equivalent to STT

We also recognize the importance of finding refactorable fragments in large models. In fact, the translation methodology presented in this paper was developed in parallel with an identification strategy that pinpoints block diagrams which are candidates for refactoring—it searches for certain patterns of logical and stateful blocks which indicate complex state update logic. An elaborated description of both translation and identification strategies will be presented in the master's thesis of the first author [29].

7 Related Work

Several papers propose translating Simulink block diagrams to formal languages to enable their verification using existing tools (e.g., [1,6,14,23,27,30]). Only a few, however, translate Simulink block diagrams to state transition diagrams. In [19], Simulink block diagrams are converted into an extended version of hybrid automata, with each block in a block diagram converted to a hybrid automaton, leading to an explosion in the number of states of the resulting model. In [31], Simulink models are converted to finite state machines, but transitions between states represent the small execution steps of individual blocks updates, not changes in the high level system modes. Both studies [19,31], as well as [16], do not aim to capture the high-level state machine of an entire block diagram. This is exactly what our approach does, with maintainability of the resulting model as a prime motivator.

Our approach to modelling Mealy machines and their interactions using the monoidal category **Mealy** follows a general trend in behavioural modelling. For example, monoidal categories have been used to describe interactions of quantum processes [5], labelled transition systems [12], and control systems [3]. The algebra of (traced symmetric) monoidal categories is similar to the algebra used to describe block diagrams in [6], but our approach uses a standard mathematical framework with a rich history and many known results. For example, the results of [9] indicate that by considering equivalence up to bisimilarity, the category **Mealy** is symmetric monoidal, meaning the appropriate axioms and resulting properties of this structure are already known.

8 Conclusion

In this paper, we proposed a method for translating Simulink block diagrams to Stateflow state charts via tabular expressions representing their respective Mealy machines update functions. A categorical framework for composing Mealy machines provides a theoretical basis for the translation. To the best of our knowledge, this is the first method for Simulink to Stateflow translation. Our proposed method is relevant to industrial development where it can help improve software maintainability and aid compliance with modelling guidelines.

References

1. Agrawal, A., Simon, G., Karsai, G.: Semantic translation of Simulink/Stateflow models to hybrid automata using graph transformations. Electron. Notes Theor. Comput. Sci. **109**, 43–56 (2004)
2. Alur, R.: Principles of Cyber-Physical Systems. MIT Press, Cambridge (2015)
3. Baez, J.C., Erbele, J.: Categories in control. Theor. Appl. Categories **30**(24), 836–881 (2015)
4. Bialy, M., Lawford, M., Pantelic, V., Wassyng, A.: A methodology for the simplification of tabular designs in model-based development. In: Proceedings of the 3rd FME Workshop on Formal Methods in Software Engineering (FormaliSE), pp. 47–53. IEEE Press, May 2015
5. Coecke, B., Kissinger, A.: Picturing Quantum Processes. Cambridge University Press, Cambridge (2017)
6. Dragomir, I., Preoteasa, V., Tripakis, S.: Translating hierarchical block diagrams into composite predicate transformers. arXiv preprint arXiv:1510.04873 (2015)
7. Goncharov, S., Schröder, L.: Guarded traced categories. In: Baier, C., Dal Lago, U. (eds.) FoSSaCS 2018. LNCS, vol. 10803, pp. 313–330. Springer, Cham (2018). https://doi.org/10.1007/978-3-319-89366-2_17
8. Hasegawa, M.: Recursion from cyclic sharing: Traced monoidal categories and models of cyclic lambda calculi. In: de Groote, P., Roger Hindley, J. (eds.) TLCA 1997. LNCS, vol. 1210, pp. 196–213. Springer, Heidelberg (1997). https://doi.org/10.1007/3-540-62688-3_37
9. Hofmann, M., Pierce, B., Wagner, D.: Symmetric lenses. In: ACM SIGPLAN Notices, vol. 46, no. 1, pp. 371–384 (2011)
10. Jin, Y., Parnas, D.L.: Defining the meaning of tabular mathematical expressions. Sci. Comput. Program. **75**(11), 980–1000 (2010)
11. Joyal, A., Street, R., Verity, D.: Traced monoidal categories. In: Mathematical Proceedings of the Cambridge Philosophical Society, vol. 119, pp. 447–468. Cambridge University Press (1996)

12. Katis, P., Sabadini, N., Walters, R.F.C.: Span(Graph): A categorical algebra of transition systems. In: Johnson, M. (ed.) AMAST 1997. LNCS, vol. 1349, pp. 307–321. Springer, Heidelberg (1997). https://doi.org/10.1007/BFb0000479
13. Lee, E.A., Varaiya, P.: Structure and Interpretation of Signals and Systems, 2nd edn. LeeVaraiya.org (2011)
14. Liebrenz, T., Herber, P., Glesner, S.: Deductive verification of hybrid control systems modeled in Simulink with KeYmaera X. In: Sun, J., Sun, M. (eds.) ICFEM 2018. LNCS, vol. 11232, pp. 89–105. Springer, Cham (2018). https://doi.org/10.1007/978-3-030-02450-5_6
15. Malherbe, O., Scott, P.J., Selinger, P.: Partially traced categories. J. Pure Appl. Algebra **216**(12), 2563–2585 (2012)
16. Manamcheri, K., Mitra, S., Bak, S., Caccamo, M.: A step towards verification and synthesis from Simulink/Stateflow models. In: Proceedings of the 14th International Conference on Hybrid systems: Computation and Control, pp. 317–318. ACM (2011)
17. MathWorks: Simulink Design Verifier. https://www.mathworks.com/products/sldesignverifier.html (2018). Accessed 18 Nov 2018
18. McSCert: Simulink-to-Stateflow. https://www.mathworks.com/matlabcentral/fileexchange/70317-simulink-to-stateflow (2019). Accessed Feb 2019
19. Minopoli, S., Frehse, G.: SL2SX translator: From Simulink to SpaceEx models, April 2016. http://www-verimag.imag.fr/~minopoli/SL2SX.pdf
20. von Mohrenschildt, M.: Algebraic composition of function tables. Formal Aspects Comput. **12**(1), 41–51 (2000)
21. Parnas, D.L.: Tabular representation of relations. McMaster University, Technical report, October 1992
22. Selinger, P.: A survey of graphical languages for monoidal categories. In: Coecke, B. (ed.) New Structures for Physics, vol. 813, pp. 289–355. Springer, Heidelberg (2010). https://doi.org/10.1007/978-3-642-12821-9_4
23. Sfyrla, V., Tsiligiannis, G., Safaka, I., Bozga, M., Sifakis, J.: Compositional translation of Simulink models into synchronous BIP. In: 2010 International Symposium on Industrial Embedded Systems (SIES), pp. 217–220. IEEE (2010)
24. Singh, N.K., Lawford, M., Maibaum, T.S., Wassyng, A.: Stateflow to tabular expressions. In: Proceedings of the Sixth International Symposium on Information and Communication Technology (SoICT), p. 47. ACM (2015)
25. The MathWorks: MathWorks Automotive Advisory Board (MAAB): Control Algorithm Modeling Guidelines Using MATLAB, Simulink, and Stateflow, Version 3.0 (2012). www.mathworks.com/solutions/automotive/standards/maab.html
26. The MathWorks: Simulink user's guide, September 2018. http://www.mathworks.com/help/releases/R2018b/pdf_doc/simulink/sl_using.pdf, http://www.mathworks.com/help/releases/R2015b/pdf_doc/simulink/sl_using.pdf, version R2018b. Accessed Feb 2019
27. Tripakis, S., Sofronis, C., Caspi, P., Curic, A.: Translating discrete-time Simulink to Lustre. ACM Trans. Embed. Comput. Syst. (TECS) **4**(4), 779–818 (2005)
28. Wassyng, A., Janicki, R.: Tabular expressions in software engineering. In: Proceedings of 2003 International Conference on Software and System Engineering ICSSEA 2003, pp. 1–46 (2003)

29. Wynn-Williams, S.: SL2SF: Refactoring Simulink to Stateflow (2019), unpublished thesis
30. Zhan, N., Wang, S., Zhao, H.: Formal Verification of Simulink/Stateflow Diagrams, Springer (2017)
31. Zhou, C., Kumar, R.: Semantic translation of Simulink diagrams to input/output extended finite automata. Discrete Event Dyn. Syst. **22**(2), 223–247 (2012)

Metric Temporal Graph Logic over Typed Attributed Graphs

Holger Giese, Maria Maximova, Lucas Sakizloglou, and Sven Schneider(✉)

Hasso Plattner Institute, University of Potsdam, Potsdam, Germany
{holger.giese,maria.maximova,lucas.sakizloglou,sven.schneider}@hpi.de

Abstract. Various kinds of typed attributed graphs can be used to represent states of systems from a broad range of domains. For dynamic systems, established formalisms such as graph transformation can provide a formal model for defining state sequences. We consider the case where time may elapse between state changes and introduce a logic, called *Metric Temporal Graph Logic* (MTGL), to reason about such timed graph sequences. With this logic, we express properties on the structure and attributes of states as well as on the occurrence of states over time that are related by their inner structure, which no formal logic over graphs concisely accomplishes so far.

Firstly, based on timed graph sequences as models for system evolution, we define MTGL by integrating the temporal operator *until* with time bounds into the well-established logic of (nested) graph conditions. Secondly, we outline how a finite timed graph sequence can be represented as a single graph containing all changes over time (called graph with history), how the satisfaction of MTGL conditions can be defined for such a graph and show that both representations satisfy the same MTGL conditions. Thirdly, we present how MTGL conditions can be reduced to (nested) graph conditions and show using this reduction that both underlying logics are equally expressive. Finally, we present an extension of the tool AutoGraph allowing to check the satisfaction of MTGL conditions for timed graph sequences, by checking the satisfaction of the (nested) graph conditions, obtained using the proposed reduction, for the graph with history corresponding to the timed graph sequence.

Keywords: Nested graph conditions · Metric temporal logic · Sequence properties · Typed attributed graphs · Symbolic graphs

1 Introduction

Various kinds of typed attributed graphs are used to represent states of systems from a broad range of domains. Also, the evolution of such systems can be described using a multitude of graph transformation formalisms in which the possible behavior in form of graph sequences is defined by a set of rules and their application. In many cases, the analysis of this induced behavior with respect to a specification in form of a temporal logic that defines the admissible graph sequences is of paramount importance.

R. Hähnle and W. van der Aalst (Eds.): FASE 2019, LNCS 11424, pp. 282–298, 2019.
https://doi.org/10.1007/978-3-030-16722-6_16

In our running example, from which we derive the lack of suitable specification formalisms, we consider a dynamic system describing an operating system, which generates timed sequences of (typed attributed) graphs to model the change of the operating system states over time. In this example, users may create tasks with identifiers *id*, the operating system may create handlers specific to task identifiers to allow for the task execution, and the handlers may produce a result when a task has been executed (marking the successful handling of the task). To model the states of the operating system, we employ graphs that store the tasks, the handlers, and the computed results. In the remainder, we refer in the context of this example to the *sequence property* **P** to be checked w.r.t. the *timed graph sequence* at hand describing systems' state changes over time.

P: Whenever a task T with identifier id is created on a system S, a handler H for this task (i.e., with a task identifier t_id equal to id of T) must exist. Moreover, within 120 timeunits, the handler must produce a result R with value *success* and, during the computation of the result, no other handler H' for the same task (i.e., with the same task identifier t_id) may exist.

We consider the problem that existing specification formalisms for graph-based systems cannot cover properties such as **P**. The available (metric) temporal logics, such as Metric Temporal Logic (MTL) [16], are defined over Kripke structures abstracting from the system states by labeling each state with a subset of the finite set of atomic propositions. The commonly used operator *until* allows then to formalize the part of property **P** stating that every graph that contains a task T is followed by some graph containing some result R before t time units. However, the existing metric temporal logics do not support the use of *bindings* of elements contained in the graphs to express how a certain matched pattern evolves in a sequence of graphs. Therefore, they are insufficient when e.g. creating different tasks T and T' must be followed by creating the *corresponding* results R and R' while also treating the deadlines for their existence separately.

As a first contribution, we define *Metric Temporal Graph Logic* (MTGL) for the concise specification of systems that generate timed graph sequences. In MTGL, we express properties on *states* using the well-known formalism of nested graph conditions [12,24] (called GCs for short). The satisfaction of a GC that states the existence of a graph pattern H in the given graph G results in a *match* m from H to G. We extend the logic of GCs to MTGL by extending GCs with the metric temporal operator *until* that may appear in the scope of a previously determined match m. Using this extension, we can express properties, such as property **P**, on the structure and attributes of states as well as on the occurrence of states over time where the preservation/extension of matches during a systems' evolution increases the expressiveness beyond the existing formal logics.

As a second contribution, we outline how a finite timed graph sequence can be represented as a single graph containing all changes over time (called *graph with history*), how the satisfaction of MTGL conditions can be defined for such a graph, and show that both representations satisfy the same MTGL conditions.

As a third contribution, we show that MTGL conditions can be reduced to GCs using attribute constraints to encode the metric temporal requirements, while preserving the satisfaction for finite timed graph sequences. This encoding enables the direct application of techniques for GCs such as [25].

As a fourth contribution, we present an extension of the tool AutoGraph [25] allowing to check the satisfaction of MTGL conditions for timed graph sequences by checking the satisfaction of the GCs obtained using the proposed reduction for the graph with history corresponding to the timed graph sequence at hand.

The paper is structured as follows. Section 2 discusses related work. Section 3 iterates on technical preliminaries. Section 4 defines timed graph sequences, MTGL, and the satisfaction of MTGL conditions for timed graph sequences. In Sect. 5, we show how to represent a finite timed graph sequence as a single graph with history, define satisfaction of MTGL conditions for a graph with history, and prove that both representations satisfy the same MTGL conditions. In Sect. 6, we introduce a reduction of MTGL conditions to GCs and show the equivalence of these two logics. Finally, Sect. 7 discusses the tool support and Sect. 8 concludes the paper with a summary and remarks on future work.

2 Related Work

There are several related formal and informal approaches for the specification and verification of different kinds of sequence properties.

In [13] the satisfaction of CTL (state/sequence) properties is checked where the tool Groove [10,26] is used to generate the finite state space of the graph transformation system (GTS) at hand. In [7] invariants are checked for a GTS with a possibly infinite state space. The validity of given pre/post conditions for a program over a GTS has been presented in [23]. In [2,15] temporal properties for GTS with infinite state space are checked using the tool Augur2.

In [19] the satisfaction of graph-based probabilistic timed CTL properties is checked where the tool Henshin [1,8] is used to generate the finite state space of a GTS and where the tool Prism [17] is used to model check translations of the given properties. In [6] a sequence of timed events are checked against sequence properties given by regular languages based on deterministic finite automata.

The use of bindings, as in this paper, is supported in [3] where bindings are part of the Metric First-Order Temporal Logic in which system states are represented by a set of relations that are adapted during the execution of the system.

A visual but informal notation for the specification of sequence properties involving time and graph bindings was introduced in [14].

In conclusion, existing approaches with a formal semantics do not support either time, bindings, or graphs in a concise manner. Thereby, our graph-based logic MTGL for graph-based systems complements existing approaches since (a) it eases usability in graph-based contexts similarly to the usage of GCs that are favored over first-order logic in these contexts, (b) it enables further developments and combinations with other graph-based techniques such as those in [25], and, (c) as to be shown by future tool-based evaluations, it can be expected that domain-specific tools for checking MTGL conditions are more efficient compared to general-purpose tools such as shown analogously for GCs in [23].

TG:

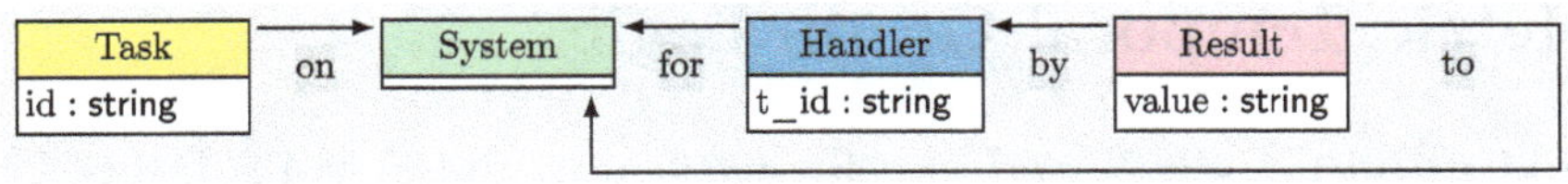

Fig. 1. The type graph TG for our running example where the attributes cts and dts of sort real used in later sections are omitted in every node and edge to improve readability

3 Typed Attributed Graphs and Graph Conditions

We now recall typed attributed graphs and nested graph conditions used for representing system states and properties on these states, respectively.

We use *symbolic graphs* [21] to encode (finite) typed attributed graphs. Symbolic graphs are an adaptation of E-GRAPHS [9] where a graph does not contain data nodes (i.e., elements that represent actual values) but instead node and edge attributes are connected to variables, which replace the data nodes. Symbolic graphs are also equipped with attribute constraints over these (sorted) variables (e.g. $x = 5$, $x \leq 5$, and $y =$ "aabb").

We consider symbolic graphs that are typed over a type graph TG using a typing morphism $type : G \to TG$. Type graphs restrict attributed graphs to an admitted subset. For our running example, we employ the type graph TG from Fig. 1. An example of a symbolic graph that is typed over TG is given in Fig. 4.

We state the existence and nonexistence of graph patterns in a given symbolic graph, which is called a *host graph*, by representing graph patterns by symbolic graphs and by using monomorphisms (called *monos* and denoted using $\hookrightarrow$ subsequently) to extend graph patterns. Formally, we rely on the notion of nested graph conditions (GCs) [12], which are expressively equivalent to first-order logic on graphs [5] as shown in [12,24].

Definition 1 (Graph Conditions (GCs)). *The class of* graph conditions (GCs) Φ_H^{GC} *for the graph H contains ψ if one of the following cases applies.*

- $\psi = \wedge S$ *and* $S = \{\phi_1, \dots, \phi_n\} \subseteq \Phi_H^{\mathrm{GC}}$.
- $\psi = \neg\phi$ *and* $\phi \in \Phi_H^{\mathrm{GC}}$.
- $\psi = \exists(a, \phi)$, $a : H \hookrightarrow H'$, *and* $\phi \in \Phi_{H'}^{\mathrm{GC}}$.

GCs allow for further abbreviations such as true, false, $\vee S$, *and* $\forall(a, \phi)$.

Intuitively, a GC is satisfied if the positive but not the negative patterns given by the GC can be found in the given host graph. For the case of the *exists* operator, a previously determined match m must be extendable using a mono q according to the mono a from the GC.

Definition 2 (Satisfaction of GCs). *A GC* $\psi \in \Phi_H^{\mathrm{GC}}$ *is* satisfied *by a mono* $m : H \hookrightarrow G$, *written* $m \models \psi$, *if one of the following cases applies.*

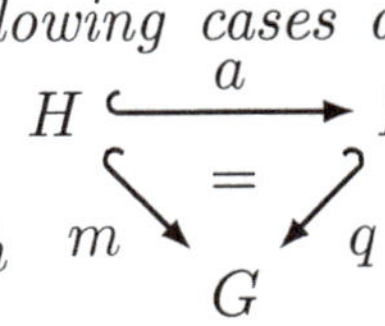

- $\psi = \wedge S$ *and* $m \models \phi$ *for each* $\phi \in S$.
- $\psi = \neg\phi$ *and not* $m \models \phi$.
- $\psi = \exists(a : H \hookrightarrow H', \phi)$ *and there exists* $q : H' \hookrightarrow G$ *such that* $q \circ a = m$ *and* $q \models \phi$ *(as depicted on the right).*

A GC ψ over the empty graph is satisfied by a graph G, written $G \models \psi$, if $\mathrm{i}_G \models \psi$ *where* $\mathrm{i}_G : \emptyset \hookrightarrow G$ *is the initial morphism to G.*

4 Metric Temporal Graph Logic

We build upon GCs [12] and the future fragment of MTL [16,22] to introduce *Metric Temporal Graph Logic* (MTGL) by defining its syntax and semantics.

We assume a graph transformation based formalism for the definition of steps changing a graph while possibly also determining a progress of time. We abstract from the actual timed graph transformation formalism employed but only assume that it is capable to generate so-called *timed graph sequences* (short TGSs), which contain the graphs, their modifications, and the elapsed time between successive graphs. In the following, we are concerned with TGSs in which either only the past states of sequences are given in the form of *finite* TGSs or where, alternatively, an *infinite* TGS describes a nonterminating evolution of a system.

A step from a graph G to a graph G' where G has remained unchanged for a duration of δ, which may be determined by a timed graph transformation formalism, is represented by $G \cdot (\delta, l, r) \cdot G'$ in our notion of TGSs. In this representation, the monos $l : IG \hookrightarrow G$ and $r : IG \hookrightarrow G'$ identify the graph elements that are preserved from G to G', i.e., $G - l(IG)$ are the nodes and edges that are present in G but are deleted to obtain G' and $G' - r(IG)$ are the nodes and edges that do not exist in G but are created to obtain G'.[1]

Definition 3 (Timed Graph Sequences (TGSs)). *We inductively define the class of finite* timed graph sequences *(TGSs)* Π_{fin} *as follows:*

- *If* $\pi = G_{init}$ *is the sequence containing only the graph* G_{init}*, then* $\pi \in \Pi_{fin}$.
- *If* $\pi \in \Pi_{fin}$ *is a TGS ending with a graph* G, $l : IG \hookrightarrow G$, $r : IG \hookrightarrow G'$ *are monos (for an* interface graph IG*), and* $\delta \in \mathbf{R}_0^+$ *is the timepoint where the graph* G *is changed relative to the previous change, then* $\pi \cdot (\delta, l, r) \cdot G' \in \Pi_{fin}$.

The class of TGSs Π *contains the finite TGSs* Π_{fin} *from above and all infinite sequences that have only finite TGSs from* Π_{fin} *as prefixes.*

Moreover, $\mathrm{dur}(\pi)$ *denotes the sum of all durations* δ *contained in* π*. Additionally, if* $\mathrm{dur}(\pi) = \infty$*,* π_t *denotes the unique graph at time* t*, i.e., if* $\pi = G$ *then* $\pi_t = G$ *and if* $\pi = G \cdot (\delta, l, r) \cdot \pi'$ *then* ($\pi_t = G$ *for* $t < \delta$) *and* ($\pi_t = \pi'_{t-\delta}$ *for* $t \geq \delta$)*. Finally, if* $\mathrm{dur}(\pi) = \infty$*,* $\pi_{[t_1,t_2]}$ *denotes the finite TGS contained in* π *between and including* π_{t_1} *and* π_{t_2}.

We do not require that every step modifies the current graph (i.e., we permit $G = G'$ possibly using $l = r = \mathrm{id}_G$). Also, time may not elapse in a step (i.e., we permit $\delta = 0$) but for well-definedness of the satisfaction relation for TGSs we require that time diverges in every infinite TGS π (i.e., $\mathrm{dur}(\pi) = \infty$).

In our running example, we simplify the presentation by using only inclusions l and r. The TGS π given in Fig. 2 contains five graphs G_i for $i \in \{0, 1, 2, 3, 4\}$ showing the system states in five different points in time, namely 0, 5, 10, 13, and 15. The corresponding durations where the respective graphs G_i remain unchanged are denoted by δ_i for $i \in \{0, 1, 2, 3\}$.

[1] The span $G \overset{l}{\hookleftarrow} IG \overset{r}{\hookrightarrow} G'$ does not correspond to a rule as used in the DPO approach but rather to a rule application describing changes between the graphs G and G'.

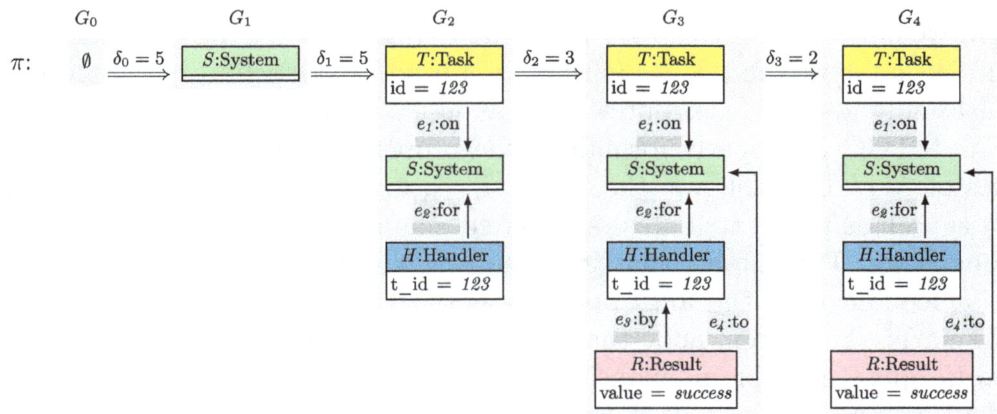

Fig. 2. A TGS π for our running example. For $i \in \{0,1,2,3\}$, the arrows $\overset{\delta_i}{\Longrightarrow}$ between graphs of the TGS describe changes $G_i \cdot (\delta_i, l_i, r_i) \cdot G_{i+1}$ where the inclusions l_i and r_i are implicitly given by the usage of the same names in all graphs.

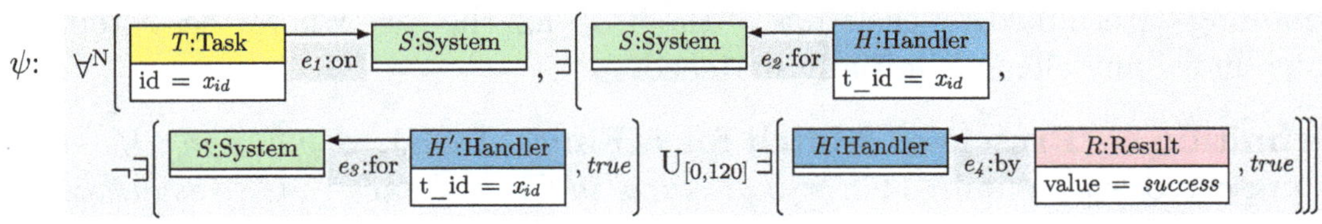

Fig. 3. The property **P** from our running example formalized by the MTGC ψ

The syntax of MTGL is given by *Metric Temporal Graph Conditions* (short MTGCs) introduced in the following definition. The distinguishing feature of MTGL is the extension of the binding of graph elements used by the operator *exists* in GCs to the *until* operator of MTL. This allows for the formalization of properties where a match into a graph is preserved/extended over multiple timepoints in the subsequently introduced semantics for TGSs.

Definition 4 (Metric Temporal Graph Conditions (MTGCs)). *The class of* metric temporal graph conditions (MTGCs) Φ_H^{MTGC} *for the graph* H *contains* ψ *if one of the following cases applies.*

- $\psi = \wedge S$ *and* $S = \{\phi_1, \ldots, \phi_n\} \subseteq \Phi_H^{\mathrm{MTGC}}$.
- $\psi = \neg\phi$ *and* $\phi \in \Phi_H^{\mathrm{MTGC}}$.
- $\psi = \exists(a, \phi)$, $a : H \hookrightarrow H'$, *and* $\phi \in \Phi_{H'}^{\mathrm{MTGC}}$.
- $\psi = \phi_1 \, \mathrm{U}_I \, \phi_2$, I *is an interval over* $\mathbf{R}_0^+$, *and* $\{\phi_1, \phi_2\} \subseteq \Phi_H^{\mathrm{MTGC}}$.

Further metric temporal operators can be defined as for MTL and GCs.

For our running example, we formalize the property **P** from Sect. 1 by the MTGC ψ depicted in Fig. 3. In this MTGC, we additionally use the *forall-new* operator in the form of $\forall^{\mathrm{N}}(a : H \hookrightarrow H', \phi)$ to match the pattern H' into the considered TGS as soon as possible, i.e., precisely at the minimal timepoint, at which all elements of H' exist. This operator can be encoded by the equivalent MTGC $\neg((\neg\exists(a, \neg\phi)) \, \mathrm{U}_{[0,\infty)} \, \exists(a, \neg\phi))$, which intuitively states that "there is no violation ever that did not exist before". Moreover, we use notational conventions to simplify our presentation of MTGCs by omitting elements in subconditions.

Firstly, we omit nodes (such as T) if no new edges or attributes are attached to them. Secondly, we omit edges (such as e_1) if no new attributes are attached to them. Finally, we omit attributes (such as *id* of T) in general.

The MTGC ψ properly formalizes the property **P** using the binding capabilities of MTGL as follows: the nodes T, S, and H (together with the edges e_1, e_2 as well as their attributes) are shared among the two subconditions of the *until* operator. This implies that the Handler node that must be matched by the right subcondition of the *until* operator is the previously bound Handler node H. Similarly, the System node that may be matched by the left subcondition of the *until* operator is the previously bound System node S.

Next we present the MTGL *semantics for TGSs* that defines when a given TGS satisfies a given MTGC. For the definition of this semantics, we first introduce the concept of a *match that is preserved over a finite number of steps* given by a finite TGS. In the following, we also call such a preserved match a *binding.* The preservation of the match is guaranteed by adapting it according to the renaming determined by the steps of the TGS for the case where these steps do not remove any element initially matched.

Definition 5 (Preserved Match for a Finite TGS). *A mono $m : H \hookrightarrow G_0$ is* preserved over a finite TGS π *that starts in G_0 and ends in G_n resulting in a mono $m' : H \hookrightarrow G_n$, written $m \overset{\pi}{\rightsquigarrow} m'$, if one of the following cases applies.*

- *$\pi = G_0 = G_n$ and $m = m'$.*
- *$\pi = G_0 \cdot (\delta, l : IG \hookrightarrow G_0, r : IG \hookrightarrow G_1) \cdot \pi'$ and there is $m'' : H \hookrightarrow IG$ such that $m = l \circ m''$ and $r \circ m'' \overset{\pi'}{\rightsquigarrow} m'$.*

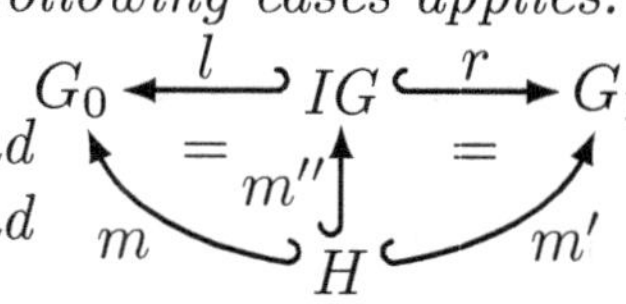

The fact that the step does not remove elements that are matched by a mono m is obtained from the existence of a mono m'' making the triangle $m = l \circ m''$ commute. The required renaming is then performed by replacing the match m by $r \circ m''$. The mono m'' is uniquely defined when it exists.

Based on the preservation of matches, we now define the semantics for TGSs.

Definition 6 (Satisfaction of MTGCs by TGSs). *A given MTGC $\psi \in \Phi_H^{\text{MTGC}}$ is* satisfied *by a TGS π, an observation timepoint $t \in \mathbf{R}_0^+$, and a mono $m : H \hookrightarrow \pi_t$, written $(\pi, t, m) \models_{\text{TGS}} \psi$, if one of the following cases applies.*

- *$\psi = \wedge S$ and $(\pi, t, m) \models_{\text{TGS}} \phi$ for each $\phi \in S$.*
- *$\psi = \neg\phi$ and not $(\pi, t, m) \models_{\text{TGS}} \phi$.*
- *$\psi = \exists(a : H \hookrightarrow H', \phi)$ and there is some $q : H' \hookrightarrow \pi_t$ such that $q \circ a = m$ and $(\pi, t, q) \models_{\text{TGS}} \phi$.*
- *$\psi = \phi_1 \, \mathrm{U}_I \, \phi_2$ and there is some $t' \in I$ such that*
  - *there is $m' : H \hookrightarrow \pi_{t+t'}$ s.t. $m \overset{\pi_{[t,t+t']}}{\rightsquigarrow} m'$ and $(\pi, t+t', m') \models_{\text{TGS}} \phi_2$ and*
  - *for every $t'' \in [0, t')$ it holds that there is an $m'' : H \hookrightarrow \pi_{t+t''}$ such that $m \overset{\pi_{[t,t+t'']}}{\rightsquigarrow} m''$ and $(\pi, t+t'', m'') \models_{\text{TGS}} \phi_1$.*

An MTGC ψ over the empty graph is satisfied by a TGS π, written $\pi \models_{\text{TGS}} \psi$, if $(\pi, 0, \mathrm{i}_{\pi_0}) \models_{\text{TGS}} \psi$ where $\mathrm{i}_{\pi_0} : \emptyset \hookrightarrow \pi_0$ is the initial morphism to the graph at timepoint 0 of π (i.e., the first graph of π).

This semantics is similar to the semantics of GCs for *conjunction*, *negation*, and the *exists* operator since for the triple (π, t, m) it always holds that the codomain of m is the graph π_t and since the checked MTGC is defined for the domain of m. The TGS π and the current timepoint t are used in the case for the *until* operator where we rely on the *preserved match* relation from above to change the codomain of a match from π_t to the graphs $\pi_{t+t'}$ and $\pi_{t+t''}$ at later timepoints.

Example 1 (TGS satisfies MTGC). Considering our running example, we argue that the MTGC given in Fig. 3 is satisfied by the TGS given in Fig. 2. Firstly, the *forall-new* operator matches the nodes T, S and the edge e_1 in G_2 at timepoint 10, which is the maximal creation timepoint of these three elements. Then, the *exists* operator matches the node H together with the edge e_2 in G_2 at the same timepoint. Finally, the *until* operator matches subsequently the node R and the edge e_3 in G_3 at the timepoint 13 and the remainder *true* is trivially satisfied for the timepoint 13. In addition, as also required by the *until* operator, for every timepoint in the interval $[10, 13)$, it is not possible to match a second Handler node H' that is connected to S. This holds because the graph in π for the timepoints in this interval is the graph G_2, which indeed does not contain such a second Handler node.

5 Mapping of TGSs to Graphs with History

Subsequently, we are concerned with finite TGSs π (which have a finite number of steps and therefore also satisfy $\mathrm{dur}(\pi) < \infty$) for which the satisfaction of an MTGC ψ is decidable [4] when replacing in ψ right-open intervals $[r, \infty)$ and (r, ∞) by $[r, \mathrm{dur}(\pi))$ and $(r, \mathrm{dur}(\pi))$, respectively. Such an adaptation of intervals leads to an MTGC ψ' that is *bounded* and for which the satisfaction by the finite TGS π is equivalent (i.e., $\pi \models_{\mathrm{TGS}} \psi \iff \pi \models_{\mathrm{TGS}} \psi'$).

To analyze the satisfaction of an MTGC by a given finite TGS, we now introduce the notion of *graphs with history* (in short, GHs) as an equivalent representation of a given finite TGS. Afterwards, we introduce a semantics operating on this alternative representation (called in the following *semantics for GHs*) that is compatible with the semantics introduced before for TGSs. The translation from finite TGSs to GHs reduces the size of the representation in terms of the stored data. Moreover, it decouples the observation of modifications, resulting in a GH, and the subsequent satisfaction check for possibly several MTGCs.

The notion of GHs for capturing the changes to a current graph over time as given by a TGS π, requires that the used type graph TG contains for all nodes and edges the attributes cts and dts of sort real to capture the total timepoint at which an element was created and (if applicable) deleted, respectively.[2]

Definition 7 (Graphs with History (GHs)). *Let TG be a type graph where all nodes and edges have attributes* cts *denoting the timepoint of their creation and* dts *denoting the timepoint of their deletion. Then G_H is a* graph with history (GH) *if it is typed over TG satisfying the following consistency requirements.*[3]

- *There is precisely one* cts *attribute for every graph node and edge.*
- *There is at most one* dts *attribute for every graph node and edge.*
- *For an edge e, the value of the* cts *attributes of the source and the target nodes of e are less or equal to the* cts *attribute of e.*
- *For an edge e, the value of the* dts *attributes of the source and the target nodes of e are greater or equal to the* dts *attribute of e.*

We now define the operation $\mathcal{F}\text{old}$, which converts a finite TGS π (i.e., a TGS with a finite number of steps) into the corresponding GH G_H. This recursive operation handles the renaming given by the monos l and r in the steps of π and, moreover, encodes the insertion of additional nodes/edges α by adding attributes cts $= t$ for these nodes/edges in the constructed G_H and by equipping removed nodes/edges α with an additional attribute dts $= t$ where t is the current total time of the considered TGS π in both cases.

Definition 8 (Map TGS to GH (Operation $\mathcal{F}\text{old}$)).

- *If $\pi = G_{init}$, then $G_H = \mathcal{F}\text{old}(\pi)$ is obtained from G_{init} by adding the attributes $\text{cts}(\alpha) = 0$ to each node or edge α in G_{init}.*
- *If $\pi = \pi' \cdot (\delta, l : IG \hookrightarrow G, r : IG \hookrightarrow G') \cdot G'$ is a TGS, $G'_H = \mathcal{F}\text{old}(\pi')$ is the GH obtained from the mapping of the TGS π' using the operation $\mathcal{F}\text{old}$, and $t = \text{dur}(\pi')$ is the total time of G'_H, then $G_H = \mathcal{F}\text{old}(\pi)$ is constructed from G'_H by adding the attributes $\text{dts}(\alpha) = t+\delta$ to each node or edge $\alpha \in G - l(IG)$, by renaming each node and edge $\alpha \in l(IG)$ according to l, by adding each node and edge $\alpha \in G' - r(IG)$, by renaming each node and edge $\alpha \in r(IG)$ according to r, and by adding the attributes $\text{cts}(\alpha) = t + \delta$ to each node or edge $\alpha \in G' - r(IG)$.*

The following example covers an application of $\mathcal{F}\text{old}$ to a finite TGS.

Example 2 (Map TGS to GH). We map the finite TGS π from Fig. 2 to the GH G_H shown in Fig. 4 using the operation $\mathcal{F}\text{old}$ as follows. Since π starts with an empty graph G_0, we first map it into the empty GH. The second state of π given by G_1 including the System node S is added to the TGS after 5 timeunits. We map this TGS state to the GH by adding S to the empty GH

[2] The total timepoints of additions and removals of attributes and their values can be encoded by moving attributes into separate nodes, for which their cts and dts attributes then encode the relevant timepoints.

[3] Note that the consistency requirements used in this definition are not guaranteed by the formalisms of E-GRAPHS or symbolic graphs.

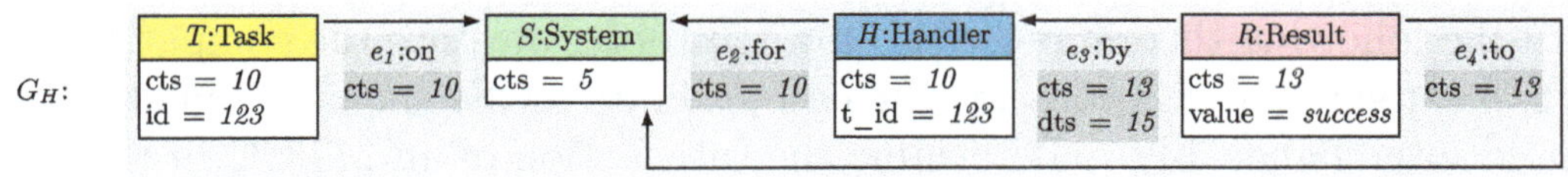

Fig. 4. Mapping of the TGS π from Fig. 2 to the GH $G_H = \mathcal{F}\text{old}(\pi)$

and by, additionally, equipping this node with the creation timepoint cts = 5. After another 5 timeunits, an additional Task node T, a Handler node H, and edges e_1, e_2 between the existing System node S and the new Task node T resp. the new Handler node H are added to the TGS resulting in the TGS state G_2. These changes are again mapped to the GH by adding the Task node T, the Handler node H, and the edges e_1, e_2 to the current version of G_H as well as by additionally equipping them with the creation timepoints cts = 10. In a similar manner the Result node R together with the edges e_3 and e_4 (see the TGS state G_3) are added to the GH with the creation timepoints cts = 13. Finally, after 2 timeunits, the edge e_3 is deleted to obtain the TGS state G_4. To reflect this in the GH, we add to the edge e_3 in G_H the additional deletion timepoint dts = 15.

For the satisfaction of an MTGC of the form $\exists(a : H \hookrightarrow H', \phi)$, where the *exists* operator is inherited from GCs, it is still required that the pattern that is found so far (given by some mono $m : G \hookrightarrow G_H$) in the host graph G_H can be extended to a larger pattern (given by some mono $m' : G' \hookrightarrow G_H$). Additionally, we have to check that all matched elements are already created (because the GH also contains the elements created with higher cts values) but not yet deleted (because the GH also contains the elements deleted at earlier timepoints). For the satisfaction of an MTGC of the form $\phi_1 \, \mathrm{U}_I \, \phi_2$, where the *until* operator is inherited from MTL, it is still required that ϕ_2 must be satisfied at some timepoint t' in the interval I relative to the current observation timepoint t and that ϕ_1 is continuously satisfied (by a possibly varying match for each timepoint) for all timepoints preceding t'.

Definition 9 (Satisfaction of MTGCs by GHs). *An MTGC $\psi \in \Phi_H^{\mathrm{MTGC}}$ is satisfied by a mono $m : H \hookrightarrow G_H$ and an observation timepoint $t \in \mathbf{R}_0^+$, written $(m, t) \models_{\mathrm{GH}} \psi$, if $\max(\{0\} \cup \mathrm{cts}(m(H))) \le t < \min(\{\infty\} \cup \mathrm{dts}(m(H)))$ and one of the following cases applies.*

- *$\psi = \wedge\{\phi_1, \dots, \phi_n\}$ and $(m, t) \models_{\mathrm{GH}} \phi_i$ (for all $1 \le i \le n$).*
- *$\psi = \neg\phi$ and not $(m, t) \models_{\mathrm{GH}} \phi$.*
- *$\psi = \exists(a : H \hookrightarrow H', \phi)$ and there is some $q : H' \hookrightarrow G_H$ such that $q \circ a = m$ and $(q, t) \models_{\mathrm{GH}} \phi$.*
- *$\psi = \phi_1 \, \mathrm{U}_I \, \phi_2$ and there is some $t' \in I$ such that $(m, t + t') \models_{\mathrm{GH}} \phi_2$ and for every $t'' \in [0, t')$ it holds that $(m, t + t'') \models_{\mathrm{GH}} \phi_1$.*

An MTGC ψ over the empty graph is satisfied by a GH G_H, written $G_H \models_{\mathrm{GH}} \psi$, if $(\mathrm{i}_{G_H}, 0) \models_{\mathrm{GH}} \psi$ where $\mathrm{i}_{G_H} : \emptyset \hookrightarrow G_H$ is the initial morphism to G_H.

Note that the reasoning for the satisfaction of the MTGC ψ from Fig. 3 by $G_H = \mathcal{F}\text{old}(\pi)$ from Fig. 4 proceeds analogously to Example 1.

In the following theorem (see [11] for its proof), we state the compatibility of the two satisfaction relations for the case of finite TGSs showing that they can be used interchangeably to determine the satisfaction of an MTGC in this case.

Theorem 1 (Soundness of Operation $\mathcal{F}$old). *If $\pi \in \Pi_{fin}$ and $\psi \in \Phi_{\emptyset}^{\mathrm{MTGC}}$ then $\pi \models_{\mathrm{TGS}} \psi$ iff $\mathcal{F}\mathrm{old}(\pi) \models_{\mathrm{GH}} \psi$.*

6 Reduction of MTGL to GCs

We now introduce a procedure for checking the satisfaction of an MTGC by a GH using a reduction of an MTGC to a corresponding GC. Based on the $\mathcal{F}$old operation from the previous section, we thereby obtain a checking procedure for finite TGSs as well. Moreover, this reduction shows that MTGL is as expressive as the logic of GCs on finite TGSs (since every GC is trivially also an MTGC).

We first present the operation $\mathcal{R}$educe for translating an MTGC into the corresponding GC and then show that this translation (also called *reduction* in the following) is compatible with our semantics for GHs and the operation $\mathcal{F}$old from before. The operation $\mathcal{R}$educe encodes in the resulting GC all parts of the satisfaction relation $\models_{\mathrm{GH}}$ that are not covered by the satisfaction relation $\models$ for GCs. In particular, the operation $\mathcal{R}$educe removes all occurrences of the *until* operator and encodes the check that the elements that are matched by the *exists* operator have all been created as well as that none of them has yet been deleted.

Technically, we translate a GH $G_H = \mathcal{F}\mathrm{old}(\pi)$ for a finite TGS π, $\psi \in \Phi_{\emptyset}^{\mathrm{MTGC}}$, and an observation timepoint $t \in \mathbf{R}_0^+$ (where G_H and ψ are typed over a type graph TG) into a graph G'_H and $\psi' \in \Phi_{\emptyset}^{\mathrm{GC}}$ (where both are typed over a changed type graph TG') using the procedure presented in Definition 10. We obtain ψ' from ψ by encoding the *until* operator suitably and by implementing the checks of cts and dts attributes according to Definition 9 for the *exists* and *until* operators using attribute constraints, for which we add variables to ψ. We also add the same variables to G_H to obtain G'_H.

Definition 10 (Reduce MTGC to GC (Operation $\mathcal{R}$educe)). *The recursive operation* $\mathcal{R}$educe *takes 3 arguments: a GH G_H that has been obtained by application of the operation $\mathcal{F}$old to a TGS π, an observation timepoint $t \in \mathbf{R}_0^+$, and an MTGC $\psi \in \Phi_{\emptyset}^{\mathrm{MTGC}}$. G_H and all graphs contained in ψ are typed over the type graph TG.*

The operation $\mathcal{R}$educe *returns a pair (G'_H, ψ') consisting of a graph G'_H (which is a slight modification of G_H) and a GC $\psi' \in \Phi_{\emptyset}^{\mathrm{GC}}$. The graph G'_H and all graphs contained in ψ' are typed over an adapted type graph TG' (called a* reduction type graph*) introduced below.*

1. *(Construction of the reduction type graph TG'):*
   We adapt the original type graph TG to TG' by adding an Encoding node with attributes num : int *and* var : real.
2. *(Construction of the MTGC ψ_{att} with* cts *and* dts *attributes):*
   We obtain ψ_{att} from ψ by adding the attributes cts $= x_{c,\alpha}$ *and* dts $= x_{d,\alpha}$ *to all nodes and edges α contained in graphs in ψ.*

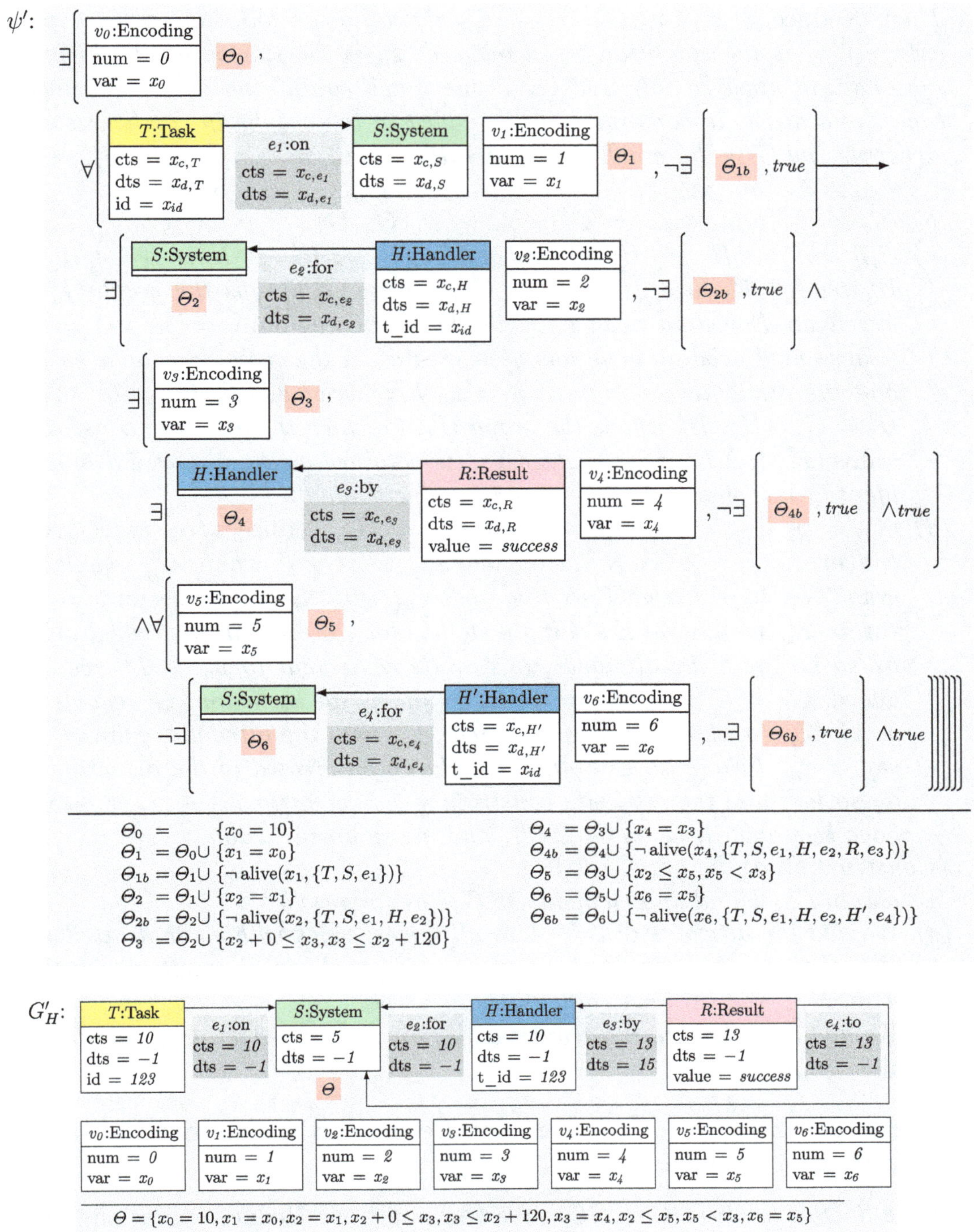

Fig. 5. The GC ψ' and the adapted graph G'_H resulting from applying the operation $\mathcal{R}$educe to the GH from Fig. 4, the timepoint $t = 10$, and the MTGC ψ from Fig. 3 (where the outermost *forall-new* operator has been simplified to the *forall* operator)

3. *(Construction of the GC* ψ'*):* $\psi' = \exists(\mathrm{i}_{G_0}, \mathcal{R}\mathrm{educe}_{\mathrm{rec}}(\psi_{att}, x_0, G_0, \emptyset))$ *where* G_0 *is the graph containing the Encoding node* v_0 *with the attributes* num $=$ *0*, var $= x_0$ *as well as the attribute constraint* $x_0 = t$ *and* $\mathrm{i}_{G_0} : \emptyset \hookrightarrow G_0$ *is the initial morphism to* G_0.

Then, $\mathcal{R}\text{educe}_{\text{rec}}(\psi_{att}, x_o, G_a, G) = \psi'_{att}$ *if one of the following cases applies (where* ψ_{att} *is the condition to be reduced,* x_o *is the timepoint at which the subcondition must be satisfied,* G_a *is the graph containing additional nodes, edges, and attribute constraints to be added to the graphs in conditions constructed, and* G *is the graph over which the condition* ψ_{att} *is defined).*

(a) $\psi_{att} = \wedge S$ *and* $\psi'_{att} = \wedge\{\mathcal{R}\text{educe}_{\text{rec}}(\phi, x_o, G_a, G) \mid \phi \in S\}$.

(b) $\psi_{att} = \neg\phi$ *and* $\psi'_{att} = \neg\,\mathcal{R}\text{educe}_{\text{rec}}(\phi, x_o, G_a, G)$.

(c) $\psi_{att} = \exists(a : H_1 \hookrightarrow H_2, \phi)$ *and* $\psi'_{att} = \exists(a' : H'_1 \hookrightarrow H'_2, \neg\exists(m : H'_2 \hookrightarrow H'_3, true) \wedge \mathcal{R}\text{educe}_{\text{rec}}(\phi, x_n, G'_a, H'_2))$ *where* G'_a *equals the graph* G_a*, to which an Encoding node* v_n *with the attributes* $\text{num} = n$*,* $\text{var} = x_n$ *(where no Encoding node has been created in the reduction for* n *so far) and the attribute constraint* $x_n = x_o$ *have been added,* $H'_1 = G_a \cup H_1$*,* $H'_2 = G'_a \cup H_2$*,* H'_3 *equals the graph* H'_2*, to which the attribute constraints* $\neg\text{alive}(x_n, H_2)$ *have been added,*[4] a' *is obtained as the union of* a *and the identity morphism* id_{G_a}*, and* m *is an inclusion.*

(d) $\psi_{att} = \phi_1 \text{ U}_I\, \phi_2$ *and* $\psi'_{att} = \exists(m_0 : G_0 \hookrightarrow G_1, \mathcal{R}\text{educe}_{\text{rec}}(\phi_2, x_{n_1}, G'_a, G_1) \wedge \forall(m_1 : G_1 \hookrightarrow G_2, \mathcal{R}\text{educe}_{\text{rec}}(\phi_1, x_{n_2}, G''_a, G_2)))$ *where* G'_a *equals the graph* G_a*, to which an Encoding node* v_{n_1} *with the attributes* $\text{num} = n_1$*,* $\text{var} = x_{n_1}$ *(where no Encoding node has been created in the reduction for* n_1 *so far) and the attribute constraints equivalent to* $x_{n_1} \in I$ *have been added,* $G_0 = G \cup G_a$*,* $G_1 = G \cup G'_a$*,* m_0 *is an inclusion,* G''_a *equals the graph* G'_a*, to which an Encoding node* v_{n_2} *with the attributes* $\text{num} = n_2$*,* $\text{var} = x_{n_2}$ *(where no Encoding node has been created in the reduction for* n_2 *so far) and the attribute constraints equivalent to* $x_{n_2} \in [x_o, x_o + x_{n_1})$ *have been added,* $G_2 = G_1 \cup G''_a$*, and* m_1 *is an inclusion.*

4. *(Construction of the graph* G'_H*):*
We obtain G'_H *by adding elements to* G_H *as follows:*
   (a) *We add the attribute* $\text{dts} = -1$ *to all nodes/edges without that attribute.*
   (b) *We insert all Encoding nodes contained in graphs in* ψ' *together with their* $\text{num} = n$ *and* $\text{var} = x_n$ *attributes.*
   (c) *We add the attribute constraints added during the reduction except for the* alive *constraints.*

We now demonstrate how the operation $\mathcal{R}$educe can be applied to the MTGC from our running example.

Example 3 (Reduce MTGC to GC). We now apply the $\mathcal{R}$educe operation to GH from Fig. 4, the timepoint $t = 10$, and the MTGC ψ from Fig. 3 resulting in G'_H and ψ' given in Fig. 5. However, to simplify the presentation, we replaced the enclosing *forall-new* operator by the *forall* operator to avoid the substitution of the *forall-new* operator by its encoding from Sect. 4.

1. We add the attribute $\text{dts} = x_{d,\alpha}$ to all nodes/edges α of G_H without dts attribute and add the attribute constraint $x_{d,\alpha} = -1$ to the set of constraints.

[4] For a graph H, $\text{alive}(x, H)$ equals $\text{alive}(x, S)$ for the disjoint union S of the nodes and edges of H. For a set S of nodes and edges, $\text{alive}(x, S)$ equals $\cup\{\text{alive}(x, \alpha) \mid \alpha \in S\}$. For a node or an edge α, $\text{alive}(x, \alpha)$ equals $\{x_{c,\alpha} \le x,\ x_{d,\alpha} = -1 \vee x < x_{d,\alpha}\}$.

With these additional attributes and the cts $=$ $x_{c,\alpha}$ attributes introduced by the operation $\mathcal{F}$old, we are able to state the existence of nodes/edges at a given timepoint x_n using attribute constraints in the resulting GC ψ'.

2. We add a unique *Encoding* node to each graph in ψ' as a container for additional variables x_n that are used in attribute constraints to encode the current observation timepoint (the num attributes are included to decrease the number of matches to be considered). Initially, we add an enclosing *exists* operator with the attribute constraint $x_0 = t$ (see Θ_0) where t is the input observation timepoint that is 10 for this application of $\mathcal{R}$educe. Further attribute constraints then relate the additional variables x_n for existential/universal quantifications (see Θ_1, Θ_2, Θ_4, and Θ_6). For the encoding of the *until* operator, these observation timepoints (x_3 in Θ_3 and x_5 in Θ_5) are restricted to some interval as described below.
3. We encode the *exists* operator $\exists(a : H_1 \hookrightarrow H_2, \phi)$ for the MTGC ϕ according to Definition 9 using an additional negative graph condition stating that the matched nodes/edges α are not violating the attribute constraints in alive(x_n, α). The set alive(x_n, α) contains the constraint $x_n \leq x_{c,\alpha}$ (to state that α was created before x_n) and the constraint $x_{d,\alpha} = -1 \vee x_n < x_{d,\alpha}$ (to state that α was not deleted or that it is deleted later than x_n).
4. We encode the *until* operator $\phi_1 \mathrm{U}_I \phi_2$ for the MTGCs ϕ_1 and ϕ_2 according to Definition 9 using the *exists* operator (the *forall* operator used in the GC below is only an abbreviation for a usage of the *exists* operator according to Definition 1). Informally, $\phi_1 \mathrm{U}_{[t_1,t_2]} \phi_2$ (the construction is similar for other kinds of intervals) is equivalent to $\exists(t' \in [x_n + t_1, x_n + t_2], \phi_2' \wedge \forall(t'' \in [x_n + t_1, t'), \phi_1'))$ where ϕ_1' and ϕ_2' are the reductions of ϕ_1 and ϕ_2, respectively. The variable x_n refers to the current observation timepoint that depends on the timepoint where an enclosing condition has been matched. In the example, the variables x_n, t', and t'' are represented in ψ' by the variables x_2, x_3, and x_5, respectively. The reduction is recursively applied to ϕ_1 and ϕ_2 resulting in ϕ_1' and ϕ_2', respectively. The replacement GC for the *until* subcondition spans the last four lines of ψ' in Fig. 5.
5. We add all *Encoding* nodes occurring in ψ' to G_H as depicted in Fig. 5. The *Encoding* nodes are used in ψ' as containers for the additional variables employed in the attribute constraints and are required in G'_H to allow for matchings from the adapted graphs of ψ' to G'_H.

In the following theorem (see [11] for its proof), we state that the operation $\mathcal{R}$educe is sound w.r.t. the satisfaction relations for MTGCs and GCs.

Theorem 2 (Soundness of Operation $\mathcal{R}$educe**).** *If* $\pi \in \Pi_{fin}$, $G_H = \mathcal{F}\mathrm{old}(\pi)$, $\psi \in \Phi_{\emptyset}^{\mathrm{MTGC}}$, $t \in \mathbf{R}_0^+$ *is a timepoint,* $\mathrm{i}_{G_H} : \emptyset \hookrightarrow G_H$ *is the initial morphism to* G_H*, and* $(G'_H, \psi') = \mathcal{R}\mathrm{educe}(G_H, t, \psi)$*, then* $(\mathrm{i}_{G_H}, t) \models_{\mathrm{GH}} \psi$ *iff* $G'_H \models \psi'$.

By application of Theorem 2, we can deduce for our running example that the MTGC ψ from Fig. 3 translated by the operation $\mathcal{R}$educe is satisfied by the graph G'_H (both given in Fig. 5). For this purpose observe that ψ from Fig. 3 (simplified as stated in Fig. 5) is satisfied by the GH from Fig. 4 for the timepoint $t = 10$

since the unique match of the Task node T, the on edge e_1, and the System node S satisfies the remaining condition starting at timepoint $t = 10$.

7 Tool Support

We provide tool support for checking finite TGSs against MTGCs as an extension of AutoGraph [25]. Firstly, we extended the support of AutoGraph to handle TGSs and MTGCs. Secondly, we implemented the operation $\mathcal{F}$old from Definition 8 to consolidate a TGS π to a GH G_H. Thirdly, we implemented the operation $\mathcal{R}$educe from Definition 10 to reduce an MTGC ψ to a GC ψ' and to adapt G_H to a graph G'_H. On the foundation of these three steps and as applications of our theoretical results (see Theorems 1 and 2), we then use the built-in support of AutoGraph for checking whether the obtained graph G'_H satisfies the reduced GC ψ'. Note that AutoGraph depends in this scenario on the constraint solver Z3 [20] to check satisfiability of expressions involving the values of cts and dts attributes of sort real as well as the additional constraints introduced by $\mathcal{R}$educe that contain further variables of sort real.

Considering our running example, we observed negligible runtime and memory consumption when verifying that the finite TGS π from Fig. 2 satisfies the MTGC ψ from Fig. 3 using our implementation due to the short length of π. Overall, the application of the AutoGraph extension *to our running example* shows promising results albeit the potential of further improvements regarding efficiency for handling more elaborate problem instances.

8 Conclusion and Future Work

We defined *Metric Temporal Graph Logic* (MTGL) by integrating the metric temporal operator *until* with time bounds into the well-established logic of (nested) graph conditions (GCs). This new logic allows to maintain an established binding of graph elements throughout the analysis of a timed sequence of (typed attributed) graphs (TGSs). Furthermore, to enable a satisfaction check for MTGL conditions by finite TGSs, we introduced a mapping of a finite TGS π into a graph with history $G_H = \mathcal{F}\mathrm{old}(\pi)$ and defined a reduction of an MTGL condition ψ to a GC ψ' given by $(G_H, \psi') = \mathcal{R}\mathrm{educe}(G_H, 0, \psi)$ where the graph with history G_H is extended to a graph G'_H. For this mapping and this reduction, we have proven that the satisfaction checks for the different representations are consistent (i.e., $\pi \models_{\mathrm{TGS}} \psi \iff G_H \models_{\mathrm{GH}} \psi \iff G'_H \models \psi'$). Finally, we presented an extension of the tool AutoGraph allowing to check the satisfaction of MTGL conditions by finite TGSs via the introduced mapping and reduction.

In the future, we want to develop checking procedures bounded MTGL conditions such that only violations that hold for any possible continuation are reported. Moreover, we intend to use our reduction of MTGL conditions to related GC counterparts for invariant checking for graph transformation systems as considered in [7]. Furthermore, we want to develop extensions of MTGL that include branching such as in timed CTL, that are applicable to the setting of probabilistic timed graph transformation systems as introduced in [19], or that support additional features e.g. permitting variables in the interval bounds of MTGL conditions or in attribute constraints. Finally, we intend to develop a model checking procedure for MTGL and these extensions. Besides these technical advancements we intend to evaluate and compare our approach based on benchmarks from applications domains such as runtime monitoring [18].

References

1. Arendt, T., Biermann, E., Jurack, S., Krause, C., Taentzer, G.: Henshin: advanced concepts and tools for in-place EMF model transformations. In: Petriu, D.C., Rouquette, N., Haugen, Ø. (eds.) MODELS 2010. LNCS, vol. 6394, pp. 121–135. Springer, Heidelberg (2010). https://doi.org/10.1007/978-3-642-16145-2_9
2. Baldan, P., Corradini, A., König, B.: A framework for the verification of infinite-state graph transformation systems. Inf. Comput. **206**(7), 869–907 (2008). https://doi.org/10.1016/j.ic.2008.04.002
3. Basin, D., Klaedtke, F., Müller, S., Zălinescu, E.: Monitoring metric first-order temporal properties. J. ACM (JACM) **62**(2), 15 (2015). http://dl.acm.org/citation.cfm?id=2699444
4. Bouyer, P., Markey, N., Ouaknine, J., Worrell, J.: The cost of punctuality. In: LICS 2007, pp. 109–120. IEEE Computer Society (2007). https://doi.org/10.1109/LICS.2007.49
5. Courcelle, B.: The expression of graph properties and graph transformations in monadic second-order logic. In: Handbook of Graph Grammars, pp. 313–400. World Scientific (1997). ISBN 9810228848
6. Dávid, I., Ráth, I., Varró, D.: Foundations for streaming model transformations by complex event processing. Softw. Syst. Model. **17**(1), 135–162 (2018). https://doi.org/10.1007/s10270-016-0533-1
7. Dyck, J., Giese, H.: k-inductive invariant checking for graph transformation systems. In: de Lara, J., Plump, D. (eds.) ICGT 2017. LNCS, vol. 10373, pp. 142–158. Springer, Cham (2017). https://doi.org/10.1007/978-3-319-61470-0_9
8. The Eclipse Foundation: EMF Henshin (2013). http://www.eclipse.org/modeling/emft/henshin
9. Ehrig, H., Ehrig, K., Prange, U., Taentzer, G.: Fundamentals of Algebraic Graph Transformation. Springer, Heidelberg (2006). https://doi.org/10.1007/3-540-31188-2
10. Ghamarian, A.H., de Mol, M., Rensink, A., Zambon, E., Zimakova, M.: Modelling and analysis using GROOVE. STTT **14**(1), 15–40 (2012). https://doi.org/10.1007/s10009-011-0186-x
11. Giese, H., Maximova, M., Sakizloglou, L., Schneider, S.: Metric temporal graph logic over typed attributed graphs: An extended version. Technical report, 127, Hasso Plattner Institute at the University of Potsdam, Potsdam, Germany (2019)
12. Habel, A., Pennemann, K.H.: Correctness of high-level transformation systems relative to nested conditions. Math. Struct. Comput. Sci. **19**, 1–52 (2009). https://doi.org/10.1017/S0960129508007202
13. Jakumeit, E., et al.: A survey and comparison of transformation tools based on the transformation tool contest. Sci. Comput. Program. **85**, 41–99 (2014). https://doi.org/10.1016/j.scico.2013.10.009
14. Klein, F., Giese, H.: Joint structural and temporal property specification using timed story scenario diagrams. In: Dwyer, M.B., Lopes, A. (eds.) FASE 2007. LNCS, vol. 4422, pp. 185–199. Springer, Heidelberg (2007). https://doi.org/10.1007/978-3-540-71289-3_16

15. König, B., Kozioura, V.: Augur 2—a new version of a tool for the analysis of graph transformation systems. ENTCS **211**, 201–210 (2008). https://doi.org/10.1016/j.entcs.2008.04.042
16. Koymans, R.: Specifying real-time properties with metric temporal logic. Real-Time Syst. **2**(4), 255–299 (1990). http://www.springerlink.com/index/X37127R758453X73.pdf
17. Kwiatkowska, M., Norman, G., Parker, D.: PRISM 4.0: verification of probabilistic real-time systems. In: Gopalakrishnan, G., Qadeer, S. (eds.) CAV 2011. LNCS, vol. 6806, pp. 585–591. Springer, Heidelberg (2011). https://doi.org/10.1007/978-3-642-22110-1_47
18. Leucker, M., Schallhart, C.: A brief account of runtime verification. J. Log. Algebr. Program. **78**(5), 293–303 (2009). https://doi.org/10.1016/j.jlap.2008.08.004
19. Maximova, M., Giese, H., Krause, C.: Probabilistic timed graph transformation systems. In: de Lara, J., Plump, D. (eds.) ICGT 2017. LNCS, vol. 10373, pp. 159–175. Springer, Cham (2017). https://doi.org/10.1007/978-3-319-61470-0_10
20. Microsoft Corporation: Z3. https://github.com/Z3Prover/z3. Accessed 19 Sept 2017
21. Orejas, F.: Symbolic graphs for attributed graph constraints. J. Symb. Comput. **46**(3), 294–315 (2011). https://doi.org/10.1016/j.jsc.2010.09.009
22. Ouaknine, J., Worrell, J.: Some recent results in metric temporal logic. In: Cassez, F., Jard, C. (eds.) FORMATS 2008. LNCS, vol. 5215, pp. 1–13. Springer, Heidelberg (2008). https://doi.org/10.1007/978-3-540-85778-5_1
23. Pennemann, K.H.: Development of correct graph transformation systems, Ph.D. thesis, Dep. Informatik, Univ. Oldenburg (2009)
24. Rensink, A.: Representing first-order logic using graphs. In: Ehrig, H., Engels, G., Parisi-Presicce, F., Rozenberg, G. (eds.) ICGT 2004. LNCS, vol. 3256, pp. 319–335. Springer, Heidelberg (2004). https://doi.org/10.1007/978-3-540-30203-2_23
25. Schneider, S., Lambers, L., Orejas, F.: Automated reasoning for attributed graph properties. STTT **20**(6), 705–737 (2018). https://doi.org/10.1007/s10009-018-0496-3
26. University of Twente: Graphs for Object-Oriented Verification (GROOVE) (2011). http://groove.cs.utwente.nl

KupC: A Formal Tool for Modeling and Verifying Dynamic Updating of C Programs

Jiaqi Qian[1], Min Zhang[1(✉)], Yi Wang[2], and Kazuhiro Ogata[3]

[1] Shanghai Key Lab of Trustworthy Computing, ECNU, Shanghai, China
zhangmin@sei.ecnu.edu.cn

[2] GCCIS, Rochester Institute of Technology, Rochester, NY, USA

[3] Japan Advanced Institute of Science and Technology, Nomi, Japan

Abstract. Dynamic Software Updating (DSU) is a useful technique for updating running software without incurring any downtime. Its correctness must be guaranteed because updating a running software is a complicated and safety-critical process. In this paper, we present a formal tool called KupC for modeling and verifying dynamic updating of C programs. The tool is built on $\mathbb{K}$–a formal semantic framework for programming languages. We formalize a patch-based dynamic updating mechanism in $\mathbb{K}$ based on the formal executable operational semantics of C. The formalization automatically yields an interpreter and several verification tools, which can be used to formally analyze the correctness of dynamic updating for C programs. To our knowledge, KupC is the first formal tool for code-level verification of dynamic software updating.

1 Introduction

Software systems require frequent updating to fixate defects, improve performance, and add new features. For those systems providing 24×7 service commitment, Dynamic Software Updating (DSU) is a useful technique as it does not incur system downtime while updating [5]. Such systems are becoming prevalent with the diffusion of Internet of Things (IoT) and Cyber-Physical Systems (CPS), where additions, modifications, and removal of behaviors could be done in a quick and localized fashion. There is a comprehensive survey on DSU [10].

The difficulty of guaranteeing the correctness of dynamic updating is a fundamental barrier when we adopt this technique widely as expected. Correctness is crucial to those systems that need dynamic updating because they are usually safety-critical and highly-dependable. Meanwhile, dynamically updating a running software system is a complicated process, and it is difficult to predict

This work was supported by NSFC Project grants 61502171 and 61872146, and China HGJ Project under Grant 2017ZX01038102-002.

R. Hähnle and W. van der Aalst (Eds.): FASE 2019, LNCS 11424, pp. 299–305, 2019.
https://doi.org/10.1007/978-3-030-16722-6_17

all possible updating results. In order to update a program successfully while it is running in practice one has to know everything about that program [6]. However, it still lacks effective methodologies and tools to help understand all possible behaviors of running programs caused by updating.

Formal methods are rigorous approaches to program verification. Some attempts have been made on applying formal methods to DSU [3,4]. The existing approaches suffer one or more difficulties as follows. In some approaches formalizing a dynamic update may require abstraction of target programs. Such abstraction is usually done manually. It requires both formal methods expertise and human intellection to interpret target programs. Some approaches [1,11] lack tool support while developing such tools needs substantial efforts.

To mitigate the above difficulties, we present a formal tool called KupC for modeling and verifying dynamic updating of C programs in this paper. KupC is built upon the formalization of a DSU tool called `Ginseng` [8] for C programs. We formalize the updating strategy of `Ginseng` atop the operational semantics of C in the formal semantic framework called $\mathbb{K}$ [9]. From the formalization, $\mathbb{K}$ automatically generates several tools that can be used for formal analysis of dynamic updating of C programs. According to our knowledge, KupC is the first tool for the code-level formal verification of dynamic software updating.

KupC has the following three features. (1) KupC is focused on the code-level verification of dynamic updating. It does not require any abstraction or transformation of target C programs that are subject to dynamic updating. (2) The verification functionalities of KupC are automatically generated from the formalization of dynamic updating mechanisms. No extra effort is needed on the implementation. (3) The formalization is built upon the operational semantics of the C language. One can easily develop similar tools for the formal analysis of dynamic updating of other languages such as Java and Python, whose operational semantics have already been formally defined in $\mathbb{K}$.

2 KupC Design

Patch-based DSU. Many DSU tools achieve dynamic updating by injecting patches into running programs [10]. A patch contains all updating contents, e.g., new functions and data. Figure 1 (left) is an overview of the patch-based updating process. An old-version program is first made updatable by attaching additional version information, wrapping user-defined types, and inserting possible updating points. They are achieved by the two operations called *Dependants Updating* and *Restriction Generating*. Next, a patch file *p1.c* is generated and complied by comparing the differences between old and new programs. After an update request is invoked, a DSU tool checks whether it is safe to inject the compiled patch whenever the running program reaches a pre-specified updating point. Safety means that the behavior of the updated program is consistent with the expectation. It is guaranteed by the adopted updating policies in DSU tools.

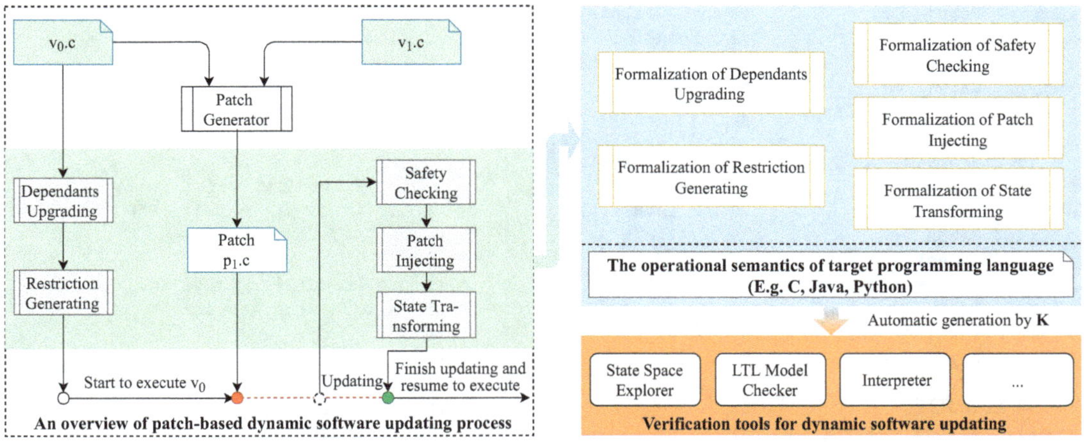

Fig. 1. Patch-based dynamic updating and its formalization using $\mathbb{K}$

If it is safe, the patch is injected and the running program state is transformed into the new version by a transformation function that is predefined in the patch. The patched program continues to execute from the new state. If updating at this point is not safe, the program continues to execute the old version.

It is worth mentioning that the entire updating process is atomically performed, that is, the execution keeps being suspended until the completion of the updating. Updating in an atomic manner is the most consistent approach that simplifies the updating process and reduces unexpected errors.

The $\mathbb{K}$ Framework. $\mathbb{K}$ [9] is a state-of-art semantic framework for programming languages. Many mainstream languages such as C and Java have been completely defined in $\mathbb{K}$. One only needs to focus on the formalization of an updating mechanism using the pre-defined operational semantics of the targeted language. After formalizing the updating mechanism, $\mathbb{K}$ automatically generates several analysis tools such as program interpreter, state space explorer, and model checker.

Formalization of dynamic updating strategy in $\mathbb{K}$. The basic idea of formalizing a dynamic updating mechanism using $\mathbb{K}$ is to formalize the functionalities of the mechanism on the basis of the operational semantics of the target programming language that the mechanism supports. The right part of Fig. 1 shows the formalization of the patch-based dynamic updating mechanism, consisting of the formalization of the five functionalities, respectively.

The functionalities of an updating mechanism are formalized by a set of rewrite rules. For instance, below is a rewrite rule that formalizes the function of checking the safety of updating a set of functions at an updating point *Loc*.

$$\left\langle \mathit{TypeSafety}(Loc, (\frac{F}{\cdot})\_)\cdots \right\rangle_k \quad \begin{array}{l} \langle \cdots Loc \mapsto (\_,\_,Re)\cdots\rangle_{restriction} \\ \langle\cdots F\mapsto T \quad F_{New}\mapsto T'\cdots\rangle_{types} \end{array}$$
$$\mathit{when}\ ((F \in Re) \wedge (T == T')) \vee (F \notin Re) \qquad (\textsc{SafetyChecking})$$

```
1 struct Road{
2   int dist;
3 };
4 struct City{
5   ... // node structure
6 };
7 struct Graph{
8   ... // Road+City..
9 };
10 struct Graph G;
11 void Shortest(int x){
12   ... // shortest path..
13 }
14 void PrintR(int x){
15   ... // print results..
16 }
17 void LoadG(){
18   ... // load graph data..
19 }
20 void Calculate(int x){
21   LoadG();
22   Shortest(x);
23 }
24 void Query(int x,int y){
25   /* point1 */
26   Calculate(x);
27   /* point2 */
28   PrintR(x,y);
29   /* point3 */
30 }
31 int main(){
32   ...
33   Query(0,6);
34   ...
35   Query(0,6);
36   ...
37 }
```

```
1 struct Road{ // modified structure
2   int dist;
3   int cost;   // new element
4 };
5 void Cheapest(int x){ // newly added
6   ... // new function
7 }
8 void PrintR(int x){ // modified
9   ... // print results and
10  ... // the cheapest path
11 }
12 void LoadG(){ // modified
13   ... // load new data
14 }
15 void Calculate(int x){  // modified
16   LoadG();
17   Shortest(x);
18   Cheapest(x);
19 }
```

Fig. 2. The snippets of old-version and new-version programs of a GPS application

In the rule, a pair of brackets is a labeled *cell*, representing a piece of program execution information. $\frac{F}{\cdot}$ means F is deleted from the set if the conduction that follows the keyword *when* is true. The condition says that either F is updatable (represented by $F \notin Re$) or it is un-updatable at the point *Loc* but its types T and T' (before and after updating, respectively) are the same. Here, *Re* is the set of un-updatable contents at *Loc*. If the second argument of *TypeSafety* becomes an empty set, it means all the functions in the set are safe to update.

We totally defined 371 rewrite rules to formalize the updating mechanism of `Ginseng`. We tested the correctness of the rules using the example dynamic updating programs provided in `Ginseng`. These rules are seamlessly compiled by $\mathbb{K}$ together with the rules defined for the operational semantics of C [2]. The compilation yields the formal tool KupC which supports formal analysis of dynamic updating of C programs in various ways such as simulation, state exploration, and LTL model checking.

3 KupC Usage

KupC is equipped with an interpreter to *execute* updatable C programs, a state space explorer to search for all possible updating results, and an LTL model checker to verify temporal properties of dynamic updating. We demonstrate the usage of KupC using a dynamic updating to a GPS application. The tool, examples and a demo video are available https://github.com/dexter-qjq/KupC.

The program in Fig. 2 (left) is the old version of a GPS system. It calculates the shortest path. In the new version in Fig. 2 (right), the new program not only shows the shortest path, but also finds the most economic path. Three update points are inserted in function `Query` from Line 24 to Line 30.

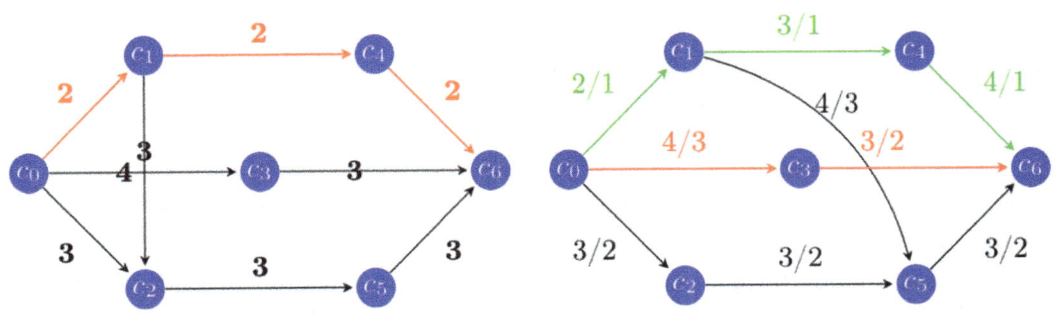

(a) Original graph (distance) (b) Updated graph (distance & cost)

Fig. 3. The shortest path before and after updating (Color figure online)

Simulating a dynamic updating scenario. Given an original C program annotated with update points, KupC can compile it with a patch file and generate binary code that is executable on $\mathbb{K}$. During execution, updating is applied once reaching a safe updating point. It simulates the behavior of a dynamic updating to a program that is running on a real-world operating system.

Figure 3 shows the results of the simulation. Figures 3(a) and (b) show the original graph and the updated graph, respectively. When the update takes place at `point1`, the output of first call is the red path in Fig. 3(a). While the second call produces two paths as shown in Fig. 3(b). The red one is the shortest path and the green one is the most economic path.

```
=========================================================================================
Case 1                          | Case 2                          | Case 3
Update at: point1               | Update at: point1               | Update at: point3
Output: "7km $3; 7km $3"        | Output: "6km; 7km $3"           | Output: "6km; 7km $3"
-----------------------------------------------------------------------------------------
Case 4                          | Case 5
Update at: point3               | Update at:
Output: "6km; 6km"              | Output: "6km; 6km"
=========================================================================================
```

Fig. 4. All possible updating results searched by the state space explorer of KupC

Exploring all dynamic updating results. In addition to simulating one possible updating scenario, KupC can search for all possible updating results by exploring each possible updating point using the state space explorer.

We compile and execute the program `map` with the option `UPSEARCH=1` to invoke the state exploration function. Figure 4 shows all five different updating results. The outputs are divided into two parts by semicolon, representing the results of the two function calls of `Query`, respectively. Case 1 and Case 2 show the results when updating occurs at `point1`. Case 3 and Case 4 are for `point3`. Case 4 shows the result when updating is not performed.

While the dynamic updating occurs during the first call of the function `Query` at `point3` in Case 3, the output of the first call is not affected by updating. The reason is that the updated content will not take effect until the next access after updating. Therefore, the outputs in Case `4` are exactly the same as the ones in Case `5`. Updating at `point2` violates the safety policies. Therefore, there is no case corresponding to `point2`. All the updating results searched are valid.

Model checking temporal properties. Dynamic updating is a temporal behavior in that the properties before and after updating may be different. Such differences can be formalized as temporal properties. Another attractive function of KupC is to verify these temporal properties using LTL model checking.

As an example, we verify whether or not updating in the GPS example can be finally deployed. First, we introduce an atomic proposition called `__update`, which is false before updating and becomes true after the program is updated. Given the command `UPLTLMC = "TrueLtl ULtl __update" ./map`, KupC returns true, indicating that updating can be eventually performed.

Another property of interest is that the shortest path must become 7 after the system is updated. It can be defined as an LTL formula `__update->(<>(x==7))`, where variable x stores the value of the shortest path. Given the command `UPLTLMC="'('~Ltl__update'\'/Ltl'('TrueLtlULtl'('x==7')'')'')'"./map`, KupC returns true, indicating that updating result is correct as expected.

4 Concluding Remarks and Ongoing Work

We have presented the design and implementation of an operational semantics-based verification tool called KupC for dynamic software updating. Three case studies showed the effectiveness of KupC for the formal analysis of the dynamic software updating of C programs by simulation, state exploration, and LTL model checking. Semantics-based formalization is promising in providing effective and practical solutions for guaranteeing the correctness of dynamic software updating. For instance, Lounas *et al.* achieved formal verification of dynamic updating of Java programs based on Java's semantics [7]. Compared with their approach, our approach is more general and extendable as $\mathbb{K}$ provides an elegant semantic framework for the definition of programming languages and an easy-to-use automated verification tool generation service.

KupC is at a good position for practical code-level verification of DSU. It is directly applicable to the code and shows the feasibility of formalizing a dynamic updating mechanism on the basis of the operational semantics of target programming languages. To verify the dynamic updating of more complex and practical programs, a complete semantics of C including those of standard libraries is needed. The efficiency of KupC also needs to examine although the efficiency of $\mathbb{K}$ has been validated [9]. There is ongoing work on these directions.

KupC has some limitations because of theoretical and practical challenges in the formal verification of DSU. Theoretically, Gutpa *et al.* have shown the undecidability of the reachability of updating points [3]. Another issue is that there is no uniform definition of *correctness* of dynamic updating. The logical correctness of dynamic updating depends on target programs and its formalization relies on programmers' interpretation. Although KupC does not require any abstraction of target programs, we suspect that certain abstraction is necessary for optimizing efficiency and scalability of the verification. For instance, a function that is not modified in a new version can be considered atomic for verification purpose. It is still an ongoing quest for an appropriate abstraction of target programs for the scalability while maintaining the validity of verification.

References

1. Duggan, D.: Type-based hot swapping of running modules. In: ICFP 2001, vol. 36, pp. 62–73. ACM (2001)
2. Ellison, C., Rosu, G.: An executable formal semantics of C with applications. In: POPL 2012. pp. 533–544. ACM (2012)
3. Gupta, D., Jalote, P., Barua, G.: A formal framework for on-line software version change. IEEE Trans. Soft. Eng. **22**(2), 120–131 (1996)
4. Hayden, C.M., Magill, S., Hicks, M., Foster, N., Foster, J.S.: Specifying and verifying the correctness of dynamic software updates. In: Joshi, R., Müller, P., Podelski, A. (eds.) VSTTE 2012. LNCS, vol. 7152, pp. 278–293. Springer, Heidelberg (2012). https://doi.org/10.1007/978-3-642-27705-4_22
5. Hicks, M., Nettles, S.: Dynamic software updating. ACM Trans. Prog. Lang. Syst. **27**(6), 1049–1096 (2005)
6. Hoare, C.A.R.: Record of a workshop on programming languages for distributed computing. In: Whitby-Strevens, C. (ed.) University of Warwick, p. 54 (1979)
7. Lounas, R., Mezghiche, M., Lanet, J.L.: A formal verification of dynamic updating in a Java-based embedded system. IJCCBS **7**(4), 303–340 (2017)
8. Neamtiu, I., Hicks, M., et al.: Practical dynamic software updating for C. In: PLDI 2006, pp. 72–83. ACM (2006)
9. Rosu, G.: 𝕂: a semantic framework for programming languages and formal analysis tools. In: Dependable Software Systems Engineering, pp. 186–206. IOS Press (2017)
10. Seifzadeh, H., Abolhassani, H., Moshkenani, M.S.: A survey of dynamic software updating. J. Softw. Evol. Process **25**(5), 535–568 (2013)
11. Zhang, M., Ogata, K., Futatsugi, K.: An algebraic approach to formal analysis of dynamic software updating mechanisms. In: APSEC 2012, pp. 664–673. IEEE (2012)

Business Process Privacy Analysis in PLEAK

Aivo Toots[1,2], Reedik Tuuling[1], Maksym Yerokhin[2], Marlon Dumas[2], Luciano García-Bañuelos[2], Peeter Laud[1], Raimundas Matulevičius[2], Alisa Pankova[1], Martin Pettai[1], Pille Pullonen[1,2](✉), and Jake Tom[2]

[1] Cybernetica AS, Tallinn, Estonia
{aivo.toots,reedik.tuuling,peeter.laud,alisa.pankova,martin.pettai, pille.pullonen}@cyber.ee

[2] University of Tartu, Tartu, Estonia
{aivo.toots,maksym.yerokhin,marlon.dumas,luciano.garcia-banuelos, raimundas.matulevicius,pille.pullonen,jake.tom}@ut.ee

Abstract. PLEAK is a tool to capture and analyze privacy-enhanced business process models to characterize and quantify to what extent the outputs of a process leak information about its inputs. PLEAK incorporates an extensible set of analysis plugins, which enable users to inspect potential leakages at multiple levels of detail.

1 Introduction

Data minimization is a core tenet of the European General Data Protection Regulation (GDPR) [2]. According to GDPR, usage of private data should be limited to the purpose for which it has been collected. To verify compliance with this principle, privacy analysts need to determine who has access to the data and what private information these data may disclose. Business process models are a rich source of metadata to support this analysis. Indeed, these models capture which tasks are performed by whom, what data are taken as input and output by each task, and what data are exchanged with external actors. Process models are usually captured using the Business Process Model and Notation (BPMN).

This paper introduces PLEAK[1] – the first tool to analyze privacy-enhanced BPMN models in order to characterize and quantify to what extent the outputs of a process leak information about its inputs. The top level (Boolean level, Sect. 2), tell us whether or not a given data in the process may reveal information about a given input. The middle level, the qualitative level (Sect. 3), goes further by indicating which attributes of (or functions over) a given input data object are potentially leaked by each output, and under what conditions this leakage may occur. The lower level quantifies to what extent a given output leaks information about an input, either in terms of a sensitivity measure (Sect. 4) or in terms of the guessing advantage that an attacker gains by having the output (Sect. 5).

[1] https://pleak.io (account: *demo@example.com*, password: *pleakdemo*, manual: https://pleak.io/wiki/, source code: https://github.com/pleak-tools/).

R. Hähnle and W. van der Aalst (Eds.): FASE 2019, LNCS 11424, pp. 306–312, 2019.
https://doi.org/10.1007/978-3-030-16722-6_18

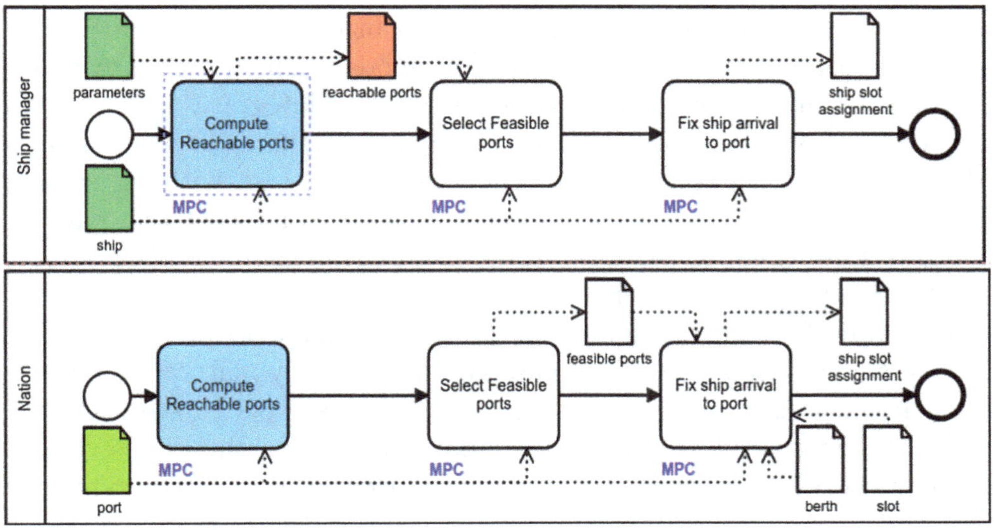

Fig. 1. Aid distribution process

To illustrate the capabilities of PLEAK, we refer to an "aid distribution" process in Fig. 1. This process starts when a nation requests aid from the international community to handle an emergency and a country offers to route a ship to help transport people and/or goods. The goal of the process is to allocate a port and a berth to the ship but not to reveal information about ships that are unable to help or the parameters of the ports. The process uses a type of privacy-enhancing technology (PET) known as secure multiparty computation (MPC). MPC allows participants to perform joint computations such that none of the parties gets to see the data of the other parties, but can learn the output depending on the private inputs. Given a ship, a deadline and the list of ports, task "Compute reachable ports" retrieves the list of ports reachable by the deadline. Tasks with identical names in different pools denote MPC computations carried out jointly by multiple stakeholders. Task "Select feasible ports" retrieves ports with the capacity to host the ship. The third task selects a port, a berth, and a slot for the ship, and discloses them to both participants.

Related Work. We are interested in privacy analysis of business processes and in this space Anica [1] is closest to our work. However, PLEAK's analysis is more fine-grained. Anica allows designers to see that a given object O1 may contain information derived from a sensitive data object O2, but it can neither explain how the data in O2 is derived from O1 (cf. Leaks-When analysis) nor to what extent the data in O2 leaks information from O1 (cf. sensitivity and guessing advantage analysis). In addition, they are interested in security levels and our high level analysis looks at PETs deployed in the process.

2 PE-BPMN Editor and Simple Disclosure Analysis

The model in Fig. 1 is captured Privacy-Enhanced BPMN (PE-BPMN) [7,8]. PE-BPMN uses stereotypes to distinguish used PETs, e.g. MPC or homomorphic encryption, that affect which data is protected in the process. The PE-BPMN editor allows users to attach stereotypes to model elements and to enter the stereotype's parameters where applicable. The editor integrates a checker, which verifies stereotype specific restrictions. For example, that: (1) when a task has an MPC stereotype, there is at least one other "twin" task with the same label in another pool, since an MPC computation involves at least two parties; (2) when one of these tasks is enabled, the other twin tasks is eventually enabled; and (3) the joint computation has at least one input and one output.

Given a valid PE-BPMN model, PLEAK runs a binary privacy analysis, which produces a *simple disclosure report* and data dependency matrix. The disclosure report in Fig. 2 tells us whether or not a stakeholder gets to see a given data object. In the report "V" indicates that a data object (in columns) is visible to a stakeholder (in rows). Marker "H" (hidden) is used for data with cryptographic protection, e.g. encrypted data. Row "shared over" refers to the network service provider, who may also see some of the data (e.g. unencrypted data objects).

#	berth	feasible ports	parameters	port	reachable ports	ship	ship slot assignment	slot
Nation	V	V	-	V	-	-	V	V
Ship manager	-	-	V	-	V	V	V	-
Shared over	-	-	-	-	-	-	-	-

Fig. 2. Simple disclosure report for the aid distribution process in Fig. 1

3 Qualitative Leaks-When Analysis

Leaks-When analysis [3] is a technique that takes as input a SQL workflow and determines, for each (output, input) pair which attributes, if any, of the input object are disclosed by the output object and under which conditions. A SQL workflow is a BPMN process model in which every data object corresponds to a database table, defined by a table schema, and every task is a SQL query that transforms the input tables of the task into its output tables. Figure 3 shows a sample collaborative SQL workflow – a variant of the "aid distribution" example where the disclosure of information about ships to the aid-requesting country is made incrementally. The figure shows the SQL workflow alongside the query corresponding to task "Select reachable ports". All data processing tasks and input data objects are specified analogously.

To perform a Leaks-When analysis, the user selects one or more output data objects and clicks the "SQL LeaksWhen" button. The Leaks-When analysis shows one tab for each output data object and one report for each column in the output table. The report is generated by extracting all runs of the workflow and applying dataflow analysis techniques to each run in order to infer all relevant data dependencies. An example of a leaks-when report (in graphical form) is shown in Fig. 4. The first input to *Filter* is the disclosed value (leaks branch), e.g. the arrival time. The second input (when branch) is the condition of outputting the first input, e.g. that the arrival time is less than the deadline and the ship has the required name. Each Leaks-When report ends with such filter but the rest of the graph aggregates the computations described in SQL.

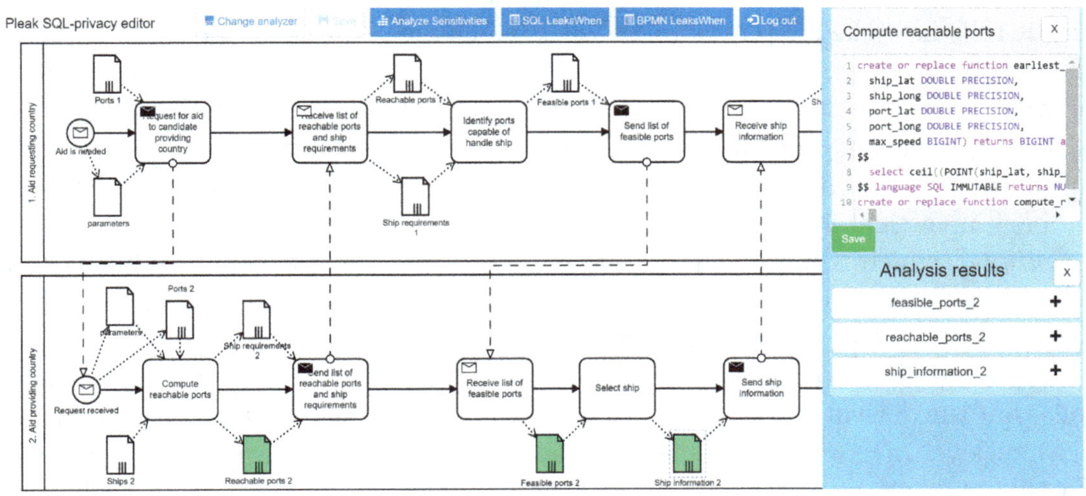

Fig. 3. Aid distribution SQL workflow in PLEAK SQL editor

4 Sensitivity Analysis and Differential Privacy

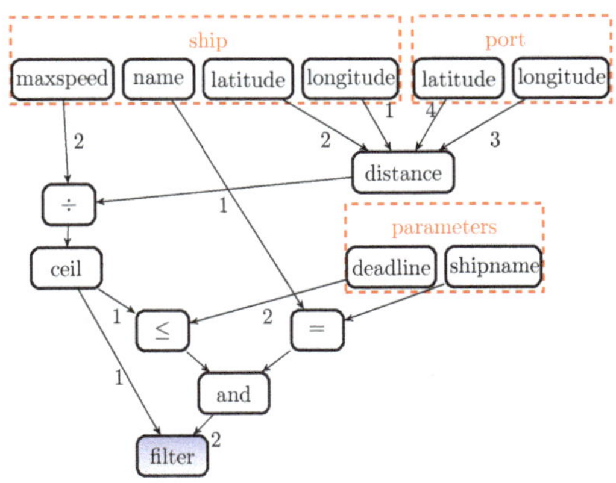

Fig. 4. Sample leaks-when report

The *sensitivity of a function* is the expected maximum change in the output, given a change in the input of the function. Sensitivity is the basis for calibrating the amount of noise to be added to prevent leakages on statistical database queries using a differential privacy mechanism [6]. Differential privacy ensures that it is difficult for an attacker, who observes the query output, to distinguish between two input databases that are sufficiently "close" to each other, e.g. differ in one row. PLEAK tells the user how to sample noise to achieve differential privacy, and how this affects the correctness of the output. PLEAK provides two methods – global and local – to quantify sensitivity of a task in a SQL workflow or of an entire SQL workflow. These methods can be applied to queries that output aggregations (e.g. count, sum, min, max).

Global sensitivity analysis [5] takes as input a database schema and a query, and computes the theoretical bounds for sensitivity, which are suitable for any instance of the database. This shows how the output changes if we add (remove)

a row to (from) some input table. The analysis output is a matrix that shows the sensitivity w.r.t. each input table separately. It supports only COUNT queries.

Sometimes, the global sensitivity may be very large or even infinite. *Local sensitivity* analysis is an alternative approach, which requires as input not only a schema and a query, but also a particular instance of the underlying database, and it tells how the output changes with the change *from the given input*. Using the database instance improves the amount of noise needed to ensure differential privacy w.r.t. the number of rows. Moreover, it supports COUNT, SUM, MIN, MAX aggregations, and allows to capture more interesting distances between input tables, such as change in a particular attribute of some row. In PLEAK, we have investigated a particular type of local sensitivity, called *derivative sensitivity* [4], which is in first place adapted to continuous functions, and is closely related to function derivative. PLEAK uses derivative sensitivity to quantify the required amount of noise as described in [4].

An example of derivative sensitivity analysis output is shown in Fig. 5a. It tells that the derivative sensitivity w.r.t. the *Ship* table is 4, and that a differential privacy level of $\varepsilon = 1$ can be achieved using smoothness parameter $\beta = 0.05$. To this end, we would have to add an amount of (Laplacian) noise such that the relative error of the output is 74%. More precisely, if the correct output is y, the noised answer will be between $0.26y$ and $1.74y$ with probability 80%. A tutorial on sensitivity analyzer can be found at https://pleak.io/wiki/sql-derivative-sensitivity-analyser. More examples can be found in the full version of this paper [9].

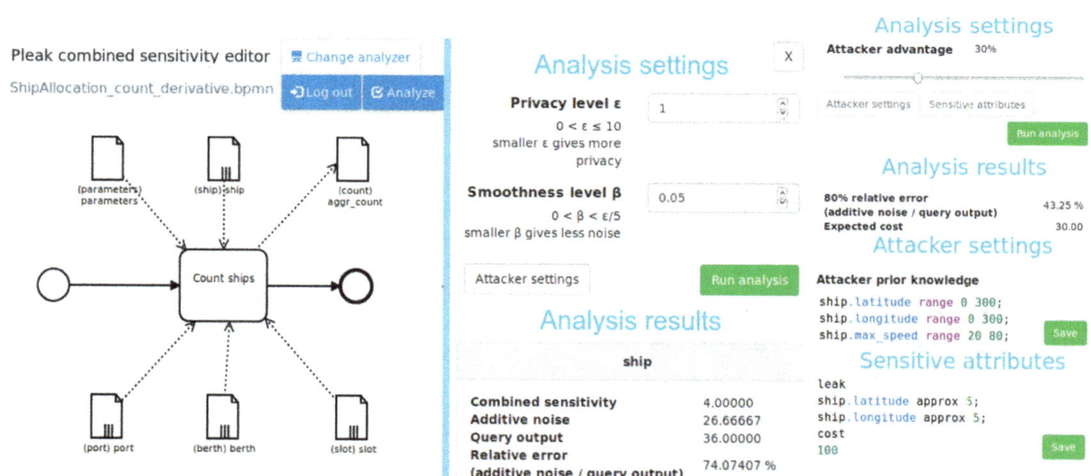

(a) Derivative sensitivity analysis (b) Guessing advantage analysis

Fig. 5. Examples of quantitative analysis

5 Attacker's Guessing Advantage

While function sensitivity as defined in Sect. 4 can be used directly to compute the noise required to achieve ε-differential privacy, it is in general not clear which ε is good enough, and the "goodness" depends on the data and the query [6]. We want a more standard security measure, such as guessing advantage, defined as the difference between the posterior (after observing the output) and prior (before observing the output) probabilities of attacker guessing the input.

The *guessing advantage* analysis of PLEAK takes as input the desired upper bound on attacker's advantage, which ranges between 0% and 100%. The user specifies particular subset of attributes that the attacker is trying to guess for some data table record, within given precision range. The user may define prior knowledge of the attacker, which is currently expressed as an upper and a lower bound on an attribute. The analyzer internally converts these values to a suitable ε, and computes the noise required to achieve the bound on attacker's advantage.

Figure 5b shows an example parameters and output of this analysis. The attacker already knows that the longitude and latitude of a ship are in the range [0...300] while the speed is in [20...80]. His goal is to learn the location of any ship with a precision of 5 units. If we want to bound the guessing advantage by 30% using differential privacy, the relative error of the output will be 43.25%. For a tutorial see https://pleak.io/wiki/sql-guessing-advantage-analyser.

Acknowledgements. The research was funded by Estonian Research Council under IUT27-1 and IUT20-55 and by the Air Force Research laboratory (AFRL) and Defense Advanced Research Projects Agency (DARPA) under contract FA8750-16-C-0011. The views expressed are those of the authors and do not reflect the official policy or position of the Department of Defense or the U.S. Government.

References

1. Accorsi, R., Lehmann, A.: Automatic information flow analysis of business process models. In: Barros, A., Gal, A., Kindler, E. (eds.) BPM 2012. LNCS, vol. 7481, pp. 172–187. Springer, Heidelberg (2012). https://doi.org/10.1007/978-3-642-32885-5_13
2. Colesky, M., Hoepman, J., Hillen, C.: A critical analysis of privacy design strategies. In: IEEE Security and Privacy Workshops (SP), pp. 33–40. IEEE (2016)
3. Dumas, M., García-Bañuelos, L., Laud, P.: Disclosure analysis of SQL workows. In: 5th International Workshop on Graphical Models for Security. Springer, Heidelberg (2018)
4. Laud, P., Pankova, A., Pettai, M.: Achieving differential privacy using methods from calculus (2018). http://arxiv.org/abs/1811.06343
5. Laud, P., Pettai, M., Randmets, J.: Sensitivity analysis of SQL queries. In: Proceedings of the 13th Workshop on Programming Languages and Analysis for Security, PLAS 2018, pp. 2–12. ACM, New York (2018)
6. Lee, J., Clifton, C.: How much is enough? Choosing ϵ for differential privacy. In: Lai, X., Zhou, J., Li, H. (eds.) ISC 2011. LNCS, vol. 7001, pp. 325–340. Springer, Heidelberg (2011). https://doi.org/10.1007/978-3-642-24861-0_22

7. Pullonen, P., Matulevičius, R., Bogdanov, D.: PE-BPMN: privacy-enhanced business process model and notation. In: Carmona, J., Engels, G., Kumar, A. (eds.) BPM 2017. LNCS, vol. 10445, pp. 40–56. Springer, Cham (2017). https://doi.org/10.1007/978-3-319-65000-5_3
8. Pullonen, P., Tom, J., Matulevičius, R., Toots, A.: Privacy-enhanced BPMN: enabling data privacy analysis in business processes models. Softw. Syst. Model. (2019). https://link.springer.com/article/10.1007/s10270-019-00718-z
9. Toots, A., et al.: Business process privacy analysis in pleak (2019). http://arxiv.org/abs/1902.05052

Specification, Design, and Implementation of Particular Classes of Systems

CLTestCheck: Measuring Test Effectiveness for GPU Kernels

Chao Peng(✉) and Ajitha Rajan

University of Edinburgh, Edinburgh, UK
{chao.peng,arajan}@ed.ac.uk

Abstract. Massive parallelism, and energy efficiency of GPUs, along with advances in their programmability with OpenCL and CUDA programming models have made them attractive for general-purpose computations across many application domains. Techniques for testing GPU kernels have emerged recently to aid the construction of correct GPU software. However, there exists no means of measuring quality and effectiveness of tests developed for GPU kernels. Traditional coverage criteria over CPU programs is not adequate over GPU kernels as it uses a completely different programming model and the faults encountered may be specific to the GPU architecture.

We address this need in this paper and present a framework, CLTestCheck, for assessing quality of test suites developed for OpenCL kernels. The framework has the following capabilities, 1. Measures kernel code coverage using three different coverage metrics that are inspired by faults found in real kernel code, 2. Seeds different types of faults in kernel code and measures fault finding capability of test suite, 3. Simulates different work-group schedules to check for potential deadlocks and data races with a given test suite. We conducted empirical evaluation of CLTestCheck on a collection of 82 publicly available GPU kernels and test suites. We found that CLTestCheck is capable of automatically measuring effectiveness of test suites, in terms of kernel code coverage, fault finding and revealing data races in real OpenCL kernels.

Keywords: Testing · Code coverage · Fault finding · Data race · Mutation testing · GPU · OpenCL

1 Introduction

Recent advances in the programmability of Graphics Processing Units (GPUs), accompanied by the advantages of massive parallelism and energy efficiency, have made them attractive for general-purpose computations across many application domains [19]. However, writing correct GPU programs is a challenge owing to many reasons [13] – a program may spawn millions of threads, which are clustered in multi-level hierarchies, making it difficult to analyse; programmer assumes responsibility for ensuring concurrently executing threads do not conflict by checking threads access disjoint parts of memory; complex striding patterns of memory accesses are hard to reason about; GPU work-group execution model and thread scheduling vary platform to platform and the assumptions are not

R. Hähnle and W. van der Aalst (Eds.): FASE 2019, LNCS 11424, pp. 315–331, 2019.
https://doi.org/10.1007/978-3-030-16722-6_19

explicit. As a consequence of these factors, GPU programs are difficult to analyse with existing static or dynamic approaches [13]. Static techniques are thwarted by the complexity of the sharing patterns. Dynamic techniques are challenged by the combinatorial explosion of thread interleavings and space of possible data inputs. Given these difficulties, it becomes important to understand the extent to which a GPU program has been analysed and tested, and the code portions that may need further attention.

In this paper, we focus on GPU program testing and address concerns with respect to quality and adequacy of tests developed for GPU programs. We present a framework, CLTestCheck, that measures test effectiveness over GPU kernels written using OpenCL programming model [7]. The framework has three main capabilities. The first capability is a technique called *schedule amplification* to check execution of test inputs over several work-group schedules. Existing GPU architecture and simulators do not provide a means to control work-group schedules. The OpenCL specification provides no execution model for inter work-group interactions [21]. As a result, the ordering of work-groups when a kernel is launched is non-deterministic and there is, presently, no means for checking the effect of schedules on test execution. We provide this monitoring capability. For a test case T_i in test suite TS, instead of simply executing it once with an arbitrary schedule of work-groups, we execute it many times with a different work-group schedule in each execution. We build a simulator that can force work-groups in a kernel execution to execute in a certain order. This is done in an attempt to reveal test executions that produce different outputs for different work-group schedules which inevitably point to problems in inter work-group interactions.

The second capability of CLTestCheck is measuring code coverage for OpenCL kernels. The structures we chose to cover were motivated by OpenCL bugs found in public repositories like Github and research papers for GPU testing. We define and measure coverage over synchronisation statements, loop boundaries and branches in OpenCL kernels.

The final capability of the framework is creating mutations by seeding different classes of faults relevant to GPU kernels. We assess the effectiveness of test suites in uncovering the seeded faults.

We empirically evaluate CLTestCheck using 82 kernels and associated test input workloads from industry standard benchmarks. The schedule amplifier in CLTestCheck was able to detect deadlocks and inter work-group data races in benchmarks. We were able to detect barrier divergence and kernel code that requires further tests using the coverage measurement capabilities of CLTestCheck. Finally, the fault seeding capability was able to expose unnecessary barriers and unsafe accesses in loops.

The CLTestCheck framework aims to help developers assess how well the OpenCL kernels have been tested, kernel regions that require further testing, uncover bugs sensitive to work-group schedules. In summary, the main contributions in this paper are:

1. Schedule amplification to evaluate test executions using different work-group schedules.
2. Definition and measurement of kernel code coverage considering synchronisation statements, loop boundaries and branch conditions.

3. Fault seeder for OpenCL kernels that seeds faults from different classes. The seeded faults are used to assess the effectiveness of test suites with respect to fault finding.
4. Empirical evaluation on a collection of 82 publicly available GPU kernels, examining coverage, fault finding and inter work-group interactions.

The rest of this paper is organised as follows. We present background on the OpenCL programming model in Sect. 2. Related work in GPU program testing and verification is discussed in Sect. 3. CLTestCheck capabilities is discussed in Sect. 4. Experiment setup and results of our empirical evaluation is discussed in Sects. 5 and 6, respectively.

2 Background

The success of GPUs in the past few years has been due to the ease of programming using the CUDA [17] and OpenCL [7] parallel programming models, which abstract away details of the architecture. In these programming models, the developer uses a C-like programming language to implement algorithms. The parallelism in those algorithms has to be exposed explicitly. We now present a brief overview of the core concepts of OpenCL, the programming model used in this paper.

OpenCL is a programming framework and standard set from Khronos, for heterogeneous parallel computing on cross-vendor and cross-platform hardware. In the OpenCL architecture, CPU-based *Host* controls multiple *Compute Devices* (for instance CPUs and GPUs are different compute devices). Each of these coarse grained compute devices consists of multiple *Compute Units* which in turn contain one or more *processing elements* (a.k.a *streaming processors*). The processing elements execute groups of individual threads, referred to as work-groups, concurrently. The functions executed by the GPU threads are called *kernels*, parameterised by thread and group id variables. OpenCL has four types of memory regions: global and constant memory shared by all threads in all work-groups, local memory shared by threads within the same work-group and private memory for each thread. Kernels cannot write to the constant memory.

GPUs have SIMT (single instruction, multiple thread) execution model that executes batches of threads (warps) in *lock-step*, i.e all threads in a work-group execute the same instruction but on different data. If the control flow of threads within the same work-group diverges, the different execution paths are scheduled sequentially until the control flows reconverge and lock-step execution resumes. Sequential scheduling caused by divergence results in a performance penalty, slowing down execution of the kernel.

Betts et al. [2] describe two specific classes of bugs that make GPU kernels harder for verification than sequential code, data races and barrier divergence. *Inter work-group data race* is referred to as a global memory location is written by one or more threads from one work-group and accessed by one or more threads from another work-group. *Intra work-group data race* is referred to as a global or local memory location is written by one thread and accessed by another from the same work-group. Barrier is a synchronisation mechanism for threads within a work-group in OpenCL and is used to prevent intra work-group data race errors.

Barrier divergence occurs if threads in the same group reach different barriers, in which case kernel behaviour is undefined [2] and may lead to intra work-group data race.

In this paper, we focus on covering barrier functions to help detect intra work-group barrier divergence errors and revealing problems with inter work-group interactions using work-group schedule amplification.

3 Related Work

We discuss related work in the context of work-group synchronisation, verification and testing of GPU programs.

Inter Work-group Synchronisation for OpenCL Kernels. Barrier functions in the OpenCL specification [7] help synchronise threads within the same work-group. There is no mechanism, however, to synchronise threads belonging to different work-groups. One solution for this problem is to split a program into multiple kernels with the CPU executing the kernels in sequence providing implicit synchronisation. The drawback with this method is the overhead incurred in launching multiple kernels. Xiao et al. [24] proposed an implementation of inter work-group barrier that relies on information on the number of work-groups. This method is not portable as the number of launched work-groups depends on the device. Sorensen et al. [22] extended it to be portable by discovering work-group occupancy dynamically. Their implementation of inter work-group barrier synchronisation is useful when the developer knows there is interaction between work-groups that needs to be synchronised. Our contribution is in detecting undesired inter work-group interactions, not intended by the developer.

GPU Kernel Verification. Verification of GPU kernels to detect data races and barrier divergence bugs has been explored in the past. Li et al. [14] introduced a Satisfiability Modulo Theories (SMT) based approach for analysing GPU kernels and developed a tool called Prover of User GPU (PUG). The main drawback of this approach is scalability. With an increasing number of threads, the number of possible thread interleavings grows exponentially, making the analysis infeasible for large number of threads. GRace [25] and GMRace [26] were developed for CUDA programs to detect data races using both static and dynamic analysis. However, they do not support detection of inter work-group data races.

GKLEE [15] and KLEE-CL [3], based on dynamic symbolic execution, provides data race checks for CUDA and OpenCL kernels, respectively. Both tools are restricted by the need to specify a certain number of threads, and the lack of support for custom synchronisation constructs. Scalability and general applicability is a challenge with these tools.

Leung et al. [13] present a flow-based test amplification technique for verifying race freedom and determinism of CUDA kernels. For a single test input under a particular thread interleaving, they log the behaviour of the kernel and check the property. They then amplify the result of the test to hold over all the inputs that have the same values for the property integrity-inputs. The test amplification approach in [13] can check the absence of data-races, not the presence. Additionally, their approach amplifies across the space of test inputs, not work-group schedules as done in our schedule amplifier. GPUVerify [2] is a static analysis tool that transforms a parallel GPU kernel into a two-threaded predicated program with lock-step execution and checks data races over this transformed model. The drawback of GPUVerify is that it may report false alarms and has limited support for atomic operations.

Test Effectiveness Measurement. Measuring effectiveness of tests in terms of code coverage and fault finding is common for CPU programs [6,18]. Support for GPU programs is scarce. GKLEE is the only tool that provides support for code coverage for CUDA GPU kernels. Given a kernel, it converts it into its sequential C program version (using Perl scripts) and applies the Gcov utility supplied with GCC for measuring code coverage. This form of coverage measurement disregards the GPU programming model. In our approach, we measure coverage conforming to the OpenCL programming model. With respect to fault seeder and schedule amplification, we are not aware of any existing work that provides these capabilities for GPU kernels to help measure effectiveness of test suites. The CLTestCheck framework is discussed in the next Sect. 4.

4 Our Approach

In this Section, we present the CLTestCheck framework that provides capabilities for kernel code coverage measurement, mutant generation and schedule amplification. To understand the kinds of programming bugs[1] encountered by OpenCL developers, we surveyed several publicly available OpenCL kernels and associated bug fix commits. A summary of our findings is shown in Table 1. We found bugs most commonly occur in the following OpenCL code constructs: barriers, loops, branches, global memory accesses and arithmetic computations. We seek to aid the developer in assessing quality of test suites in revealing these bug types using CLTestCheck. A detailed discussion of CLTestCheck capabilities is presented in the following sections.

4.1 Kernel Code Coverage

We define coverage over barriers, loops and branches in OpenCL code to check rigour of test suites in exercising these code structures.

Branch Coverage. GPU programs are highly parallelised, executed by numerous processing elements, each of them executing groups of threads in lock step, which is very different from parallelism in CPU programs, where each thread executes different instructions with no implicit synchronisation, as seen in lock-step execution. Kernel code for all the threads is the same, however, the threads may diverge, following different branches based on the input data they process. As seen in Table 1, uncovered branches and branch conditions are an important class of OpenCL bugs. Lidbury et al. [16] report in their work that branch coverage

[1] These are kernel bugs that violate the specification of the program or are associated with executions that lead to undefined behaviour.

Table 1. Summary of bug fixing commits we collected

#	Code Structure	Bug Type	Repository
1	Barrier	Missing barriers	Winograd-OpenCL [10], histogram [13], reduction [13], OP2 [3]
2		Removing unnecessary barriers	Winograd-OpenCL [10]
3	Loop	Incorrect condition	mcxcl [5], particles [8]
4		Incorrect boundary value	clSPARSE [1]
5		Missing loop boundary	Pannotia [21]
6	Branch	Missing else branch	liboi [11]
7		Incorrect condition	mcxcl [5], ClGaussianPyramid [4]
8	Global memory access	Inter work-group data race	Parboil-spmv [16], lonestar-bfs [21], lonestar-sssp [21]
9	Arithmetic Computations	Incorrect arithmetic operators	mcxcl [5], ClGaussianPyramid [4]

measurement is crucial for GPU programs but is currently lacking. To address this need, we define branch coverage for GPU programs as follows,

$$branch\ coverage = \frac{\#covered\ branches}{total\ \#branches} \times 100\% \tag{1}$$

Branch coverage measures adequacy of a test suite by checking if each branch of each control structure in GPU code has been executed by at least one thread.

Loop Boundary Coverage. In our survey of kernel bugs shown in Table 1, we found bugs related to loop boundary values and loop conditions were fairly common. For instance, bug #3 found in the `mcxcl` program allowed the loop index to access memory locations beyond the end of the array due to an erroneous loop condition. We assess adequacy of test executions with respect to loops by considering the following cases,

1. Loop body is not executed,
2. Loop body is executed exactly once,
3. Loop body is executed more than once
4. Loop boundary value is reached

$$Loop\ boundary\ coverage_{case\_i} = \frac{\#loops\ satisfying\ case\_i}{total\ \#loops} \times 100\% \tag{2}$$

where $case_i$ refers to one of the four loop execution cases listed above.

Barrier Coverage. Barrier divergence occurs when the number of threads within a work-group executing a barrier is not the same as the total number of threads in that work-group. Kernel behaviour with barrier divergence is undefined. Barrier related bugs, missing barriers and unnecessary barriers, is a common class of GPU bugs according to our survey. We define barrier coverage as follows.

$$barrier\ coverage = \frac{\#covered\ barriers}{total\ \#barriers} \times 100\% \tag{3}$$

Barrier coverage measures adequacy of a test suite by checking if each barrier in GPU code is executed correctly. Correct execution of a barrier without barrier divergence, *covered barrier*, is when it is executed by *all* threads in any given work-group.

4.2 Fault Seeding

Mutation testing is known to be an effective means of estimating the fault finding effectiveness of test suites for CPU programs [9]. We generate mutations using traditional mutant operators, namely, arithmetic, relational, bitwise, logical and assignment operator types. In Table 1, bug fixes #3, #7 and #8 show that traditional arithmetic and relational operator mutations remain applicable to GPU programs. In addition, we define three mutations specifically for OpenCL kernels: barrier mutation, image access mutation and loop boundary mutation inspired by bug fixes #1 to #5.

The barrier mutation operator we define is deletion of an existing barrier function call, to reproduce bugs similar to #1 and #2 in Table 1. OpenCL provides 2D and 3D image data structures to facilitate access to images. Multi-dimensional arrays are not supported in OpenCL. Image structures are accessed using read and write functions that take the pixel coordinates in the image as parameter. We perform image access mutations for 2D or 3D coordinates by increasing or decreasing one of the coordinates or exchanging coordinates. Finally, we define loop boundary mutations as either (1) skipping the loop, (2) allowing n-1 iterations of the loop and (3) allowing n+1 iterations of the loop where n is the number of iterations when the loop boundary is reached. The mutant operators we use in this paper are summarised in Table 2.

Table 2. Summary of mutation operators

Type of Operator		Mutants
Arithmetic	Binary	+, −, *, /, %
	Unary	-(negation), ++, --
Relational		<, >, ==, <=, >=, !=
Logical		&&, $\vert\vert$, !
Bitwise		&, $\vert$, ^, ~, <<, >>
Assignment		=, +=, −=, *=, /=, %=, <<=, >>=, &=, $\vert$=, ^=
Barrier		Delete barrier function call
Image coordinates		Change coordinates when accessing images
Loop boundary		Change the boundary value in loop condition check

4.3 Schedule Amplification

When a kernel execution is launched the GPU schedules work-groups on compute units in a certain order. Presently, there is no provision for determining this schedule or setting it in advance. The scheduler makes the decision on the fly subject to availability of compute units and readiness of work-groups for execution. The order in which work-groups are executed with the same test input can differ every time the kernel is executed. OpenCL specification has no execution model for inter work-group interactions and provides no guarantees on how work-groups are mapped to compute units. In our approach, we execute each test input over a set of schedules. In each schedule, we fix the work-group that should execute first. All other work-groups wait till it has finished execution. The work-group going first is picked so that we achieve a uniform distribution over the entire range of work-groups in the set of schedules. The order of execution for the remaining work-groups is left to the scheduler. For a test case, T over a kernel with G work-groups, we will generate N schedules, with $N < G$, such that a different work-group is executed first in each of the N schedules. The number of schedules, N, we generate is much lesser than the total number of schedules which is typically infeasible to check. The reason we only fix the first work-group in the schedule is because, most data races or deadlocks involve interactions between two work-groups. Fixing one of them and picking a different work-group each time, significantly reduces the search space of possible schedules. We cannot provide guarantees with this approach. However, with little extra cost we are able to check significantly more number of schedules than is currently possible. We believe this approach will be effective in revealing issues, if any, in inter work-group interactions.

To illustrate this, we consider a kernel co running on four work-groups. The CLTestCheck schedule amplifier will insert code on the host and GPU side, shown in Listings 1.1 and 1.2, to generate different work-group schedules.

Listing 1.1: Schedule OpenCL kernel (CPU-side)

```
// Generate a value in the range of [0,4)
int target_group = randint(4);
// Pass the value as a macro to GPU code
sprintf(clOptions,"-DTARGET_GROUP=%d", target_group);
```

Listing 1.2: Schedule OpenCL kernel (GPU-side)

```
if (my_group_id == TARGET_GROUP){
  // Original code here executed by target group
  A[(1 - buf) * 4 + tid] = A[buf * 4 + (tid + 1) % 4];
  atom_increase(num_threads_finishes);
} else {
  while (num_threads_finishes != group_size) continue;
  // Original code executed by other groups
  A[(1 - buf) * 4 + tid] = A[buf * 4 + (tid + 1) % 4];
}
```

In this example, before the GPU kernel is launched, the host side generates a random value in the range of available work-group ids. This value is the id of the selected work-group to be executed first and is passed to the kernel code using a macro definition. On the kernel side, each thread determines if it belongs to the selected work-group. Threads in the selected work-group proceed with executing the kernel code while threads belonging to other work-groups wait. After the selected work-group completes execution, the remaining work-groups execute the original kernel in an order based on mapping to available compute units (occupancy bound execution model [22]). With different work-group schedules generated by the schedule amplifier, we were able to detect the presence of *inter* work-group data races using a *single* GPU platform. Betts et al. [2], on the other hand, focus on intra work-group data races on different GPU platforms.

4.4 Implementation

CLTestCheck is implemented using Clang LibTooling [12]. We instrument OpenCL kernel source code to measure coverage, generate mutations and multiple work-group schedules automatically. Our implementation is available at https://github.com/chao-peng/CLTestCheck.

Coverage Measurement. To record branches, loops and barriers executed within each kernel when running tests, we instrument the kernel code with data structures and statements recording the execution of these code structures. For each work-group, we introduce three local arrays, whose size is determined by the number of branches, loops and barriers accessible by threads in that work-group. To measure branch coverage, we add statements at the beginning of each then- and else-branch to record whether that branch is enabled. Similarly, statements to record the number of iterations of loops are added at the beginning of each loop body. At the end of the kernel, the information contained in the data structures is processed to compute coverage.

Fault Seeder and Mutant Execution. The CLTestCheck fault seeder generates mutants and executes them with each of the tests in the test suite to compute mutation score, as the fraction of mutants killed. The CLTestCheck fault seeder translates the target kernel source code into an intermediate form where all the applicable operators are replaced by a template string containing the original operator, its ID and type. The tool then generates mutants from this intermediate form. Once mutants are generated, the tool executes each of the mutant files and checks if the test suite kills the mutant. We term the mutant as killed if one of the following occurs: program crashes, deadlocks or produces a result different from the original kernel code.

Schedule Amplification. As mentioned earlier, we generate several schedules for each test execution by requiring a target work-group to execute the kernel code first and then allowing other work-groups to proceed. The target work-group is selected uniformly across the input space of work-group ids. To achieve coverage of this input space, we partition work-group ids into sets of 10 work-groups. Thus if we have N work-groups, we partition them into $N/10$ sets. The first set has work-group ids 0 to 9, the second set has ids 10 to 19 and so on. We then randomly pick a target work-group, W_t, from each of these sets to go first and generate a corresponding schedule of work-groups, $\{W_t, S_{N-1}\}$, where S_{N-1} refers to the schedule of remaining $N-1$ work-groups generated by the GPU execution model which is non-deterministic. For $N/10$ sets of work-groups, we will have $N/10$ schedules of the form $\{W_t, S_{N-1}\}$ (a W_t first schedule). The test input is executed using each of these $N/10$ W_t first schedules. Due to the non-deterministic nature of S_{N-1}, we repeat the test execution with a chosen W_t first schedule 20 times. This will enable us to check if the execution model generates different S_{N-1} and evaluate executions with 20 such orderings.

5 Experiment

In our experiment, we evaluate the feasibility and effectiveness of the coverage metrics, fault seeder and work-group schedule amplifier proposed in Sect. 4 using OpenCL kernels from industry standard benchmark families and their associated test suites. We investigate the following questions:

Q1. Coverage Achieved: *What is the branch, barrier and loop coverage achieved by test suites over OpenCL kernels in our subject benchmarks?* To answer this question, we use our implementation to instrument and analyse kernel source code to record visited branches, barrier functions, loop iterations along with information on executing work-group and threads.

Q2. Fault Finding: *What is the mutation score of test suites associated with the subject programs?* For each benchmark, we generate all possible mutants by analysing the kernel source code and applying the mutation operators, discussed in Sect. 4, to eligible locations. We then assess number of mutants killed by the tests associated with each benchmark. To check if a mutant is killed, we compared execution results between the original program and mutant.

Q3. Deadlocks and Data Races: *Can the tests in the test suite give rise to unusual behaviour in the form of deadlocks or data races?* Deadlocks occur when two or more work-groups are waiting on each other for a resource. Inter work-group data races occur when test executions produce different outputs for different work-group schedules. For each test execution in each benchmark, we generate $20 * N/10$ different work-group schedules, where N is total number of work-groups for the kernel, and check if the outputs from the execution change based on work-group schedule.

Subject Programs. We used the following benchmarks for our experiments, 1. Nine scientific benchmarks with 23 OpenCL kernels from Parboil benchmark suite [23], 2. `scan` benchmark [20], with 3 kernels, that computes parallel prefix sum, 3. Five applications containing 13 kernels from Rodinia benchmark suite for heterogeneous computing, 4. 20 benchmarks from PolyBench with 43 kernels spanning linear algebra, data mining and stencil computations.

We ran our experiments on Intel CPU (i5-6500) and GPU (HD Graphics 530) using OpenCL SDK 2.0.

6 Results and Analysis

For each of the subject programs presented in Sect. 5, we ran the associated test suites and report results in terms of coverage achieved, fault finding and overhead incurred with CLTestCheck framework. We executed the test suites 20 times for each measurement. Our results in the context of the questions in Sect. 5 is presented below.

6.1 Coverage Achieved

Branch and Loop coverage (with 0, exactly 1 and >1 iterations) for each of the subject programs in the three benchmark suites[2] is shown in the plots in Fig. 1. The first row shows branch coverage, the second loop coverage. Mutation score and surviving mutation types shown in the last two rows of Fig. 1 is discussed in the next Sect. 6.2.

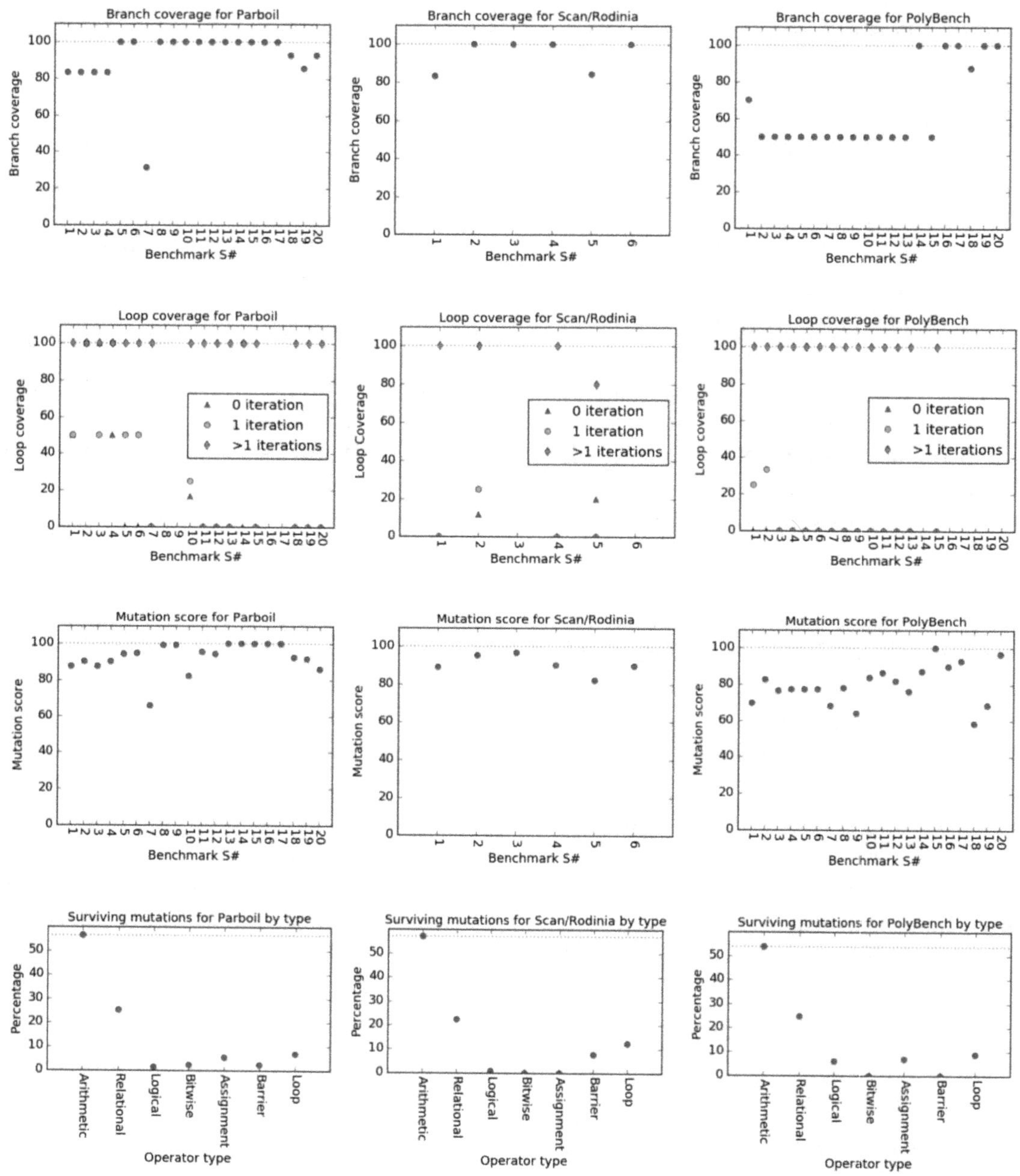

Fig. 1. Coverage achieved - Branch and Loop, mutation score and percentage of surviving mutations by type for each subject program in the 3 benchmark suites.

---

[2] 20 applications in Parboil counting different test suites separately, 6 in Scan/Rodinia, and 20 in PolyBench.

Barrier Coverage is not shown in the plots since for all, except one, applications with barriers, the associated test suites achieved 100% barrier coverage. The only subject program with less than 100% barrier coverage was `scan`, which had 87.5% barrier coverage. The uncovered barrier is in a loop whose condition does not allow some threads to enter the loop, resulting in barrier divergence between threads. We find that less than 100% barrier coverage is a useful indicator of barrier divergence in code.

Branch Coverage. For most subject programs in Parboil and Scan/Rodinia, test suites achieve high branch coverage (>83%). The `histo` benchmark is an outlier with a low branch coverage of 31.6%. Its kernel function, `histo_main`, contains 20 branches in a code block handling an exception condition (overflow). The test suite provided with `histo` does not raise the overflow exception, and as a result, these branches are never executed. We found uncovered branches in other applications, with >80% coverage, in Parboil and Scan/Rodinia to also result from exception handing code that is not exercised by the associated test data.

Branch coverage achieved for 13 of the 20 applications in PolyBench is at 50%. This is very low compared with other benchmark suites. Upon investigating the kernel code, we found that all the uncovered branches reside within a condition check for out of range array index. Tests associated with a majority of the applications did not check out of range array index access, resulting in low branch coverage.

Loop Coverage. Test suites for nearly all applications (with loops) execute loops more than once. Thus, coverage for >1 iterations is 100% for all but one of the applications, `srad` in Rodinia suite, that has 80%. The uncovered loop in `srad` is in an uncovered then-branch that checks exception conditions. We also checked if the boundary value in loop conditions is reached when >1 iterations is covered by test executions. We found `pathfinder` in Rodinia to be the only application to have full coverage for >1 iterations but not reach the boundary value. The unusual scenario in `pathfinder` is because one of the loops is exited using a break statement.

We find that test suites for most applications are unable to achieve any loop coverage for 0 and exactly 1 iteration. The boundary condition for most loops is based on the size of the work-groups which is typically much greater than 1. As a result, test suites have been unable skip the loop or execute it exactly once. The only exceptions were applications in the Parboil suite - `bfs, cutcp, mri-gridding, spmv`, and two applications in Rodinia - `lud, srad`, that have boundary values dependent on variables that maybe set to 0 or 1.

Overhead. For each benchmark and associated test suite, we assessed overhead introduced by our approach. We compared time needed for executing the benchmark with instrumentation and additional data structures that we introduced for coverage measurement against the original unchanged benchmark. Overhead varied greatly across benchmarks and test suites. Overhead for Parboil and Rodinia benchmarks was in the range of 2% to 118%. Overhead was lower for benchmarks that took longer to execute as the additional execution time from instrumentation is a smaller fraction of the overall time. Overhead for most programs in PolyBench ranges from 2% to 70%, which is similar to Parboil and Rodinia benchmarks. The overhead for `lu`, `fdtd-2d` and `jacobi-2d-imper` programs are >100%. The code for kernel computations in these benchmarks is small with fast execution. Consequently, the relative increase in code size and execution time after instrumentation with CLTestCheck is high.

6.2 Fault Finding

Fault finding for the subject programs is assessed using the mutants we generate with the fault seeder, described in Sect. 4. The mutation score, percentage of mutants killed, is used to estimate fault finding capability of test suites associated with the subject programs. Each test suite associated with a benchmark is run 20 times to determine the killed mutants. A mutant is considered killed if the test suite generates different outputs on the mutant than the original program in *all* 20 repeated runs of the test suite. In addition to killed mutants, we also report results on "Undecided Mutants", that refers to mutants that are killed in at least one of the executions of the test suite, but *not all* 20 repeated executions. Changes in GPU thread scheduling between runs causes this uncertainty. We do not count the undecided mutants towards killed mutants in the mutation score. Mutation score for all subject programs in each benchmark suite is shown in the third row of plots in Fig. 1.

Mutation Score. In general, we find that test suites for subject programs achieving high branch, barrier and loop coverage also have high mutation score. For instance, for `spmv` and `stencil`, their test suites achieving 100% coverage, also achieved 100% mutation score. An instance of a program that does not follow this trend is `mri-gridding` that has 100% branch, barrier, and loop (>1 iterations) coverage but only 82% mutation score. On analysing the survived mutants, we found a significant fraction (160 out of 232) were arithmetic operator mutations within a function named *kernel_value* that contained variables defining a fourteenth-order polynomial and a cubic polynomial. Effect of mutations on the polynomials did not propagate to the output of the benchmark with the given test suite. The `histo` program with low branch coverage, 100% barrier and loop coverage has 65.9% mutation score. Nearly two thirds of the branches in `histo` cannot be reached by the input data, as a result, all the mutations in the untouched branches is not killed, resulting in a low mutation score. A few of the programs in PolyBench have mutation scores that are between 60–70%. In these programs, most surviving mutations are arithmetic operator mutations.

As seen in the last row of Fig. 1 showing surviving mutations by operator type, arithmetic operators are the dominant surviving mutations in all three benchmark suites. Control flow adequate tests can kill arithmetic operator mutations only if they propagate to a control condition or the output. Data flow coverage may be better suited for estimating these mutations. Around 20% of relational operator mutations also survive in our evaluation. Most of the surviving relational operator mutations made slight changes to operators, such as $<$ to $<=$, or $>$ to $>=$ and vice versa. The test suites provided with the benchmarks missed such boundary mutations.

Undecided mutants occur during executions of 9, out of the 46 subject programs and test suites across all three benchmark suites. Number of undecided mutants during the 9 executions is generally small ($<= 5$). The only exception is `tpacf` in the Parboil benchmark suite, that resulted in 18 undecided mutants when executing one of its test suite. Undecided mutants point to non-deterministic behaviour in the kernel, that is dependent on GPU thread execution model. A large number of undecided mutants is alarming and developers should examine kernel code more closely to ensure that the behaviour observed is as intended.

Barriers were not used in all benchmarks. Only 5 out of the 9 benchmarks in Parboil, and 4 of the 6 in Scan/Rodinia had barriers. PolyBench programs did not use any barriers. Mutations removed barrier function calls in these benchmarks and we ecorded the number of mutants killed by test suites. Percentage of killed barrier mutations is generally low across all benchmarks with barriers. For instance, removing 2 out of 3 barriers in the `histo` program in Parboil, and removing all barriers in the `cutcp` program had no effect on outputs of the respective program executions. This may either mean that the test suites are inadequate with respect to the barrier mutations or it could be an indication that these barriers are superfluous with respect to program outputs, and the need for synchronisation should be further justified. For the programs in our experiment, we found barriers, whose mutations survived, to be unnecessary.

Coverage versus Mutation Score. The plots in Fig. 1 illustrate total mutation score over all types of mutations for each subject program and test suite. We also compute mutation scores specifically for branches, barriers, and loops using mutations relevant to them. We do this to compare against branch, barrier and loop coverage achieved for each of the subject programs. We found that mutation score for branches closely follows branch coverage for most subject programs. Outliers include `adi`, `nn`, `convolution-2d` and `convolution-3d`. Mutations that change $<$ to $<=$ are not killed in these kernels; these comprise one third of all branch mutations.

Mutation score for barriers is quite different from barrier coverage. This is because test suites are able to execute the barriers and achieve coverage. However, they are unable to produce different outputs when the barriers are removed. This may be a problem with the superfluous manner in which barriers are used in these programs.

Loop coverage with >1 iterations is 100% for all but one subject program (`srad` in Rodinia). Mutation score for loops on the other hand is variable. In general, tests achieving loop coverage are unable to reveal loop boundary mutations. Histo and srad are worth noting with high loop coverage but low loop mutation scores. We find that mutations to the loop boundary value in these two benchmarks survive, which implies that access to loop indices outside the boundary go unchecked in these programs. These unsafe values of loop indices should be disallowed in these kernels and loop boundary mutations in our fault seeder help reveal them.

6.3 Schedule Amplification: Deadlocks and Data Races

Kernel Deadlocks: When we used the CLTestCheck schedule amplifier on our benchmarks, we found kernel executions deadlock when the work-group ID selected to go first exceeds the number of available compute units. As there are no guarantees on how work-groups are mapped to compute units, we allow work-group IDs exceeding number of compute units to go first in some test executions using our schedule amplifier. However, it appears that the GPU makes unstated assumptions on what work-group IDs are allowed to go first. As noted by Sorenson et al. [22], "execution of large number of work-groups is in any *occupancy* *bound* fashion, by delaying the scheduling of some work-groups until others have executed to completion". They observed deadlocks in kernel execution due to inter work-group barriers. However, in the benchmarks in our evaluation, there is no explicit inter work-group barrier. It may be the case that developers made implicit assumptions on inter work-group barriers using the occupancy bound model and our schedule amplification approach violates this assumption. Nevertheless, our finding exposes the need for an inter work-group execution model that explicitly states the details and assumptions related to mapping of work-groups to compute units for a given kernel on a given GPU platform.

Inter Work-group Data Races: We were able to reveal a data race in the `spmv` application from the Parboil benchmark suite. We found that when work-groups 0 or 1 are chosen to go first in our schedules, the kernels execution always produces the same result. However, when we pick other work-group ids to go first, the test output is not consistent. Among twenty executions for each schedule, the frequency of producing correct output varies from 45% to 70%.

We observe similar behaviour in the `tpacf` application in Parboil when we delete the last barrier function call in the kernel. The kernel execution produces consistent outputs when we pick work-group 0 or 1 to go first. When we pick other work-groups to go first using our schedule amplifier, the kernel execution results are non-deterministic.

We observe no unusual behaviour in any of the PolyBench programs. These programs split the computation into multiple kernels and the CPU program launches GPU kernels one by one. The transfer of control from the GPU to the CPU between kernels acts like a barrier as the CPU will wait until a kernel finishes before launching the next kernel. In addition, care has been taken in the kernel code to ensure threads do not access the same memory location. As a result, we observe no data races in PolyBench with our schedule amplifier.

7 Conclusion

We have presented the CLTestCheck framework for measuring test effectiveness over OpenCL kernels with capabilities to measure code coverage, fault seeding and mutation score measurement, and finally amplify the execution of a test input with multiple work-group schedules to check inter work-group interactions. Our empirical evaluation of CLTestCheck capabilities with 82 publicly available kernels revealed the following,

1. The schedule amplifier was able to detect deadlocks and inter work-group data races in Parboil benchmarks when higher work-group ids were forced to execute first. This finding emphasizes the need for transparency and clearly stated assumptions on how work-groups are mapped to compute units.
2. Barrier coverage served as a useful measure in identifying barrier divergence in benchmarks (`scan`).
3. Branch coverage pointed to inadequacies in existing test suites and found test inputs for exercising error handling code were missing.
4. Across all benchmark suites, we found arithmetic operator and relational operator mutations that changed $<$ to $<=$, $>$ to $>=$ or vice versa were hard to kill. More rigorous test suites to handle these mutations are needed.

5. The use of barrier mutations revealed several instances of unnecessary barrier use. Barrier usage and its implications is not well understood by developers. Barrier mutations can help reveal incorrect barrier uses.
6. Loop boundary mutations helped reveal unsafe accesses to loop indices outside the loop boundary.

In sum, the CLTestCheck framework is an automated, effective and useful tool that will help developers assess how well OpenCL kernels have been tested, kernel regions that require further testing, uncover bugs with respect to work-group schedules. In the future, we plan to add further metrics, like data flow coverage with work-group schedule, to strengthen test adequacy measurement.

References

1. AMD Inc. and Vratis Ltd.: clSPARSE: a software library containing sparse functions written in OpenCL (2016). https://github.com/clMathLibraries/clSPARSE
2. Betts, A., Chong, N., Donaldson, A., Qadeer, S., Thomson, P.: GPUVerify: a verifier for GPU kernels. In: Proceedings of the ACM International Conference on Object Oriented Programming Systems Languages and Applications, OOPSLA 2012, pp. 113–132. ACM, New York (2012)
3. Collingbourne, P., Cadar, C., Kelly, P.H.J.: Symbolic testing of OpenCL code. In: Eder, K., Lourenço, J., Shehory, O. (eds.) HVC 2011. LNCS, vol. 7261, pp. 203–218. Springer, Heidelberg (2012). https://doi.org/10.1007/978-3-642-34188-5_18
4. Emonet, R.: Experiments on Gaussian pyramid implemented using OpenCL (2010). https://github.com/twitwi/ClGaussianPyramid
5. Fang, Q.: Monte Carlo eXtreme for OpenCL (MCXCL) (2017). https://github.com/fangq/mcxcl
6. Gay, G., Rajan, A., Staats, M., Whalen, M., Heimdahl, M.P.: The effect of program and model structure on the effectiveness of MC/DC test adequacy coverage. ACM Trans. Softw. Eng. Methodol. (TOSEM) **25**(3), 25 (2016)
7. Group, K.O.W.: The OpenCL specification version 2.2 (2017)
8. Horton, T.: Cinematic particle effects with OpenCL (2010). https://github.com/hortont424/particles
9. Jia, Y., Harman, M.: An analysis and survey of the development of mutation testing. IEEE Trans. Softw. Eng. **37**(5), 649–678 (2011)
10. Kim, H.H.: Winograd-based convolution implementation in OpenCL (2017). https://github.com/csehydrogen/Winograd-OpenCL
11. Kloppenborg, B., Baron, F.: LibOI: the OpenCL interferometry library (2012). https://github.com/bkloppenborg/liboi
12. Lattner, C., Adve, V.: LLVM: a compilation framework for lifelong program analysis & transformation. In: Proceedings of the International Symposium on Code Generation and Optimization: Feedback-directed and Runtime Optimization, p. 75. IEEE Computer Society (2004)
13. Leung, A., Gupta, M., Agarwal, Y., Gupta, R., Jhala, R., Lerner, S.: Verifying GPU kernels by test amplification. In: Proceedings of the 33rd ACM SIGPLAN Conference on Programming Language Design and Implementation, PLDI 2012, pp. 383–394. ACM, New York (2012)
14. Li, G., Gopalakrishnan, G.: Scalable SMT-based verification of GPU kernel functions. In: Proceedings of the Eighteenth ACM SIGSOFT International Symposium on Foundations of Software Engineering, pp. 187–196. ACM (2010)

15. Li, G., Li, P., Sawaya, G., Gopalakrishnan, G., Ghosh, I., Rajan, S.P.: GKLEE: concolic verification and test generation for GPUs. In: Proceedings of the 17th ACM SIGPLAN Symposium on Principles and Practice of Parallel Programming, PPoPP 2012, pp. 215–224. ACM, New York (2012)
16. Lidbury, C., Lascu, A., Chong, N., Donaldson, A.F.: Many-core compiler fuzzing. ACM SIGPLAN Not. **50**(6), 65–76 (2015)
17. NVIDIA Corporation: CUDA zone, September 2017. https://developer.nvidia.com/cuda-zone
18. Rajan, A., Heimdahl, M.P.: Coverage metrics for requirements-based testing. University of Minnesota (2009)
19. Rajan, A., Sharma, S., Schrammel, P., Kroening, D.: Accelerated test execution using GPUs. In: Proceedings of the 29th ACM/IEEE International Conference on Automated Software Engineering, pp. 97–102. ACM (2014)
20. Sengupta, S., Harris, M., Zhang, Y., Owens, J.D.: Scan primitives for GPU computing. In: Graphics Hardware, vol. 2007, pp. 97–106 (2007)
21. Sorensen, T., Donaldson, A.F.: The Hitchhiker's guide to cross-platform OpenCL application development. In: Proceedings of the 4th International Workshop on OpenCL, p. 2. ACM (2016)
22. Sorensen, T., Donaldson, A.F., Batty, M., Gopalakrishnan, G., Rakamarić, Z.: Portable inter-workgroup barrier synchronisation for GPUs. In: Proceedings of the 2016 ACM SIGPLAN International Conference on Object-Oriented Programming, Systems, Languages, and Applications, OOPSLA 2016, pp. 39–58. ACM, New York (2016)
23. Stratton, J.A., et al.: Parboil: a revised benchmark suite for scientific and commercial throughput computing. Center Reliable High-Perform. Comput. **127** (2012)
24. Xiao, S., Feng, W.C.: Inter-block GPU communication via fast barrier synchronization. In: 2010 IEEE International Symposium on Parallel & Distributed Processing (IPDPS), pp. 1–12. IEEE (2010)
25. Zheng, M., Ravi, V., Qin, F., Agrawal, G.: GRace: a low-overhead mechanism for detecting data races in GPU programs. In: Proceedings of the ACM SIGPLAN Symposium on Principles and Practice of Parallel Programming, PPOPP, vol. 46, pp. 135–146, August 2011
26. Zheng, M., Ravi, V.T., Qin, F., Agrawal, G.: GMRace: detecting data races in GPU programs via a low-overhead scheme. IEEE Trans. Parallel Distrib. Syst. **25**(1), 104–115 (2014)

Implementing SOS with Active Objects: A Case Study of a Multicore Memory System

Nikolaos Bezirgiannis[1], Frank de Boer[1], Einar Broch Johnsen[2(✉)], Ka I Pun[2,3], and S. Lizeth Tapia Tarifa[2]

[1] CWI, Amsterdam, The Netherlands
{n.bezirgiannis,f.s.de.boer}@cwi.nl
[2] Department of Informatics, University of Oslo, Oslo, Norway
{einarj,violet,sltarifa}@ifi.uio.no
[3] Western Norway University of Applied Sciences, Bergen, Norway

Abstract. This paper describes the development of a parallel simulator of a multicore memory system from a model formalized as a structural operational semantics (SOS). Our implementation uses the Abstract Behavioral Specification (ABS) language, an executable, active object modelling language with a formal semantics, targeting distributed systems. We develop general design patterns in ABS for implementing SOS, and describe their application to the SOS model of multicore memory systems. We show how these patterns allow a formal correctness proof that the implementation simulates the formal operational model and discuss further parallelization and fairness of the simulator.

1 Introduction

Structural operational semantics (SOS) [1], introduced by Plotkin in 1981, describes system behavior as transition relations in a syntax-oriented, compositional way, using inference rules for local transitions and their composition. Process synchronization in SOS rules is expressed abstractly using, e.g., assertions over system states and reachability conditions over transition relations as premises, and label synchronization for parallel transitions. This high level of abstraction greatly simplifies the verification of system properties, but not the simulation of system behavior as execution quickly becomes a reachability problem with a lot of backtracking. In this paper, we study how to implement a parallel simulator with a formal correctness proof from a SOS model, in terms of a case study of a multicore memory system. Such a correctness proof requires that the implementation language is also defined formally by an operational semantics.

Supported by *SIRIUS: Centre for Scalable Data Access* (www.sirius-labs.no) and *ADAPt: Exploiting Abstract Data-Access Patterns for Better Data Locality in Parallel Processing* (www.mn.uio.no/ifi/english/research/projects/adapt/).

R. Hähnle and W. van der Aalst (Eds.): FASE 2019, LNCS 11424, pp. 332–350, 2019.
https://doi.org/10.1007/978-3-030-16722-6_20

A major challenge in software engineering is the exploitation of the computational power of multicore (and manycore) architectures. One important aspect of this challenge is the memory systems of these architectures. These memory systems generally use caches to avoid bottlenecks in data access from main memory, but caches introduce data duplication and require protocols to ensure coherence. Although data duplication is usually not visible to the programmer, the way a program interacts with these copies largely affects performance by moving data around to maintain coherence. To develop, test and optimize software for multicore architectures, we need correct, executable models of the underlying memory systems. A SOS model of multicore memory systems with correctness proofs for cache coherency has been described in [2], together with a prototype implementation in the rewriting logic system Maude [3]. However, this fairly direct implementation of the SOS model is not well suited to simulate large systems.

This paper considers an implementation of the SOS model in ABS [4], a language tailored to the description of distributed systems based on active objects [5]. ABS is formally defined by an operational semantics and supports parallel execution on backends in Erlang, Haskell, and Java. The following features of ABS allow a high-level, coarse-grained view of the execution of different method invocations by different active objects: encapsulation of local state in active objects, communication using asynchronous method calls and futures, and cooperative scheduling of the method invocations of an active object. Our case study fully exploits these features and the resulting abstractions to correctly implement the complex process synchronization of the original SOS model.

The main contributions of this paper are as follows:

- We provide general design patterns in ABS for implementing structural operational semantics with active objects, and apply these patterns to the implementation in ABS of a structural operational semantics of multicore memory systems.
- We show how these patterns allow a formal correctness proof of this implementation by means of a simulation relation between the formal operational semantics of the ABS implementation and the operational model of multicore memory systems.
- We discuss how these ABS design patterns can be used to further parallelize the implementation while preserving correctness.
- Finally, we show how the ABS modeling concepts of symbolic time and virtual resources can be used to obtain a parallel implementation of the SOS model which abstractly ensures fairness between the progress of different parallel components, independently of the number of cores that are used in the simulation.

2 An Abstract Model of a Multicore Memory System

Design decisions for a program running on top of a multicore memory systems can be explored using simulators based on abstract models. Bijo et al. [2,6] developed a model which takes as input tasks (expressed as data access) to be executed, the corresponding data layout in main memory (indicating where data is allocated), and a parallel architecture consisting of cores with private multi-level caches and shared memory (see Fig. 1). Additionally, the model is configurable in the number of cores, the number and size of caches, and the associativity and replacement policy. Memory is organized in blocks which move between caches and main memory. For simplicity, the model assumes that the size of cache lines and memory blocks in main memory coincide, abstracts from the data content of memory blocks, and transfers memory blocks from the caches of one core to the caches of another core via main memory.

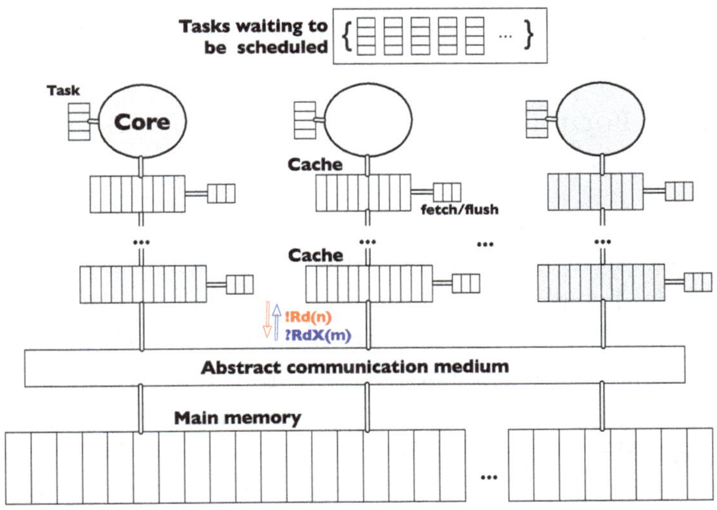

Fig. 1. Abstract model of a multicore memory system.

Tasks from the program are scheduled for execution from a shared task pool. Task execution on a core requires memory blocks to be transferred from main memory to the closest cache. Each cache has a pool of fetch/flush instructions to move blocks among caches and between caches and main memory. Consistency between multiple copies of a memory block is ensured using the standard cache coherence protocol MSI (e.g., [7]), with which a cache line is either modified, shared or invalid. A *modified* cache line has the most recent value of the memory block, therefore all other copies are *invalid* (including the one in main memory). A *shared* cache line indicates that all copies of the block are consistent. The protocol's messages are broadcast to the cores. The details of the broadcast (e.g., on a mesh or a ring) can be abstracted into an *abstract communication medium*. Following standard nomenclature, *Rd* messages request *read* access and *RdX* messages *read exclusive* access to a memory block. The latter invalidates other copies of the same block in other caches to provide write access.

To access data from a block n, a core looks for n in its local caches. If n is not found in shared or modified state, a *read request* $!Rd(n)$ is broadcast to the other cores and to main memory. The cache can *fetch* the block when it is available in main memory. Eviction is required if the cache is full. Writing to block n requires n to be in shared or modified state in the local cache; if it is in shared state, an *invalidation request* $!RdX(n)$ is broadcast to obtain exclusive access. If a cache with block n in modified state receives a read request $?Rd(n)$, it *flushes* the block to main memory; if a cache with block n in shared state receives an invalidation request $?RdX(n)$, the cache line will be *invalidated*; the requests are discarded otherwise. Read and invalidation requests are broadcast instantaneously in the abstract model, reflecting that signalling on the communication medium is order of magnitude faster than moving data to or from main memory.

Syntactic categories.	***Definitions.***	
$cid \in CoreId$	$cf \in Config$	$::= M \circ \overline{dap} \circ \overline{Ca} \circ \overline{CR}$
$caid \in CacheId$	$CR \in Core$	$::= cid \bullet rst$
$n \in Address$	$Ca \in Cache$	$::= caid \bullet M \bullet dst$
$r \in Ref$	$st \in Status$	$::= \{mo, sh, inv\}$
	$dap \in AccessPtns$	$::= \varepsilon \mid dap; dap \mid \mathbf{read}(r) \mid \mathbf{write}(r) \mid \mathbf{commit}(r)$ $\mid \mathbf{commit} \mid dap \sqcap dap \mid dap^* \mid \mathbf{skip} \mid \mathbf{spawn}(dap)$
	$rst \in RunLang$	$::= dap \mid rst; rst \mid \mathbf{readBl}(r) \mid \mathbf{writeBl}(r)$
	$dst \in DataLang$	$::= \varepsilon \mid \overline{dst} \mid \mathbf{fetch}(n) \mid \mathbf{flush}(n) \mid \mathbf{fetchBl}(n) \mid \mathbf{flush}$

Fig. 2. Syntax of runtime configurations, where over-bar denotes sets (e.g., $\overline{CR}$).

2.1 Formalization of the Multicore Memory System as an SOS Model

An operational meaning for the abstract model described above has be defined using structural operational semantics (SOS) [1] with labeled transitions to model broadcast in the abstract communication medium. The resulting formalization [2,6] is shown to guarantee standard correctness properties for data consistency and cache coherence from the literature [8,9], including the preservation of program order in each core, the absence of data races, and no access to stale data. We briefly outline the main aspects of the formal model. The runtime syntax is given in Fig. 2. A configuration cf consists of main memory M, cores $\overline{CR}$, caches $\overline{Ca}$, and tasks $\overline{dap}$ to be scheduled. (We syntactically abuse set operations for multisets, including union $\cup$ and subtraction $\setminus$.) A core $cid \bullet rst$ with identifier cid executes runtime statements rst. A cache with identifier $caid$ has a local cache memory M and data instructions dst. We assume that $caid$ encodes the cid of the core to which the cache belongs and its level in the cache hierarchy. We denote by $Status \cup \{\perp\}$ the extension of the set of status tags with the undefined value $\perp$. Thus, a memory $M : Address \rightarrow Status \cup \{\perp\}$ maps addresses n to either a status tags $Status$ or to $\perp$ if the memory block with address n is not found in M.

Data access patterns dap model tasks consisting of $\mathbf{read}(r)$ and $\mathbf{write}(r)$ operations to references r and control flow operations for sequential composition $dap_1; dap_2$, non-deterministic choice $dap_1 \sqcap dap_2$, repetition dap^*, task creation $\mathbf{spawn}(dap)$, and **commit** which flushes the entire cache after task execution. The empty access pattern is denoted ε. Cores execute *runtime statements rst*, which extend dap with $\mathbf{readBl}(r)$ and $\mathbf{writeBl}(r)$ to block execution while waiting for data. Caches execute *data instructions dst* to fetch and flush the memory block with address n, here $\mathbf{fetchBl}(n)$ blocks execution while waiting for data, and **flush** flushes the entire cache.

The *abstract communication medium* allows messages from one cache to be transmitted to the other caches and to main memory in a parallel instantaneous broadcast. Communication in the abstract communication medium is formalized in terms of label matching on transitions. The formal syntax for this label mechanism is as follows:

$$S ::= !Rd(n) \mid !RdX(n) \qquad R ::= ?Rd(n) \mid ?RdX(n)$$

Here, for any address n, a request of the form $!Rd(n)$ or $!RdX(n)$ is sent by one node and its dual of the form $dual(!Rd(n)) = ?Rd(n)$ or $dual(!RdX(n)) = ?RdX(n)$ is broadcast to the rest of nodes and main memory. The syntax of the model is further detailed in [2,6].

2.2 Local and Global SOS Rules

The semantics is divided into local and global rules. Local rules capture interaction inside a node containing a core and the hierarchy of caches. Global rules capture synchronization and coordination between different nodes and main memory. In an *initial* configuration cf_0, all blocks in main memory M have status sh, all cores are idle, all caches are empty, and the task pool in $\overline{dap}$ has a single task representing the main block of a program. Let $cf \xrightarrow{*} cf'$ denote an execution starting from cf and reaching cf' by applying global transition rules, which in turn apply local transition rules for each core and its cache hierarchy. In the rules, let the auxiliary function $addr(r)$ return the address n of the block containing reference r, $cid(caid)$ the identity of the core associated with cache $caid$, $lid(caid)$ the cache level of $caid$, and $status(M, n)$ the status of block n in map M. Let the predicate $first(caid)$ hold when $caid$ is the first level and $last(caid)$ when $caid$ is the last level cache. Note that unlabelled transitions $\rightarrow$ can be executed asynchronously, while labelled transitions $\xrightarrow{S}$ require synchronization between all the nodes and main memory (see Figs. 3 and 4). We discuss some representative rules for local and global level of the SOS model. The full SOS formalization can be found in [6].

Local semantics. The first rules of Fig. 3 involve a core and its first level cache. In PrRd$_1$, reading reference r succeeds if the block containing r is available. Otherwise, in PrRd$_2$ a **fetch**(n) instruction is added to the data instructions dst of the first level cache and further execution of the core is blocked by **readBl**(r). Writing to r only succeeds if the associated memory block has mo status in the first level cache. If the cache line is shared, the core broadcasts a $!RdX(n)$ request to acquire exclusive access, where the broadcast appears as a label on the transition in PrWr$_2$. Otherwise, the block must be fetched from main memory in PrWr$_3$ and **writeBl**(r) blocks execution.

For the remaining rules of Fig. 3, LC-Hit$_1$ and LC-Miss$_1$ capture interactions between adjacent levels of caches, and LCC-Miss$_1$ local state change in a cache line. If cache $caid_i$ needs a block n that is sh or mo in the next level cache, the address where block n should be placed is decided by a function $select(M_i, n)$ which reflects the cache associativity and the replacement policy. If eviction is needed, block n in $caid_j$ will be swapped with the selected block in $caid_i$ in LC-Hit$_1$. LC-Miss$_1$ shows how **fetch**(n)-instructions propagate to lower cache levels: **fetch**(n) is replaced by **fetchBl**(n) in $caid_i$ and added to the data instructions in $caid_j$. If the block cannot be found in any local cache, we have a *cache miss*: Execution is blocked by **fetchBl**(n) and a read request $!Rd(n)$ is broadcast, represented by the label in LLC-Miss$_1$.

$$(\textsc{PrRd}_1)\quad \frac{n = addr(r) \quad first(caid) = true \qquad cid(caid) = c \quad status(M,n) \in \{sh, mo\}}{(caid \bullet M \bullet \overline{dst}) \circ (c \bullet \texttt{\textbf{read}}(r); rst) \to (caid \bullet M \bullet \overline{dst}) \circ (c \bullet rst)}$$

$$(\textsc{PrRd}_2)\quad \frac{n = addr(r) \quad first(caid) = true \qquad cid(caid) = c \quad status(M,n) \in \{inv, \bot\}}{(caid \bullet M \bullet \overline{dst}) \circ (c \bullet \texttt{\textbf{read}}(r); rst) \to (caid \bullet M[n \mapsto \bot] \bullet \overline{dst} \cup \{\texttt{\textbf{fetch}}(n)\}) \circ (c \bullet \texttt{\textbf{readBl}}(r); rst)}$$

$$(\textsc{PrWr}_2)\quad \frac{n = addr(r) \quad first(caid) = true \qquad cid(caid) = c \quad status(M,n) = sh}{(caid \bullet M \bullet \overline{dst}) \circ (c \bullet \texttt{\textbf{write}}(r); rst) \xrightarrow{!RdX(n)} (caid \bullet M[n \mapsto mo] \bullet \overline{dst}) \circ (c \bullet rst)}$$

$$(\textsc{PrWr}_3)\quad \frac{n = addr(r) \quad first(caid) = true \qquad cid(caid) = c \quad status(M,n) \in \{inv, \bot\}}{(caid \bullet M \bullet \overline{dst}) \circ (c \bullet \texttt{\textbf{write}}(r); rst) \to (caid \bullet M[n \mapsto \bot] \bullet \overline{dst} \cup \{\texttt{\textbf{fetch}}(n)\}) \circ (c \bullet \texttt{\textbf{writeBl}}(r); rst)}$$

$$(\textsc{LC-Hit}_1)\quad \frac{status(M_i,n_i) = s_i \quad status(M_j,n) = s_j \quad s_j \in \{sh, mo\} \qquad lid(caid_j) = lid(caid_i) + 1 \quad cid(caid_i) = cid(caid_j) \quad select(M_i,n) = n_i}{(caid_i \bullet M_i \bullet \overline{dst_i} \cup \{\texttt{\textbf{fetch}}(n)\}) \circ (caid_j \bullet M_j \bullet \overline{dst_j}) \to (caid_i \bullet M_i[n_i \mapsto \bot, n \mapsto s_j] \bullet \overline{dst_i}) \circ (caid_j \bullet M_j[n \mapsto \bot, n_i \mapsto s_i] \bullet \overline{dst_j})}$$

$$(\textsc{LC-Miss}_1)\quad \frac{lid(caid_j) = lid(caid_i) + 1 \quad cid(caid_i) = cid(caid_j) \quad status(M_j,n) \in \{inv, \bot\}}{(caid_i \bullet M_i \bullet \overline{dst_i} \cup \{\texttt{\textbf{fetch}}(n)\}) \circ (caid_j \bullet M_j \bullet \overline{dst_j}) \to (caid_i \bullet M_i \bullet \overline{dst_i} \cup \{\texttt{\textbf{fetchBl}}(n)\}) \circ (caid_j \bullet M_j[n \mapsto \bot] \bullet \overline{dst_j} \cup \{\texttt{\textbf{fetch}}(n)\})}$$

$$(\textsc{LLC-Miss}_1)\quad \frac{last(caid) = true \quad status(M,n) \in \{inv, \bot\}}{(caid \bullet M \bullet \overline{dst} \cup \{\texttt{\textbf{fetch}}(n)\}) \xrightarrow{!Rd(n)} (caid \bullet M[n \mapsto \bot] \bullet \overline{dst} \cup \{\texttt{\textbf{fetchBl}}(n)\})}$$

Fig. 3. Local transition rules.

$$(\textsc{Synch}_1)\quad \frac{S \neq \emptyset \quad R = dual(S) \qquad M \xrightarrow{R} M' \quad \overline{Ca} \circ \overline{CR} \xrightarrow{S} \overline{Ca'} \circ \overline{CR'}}{M \circ \overline{dap} \circ \overline{Ca} \circ \overline{CR} \to M' \circ \overline{dap} \circ \overline{Ca'} \circ \overline{CR'}}$$

$$(\textsc{Synch}_2)\quad \frac{\begin{array}{c} \overline{CR} = \{CR_1\} \uplus \overline{CR_2} \qquad \overline{Ca} = \overline{Ca_1} \uplus \overline{Ca_2} \\ belongs(\overline{Ca_1}, \{CR_1\}) \quad belongs(\overline{Ca_2}, \overline{CR_2}) \quad R = dual(S) \\ \overline{Ca_1} \circ CR_1 \xrightarrow{S} \overline{Ca_1'} \circ CR_1' \quad \overline{Ca_2} \xrightarrow{R} \overline{Ca_2'} \\ \overline{CR'} = \{CR_1'\} \cup \overline{CR_2} \qquad \overline{Ca'} = \overline{Ca_1'} \cup \overline{Ca_2'} \end{array}}{\overline{Ca} \circ \overline{CR} \xrightarrow{S} \overline{Ca'} \circ \overline{CR'}}$$

$$(\textsc{Asynch})\quad \frac{\begin{array}{c} \overline{CR} = \overline{CR_1} \uplus \overline{CR_2} \uplus \overline{CR_3} \quad \overline{Ca} = \overline{Ca_1} \uplus \overline{Ca_2} \uplus \overline{Ca_3} \uplus \overline{Ca_4} \qquad belongs(\overline{Ca_3}, \overline{CR_3}) \\ M \circ \overline{Ca_1} \to M' \circ \overline{Ca_1'} \quad \overline{Ca_2} \to \overline{Ca_2'} \quad \overline{dap} \circ \overline{CR_2} \to \overline{dap'} \circ \overline{CR_2'} \quad \overline{Ca_3} \circ \overline{CR_3} \to \overline{Ca_3'} \circ \overline{CR_3'} \\ \overline{CR'} = \overline{CR_1} \cup \overline{CR_2'} \cup \overline{CR_3'} \quad \overline{Ca'} = \overline{Ca_1'} \cup \overline{Ca_2'} \cup \overline{Ca_3'} \cup \overline{Ca_4} \end{array}}{M \circ \overline{dap} \circ \overline{Ca} \circ \overline{CR} \to M' \circ \overline{dap'} \circ \overline{Ca'} \circ \overline{CR'}}$$

Fig. 4. Global transition rules.

Global semantics. The global rules synchronize the cache hierarchies of different cores and main memory, and ensures coherence. Selected global rules are given in Fig. 4. Rule $\textsc{Synch}_1$ captures a global step with synchronization on a label S, which can be either $!Rd(n)$ or $!RdX(n)$. The request will be broadcast to other caches. To maintain data consistency, these caches must process the requests at the same time. The receiving label R is the *dual* of S. For synchronization, the transition is decomposed into a premise for main memory with label R and another premise for the caches with label S. Rule SYNCH$_2$ distributes the receiving label to caches $\overline{Ca}_2$, which do not belong to the cache hierarchy of the sender core CR_1. The predicate $belongs(\overline{Ca}, \overline{CR})$ expresses that any cache in $\overline{Ca}$ belongs to exactly one core in $\overline{CR}$. Rule ASYNCH captures parallel transitions without label. These transitions can be local to individual nodes and caches, parallel memory accesses, or the parallel spawning and scheduling of new tasks.

3 The ABS Model of the Multicore Memory System

In this section we outline the translation of the formal model into an executable object-oriented model using the ABS modeling language. We first briefly introduce the language and later explain the structural and behavioural correspondence between these two models, with a focus on the main challenges.

3.1 The ABS Language

ABS is a modeling language for designing, verifying, and executing concurrent software [4]. The language combines the syntax and object-oriented style of Java with the Actor model of concurrency [10] into active objects which decouple communication and synchronization using asynchronous method calls, futures and cooperative scheduling [5]. Although only one thread of control can execute in an active object at any time, cooperative scheduling allows different threads to interleave at explicitly declared points in the code. Access to an object's fields is encapsulated, so any non-local (outside of the object) read or write to fields must happen explicitly via asynchronous method calls so as to mitigate race-conditions or the need for mutual exclusion (locks).

```
class Bus {
  Bool unlocked = True;
  Unit lock_bus{await unlocked; unlocked = False;}
  Unit release_bus{unlocked = True;} }
```

Fig. 5. Bus lock implementation in ABS using await on Booleans.

We explain the basic mechanism of asynchronous method calls and cooperative scheduling in ABS by the simple code example of a class Bus. First, the execution of a statement res = **await** o!m(args) consists of storing a message m(args) corresponding to the asynchronous call to the message pool of the callee object o. This **await** statement *releases the control* of the caller until the return value of that method has been received. Releasing the control means that the caller can execute other messages from its own message pool in the meantime. ABS supports the shorthand o.m(args) to make an asynchronous call f=o!m(args) followed by the operation f.**get** which *blocks* the caller object (does not release control) until the future f has received the return value from the call. As a special case the statement **this**.m(args) models a self-call, which corresponds to a standard subroutine call and avoids this blocking mechanism. The code in Fig. 5 illustrates the use of the **await** statement

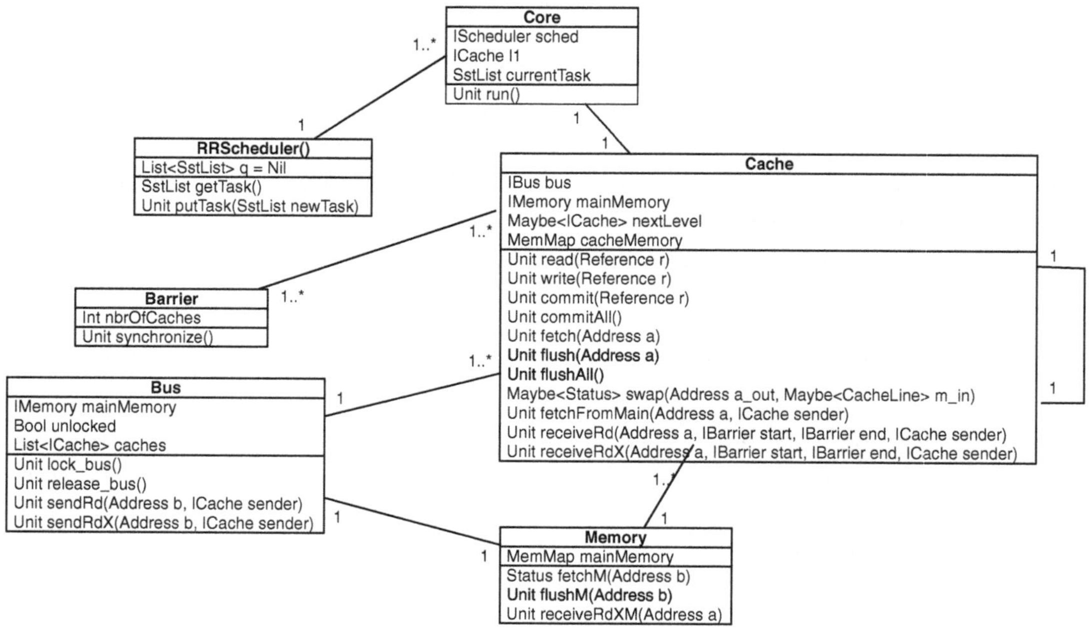

Fig. 6. Class diagram of the ABS model.

on a Boolean condition to model a binary semaphore, which is used to enforce exclusive access to a communication medium implemented as a "bus". Thus, the statement **await** bus!lock_bus() will suspend the calling method invocation (and release control in the caller object) and will be resumed when the generated invocation of the method lock_bus of the "bus" itself has been resumed when the local condition unlocked (of the "bus") has become true.

3.2 The Structural View

The runtime syntax of the SOS is represented by ABS classes, as outlined in Fig. 6. We briefly overview the translation. In ABS, object identifiers guarantee unique names and object references are used to capture how cores and caches are related. These references are encoded in a one-to-one correspondence with the naming scheme of the SOS.

A core $cid \bullet rst$ is translated into a class Core with a field currentTask representing the current task rst. Each core holds a reference to the first level cache. A cache memory $caid \bullet M \bullet dst$ is translated into a class Cache with an interface ICache and a class parameter nextLevel. In a cache, nextLevel holds a reference to the next level cache. If this reference is Nothing, it is last level cache (in the SOS, a predicate *last* is used to identify the last level). The field cacheMemory models the cache's memory M in SOS. The process pool of each cache object in ABS represents the data instruction set dst.

An ABS configuration consists of a number of cores with their corresponding cache hierarchies, the main memory, a scheduler with tasks waiting to be scheduled, and the ABS classes Bus and Barrier, which model the abstract communication medium and the global synchronization with labels $!Rd(n)$ and $!RdX(n)$

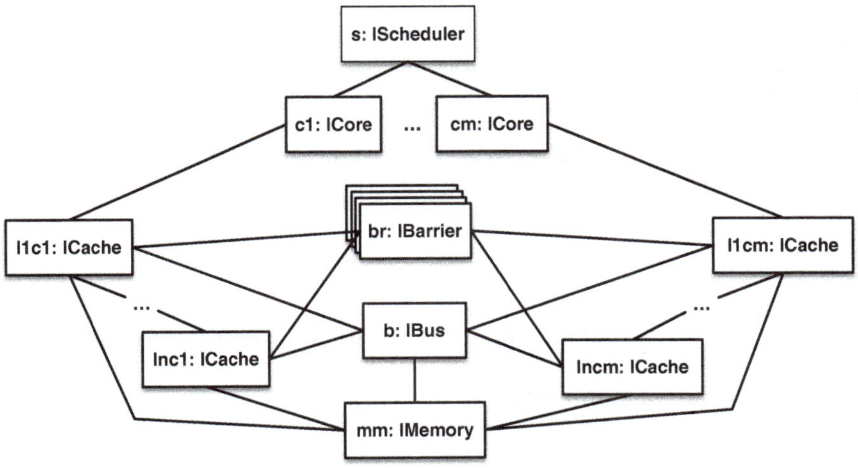

Fig. 7. Object diagram of an initial configuration.

in the SOS. The object diagram in Fig. 7 shows an initial configuration corresponding to the one depicted in Fig. 1.

3.3 The Behavioral View

We discuss in this section the design patterns in ABS that implement the synchronization inherent in the SOS model. We observe here that the combination of asynchronous method calls and cooperative scheduling is crucial because of the *multitasking* inherent in the SOS model, which requires that objects need to be able to process other requests; e.g., caches need to flush memory blocks while waiting for a fetch to succeed.

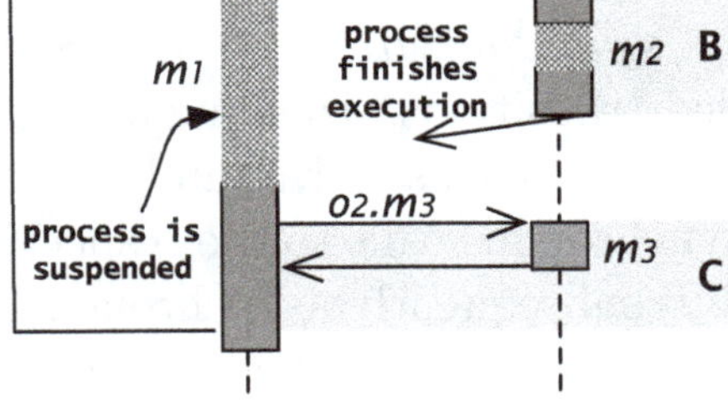

Fig. 8. Local synchronization between two ABS objects.

Local synchronization in the SOS model between two structural entities (e.g., two caches in rule LC-HIT$_1$ of Fig. 3), is implemented by the following synchronization pattern in ABS (see Fig. 8). Given two objects o_1 and o_2, let o_1 execute method m_1, which checks the local conditions of o_1 (highlighted as region **A** in Fig. 8). If these local conditions hold, method m_2 on o_2 is called asynchronously. Method m_2 completes when the local conditions of o_2 hold (highlighted as region **B** in Fig. 8). However, when m_2 has returned and object o_1 again schedules method m_1, the conditions on object o_2 need no longer hold. Therefore, o_1 next calls the method m_3 *synchronously* to check these conditions again. If these condition still hold, method m_3 returns successfully (in general, having updated o_2), and we can proceed to do the local changes in o_1 (highlighted

```
Just(nextCache) => {
  Maybe<Status> s = Nothing;
  Maybe<CacheLine> selected = Nothing;
  while (s == Nothing) {
    retValue = await nextCache!fetch(n);
    selected = select(cacheMemory, maxSize, n);
    s = nextCache.swap(n,selected,name);
  }
  case selected {
    Nothing => skip;
    Just(Pair(n1,_)) => cacheMemory = removeKey(cacheMemory,n1);
  }
  cacheMemory = put(cacheMemory, n, fromJust(s));
```

Fig. 9. Extract of ABS method fetch. When this code is reached, the requested cache line n has status invalid or it is not in the cache. The function select chooses a cache line to be swapped with n. If there is still free space in the cache, select returns Nothing. If n has either shared or modified status in the next level cache, the method swap removes the cache line with address n, inserts the selected cache line and returns the current status of n; otherwise, swap simply returns Nothing.

as region **C** in Fig. 8). Otherwise, the process needs to be repeated until we succeed. Note that method m_3 should not contain release points; because this method is called synchronously from a different object, a release point will in general have the potential of introducing deadlocks in the caller object.

To illustrate the above protocol, consider the code snippet in Fig. 9, which corresponds to part of several rules in the SOS (in particular, rule LC-HIT$_1$). Here, the current object **this** corresponds to $caid_i$ in the SOS, running method fetch, and the referenced object in nextCache corresponds to $caid_j$. When fetch from nextCache returns, all the required conditions in nextCache are *True*. However, since the call is asynchronous, (some of) the conditions may no longer hold when execution continues in **this**. This is addressed by checking the return value of method swap: If swap returns an address, it means the conditions still hold and the necessary updates are performed both locally and in nextCache; otherwise (when swap returns Nothing) fetch will be called again.

Global synchronization in the SOS (see Fig. 10a) is modelled by matching labelled transitions. To simulate this instantaneous communication in ABS, we introduced the classes Bus and Barrier. The synchronization protocol is activated by asynchronous calls to the respective methods sendRd and sendRdX of the bus. The bus subsequently asynchronously calls the corresponding methods receiveRd and receiveRdX of the caches. Two barriers start and end are used by the caches to synchronize the start, as well as the completion, of the local executions of methods receiveRd and receiveRdX.

However, observe that objects in ABS are input enabled: it is always possible to call a method on an object. In our model, this scheme may give rise

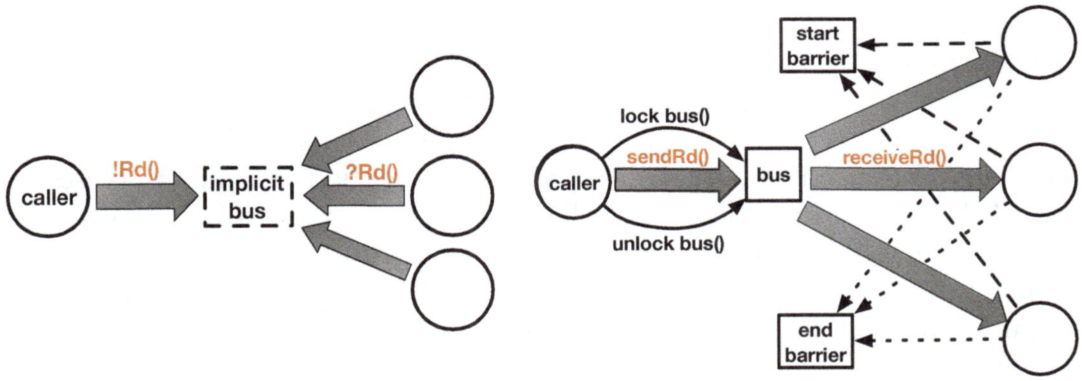

(a) State machine of the global synchronization using labels in the SOS model.

(b) State machine of the global synchronization using a bus and barriers in the ABS model.

Fig. 10. Synchronization in SOS vs ABS. In the SOS model (a), circles represent nodes in the memory system and shaded arrows labelled transitions. Note that the bus is *implicit* in the SOS model, as synchronization is captured by label matching. In the ABS model (b), circles represent the same nodes as in the SOS model, shaded arrows method invocations, solid arrows mutual access to the bus object and dotted arrows barrier synchronizations.

to inconsistent states: the local status of a memory location which triggers an asynchronous call of one of the methods sendRd and sendRdX of the bus may be invalidated by other bus synchronizations. Therefore, we add a lock to the bus (see Figs. 5 and 6), which is used to ensure exclusive access to the *message pool* of the bus when one of the methods read, write, and fetch are executed. The lock is released in case bus synchronization is not needed. The overall scheme is depicted in Fig. 10b. The exclusive access to the message pool of the bus guarantees that the message pool of the bus contains at most one call to one of the methods sendRd and sendRdX. Consequently, the triggering condition of the call cannot be invalidated before the call has been executed. This *strict* locking strategy, however, decreases concurrency in the distributed system, but reduces the complexity of the proof of equivalence between the SOS and the distributed implementation. We discuss how to further enhance the parallelization in Sect. 5.

4 Correctness

In this section we discuss the correctness of the ABS model by means of a simulation relation between the transition system describing the semantics of the ABS model of the multicore memory system and the transition system described by the SOS model.

The semantics of an ABS model can be described by a transition relation between global configurations. A global configuration is a (finite) set of object configurations. An object configuration is a tuple of the form $\langle oid, \sigma, p, Q\rangle$, where oid denotes the unique identity of the object, σ assigns values to the instance variables (fields) of the object, p denotes the currently executing process, and Q

denotes a set of (suspended) processes. A process is a closure (τ, S) consisting of an assignment τ of values to the local variables of the statement S.

We refer to [4] for the details of the structural operational semantics for deriving transitions $G \to G'$ between global configurations in ABS. Since in ABS concurrent objects only interact via asynchronous method calls and processes are scheduled non-deterministically (which provides an abstraction from the order in which the processes are generated by method calls), the ABS semantics satisfies the following global confluence property that allows to commute consecutive computations steps of *independent* processes which belong to *different* objects. Two processes are independent if neither one is generated by the other by an asynchronous call.

Lemma 1 (Global confluence). *For any two transitions $G \to G_1$ and $G \to G_2$ that describe execution steps of independent processes of different objects, there exists a global configuration G' such that $G_1 \to G'$ and $G_2 \to G'$.*

An object configuration is *stable* if the statement S to be executed has terminated or starts either with a **get** operation on a future or with an **await** statement on a Boolean condition or a future. A global ABS configuration is *stable* if all its object configurations are stable. Observe that our ABS model does not give rise to local divergent computations without passing through stable configurations; i.e., every local computation eventually enters a stable configuration. Together with the global confluence property in Lemma 1, this allows to restrict the semantics of the ABS model in the simulation relation to stable global configurations; i.e., transitions $G \Rightarrow G'$ between stable global configurations G and G' which result from a (non-empty) sequence of local execution steps of a *single* process from one stable configuration to a next one.

Because of the global synchronization with the bus in ABS described above, we may also represent without loss of generality the synchronization on the bus by a *single* global transition $G \Rightarrow G'$ which involves a completed execution of the method sendRd(...) (or sendRdX(...)) by the bus. This is justified because the global confluence allows for a scheduling policy such that the execution of the processes that are generated by these methods, i.e., the calls of the methods receiveRd(...) (or receiveRd(...)) are not interleaved with any other processes.

The simulation relation. The structural correspondence between a global configuration of the ABS model and a configuration of the SOS model is described in Sect. 3.2. For each method we have constructed a table which, among others, associates with some, so-called *observable*, occurrences of **await** statements (appearing in the method body) a corresponding **dst** instruction. In general, the execution of the remaining (occurrences of) **await** statements, for which there does not exist a corresponding **dst** instruction, involves some asynchronous messaging *preparing* for the corresponding synchronous exchange of information in the SOS model. In some cases, the execution of these unobservable statements (e.g., the read and write methods) also does not correspond to a change of the SOS configuration. Let α map every stable global configuration G of the ABS model to a structurally equivalent configuration $\alpha(G)$ of the SOS model, which additionally maps every observable process (either queued or active) to the associated **dst** instruction (a process is observable if its corresponding statement is observable).

We arrive at the following theorem which expresses that the ABS model is a correct implementation of the abstract model.

Theorem 1. *Let G be a stable global configuration of the ABS model. If $G \Rightarrow G'$ then $\alpha(G) \rightarrow^* \alpha(G')$, where $\rightarrow^*$ denotes the reflexive, transitive closure of $\rightarrow$.*

Proof. The proof proceeds by a case analysis of the given transition $G \Rightarrow G'$, which, as discussed above, involves the local execution of some basic sequential code by a single object. For example, for the case of a completed execution of a method sendRd(...) (or sendRdX(...)) by the bus, a simple inspection of the sequential code of the methods that have been executed, e.g., sendRd(...) and receiveRd(...), suffices to establish the existence of a corresponding transition $\alpha(G) \rightarrow \alpha(G')$.

The remaining cases are captured by tables (as mentioned above) which provide for each method the following information. The statements in the **Location** column of each table represent for the respective method all possible processes generated by a call, i.e., a call to the method itself, and the processes which correspond to the **await** statements appearing in its body. In each row the **Next release point** statement indicates the next **await** statement or **return** statement that can be reached (statically). The **dst** instruction in each row specifies the instruction which corresponds to the **Location** statement in the simulation. Finally, **Enable condition** in each row specifies the enabling conditions (expressed in the abstract model) of the rule applications (of the abstract model) specified in **Rules**. In general these rule applications involve the sequential application of one or more rules. For unobservable statements, for which there is no corresponding **dst** instruction, the latter two columns are left unspecified.

The case analysis then consists of checking statically for each row the *local* structural correspondence between the resulting ABS process (the **Next release point**) and the resulting SOS configuration described by the specified rule applications.

5 Parallelism and Fairness of the ABS Model

This section discusses how to relax the eager locking policy of the bus implementation, without generating inconsistent states. Instead of locking the bus unconditionally when executing the read, write, and fetch methods in the ABS model, and releasing the lock when no bus synchronization is required, we only lock the bus when the triggering conditions of the bus synchronization may be invalidated. For example, an *optimistic* write implementation (see Fig. 11) tries to acquire the lock of the bus, and only after the acquisition checks if a race-condition has happened and invalidated the shared status of the address n; in this case, the write method will *backtrack* and retry (by calling itself); otherwise the write operation can safely be performed.

```
Int write(Ref r) {
 case lookup(cacheMemory, addr(r)) {
    Just(Sh) => {
      await bus!lock_bus();
      // after waking up do RACE DETECTION
      if (lookup(cacheMemory,addr(r)) == Just(Sh)) { // NO RACE
        await bus!sendRdX(addr(r),this);
        await bus!release_bus();
        cacheMemory = put(cacheMemory,addr(r),Mo);
      }
      else { // RACE CONDITION
        await bus!release_bus();
        await this!write(r); // RETRY
      } } ... } }
```

Fig. 11. Alternative, optimistic implementation of the write method to detect a bus race-condition and, in that case, retry the operation.

The strict and relaxed variations of the global synchronization bear strong resemblance respectively to conservative [11,12] and optimistic [13] algorithms in parallel and distributed discrete-event simulation (PDES) [14]. As with PDES, there is no clear winner between the strict (conservative) and relaxed (optimistic) versions of our cache simulator; certain computer programs (input-models) will be simulated faster using one version or the other, depending on the inter-dependency of the parallel components (for us, the caches). For the contrived experiment, we implemented a penalty system in the ABS model. A cache penalty is the cost (delay) incurred by failing to read or write to a particular level of cache—set here to $(L_1, L_2, L_3) =_{cost} (1, 10, 100)$ [15]. We compared the two versions for a scenario with full inter-dependency (simultaneous write instructions on the same memory block) and a scenario with minimal inter-dependency (write instructions on separate memory blocks) between 16 simulated cores. In these experiments the strict version was slightly faster up to 2% for the first case and losing out by up to 12% in the second case. The experiments were executed using the ABS-Erlang backend [16] and Erlang version 21, running on quad-socket 8-cores 16-hyperthreads Xeon®L7555, which yielded in total 64 hardware threads.

Fairness. A concern that often arises in parallel execution is fairness: the degree of variability when distributing the computing resources among different parallel components—here, the simulated cores. Fairness of parallel execution can affect the simulation's accuracy in approximating the intended (or idealized) many-core hardware. To ensure fairness of the simulation, we make use of *deployment components* [17] in ABS.

A *Deployment Component* (DC) is an ABS execution location that is created with a number of virtual resources (e.g., execution speed, memory use, network bandwidth), which are shared among its deployed objects. Any annotated statement [Cost: x] S decrements by x the resources of its DC and then completes, or

Table 1. Total cache penalties between strict/relaxed, with/without DC configurations.

	Strict with DC	Relaxed with DC	Strict	Relaxed
$\sum_{penalty}$	43068	43290	39183	24956

it will stall its computation if there are currently not enough resources remaining; the statement S may continue on the next passage of the global symbolic time where all the resources of the DCs have been renewed, and will eventually complete when its Cost has reached zero.

We make use of this resource modeling of ABS to assign equal (fair) resources of virtual execution speed to the simulated cores of the system. Each Core object is deployed onto a separate DC with fixed Speed(1) resources. The processing of each instruction has the same cost [Cost: 1]—a generalization, since common processor architectures execute different instructions in different speeds (cycles per instruction); e.g., `JUMP` is faster than `LOAD`. The result is that all Cores can execute maximum one instruction in every time interval of the global symbolic clock, and thus no Core can get too far ahead with processing its own instructions—a problem that manifests upon the parallel simulation of N number of cores using a physical machine of M cores, where N is vastly greater than M. To test this, we performed a write-congested experiment with a configuration of 20 simulated cores and 3 cache levels, comparing the strict and relaxed variations, with and without the use of deployment components. The results (shown in Table 1) were measured on a quad-core system running ABS-Erlang, counting the total cache penalties of all the cores. With respect to the strict variation, the results with and without DC have similar penalties; this can be attributed to the lock-step nature of strict bus synchronization, where no cache (and thus core) can unfairly stride forward. In the relaxed variation, however, where synchronization is less strict, we see that without the fairness imposed by DC, the penalties are almost halved, which means some cores are allowed to do multiple (successful) write operations while other cores are still waiting on the "backlog" to be simulated. This gives rise to less penalties, because of less runtime interleavings of the simulated cores and thus less competition between them.

6 Related Work

There is in general a significant gap between a formal model and its implementation [18]. SOS [1] succinctly formalizes operational models and are well-suited for proofs, but direct implementations of SOS quickly lead to very inefficient implementations. Executable semantic frameworks such as Redex [19], rewriting logic [20,21], and $\mathbb{K}$ [22] reduce this gap, and have been used to develop executable formal models of complex languages like C [23] and Java [24]. The relationship between SOS and rewriting logic semantics has been studied [25] without proposing a general solution for label matching. Bijo et al. implemented their SOS multicore memory model [26] in the rewriting logic system Maude

[3] using an orchestrator for label matching, but do not provide a correctness proof wrt. the SOS. Different semantic styles can be modeled and related inside one framework; for example, the correctness of distributed implementations of KLAIM systems in terms of simulation relations have been studied in rewriting logic [27]. Compared to these works on semantics, we implemented an SOS model in a distributed active object setting, and proved the correctness of this implementation.

Correctness-preserving compilation is related to correctness proofs for implementations, and ensures that the low-level representation of a program preserves the properties of the high-level model. Examples of this line of work include type-preserving translations into typed assembly languages [28] and formally verified compilers [29,30], which proves the semantic preservation of a compiler from C to assembler code, but leaves shared-variable concurrency for future work. In contrast to this work which studies compilation from one language to another, our work focuses on a specific model and its implementation and specifically targets parallel systems.

Simulation tools for cache coherence protocols can evaluate performance and efficiency on different architectures (e.g., gems [31] and gem5 [32]). These tools perform evaluations of, e.g., the cache hit/miss ratio and response time, by running benchmark programs written as low-level read and write instructions to memory. Advanced simulators such as Graphite [33] and Sniper [34] run programs on distributed clusters to simulate executions on multicore architectures with thousands of cores. Unlike our work, these simulators are not based on a formal semantics and correctness proofs. Our work complements these simulators by supporting the executable exploration of design choices from a programmer perspective rather from hardware design. Compared to worst-case response time analysis for concurrent programs on multicore architectures [35], our focus is on the underlying data movement rather than the response time.

7 Conclusion

We have introduced in this paper a methodology for implementing SOS models in the active object language ABS, and applied this methodology to the implementation of a SOS model of an abstraction of multicore memory systems, resulting in a parallel simulator for these systems. A challenge for this implementation is to correctly implement the synchronization patterns of the SOS rules, which may cross encapsulation barriers in the active objects, and in particular label synchronization on parallel transitions steps. We prove the correctness of this particular implementation, exploiting that the ABS model allows for a high-level coarse-grained semantics. We investigated the further parallelization and fairness of the ABS model.

The results obtained in this paper provide a promising basis for further development of the ABS model for simulating the execution of (object-oriented) programs on multicore architectures. A first such development concerns an extension of the abstract memory model with data. In particular, having the addresses of the memory locations themselves as data allows to model and simulate different data layouts of the dynamically generated object structures.

References

1. Plotkin, G.D.: A structural approach to operational semantics. J. Log. Algebr. Program. **60–61**, 17–139 (2004)
2. Bijo, S., Johnsen, E.B., Pun, K.I, Tapia Tarifa, S.L.: A formal model of parallel execution on multicore architectures with multilevel caches. In: Proença, J., Lumpe, M. (eds.) FACS 2017. LNCS, vol. 10487, pp. 58–77. Springer, Cham (2017). https://doi.org/10.1007/978-3-319-68034-7_4
3. Clavel, M., et al. (eds.): All About Maude - A High-Performance Logical Framework, How to Specify, Program and Verify Systems in Rewriting Logic, vol. 4350. Springer, Heidelberg (2007). https://doi.org/10.1007/978-3-540-71999-1
4. Johnsen, E.B., Hähnle, R., Schäfer, J., Schlatte, R., Steffen, M.: ABS: a core language for abstract behavioral specification. In: Aichernig, B.K., de Boer, F.S., Bonsangue, M.M. (eds.) FMCO 2010. LNCS, vol. 6957, pp. 142–164. Springer, Heidelberg (2011). https://doi.org/10.1007/978-3-642-25271-6_8
5. Boer, F.D., et al.: A survey of active object languages. ACM Comput. Surv. **50**(5), 76:1–76:39 (2017)
6. Bijo, S., Johnsen, E.B., Pun, K.I, Tapia Tarifa, S.L.: A formal model of parallel execution in multicore architectures with multilevel caches (long version). Research report, Department of Informatics, University of Oslo (2018). Under revision for journal publication. http://violet.at.ifi.uio.no/papers/mc-rr.pdf
7. Solihin, Y.: Fundamentals of Parallel Multicore Architecture, 1st edn. Chapman & Hall/CRC, Boca Raton (2015)
8. Culler, D.E., Gupta, A., Singh, J.P.: Parallel Computer Architecture: A Hardware/Software Approach, 1st edn. Morgan Kaufmann Publishers Inc., Los Altos (1997)
9. Sorin, D.J., Hill, M.D., Wood, D.A.: A Primer on Memory Consistency and Cache Coherence, 1st edn. Morgan & Claypool Publishers, San Francisco (2011)
10. Hewitt, C., Bishop, P., Steiger, R.: A universal modular ACTOR formalism for artificial intelligence. In: Proceedings of the 3rd International Joint Conference on Artificial Intelligence, IJCAI 1973, pp. 235–245. Morgan Kaufmann Publishers Inc., San Francisco (1973)
11. Bryant, R.E.: Simulation of packet communication architecture computer systems. Technical report MIT/LCS/TR-188, MIT, Lab for Computer Science, November 1977
12. Chandy, K.M., Misra, J.: Distributed simulation: a case study in design and verification of distributed programs. IEEE Trans. Softw. Eng. **SE–5**(5), 440–452 (1979)
13. Jefferson, D.R.: Virtual time. ACM Trans. Program. Lang. Syst. **7**(3), 404–425 (1985)
14. Fujimoto, R.M.: Parallel and Distributed Simulation Systems. Wiley, Hoboken (2000)
15. Schmidl, D., Vesterkjær, A., Müller, M.S.: Evaluating OpenMP performance on thousands of cores on the numascale architecture. In: Parallel Computing: On the Road to Exascale, Proceedings of the International Conference on Parallel Computing (ParCo 2015). Advances in Parallel Computing, vol. 27, pp. 83–92. IOS Press (2016)

16. Wong, P.Y.H., Albert, E., Muschevici, R., Proença, J., Schäfer, J., Schlatte, R.: The ABS tool suite: modelling, executing and analysing distributed adaptable object-oriented systems. STTT **14**(5), 567–588 (2012)
17. Johnsen, E.B., Schlatte, R., Tapia Tarifa, S.L.: Integrating deployment architectures and resource consumption in timed object-oriented models. J. Log. Algebr. Methods Program. **84**(1), 67–91 (2015)
18. Schlatte, R., Johnsen, E.B., Mauro, J., Tapia Tarifa, S.L., Yu, I.C.: Release the beasts: when formal methods meet real world data. In: de Boer, F., Bonsangue, M., Rutten, J. (eds.) It's All About Coordination. LNCS, vol. 10865, pp. 107–121. Springer, Cham (2018). https://doi.org/10.1007/978-3-319-90089-6_8
19. Felleisen, M., Findler, R.B., Flatt, M.: Semantics Engineering with PLT Redex. The MIT Press, Cambridge (2009)
20. Meseguer, J., Rosu, G.: The rewriting logic semantics project: a progress report. Inf. Comput. **231**, 38–69 (2013)
21. Meseguer, J., Rosu, G.: The rewriting logic semantics project. Theor. Comput. Sci. **373**(3), 213–237 (2007)
22. Rosu, G.: $\mathbb{K}$: a semantic framework for programming languages and formal analysis tools. In: Dependable Software Systems Engineering, pp. 186–206. IOS Press (2017)
23. Ellison, C., Rosu, G.: An executable formal semantics of C with applications. In: Field, J., Hicks, M. (eds.) Proceedings of the 39th ACM SIGPLAN-SIGACT Symposium on Principles of Programming Languages (POPL 2012), pp. 533–544. ACM (2012)
24. Bogdanas, D., Rosu, G.: K-Java: a complete semantics of Java. In: Rajamani, S.K., Walker, D. (eds.) Proceedings of the 42nd Annual ACM SIGPLAN-SIGACT Symposium on Principles of Programming Languages (POPL 2015), pp. 445–456. ACM (2015)
25. Serbanuta, T., Rosu, G., Meseguer, J.: A rewriting logic approach to operational semantics. Inf. Comput. **207**(2), 305–340 (2009)
26. Bijo, S., Johnsen, E.B., Pun, K.I, Tapia Tarifa, S.L.: A maude framework for cache coherent multicore architectures. In: Lucanu, D. (ed.) WRLA 2016. LNCS, vol. 9942, pp. 47–63. Springer, Cham (2016). https://doi.org/10.1007/978-3-319-44802-2_3
27. Eckhardt, J., Mühlbauer, T., Meseguer, J., Wirsing, M.: Semantics, distributed implementation, and formal analysis of KLAIM models in Maude. Sci. Comput. Program. **99**, 24–74 (2015)
28. Morrisett, J.G., Walker, D., Crary, K., Glew, N.: From system F to typed assembly language. ACM Trans. Program. Lang. Syst. **21**(3), 527–568 (1999)
29. Leroy, X.: Formal verification of a realistic compiler. Commun. ACM **52**(7), 107–115 (2009)
30. Leroy, X.: A formally verified compiler back-end. J. Autom. Reason. **43**(4), 363–446 (2009)
31. Martin, M.M.K., et al.: Multifacet's general execution-driven multiprocessor simulator (GEMS) toolset. SIGARCH Comput. Arch. News **33**(4), 92–99 (2005)
32. Binkert, N., et al.: The gem5 simulator. SIGARCH Comput. Arch. News **39**(2), 1–7 (2011)
33. Miller, J.E., et al.: Graphite: a distributed parallel simulator for multicores. In: Proceedings of the 16th International Symposium on High-Performance Computer Architecture (HPCA), pp. 1–12. IEEE Computer Society (2010)

34. Carlson, T.E., Heirman, W., Eeckhout, L.: Sniper: exploring the level of abstraction for scalable and accurate parallel multi-core simulation. In: Proceedings of International Conference for High Performance Computing, Networking, Storage and Analysis (SC), pp. 52:1–52:12. ACM (2011)
35. Li, Y., Suhendra, V., Liang, Y., Mitra, T., Roychoudhury, A.: Timing analysis of concurrent programs running on shared cache multi-cores. In: Proceedings of the 30th IEEE Real-Time Systems Symposium (RTSS), pp. 57–67. IEEE Computer Society (2009)

Optimal and Automated Deployment for Microservices

Mario Bravetti[1], Saverio Giallorenzo[2(✉)], Jacopo Mauro[2], Iacopo Talevi[1], and Gianluigi Zavattaro[1]

[1] FOCUS Research Team, University of Bologna/Inria, Bologna, Italy
[2] University of Southern Denmark, Odense, Denmark
saverio@imada.sdu.dk

Abstract. Microservices are highly modular and scalable Service Oriented Architectures. They underpin automated deployment practices like Continuous Deployment and Autoscaling. In this paper we formalize these practices and show that automated deployment — proven undecidable in the general case — is algorithmically treatable for microservices. Our key assumption is that the configuration life-cycle of a microservice is split into two phases: (i) creation, which entails establishing initial connections with already available microservices, and (ii) subsequent binding/unbinding with other microservices. To illustrate the applicability of our approach, we implement an automatic optimal deployment tool and compute deployment plans for a realistic microservice architecture, modeled in the Abstract Behavioral Specification (ABS) language.

1 Introduction

Inspired by service-oriented computing, Microservices structure software applications as highly modular and scalable compositions of fine-grained and loosely-coupled services [18]. These features support modern software engineering practices, like continuous delivery/deployment [30] and application autoscaling [3]. Currently, these practices focus on single microservices and do not take advantage of the information on the interdependencies within an architecture. On the contrary, architecture-level deployment supports the global optimization of resource usage and avoids "domino" effects due to unstructured scaling actions that may cause cascading slowdowns or outages [27,35,39].

In this paper, we formalize the problem of automatic deployment and reconfiguration (at the architectural level) of microservice systems, proving formal properties and presenting an implemented solution.

In our work, we follow the approach taken by the *Aeolus component model* [13–15], which was used to formally define the problem of deploying component-based software systems and to prove that, in the general case, such problem is undecidable [15]. The basic idea of Aeolus is to enrich the specification of components with a finite state automaton that describes their deployment life cycle. Previous work identified decidable fragments of the Aeolus model: e.g.,

R. Hähnle and W. van der Aalst (Eds.): FASE 2019, LNCS 11424, pp. 351–368, 2019.
https://doi.org/10.1007/978-3-030-16722-6_21

removing from Aeolus replication constraints (e.g., used to specify a minimal amount of services connected to a load balancer) makes the deployment problem decidable, but non-primitive recursive [14]; removing also conflicts (e.g., used to express the impossibility to deploy in the same system two types of components) makes the problem PSpace-complete [34] or even poly-time [15], but under the assumption that every required component can be (re)deployed from scratch.

Our intuition is that the Aeolus model can be adapted to formally reason on the deployment of microservices. To achieve our goal, we significantly revisit the formalization of the deployment problem, replacing Aeolus components with a model of *microservices*. The main difference between our model of microservices and Aeolus components lies in the specification of their deployment life cycle. Here, instead of using the full power of finite state automata (like in Aeolus and other TOSCA-compliant deployment models [10]), we assume microservices to have two states: (i) creation and (ii) binding/unbinding. Concerning creation, we use *strong* dependencies to express which microservices must be immediately connected to newly created ones. After creation, we use *weak* dependencies to indicate additional microservices that can be bound/unbound. The principle that guided this modification comes from state-of-the-art microservice deployment technologies like Docker [36] and Kubernetes [29]. In particular, the weak and strong dependencies have been inspired by Docker Compose [16] (a language for defining multi-container Docker applications) where it is possible to specify different relationships among microservices using, e.g., the depends_on (resp. external_links) modalities that force (resp. do not force) a specific startup order similarly to our strong (resp. weak) dependencies. Weak dependencies are also useful to model horizontal scaling, e.g., a load balancer that is bound to/unbound from many microservice instances during its life cycle.

In addition, w.r.t. the Aeolus model, we also consider resource/cost-aware deployments, taking inspiration from the memory and CPU resources found in Kubernetes. Microservice specifications are enriched with the amount of resources they need to run. In a deployment, a system of microservices runs within a set of computation *nodes*. Nodes represent computational units (e.g., virtual machines in an Infrastructure-as-a-Service Cloud deployment). Each node has a cost and a set of resources available to the microservices it hosts.

On the model above, we define the *optimal deployment problem* as follows: given an initial microservice system, a set of available nodes, and a new target microservice to be deployed, find a sequence of reconfiguration actions that, once applied to the initial system, leads to a new deployment that includes the target microservice. Such a deployment is expected to be *optimal*, meaning that the total cost (i.e., the sum of the costs) of the nodes used is minimal. We show that this problem is decidable by presenting an algorithm working in three phases: (1) generate a set of constraints whose solution indicates the microservices to be deployed and their distribution over the nodes; (2) generate another set of constraints whose solution indicates the connections to be established; (3) synthesize the corresponding deployment plan. The set of constraints includes optimization metrics that minimize the overall cost of the computed deployment.

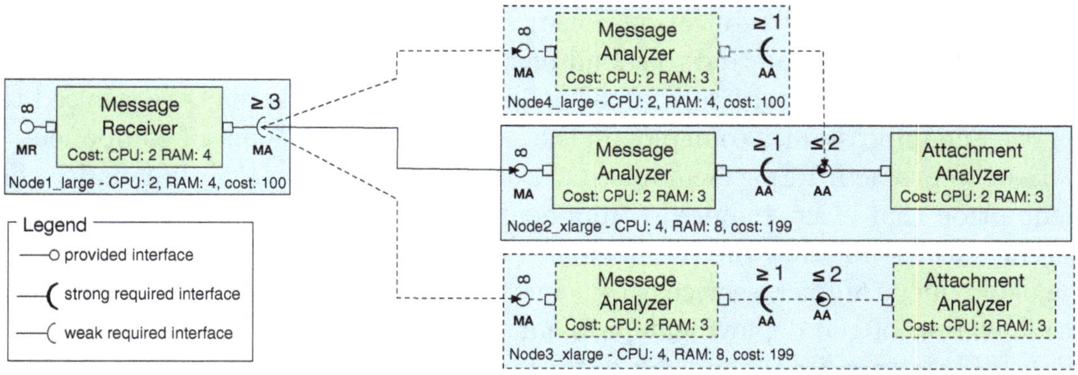

Fig. 1. Example of microservice deployment (blue boxes: nodes; green boxes: microservices; continuous lines: the initial configuration; dashed lines: full configuration). (Color figure online)

The algorithm has NEXPTIME complexity because, in the worst-case, the length of the deployment plan could be exponential in the size of the input. However, we consider this worst-case unfeasible in practice, as the number of microservices deployable on one node is limited by the available resources. Under the assumption that each node can host at most a polynomial amount of microservices, the deployment problem is NP-complete and the problem of deploying a system minimizing its total cost is an NP-optimization problem. Moreover, having reduced the deployment problem in terms of constraints, we can exploit state-of-the-art constraint solvers [12,23,24] that are frequently used in practice to cope with NP-hard problems.

To concretely evaluate our approach, we consider a real-world microservice architecture, inspired by the reference email processing pipeline from Iron.io [22]. We model that architecture in the Abstract Behavioral Specification (ABS) language, a high-level object-oriented language that supports deployment modeling [31]. We use our technique to compute two types of deployments: an initial one, with one instance for each microservice, and a set of deployments to horizontally scale the system depending on small, medium or large increments in the number of emails to be processed. The experimental results are encouraging in that we were able to compute deployment plans that add more than 30 new microservice instances, assuming availability of hundreds of machines of three different types, and guaranteeing optimality.

2 The Microservice Optimal Deployment Problem

We model microservice systems as aggregations of components with ports. Each port exposes provided and required interfaces. Interfaces describe offered and required functionalities. Microservices are connected by means of bindings indicating which port provides the functionality required by another port. As discussed in the Introduction, we consider two kinds of requirements: strong required interfaces, that need to be already fulfilled when the microservice is created, and weak required interfaces, that must be fulfilled at the end of a deployment (or reconfiguration) plan. Microservices are enriched with the specification of the resources they need to properly run; such resources are provided to the microservices by nodes. Nodes can be seen as the unit of computation executing the tasks associated to each microservice.

As an example, in Fig. 1 we have reported the representation of the deployment of a microservice system inspired by the email processing pipeline that we will discuss in Sect. 3. Here, we consider a simplified pipeline. A Message Receiver microservice handles inbound requests, passing them to a Message Analyzer that checks the email content and sends the attachments for inspection to an Attachment Analyzer. The Message Receiver has a port with a *weak* required interface that can be fulfilled by Message Analyzer instances. This requirement is weak, meaning that the Message Receiver can be initially deployed without any connection to instances of Message Analyzer. These connections can be established afterwards and reflect the possibility to horizontally scale the application by adding/removing instances of Message Analyzer. This last microservice has instead a port with a *strong* required interface that can be fulfilled by Attachment Analyzer instances. This requirement is strong to reflect the need to immediately connect a Message Analyzer to its Attachment Analyzer.

Figure 1 presents a reconfiguration that, starting from the initial deployment depicted in continuous lines, adds the elements depicted with dashed lines. Namely, a couple of new instances of Message Analyzer and a new instance of Attachment Analyzer are deployed. This is done in order to satisfy numerical constraints associated to both required and provided interfaces. For required interfaces, the numerical constraints indicate lower bounds to the outgoing bindings, while for provided interfaces they specify upper bounds to the incoming connections. Notice that the constraint ≥ 3 associated to the weak required interface of Message Receiver is not initially satisfied; this is not problematic because constraints on weak interfaces are relevant only at the end of a reconfiguration. In the final deployment, such a constraint is satisfied thanks to the two new instances of Message Analyzer. These two instances need to be immediately connected to an Attachment Analyzer: only one of them can use the initially available Attachment Analyzer, because of the constraint ≤ 2 associated to the corresponding provided interface. Hence, a new instance of Attachment Analyzer is added.

We also model resources: each microservice has associated resources that it consumes (see the CPU and RAM quantities associated to the microservices in Fig. 1). Resources are provided by nodes, that we represent as containers for the microservice instances, providing them the resources they require. Notice that nodes have also costs: the total cost of a deployment is the sum of the costs of the used nodes (e.g., in the example the total cost is 598 cents per hour, corresponding to the cost of 4 nodes: 2 C4 large and 2 C4 xlarge virtual machine instances of the Amazon public Cloud).

We now move to the formal definitions. We assume the following disjoint sets: $\mathcal{I}$ for interfaces, $\mathcal{Z}$ for microservices, and a finite set $\mathcal{R}$ for kinds of resources. We use $\mathbb{N}$ to denote natural numbers, $\mathbb{N}^+$ for $\mathbb{N} \setminus \{0\}$, and $\mathbb{N}^+_\infty$ for $\mathbb{N}^+ \cup \{\infty\}$.

Definition 1 (Microservice type). *The set Γ of* microservice types*, ranged over by $\mathcal{T}_1, \mathcal{T}_2, \ldots$, contains 5-ples $\langle P, D_s, D_w, C, R\rangle$ where:*

- $P = (\mathcal{I} \nrightarrow \mathbb{N}^+_\infty)$ *are the provided interfaces, defined as a partial function from interfaces to corresponding numerical constraints (indicating the maximum number of connected microservices);*
- $D_s = (\mathcal{I} \nrightarrow \mathbb{N}^+)$ *are the* strong *required interfaces, defined as a partial function from interfaces to corresponding numerical constraints (indicating the minimum number of connected microservices);*
- $D_w = (\mathcal{I} \nrightarrow \mathbb{N})$ *are the* weak *required interfaces (defined as the strong ones, with the difference that also the constraint 0 can be used indicating that it is not strictly necessary to connect microservices);*
- $C \subseteq \mathcal{I}$ *are the conflicting interfaces;*
- $R = (\mathcal{R} \rightarrow \mathbb{N})$ *specifies resource consumption, defined as a total function from resources to corresponding quantities indicating the amount of required resources.*

We assume sets $\mathtt{dom}(D_s)$, $\mathtt{dom}(D_w)$ *and C to be pairwise disjoint.*[1]

Notation: given a microservice type $\mathcal{T} = \langle P, D_s, D_w, C, R\rangle$, we use the following postfix projections $\mathtt{.prov}$, $\mathtt{.req_s}$, $\mathtt{.req_w}$, $\mathtt{.conf}$ and $\mathtt{.res}$ to decompose it; e.g., $\mathcal{T}\mathtt{.req_w}$ returns the partial function associating arities to weak required interfaces. In our example, for instance, the Message Receiver microservice type is such that Message Receiver$\mathtt{.req_w}$(MA) $= 3$ and Message Receiver$\mathtt{.res}$(RAM) $= 4$. When the numerical constraints are not explicitly indicated, we assume as default value ∞ for provided interfaces (i.e., they can satisfy an unlimited amount of ports requiring the same interface) and 1 for required interfaces (i.e., one connection with a port providing the same interface is sufficient).

Inspired by [14], we allow a microservice to specify a conflicting interface that, intuitively, forbids the deployment of other microservices providing the same interface. Conflicting interfaces can be used to express conflicts among microservices, preventing both of them to be present at the same time, or cases in which only one microservice instance can be deployed (e.g., a consistent and available microservice that can not be replicated).

Since the requirements associated with strong interfaces must be immediately satisfied, it is possible to deploy a configuration with circular dependencies only if at least one weak required interface is involved in the cycle. In fact, having a cycle with only strong required interfaces would mean to deploy all the microservices involved in the cycle simultaneously. We now formalize a well-formedness condition on microservice types to guarantee the absence of such configurations.

Definition 2 (Well-formed Universe). *Given a finite set of microservice types U (that we also call* universe*), the strong dependency graph of U is as follows: $G(U) = (U, V)$ with $V = \{(\mathcal{T}, \mathcal{T}') | \mathcal{T}, \mathcal{T}' \in U \wedge \exists p \in \mathcal{I}.p \in$ $\mathtt{dom}(\mathcal{T}\mathtt{.req_s}) \cap \mathtt{dom}(\mathcal{T}'\mathtt{.prov})\}$. The universe U is well-formed if $G(U)$ is acyclic.*

[1] Given a partial function f, we use $\mathtt{dom}(f)$ to denote the domain of f, i.e., the set $\{e \mid \exists e' : (e, e') \in f\}$.

In the following, we always assume universes to be well-formed. Well-formedness does not prevent the specification of microservice systems with circular dependencies, which are captured by cycles with at least one weak required interface.

Definition 3 (Nodes). *The set* $\mathcal{N}$ *of* nodes *is ranged over by* $o_1, o_2, \ldots$ *We assume the following information to be associated to each node* o *in* $\mathcal{N}$.

- *A function* $R = (\mathcal{R} \to \mathbb{N})$ *that specifies node* resource availability*: we use* $o.\mathtt{res}$ *to denote such a function.*
- *A value in* $\mathbb{N}$ *that specifies node* cost*: we use* $o.\mathtt{cost}$ *to denote such a value.*

As example, in Fig. 1, the node Node1_large is such that Node1_large.$\mathtt{res}$(RAM) = 4 and Node1_large.$\mathtt{cost}$ = 100.

We now define configurations that describe systems composed of microservice instances and bindings that interconnect them. A configuration, ranged over by $\mathcal{C}_1, \mathcal{C}_2, \ldots$, is given by a set of microservice types, a set of deployed microservices (with their associated type), and a set of bindings. Formally:

Definition 4 (Configuration). *A* configuration $\mathcal{C}$ *is a 4-ple* $\langle Z, T, N, B\rangle$ *where:*

- $Z \subseteq \mathcal{Z}$ *is the set of the currently deployed* microservices*;*
- $T = (Z \to \mathcal{T})$ *are the* microservice types*, defined as a function from deployed microservices to microservice types;*
- $N = (Z \to \mathcal{N})$ *are the* microservice nodes*, defined as a function from deployed microservices to nodes that host them;*
- $B \subseteq \mathcal{I} \times Z \times Z$ *is the set of* bindings*, namely 3-ples composed of an interface, the microservice that requires that interface, and the microservice that provides it; we assume that, for* $(p, z_1, z_2) \in B$*, the two microservices* z_1 *and* z_2 *are distinct and* $p \in (\mathtt{dom}(T(z_1).\mathtt{reqs}) \cup \mathtt{dom}(T(z_1).\mathtt{reqw})) \cap \mathtt{dom}(T(z_2).\mathtt{prov})$.

In our example, if we use mr to refer to the instance of Message Receiver, and ma for the initially available Message Analyzer, we will have the binding (MA, mr, ma). Moreover, concerning the microservice placement function N, we have N(mr) = Node1_large and N(ma) = Node2_xlarge.

We are now ready to formalize the notion of correctness of configuration. We first define a *provisional correctness*, considering only constraints on strong required and provided interfaces, and then we define a general notion of configuration correctness, considering also weak required interfaces and conflicts. The former is intended for transient configurations traversed during the execution of a reconfiguration, while the latter for the final configuration.

Definition 5 (Provisionally correct configuration). *A configuration* $\mathcal{C} = \langle Z, T, N, B\rangle$ *is* provisionally correct *if, for each node* $o \in \mathtt{ran}(N)$*, it holds*[2]

$$\forall r \in \mathcal{R}.\ \ o.\mathtt{res}(r) \geq \sum_{z \in Z, N(z)=o} T(z).\mathtt{res}(r)$$

and, for each microservice $z \in Z$*, both following conditions hold:*

[2] Given a (partial) function f, we use $\mathtt{ran}(f)$ to denote the range of f, i.e., the function image set $\{f(e) \mid e \in \mathtt{dom}(f)\}$.

- $(p \mapsto n) \in T(z).\mathtt{req_s}$ *implies that there exist* n *distinct microservices* $z_1, \ldots, z_n \in Z \setminus \{z\}$ *such that, for every* $1 \leq i \leq n$*, we have* $\langle p, z, z_i \rangle \in B$*;*
- $(p \mapsto n) \in T(z).\mathtt{prov}$ *implies that there exist no* m *distinct microservices* $z_1, \ldots, z_m \in Z \setminus \{z\}$*, with* $m > n$*, such that, for every* $1 \leq i \leq m$*, we have* $\langle p, z_i, z \rangle \in B$*.*

Definition 6 (Correct configuration). *A configuration* $\mathcal{C} = \langle Z, T, N, B \rangle$ *is* correct *if* $\mathcal{C}$ *is provisionally correct and, for each microservice* $z \in Z$*, both following conditions hold:*

- $(p \mapsto n) \in T(z).\mathtt{req_w}$ *implies that there exist* n *distinct microservices* $z_1, \ldots, z_n \in Z \setminus \{z\}$ *such that, for every* $1 \leq i \leq n$*, we have* $\langle p, z, z_i \rangle \in B$*;*
- $p \in T(z).\mathtt{conf}$ *implies that, for each* $z' \in Z \setminus \{z\}$*, we have* $p \notin \mathtt{dom}(T(z').\mathtt{prov})$*.*

Notice that, in the example in Fig. 1, the initial configuration (in continuous lines) is only provisionally correct in that the weak required interface MA (with arity 3) of the Message Receiver is not satisfied (because there is only one outgoing binding). The full configuration — including also the elements in dotted lines — is instead correct: all the constraints associated to the interfaces are satisfied.

We now formalize how configurations evolve by means of atomic actions.

Definition 7 (Actions). *The set* $\mathcal{A}$ *contains the following actions:*

- $bind(p, z_1, z_2)$ *where* $z_1, z_2 \in \mathcal{Z}$*, with* $z_1 \neq z_2$*, and* $p \in \mathcal{I}$*: add a binding between* z_1 *and* z_2 *on port* p *(which is supposed to be a weak-require port of* z_1 *and a provide port of* z_2*);*
- $unbind(p, z_1, z_2)$ *where* $z_1, z_2 \in \mathcal{Z}$*, with* $z_1 \neq z_2$*, and* $p \in \mathcal{I}$*: remove the specified binding on* p *(which is supposed to be a weak required interface of* z_1 *and a provide port of* z_2*);*
- $new(z, \mathcal{T}, o, B_s)$ *where* $z \in \mathcal{Z}$*,* $\mathcal{T} \in \Gamma$*,* $o \in \mathcal{N}$ *and* $B_s = (\mathtt{dom}(\mathcal{T}.\mathtt{req_s}) \rightarrow 2^{\mathcal{Z} - \{z\}})$*; with* B_s *(representing bindings from strong required interfaces in* $\mathcal{T}$ *to sets of microservices) being such that, for each* $p \in \mathtt{dom}(\mathcal{T}.\mathtt{req_s})$*, it holds* $|B_s(p)| \geq \mathcal{T}.\mathtt{req_s}(p)$*: add a new microservice* z *of type* $\mathcal{T}$ *hosted in* o *and bind each of its strong required interfaces to a set of microservices as described by* B_s*;*[3]
- $del(z)$ *where* $z \in \mathcal{Z}$*: remove the microservice* z *from the configuration and all bindings involving it.*

In our example, assuming that the initially available Attachment Analyzer is named aa, we have that the action to create the initial instance of Message Analyzer is $new(\mathsf{ma}, \mathsf{MessageAnalyzer}, \mathsf{Node2\_xlarge}, (\mathsf{AA} \mapsto \{\mathsf{aa}\}))$. Notice that it is necessary to establish the binding with the Attachment Analyzer because of the corresponding strong required interface.

The execution of actions can now be formalized using a labeled transition system on configurations, which uses actions as labels.

---

[3] Given sets S and S' we use: 2^S to denote the power set of S, i.e., the set $\{S' \mid S' \subseteq S\}$; $S - S'$ to denote set difference; and $|S|$ to denote the cardinality of S.

Definition 8 (Reconfigurations). *Reconfigurations are denoted by transitions* $\mathcal{C} \xrightarrow{\alpha} \mathcal{C}'$ *meaning that the execution of* $\alpha \in \mathcal{A}$ *on the configuration* $\mathcal{C}$ *produces a new configuration* $\mathcal{C}'$. *The transitions from a configuration* $\mathcal{C} = \langle Z, T, N, B \rangle$ *are defined as follows:*

$$\mathcal{C} \xrightarrow{bind(p,z_1,z_2)} \langle Z, T, N, B \cup \langle p, z_1, z_2 \rangle \rangle \quad \textit{if } \langle p, z_1, z_2 \rangle \notin B \textit{ and } p \in \mathtt{dom}(T(z_1).\mathtt{req_w}) \cap \mathtt{dom}(T(z_2).\mathtt{prov})$$

$$\mathcal{C} \xrightarrow{unbind(p,z_1,z_2)} \langle Z, T, N, B \backslash \langle p, z_1, z_2 \rangle \rangle \quad \textit{if } \langle p, z_1, z_2 \rangle \in B \textit{ and } p \in \mathtt{dom}(T(z_1).\mathtt{req_w}) \cap \mathtt{dom}(T(z_2).\mathtt{prov})$$

$$\mathcal{C} \xrightarrow{new(z,\mathcal{T},o,B_s)} \langle Z \cup \{z\}, T', N', B' \rangle \quad \textit{if } z \notin Z \textit{ and } \forall p \in \mathtt{dom}(\mathcal{T}.\mathtt{req_s}).\ \forall z' \in B_s(p).\ p \in \mathtt{dom}(T(z').\mathtt{prov}) \textit{ and } T' = T \cup \{(z \mapsto \mathcal{T})\} \textit{ and } N' = N \cup \{(z \mapsto o)\} \textit{ and } B' = B \cup \{\langle p, z, z' \rangle \mid z' \in B_s(p)\}$$

$$\mathcal{C} \xrightarrow{del(z)} \langle Z \backslash \{z\}, T', N', B' \rangle \quad \textit{if } T' = \{(z' \mapsto \mathcal{T}) \in T \mid z \neq z'\} \textit{ and } N' = \{(z' \mapsto o) \in N \mid z \neq z'\} \textit{ and } B' = \{\langle p, z_1, z_2 \rangle \in B \mid z \notin \{z_1, z_2\}\}$$

A *deployment plan* is simply a sequence of actions that transform a provisionally correct configuration (without violating provisional correctness along the way) and, finally, reach a correct configuration.

Definition 9 (Deployment plan). *A* deployment plan P *from a provisionally correct configuration* $\mathcal{C}_0$ *is a sequence of actions* $\alpha_1, \ldots, \alpha_m$ *such that:*

- *there exist* $\mathcal{C}_1, \ldots, \mathcal{C}_m$ *provisionally correct configurations, with* $\mathcal{C}_{i-1} \xrightarrow{\alpha_i} \mathcal{C}_i$ *for* $1 \leq i \leq m$, *and*
- $\mathcal{C}_m$ *is a correct configuration.*

Deployment plans are also denoted with $\mathcal{C}_0 \xrightarrow{\alpha_1} \mathcal{C}_1 \xrightarrow{\alpha_2} \cdots \xrightarrow{\alpha_m} \mathcal{C}_m$.

In our example, a deployment plan that reconfigures the initial provisionally correct configuration into the final correct one is as follows: a *new* action to create the new instance of Attachment Analyzer, followed by two *new* actions for the new Message Analyzers (as commented above, the connection with the Attachment Analyzer is part of these *new* actions), and finally two *bind* actions to connect the Message Receiver to the two new instances of Message Analyzer.

We now have all the ingredients to define the *optimal deployment problem*, that is our main concern: given a universe of microservice types, a set of available nodes and an initial configuration, we want to know whether and how it is possible to deploy at least one microservice of a given microservice type $\mathcal{T}$ by optimizing the overall cost of nodes hosting the deployed microservices.

Definition 10 (Optimal deployment problem). *The* optimal deployment problem *has, as input, a finite well-formed universe* U *of microservice types, a finite set of available nodes* O, *an initial provisionally correct configuration* $\mathcal{C}_0$ *and a microservice type* $\mathcal{T}_t \in U$. *The output is:*

- *A* **deployment plan** $\mathsf{P} = \mathcal{C}_0 \xrightarrow{\alpha_1} \mathcal{C}_1 \xrightarrow{\alpha_2} \cdots \xrightarrow{\alpha_m} \mathcal{C}_m$ *such that*
  - *for all* $\mathcal{C}_i = \langle Z_i, T_i, N_i, B_i \rangle$*, with* $1 \leq i \leq m$*, it holds* $\forall z \in Z_i.\ T_i(z) \in U \wedge N_i(z) \in O$*, and*
  - $\mathcal{C}_m = \langle Z_m, T_m, N_m, B_m \rangle$ *satisfies* $\exists z \in Z_m : T_i(z) = \mathcal{T}_t$*;*

  if there exists one. In particular, among all deployment plans satisfying the constraints above, one that minimizes $\sum_{o \in O.(\exists z.N_m(z)=o)} o.\mathtt{cost}$ *(i.e., the overall cost of nodes in the last configuration* $\mathcal{C}_m$*), is outputted.*
- **no** *(stating that no such plan exists); otherwise.*

We are finally ready to state our main result on the decidability of the optimal deployment problem. To prove the result we describe an approach that splits the problem in three incremental phases: (1) the first phase checks if there is a possible solution and assigns microservices to deployment nodes, (2) the intermediate phase computes how the microservices need to be connected to each other, and (3) the final phase synthesizes the corresponding deployment plan.

Theorem 1. *The optimal deployment problem is decidable.*

Proof. The proof is in the form of an algorithm that solves the optimal deployment problem. We assume that the input to the problem to be solved is given by U (the microservice types), O (the set of available nodes), $\mathcal{C}_0$ (the initial provisionally correct configuration), and $\mathcal{T}_t \in U$ (the target microservice type). We use $\mathcal{I}(U)$ to denote the set of interfaces used in the considered microservice types, namely $\mathcal{I}(U) = \bigcup_{\mathcal{T} \in U} \mathtt{dom}(\mathcal{T}.\mathtt{req_s}) \cup \mathtt{dom}(\mathcal{T}.\mathtt{req_w}) \cup \mathtt{dom}(\mathcal{T}.\mathtt{prov}) \cup \mathcal{T}.\mathtt{conf}$. The algorithm is based on three phases.

Phase 1 The first phase consists of the generation of a set of constraints that, once solved, indicates how many instances should be created for each microservice type $\mathcal{T}$ (denoted with $\mathtt{inst}(\mathcal{T})$), how many of them should be deployed on node o (denoted with $\mathtt{inst}(\mathcal{T}, o)$), and how many bindings should be established for each interface p from instances of type $\mathcal{T}$ — considering both weak and strong required interfaces — and instances of type $\mathcal{T}'$ (denoted with $\mathtt{bind}(p, \mathcal{T}, \mathcal{T}')$). We also generate an optimization function that guarantees that the generated configuration is minimal w.r.t. its total cost.

We now incrementally report the generated constraints. The first group of constraints deals with the number of bindings:

$$\bigwedge_{p \in \mathcal{I}(U)} \quad \bigwedge_{\mathcal{T} \in U,\ p \in \mathtt{dom}(\mathcal{T}.\mathtt{req_s})} \mathcal{T}.\mathtt{req_s}(p) \cdot \mathtt{inst}(\mathcal{T}) \leq \sum_{\mathcal{T}' \in U} \mathtt{bind}(p, \mathcal{T}, \mathcal{T}') \tag{1a}$$

$$\bigwedge_{p \in \mathcal{I}(U)} \quad \bigwedge_{\mathcal{T} \in U,\ p \in \mathtt{dom}(\mathcal{T}.\mathtt{req_w})} \mathcal{T}.\mathtt{req_w}(p) \cdot \mathtt{inst}(\mathcal{T}) \leq \sum_{\mathcal{T}' \in U} \mathtt{bind}(p, \mathcal{T}, \mathcal{T}') \tag{1b}$$

$$\bigwedge_{p \in \mathcal{I}(U)} \quad \bigwedge_{\mathcal{T} \in U,\ \mathcal{T}.\mathtt{prov}(p) < \infty} \mathcal{T}.\mathtt{prov}(p) \cdot \mathtt{inst}(\mathcal{T}) \geq \sum_{\mathcal{T}' \in U} \mathtt{bind}(p, \mathcal{T}', \mathcal{T}) \tag{1c}$$

$$\bigwedge_{p \in \mathcal{I}(U)} \quad \bigwedge_{\mathcal{T} \in U,\ \mathcal{T}.\mathtt{prov}(p) = \infty} \mathtt{inst}(\mathcal{T}) = 0 \ \Rightarrow \ \sum_{\mathcal{T}' \in U} \mathtt{bind}(p, \mathcal{T}', \mathcal{T}) = 0 \tag{1d}$$

$$\bigwedge_{p \in \mathcal{I}(U)} \quad \bigwedge_{\mathcal{T} \in U,\ p \notin \mathtt{dom}(\mathcal{T}.\mathtt{prov})} \sum_{\mathcal{T}' \in U} \mathtt{bind}(p, \mathcal{T}', \mathcal{T}) = 0 \tag{1e}$$

Constraint 1a and 1b guarantee that there are enough bindings to satisfy all the required interfaces, considering both strong and weak requirements. Symmetrically, constraint 1c guarantees that the number of bindings is not greater than the total available capacity, computed as the sum of the single capacities of each provided interface. In case the capacity is unbounded (i.e., ∞), it is sufficient to have at least one instance that activates such port to support any possible requirement (see constraint 1d). Finally, constraint 1e guarantees that no binding is established connected to provided interfaces of microservice types that are not deployed.

The second group of constraints deals with the number of instances of microservices to be deployed.

$$\texttt{inst}(\mathcal{T}_t) \geq 1 \tag{2a}$$

$$\bigwedge_{p\in\mathcal{I}(U)} \bigwedge_{\substack{\mathcal{T}\in U,\\ p\in\mathcal{T}.\texttt{conf}}} \bigwedge_{\substack{\mathcal{T}'\in U-\{\mathcal{T}\},\\ p\in\texttt{dom}(\mathcal{T}'.\texttt{prov})}} \texttt{inst}(\mathcal{T}) > 0 \;\Rightarrow\; \texttt{inst}(\mathcal{T}') = 0 \tag{2b}$$

$$\bigwedge_{p\in\mathcal{I}(U)} \bigwedge_{\substack{\mathcal{T}\in U,\, p\in\mathcal{T}.\texttt{conf}\,\wedge\\ p\in\texttt{dom}(\mathcal{T}.\texttt{prov})}} \texttt{inst}(\mathcal{T}) \leq 1 \tag{2c}$$

$$\bigwedge_{p\in\mathcal{I}(U)} \bigwedge_{\mathcal{T}\in U} \bigwedge_{\mathcal{T}'\in U-\{\mathcal{T}\}} \texttt{bind}(p,\mathcal{T},\mathcal{T}') \leq \texttt{inst}(\mathcal{T}) \cdot \texttt{inst}(\mathcal{T}') \tag{2d}$$

$$\bigwedge_{p\in\mathcal{I}(U)} \bigwedge_{\mathcal{T}\in U} \texttt{bind}(p,\mathcal{T},\mathcal{T}) \leq \texttt{inst}(\mathcal{T}) \cdot (\texttt{inst}(\mathcal{T}) - 1) \tag{2e}$$

The first constraint 2a guarantees the presence of at least one instance of the target microservice. Constraint 2b guarantees that no two instances of different types will be created if one activates a conflict on an interface provided by the other one. Constraint 2c, consider the other case in which a type activates the same interface both in conflicting and provided modality: in this case, at most one instance of such type can be created. Finally, the constraints 2d and 2e guarantee that there are enough pairs of distinct instances to establish all the necessary bindings. Two distinct constraints are used: the first one deals with bindings between microservices of two different types, the second one with bindings between microservices of the same type.

The last group of constraints deals with the distribution of microservice instances over the available nodes O.

$$\texttt{inst}(\mathcal{T}) = \sum_{o\in O} \texttt{inst}(\mathcal{T},o) \tag{3a}$$

$$\bigwedge_{r\in\mathcal{R}} \bigwedge_{o\in O} \sum_{\mathcal{T}\in U} \texttt{inst}(\mathcal{T},o) \cdot \mathcal{T}.\texttt{res}(r) \leq o.\texttt{res}(r) \tag{3b}$$

$$\bigwedge_{o\in O} \Big(\sum_{\mathcal{T}\in U} \texttt{inst}(\mathcal{T},o) > 0\Big) \Leftrightarrow \texttt{used}(o) \tag{3c}$$

$$\min \sum_{o\in O,\, \texttt{used}(o)} o.\texttt{cost} \tag{3d}$$

Constraint 3a simply formalizes the relationship among the variables $\mathtt{inst}(\mathcal{T})$ and $\mathtt{inst}(\mathcal{T}, o)$ (the total amount of all instances of a microservice type, should correspond to the sum of the instances locally deployed on each node). Constraint 3b checks that each node has enough resources to satisfy the requirements of all the hosted microservices. The last two constraints define the optimization function used to minimize the total cost: constraint 3c introduces the boolean variable $\mathtt{used}(o)$ which is true if and only if node o contains at least one microservice instance; constraint 3d is the function to be minimized, i.e., the sum of the costs of the used nodes.

These constraints, and the optimization function, are expected to be given in input to a constraint/optimization solver. If a solution is not found it is not possible to deploy the required microservice system; otherwise, the next phases of the algorithm are executed to synthesize the optimal deployment plan.

Phase 2 The second phase consists of the generation of another set of constraints that, once solved, indicates the bindings to be established between any pair of microservices to be deployed. More precisely, for each type $\mathcal{T}$ such that $\mathtt{inst}(\mathcal{T}) > 0$, we use $s_i^{\mathcal{T}}$, with $1 \leq i \leq \mathtt{inst}(\mathcal{T})$, to identify the microservices of type $\mathcal{T}$ to be deployed. We also assume a function N that associates microservices to available nodes O, which is compliant with the values $\mathtt{inst}(\mathcal{T}, o)$ already computed in Phase 1, i.e., given a type $\mathcal{T}$ and a node o, the number of $s_i^{\mathcal{T}}$, with $1 \leq i \leq \mathtt{inst}(\mathcal{T})$, such that $N(s_i^{\mathcal{T}}) = o$ coincides with $\mathtt{inst}(\mathcal{T}, o)$.

In the constraints below we use the variables $\mathtt{b}(p, s_i^{\mathcal{T}}, s_j^{\mathcal{T}'})$ (with $i \neq j$, if $\mathcal{T} = \mathcal{T}'$): its value is 1 if there is a connection between the required interface p of $s_i^{\mathcal{T}}$ and the provided interface p of $s_j^{\mathcal{T}'}$, 0 otherwise. We use n and m to denote $\mathtt{inst}(\mathcal{T})$ and $\mathtt{inst}(\mathcal{T}')$, respectively, and an auxiliary total function $\mathit{limProv}(\mathcal{T}', p)$ that extends $\mathcal{T}'.\mathtt{prov}$ associating 0 to interfaces outside its domain.

$$\bigwedge_{\mathcal{T}\in U} \bigwedge_{p\in\mathcal{I}(U)} \bigwedge_{i\in 1\ldots n} \sum_{j\in(1\ldots m)\setminus\{i|\mathcal{T}=\mathcal{T}'\}} \mathtt{b}(p, s_i^{\mathcal{T}}, s_j^{\mathcal{T}'}) \leq \mathit{limProv}(\mathcal{T}', p) \tag{4a}$$

$$\bigwedge_{\mathcal{T}\in U} \bigwedge_{p\in\mathtt{dom}(\mathcal{T}.\mathtt{reqs})} \bigwedge_{i\in 1\ldots n} \sum_{j\in(1\ldots m)\setminus\{i|\mathcal{T}=\mathcal{T}'\}} \mathtt{b}(p, s_i^{\mathcal{T}}, s_j^{\mathcal{T}'}) \geq \mathcal{T}.\mathtt{reqs}(p) \tag{4b}$$

$$\bigwedge_{\mathcal{T}\in U} \bigwedge_{p\in\mathtt{dom}(\mathcal{T}.\mathtt{reqw})} \bigwedge_{i\in 1\ldots n} \sum_{j\in(1\ldots m)\setminus\{i|\mathcal{T}=\mathcal{T}'\}} \mathtt{b}(p, s_i^{\mathcal{T}}, s_j^{\mathcal{T}'}) \geq \mathcal{T}.\mathtt{reqw}(p) \tag{4c}$$

$$\bigwedge_{\mathcal{T}\in U} \bigwedge_{p\notin\mathtt{dom}(\mathcal{T}.\mathtt{reqs})\cup\mathtt{dom}(\mathcal{T}.\mathtt{reqw})} \bigwedge_{i\in 1\ldots n} \sum_{j\in(1\ldots m)\setminus\{i|\mathcal{T}=\mathcal{T}'\}} \mathtt{b}(p, s_i^{\mathcal{T}}, s_j^{\mathcal{T}'}) = 0 \tag{4d}$$

Constraint 4a considers the provided interface capacities to fix upper bounds to the bindings to be established, while constraints 4b and 4c fix lower bounds based on the required interface capacities, considering both the weak (see 4b) and the strong (see 4c) ones. Finally, constraint 4d indicates that it is not possible to establish connections on interfaces that are not required.

A solution for these constraints exists because, as also shown in [13], the constraints 1a ... 2e (already solved during Phase 1) guarantee that the configuration to be synthesized contains enough capacity on the provided interfaces to satisfy all the required interfaces.

Phase 3 In this last phase we synthesize the deployment plan that, when applied to the initial configuration $\mathcal{C}_0$, reaches a new configuration $\mathcal{C}_t$ with nodes, microservices and bindings as computed in the first two phases of the algorithm. Without loss of generality, in this decidability proof we show the existence of a simple plan that first removes the elements in the initial configuration and then deploys the target configuration from scratch. However, as also discussed in Sect. 3, in practice it is possible to define more complex planning mechanisms that re-use microservices already deployed.

Reaching an empty configuration is a trivial task since it is always possible to perform in the initial configuration unbind actions for all the bindings connected to weak required interfaces. Then, the microservices can be safely deleted. Thanks to the well-formedness assumption (Definition 2) and using a topological sort, it is possible to order the microservices to be removed without violating any strong required interface (e.g., first remove the microservice not requiring anything and repeat until all the microservices have been deleted).

The deployment of the target configuration follows a similar pattern. Given the distribution of microservices over nodes (computed in the first phase) and the corresponding bindings (computed in the second phase), the microservices can be created by following a topological sort considering the microservices dependencies following from the strong required interfaces. When all the microservices are deployed on the corresponding nodes, the remaining bindings (on weak required ports) may be added in any possible order. □

Remark 1. The constraints generated during Phase 2 of the algorithm, in order to establish the microservice bindings, are expected to be given in input to a constraint/optimization solver. One can enrich such constraints with metrics to optimize, e.g., the number of local bindings (i.e., give a preference to the connections among microservices hosted in the same node):

$$\min \sum_{\mathcal{T},\mathcal{T}'\in U, i\in 1\ldots\mathtt{inst}(\mathcal{T}), j\in 1\ldots\mathtt{inst}(\mathcal{T}'), p\in\mathcal{I}(U), N(s_i^{\mathcal{T}})\neq N(s_j^{\mathcal{T}'})} \mathtt{b}(p, s_i^{\mathcal{T}}, s_j^{\mathcal{T}'})$$

Another example, used in the case study discussed in Sect. 3, is the following metric that maximizes the number of bindings[4]:

$$\max \sum_{s_i^{\mathcal{T}}, s_j^{\mathcal{T}'}, p\in\mathcal{I}(U)} \mathtt{b}(p, s_i^{\mathcal{T}}, s_j^{\mathcal{T}'})$$

From the complexity point of view, it is possible to show that the decision versions of the optimization problem solved in Phase 1 is NP-complete, in Phase

[4] We model a load balancer as a microservice having a weak required interface, with arity 0, that can be provided by its back-end service. By adopting the above maximization metric, the synthesized configuration connects all possible services to such required interface, thus allowing the load balancer to forward requests to all of them.

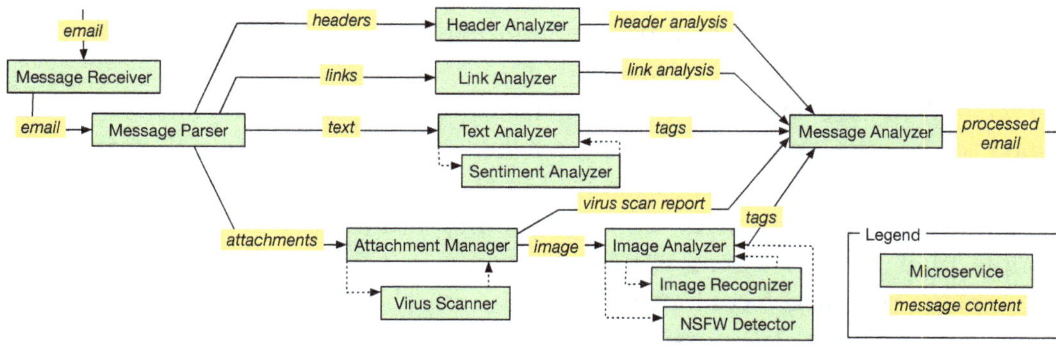

Fig. 2. Microservice architecture for email processing.

2 is in NP, while the planning in Phase 3 is synthesized in polynomial time. Unfortunately, due to the fact that numeric constraints can be represented in log space, the output of Phase 2 requiring the enumeration of all the microservices to deploy can be exponential in the size of the output of Phase 1 (indicating only the total number of instances for each type). For this reason, the optimal deployment problem is in NEXPTIME. However, we consider unfeasible in practice the deployment of an exponential number of microservices on one node having limited resources. If at most a polynomial number of microservices can be deployed on each node, we have that the optimal deployment problem becomes an NP-optimization problem and its decision version is NP-complete. See the companion technical report [8] for the formal proofs of complexity.

3 Application of the Technique to the Case-Study

Given the asymptotic complexity of our solution (NP under the assumption of polynomial size of the target configuration) we have decided to evaluate its applicability in practice by considering a real-world microservice architecture, namely the email processing pipeline described in [22]. The considered architecture separates and routes the components found in an email (headers, links, text, attachments) into distinct, parallel sub-pipelines with specific tasks (e.g., remove malicious attachments, tag the content of the mail). We report in Fig. 2 a depiction of the architecture. When an email reaches the Message Receiver it is forwarded to the Message Parser, which sends each component into a specific sub-pipeline. In the sub-pipelines, some microservices — e.g., Text Analyzer and Attachment Analyzer — coordinate with other microservices — e.g., Sentiment Analyzer and Virus Scanner — to process their inputs. Each microservice in the architecture has a given resource consumption (expressed in terms of CPU and memory). As expected, the processing of each email component entails a specific load. Some microservices can handle large inputs, e.g., in the range of 40K simultaneous requests (e.g., Header Analyzer that processes short and uniform inputs). Other microservices sustain heavier computations (e.g., Image Recognizer) and can handle smaller simultaneous inputs, e.g., in the range of 10K requests.

To model the system above, we use the Abstract Behavioral Specification (ABS) language, a high-level object-oriented language that supports deployment modeling [31]. ABS is agnostic w.r.t. deployment platforms (Amazon AWS, Microsoft Azure) and technologies (e.g., Docker or Kubernetes) and it offers high-level deployment primitives for the creation of new *deployment components* and the instantiation of objects inside them. Here, we use ABS deployment components as computation nodes, ABS objects as microservice instances, and ABS object references as bindings. Finally, to describe the requirements in our model, we use ABS with SmartDepl [25], an extension that supports deployment annotations. Strong required interfaces are modeled as class annotations indicating mandatory parameters for the class constructor: such parameters contain the references to the objects corresponding to the microservices providing the strongly required interfaces. Weak required interfaces are expressed as annotations concerning specific methods used to pass, to an already instantiated object, the references to the objects providing the weakly required interfaces. We define a class for each microservice type, plus one *load balancer* class for each microservice type. A load balancer distributes requests over a set of instances that can scale horizontally. Finally, we model nodes corresponding to Amazon EC2 instances: `c4_large`, `c4_xlarge`, and `c4_2xlarge` (with the corresponding provided resources and costs).

Microservice (max computational load)	Initial (10K)	+20K	+50K	+80K
MessageReceiver(∞)	1	-	-	-
MessageParser(40K)	1	-	+1	-
HeaderAnalyzer(40K)	1	-	+1	-
LinkAnalyzer(40K)	1	-	+1	-
TextAnalyzer(15K)	1	+1	+2	+2
SentimentAnalyzer(15K)	1	+3	+4	+6
AttachmentsManager(30K)	1	+1	+2	+2
VirusScanner(13K)	1	+3	+4	+6
ImageAnalyzer(30K)	1	+1	+2	+2
NSFWDetector(13K)	1	+3	+4	+6
ImageRecognizer(13K)	1	+3	+4	+6
MessageAnalyzer(70K)	1	+1	+2	+2

In the table above, we report the result of our algorithm w.r.t. four incremental deployments: the initial in column 2 and under incremental loads in 3–5. We also consider an availability of 40 nodes for each of the three node types. In the first column of the Table, next to a microservice type, we report its corresponding maximum computational load, i.e., the maximal number of simultaneous requests that it can manage. As visible in columns 2–5, different maximal computational loads imply different scaling factors w.r.t. a given number of simultaneous requests. In the initial configuration we consider 10K simultaneous requests and we have one instance of each microservice type (and of the corresponding load balancer). The other deployment configurations deal with three scenarios of horizontal scaling, assuming three increasing increments of inbound messages (20K, 50K, and 80K). In the three scaling scenarios, we do not implement the planning algorithm described in Phase 3 of the proof of Theorem 1. Contrarily, we take advantage of the presence of the load balancers and, as described in Remark 1, we achieve a similar result with an optimization function that maximizes the number of bindings of the load balancers. For every scenario, we use SmartDepl [33] to generate the ABS code for the plan that deploys an optimal configuration, setting a timeout of 30 min for the computation of every deployment scenario.[5] The ABS code modeling the system and the generated code are publicly available at [7]. A graphical representation of the initial configuration is available in the companion technical report [8].

4 Related Work and Conclusion

In this work, we consider a fundamental building block of modern Cloud systems, microservices, and prove that the generation of a deployment plan for an architecture of microservices is decidable and fully automatable; spanning from the synthesis of the optimal configuration to the generation of the deployment actions. To illustrate our technique, we model a real-world microservice architecture in the ABS [31] language and we compute a set of deployment plans.

The context of our work regards automating Cloud application deployment, for which there exist many specification languages [5,11], reconfiguration protocols [6,19], and system management tools [26,32,37,38]. Those tools support the specification of deployment plans but they do not support the automatic distribution of software instances over the available machines. The proposals closest to ours are those by Feinerer [20] and by Fischer et al. [21]. Both proposals rely on a solver to plan deployments. The first is based on the UML component model, which includes conflicts and dependencies, but lacks the modeling of nodes. The second does not support conflicts in the specification language. Neither proposals support the computation of optimal deployments.

Three projects inspire our proposal: Aeolus [13,14], Zephyrus [1], and ConfSolve [28]. The Aeolus model paved the way to reason on deployment and reconfiguration, proving some decidability results. Zephyrus is a configuration tool based on Aeolus and it constitutes the first phase of our approach. ConfSolve is a tool for the optimal allocation of virtual machines to servers and of applications to virtual machines. Both tools do not synthesize deployment plans.

[5] Here, 30 min are a reasonable timeout since we predict different system loads and we compute in advance a different deployment plan for each of them. An interesting future work would aim at shortening the computation to a few minutes (e.g., around the average start-up time of a virtual machine in a public Cloud) to obtain on-the-fly deployment plans tailored to unpredictable system loads.

Regarding autoscaling, existing solutions [2,4,17,29] support the automatic increase or decrease of the number of instances of a service/container, when some conditions (e.g., CPU average load greater than 80%) are met. Our work is an example of how we can go beyond single-component horizontal scaling policies (as analyzed, e.g., in [9]).

As future work, we want to investigate local search approaches to speed-up the solution of the optimization problems behind the computation of a deployment plan. Shorter computation times would open our approach to contexts where it is unfeasible to compute plans ahead of time, e.g., due to unpredictable loads.

References

1. Ábrahám, E., Corzilius, F., Johnsen, E.B., Kremer, G., Mauro, J.: Zephyrus2: on the fly deployment optimization using SMT and CP technologies. In: Fränzle, M., Kapur, D., Zhan, N. (eds.) SETTA 2016. LNCS, vol. 9984, pp. 229–245. Springer, Cham (2016). https://doi.org/10.1007/978-3-319-47677-3_15
2. Amazon: Amazon CloudWatch. https://aws.amazon.com/cloudwatch/. Accessed Jan 2019
3. Amazon: AWS auto scaling. https://aws.amazon.com/autoscaling/. Accessed Jan 2019
4. Apache: Apache Mesos. http://mesos.apache.org/. Accessed Jan 2019
5. Bergmayr, A., et al.: A systematic review of cloud modeling languages. ACM Comput. Surv. **51**(1), 22:1–22:38 (2018)
6. Boyer, F., Gruber, O., Pous, D.: Robust reconfigurations of component assemblies. In: ICSE, pp. 13–22. IEEE Computer Society (2013)
7. Bravetti, M., Giallorenzo, S., Mauro, J., Talevi, I., Zavattaro, G.: Code repository for the email processing example. https://github.com/IacopoTalevi/SmartDeploy-ABS-ExampleCode. Accessed Jan 2019
8. Bravetti, M., Giallorenzo, S., Mauro, J., Talevi, I., Zavattaro, G.: Optimal and automated deployment for microservices. Technical Report (2019). https://arxiv.org/abs/1901.09782
9. Bravetti, M., Gilmore, S., Guidi, C., Tribastone, M.: Replicating web services for scalability. In: Barthe, G., Fournet, C. (eds.) TGC 2007. LNCS, vol. 4912, pp. 204–221. Springer, Heidelberg (2008). https://doi.org/10.1007/978-3-540-78663-4_15
10. Brogi, A., Canciani, A., Soldani, J.: Modelling and analysing cloud application management. In: Dustdar, S., Leymann, F., Villari, M. (eds.) ESOCC 2015. LNCS, vol. 9306, pp. 19–33. Springer, Cham (2015). https://doi.org/10.1007/978-3-319-24072-5_2
11. Chardet, M., Coullon, H., Pertin, D., Pérez, C.: Madeus: a formal deployment model. In: HPCS, pp. 724–731. IEEE (2018)
12. Chuffed Team: The CP solver. https://github.com/geoffchu/chuffed. Accessed Jan 2019
13. Di Cosmo, R., Lienhardt, M., Mauro, J., Zacchiroli, S., Zavattaro, G., Zwolakowski, J.: Automatic application deployment in the cloud: from practice to theory and back (invited paper). In: CONCUR. LIPIcs, vol. 42, pp. 1–16. Schloss Dagstuhl - Leibniz-Zentrum fuer Informatik (2015)

14. Di Cosmo, R., Mauro, J., Zacchiroli, S., Zavattaro, G.: Aeolus: a component model for the cloud. Inf. Comput. **239**, 100–121 (2014)
15. Di Cosmo, R., Zacchiroli, S., Zavattaro, G.: Towards a formal component model for the cloud. In: Eleftherakis, G., Hinchey, M., Holcombe, M. (eds.) SEFM 2012. LNCS, vol. 7504, pp. 156–171. Springer, Heidelberg (2012). https://doi.org/10.1007/978-3-642-33826-7_11
16. Docker: Docker compose documentation. https://docs.docker.com/compose/. Accessed Jan 2019
17. Docker: Docker swarm. https://docs.docker.com/engine/swarm/. Accessed Jan 2019
18. Dragoni, N., et al.: Microservices: yesterday, today, and tomorrow. In: Mazzara, M., Meyer, B. (eds.) Present and Ulterior Software Engineering, pp. 195–216. Springer, Cham (2017). https://doi.org/10.1007/978-3-319-67425-4_12
19. Durán, F., Salaün, G.: Robust and reliable reconfiguration of cloud applications. J. Syst. Softw. **122**, 524–537 (2016)
20. Feinerer, I.: Efficient large-scale configuration via integer linear programming. AI EDAM **27**(1), 37–49 (2013)
21. Fischer, J., Majumdar, R., Esmaeilsabzali, S.: Engage: a deployment management system. In: PLDI (2012)
22. Fromm, K.: Thinking Serverless! How New Approaches Address Modern Data Processing Needs. https://read.acloud.guru/thinking-serverless-how-new-approaches-address-modern-data-processing-needs-part-1-af6a158a3af1. Accessed Jan 2019
23. GECODE: an open, free, efficient constraint solving toolkit. http://www.gecode.org. Accessed Jan 2019
24. Google: Optimization tools. https://developers.google.com/optimization/. Accessed Jan 2019
25. de Gouw, S., Mauro, J., Nobakht, B., Zavattaro, G.: Declarative elasticity in ABS. In: Aiello, M., Johnsen, E.B., Dustdar, S., Georgievski, I. (eds.) ESOCC 2016. LNCS, vol. 9846, pp. 118–134. Springer, Cham (2016). https://doi.org/10.1007/978-3-319-44482-6_8
26. Red Hat Ansible. https://www.ansible.com/. Accessed Jan 2019
27. Hellerstein, J.M., et al.: Serverless computing: one step forward, two steps back. arXiv preprint arXiv:1812.03651 (2018)
28. Hewson, J.A., Anderson, P., Gordon, A.D.: A declarative approach to automated configuration. In: LISA (2012)
29. Hightower, K., Burns, B., Beda, J.: Kubernetes: Up and Running Dive into the Future of Infrastructure, 1st edn. O'Reilly Media, Inc., Sebastopol (2017)
30. Humble, J., Farley, D.: Continuous Delivery: Reliable Software Releases Through Build, Test, and Deployment Automation. Addison-Wesley Professional, Boston (2010)
31. Johnsen, E.B., Hähnle, R., Schäfer, J., Schlatte, R., Steffen, M.: ABS: a core language for abstract behavioral specification. In: Aichernig, B.K., de Boer, F.S., Bonsangue, M.M. (eds.) FMCO 2010. LNCS, vol. 6957, pp. 142–164. Springer, Heidelberg (2011). https://doi.org/10.1007/978-3-642-25271-6_8
32. Kanies, L.: Puppet: next-generation configuration management. `;login`: USENIX Mag. **31**(1), 19–25 (2006)
33. Mauro, J.: Smartdepl. https://github.com/jacopoMauro/abs_deployer. Accessed Jan 2019

34. Mauro, J., Zavattaro, G.: On the complexity of reconfiguration in systems with legacy components. In: Italiano, G.F., Pighizzini, G., Sannella, D.T. (eds.) MFCS 2015. LNCS, vol. 9234, pp. 382–393. Springer, Heidelberg (2015). https://doi.org/10.1007/978-3-662-48057-1_30
35. Mccombs, S.: Outages? Downtime? https://sethmccombs.github.io/work/2018/12/03/Outages.html. Accessed Jan 2019
36. Merkel, D.: Docker: lightweight Linux containers for consistent development and deployment. Linux J. **2014**(239), 2 (2014)
37. Opscode: Chef. https://www.chef.io/chef/. Accessed Jan 2019
38. Puppet Labs: Marionette collective. http://docs.puppetlabs.com/mcollective/. Accessed Jan 2019
39. Woods, D.: On infrastructure at scale: a cascading failure of distributed systems. https://medium.com/@daniel.p.woods/on-infrastructure-at-scale-a-cascading-failure-of-distributed-systems-7cff2a3cd2df. Accessed Jan 2019

A Data Flow Model with Frequency Arithmetic

Paul Dubrulle(✉), Christophe Gaston, Nikolai Kosmatov, Arnault Lapitre, and Stéphane Louise

CEA, List, 91191 Gif-sur-Yvette, France
{paul.dubrulle,christophe.gaston,nikolai.kosmatov, arnault.lapitre,stephane.louise}@cea.fr

Abstract. Data flow formalisms are commonly used to model systems in order to solve problems of buffer sizing and task scheduling. A prerequisite for static analysis of a modeled system is the existence of a periodic schedule in which the sizes of communication channels can be bounded for an unbounded execution (consistency), and that communication dependencies do not introduce a deadlock in such an execution (liveness). In the context of Cyber-Physical Systems, components are often interfaced with the physical world and have frequency constraints. The existing data flow formalisms lack expressiveness to fully cover the expected behavior of these components. We propose an extension to Synchronous Data Flow (SDF) formalism, called Polygraph, that includes frequency constraints and adjustable communication rates. We show that with these extensions, the conditions for a model to be consistent and live are no longer sufficient, and we extend the corresponding theorems with necessary and sufficient conditions to preserve these properties. We also introduce a framework to check the liveness of a Polygraph model, implemented in the tool DIVERSITY, along with preliminary experiments to validate this approach.

1 Introduction

Context. Cyber-Physical Systems (CPS) are increasingly present in everyday life. In these systems, the components require a certain amount of input data to produce a known amount of output data, and some of them must do so in synchrony with a reference time scale. For example, the next generation of autonomous vehicles will heavily rely on sensor fusion systems to operate the car. Sensors and actuators have specified frequencies. To produce its output, the fusion kernel requires a certain number of samples from several sources, with a temporal correlation between them.

Often, when implementing this kind of system, the prediction of its performance is important to the system designer. The performance prediction covers different characteristics of the system, including its throughput, memory footprint, and latency. In distributed implementations of such systems, an analysis of

R. Hähnle and W. van der Aalst (Eds.): FASE 2019, LNCS 11424, pp. 369–385, 2019.
https://doi.org/10.1007/978-3-030-16722-6_22

the communications between the components is necessary to configure a network capable to respect the application's real-time requirements.

Data flow formalisms [3,14] can be used to perform this kind of performance analysis [4,5,10–12]. A prerequisite to analyze a model is the existence of a periodic schedule with two properties. The first property, *consistency*, requires that the sizes of the communication buffers remain bounded for an unbounded execution of the periodic schedule. In practice, if a model is not consistent, it is not possible to implement the communications without losing data samples. The second property, *liveness*, requires the absence of deadlocks in the schedule.

Motivation and Goals. The limitation of the existing data flow formalisms to model the considered systems is the lack of expressiveness regarding the synchronization on a common time scale for different components. Overcoming this limitation is the subject of recent research work [6]. Our goal is to extend an existing data flow formalism for which the consistency and liveness properties of a given model are decidable. In doing so, we want to ensure that the expressiveness extension does not impact the decidability of these properties. With this extension, all applicative constraints are taken into account when checking the prerequisites for a performance analysis. The verification can be performed in abstraction of a particular implementation's characteristics (like execution times or mapping), and the results are the same for different implementations. Moreover, the performance analysis can benefit from the additional information on the system provided by the extension.

Approach and Main Results. This paper introduces Polygraph, an extension to Synchronous Data Flow (SDF) [14] for specification of frequency constraints on the components. We use an arithmetic based on rational numbers to reason on data exchanges between components. We show that the theorems that provide a theoretical foundation for practical verification of consistency and liveness for an SDF model can be generalized to this new formalism. Finally, we propose a symbolic execution framework to decide the liveness of models expressed in Polygraph, in a way similar to [11,14].

The contributions of this work include:

- a data flow formalism, called Polygraph, extending the well-known SDF [14] formalism, to support the synchronization of data production and consumption on a reference time scale;
- a demonstration that the decidability of two classical properties of dataflow models, namely consistency and liveness, is preserved for this new formalism;
- an adaptation to the new formalism of an existing symbolic execution technique for evaluation of liveness in the DIVERSITY tool and initial experiments to validate this approach.

Outline. The remainder of this paper is organized as follows. Section 2 gives an informal introduction to the proposed modeling approach, with a step-by-step explanation relying on an illustrative system. In Sect. 3, we formalize Polygraph

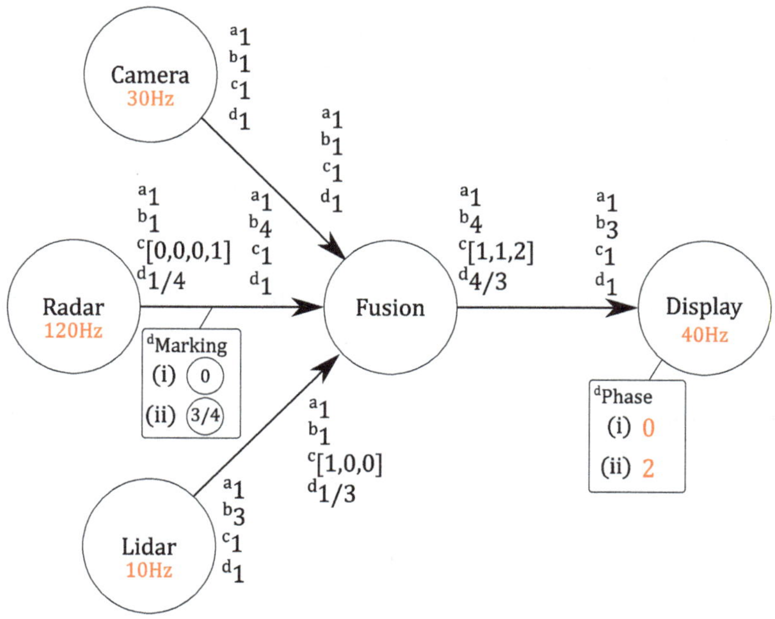

Fig. 1. Motivating example: a data fusion system modeled as a data flow graph. The upper indexes "a" to "d" denote an amount of data exchanged by the components in different variants of the model. The rates denoted by upper index "d" are those of Polygraph, and initial conditions for this configuration are denoted by (i) and (ii).

and provide extended statements and a sketch of proof for the consistency and liveness theorems. Section 4 presents a framework to check the liveness property for Polygraph and a preliminary evaluation. In Sect. 5, we discuss related work, while Sect. 6 presents conclusion and perspectives.

2 Motivation and Running Example

Running Example. To introduce the modeling approach behind Polygraph, we use a toy example of a data fusion system that could be integrated into the cockpit display of a car, depicted in Fig. 1. The system is composed of three sensors producing data samples to be used by a data fusion component, and a display component. The function of the sensor components is to read the data from their sensors, while the function of the data fusion component is to compute a result based on this data. The function of the display component is to render the fusion result on a screen. To do so, the sensor components send the data to the fusion component, and the fusion component sends the result to the display component. The first sensor component is a video camera producing frames. The other two sensor components analyze radar and lidar based samples to produce a descriptor of the closest detected obstacles. The fusion component uses this information to draw the obstacle descriptors on the corresponding frame.

The first step to model this system is to build a graph capturing data dependencies between the components. Each vertex of this graph models an *actor*, an abstract entity representing the function of a component. Each directed edge of the graph models a communication *channel*, the source actor being the producer of data consumed by the destination actor. The structure of the graph in Fig. 1 illustrates the dependencies in our example. The communication policy on the channels is First-In First-Out (FIFO), the write operation is non-blocking, and the read operation is blocking. On each channel, the atomic amount of data exchanged by the connected actors is called a *token*, and all write and read operations are measured in tokens. An actor *produces* (resp. *consumes*) a certain number of tokens on a channel when it writes (resp. reads) the corresponding amount of data. With this policy, the graph can be assimilated to a Kahn Process Network (KPN) [13]. In a KPN, the communications are determinate, but in general it is not possible to decide if the sizes of the channels can be bounded for an unbounded execution of the system.

Synchronous and Asynchronous Constraints. In practice, sensors and actuators have a fixed sampling rate, and the production of each data sample occurs at that specified frequency. To model these constraints, we propose to label some actors with *frequencies*, corresponding to the real-life constraint. An actor with a frequency label must *fire* at that frequency. We further detail this notion of firing below, but for now it is sufficient to say that the firing of an actor is an atomic process, during which it performs the actions and communications expected from the modeled component. A global clock provides ticks to synchronize the firing of frequency labeled actors. For our example, we consider the frequency labeling illustrated by Fig. 1.

Generally, in real-life systems, computation kernels compute when input data is available and do not have frequency constraints. In our frequency labeling, the actors modeling such components can be left without a frequency label. In our example, this is the case for the fusion actor.

The possibility to have unlabeled actors is an important part of our approach, as further discussed in Sect. 5. It allows to mix a synchronous firing policy for labeled actors, and an asynchronous firing policy for unlabeled actors. This means that the scheduling of firings has periodic constraints only where needed, which offers more options for optimization algorithms.

Static Rates. Another characteristic of real-life software components in our context is that they require a fixed number of input samples from each different source. Also, there must be a correlation between the production time of the samples consumed from different sources. In our example, the fusion component requires one token from each sensor, and these samples must have a close-enough production time. This constraint can be captured by KPN restrictions, such as Synchronous Data Flow (SDF) [14]. In SDF, both ends of each channel are assigned a communication rate, denoting the fixed number of tokens produced or consumed by the connected actors' firings. This characteristic allows to decide whether the sizes of the channels are bounded for an unbounded execution. Graphs respecting this property are said to be *consistent*.

Without taking frequencies into account, the communication rates denoted by an upper index "a" in Fig. 1 match the description of the system. Indeed, the sensor actors produce one token each, the fusion actor consumes these tokens, and in turn produces one token to be consumed by the display actor. With these rates, considering a marking of the graph with any number of tokens stored in the channels, if firing all the actors once, the same number of tokens remains in the channels. Hence, the SDF graph is consistent. But when taking frequencies into account, the graph is no longer consistent. In this example, the camera produces 30 tokens per second, the radar produces 120 tokens per second, and the lidar produces 10 tokens per second. This means that per second, because of the production rate and frequency of the lidar, the fusion actor will be able to fire only 10 times. It will consume only 10 tokens from the camera and radar actors, leaving 20 and 110 unconsumed tokens per second on their respective channels. Hence, it is no longer possible to bound the size of these channels for an unbounded execution of the graph. This shows that to achieve consistency, for any frequency labeled actor, the number of asynchronous firings of its unlabeled predecessors and successors should be limited.

A possible adaptation of communication rates, denoted by upper index "b" in Fig. 1, takes frequency inheritance into account and restores the consistency property. With the production and consumption rates both set to 1 on the channel connecting the camera and the fusion actors, the fusion actor basically inherits a frequency constraint of 30 Hz. It inherits the same frequency constraint from the radar and lidar actors since it now consumes $4 \times 30 = 1 \times 120$ tokens per second from the radar, and $1 \times 30 = 3 \times 10$ tokens per second from the lidar. The rates on the channel connecting the fusion and display actors are also balanced. But with these rates, the number of tokens does not reflect accurately the expected behavior of the modeled components. For example, the fusion actor would consume 4 tokens per activation from the radar actor, while in reality the component only requires 1.

Cyclo-Static Rates. It is possible to use Cyclo-Static Data Flow (CSDF) [3] to get closer to the real communication requirements. In CSDF, the rates of the actors are fixed as in SDF, but the successive firings of an actor cyclically consume and produce a different number of tokens on every connected channel. The successive rates on each channel are expressed as a sequence of natural numbers. For example, an actor with a cyclo-static sequence of output rates $[1, 2]$ produces 1 token for its first firing, 2 tokens for the second, 1 for the third and so on. A zero rate may occur in the sequence, meaning that the actor does not push or pull tokens on the channel for the corresponding firing.

A cyclo-static sequence is necessary on a channel if the connected actors have frequency constraints conflicting with the expected communication behavior. In this case, we propose that one of the actors must be chosen as having the reference frequency for the communication, and the other actor must adapt its communication rate to a cyclo-static sequence accordingly. Back to our example (see variant "c" in Fig. 1), the fusion actor requires one token from each sensor every firing. Since the component is synchronized on camera frames, we decide that the actor's reference frequency should be 30 Hz. In this case, the frequency constraints do not conflict with the expected communication behavior, and we

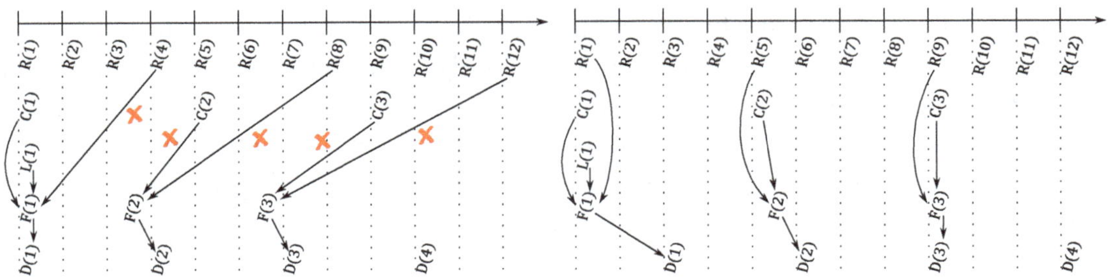

(a) Initial conditions (i). (b) Initial conditions (ii).

Fig. 2. Firings of actors of the motivating example: the firings are identified by the initial letter of the corresponding actor and the rank of the firing, arrows show data dependencies between firings, and a reference time scale constrains the firing of timed actors. The data dependencies marked by a cross in (a) introduce a causality issue.

assign production and consumption rates of 1 on the channel connecting the fusion and camera actors. Now, considering the radar actor, the fusion actor only requires 30 tokens per second out of 120. Considering this ratio, we assign the sequence $[0, 0, 0, 1]$ as production rates for the radar actor, and the rate 1 for the fusion actor. The same logic applies for the lidar actor, the fusion actor requires 30 tokens per second, but only 10 tokens per second are produced. We then assign the cyclo-static sequence $[1, 0, 0]$ as consumption rates for the fusion actor, and the rate 1 for the lidar actor. A similar logic is applied for the display actor. The consequence on the stream of actual data values highly depends on the implemented function, and is therefore out of the scope of the data flow modeling. In the particular case of the radar actor in our example, the software implementation could perform a downsampling of the sensed data, or just send the latest sample.

The corresponding communication rates, denoted by upper index "c" in Fig. 1, give a graph where only the required tokens are exchanged on the channels, and the consistency property is preserved. But in all generality, choosing the appropriate cyclic rate sequences for all the channels in a graph is time consuming and error prone.

Rational Rates. We propose instead to extend the SDF model with rational communication rates. A rational communication rate $r = p/q$ specifies that the actor produces or consumes p tokens every q firings, and the natural number of tokens produced or consumed by any firing is r rounded either up or down, denoted $\lceil r \rceil$ and $\lfloor r \rfloor$ respectively. With the semantic formalized in the next section, there is a unique default cyclo-static sequence that corresponds to a given rational rate. The default sequences for the rates denoted by an upper index "d" in Fig. 1 are those denoted by upper index "c". As explained earlier when assigning cyclo-static sequences, in this extension, only one rate on a given channel can be a rational number with denominator greater than one. The methodology remains the same, for any channel, one actor's frequency is considered as a reference, and the other one adapts its rates according to that reference.

Initial Conditions. With the frequency labeling and rational communication rates, we obtain a model that describes as closely as possible the communication and timing requirements of our illustrative example. But there are causality issues in this model. Figure 2(a) illustrates the timing of actor firings in our example, and the data dependencies between them, according to the semantic defined in the next section. It is obvious that the data dependencies marked by a cross are not satisfied in time.

This kind of causality issue can also appear in SDF: in the case of cyclic graphs, the firings of the actors in a cycle all depend on each other. To prevent this, it is possible to *mark* the channels with an initial number of tokens, allowing sufficient initial firings to complete the firing of all actors in the cycle. The liveness property of an SDF graph is verified when all the cycles in the graph are marked with enough tokens to prevent a deadlock [14]. With the SDF extensions we propose, this condition is no longer sufficient. We need to be able to shift the production or consumption of tokens in order to make sure that when a firing requires input tokens, they are produced at an earlier tick of the global clock.

One way to achieve this is to rotate the default sequences defined by the rational rates. For this, we propose a rational initial marking of the graph. Each channel with natural rates at both ends can be marked with an initial number of tokens as in SDF. Each other channel with rational rate $r = p/q$ on either end can be initially marked with a rational number $n + k/q$ with $k < q$, which denotes that the channel initially holds n tokens (as in SDF), and the default sequence is rotated by k. If the rational rate is on the producer, the default sequence is rotated left, otherwise it is rotated right. In Fig. 1, considering the default sequences denoted by "c", the corresponding rational rates denoted by upper index "d", and the initial marking (ii), the marking of 3/4 on the channel connecting the radar and fusion actors rotates the default sequence $[0, 0, 0, 1]$ by 3 elements to the right, yielding the sequence $[1, 0, 0, 0]$.

Another way to prevent unsatisfied data dependencies is to shift the first tick on which a frequency labeled actor must fire. We propose to add a *phase* to each of these actors, giving the offset from the first tick at which it must fire. With the semantic formalized in the next section, that phase is constrained in order to have a periodic global clock. Figure 2(b) takes into account the marking and phase denoted (ii) in Fig. 1. With the rational marking, the dependencies between the radar and fusion firings are now satisfied, and with the phase on the display actor, the dependencies between the camera and display firings are also satisfied.

3 Formalization of the Polygraph Model

We denote by $\mathbb{B}$ the set $\{0, 1\}$, by $\mathbb{Z}$ the set of integers, by $\mathbb{N} = \{n \in \mathbb{Z} \mid n \geqslant 0\}$ the set of natural integers, and by $\mathbb{Q}$ the set of rational numbers. For any set S, the free semigroup on S is denoted S^+.

System graph. A *system graph* is a structure used to represent the topology of the communications. Formally, it is a connected finite directed graph $G = (V, E)$

with set of vertices V and set of edges $E \subseteq V \times V$ such that V is the set of *actors* and E is the set of *channels*. We use an index notation to identify elements with respect to a given actor or channel, considering that E and V are sets indexed respectively in $\{1, \cdots, |E|\}$ and $\{1, \cdots, |V|\}$. We denote v_i (resp. e_j) the actor (resp. channel) of index i (resp. j). For an actor $v \in V$, let $\text{in}(v) = \{\langle v', v\rangle \in E \mid v' \in V\}$ denote the set of *input channels* of v and $\text{out}(v) = \{\langle v, v'\rangle \in E \mid v' \in V\}$ the set of *output channels* of v.

Topology matrix and channel states. As for SDF and its derivations [3,14], the communication rates are defined by a topology matrix with one row per channel and one column per actor. The only difference in this definition is that we rely on rational numbers. The absolute value of a rate in the matrix defines how many tokens are produced or consumed per firing of the corresponding actor on the corresponding channel, and the sign of that rate indicates if the tokens are produced (positive rate) or consumed (negative rate). For a given actor and channel, the rate must be 0 if the actor is not connected to the channel, or if the actor is connected to both ends of the channel.

Definition 1 (Topology matrix). *A matrix* $\mathbf{\Gamma} = (\gamma_{ij}) \in \mathbb{Q}^{|E| \times |V|}$ *is a* topology matrix *of a system graph* G *if for every channel* $e_i = \langle v_j, v_k\rangle \in E$ *we have:*

- $\gamma_{il} = 0$ *for all* $l \neq j, k$*;*
- *if* $j \neq k$*, then* $\gamma_{ij} > 0$ *and* $\gamma_{ik} < 0$ *are irreducible fractions, and at most one of them has a denominator greater than 1;*
- *if* $j = k$*, then* $\gamma_{ij} = 0$*.*

We also use a rational number per channel to track the communication state of the system during an execution. A channel state is a vector with one row per channel. Each coordinate in the vector tracks the respective number of firings of the connected actors, by addition of their rates when they fire, and that coordinate rounded down is the number of tokens in the channel.

Definition 2 (Channel state). *A vector* $\mathbf{c} \in \mathbb{Q}^{|E| \times 1}$ *is a* channel state *of a system graph* G *with topology matrix* $\mathbf{\Gamma}$ *if for every channel* $e_i = \langle v_j, v_k\rangle \in E$*, the denominator of* c_i *is the maximum between the denominators of* γ_{ij} *and* γ_{ik}*, and* $\lfloor c_i \rfloor$ *is the number of tokens in the channel. We denote* $C \subseteq \mathbb{Q}^{|E| \times 1}$ *the set of all these possible states.*

Timed actors and global clock. A subset $V_F \subseteq V$ of *timed actors* are constrained by a *frequency*, expressed as a strictly positive natural number. We use a frequency mapping $\omega : V_F \longrightarrow \mathbb{N}^{>0}$ in order to map the timed actors to their frequency. There is an implicit system time unit, and each timed actor $v_i \in V_F$ is supposed to be fired exactly $\omega_i := \omega(v_i)$ times per system time unit. In order to have a minimal system time unit, we consider that the greatest common divisor of all the frequencies is $\gcd(\omega[V_F]) = 1$. This is not limiting, since any set of frequencies and system time unit can be adjusted to fit this constraint.

In addition, the timed actors must fire synchronously with respect to a global clock. The *resolution* of that global clock is a sufficient number of *ticks* per system time unit to associate to each tick the set of timed actors that must fire at the corresponding date. For this, we consider the ticks $0, 1, \ldots, \pi - 1$ per system time unit, where π is the least common multiple of all the actor frequencies $\pi = \mathrm{lcm}(\{\omega_i | v_i \in V_F\})$. Note that if V_F is empty, $\pi = 1$, and the global clock does not constrain the firing of any actor.

Given a timed actor $v_i \in V_F$, there should be ω_i out of π ticks associated with that actor's firings. To reflect the periodic nature of the firing of timed actors, for a timed actor v_i of period $p_i = \pi/\omega_i$, it fires every p_i-th tick.

As mentioned in Sect. 2, all the timed actors have a *phase*. We use a phase mapping $\varphi : V_F \longrightarrow \mathbb{N}$ to map the timed actors to their phase. The first firing of each timed actor $v_i \in V_F$ occurs at the tick $\varphi_i := \varphi(v_i)$. The only constraint to respect the expected frequency of the firings is that $\forall v_i \in V_F$ we have $0 \leqslant \varphi_i < \pi/\omega_i$.

Definition 3 (Global clock, firing ticks). *For a system graph G with frequency mapping ω, resolution π, and phase mapping φ, the* global clock *is a set* $\mathrm{T} = \{0, 1, \ldots, \pi - 1\}$ *and for each timed actor $v_i \in V_F$ there is a subset of* firing ticks $\mathrm{T}_i = \{\tau \in \mathrm{T} \,|\, \tau \equiv \varphi_i \pmod{\pi/\omega_i}\}$.

Polygraphs. We now define the notion of *polygraph* which introduces a basic communication topology, a topology matrix, a frequency and phase mapping for all timed actors, and an initial marking of the graph.

Definition 4 (Polygraph, initial marking). *A* polygraph *is a tuple* $\mathcal{P} = \langle G, \mathbf{\Gamma}, \omega, \varphi, \mathbf{m}\rangle$ *where G is a system graph, $\mathbf{\Gamma}$ is a topology matrix, ω is a frequency mapping, φ is a phase mapping and $\mathbf{m} \in C$ is an* initial marking *such that $\forall e_i \in E$ we have $m_i \geqslant 0$.*

In the following, we consider that a polygraph $\mathcal{P} = \langle G, \mathbf{\Gamma}, \omega, \varphi, \mathbf{m}\rangle$ is given, with its global clock T and sets of firing ticks T_i for all the timed actors $v_i \in V_F$.

States and transitions. The state of a polygraph is composed of a channel state, the current tick of the global clock, and a vector with one row per actor used to track the number of firings of the timed actors since the last change in the current tick. This *tracking vector* is used to check that the timed actors respect their synchronous firing constraints.

Definition 5 (State). *A* state *of a polygraph $\mathcal{P}$ is a tuple $s = \langle \mathbf{c}, \tau, \mathbf{a}\rangle$ where $\mathbf{c} \in C$ is a channel state, $\tau \in \mathrm{T}$ is a tick, and $\mathbf{a} \in \mathbb{N}^{|V| \times 1}$ is a tracking vector. We denote $S \subseteq C \times \mathrm{T} \times \mathbb{N}^{|V| \times 1}$ the set of all possible states for $\mathcal{P}$.*

The effect of the firing of an actor on the channel state is to add its rates to the respective coordinate of all the channels. For an actor v_i, the i-th column of $\mathbf{\Gamma}$ gives all the rates per channel. Therefore, to extract that column from the matrix for each actor $v_i \in V$, we use a *unitary firing vector* $\mathbf{u} \in \mathbb{B}^{|V| \times 1}$, such that $u_i = 1$, and for all $j \neq i$ we have $u_j = 0$. We denote $U \subset \mathbb{B}^{|V| \times 1}$ the set of these vectors, and for convenience we denote the unitary activation vector of actor v_i by $\mathbf{u}_i$. With the unitary firing vector of any actor v_i, the product $\mathbf{\Gamma}\mathbf{u}_i$

gives a vector holding for each channel e_j the rate of v_i on e_j. For any channel state $\mathbf{c}$, the channel state after the atomic firing of v_i is then $\mathbf{c} + \mathbf{\Gamma u^i}$. Also, the firing of a timed actor is tracked by adding its unitary firing vector to the tracking vector. The firing of an actor has no effect on the current tick.

Definition 6 (Fire). *For a polygraph $\mathcal{P}$, the mapping* fire : $U \times S \longrightarrow S$ *maps a unitary activation vector $\mathbf{u}_i$ and a state $s = \langle \mathbf{c}, \tau, \mathbf{a} \rangle$ to the state $s' = \langle \mathbf{c}', \tau', \mathbf{a}' \rangle$ such that we have $\mathbf{c}' = \mathbf{c} + \mathbf{\Gamma u}_i$, $\tau' = \tau$, and if $v_i \in V_F$ then $\mathbf{a}' = \mathbf{a} + \mathbf{u}_i$, otherwise $\mathbf{a}' = \mathbf{a}$.*

Remark 1. For two consecutive firings of any actors v_i and v_j from a state $s = \langle \mathbf{c}, \tau, \mathbf{a} \rangle$, the resulting state $s'' = \langle \mathbf{c}'', \tau'', \mathbf{a}'' \rangle$ does not depend on the order of the firings, and $\mathbf{c}'' = \mathbf{c} + \mathbf{\Gamma}(\mathbf{u}_i + \mathbf{u}_j)$. This property can be generalized to any finite number of consecutive firings.

The other possible transition between two states occurs when the global clock ticks. When the global clock ticks, the channel state is not changed, the current tick is adjusted, and the tracking vector is reset.

Definition 7 (Tick). *For a polygraph $\mathcal{P}$, the mapping* tick : $S \longrightarrow S$ *maps a state $s = \langle \mathbf{c}, \tau, \mathbf{a} \rangle$ to the state $s' = \langle \mathbf{c}', \tau', \mathbf{a}' \rangle$ such that we have $\mathbf{c}' = \mathbf{c}$, $\tau' = (\tau + 1) \bmod \pi$, and $\mathbf{a}' = \mathbf{0}$.*

Executions. The state of $\mathcal{P}$ can evolve by successive application of either $fire$ or *tick*. An *execution* of $\mathcal{P}$ is a sequence of such applications starting from a state $s_1 \in S$ and leading to states $e = s_1 \cdots s_n \in S^+$. However, with the frequency constraints, there are some conditions for the applications.

Consider the firing fire$(\mathbf{u}_i, s)$ of a timed actor v_i in a state $s = \langle \mathbf{c}, \tau, \mathbf{a} \rangle$. In this case, v_i may fire only if the current tick τ is one of its firing ticks, *i.e.* $\tau \in \mathrm{T}_i$. Since it must fire exactly once on such a tick, an additional constraint to fire a timed actor v_i is that it has not fired yet, *i.e.* its coordinate in the tracking vector $\mathbf{a}$ is $a_i = 0$. To capture this constraint, we define a *tick firing vector* $\mathbf{t}^\tau \in \mathbb{B}^{|V| \times 1}$ for each tick $\tau \in \mathrm{T}$, in which a coordinate is set to one if the corresponding actor is expected to fire at tick τ. More formally, for any $v_i \in V \setminus V_F$ we have $t_i^\tau = 0$, and for any $v_j \in V_F$ we have $t_j^\tau = 1$ if $\tau \in \mathrm{T}_j$, and $t_j^\tau = 0$ otherwise. The constraint to fire $v_i \in V_F$ in a state with current tick τ and tracking vector $\mathbf{a}$ is then $a_i < t_i^\tau$.

The clock update tick(s) in a state $s = \langle \mathbf{c}, \tau, \mathbf{a} \rangle$ is also subject to a constraint: the timed actors that were supposed to fire synchronously with the current tick have done so exactly once, *i.e.* $\mathbf{a} = \mathbf{t}^\tau$.

Definition 8 (Synchronous execution). *An execution $e = s_1 \cdots s_n \in S^+$ of a polygraph $\mathcal{P}$ is* synchronous *if $\forall 1 \leqslant k < n$, we have $s_k = \langle \mathbf{c}, \tau, \mathbf{a} \rangle$ such that:*

- *either $s_{k+1} =$ fire$(\mathbf{u}_i, s_k)$ for some $v_i \in V$, and in addition, if $v_i \in V_F$, then $a_i < t_i^\tau$,*
- *or $s_{k+1} =$ tick(s_k), and in addition, $\mathbf{a} = \mathbf{t}^\tau$.*

Until now, we considered executions of a polygraph where the order of the firings is constrained only by the frequencies. However, for an actor to fire, there must be enough tokens on its input channels, or its rational communication rate must allow firings consuming 0 tokens. In order to fire an actor v_i in a state $s = \langle \mathbf{c}, \tau, \mathbf{a} \rangle$, we require that for each input channel e_j of v_i, since the rate γ_{ji} is negative, the channel state c_j must be large enough to avoid reaching a negative state, *i.e.* $c_j + \gamma_{ji} \geqslant 0$, or equivalently $c_j \geqslant |\gamma_{ji}|$. This constraint requires an ordering of the actor firings such that a producer is fired a sufficient number of times for a consumer to be able to fire in turn.

Definition 9 (Non-blocking execution). *An execution* $e = s_1 \cdots s_n \in S^+$ *of a polygraph* $\mathcal{P}$ *is* non-blocking *if* $\forall 1 \leqslant k < n$, *we have* $s_k = \langle \mathbf{c}, \tau, \mathbf{a} \rangle$ *such that:*

- *either* $s_{k+1} = \text{fire}(\mathbf{u}_i, s_k)$ *for some* $v_i \in V$, *and in addition,* $\forall e_j \in \text{in}(v_i)$, $c_j \geqslant |\gamma_{ji}|$,
- *or* $s_{k+1} = \text{tick}(s_k)$.

Consistency property. If verified, the *consistency* property of $\mathcal{P}$ guarantees that it is possible to build a synchronous execution $e = s_1 \cdots s_n \in S^+$ such that $s_1 = \langle \mathbf{m}, 0, \mathbf{0} \rangle$ and $s_1 = s_n$. Such an execution is called a *consistent* execution of $\mathcal{P}$, and can obviously be repeated an indefinite number of times to build a consistent execution of arbitrary length. [14, Theorem 1] states that a necessary and sufficient condition for a given SDF graph to be consistent is that there is a non-trivial solution $\mathbf{x}$ to $\mathbf{\Gamma x} = \mathbf{0}$.

To extend this result to polygraphs, as explained in the previous section, we need to take into account the frequencies of the timed actors. In other words, we need to make sure that it is possible to have a synchronous execution with x_i firings per actor v_i. The additional constraint due to the frequencies is that the number of firings x_i of all the timed actors v_i corresponds to a number $r \in \mathbb{N}$ of repetitions of the global clock period.

To state the conditions for a polygraph to be consistent, we thus want to separate the number of firings of the timed actors from the others. We define the vector $\mathbf{t} = \sum_{\forall \tau \in T} \mathbf{t}^{\tau}$ giving for each timed actor v_i the number t_i of expected firings per period of the global clock. We then define the set $Y \subset \mathbb{N}^{|V| \times 1}$ of vectors $\mathbf{y}$ such that we have a number of firings $y_i \neq 0$ only for $v_i \in V \setminus V_F$.

Theorem 1. *A polygraph* $\mathcal{P}$ *has a consistent execution if and only if there exists a non-trivial solution* $\mathbf{x} \in \mathbb{N}^{|V| \times 1}$ *to* $\mathbf{\Gamma x} = \mathbf{0}$ *such that* $\mathbf{x} = \mathbf{y} + r\mathbf{t}$ *for some* $\mathbf{y} \in Y$ *and* $r \in \mathbb{N}$. *Any such solution is called a* repetition vector *of* $\mathcal{P}$. *Moreover, there exists a* minimal repetition vector $\mathbf{x}$ *such that for any other repetition vector* $\mathbf{x}'$ *we have* $\mathbf{x}' = k\mathbf{x}$ *for some* $k \in \mathbb{N}$.

Sketch of proof. First, we prove that the condition is sufficient, and suppose that there exists such a solution $\mathbf{x}$. Then we can decompose:

$$\mathbf{x} = \mathbf{y} + \underbrace{\underbrace{(\mathbf{t}^{\mathbf{0}} + \ldots + \mathbf{t}^{\pi-\mathbf{1}})}_{=\mathbf{t}} + \ldots + \underbrace{(\mathbf{t}^{\mathbf{0}} + \ldots + \mathbf{t}^{\pi-\mathbf{1}})}_{=\mathbf{t}}}_{=r\mathbf{t}}$$

The required consistent execution can be obtained by constructing sub-executions corresponding to this decomposition, relying on Definition 8 and Remark 1.

Claim (1). There exists a synchronous execution $e_1 \in S^+$ with starting state $s = \langle \mathbf{m}, 0, \mathbf{0} \rangle$ and ending state $s' = \langle \mathbf{m} + \mathbf{\Gamma y}, 0, \mathbf{0} \rangle$.

The execution e_1 is constructed by applying y_i firings of each actor $v_i \in V \setminus V_F$ (in any order). Since the fired actors are not timed actors, any such sequence is synchronous. The resulting channel state is $\mathbf{m} + \mathbf{\Gamma y}$ as per Remark 1.

Claim (2). For any starting state $s = \langle \mathbf{c}, \tau, \mathbf{0} \rangle$, there exists a synchronous execution $e_2 \in S^+$ starting from s with ending state $s' = \langle \mathbf{c} + \mathbf{\Gamma t}^{\tau}, (\tau + 1) \bmod \pi, \mathbf{0} \rangle$.

The execution e_2 for τ is constructed by firing exactly once each timed actor supposed to do so at tick τ, and then applying the tick mapping.

Claim (3). For any starting state $s = \langle \mathbf{c}, 0, \mathbf{0} \rangle$, there exists a synchronous execution $e_3 \in S^+$ starting from s with ending state $s' = \langle \mathbf{c} + \mathbf{\Gamma t}, 0, \mathbf{0} \rangle$.

The execution e_3 is obtained by successively executing e_2 for $\tau = 0, \ldots, \pi - 1$.

Claim (4). There exists a synchronous execution $e_4 \in S^+$ with starting state $s = \langle \mathbf{m}, 0, \mathbf{0} \rangle$ and ending state $s' = \langle \mathbf{m} + \mathbf{\Gamma}(\mathbf{y} + r\mathbf{t}), 0, \mathbf{0} \rangle$.

The sequence e_4 is constructed by executing e_1, followed by e_3 repeated r times. Hence, given that $\mathbf{\Gamma x} = \mathbf{0}$ and $\mathbf{x} = \mathbf{y} + r\mathbf{t}$, it can be easily checked that the ending state of e_4 is the same as its starting state, and e_4 is consistent. The fact that the condition is also necessary follows from the definitions. Since the current tick must return to 0 after a consistent execution, such an execution must perform a number r of periods of the global clock for some $r \in \mathbb{N}$, in other words it must contain $r\pi$ applications of the tick mapping and rt_i firings of each timed actor v_i. The existence of a minimal solution immediately follows from the fact that in this case $\operatorname{rank}(\mathbf{\Gamma}) = |V| - 1$ according to [14, Corollary of Lemma 2].

Due to lack of space, a detailed proof is left to the reader. □

Liveness property. If verified, the *liveness* property of $\mathcal{P}$ guarantees that it is possible to build a consistent execution $e = s_1 \cdots s_n \in S^+$ such that e is also a non-blocking execution. Such an execution e is called a *live execution.*

In a way similar to [14, Theorem 3], we define the notion of a scheduler building only synchronous and non-blocking executions. Our goal is to show that $\mathcal{P}$ has a live execution if and only if any such scheduler can build a consistent execution.

From now on, we consider that $\mathcal{P}$ is consistent with minimal repetition vector $\mathbf{x}$. We define the mapping *count* : $V \times S^+ \longrightarrow \mathbb{N}$ that given an actor v_i and an execution $e = s_1 \cdots s_n \in S^+$ returns the number of firings of v_i in e, *i.e.* the number of k such that $1 \leqslant k < n$ and $s_{k+1} = \text{fire}(\mathbf{u}_i, s_k)$. Notice that since a live execution e of $\mathcal{P}$ is also consistent, by definition we have $\forall v_i \in V, \text{count}(v_i, e) = x_i$. Also, we say that an actor $v_i \in V$ is *runnable* after an execution $e \in S^+$ with ending state s if $\text{count}(v_i, e) < x_i$ and the one-step execution $ss' \in S^+$ with $s' = \text{fire}(\mathbf{u}_i, s)$ is synchronous and non-blocking.

Definition 10 (Scheduler). *A* scheduler *of $\mathcal{P}$ is a mapping $\sigma : S^+ \longrightarrow S^+$ that maps an execution $e = s_1 \cdots s_n \in S^+$ to an execution $e' \in S^+$ such that if we denote $s_n = \langle \mathbf{c}, \tau, \mathbf{a} \rangle$ we have:*

- *either $e' = s_1 \cdots s_n s' \in S^+$ with $s' = \text{fire}(\mathbf{u}_i, s_n)$ for some actor v_i runnable after e;*
- *or $e' = s_1 \cdots s_n s' \in S^+$ with $s' = \text{tick}(s_n)$ and $\mathbf{a} = \mathbf{t}^\tau$;*
- *or $e' = e$ if there is no runnable actor after e and $\mathbf{a} \neq \mathbf{t}^\tau$.*

An execution defined by a scheduler σ is the fixed point constructed by recursive application[1] of σ starting from an initial execution $e = (\langle \mathbf{m}, 0, \mathbf{0} \rangle)$.

Theorem 2. *Let $\mathcal{P}$ be a consistent polygraph with minimal repetition vector $\mathbf{x}$, σ a scheduler of $\mathcal{P}$, and e the execution defined by σ. Then $\mathcal{P}$ has a live execution if and only if $\forall v_i \in V, \text{count}(v_i, e) = x_i$.*

Sketch of proof. The condition is obviously sufficient. The proof that it is also necessary can be easily made by induction. If e is a live execution and e' is a synchronous and non-blocking execution constructed by σ so far, with $|e'| < |e|$, we can show that e' can be extended by one more step (*e.g.* by taking the first step present in e but not in e', since its preconditions are necessarily satisfied). □

4 Tool Support for Liveness Checking

DIVERSITY is a customizable model analysis tool based on symbolic execution, available in the *Eclipse Formal Modeling Project* [17]. DIVERSITY provides a pivot language called *xLIA* (eXecutable Language for Interaction and Architecture) introducing a set of communication and execution primitives allowing one to encode a wide class of dynamic model semantics [2,9], Communicating STS [1], and abstractions of hybrid systems [15]. In this work, we use it to analyze Polygraph models, to check their liveness in a similar way to that defined by a scheduler as per Definition 10.

The root entity in an xLIA model is a so-called *system*. A system is an executable entity that can be atomic (state-machine) or compositional or hierarchical. A Polygraph model translated to xLIA is a system where the actors are state-machines with input/output ports associated with the ends of the channels. They communicate asynchronously over FIFO queues, bounded or not, using xLIA connectors. Variables are used to store received tokens on input instructions in transitions, with guards conditioning their firing, and output statements to model their token productions.

Figure 3 represents such a state machine for any actor of the polygraph in Fig. 1. Each transition is labeled with xLIA macros representing the actions performed. The *init* macro moves the initial marking from the input queues to the

[1] Hence, a scheduler can be also defined as a *partial* mapping on $\sigma^*(\langle \mathbf{m}, 0, \mathbf{0} \rangle)$.

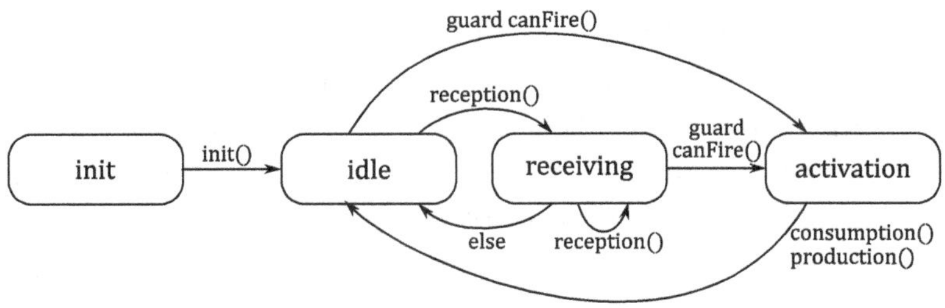

Fig. 3. xLIA state machine pattern for an actor of a polygraph

counter of available input tokens, *canFire()* tests if enough tokens are present for a non-blocking firing, *consumption* decrements the counter of available input tokens, *production* sends the production rate on the successor's queue, and *reception* reads that rate and adds it to the number of available tokens. Regarding state machine semantics, all the states are pseudo-states, except *idle* which is stable. This means that any fired transition must be completed until returning to the idle state. The *else* transition will be evaluated if there is no possible *reception*.

The xLIA language allows a fine-grained definition of an execution model for the actors of a polygraph. Some instructions associate a sequence of actors to fire with each tick of a clock. When attempting to fire a timed actor, only one firing is triggered if possible, and when attempting the same for other actors, as many firings as possible are triggered. Hence, the timed actors are only fired at the expected tick, and cause a deadlock result if it's not possible. For the other actors, a counter limits their number of firings to their coordinate in the minimal repetition vector, as required by Theorem 2. With this setup, for a polygraph $\mathcal{P}$ with minimal repetition vector $\mathbf{x} = \mathbf{y} + r\mathbf{t}$, the length of a live execution path is $r\pi$, plus one for the initialization step handling the initial marking. Any path with less steps leads to a deadlock.

We tested this technique using DIVERSITY on an *Intel core i7*. For the polygraph of Fig. 1 with initial marking (ii), the tool finds that the liveness property is verified. We also tested the initial marking (i), and the tool correctly identified a deadlock in less than 200 ms. This example is extracted from a more complex polygraph modeling an Advanced Driver-Assistance System (ADAS), that we also used to evaluate the liveness checking tool. The considered polygraph has 18 actors (5 of which are timed actors), 32 channels (6 of which have an initial marking), where 10 actors have rational communication rates. For a correctly marked model, we find a live execution sequence in 4s.

5 Discussion and Related Work

In [16], an extension to SDF is proposed to add a single throughput constraint on a channel of a consistent graph. From this constraint, a firing frequency is derived for the actors by transitivity. This approach, while preserving the consistency property by construction, does not allow the expression of a frequency constraint per actor, based on a real-life constraint on the modeled component, nor the explicit synchronization of the firings on a reference time scale.

The programming model PTIDES [18] combines a real-time semantic for sensors and actuators, and a discrete event semantic for other components like computation kernels. These other components have an awareness of the real time through a logical time abstraction. The resulting execution semantic has similarities with Polygraph, since some components are constrained by real-time and others only react to their stimuli. The semantic of PTIDES is much more flexible than Polygraph, since it does not require fixed production or consumption rates. On the other hand, and as opposed to Polygraph, there is no way to derive a consistent and live periodic schedule in PTIDES, which makes static performance prediction more difficult. Nevertheless, since the semantics are similar, we believe that the notion of logical time as defined in PTIDES is applicable to practical distributed implementations of polygraphs.

Synchronous programming languages [7,8] can be used to express a data flow between synchronous periodic nodes, in order to generate correct-by-construction programs. In these approaches, all the nodes are synchronous, while in Polygraph, some actors fire asynchronously when enabled. Also, the goal of our approach is to be able to reason formally on the modeled systems, and automate as many tasks as possible in its design, implementation and validation. Such a task could be the association of the asynchronous firings to ticks of the global clock, and the generation of a synchronous program for automatic code generation.

Recently published research [6] follows a similar approach to ours. By mixing elements from two existing formalisms, one allowing the specification of time-triggered tasks and the other the specification of data flow actors, the expressiveness of the resulting modeling framework is comparable to that of Polygraph. The main difference is that Polygraph is a single formalism with decidable properties and algorithms to check them in practice. In [6], the impact of the combination of constraints from two different formalisms on their respective properties is not discussed, as the proposed approach is more focused on the performance evaluation. The experimental results the authors obtained are in favor of the modeling approach we have in common.

6 Conclusion

We have introduced Polygraph, a data flow formalism extending SDF with synchronous firing semantics for the actors. We have shown that with this extension, the existing conditions to decide of a given SDF graph's consistency and liveness were no longer sufficient. We have extended the corresponding theorems and shown that the expressiveness extensions we proposed do not impact the decidability of these properties. Finally, as a first step towards tool assisted modeling of polygraphs, we have introduced a framework relying on DIVERSITY to verify their liveness.

Our next step is to further extend Polygraph to add flexibility in the execution semantic, with the same objective to preserve the capability to perform accurate static analysis of a system's performance. Still, with this first extension, there are already interesting research perspectives regarding the applicability of existing static performance analysis techniques, and their potential extensions to take into account the specifics of a polygraph's scheduling.

Acknowledgement. Part of this work has been realized in the FACE project, involving CEA List and Renault. The Polygraph formalism has been used as a theoretical foundation for the software methodology in the project.

References

1. Arnaud, M., Bannour, B., Lapitre, A.: An illustrative use case of the DIVERSITY platform based on UML interaction scenarios. Electr. Notes Theor. Comput. Sci. **320**, 21–34 (2016)
2. Bannour, B., Escobedo, J.P., Gaston, C., Le Gall, P.: Off-line test case generation for timed symbolic model-based conformance testing. In: Nielsen, B., Weise, C. (eds.) ICTSS 2012. LNCS, vol. 7641, pp. 119–135. Springer, Heidelberg (2012). https://doi.org/10.1007/978-3-642-34691-0_10
3. Bilsen, G., Engels, M., Lauwereins, R., Peperstraete, J.A.: Cyclo-static data flow. In: Proceedings of the 1995 International Conference on Acoustics, Speech, and Signal Processing, vol. 5, pp. 3255–3258 (1995)
4. Bodin, B., Munier-Kordon, A., de Dinechin, B.D.: K-periodic schedules for evaluating the maximum throughput of a synchronous dataflow graph. In: Proceedings of the 2012 International Conference on Embedded Computer Systems (SAMOS), pp. 152–159 (2012)
5. Bouakaz, A., Fradet, P., Girault, A.: Symbolic buffer sizing for throughput-optimal scheduling of dataflow graphs. In: Proceedings of the 22nd IEEE Real-Time Embedded Technology and Applications Symposium (RTAS 2016) (2016)
6. Breaban, G., Stuijk, S., Goossens, K.: Efficient synchronization methods for LET-based applications on a multi-processor system on chip. In: Design, Automation Test in Europe Conference Exhibition (DATE) 2017, pp. 1721–1726 (2017)
7. Cohen, A., Duranton, M., Eisenbeis, C., Pagetti, C., Plateau, F., Pouzet, M.: N-synchronous Kahn networks: a relaxed model of synchrony for real-time systems. SIGPLAN Not. **41**(1), 180–193 (2006)
8. Forget, J., Boniol, F., Lesens, D., Pagetti, C.: A multi-periodic synchronous data-flow language. In: 2008 11th IEEE High Assurance Systems Engineering Symposium, pp. 251–260 (2008)
9. Gaston, C., Le Gall, P., Rapin, N., Touil, A.: Symbolic execution techniques for test purpose definition. In: Uyar, M.Ü., Duale, A.Y., Fecko, M.A. (eds.) TestCom 2006. LNCS, vol. 3964, pp. 1–18. Springer, Heidelberg (2006). https://doi.org/10.1007/11754008_1
10. Geilen, M., Basten, T., Stuijk, S.: Minimising buffer requirements of synchronous dataflow graphs with model checking. In: Proceedings of the 42nd Design Automation Conference, pp. 819–824. IEEE (2005)
11. Ghamarian, A.H., et al.: Throughput analysis of synchronous data flow graphs. In: Proceedings of the Sixth International Conference on Application of Concurrency to System Design (ACSD 2006), pp. 25–36 (2006)

12. Ghamarian, A.H., Stuijk, S., Basten, T., Geilen, M.C.W., Theelen, B.D.: Latency minimization for synchronous data flow graphs. In: Proceedings of the 10th Euromicro Conference on Digital System Design Architectures, Methods and Tools (DSD 2007), pp. 189–196 (2007)
13. Kahn, G., MacQueen, D., Laboria, I.: Coroutines and Networks of Parallel Processes. IRIA Research Report, IRIA laboria (1976)
14. Lee, E.A., Messerschmitt, D.G.: Static scheduling of synchronous data flow programs for digital signal processing. IEEE Trans. Comput. **C–36**(1), 24–35 (1987)
15. Medimegh, S., Pierron, J.Y., Gallois, J., Boulanger, F.: A new approach of qualitative simulation for the validation of hybrid systems. In: Proceedings of the workshop on Model Driven Engineering Languages and Systems (MODELS). ACM (2016)
16. Selva, M.: Performance monitoring of throughput constrained dataflow programs executed on shared-memory multi-core architectures. Theses, INSA de Lyon (2015)
17. The List Institute: CEA Tech: The DIVERSITY Tool. http://projects.eclipse.org/proposals/eclipse-formal-modeling-project/
18. Zhao, Y., Liu, J., Lee, E.A.: A programming model for time-synchronized distributed real-time systems. In: Proceedings of the 13th IEEE Real Time and Embedded Technology and Applications Symposium (RTAS 2007), pp. 259–268. IEEE (2007)

Software Testing

CoVeriTest: Cooperative Verifier-Based Testing

Dirk Beyer and Marie-Christine Jakobs

LMU Munich, Munich, Germany

Abstract. Testing is a widely used method to assess software quality. Coverage criteria and coverage measurements are used to ensure that the constructed test suites adequately test the given software. Since manually developing such test suites is too expensive in practice, various automatic test-generation approaches were proposed. Since all approaches come with different strengths, combinations are necessary in order to achieve stronger tools. We study cooperative combinations of verification approaches for test generation, with high-level information exchange.

We present CoVeriTest, a hybrid approach for test-case generation, which iteratively applies different conditional model checkers. Thereby, it allows to adjust the level of cooperation and to assign individual time budgets per verifier. In our experiments, we combine explicit-state model checking and predicate abstraction (from CPAchecker) to systematically study different CoVeriTest configurations. Moreover, CoVeriTest achieves higher coverage than state-of-the-art test-generation tools for some programs.

Keywords: Test-case generation · Software testing · Test coverage · Conditional model checking · Cooperative verification · Model checking

1 Introduction

Testing is a commonly used technique to measure the quality of software. Since manually creating such test suites is laborious, automatic techniques are used: e.g., model-based techniques for black-box testing and techniques based on control-flow coverage for white-box testing. Many automatic techniques have been proposed, ranging from random testing [36,57] and fuzzing [26,52,53], over search-based testing [55] to symbolic execution [23,24,58] and reachability analyses [5,12,45,46]. The latter are well-suited to find bugs and derive test suites that achieve high coverage, and several verification tools support test generation (e.g., Blast [5], PathFinder [61], CPAchecker [12]). The reachability checks for all test goals seem too expensive, but in practice, those approaches can be made pretty efficient.

Encouraged by tremendous advances in software verification [3] and a recent case study that compared model checkers with test tools w.r.t. bug finding [17], we study a new kind of combination of reachability analyses for test generation. Combinations are necessary because different analysis techniques have different strength and weaknesses. For example, consider function `foo` in Listing 1. Explicit state model checking [18,33] tracks the values of variables i and s and easily

R. Hähnle and W. van der Aalst (Eds.): FASE 2019, LNCS 11424, pp. 389–408, 2019.
https://doi.org/10.1007/978-3-030-16722-6_23

detects the reachability of the statements in the outermost `if` branch (lines 3–6), while it has difficulties with the complex condition in the else-branch (line 8). In contrast, predicate abstraction [33,39] can easily derive test values for the complex condition in line 8, but to handle the `if` branch (lines 3–6) it must spent effort on the detection of the predicates $s = 0$, $s = 1$, and $i = 0$. Independently of each other, test approaches [1,34,47,54] and verification approaches [9,10,29,37] employ combinations to tackle such problems. However, there are no approaches yet that combine different reachability analyses for test generation.

```
0 void foo(int i, int n) {
1   int s=0;
2   if(i==0)
3     while (i==0)   {
4       if(s==0) init();
5       if(s==1) i = exec();
6       s=(s+1)%2;
7     }
8   else if(2*i<n && i>0) exec();
9 }
```

Fig. 1. Example program foo

Inspired by abstraction-driven concolic testing [32], which interleaves concolic execution and predicate abstraction, we propose CoVeriTest, which stands for cooperative verifier-based testing. CoVeriTest iteratively executes a given sequence of reachability analyses. In each iteration, the analyses are run in sequence and each analysis is limited by its individual, but configurable time limit. Furthermore, CoVeriTest allows the analysis to share various types of analysis information, e.g., which paths are infeasible, have already been explored, or which abstraction level to use. To get access to a large set of reachability analyses, we implemented CoVeriTest in the configurable software-analysis framework CPAchecker [15]. We used our implementation to evaluate different CoVeriTest configurations on a large set of well-established benchmark programs and to compare CoVeriTest with existing state-of-the-art test-generation techniques. Our experiments confirm that reachability analyses are valuable for test generation.

Contributions. In summary, we make the following contributions:

- We introduce CoVeriTest, a flexible approach for high-level interleaving of reachability analyses with information exchange for test generation.
- We perform an extensive evaluation of CoVeriTest studying 54 different configurations and two state-of-the-art test-generation tools[1].
- CoVeriTest and all our experimental data are publically available[2] [13].

2 Testing with Verifiers

The basic idea behind testing with verifiers is to derive test cases from counterexamples [5,61]. Thus, meeting a test goal during verification has to trigger a specification violation. First, we remind the reader of some basic notations.

[1] We choose the best two tools VeriFuzz and Klee from the international competition on software testing (Test-Comp 2019) [4]. https://test-comp.sosy-lab.org/2019/

[2] https://www.sosy-lab.org/research/coop-testgen/

Programs. Following literature [9], we represent programs by control-flow automata (CFAs). A CFA $P = (L, \ell_0, G)$ consists of a set L of program locations (the program-counter values), an initial program location $\ell_0 \in L$, and a set of control-flow edges $G \subseteq L \times Ops \times L$. The set Ops describes all possible operations, e.g., assume statements (resulting from conditions in `if` or `while` statements) and assignments. For the program semantics, we rely on an operational semantics, which we do not further specify.

Abstract Reachability Graph (ARG). ARGs record the work done by reachability analyses. An ARG is constructed for a program $P = (L, \ell_0, G)$ and stores (a) the abstract state space that has been explored so far, (b) which abstract states must still be explored, and (c) what abstraction level (tracked variables, considered predicates, etc.) is used. Technically, an ARG is a five-tuple $(N, succ, root, F, \pi)$ that consists of a set N of abstract states, a special node $root \in N$ that represents the initial states of program P, a relation $succ \subseteq N \times G \times N$ that records already explored successor relations, a set $F \subseteq N$ of frontier nodes, which remembers all nodes that have not been fully explored, and a precision π describing the abstraction level. Every ARG must ensure that a node n is either contained in F or completely explored, i.e., all abstract successors have been explored. We use ARGs for information exchange between reachability analyses.

Test Goals. In this paper, we are interested in structural coverage, e.g., branch coverage. Transferred to our notion of programs, this means that our test goals are a subset of the program's control-flow edges. For using a verifier to generate tests, we have to encode the test goals as a specification violation. Figure 2 shows a possible encoding, which uses a protocol automaton. Whenever a test goal is executed, the automaton transits from the initial, safe state q_0 to the accepting state q_e, which marks a property violation. Note that reachability analyses, which we consider for test generation, can easily monitor such specifications during exploration.

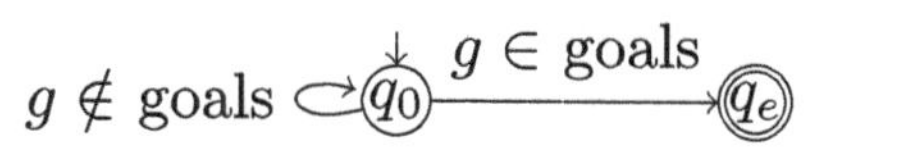

Fig. 2. Encoding test goals as specification violation

Now, we have everything at hand to describe how reachability analyses generate tests. Algorithm 1 shows the test-generation process. The algorithm gets as input a program, a set of test goals, and a time limit for test generation. For cooperative test generation, we need to guide state-space explorations. To this end, we also provide an initial ARG and a condition. A condition is a concept known from conditional model checking [10] and describes which parts of the state space have already been explored by other verifiers. A verifier, e.g., a reachability analysis, can use a condition to ignore the already explored parts of the state space. Verifiers that do not understand conditions can safely ignore them.

At the beginning, Alg. 1 sets up the data structures for the test suite and the set of covered goals. To set up the specification, it follows the idea of Fig. 2. As long as not all test goals are covered, there exist abstract states that must be explored, and the time limit has not elapsed, the algorithm tries to generate new tests. Therefore, it resumes the exploration of the current ARG [5] taking into

Algorithm 1. Generating tests with a (conditional) reachability analysis

Input: prog = (L, ℓ_0, G), goals $\subseteq G$, limit $\in \mathbb{N}$, arg =(N,succ, root, F, π), condition ψ

Output: generated test_suite, covered goals, updated arg

```
test_suite=∅;   covered=∅;
φ=generate_specification(goals);

while (goals ≠ ∅ and arg.F ≠ ∅ and elapsed_time<limit) do
    arg = explore(prog, φ, arg, ψ, limit − elapsed_time);

    if (arg.F ≠ ∅ and elapsed_time<limit) then
        τ = extract_counterexample_trace(arg);
        test_suite = test_suite ∪ generate_test_from_trace(τ);

        goals = goals\{last_edge(τ)};   covered = covered ∪ {last_edge(τ)}

    φ=generate_specification(goals);
return (test_suite, covered, arg);
```

account program prog, specification φ, and (if understood) the condition ψ. If the exploration stops, then it returns an updated ARG. Exploration stops due to one of three reasons: (1) the state space is explored completely ($F = \emptyset$), (2) the time limit is reached, or (3) a counterexample has been found.[3] In the latter case, a new test is generated. First, a counterexample trace is extracted from the ARG. The trace describes a path through the ARG that starts at the root and its last edge is a test goal (the reason for the specification violation). Next, a test is constructed from the path and added to the test suite. Basically, the path is converted into a formula and a satisfying assignment[4] is used as the test case. For the details, we refer the reader to the work that defined the method [5]. Additionally, the covered goal (last edge on the counterexample path) is removed from the set of open test goals and added to the set of covered goals. Finally, the specification is updated to no longer consider the covered goal. When the algorithm finishes, it returns the generated test suite, the set of covered goals and the last ARG considered. The ARG is returned to enable cooperation.

3 CoVeriTest

The previous section described how to use a single reachability analysis to produce tests for covering a set of test goals. Due to different strengths and weaknesses, some test goals are harder to cover for one analysis than for another. To

[3] We assume that an exploration is only complete if no counterexample exists.

[4] We assume that only feasible counterexamples are contained and infeasible counterexamples were eliminated by the reachability analysis during exploration.

Algorithm 2. CoVeriTest: alternating reachability analyses to generate tests

```
Input: prog = (L, ℓ0, G), goals ⊆ G, total_limit ∈ ℕ, configs ∈ (analysis × ℕ)+
Output: test_suite
 1: test_suite=∅;  args=⟨⟩;  current=0;
 2: while (goals ≠ ∅ and elapsed_time<total_limit) do
 3:     analysis = configs[current].first;  limit = configs[current].second;
 4:     (arg,ψ) = cooperateAndInit(prog, args, configs.length);
 5:     (tests, covered, arg) = analysis(prog, goals, limit, arg, ψ);
 6:     test_suite=test_suite ∪ tests; goals=goals\covered; args=args ∘⟨arg⟩;
 7:     if (arg.F=∅) then
 8:         return test_suite;
 9:     current = (current+1) % configs.length;
10: return test_suite;
```

maximize the number of covered goals, different analyses should be combined. In CoVeriTest, we rotate analyses for test generation. Thus, we avoid that analyses try to cover the same goal in parallel and we do not need to know in advance which analysis can cover which goals. Moreover, analyses that get stuck trying to cover goals that other analyses handle later, get a chance to recover. Additionally, CoVeriTest supports cooperation among analyses. More concrete: analyses may extract and use information from ARGs constructed by previous analysis runs.

Algorithm 2 describes the CoVeriTest workflow. It gets four inputs. Program, test goals, and time limit are already known from Alg. 1 (test generation with a single analysis). Additionally, CoVeriTest gets a sequence of configurations, namely pairs of reachability analysis and time limit. The time limit accompanied with the analysis restricts the runtime of the respective analysis per call (see line 5). In contrast to Alg. 1, CoVeriTest does not get an ARG or condition. To enable cooperation between analyses, CoVeriTest constructs these two elements individually for each analysis run. During construction, it may extract and use information from results of previous analysis runs.

After initializing the test suite and the data structure to store analysis results (`args`), CoVeriTest repeatedly iterates over the configurations. It starts with the first pair in the sequence and finishes iterating when its time limit exceeded or all goals are covered. In each iteration, CoVeriTest first extracts the analysis to execute and its accompanied time limit (line 3). Then, it constructs the remaining inputs of the analysis: ARG and condition. Details regarding the construction are explained later in Alg. 3. Next, CoVeriTest executes the current analysis with the given program, the remaining test goals, the accompanied time limit, and the constructed ARG and condition. When the analysis has finished, CoVeriTest adds the returned tests to its test suite, removes all test goals covered by the analysis run from the set of goals, and stores the analysis result for cooperation (concatenates `arg` to the sequence of ARGs). If the analysis finished its exploration (`arg`.F=∅), any remaining test goal should be unreachable and

Algorithm 3. cooperateAndInit: set up start point for analysis exploration, possibly transferring knowledge from previous analysis runs

Input: prog = (L, ℓ_0, G), args $\in (arg)^+$, numAnalyses $\in \mathbb{N}$
Output: ARG for program prog, condition describing explored state space

```
ψ=false;    π = ∅;    root = (ℓ0, ⊤);
if (length(args)≥numAnalyses) then
    if (reuse-arg) then
        return (last_arg_of_analysis(numAnalyses, args), ψ);
    if (reuse-precision) then
        π = last_arg_of_analysis(numAnalyses, args).π;
if (use-condition ∧ length(args)>0) then
    ψ = extract_condition(args[length(args)-1]);
return (({root}, ∅, root, {root}, π), ψ);
```

CoVeriTest returns its test suite. Otherwise, CoVeriTest determines how to continue in the next iteration (i.e., which configuration to consider). At the end of all iterations, CoVeriTest returns its generated test suite.

Next, we explain how to construct the ARG and the condition input for an analysis. The ARG describes the level of abstraction and where to continue exploration while the condition describes which parts of the state space have already been explored. Both guide the exploration of an analysis, which makes them well-suited for cooperation. While there are plenty of possibilities for cooperation, we currently only support three basic options: continue exploration of the previous ARG of the analysis (`reuse-arg`), reuse the analysis' abstraction level (`reuse-precision`), and restrict the exploration to the state space left out by the previous analysis (`use-condition`). The first two options only ensure that an analysis does not loose too much information due to switching. The last option, which is inspired by abstraction-driven concolic execution [32], indeed realizes cooperation between different analyses. Note that the last two options can also be combined.[5] If all options are turned off, no information will be exchanged.

Algorithm 3 shows the cooperative initialization of ARG and condition discussed above. It gets three inputs: the program, a sequence of args needed to realize cooperation, and the number of analyses used. At the beginning, it initializes the ARG components and the condition assuming no cooperation should be done. The condition states that nothing has been explored, the abstraction level becomes the coarsest available, and the ARG root considers the start of all program executions (initial program location and arbitrary variable values). If no cooperation is configured or the ARG required for cooperation is not available (e.g., in the first round), the returned ARG and condition tell the analysis to explore the complete state space from scratch. In all other cases, the analysis will be guided by information obtained in previous iterations. Option `reuse-arg`

[5] In contrast, the options `reuse-arg` and `use-conditions` cannot be combined because they are incompatible. The existing ARG does not fit to the constructed condition. Since `reuse-arg` subsumes `reuse-precision`, a combination makes no sense.

looks up the last ARG of the analysis stored in `args`. `Reuse-precision` considers the same ARG as `reuse-arg`, but only provides the ARG's precision π. For `use-condition`, a condition is constructed from the last ARG in args. For the details of the condition construction, we refer to conditional model checking [10].

Next, we study the effectiveness of different CoVeriTest configurations and compare CoVeriTest with existing test-generation tools.

4 Evaluation

We systematically evaluate CoVeriTest along the following claims:

Claim 1. For analyses that discard their own results from previous iterations (i.e., `reuse-arg` and `reuse-precision` turned off), CoVeriTest achieves higher coverage if switches between analyses happen rarely. *Evaluation Plan:* We look at CoVeriTest configurations in which analyses discard their own, previous results and compare the number of covered test goals reported by configurations that only differ in the analyses' time limits.

Claim 2. For analyses that reuse knowledge from their own, previous execution (i.e., `reuse-arg` or `reuse-precision` turned on), CoVeriTest achieves higher coverage if favoring more powerful analyses. *Evaluation Plan:* We look at CoVeriTest configurations in which analyses reuse their own, previous knowledge and compare the number of covered test goals reported by configurations that only differ in the analyses' time limits.

Claim 3. CoVeriTest performs better if analyses reuse knowledge from their own, previous execution (i.e., `reuse-arg` or `reuse-precision` turned on). *Evaluation Plan:* From all sets of CoVeriTest configurations that only differ in the analyses' time limits, we select the best and compare these.

Claim 4. Interleaving multiple analyses with CoVeriTest often achieves better results than using only one of the analyses for test generation. *Evaluation Plan:* We compare the number of covered goals reported by the best CoVeriTest configuration with those numbers achieved when running only one analysis of the CoVeriTest configuration for the total time limit.

Claim 5. Interleaving verifiers for test generation is often better than running them in parallel. *Evaluation Plan:* We compare the number of covered goals reported by the best CoVeriTest configuration with the number achieved when running all analyses of the CoVeriTest configuration in parallel.

Claim 6. CoVeriTest complements existing test-generation tools. *Evaluation Plan:* We use the same infrastructure and resources as used by the International Competition on Software Testing (Test-Comp'19)[6] and let the best CoVeriTest configuration construct test suites. These test suites are executed by the Test-Comp'19 validator to measure the achieved branch coverage. Then, we compare the coverage achieved by CoVeriTest with the coverage of the best two test-generation tools from Test-Comp'19.

[6] https://test-comp.sosy-lab.org/2019/

4.1 Setup

CoVeriTest Configurations. We implemented CoVeriTest in the software analysis framework CPAchecker [15]. Basically, we implemented Algs. 1, 2 and integrated Alg. 3 into Alg. 2. For condition construction, we reuse the code from conditional model checking [10]. For our experiments, we combine value [18] and predicate analysis [16]. Both have been used in cooperative verification [10,11,21].

Value analysis. CPAchecker's value analysis [18] tracks the values of variables stored in its current precision explicitly while assuming that the remaining variables may have any possible value. It iteratively increases its precision, i.e., the variables to track, combining counterexample-guided abstraction [28] with path-prefix slicing [22], and refinement selection [21]. Value analysis is efficient if few variable values need to be tracked, but it may get stuck in loops or suffers from a large state space in case variables are assigned many different values.

Predicate analysis. CPAchecker's predicate analysis uses predicate abstraction with adjustable-block encoding (ABE) [16]. ABE is configured to abstract at loop heads and uses the strongest postcondition at all remaining locations. To compute the set of predicates—its precision—, it uses counterexample-guided abstraction refinement [28] combined with lazy refinement [43] and interpolation [41]. While the predicate analysis is powerful and often summarizes loops easily, successor computation may require expensive SMT solver calls.

For both analyses, a CoVeriTest configuration specifies how Alg. 3 reuses the ARGs returned by previous analysis runs to set up the initial ARG and condition. In our experiments, we consider the following types of reuses.

plain Ignores all ARGs returned by previous analysis runs, i.e., `reuse-arg`, `reuse-prec`, and `use-condition` are turned off.

cond$_\mathrm{v}$ The value analysis does not obtain information from previous ARGs and the predicate analysis is only steered by the condition extracted from the ARG returned by the previous value analysis.

cond$_\mathrm{p}$ The value analysis is steered by the condition extracted from the ARG returned by the previous run of the predicate analysis and the predicate analysis ignores all previous ARGs.

cond$_\mathrm{v,p}$ Value and predicate analysis are steered by the condition extracted from the last ARG returned, i.e., only `use-condition` turned on.

reuse-prec In each round, each analysis resumes its precision from the previous round, but restarts exploration, i.e., only `reuse-prec` is turned on.

reuse-arg In each round, each analysis continues to explore the ARG it returned in the previous round, i.e., only `reuse-arg` is turned on.

cond$_\mathrm{v}$+r Similar to cond$_\mathrm{v}$, but additionally the value analysis continues to explore the ARG it returned in the previous round and the predicate analysis restarts exploration with its precision from the previous round.

cond$_\mathrm{p}$+r Similar to cond$_\mathrm{p}$, but additionally the value analysis restarts exploration with its precision from the previous round and the predicate analysis continues to explore the ARG it returned in the previous round.

cond$_\mathrm{v,p}$+r Like cond$_\mathrm{v,p}$, but additionally the value and predicate analysis reuse their previous precision, i.e., `reuse-prec` and `use-condition` are turned on.

Finally, we need to fix the time limit for each analysis. We want to find out whether switches between analyses are important to the CoVeriTest approach. Therefore, we chose four limits (10 s, 50 s, 100 s, 250 s) that are applied to both analyses and trigger switches often, sometimes, or rarely. Additionally, we want to study whether it is advantageous if the time CoVeriTest spends in a round is not equally spread among the analyses. Thus, we come up with two additional time limit pairs: (20 s, 80 s) and (80 s, 20 s).

We combine all nine reuse types with the six time limit pairs, which results in 54 CoVeriTest configurations. All 54 configurations aim at generating tests to cover the assume edges of a program.

Tools. For CoVeriTest, we used the implementation in CPAchecker version 29 347. Moreover, we compare CoVeriTest against the two best tools VeriFuzz [26] and Klee [23] from Test-Comp'19 (in the versions submitted to Test-Comp'19[7]). The tool VeriFuzz is based on the evolutionary fuzzer AFL and uses verification techniques to compute initial input values and parameters for AFL. Klee applies symbolic execution. To compare CoVeriTest against Klee and VeriFuzz, we use the validator TBF Test-Suite Validator v1.2[8] to measure branch coverage. TBF Test-Suite Validator is based on gcov[9].

Programs. CoVeriTest, Klee, and VeriFuzz produce tests for C programs. All three tools participated in TestComp'19. Thus, for comparison of the three tools, we consider all 1 720 tasks of the TestComp'19 benchmark set[10] that support the branch-coverage property. Since we do not need to execute tests for the comparison of the different CoVeriTest configurations, we evaluated them on a larger benchmark set, which contains all 6 703 C programs from the well-established SV-benchmark set[11] in the version tagged svcomp18.

Computing Resources. We run our experiments on machines with 33 GB of memory and an Intel Xeon E3-1230 v5 CPU with 8 processing units and a frequency of 3.4 GHz. The underlying operating system is Ubuntu 18.04 with Linux kernel 4.15. As in TestComp'19, for test generation we grant each run a maximum of 8 processing units, 15 min of CPU time, and 15 GB of memory, and for test-suite execution (required to compare against Klee and VeriFuzz), the TBF Test-Suite Validator is granted 2 processing units, 3 h of CPU time, and 7 GB of memory per run. We use BenchExec [20] to enforce the limits of a run.

Availability. Our experimental data are available online[12] [13].

---

7 https://gitlab.com/sosy-lab/test-comp/archives-2019/tree/testcomp19/2019
8 https://gitlab.com/sosy-lab/test-comp/archives-2019/blob/testcomp19/2019/tbf-testsuite-validator.zip
9 https://gcc.gnu.org/onlinedocs/gcc/Gcov.html
10 https://github.com/sosy-lab/sv-benchmarks/tree/testcomp19
11 https://github.com/sosy-lab/sv-benchmarks
12 https://www.sosy-lab.org/research/coop-testgen/

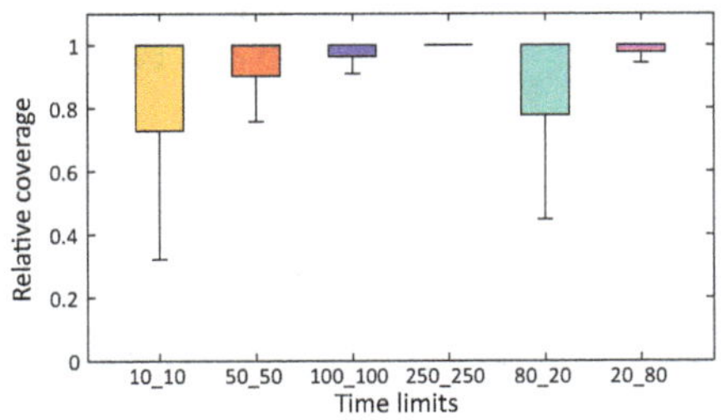

(a) Reuse type plain

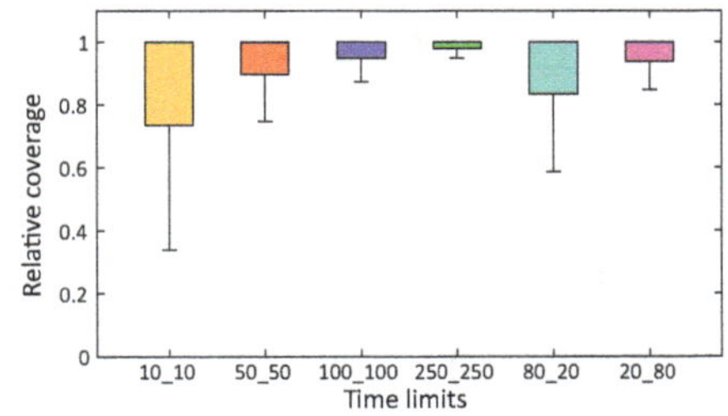

(b) Reuse type $\text{cond}_{\text{v,p}}$

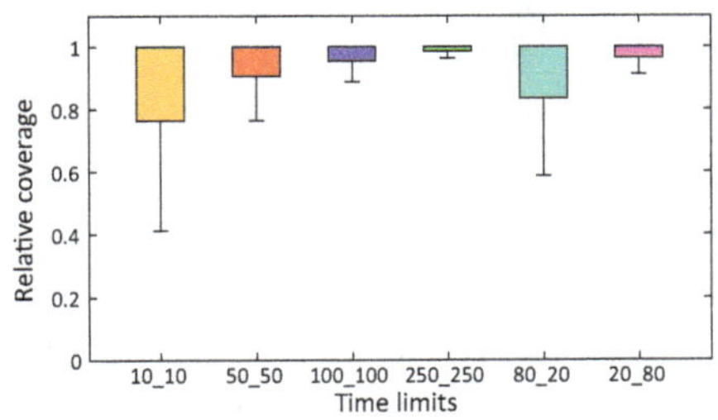

(c) Reuse type cond_{v}

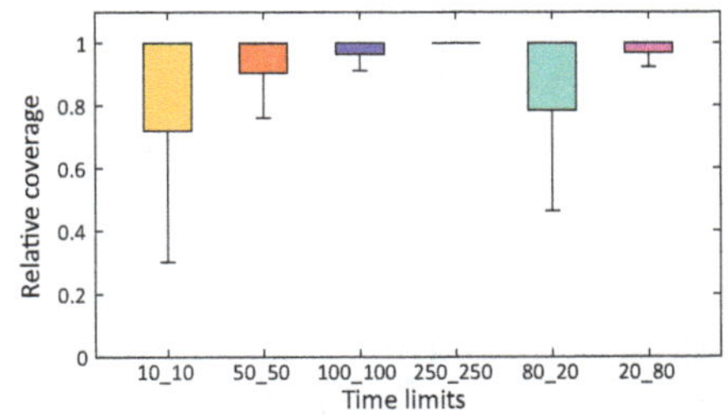

(d) Reuse type cond_{p}

Fig. 3. Comparing relative coverage (number of covered goals divided by maximal number of covered goals) achieved by CoVeriTest configurations with different time limits. All configurations let analyses discard their own knowledge gained in previous executions.

4.2 Experiments

Claim 1 (Reduce switching when discarding own results). Four types of reuse (namely, plain, cond_{v}, cond_{p}, and $\text{cond}_{\text{v,p}}$) let the analyses discard their own knowledge from their previous executions. For each of these types, we compare the coverage achieved by all six CoVeriTest configurations that use this type[13]. More concrete, for all six CoVeriTest configurations applying the same reuse type, we first compute for each program the maximum over the number of covered goals achieved by each of these six configurations for that program. Then, for each of the six CoVeriTest configurations that use that reuse type, we divide the number of covered goals achieved for a program by the respective maximum computed. We call this measure *relative coverage* because the value is relative to the maximum and not the total number of goals. Figure 3 shows box plots per reuse type. The box plots show the distribution of the relative coverage. The closer the bottom border of a box is to value one, the higher coverage is achieved. For all four reuse types, the fourth box plot has the bottom border closest to value one. Since the fourth box plot is a configuration that grants each analysis 250 s per round (highest limit considered, only three switches), the claim holds.

Claim 2 (Favor powerful analysis when reusing own results). Five types of reuse (namely, reuse-prec, reuse-arg, cond_{v}+r, cond_{p}+r, and $\text{cond}_{\text{v,p}}$+r) let analyses reuse knowledge from their own, previous execution. Similar to the previous claim, we compute for each of these types the relative coverage of all six configurations using this particular type of reuse. For each reuse type,

[13] Note that those six configurations only differ in the analyses' time limits.

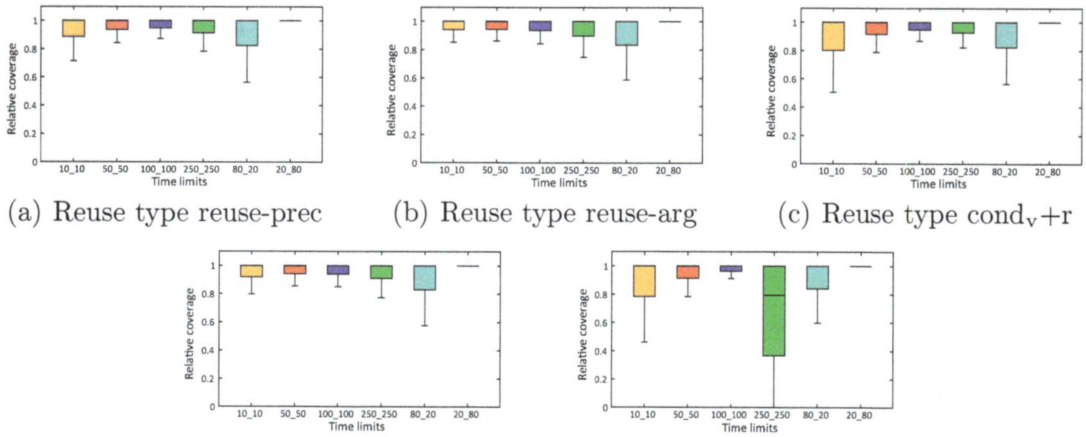

(a) Reuse type reuse-prec (b) Reuse type reuse-arg (c) Reuse type cond_v+r

(d) Reuse type cond_p+r (e) Reuse type $\text{cond}_{\text{v,p}}$+r

Fig. 4. Comparing relative coverage (number of covered goals divided by maximal number of covered goals) achieved by CoVeriTest configurations when using different time limits and a fixed reuse type. All considered configurations let analyses reuse knowledge from their own, previous execution.

Fig. 4 shows box plots of the distributions of the relative coverage. As before, a bottom border closer to value one reflects higher coverage. In all five cases, the last box plot has the bottom border closest to value one. The last box plots represent CoVeriTest configurations that grant the value analysis 20 s and the predicate analysis 80 s in each round. Since the predicate analysis, which gets more time per round, is more powerful than the value analysis, our claim is valid.[14]

Claim 3 (Better reuse own results). So far, we know how to configure time limits. Now, we want to find out how to reuse information from previous analysis runs. For each reuse type, we select from the six available configurations the configuration that performed best. Again, we use the relative coverage to compare the resulting nine configurations. Figure 5 shows box plots of the distributions of the relative coverage. The first four box plots show configurations in which analyses discard their own results, while the last five box plots refer to configurations in which analyses reuse knowledge from their own, previous executions. Since the last five boxes are smaller than the first four and their bottom borders are closer to one, the last five configurations achieve higher coverage. Hence, our claim holds. Moreover, from Fig. 5 we conclude that it is best to reuse the ARG (although cond_v+r and cond_p+r are close by).

Claim 4 (Interleave multiple analyses rather than use one of them). To evaluate whether CoVeriTest benefits from interleaving, we compare CoVeriTest against the analyses used by it. CoVeriTest interleaves value and predicate analysis. Figure 6(a) and 6(b) show scatter plots that compare for each program the coverage, i.e., number of covered goals divided by number of total goals, achieved by the best CoVeriTest configuration (x-axis) with the coverage achieved when only using either value or predicate analysis for test generation. Note that we excluded those programs from the scatter plots, for which we miss

[14] This insight is independently partially backed by a sequential combination of explicit-value analysis and predicate analysis that performed well in SV-COMP 2013 [62].

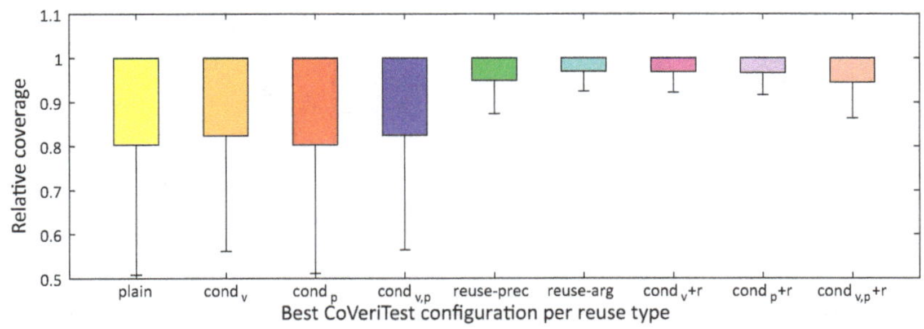

Fig. 5. Comparing relative coverage achieved by CoVeriTest configurations applying different strategies to reuse information gained by previous verifier runs.

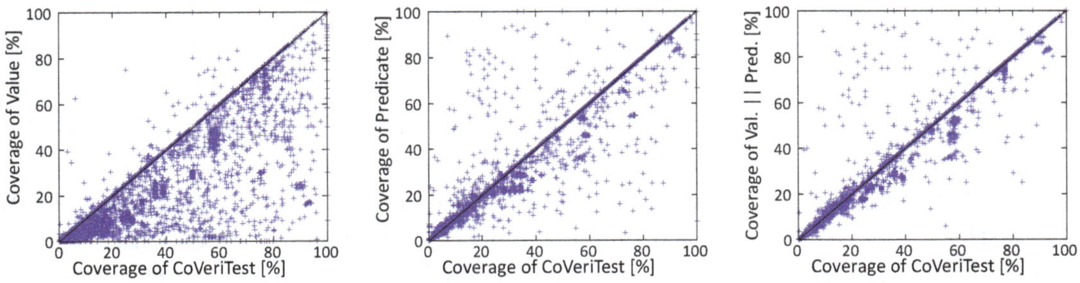

(a) CoVeriTest (x-axis) vs. value analysis

(b) CoVeriTest (x-axis) vs. predicate analysis

(c) CoVeriTest (x-axis) vs. value and predicate analysis in parallel

Fig. 6. Compares the coverage achieved by CoVeriTest (best configuration) with the coverage achieved when running CoVeriTest's analyses alone or in parallel

the number of covered goals for at least one test generator, e.g., due to timeout of the analysis. Figure 6(a) compares CoVeriTest and value analysis; we see that almost all points are in the lower right half. Thus, CoVeriTest typically achieves higher coverage than value analysis alone. Figure 6(b), comparing CoVeriTest with predicate analysis, is more diverse. About 54% of the points are on the diagonal, i.e., CoVeriTest and predicate analysis cover the same number of goals. The upper left half contains 19% of the points, i.e., predicate analysis alone achieves higher coverage. These points for example reflect float programs and ECA programs without arithmetic computations. In contrast, CoVeriTest achieves higher coverage in 27% of the programs. CoVeriTest is beneficial for programs that only need few variable values to trigger the branches, like ssh programs or programs from the product-lines subcategory. CoVeriTest also profits from the value analysis when considering ECA programs with arithmetic computations, since the variables have a fixed value in each loop iteration. All in all, CoVeriTest performs slightly better than predicate analysis alone.

Claim 5 (Interleave rather than parallelize). Figure 6(c) shows a scatter plot that compares for each program the coverage achieved by CoVeriTest (x-axis) and a test generator that runs the value analysis and the predicate analysis in parallel[15]. As before, we exclude programs for which

[15] The test generator uses CPAchecker's parallel algorithm and lets the two analyses share information about covered test goals.

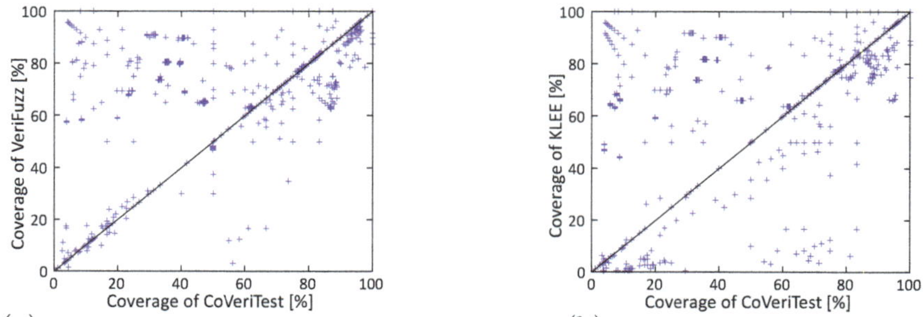

(a) CoVeriTest vs. VeriFuzz (b) CoVeriTest vs. Klee

Fig. 7. Compares the branch coverage achieved by CoVeriTest (best configuration) with the branch coverage achieved by existing state-of-the-art test-generation tools

we could not get the number of covered goals for at least one of the analyses. Looking at Fig. 6(c), we observe that many points (60%) are on the diagonal, i.e., the achieved coverage is identical. Moreover, CoVeriTest performs better for 30% (lower right half), while approximately 10% of the points are in the upper left half. Since CoVeriTest achieves the same or better coverage results in about 90% of the cases, it should be preferred over parallelization. This is no surprise since we showed that a test generator should favor the more powerful analysis (which CoVeriTest does, but parallelization evenly distributes CPU time).

Claim 6 (CoVeriTest complementary). Our goal is to compare CoVeriTest and the two best tools of Test-Comp'19 [4]: VeriFuzz and Klee. All three tools aim at constructing test suites with high branch coverage. Thus, we use branch coverage as comparison criterion. We measure branch coverage with TBF Test-Suite Validator. Figure 7 shows two scatter plots. Each plot compares branch coverage achieved by CoVeriTest and by one of the other techniques.[16] Points in the lower right half indicate that CoVeriTest achieved higher coverage. Looking at the two scatter plots, we observe that there exist programs for which CoVeriTest performs better and vice versa. Generally, we observed that CoVeriTest has problems with array tasks and ECA tasks. We already know from verification that CPAchecker sometimes lacks refinement support for array tasks. Moreover, the problem with the ECA tasks is that CPAchecker splits conditions with conjunctions or disjunctions—which ECA tasks contain a lot—into multiple assume edges. Thus, the number of test goals is much larger than the actual branches to be covered. However, CoVeriTest seems to benefit from splitting for some of the float tasks. Additionally, CoVeriTest is often better on tasks of the sequentialized subcategory. We think that CoVeriTest benefits from the value analysis since the tasks of the sequentialized subcategory contain lots of branch conditions checking for a specific value or interpreting variable values as booleans. All in all, CoVeriTest is not always best, but is also not dominated. Thus, CoVeriTest complements the existing approaches.

[16] Note that the scatter plots only contain points that have a positive x and y value because there exist different reasons (timeout, out of memory, tool failure, etc.) why we might get no or a zero coverage value from the test validator. The plots contain points for about 98% of the 1 720 programs.

4.3 Threats to Validity

All our CoVeriTest configurations consider the same two analyses. Our results might not apply if using CoVeriTest with a different set of analyses. In our experiments, we used benchmark programs instead of real-world applications. Although the benchmark set is diverse and well-established, our results may not carry over into practice.

The validator TBF Test-Suite Validator might contain bugs that result in wrong coverage numbers. However, the validator was used in Test-Comp'19 already, and is based on the well-established coverage-measurement tool `gcov`.

For the comparison of the CoVeriTest configurations as well as the comparison of CoVeriTest with the single analyses and the parallel approach, we relied on the number of covered goals reported by CoVeriTest. Invalid counterexamples could be used to cover test goals. The analyses used by CoVeriTest apply CEGAR approaches and should detect spurious counterexamples. Moreover, these analyses run in the SV-COMP configuration of CPAchecker and are tuned to not report false results. Another problem is that whenever CPAchecker does not output statistics (due to timeout, out of memory, etc.), we use the last number of covered goals reported in the log. However, this might be an underapproximation of the number of covered goals. All these problems do not occur in the comparison of CoVeriTest with Klee and VeriFuzz, in which the coverage is measured by the validator. Thus, this comparison still supports the value of CoVeriTest.

5 Related Work

CoVeriTest interleaves reachability analyses to construct tests for C programs. To enable cooperation, CoVeriTest extracts information from ARGs constructed by previous analysis runs.

A few tools use reachability analyses for test generation. Blast [5] considers a target predicate p and generates a test for each program location that can be reached with a state fulfilling the predicate p. For test generation, Blast uses predicate abstraction. FShell [44–46] and CPA/Tiger [12] generate tests for a coverage criterion specified in the FShell query language (FQL) [46]. Both transform the FQL specification into a set of test-goal automata and check for each automaton whether its final state can be reached. FShell uses CBMC to answer those reachability queries and CPA/Tiger uses predicate abstraction.

Various combinations have been proposed for verification [2,10,11,14,25,27, 29–31,35,37,40,50,64] and test-suite generation [1,32,34,36,38,47,51,54,56,59, 60,63]. We focus on combinations that interleave approaches. SYNERGY [40] and DASH [2] alternate test generation and proof construction to (dis)prove a property. Similarly, SMASH [37] combines underapproximation with overapproximation. Interleaving is also used in test generation. Hybrid concolic testing [54] interleaves random testing with symbolic execution. When random testing gets stuck, symbolic execution is started from the current state. As soon as a new goal is covered, symbolic execution hands over to random testing providing the values used to cover the goal. Similarly, Driller [60] and Badger [56] combine fuzzing with concolic execution. However, they only exchange inputs. Xu et al. [51,63] interleave different approaches to augment test suites. The approach closest to CoVeriTest is abstraction-driven concolic testing [32]. Abstraction-driven concolic testing interleaves concolic execution and predicate analysis. Furthermore, it uses conditions extracted from the ARGs generated by the predicate analysis to direct the concolic execution towards feasible paths. Abstraction-driven concolic testing can be seen as one particular configuration of CoVeriTest.

Also, ARG information has been reused in different contexts. Precision reuse [19] uses the precision determined in a previous analysis run to reverify a modified program. Similarly, extreme model checking [42] adapts an ARG constructed in a previous analysis to fit to the modified program. CPA/Tiger [12] transforms an ARG that was constructed for one test goal such that it fits to a new test goal. Lazy abstraction refinement [43] adapts an ARG to continue exploration after abstraction refinement. Configurable program certification [48,49] constructs a certificate from an ARG, which can be used to reverify a program. Similarly, reachability tools like CPAchecker construct witnesses [6,7] from ARGs. Conditional model checking [10,14] constructs a condition from an ARG when a verifier gives up. The condition describes the remaining verification task and is used by a subsequent verifier to restrict its exploration.

6 Conclusion

Testing is a standard technique for software quality assurance. But state-of-the-art techniques still miss many bugs that involve sophisticated branching conditions [17]. It turns out that techniques performing abstract reachability analyses are well-suited for this task. They simply need to check the reachability of every branch and generate a test for each positive check. However, in practice, for every such technique there exist reachability queries on which the technique is inefficient or fails [8]. We propose CoVeriTest to overcome these practical limitations. CoVeriTest interleaves different reachability analyses for test generation. We experimented with various configurations of CoVeriTest, which vary in the time limits of the analyses and the type of information exchanged between different analysis runs. CoVeriTest works best when each analysis resumes its exploration, different analyses only share test goals, and more powerful analyses get larger time budgets. Moreover, a comparison of CoVeriTest with (a) the reachability analyses used by CoVeriTest and (b) state-of-the-art test-generation tools witness the benefits of the new CoVeriTest approach.

CoVeriTest participated in Test-Comp 2019 [4] and achieved rank 3 (out of 9) in both categories, bug finding and branch coverage.[17]

In future, we plan to integrate further analyses, e.g., bounded model checking or symbolic execution, into CoVeriTest and to evaluate CoVeriTest on real-world applications.

[17] https://test-comp.sosy-lab.org/2019/results/

References

1. Baars, A.I., Harman, M., Hassoun, Y., Lakhotia, K., McMinn, P., Tonella, P., Vos, T.E.J.: Symbolic search-based testing. In: Proc. ASE, pp. 53–62. IEEE (2011). https://doi.org/10.1109/ASE.2011.6100119
2. Beckman, N., Nori, A.V., Rajamani, S.K., Simmons, R.J.: Proofs from tests. In: Proc. ISSTA, pp. 3–14. ACM (2008). https://doi.org/10.1145/1390630.1390634
3. Beyer, D.: Software verification with validation of results (Report on SV-COMP 2017). In: Proc. TACAS, LNCS, vol. 10206, pp. 331–349. Springer, Heidelberg (2017). https://doi.org/10.1007/978-3-662-54580-5_20
4. Beyer, D.: International competition on software testing (Test-Comp). In: Proc. TACAS, Part 3, LNCS, vol. 11429, pp. 167–175. Springer, Cham (2019). https://doi.org/10.1007/978-3-030-17502-3_11
5. Beyer, D., Chlipala, A.J., Henzinger, T.A., Jhala, R., Majumdar, R.: Generating tests from counterexamples. In: Proc. ICSE, pp. 326–335. IEEE (2004). https://doi.org/10.1109/ICSE.2004.1317455
6. Beyer, D., Dangl, M., Dietsch, D., Heizmann, M.: Correctness witnesses: Exchanging verification results between verifiers. In: Proc. FSE, pp. 326–337. ACM (2016). https://doi.org/10.1145/2950290.2950351
7. Beyer, D., Dangl, M., Dietsch, D., Heizmann, M., Stahlbauer, A.: Witness validation and stepwise testification across software verifiers. In: Proc. FSE, pp. 721–733. ACM (2015). https://doi.org/10.1145/2786805.2786867
8. Beyer, D., Dangl, M., Wendler, P.: A unifying view on SMT-based software verification. J. Autom. Reasoning **60**(3), 299–335 (2018). https://doi.org/10.1007/s10817-017-9432-6
9. Beyer, D., Gulwani, S., Schmidt, D.: Combining model checking and data-flow analysis. In: Clarke, E.M., Henzinger, T.A., Veith, H. (eds.) Handbook on Model Checking, pp. 493–540. Springer, Cham (2018). https://doi.org/10.1007/978-3-319-10575-8_16
10. Beyer, D., Henzinger, T.A., Keremoglu, M.E., Wendler, P.: Conditional model checking: A technique to pass information between verifiers. In: Proc. FSE, pp. 57:1–57:11. ACM (2012). https://doi.org/10.1145/2393596.2393664
11. Beyer, D., Henzinger, T.A., Théoduloz, G.: Program analysis with dynamic precision adjustment. In: Proc. ASE, pp. 29–38. IEEE (2008). http://dx.doi.org/10.1109/ASE.2008.13
12. Beyer, D., Holzer, A., Tautschnig, M., Veith, H.: Information reuse for multi-goal reachability analyses. In: Proc. ESOP, LNCS, vol. 7792, pp. 472–491. Springer, Heidelberg (2013). https://doi.org/10.1007/978-3-642-37036-6_26
13. Beyer, D., Jakobs, M.C.: Replication package for article "CoVeriTest: Cooperative verifier-based testing" in Proc. FASE 2019. Zenodo (2019). https://doi.org/10.5281/zenodo.2566735
14. Beyer, D., Jakobs, M.C., Lemberger, T., Wehrheim, H.: Reducer-based construction of conditional verifiers. In: Proc. ICSE, pp. 1182–1193. ACM (2018). https://doi.org/10.1145/3180155.3180259
15. Beyer, D., Keremoglu, M.E.: CPAchecker: A tool for configurable software verification. In: Proc. CAV, LNCS, vol. 6806, pp. 184–190. Springer, Heidelberg (2011). https://doi.org/10.1007/978-3-642-22110-1_16

16. Beyer, D., Keremoglu, M.E., Wendler, P.: Predicate abstraction with adjustable-block encoding. In: Proc. FMCAD, pp. 189–197. FMCAD (2010). http://ieeexplore.ieee.org/document/5770949/
17. Beyer, D., Lemberger, T.: Software verification: Testing vs. model checking. In: Proc. HVC, LNCS, vol. 10629, pp. 99–114. Springer, Cham (2017). https://doi.org/10.1007/978-3-319-70389-3_7
18. Beyer, D., Löwe, S.: Explicit-state software model checking based on CEGAR and interpolation. In: Proc. FASE, LNCS, vol. 7793, pp. 146–162. Springer, Heidelberg (2013). https://doi.org/10.1007/978-3-642-37057-1_11
19. Beyer, D., Löwe, S., Novikov, E., Stahlbauer, A., Wendler, P.: Precision reuse for efficient regression verification. In: Proc. FSE, pp. 389–399. ACM (2013). https://doi.org/10.1145/2491411.2491429
20. Beyer, D., Löwe, S., Wendler, P.: Benchmarking and resource measurement. In: Proc. SPIN, LNCS, vol. 9232, pp. 160–178. Springer, Cham (2015). https://doi.org/10.1007/978-3-319-23404-5_12
21. Beyer, D., Löwe, S., Wendler, P.: Refinement selection. In: Proc. SPIN, LNCS, vol. 9232, pp. 20–38. Springer, Cham (2015). https://doi.org/10.1007/978-3-319-23404-5_3
22. Beyer, D., Löwe, S., Wendler, P.: Sliced path prefixes: An effective method to enable refinement selection. In: Proc. FORTE, LNCS, vol. 9039, pp. 228–243. Springer, Cham (2015). https://doi.org/10.1007/978-3-319-19195-9_15
23. Cadar, C., Dunbar, D., Engler, D.R.: KLEE: Unassisted and automatic generation of high-coverage tests for complex systems programs. In: Proc. OSDI, pp. 209–224. USENIX Association (2008). http://www.usenix.org/events/osdi08/tech/full_papers/cadar/cadar.pdf
24. Chalupa, M., Vitovská, M., Strejcek, J.: SYMBIOTIC 5: Boosted instrumentation (competition contribution). In: Proc. TACAS, LNCS, vol. 10806, pp. 442–446. Springer, Cham (2018). https://doi.org/10.1007/978-3-319-89963-3_29
25. Chebaro, O., Kosmatov, N., Giorgetti, A., Julliand, J.: Program slicing enhances a verification technique combining static and dynamic analysis. In: Proc. SAC, pp. 1284–1291. ACM (2012). http://doi.acm.org/10.1145/2245276.2231980
26. Chowdhury, A.B., Medicherla, R.K., Venkatesh, R.: VeriFuzz: Program aware fuzzing. In: Proc. TACAS, Part 3, LNCS, vol. 11429, pp. 244–249. Springer, Cham (2019). https://doi.org/10.1007/978-3-030-17502-3_22
27. Christakis, M., Müller, P., Wüstholz, V.: Guiding dynamic symbolic execution toward unverified program executions. In: Proc. ICSE, pp. 144–155. ACM (2016). http://doi.acm.org/10.1145/2884781.2884843
28. Clarke, E.M., Grumberg, O., Jha, S., Lu, Y., Veith, H.: Counterexample-guided abstraction refinement for symbolic model checking. J. ACM **50**(5), 752–794 (2003). http://doi.acm.org/10.1145/876638.876643
29. Cousot, P., Cousot, R.: Systematic design of program-analysis frameworks. In: Proc. POPL, pp. 269–282. ACM (1979). http://doi.acm.org/10.1145/567752.567778
30. Csallner, C., Smaragdakis, Y.: Check 'n' crash: Combining static checking and testing. In: Proc. ICSE, pp. 422–431. ACM (2005). http://doi.acm.org/10.1145/1062455.1062533
31. Czech, M., Jakobs, M.C., Wehrheim, H.: Just test what you cannot verify! In: Proc. FASE, LNCS, vol. 9033, pp. 100–114. Springer, Heidelberg (2015). https://doi.org/10.1007/978-3-662-46675-9_7

32. Daca, P., Gupta, A., Henzinger, T.A.: Abstraction-driven concolic testing. In: Proc. VMCAI, LNCS, vol. 9583, pp. 328–347. Springer, Heidelberg (2016). https://doi.org/10.1007/978-3-662-49122-5_16
33. D'Silva, V., Kröning, D., Weissenbacher, G.: A survey of automated techniques for formal software verification. IEEE Trans. CAD Integr. Circ. Syst. **27**(7), 1165–1178 (2008). https://doi.org/10.1109/TCAD.2008.923410
34. Galeotti, J.P., Fraser, G., Arcuri, A.: Improving search-based test suite generation with dynamic symbolic execution. In: Proc. ISSRE, pp. 360–369. IEEE (2013). https://doi.org/10.1109/ISSRE.2013.6698889
35. Ge, X., Taneja, K., Xie, T., Tillmann, N.: DyTa: Dynamic symbolic execution guided with static verification results. In: Proc. ICSE, pp. 992–994. ACM (2011). http://doi.acm.org/10.1145/1985793.1985971
36. Godefroid, P., Klarlund, N., Sen, K.: DART: Directed automated random testing. In: Proc. PLDI, pp. 213–223. ACM (2005). http://doi.acm.org/10.1145/1065010.1065036
37. Godefroid, P., Nori, A.V., Rajamani, S.K., Tetali, S.: Compositional may-must program analysis: Unleashing the power of alternation. In: Proc. POPL, pp. 43–56. ACM (2010). http://doi.acm.org/10.1145/1706299.1706307
38. Godefroid, P., Levin, M.Y., Molnar, D.A.: Automated whitebox fuzz testing. In: Proc. NDSS. The Internet Society (2008)
39. Graf, S., Saïdi, H.: Construction of abstract state graphs with PVS. In: Proc. CAV, LNCS, vol. 1254, pp. 72–83. Springer, Heidelberg (1997). https://doi.org/10.1007/3-540-63166-6_10
40. Gulavani, B.S., Henzinger, T.A., Kannan, Y., Nori, A.V., Rajamani, S.K.: SYNERGY: A new algorithm for property checking. In: Proc. FSE, pp. 117–127. ACM (2006). https://doi.org/10.1145/1181775.1181790
41. Henzinger, T.A., Jhala, R., Majumdar, R., McMillan, K.L.: Abstractions from proofs. In: Proc. POPL, pp. 232–244. ACM (2004). http://doi.acm.org/10.1145/964001.964021
42. Henzinger, T.A., Jhala, R., Majumdar, R., Sanvido, M.A.A.: Extreme model checking. In: Verification: Theory and Practice, pp. 332–358. Springer, Heidelberg (2003). https://doi.org/10.1007/978-3-540-39910-0_16
43. Henzinger, T.A., Jhala, R., Majumdar, R., Sutre, G.: Lazy abstraction. In: Proc. POPL, pp. 58–70. ACM (2002). https://doi.org/10.1145/503272.503279
44. Holzer, A., Schallhart, C., Tautschnig, M., Veith, H.: FShell: Systematic test case generation for dynamic analysis and measurement. In: Gupta, A., Malik, S. (eds.) Proc. CAV, LNCS, vol. 5123, pp. 209–213. Springer, Heidelberg (2008). https://doi.org/10.1007/978-3-540-70545-1_20
45. Holzer, A., Schallhart, C., Tautschnig, M., Veith, H.: Query-driven program testing. In: Proc. VMCAI, LNCS, vol. 5403, pp. 151–166. Springer, Heidelberg (2009). https://doi.org/10.1007/978-3-540-93900-9_15
46. Holzer, A., Schallhart, C., Tautschnig, M., Veith, H.: How did you specify your test suite. In: Proc. ASE, pp. 407–416. ACM (2010). https://doi.org/10.1145/1858996.1859084
47. Inkumsah, K., Xie, T.: Improving structural testing of object-oriented programs via integrating evolutionary testing and symbolic execution. In: Proc. ASE, pp. 297–306. IEEE (2008). https://doi.org/10.1109/ASE.2008.40

48. Jakobs, M.C.: Speed up configurable certificate validation by certificate reduction and partitioning. In: Proc. SEFM, LNCS, vol. 9276, pp. 159–174. Springer, Cham (2015). https://doi.org/10.1007/978-3-319-22969-0_12
49. Jakobs, M.C., Wehrheim, H.: Certification for configurable program analysis. In: Proc. SPIN, pp. 30–39. ACM (2014). https://doi.org/10.1145/2632362.2632372
50. Jalote, P., Vangala, V., Singh, T., Jain, P.: Program partitioning: A framework for combining static and dynamic analysis. In: Proc. WODA, pp. 11–16. ACM (2006). http://doi.acm.org/10.1145/1138912.1138916
51. Kim, Y., Xu, Z., Kim, M., Cohen, M.B., Rothermel, G.: Hybrid directed test suite augmentation: An interleaving framework. In: Proc. ICST, pp. 263–272. IEEE (2014). https://doi.org/10.1109/ICST.2014.39
52. Lemieux, C., Sen, K.: FairFuzz: A targeted mutation strategy for increasing greybox fuzz testing coverage. In: Proc. ASE, pp. 475–485. ACM (2018). https://doi.org/10.1145/3238147.3238176
53. Li, J., Zhao, B., Zhang, C.: Fuzzing: A survey. Cybersecurity **1**(1), 6 (2018). https://doi.org/10.1186/s42400-018-0002-y
54. Majumdar, R., Sen, K.: Hybrid concolic testing. In: Proc. ICSE, pp. 416–426. IEEE (2007). https://doi.org/10.1109/ICSE.2007.41
55. McMinn, P.: Search-based software test data generation: A survey. Softw. Test. Verif. Reliab. **14**(2), 105–156 (2004). https://doi.org/10.1002/stvr.294
56. Noller, Y., Kersten, R., Pasareanu, C.S.: Badger: Complexity analysis with fuzzing and symbolic execution. In: Proc. ISSTA, pp. 322–332. ACM (2018). http://doi.acm.org/10.1145/3213846.3213868
57. Pacheco, C., Lahiri, S.K., Ernst, M.D., Ball, T.: Feedback-directed random test generation. In: Proc. ICSE, pp. 75–84. IEEE (2007). https://doi.org/10.1109/ICSE.2007.37
58. Pasareanu, C.S., Visser, W.: A survey of new trends in symbolic execution for software testing and analysis. STTT **11**(4), 339–353 (2009). https://doi.org/10.1007/s10009-009-0118-1
59. Sakti, A., Guéhéneuc, Y., Pesant, G.: Boosting search based testing by using constraint based testing. In: Proc. SSBSE, LNCS, vol. 7515, pp. 213–227. Springer, Heidelberg (2012). https://doi.org/10.1007/978-3-642-33119-0_16
60. Stephens, N., Grosen, J., Salls, C., Dutcher, A., Wang, R., Corbetta, J., Shoshitaishvili, Y., Kruegel, C., Vigna, G.: Driller: Augmenting fuzzing through selective symbolic execution. In: Proc. NDSS. The Internet Society (2016). http://wp.internetsociety.org/ndss/wp-content/uploads/sites/25/2017/09/driller-augmenting-fuzzing-through-selective-symbolic-execution.pdf
61. Visser, W., Păsăreanu, C.S., Khurshid, S.: Test input generation with Java PathFinder. In: Proc. ISSTA, pp. 97–107. ACM (2004). http://doi.acm.org/10.1145/1007512.1007526
62. Wendler, P.: CPAchecker with sequential combination of explicit-state analysis and predicate analysis (competition contribution). In: Proc. TACAS, LNCS, vol. 7795, pp. 613–615. Springer, Heidelberg (2013). https://doi.org/10.1007/978-3-642-36742-7_45

63. Xu, Z., Kim, Y., Kim, M., Rothermel, G.: A hybrid directed test suite augmentation technique. In: Proc. ISSRE, pp. 150–159. IEEE (2011). https://doi.org/10.1109/ISSRE.2011.21
64. Yorsh, G., Ball, T., Sagiv, M.: Testing, abstraction, theorem proving: Better together! In: Proc. ISSTA, pp. 145–156. ACM (2006). http://doi.acm.org/10.1145/1146238.1146255

PARDIS: Priority Aware Test Case Reduction

Golnaz Gharacharlu(✉) and Nick Sumner

Simon Fraser University, Burnaby, BC, Canada
{ggharach,wsumner}@sfu.ca

Abstract. Test cases play an important role in testing and debugging software. Smaller tests are easier to understand and use for these tasks. Given a test that demonstrates a bug, *test case reduction* finds a smaller variant of the test case that exhibits the same bug. Classically, one of the challenges for test case reduction is that the process is slow, often taking hours. For hierarchically structured inputs like source code, the state of the art is Perses, a recent grammar aware and queue driven approach for test case reduction. Perses traverses nodes in the abstract syntax tree (AST) of a program (test case) based on a priority order and tries to reduce them while preserving syntactic validity.

In this paper, we show that Perses' reduction strategy suffers from *priority inversion*, where significant time may be spent trying to perform reduction operations on lower priority portions of the AST. We show that this adversely affects the reduction speed. We propose PARDIS, a technique for priority aware test case reduction that avoids priority inversion. We implemented PARDIS and evaluated it on the same set of benchmarks used in the Perses evaluation. Our results indicate that compared to Perses, PARDIS is able to reduce test cases 1.3x to 7.8x faster and with 46% to 80% fewer queries.

Keywords: Test case reduction · Automated debugging · Priority aware reduction

1 Introduction

Test case reduction is a technique that aids in testing and debugging software. When an input for a program causes the program to exhibit a property of interest, like a bug, finding a smaller input that also exhibits the property can help to explain the behavior [1–3]. Given an input $I \in \mathbb{I}$ and an oracle $\psi : \mathbb{I} \to \mathbb{B}$ that performs a test and returns true iff a property holds, test case reduction aims to find a smaller input I' such that $\psi(I') = \text{true}$. Often, this problem is approached through Delta Debugging (DD), a longstanding and effective algorithm for test case reduction that essentially generalizes binary search [2]. However, for inputs with significant structure, generic DD can perform poorly, requiring significant time and not performing much reduction [3,4]. For compilers in particular, where

R. Hähnle and W. van der Aalst (Eds.): FASE 2019, LNCS 11424, pp. 409–426, 2019.
https://doi.org/10.1007/978-3-030-16722-6_24

the inputs must be valid programs, this has led to specialized techniques like Hierarchical Delta Debugging [3,4], language specific reducers like C-Reduce [5], and most recently to Syntax Guided Program Reduction as seen in Perses [6].

Syntax Guided Program Reduction (SGPR) is the present state of the art for compiler targeted test case reduction. The intuition behind SGPR is that the grammar defining the language of inputs eliminates many invalid sub-inputs from the search space. For example, when an input must adhere to the C programming language [7], removing the return type of a function declaration would not be valid because the C grammar specifies that the return type is required. Such syntactically invalid inputs are removed from the search space by SGPR.

Perses, a form of SGPR, takes as arguments not only a program p and oracle ψ, but also the context free grammar G of valid inputs [6]. It transforms the grammar so that removable parts of the input can be identified by the names of the grammar rules used to parse them. This also normalizes the grammar so that all removable components are expressed through quantifiers in an extended context free grammar [8], i.e. optionality (?) and lists (*, +). This transformation is illustrated in Fig. 1. Notice, for instance, that the recursive rule BAR denoting a list is transformed ($\Longrightarrow$) into a Kleene-+ quantified list. Individual elements of the list may be removed while preserving syntactic validity. Perses then parses the input of interest into an abstract syntax tree (AST) and traverses the AST while trying to (1) remove optional nodes and (2) perform DD to minimize the children of nodes representing lists. The grammar transformations have the benefit of making many syntactically correct removals easy and efficient to locate.

FOO → a | a b ⟹ FOO → a FOO_opt
FOO_opt → b?

(a) Optional elements like b are refactored into rules with ? quantifiers.

BAR → c | c BAR ⟹ BAR → BAR_plus
BAR_plus → c+

(b) Lists of elements are refactored into rules with * or + quantifiers.

Fig. 1. Overview of Perses grammar transformations for SGPR.

Perses has significantly improved the speed of program reduction. However, it still takes several hours to reduce some inputs. Consider the code in Listing 1.1 along with its AST in Fig. 3. This example is similar to a C program generated by the compiler testing tool CSmith [9]. In this example, Perses first considers the root node with ID ① of the AST. Since the rule for this node ends in _star, it is a list node, and its children are the elements of the list. Thus, Perses applies DD to the list of children for node ① to minimize the number of children. When such lists are long, significant time can be devoted to this task. We show in Sect. 4 that this can lead to substantial *stalls* in reduction, where no progress is made while a list is being processed. However, most of the children of this node have low *token weight*, the number of tokens beneath a given node that is denoted by `w:` in Fig. 3. Indeed, greater value would be found by focusing on just *one* of its children, node ⑤, which contains the majority of the input beneath it. By spending greater effort up front on portions of the AST of lesser value, Perses suffers from a form of *priority inversion.* Priority inversion occurs when a low priority task is scheduled instead of a high priority task. In this case, Perses focuses on removing low token weight nodes instead of high token weight nodes. Indeed, Perses may even fail to remove elements that would enable better reduction success overall. In this case, the declarations of `foo`, `S`, and `d` are used within the code beneath node ⑤. Thus, those uses need to be eliminated *before* any of the declarations can be removed successfully. In practice, we find that priority inversion has a significant impact on reduction time in SGPR.

To address priority inversion, we have developed *priority aware reduction strategies* for program reduction. By focusing the reduction effort on the nodes of the AST that cover the greatest number of tokens, we prioritize reduction of the most complex parts of the input first. This has multiple important benefits: (1) Dependencies between program elements are more likely to be broken by eliminating the complex uses first. (2) Stalls in reduction from unsuccessful rounds of DD can be mitigated. (3) By removing large portions of an input earlier on, each oracle query to ψ can take less time because smaller inputs tend to be faster to check. We have designed and evaluated a tool, PARDIS, that makes use of these techniques and found that it leads to consistent and significant performance improvements over Perses on the Perses benchmarks [6].

In summary, this paper makes the following contributions:

1. **Priority awareness.** We identify *priority inversion* as a key problem facing SGPR techniques and develop priority aware reduction strategies as a potential solution. *Priority aware reduction strategies* focus the reduction effort on the complex portions of an input first, enabling earlier and thus faster test case reduction (Sects. 3, 4.1).
2. **Optimization.** We identify redundancies in the reduction process when using Perses' transformed grammars and develop a solution to prune them from the candidate search space (Sect. 3.2).
3. **Significant performance improvement.** We implemented our strategies in a tool, PARDIS, and evaluated it on the same benchmarks used by Perses. Experimental results show that PARDIS both removes more of the input earlier on and is faster overall. Compared to Perses, PARDIS reduces test cases 1.3x to 7.8x faster and with 46% to 80% fewer oracle queries (Sect. 4.1).

2 Background and Motivation

Consider again the example in Fig. 3 and suppose that the oracle (ψ) checks that this program p should print `"Hello World!"` on line 24 (marked with $*$). Thus, the smallest subprogram for which ψ returns true is the main function with the desired `print` statement.

To search for this smaller input inside the original input, Perses traverses the AST using a priority queue ordered by the token weight. In each trial, the node

Listing 1.1: A C program with property of interest on line 24.

```
1  double d = 0.10;
2  struct S {
3    int f1;
4    int f2;
5  };
6  void foo(struct S s, char str[]){
7    double v = s.f2 + s.f2 * d;
8    printf("%s %f\n",str,v);
9  }
10 int main() {
11   unsigned int a = 1;
12   char b[] = "first";
13   char c[] = "second";
14   if (a) {
15     struct S s1;
16     s1.f1 = 1;
17     s1.f2 = 4000;
18     struct S s2;
19     s2.f1 = 2;
20     s2.f2 = 2000;
21     foo(s1, b);
22     foo(s2, c);
23   }
24   printf("Hello World!\n"); (*)
25   return 0;
26 }
```

node(s) to remove	removed
{2,3,4,5}	F
{2,3}	F
{4,5}	F
{2}	F
{3}	F
{4}	F
{5}	F
{3,4,5}	F
{2,4,5}	F
{2,3,4}	F
{2,3,5}	F
{8,9,10,11,12,13}	F
{8,9,10}	F
{11,12,13}	F
{8,9}	F
{10,11}	T
{12,13}	F
{8}	T
{9}	T
{12}	F

(a) Perses

node to remove	removed
{1}	F
{5}	F
{7}	F
{11}	T
{4}	T
{3}	T
{10}	T
{9}	T
{8}	T
{12}	F
{2}	T

(b) PARDIS

node(s) to remove	removed
{1}	F
{5}	F
{7}	F
{11}	T
{4}	T
{3}	T
{9,10}	T
{8}	T
{12}	F
{2}	T

(c) PARDIS HYBRID

Fig. 2. One round of removal trials in Perses, PARDIS and PARDIS HYBRID for the AST in Fig. 3. Numbers are node IDs.

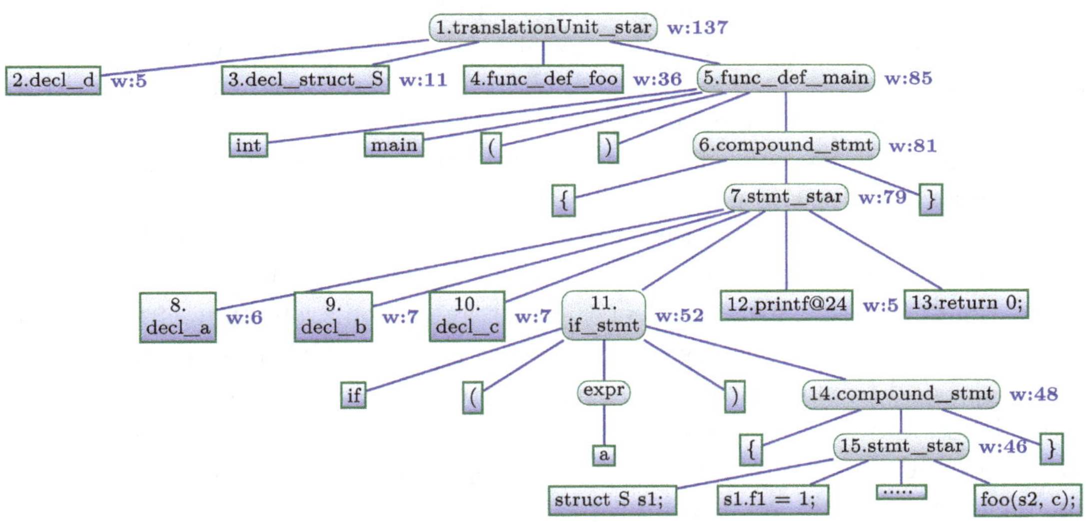

Fig. 3. AST of the program in Listing 1.1. `w` denotes the token weight of each node.

with the maximum weight is removed from the work queue and traversed. In our example, the queue starts out containing only the root of the AST, node ①. Perses performs specific reduction operations on different types of nodes during traversal. For instance, on optional nodes, Perses tries to remove the optional child node. For list nodes, Perses minimizes the list of children using DD. Any *remaining* children of the traversed node are then added to the priority queue in order to be traversed in the future.

Observe that in this example, Perses will first examine node ① and remove it from the queue. Because ① is a list node, DD is applied to the children of ①. Different combinations of children are removed from ① and the result is checked by ψ to find a smaller input. First, all children are removed and ψ is checked. After this fails, the first half of the children (② and ③) are removed, but ψ returns false again because this removes required declarations. Since removing the second half of the children (④ and ⑤) also fails, the process continues recursively. First DD tries shrinking the list by *removing* each individual child, and next it tries *only keeping* each individual child. Ultimately none of the trials succeed, so all children are added to the queue, and reduction continues with node ⑤. The intervening node ⑥ is not tested by SGPR because it is not syntactically removable. The next node removed from the work queue is node ⑦. This continues until the queue is empty. The precise trials exercised in this process are illustrated in Fig. 2(a). Note that 16 steps elapse until a successful trial occurs.

While the priorities used by Perses are controlled by the token weight, they determine how the *children* of the traversed nodes are removed. Thus, any node whose *parent* in the AST is a list is given the same priority as all other elements in the list. This is because DD recursively tries to minimize the entire list until no single element can be removed, regardless of the priorities of individual list elements. As a result, Perses must employ DD on the entirety of the children of ① even though it would be more beneficial to focus on just one child, node ⑤.

Instead, PARDIS more directly models the priorities. We note that in an optional or list node, such as ①, each child may be removed in a syntactically valid fashion. We call such removable nodes *nullable.* When traversing a nullable node in the AST, we can simply try directly to remove it, adding its children if the removal fails. For instance, in the running example, we would visit ① first. Because ① cannot get removed, we would simply add its children to the priority queue. Note that all children of ① are nullable, but ⑤ has the highest *token weight.* Thus, we next select ⑤ to traverse but removing ⑤ also fails. From the given token weights, we next traverse ⑥, which is syntactically not removable, and then ⑦, which we attempt to remove but is unsuccessful. Next ⑪ is visited and successfully removed. Removing ⑪ *enables the removal of* ④, ③ *and* ②. Thus, they are removed in a single pass of the tree using PARDIS, whereas Perses would require multiple traversals of the AST to remove them. This process continues until the desired output is achieved. As seen in Fig. 2(b), just 4 steps elapse until the first successful trial removes node ⑪.

Note that in this example, PARDIS is able to reduce to the desired output in a *single pass*, while Perses requires multiple passes of the AST. In practice, all program reduction techniques continue until a fixed point is reached, including PARDIS, however PARDIS can achieve greater reduction in a single traversal of the AST, accelerating convergence on the fixed point.

This priority aware approach can still have drawbacks, however. After focusing on the highest priority nodes, there may be many lower priority nodes remaining. For example, there are multiple remaining nodes of weight 7 in the tree after performing the reduction by PARDIS as described above. We also show experimentally that these lower priority nodes occur in practice in Sect. 5. The above approach of PARDIS considers each node *one at a time*, which can have poor performance when reducing such long lists. In addition, we thus propose a *hybrid* approach that still prioritizes nodes by maximum token weight but also uses a list based reduction technique for spans of nodes that have *the same* token weight. This hybrid approach is able to achieve the benefits of being priority aware while still avoiding the cost of considering each node of the AST individually.

Section 3 presents the algorithms behind these techniques in detail.

3 Approach

Recall that the core of PARDIS, similar to Perses, maintains a priority queue of the nodes in an AST and traverses the nodes in order to process them. It also makes use of Perses Normal Form, the result of the grammar transformations that Perses introduced [6]. The key difference is that instead of using the token weight of a parent node to determine when its nullable children may be removed, PARDIS identifies all nullable nodes (see Sect. 3.2) and uses their token weights directly to prioritize the search. The core algorithm for this process is quite straightforward and presented in Algorithm 1.

Algorithm 1: Priority queue driven program reduction.

```
  Input: P : ℙ – The program to reduce as an AST
  Input: ψ : ℙ → 𝔹 – Oracle for the property to preserve
  Input: ρ : 𝕍 → ℕ × ··· × ℕ – Prioritizer for AST nodes
  Result: A minimum program p ∈ ℙ s.t. ψ(p)
1 work ← MaxPriorityQueue({p.root}, ρ)
2 while !work.empty() do
3     node ← work.takeMax()
4     if node.isNullable && ψ(p − node) then
5         p ← p - node
6     else
7         work.insert(node.children)
8 return p
```

Line 1 of the algorithm constructs the priority queue (a max-heap), initializing it with the root of the AST and using a parameterizable priority ρ. ρ is simply a function that takes a node and returns its priority as a tuple. The priority queue selects the element with a lexicographically maximal priority, so ties on the *first* element of the priority tuple are broken by the *second* element and so on. As seen in Fig. 4, for PARDIS, ρ_{PARDIS} returns a pair of numbers, the token weight of the node and the position of the node in a decreasing, right-to-left, breadth first search. The specific breadth first order means that for an AST with n nodes, bfsOrder(p.root)=n, the last child c of p.root has bfsOrder(c)=n-1, and so on. Thus, if several nodes have the same token weight, the one highest in the AST and furthest to the right is selected next. This ordering decreases the chances of trying to remove a declaration before its uses [10].

Line 2 starts the core of the algorithm. While there are more nodes to explore in the queue, the node with the next highest priority is considered. If it is nullable and can be successfully removed, we remove it from the AST, otherwise we add its children to the queue so that they will also be traversed.

While the algorithm is surprisingly simple, we have found it to perform significantly better than the state of the art in practice. As we explore in Sect. 4.2, this results from prioritizing the search toward those portions of the input where reduction can have the greatest impact. To more closely compare with Perses, consider a version of Perses that upon visiting a list or optional node only tries removing each child of that node once[1]. This "one node at a time" variant of Perses can also be implemented using Algorithm 1 by carefully choosing the priority formula ρ. Because Perses considers removing the *children* of the nodes it traverses, it actually prioritizes the work queue using the token weight of the *parent* rather than the token weight of nullable nodes being considered for removal. This leads to the alternative prioritizer ρ_{perses} presented in Fig. 4. Observe that all children of a list node receive the same token weight, that of the entire list. This can inflate the priority of some nodes in the work queue and leads to poor performance.

Definitions:

tokensBelow(n) – returns the number of tokens beneath an AST node n.

bfsOrder(n) – returns the position of an AST node n in a decreasing, right to left, breadth first search.

Prioritizers:

$$\rho_{\text{PARDIS}} = (\mathsf{tokensBelow(n)},\ \mathsf{bfsOrder(n)})$$

$$\rho_{perses} = \begin{cases} \textbf{let}\ \mathsf{parentWeight} \leftarrow \mathsf{tokensBelow(n.parent)}\ \textbf{if}\ \mathsf{n.parent}\ \textbf{else}\ \infty\ \textbf{in} \\ \textbf{let}\ \mathsf{parentOrder} \leftarrow \mathsf{bfsOrder(n.parent)}\ \textbf{if}\ \mathsf{n.parent}\ \textbf{else}\ \infty\ \textbf{in} \\ (\mathsf{parentWeight},\ \mathsf{parentOrder}) \end{cases}$$

$$\rho_{\text{PARDIS HYBRID}} = \begin{cases} \textbf{let}\ \mathsf{parentOrder} \leftarrow \mathsf{bfsOrder(n.parent)}\ \textbf{if}\ \mathsf{n.parent}\ \textbf{else}\ \infty\ \textbf{in} \\ (\mathsf{tokensBelow(n)},\ \mathsf{parentOrder},\ \mathsf{bfsOrder(n)}) \end{cases}$$

Fig. 4. Prioritizers used for PARDIS, node at a time Perses, and PARDIS HYBRID.

Like other program reduction algorithms [3,5,6,11,12], Algorithm 1 is used to compute a fixed point. That is, in practice the algorithm is repeated until no further reductions can be made. As in prior work, we omit this from our presentation for clarity. In theory, this means that the worst case complexity of the technique is $O(n^2)$ where n is the number of nodes in the AST. This arises when only one leaf of the AST is removed in each pass through the algorithm. In practice, most nodes are not syntactically nullable, and we show in Sect. 4.1 that performance of PARDIS exceeds the state of the art.

In addition, while we focus on *removing* nodes of the AST, Perses also tries to *replace* non-list and -optional nodes with compatible nodes in their subtrees. We do not focus on this aspect of the algorithm. In practice, we found it to

[1] We compare against *both* versions of Perses in Sect. 4.1.

significantly hurt performance (see Sect. 4.1) and we consider efficient replacement strategies to be orthogonal to and outside the scope of this work.

3.1 Pardis Hybrid

The initial priority aware technique from Algorithm 1 can also encounter performance bottlenecks, however. The original motivation for using DD on lists of children in the AST was that its best case behavior is $O(log(n))$ where n is the number of children in the list. This is because it tries removing multiple children at the same time. Processing one node at a time, however, requires that every list element is considered individually, guaranteeing $O(n)$ time for one round of Algorithm 1. Priority aware reduction that proceeds one node at a time faces a different set of inefficiencies that can still cause stalls in the reduction process.

Thus, we desire a means of removing multiple elements from lists at the same time while *still* preserving priority awareness. In order to achieve this, we developed Pardis Hybrid, as presented in Algorithm 2. This approach uses a modified prioritizer as presented in Fig. 4 that first orders by token weight, then by parent traversal order, then by node traversal order. The effect this has is that all children of the same parent with the same weight are grouped together. As a result, we can remove them from the priority queue together and perform list based reduction (like DD) to more efficiently remove groups of elements in a list that have the same priority (for instance, nodes ⑨ and ⑩ get removed as a group in one trial using Pardis Hybrid as shown in Fig. 2(c)). Because the search is still primarily directed by the token weights of the removed nodes, the technique still fully respects the priorities of the removed nodes.

Algorithm 2: Pardis Hybrid algorithm with priority aware list reduction.

```
  Input: p : ℙ – The program to reduce as an AST
  Input: ψ : ℙ → 𝔹 – Oracle for the property to preserve
  Result: A minimum program p ∈ ℙ s.t. ψ(p)
1 work ← MaxPriorityQueue({p.root}, ρ_PARDIS HYBRID)
2 while !work.empty() do
3     nodes ← work.takeWithSameWeightAndParent()
4     nullable, nonnullable ← partitionNullable(nodes)
5     removed, retained ← minimize(p, nullable, ψ)
6     p ← p - removed
7     work.insert(⋃_{x∈retained∪nonnullable} x.children)
8 return p
```

Similar to the previous approach, line 1 of Algorithm 2 starts by creating the priority queue. Note that it specifically uses the prioritizer $\rho_{\text{Pardis Hybrid}}$, which groups children having the same token weight in the priority queue. As long as there are more nodes to consider, line 3 takes all nodes from the queue with the same weight and parent. If the weight of a node is unique, this simply returns a list of length 1. Line 4 filters out non-nullable nodes from the trial, and line 5 just applies list based reduction to any nullable nodes. Lines 6 and 7 then remove the eliminated nodes from the tree and add the children of remaining nodes to the work queue. Again, this algorithm actually runs to a fixed point.

While the worst case behavior of DD is $O(n^2)$ [2], this can be improved to $O(n)$ by giving up hard *guarantees* on minimality [13]. Since this reduction process is performed to a fixed point anyway, minimize on line 5 makes use of this $O(n)$ approach to list based reduction (OPDD) without losing 1-minimality. As a result, the theoretical complexity of PARDIS HYBRID is the same as PARDIS.

3.2 Nullability Pruning

Finally, we observed that many oracle queries were simply unnecessary. Specifically, recall that a node can be tagged nullable because it is an element of a list or a child of an optional node, as previously defined by Perses grammar transformations [6]. The complete algorithm for this tagging is in *TagNullable* of Algorithm 3. However, for example, a list of one element could contain another list of one element. In the AST, this appears as a chain of nodes, at least two of which are nullable. Removing *any one* of these nodes removes the same tokens from the AST. Thus, it is only necessary to select a single nullable node from any *chain* of nodes, and the others can be disregarded.

We exploit this through an optimization called *nullability pruning*. We traverse every chain of nodes in the AST, preserving the nullability of the highest node in the chain and removing nullability from those below it. The complete algorithm is presented in *PruneNullable* of Algorithm 3. In effect, it is just a depth first search that removes redundant nullability from nodes along the way instantaneously.

In practice, we find that this can statically (ahead of time) prune most of the AST from the search space. Specifically, in the benchmarks we examine in Sect. 4, we find that of 1,593,875 total nullable nodes, 17% are redundant optional nodes and 44% are redundant list element nodes. We observe the impact of this pruning on the actual reduction process in Sect. 4.1.

Algorithm 3: Nullability tagging and pruning.

```
Function TagNullable(p)
    Input: p : ℙ – The program to reduce as an AST
    foreach Node n ∈ p do
        if n ∈ KleeneStar ∪ KleenePlus ∪ Optional then
            foreach c ∈ n.children do c.isNullable ← true

Function PruneNullable(p)
    Input: p : ℙ – The program to reduce as an AST
    Function OptimizeBelow(n)
        hasNullable ← false
        Loop
            if hasNullable then
                n.isNullable ← false
            else if n.isNullable then
                hasNullable ← true
            if 1 == |n.children| then
                break
            n ← n.getOnlyChild()
        foreach c ∈ n.children do OptimizeBelow(n)
    OptimizeBelow(p.root)
```

4 Evaluation

We evaluate PARDIS's performance and examine the impact of priority inversion on reduction by answering the following research questions:

- **RQ1.** How does PARDIS perform compared to Perses in terms of reduction time and speed, number of oracle queries, and size of the reduced test case?
- **RQ2.** Does priority inversion adversely affect the reduction efficiency? In particular, does reduction require more work with a traversal order suffering from priority inversion?

4.1 RQ1. Performance: PARDIS vs. Perses

Experimental Set-Up. We evaluate PARDIS on the set of C test cases used in the evaluation of Perses, including the oracle scripts provided by authors of Perses. While using these, we observed that they still allowed for some undefined behavior [5,14], so we updated all oracles to reject test case variants with undefined behavior. As a result, we were able to reproduce bugs for 14 out of 20 original test cases. The remaining benchmarks that could not reproduce their original failures were elided for this study. Since the implementation of Perses' components is not publicly available, we implemented the Perses grammar transformations and reduction based on the algorithms available in the paper [6] using the C++ bindings of ANTLR [15]. All of our implementations have been made available[2]. Our experiments were conducted on an Intel Xeon E5-2630 CPU and 64 GB memory running Ubuntu.

Variants of Reduction Techniques. To better explain performance differences, we benchmark several algorithms that each add one difference. All approaches compute fixed points as previously described.

- *Perses DD*- The removal-based algorithm of Perses that applies DD on children of list nodes [6].
- *Perses OPDD*- The same as Perses DD but using the $O(n)$ reduction algorithm of OPDD [13]. It is faster than Perses DD in practice.
- *Perses N*- The one node at a time Perses that does not apply DD on list elements but removes them one by one using Perses' parent oriented priorities.
- PARDIS W/O PRUNING- This uses the PARDIS algorithm but does not apply nullability pruning optimization proposed in Sect. 3.2.
- PARDIS- Our proposed removal algorithm that also applies nullability pruning.
- PARDIS HYBRID- The hybrid version of PARDIS with nullability pruning and OPDD as its version of DD.

[2] https://github.com/golnazgh/PARDIS.

Table 1. Original and reduced test case size and number of oracle queries.

Bug	$O(\#)$	Perses DD		Perses OPDD		Perses N		PARDIS w/o PRUNING		PARDIS		PARDIS HYBRID	
		$R(\#)$	$Q(\#)$	$R(\#)$	$Q(\#)$	$R(\#)$	$Q(\#)$	$R(\#)$	$Q(\#)$	$R(\#)$	$Q(\#)$	$R(\#)$	$Q(\#)$
clang-22382	21,068	597	5,323	597	4,865	354	3,203	354	2,702	354	2,011	354	2,319
clang-22704	184,444	250	4,181	250	3,775	220	5,083	236	4,956	236	4,342	236	2253
clang-23309	38,647	1,624	8,688	1,624	8,095	1,522	6,106	1,726	4,618	1,726	3,004	1,726	3,684
clang-25900	78,960	618	4,455	618	4,020	600	2,816	618	2,343	618	1,652	618	1,997
clang-27137	174,538	725	9,035	725	8,299	681	6,858	807	5,889	807	4,293	807	4,891
clang-27747	173,840	379	3,171	379	2,845	311	1,773	313	1,418	313	1,074	308	1,218
clang-31259	48,799	821	4,457	821	4,073	821	3,282	538	2,464	538	1,662	538	1,853
gcc-64990	148,931	776	5,913	776	5,438	1,215	5,165	776	3,781	776	2,632	776	3,148
gcc-65383	43,942	462	5,503	462	5,002	486	3,502	598	2,559	598	1,839	598	2,204
gcc-66186	47,481	1,176	6,101	1,176	5,727	1,178	4,532	1,176	3,944	1,176	2,562	1,176	3,167
gcc-66375	65,488	1,232	7,989	1,232	6,780	1,198	4,202	1,232	4,512	1,232	3,036	1,232	3,851
gcc-70127	154,816	600	5,610	600	5,201	593	3,700	600	3,063	600	2,240	600	2,723
gcc-70586	212,259	1,583	7,671	1,583	7,276	1,489	5,582	1,497	5,233	1,497	3,491	1,497	4,318
gcc-71626	6,133	58	1,151	58	1,135	58	1,013	58	330	58	264	58	228
geomean	70300	609	5126	609	4705	583	3670	574	2881	574	2066	574	2270
median	72,224	672	5,556	672	5,102	640	3,951	609	3,422	609	2,401	609	2,521

O, R and Q denote number of tokens in the original test case, reduced one and total number of oracle queries performed by the reduction technique, respectively.

Reduction Performance. We compare these techniques in terms of *the number of oracle queries* (Q), *reduction quality* or size of the final reduced test case (R), *reduction time* (T), and *reduction speed* or the average number of tokens removed per second (E). Results are presented in Tables 1 and 2. The best values of queries, time, and speed are highlighted for each test case. As can be seen, in all cases, either PARDIS or PARDIS HYBRID outperform all variants of Perses. Compared to the full removal-based Perses algorithm (Perses DD), our proposed algorithms reduce **1.3x** to **7.8x** faster and with **46%** to **80%** fewer queries. The results across variants suggest that these benefits arise from priority awareness and nullability pruning. Due to fixed point computation, all approaches produce test

Table 2. Reduction time and speed for different variants of reduction techniques.

Bug	Perses DD		Perses OPDD		Perses N		PARDIS w/o PRUNING		PARDIS		PARDIS HYBRID	
	$T(s)$	$E(\#/s)$	$T(s)$	$E(\#/s)$	$T(s)$	$E(\#/s)$	$T(s)$	$E(\#/s)$	$T(s)$	$E(\#/s)$	$T(s)$	$E(\#/s)$
clang-22382	3,198	6	3,122	7	3,489	6	3,057	7	2,977	7	2,094	10
clang-22704	1,527	121	1,304	141	5,243	35	3,323	55	3,219	57	1,160	159
clang-23309	2,571	14	2,414	15	1,920	19	1,423	26	1,007	37	1,062	35
clang-25900	1,375	57	1,220	64	1,025	76	690	114	526	149	518	151
clang-27137	6,972	25	6,379	27	5,717	30	4,428	39	3,423	51	3,538	49
clang-27747	1,194	145	1,060	164	771	225	571	304	463	375	453	383
clang-31259	1,698	28	1,577	30	1,471	33	1,239	39	814	59	800	60
gcc-64990	1,980	75	1,768	84	1,981	75	1,237	120	932	159	916	162
gcc-65383	1,762	25	1,615	27	1,304	33	892	49	704	62	699	62
gcc-66186	1,583	29	1,493	31	1,299	36	1,016	46	691	67	741	62
gcc-66375	2,782	23	2,568	25	1,851	35	1,705	38	1,173	55	1,311	49
gcc-70127	3,083	50	2,812	55	2,265	68	1,520	101	1,124	137	1,173	131
gcc-70586	4,417	48	4,119	51	3,450	61	2,545	83	1,791	118	1,984	106
gcc-71626	156	39	156	39	206	29	57	107	54	112	20	304
geomean	1900	36	1750	40	1740	40	1202	58	933	75	807	86
median	1,871	34	1,692	35	1,886	35	1,331	52	970	64	989	84

T is reduction time in seconds. E is the efficiency of removal (number of tokens removed per second).

cases from which no one token can be removed while satisfying ψ (1-minimal) [2], but they can produce different final reduced test cases [2]. On average, PARDIS yields reduced test cases with 574 tokens compared to Perses DD with 609 tokens.

In addition, we graphed the reduction progress of each test case for the different variants. Fig. 5 shows the percentage of remaining tokens over time during reduction. For sake of space, we only include graphs for six of the test cases. Note that the y-axis is log scaled. PARDIS and PARDIS HYBRID show much faster convergence to a reduced test case compared to Perses variants. Recall that the only factor differentiating Perses N from PARDIS W/O PRUNING is the order in which the queue of nodes is traversed. Unlike Perses N, PARDIS W/O PRUNING does not suffer from priority inversion and guides the reduction process based on token weights of the nodes to remove. As can be seen, this advantage leads to faster convergence to a reduced test case. We examine the impact of priority inversion on reduction speed more rigorously in Sect. 4.2.

Replacement. As mentioned in Sect. 3, Perses also considers a replacement strategy for non-list or -optional nodes in addition to removal for other nodes. For instance, in Fig. 3, Perses will attempt to replace node ⑥ with node ⑭ because they both match the same grammar rule (`compound_stmt`). This replacement fails since required declarations will get removed and ψ will return false.

Including replacement significantly increases the work done by reduction. For completeness, we implemented Perses DD with replacement as described in their paper [6] and defined a four-hour timeout for the reduction process. In 11 out of 14 cases, Perses DD with replacement could not finish the reduction process before reaching the timeout. In the remaining three, it generated reduced test cases with the same size or slightly smaller while performing a significantly larger number of oracle queries (more than 3× over Perses DD without replacement).

4.2 RQ2. The Impact of Priority Inversion

As shown in Fig. 5, avoiding priority inversion leads to faster convergence. One explanation for this is that priority awareness may decrease the amount of work required to remove a token (as seen in the motivating example). We explore this in a case study on `gcc-64990` with 148,931 tokens. The *number of removal attempts* for a token is number of times a single token is considered for removal. Removing any ancestor of a token in the AST will remove that token, so if a first attempt fails, a deeper ancestor may be attempted. We compute this for every token of the test case to get a sense of the work required for each token. A better traversal order of the AST should cause fewer overall token removal attempts. To measure only the impact of different traversal orders, we compare PARDIS W/O PRUNING with Perses N. As described in Sect. 4.1, they follow the exact same reduction rules and differ only in their traversal orders.

Figure 6 depicts histograms of the distributions of token removal attempts for PARDIS W/O PRUNING and Perses N. For clearer visualization, we show only the distributions for the number of attempts less than or equal to 20. We can see how Perses N distribution is inclined toward a larger number of removal attempts,

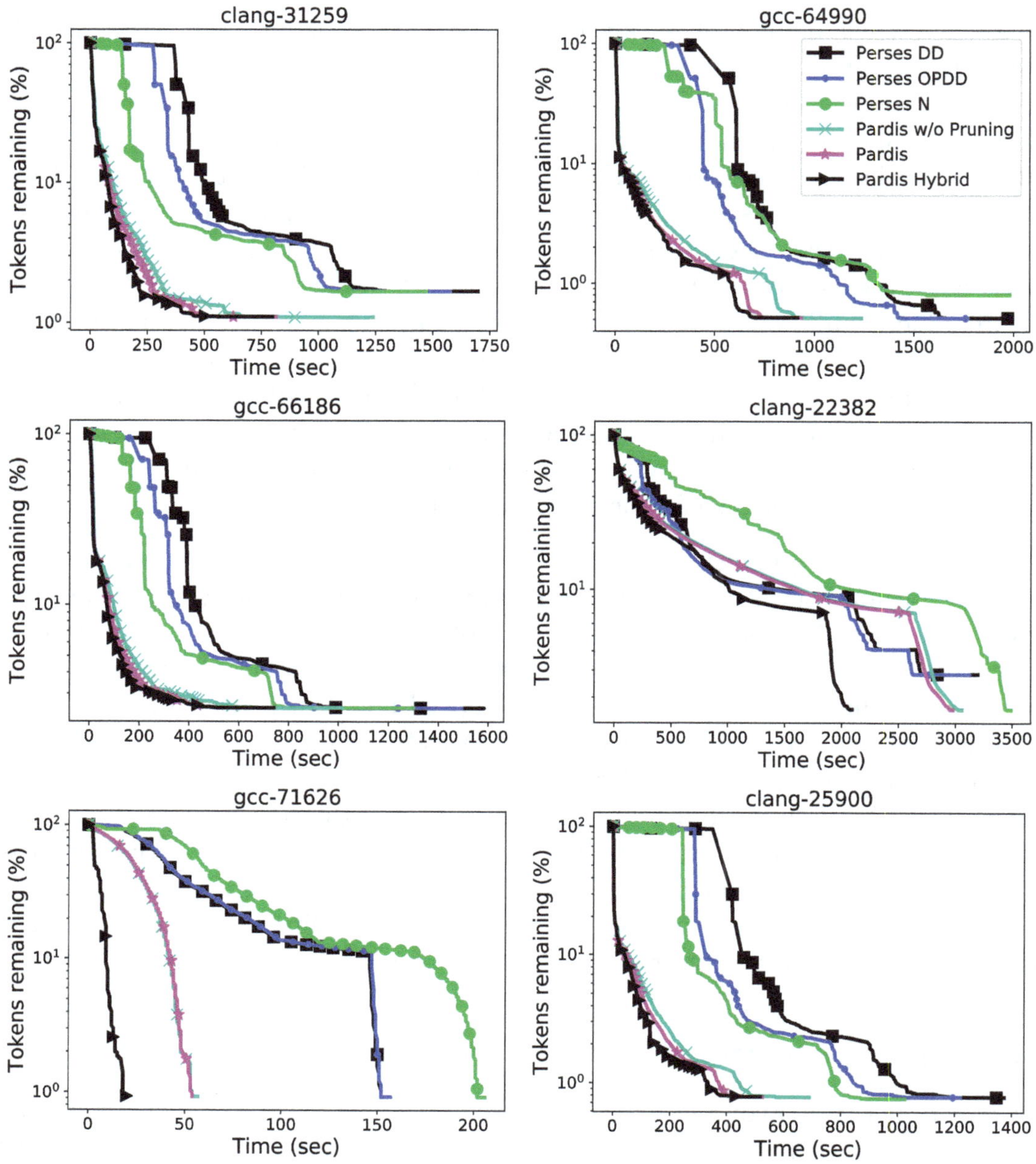

Fig. 5. Converging to a reduced test case in six variants of reduction techniques.

an indicator of more work required in order to remove individual tokens. In addition, we statically measure that the difference between the removal attempt distributions is significant. We use a one sided Wilcoxon rank-sum test [16] to determine whether the distribution of Perses N is indeed greater than that of PARDIS W/O PRUNING. The p-value computed for our data was less than $2.2e^{-16}$ which strongly supports this observation.

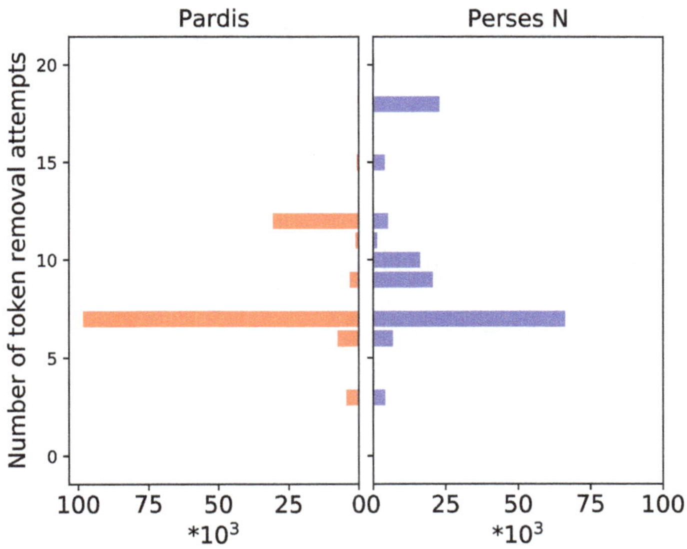

Fig. 6. Distributions of token removal attempts for PARDIS W/O PRUNING and Perses N.

5 Discussion

PARDIS HYBRID **as a *sweet spot* in reducing test cases:** As discussed earlier, unlike Perses, PARDIS HYBRID does not suffer from priority inversion because it prioritizes the search primarily on the token weight of nodes being considered for removal. Moreover, unlike PARDIS, it does not strictly remove one node at a time and allows the removal of nodes with the same weight and the same parent as a group. Hence, it can be considered a sweet spot in reducing test cases. We conduct two studies that can further explore this idea.

(1) Oracle Verification Time. The number of oracle queries is a common metric used in similar studies to reason about reduction efficiency since it directly impacts the total reduction time [2,3,6,13,17]. For instance, both PARDIS and PARDIS HYBRID perform fewer oracle queries and take less time than Perses. However, the number of oracle queries is not the only factor involved. The time required to run each of these queries, or *oracle verification time*, also affects the total running time. For instance, as presented in Sect. 4.1, PARDIS has the smallest number of oracle queries in 12 out of 14 test cases. However, in terms of total reduction time and speed, PARDIS HYBRID is the fastest in 8 out of 14 cases, even while performing *more* queries compared to PARDIS in 6 of them. Oracle verification time can depend on multiple elements such as the size and complexity of the test case. Since PARDIS HYBRID takes advantage of the possibility to remove more than one node at a time, it may try variants of the test case that are smaller and may be faster to verify compared to PARDIS. To check this hypothesis, we conducted a case study on `gcc-64990` and recorded the running time of each oracle query during reduction. As shown in Tables 1 and 2, PARDIS reduces this test case in 932 s with 2,632 queries, and PARDIS HYBRID

has a total reduction time of 916 s (16 s shorter) while performing 3,148 oracle queries (516 more queries). Both techniques yield the same final test case.

Figure 7 depicts the distribution of oracle verification times in PARDIS and PARDIS HYBRID, showing that PARDIS has more queries that take longer compared to PARDIS HYBRID. The shorter queries in PARDIS HYBRID directly decrease its overall reduction time making it reduce test cases with fewer queries compared to Perses and shorter queries compared to PARDIS.

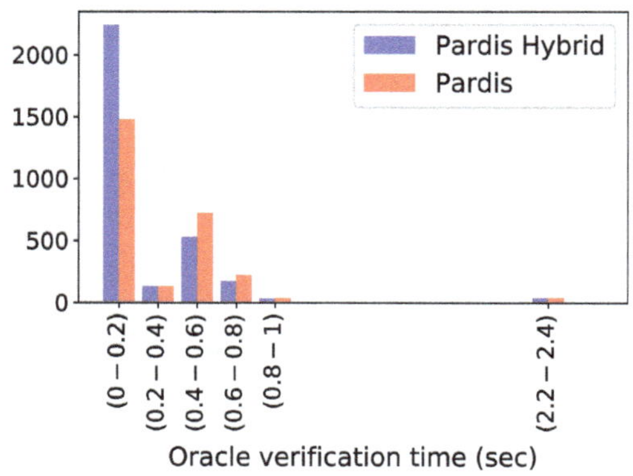

Fig. 7. Distribution of oracle verification time for PARDIS and PARDIS HYBRID.

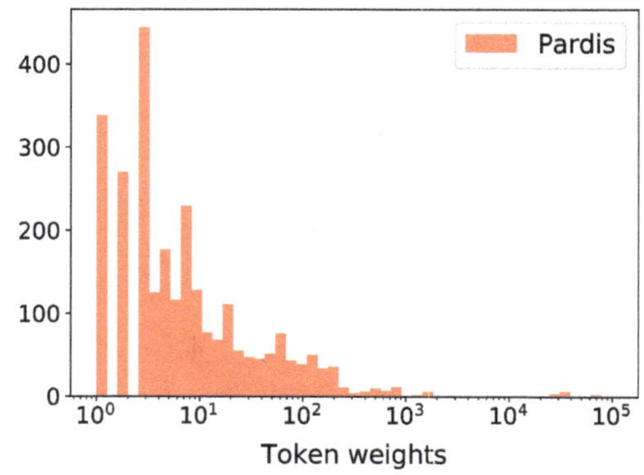

Fig. 8. Distribution of token weights of nodes visited during PARDIS reduction.

(2) Distribution of Token Weights. The motivation behind proposing PARDIS HYBRID as discussed in Sect. 3.1 was that if lists in a test case shrink after removing nodes with large unique token weights, applying DD on list elements with the same weight can be beneficial. In fact, the more of the remaining nodes that share token weights, the more beneficial using DD becomes since it provides the opportunity to remove those nodes in just one trial. This can avoid the possibly time-consuming process of visiting nodes one by one. To understand the distribution of token weights in practice, we perform PARDIS (the one node at a time removal) on `gcc-64990` and record token weights of nodes visited during the removal process. Figure 8 shows the distribution with **5** as the median of token weights of nodes visited during the reduction. The small median motivates the use of PARDIS HYBRID in practice since it indicates that half of the nodes have one of only five different token weights and can benefit from the grouped removals.

Syntactic vs Semantic Validity: Perses and PARDIS discard *syntactically* invalid variants of the test case during reduction. However, there are also *semantically* invalid queries such as removing the declaration of a variable before removing its use. SGPR techniques cannot entirely avoid these queries since they guide the reduction process based on the syntax of the grammar. However, the priority order of PARDIS can mitigate this problem. By prioritizing by token weight, it is more likely to visit and remove uses before spending effort on declarations. One reason for this is that a higher token weight tends to mean that there are more uses beneath that node. For instance, in Fig. 3, uses of variables `a`, `b` and c are descendants of node ⑪ with nodes ⑧, ⑨ and ⑩ as their declarations. Pardis removes the uses by first removing ⑪ while Perses tries to remove the declarations first due to priority inversion. Hence, Pardis prunes nodes in one pass of the AST that Perses may require a fixed point mode to remove.

Threats to Validity: We evaluated Pardis on the same set of C test cases used in the evaluation of Perses. The implementation of Perses' grammar transformations and reduction is not publicly available, so we reimplemented Perses as described in its paper. Our implementation has been made available to provide a consistent platform for future work. However, the exact implementations, environmental settings and the scripts to check the property of interest can all impact the final results. For instance, the final sizes of the reduced test cases reported for the original Perses' implementation [6] are smaller than those using our reimplemented version of Perses. As discussed in Sect. 4.1, this may be because Perses' oracles allowed for undefined behavior, which can lead through smaller but invalid reduced test cases. To mitigate this problem, we made the oracles strictly prevent undefined behavior for both Pardis and Perses. Note that Pardis significantly outperforms both Perses' original implementation [6] and our reimplementation in terms of number of oracle queries.

While the techniques presented in Pardis are general in ability, our evaluation focuses on C in order to compare with Perses. Further investigation is required to claim that the performance benefits extend to other languages.

6 Related Work

The closest work to this paper is Perses [6]. Unlike Pardis, it suffers from priority inversion that adversely affects the reduction speed. Other generic test case reduction techniques are Delta Debugging (DD) [2], its $O(n)$ variant [13], and Berkeley Delta [18]. These face challenges when reducing hierarchical inputs. Several techniques focus on reducing hierarchically structured test cases [3,4,6,11,12,19,20]. Among these, only Perses is priority aware, in spite of its priority inversion. Indeed, most techniques process the input level by level. Like Pardis, Perses and Simp [20] are notable exceptions in that they can search across levels when deciding how to reduce. However, Simp is specific to SQL Queries. GTR [12] is notable in that it is trained when to apply different reduction operations. Finally, C-Reduce [5] is a tool for reducing C/C++ test cases that requires extensive domain-specific knowledge.

7 Conclusions

We have shown that the prior state of the art for test case reduction suffers from *priority inversion* and that this causes a significant increase in reduction time. We proposed priority aware reduction techniques, Pardis and Pardis Hybrid, that focus reduction effort where they can have the most impact. These techniques can speed reduction by 1.3× to 7.8× over the prior state of the art.

Acknowledgements. This research was partially supported by the Natural Sciences and Engineering Research Council of Canada.

References

1. Clapp, L., Bastani, O., Anand, S., Aiken, A.: Minimizing GUI event traces. In: Proceedings of the 24th ACM SIGSOFT International Symposium on Foundations of Software Engineering, FSE 2016, Seattle, WA, USA, 13–18 November 2016, pp. 422–434 (2016)
2. Zeller, A., Hildebrandt, R.: Simplifying and isolating failure-inducing input. IEEE Trans. Softw. Eng. **28**(2), 183–200 (2002)
3. Misherghi, G., Su, Z.: HDD: hierarchical delta debugging. In: 28th International Conference on Software Engineering (ICSE 2006), Shanghai, China, 20–28 May 2006, pp. 142–151 (2006)
4. Misherghi, G.S.: Hierarchical delta debugging. Master's thesis, University of California Davis (2007, Approved)
5. Regehr, J., Chen, Y., Cuoq, P., Eide, E., Ellison, C., Yang, X.: Test-case reduction for C compiler bugs. In: ACM SIGPLAN Conference on Programming Language Design and Implementation, PLDI 2012, Beijing, China, 11–16 June 2012, pp. 335–346 (2012)
6. Sun, C., Li, Y., Zhang, Q., Gu, T., Su, Z.: Perses: syntax-guided program reduction. In: Proceedings of the 40th International Conference on Software Engineering, ICSE 2018, Gothenburg, Sweden, 27 May–03 June 2018, pp. 361–371 (2018)
7. Kernighan, B.W., Ritchie, D.: The C Programming Language, 2nd edn. Prentice-Hall, Upper Saddle River (1988)
8. Albert, J., Giammaressi, D., Wood, D.: Extended context-free grammars and normal form algorithms. In: Champarnaud, J.-M., Ziadi, D., Maurel, D. (eds.) WIA 1998. LNCS, vol. 1660, pp. 1–12. Springer, Heidelberg (1999). https://doi.org/10.1007/3-540-48057-9_1
9. Yang, X., Chen, Y., Eide, E., Regehr, J.: Finding and understanding bugs in C compilers. In: Proceedings of the 32nd ACM SIGPLAN Conference on Programming Language Design and Implementation, PLDI 2011, San Jose, CA, USA, 4–8 June 2011, pp. 283–294 (2011)
10. IBM Support, Test Case Reduction Techniques. http://www-01.ibm.com/support/docview.wss?uid=swg21084174
11. Hodován, R., Kiss, Á.: Coarse hierarchical delta debugging. In: Proceedings of the 33rd IEEE International Conference on Software Maintenance and Evolution, ICSME 2017, Shanghai, China, 20–22 September 2017, pp. 194–203 (2017)
12. Herfert, S., Patra, J., Pradel, M.: Automatically reducing tree-structured test inputs. In: Proceedings of the 32nd IEEE/ACM International Conference on Automated Software Engineering, ASE 2017, Urbana, IL, USA, 30 October–03 November 2017, pp. 861–871 (2017)
13. Gharachorlu, G., Sumner, N.: Avoiding the familiar to speed up test case reduction. In: 2018 IEEE International Conference on Software Quality, Reliability and Security, QRS 2018, Lisbon, Portugal, 16–20 July 2018, pp. 426–437 (2018)
14. Hathhorn, C., Ellison, C., Rosu, G.: Defining the undefinedness of C. In: Proceedings of the 36th ACM SIGPLAN Conference on Programming Language Design and Implementation, Portland, OR, USA, 15–17 June 2015, pp. 336–345 (2015)
15. Parr, T.: The Definitive ANTLR 4 Reference, 2nd edn. Pragmatic Bookshelf, Raleigh (2013)

16. Wild, C., Seber, G.: Chance Encounters: A First Course in Data Analysis and Inference, 1st edn. Wiley, New York (1999)
17. Hodován, R., Kiss, Á.: Practical improvements to the minimizing delta debugging algorithm. In: Proceedings of the 11th International Joint Conference on Software Technologies (ICSOFT 2016) - Volume 1: ICSOFT-EA, Lisbon, Portugal, 24–26 July 2016, pp. 241–248 (2016)
18. McPeak, S., Wilkerson, D.S., Goldsmith, S.: Delta, July 2003. http://delta.stage.tigris.org/
19. Kiss, Á., Hodován, R., Gyimóthy, T.: HDDr: a recursive variant of the hierarchical delta debugging algorithm. In: Proceedings of the 9th ACM SIGSOFT International Workshop on Automating TEST Case Design, Selection, and Evaluation, A-TEST 2018, pp. 16–22 (2018)
20. Bruno, N.: Minimizing database repros using language grammars. In: Proceedings of 13th International Conference on Extending Database Technology, EDBT 2010, Lausanne, Switzerland, 22–26 March 2010, pp. 382–393, 2010

Automatically Identifying Sufficient Object Builders from Module APIs

Pablo Ponzio[1,3(✉)], Valeria S. Bengolea[1], Mariano Politano[1,3], Nazareno Aguirre[1,3], and Marcelo F. Frias[2,3]

[1] Universidad Nacional de Río Cuarto, Río Cuarto, Argentina
{pponzio,vbengolea,mpolitano,naguirre}@dc.exa.unrc.edu.ar
[2] Instituto Tecnológico de Buenos Aires (ITBA), Buenos Aires, Argentina
mfrias@itba.edu.ar
[3] Consejo Nacional de Investigaciones Científicas y Técnicas (CONICET), Buenos Aires, Argentina

Abstract. Various approaches to software analysis (e.g. test input generation, software model checking) require engineers to (manually) identify a subset of a module's methods in order to drive the analysis. Given a module to be analyzed, engineers typically select a subset of its methods to be considered as object builders to define a so-called *driver*, that will be used to automatically build objects for analysis, e.g., combining them non-deterministically, randomly, etc. This requires a careful inspection of the module and its API, since both the relative exhaustiveness of the analysis (leaving important methods out may systematically avoid generating different objects), as well as its efficiency (the different bounded combinations of methods grows exponentially as the number of methods increases), are affected by the selection.

We propose an approach for automatically selecting a set of builders from a module's API, based on an evolutionary algorithm that favors sets of methods whose combinations lead to producing larger sets of objects. The algorithm also takes into account other characteristics of these sets of methods, trying to prioritize the selection of methods with less and simpler parameters. As the implementation of this evolutionary mechanism requires in principle handling and comparing large sets of objects, and this grows very quickly both in terms of space and running times, we employ an *abstraction* of sets of objects, called field extensions, that involves using the field values of the objects in the set instead of the actual objects, and enables us to effectively implement our mechanism. An experimental assessment on a benchmark of stateful classes shows that our approach can automatically identify sets of builders that are *sufficient* (can be used to create any instance of the module) and *minimal* (do not contain superfluous methods), in a reasonable time.

1 Introduction

As software is becoming more ubiquitous thanks to the rapid advances in technology, guaranteeing the functional correctness of software is more crucial than

R. Hähnle and W. van der Aalst (Eds.): FASE 2019, LNCS 11424, pp. 427–444, 2019.
https://doi.org/10.1007/978-3-030-16722-6_25

ever. Thus, a research area of growing importance is that of automated software analysis, whose goal is to assist engineers, through the provision of tools for automated analysis, in finding deficiencies both in software and software related models. Automated test generation [1,11,13,17,24,25,28,29,32], software model checking [9,34,35], and static analyses [6,16], among many others, are prominent approaches in this line of research.

While these techniques involve in many cases fully automated analyses, their application often requires some effort from the engineers. Software model checkers rely on the definition of *drivers*, programs that allow one to build inputs for the code under analysis. Similarly, in parameterized-unit testing approaches [33] a mechanism for building inputs is mandatory. Some symbolic execution based tools require the so-called *"object factories"* to build tests cases involving inputs with non-primitive types [32]. Automated test generation techniques based on a module's API can be used for building inputs for non-primitive types [11,24], thus automating the above-mentioned input-generation issues. But they usually present difficulties in generating a good set of diverse inputs for stateful, complex structures. This is even more difficult for structures with rich APIs [26]. Many authors have addressed this problem by defining different approaches for guiding test generation, to create more diverse sets of inputs [7,26].

In this paper, we take a different approach to address the problem of generating better inputs for stateful modules. We observe that the selection of routines from a module API, to feed an input generation tool so as to build input structures for program analysis (drivers for model checking, input structures for parameterized unit tests, etc.), has a crucial impact on the analysis. We call *builders* a set of routines B, drawn from a module's M API, that can be employed to create input structures in an automated program analysis for M (e.g. a driver for model checking). Clearly, the higher the number of different structures that can be created with B, the better the chances to find bugs in M. As the number of instances of a software module is potentially infinite, and the program analyses we target are also limited in the number of structures they can employ, we limit ourselves to a bounded-exhaustive set of structures for M [4] (e.g. all the instances of a linked list with up to k nodes). We denote this set by $BE(M,k)$. We say that a builders are *sufficient* if they can combined to build all the instances in $BE(M,k)$. Thus, sufficient builders are the best possible choice for bug finding (in a bounded setting). Notice that B can contain superfluous routines. A superfluous routine s is such that $BE(M,k)$ can be built using routines in $B - \{s\}$ (the simplest example being routines that never change the state of their parameters). These routines provide no benefits in terms of bug finding capabilities of the analysis. We call *minimal* a set of builders with no superfluous routines. Minimality is important because providing an analysis tool with superfluous routines often negatively impacts its efficiency (the number of ways k routines can be combined usually increases exponentially with k).

Manually selecting sufficient and minimal builders is not an easy task: it requires a thorough analysis of the available routines and a deep understanding of the program semantics. This is especially hard for programs with rich APIs, where there are many routines and a lot of redundancy in the API (see Sect. 2). We propose an automated approach for identifying such a sufficient and minimal set of builders, based on an evolutionary algorithm that searches for a minimal set of routines that is capable of generating the maximum number of different (bounded) objects (i.e., $BE(M, k)$). Moreover, our evolutionary approach also takes into account other characteristics of the builders, such as the number and complexity of their parameters, so that "simpler" routines are favored in the search. The goal is to choose builders that can be more easily and more efficiently used by the subsequent program analyses.

The fitness value for a set of routines R is based on the number of bounded structures that can be generated using combinations of these routines. To compute the fitness we use a modified version of a random test case generation tool (Randoop [24]) to generate as many bounded structures as possible from R, allowing at most k of objects of each type in the structures (a parameter to our algorithm). As sets of objects are very expensive to maintain and manipulate, both in terms of space and running time, we employ an efficient abstraction of a set of objects, called *field extensions*, defined as the set of field values appearing in any of the objects in the set [25]. Thus, instead of counting the number of different objects achieved by a candidate, the fitness function will compute the field extensions as objects are generated, and return the number of field values in the extensions. Intuitively, a higher number of field values in the field extensions means that the builders can be used to construct a more diverse set of objects, and therefore they should be preferred over other sets of builders.

We assess our approach experimentally on a benchmark of stateful Java classes drawn from the literature. The results show that in our case studies our approach identifies sets of routines that are sufficient and minimal, in a reasonable time. We also assess the impact of our approach in an automated analysis, namely, in the generation of test cases for parameterized tests. We compare how the random test case generation tool Randoop behaves when fed with the full module API, against providing the tool with only the builders identified by our approach. The results indicate that in the latter case Randoop generated more (and larger) objects, within a fixed time budget.

2 Motivating Example

In this section, we motivate our approach by means of a running example. The Apache NodeCachingLinkedList (NCL for short) [36] consists of a main circular doubly linked list, that holds the elements of the collection, and a secondary singly linked list that acts as a cache for nodes that have been removed from the main list. Nodes stored in the cache can be reused, and added again to the main list when inserting elements in the main list. Thanks to its cache, in applications where insertions and removals from the list are very frequent, NCL can significantly reduce the overhead needed for memory allocation and garbage collection of nodes. As an illustration, Fig. 1 shows the three NCL instances that can be built with exactly two nodes.

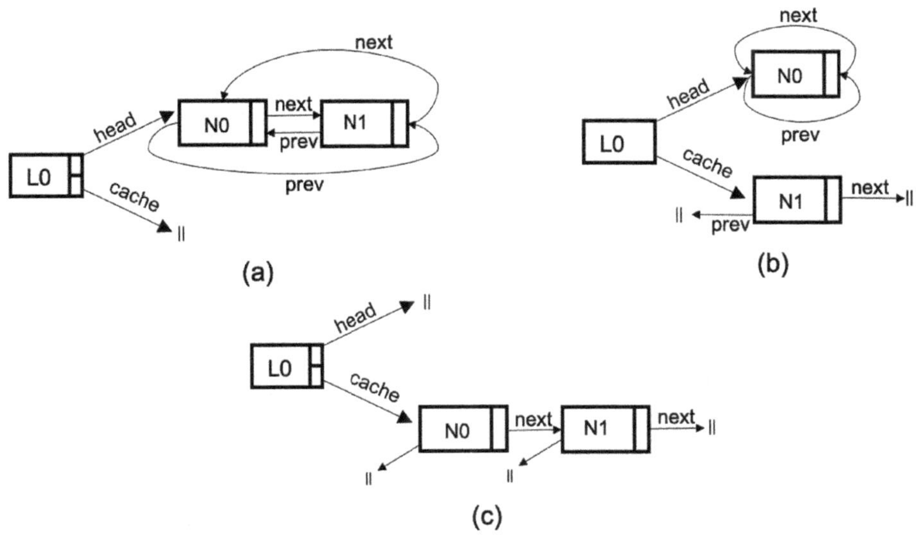

Fig. 1. Three NodeCachingLinkedList instances with exactly two nodes

Table 1. Apache's NodeCachingLinkedList API

No.	Return type	Method name	Obs?	No.	Return type	Method name	Obs?
0		NCL()	no	17	boolean	isEmpty()	yes
1		NCL(int)	no	18	Iterator	iterator()	no
2		NCL(Collection)	no	19	int	lastIndexOf(Object)	yes
3	boolean	add(Object)	no	20	ListIterator	listIterator()	no
4	void	add(int,Object)	no	21	ListIterator	listIterator(int)	no
5	boolean	addAll(Collection)	no	22	Object	remove(int)	no
6	boolean	addAll(int,Collection)	no	23	boolean	remove(Object)	no
7	boolean	addFirst(Object)	no	24	boolean	removeAll(Collection)	no
8	boolean	addLast(Object)	no	25	Object	removeFirst()	no
9	void	clear()	no	26	Object	removeLast()	no
10	boolean	contains(Object)	yes	27	boolean	retainAll(Collection)	no
11	boolean	containsAll(Collection)	yes	28	Object	set(int,Object)	no
12	boolean	equals(Object)	yes	29	int	size()	yes
13	Object	get(int)	yes	30	List	subList(int,int)	no
14	Object	getFirst()	yes	31	Object[]	toArray()	yes
15	Object	getLast()	yes	32	Object[]	toArray(Object[])	yes
16	int	indexOf(Object)	yes	33	String	toString()	yes

NCL has a very rich API, as shown in Table 1. However, for building any feasible NCL object only a few methods from the API suffice. For example, combinations of the methods in Fig. 1.1, when instantiated with appropriate parameters, can be used to build any desired (finite) NCL object. Thus, the methods therein are an example of a sufficient set of builders. Notice that, after using the constructor, the main list of NCL can be populated just by using the `addFirst` method. However, if we want to generate instances where the cache is not empty, we can do so through the `removeFirst` method, as the sufficient set of builders suggests. For most automated analyses, we would like to consider as varying scenarios (inputs) as possible, hence the motivation to build sufficient sets of builders. Furthermore, the builders in Fig. 1.1 are also minimal, since the lack of any one of them would imply that some NCL's objects cannot be constructed anymore with the routines.

```
(0)  NodeCachingLinkedList()
(7)  addFirst(Object)
(25) removeFirst()
```

Figure 1.1. A sufficient set of builders for NCL

```
(3) add(Object)
(4) add(int,Object)
(7) addFirst(Object)
(8) addLast(Object)
```

Figure 1.2. Add variants that can be used to populate NCL's main list

Notice that there can be many sets of sufficient and minimal builders. For example, we get sufficient and minimal builders by replacing `addFirst` in Fig. 1.1 with any of the other add variants shown in Fig. 1.2, as for any way of filling up NCL's main list with `addFirst` there exists a different way to build the same object using another add variant (perhaps invoked with different parameters and changing the execution order).

We also observe that the simpler the parameters of a routine, the easier to use the routine is for generating inputs in the context of a program analysis. For instance, among the alternative add routines for NCL (Fig. 1.2), `add(int,Object)` receives more parameters than the other three methods, therefore it is harder to generate parameters for it when generating inputs. This makes the other three alternatives preferred over it. Thus, our approach takes into account the number of parameters and their complexities for selecting the best possible builders.

Many methods in Table 1 are marked as observers (column Obs?), meaning that they do not modify the objects they operate on, nor they are useful for creating non-primitive objects. Hence, observers are always superfluous, and should never be included in a set of minimal builders. Our approach tries to recognize them beforehand, and discards them from the search to significantly reduce the search space.

To conclude this section we remark that, when fed with the whole NCL's API, our approach automatically identified the sufficient and minimal set of builders for NCL shown in Fig. 1.1.

3 Background

3.1 Field Extensions

The idea behind field extensions [25] is to define a representation for a set of objects that is smaller in size and easier to manipulate algorithmically. This representation implies some loss of information, but for certain applications (like the one in this paper) they are precise enough to be useful in practice [1,12,25, 26,29].

$head = (L_0, null), (L_0, N_0)$
$cache = (L_0, null), (L_0, N_1), (L_0, N_0)$
$next = (N_0, N_1), (N_1, N_0), (N_0, N_0), (N_1, null)$
$prev = (N_0, N_1), (N_0, N_0), (N_1, null), (N_0, null)$

Figure 1.3. Field extensions for the set of instances in Fig. 1

Given a set S of objects, its field extensions representation consist of a set of pairs for each field f, such that (obj,val) belongs to the field extensions of f if obj.f = val (i.e., the value of f for obj equals to val), for some object obj in S. As an example, consider the instances displayed in Fig. 1. Its corresponding field extensions are shown in Fig. 1.3. We omit the values stored in the nodes for the sake of clarity. Notice that structure (a) in Fig. 1 can be built using only add methods, whereas for (b) and (c) we have to also employ some kind of remove operation, to move nodes from the main list to the cache. Notice that values (L_0, N_0) and (L_0, N_1) for the cache field only appear in the field extensions when the structures have nodes in the cache, like (b) and (c). In addition, prev fields of nodes in the cache are always *null*, but prev fields can never be *null* in the main list (due to its circularity). This means that field extensions for structures that have non-empty caches have the potential of having a larger number of values than those for structures with no caches.

It is important to canonicalize structures before computing field extensions [12]. Canonicalization involves assigning unique identifiers $N_0, N_1, ...$ to each of its nodes during a traversal of the structure (we employ a breadth first traversal), starting at the root. Nodes visited first receive smaller identifiers than those visited afterwards during the traversal. Fields must be visited in a fixed order. Note that structures in Fig. 1 are all in canonical breadth-first form.

3.2 Random Test Case Generation

Random test generation consists of randomly producing inputs in order to test software [8,21,24]. Random input generation is straightforward when considering basic (numeric) data types, but producing inputs of other more complex types, in particular instances of *stateful* classes, is less obvious and calls for a more complex mechanism, other than just using random number generators. One such mechanism, that has been implemented by various tools for random test generation for object-oriented code, is based on randomly combining method sequences, that produce inputs of different types [8,21,24]. The process associated with the Randoop tool [24] that we use here, works essentially as follows. For every datatype, a set of sequences that produce inputs of such datatype, is maintained. To start with, for basic data types, a set of initial values is considered, and for class types, only null is considered at first (these can be considered test sequences of size one). The procedure to build a new test sequence starts by randomly selecting a method m, among all methods in the software under test. For example, one could randomly choose one of the methods for the NCL's API (Table 1), say add(Object). To actually build the test sequence, values for each of the parameters of the method m, of the corresponding types, have to be provided. These are obtained by randomly selecting test sequences, from the sets of sequences of the corresponding types, and sequentially composing them, with method m as a last statement. As an example, say that a sequence containing only the constructor of NCL is randomly selected, from the available sequences for the NCL type, and for the parameter of add, an Integer with value 0 is randomly chosen. Combining all these sequences together results in:

```
NodeCachingLinkedList l = NodeCachingLinkedList();
l.add(new Integer(0));
```

This new sequence can now be stored for later use a as parameter for other methods that operate on NCL objects.

This process is repeated until either a time budget is exhausted, or the desired number of tests (set by the user) is generated. Randoop uses guidance from the execution of tests to avoid generating illegal tests. We refer the interested reader to the article introducing Randoop [24], for further details.

An important issue to remark here is that the execution of each test sequence generated by Randoop produces a number of objects for the given type (NCL in the example). We exploit this characteristic of Randoop to compute the fitness function for a set of methods, although instead of storing actual objects we will maintain field extensions, as we explain in more detail in Sect. 4.

4 An Evolutionary Algorithm for Identifying Sufficient Object Builders

As mentioned before, to find a sufficient set of builders from a program API we design a genetic algorithm, that we describe below. Genetic algorithms [14] are non-exhaustive guided search algorithms, based on a hill climbing strategy [30]. The search space is composed of a generally very large set of individuals (the candidates), and the search objective is to find an individual with sought-for features. As opposed to classic search algorithms, genetic algorithms maintain a set of individuals, called the population, and search progresses by iteratively selecting a number of individuals in the population, using these for evolution (building new individuals out of these), and leaving out some individuals of the whole set (the "old" ones and the "new" ones). Selection of individuals for population evolution, as well as individuals' removal, are guided by a fitness function, the heuristic function used to guide the search. This function applies to individuals, and its result is generalizable to the population too (e.g., the fitness of the population may be taken as the fitness of its "fittest" individual). This function captures the features sought for in the search, and thus can be used as a halting criterion (e.g., algorithm stops after finding an individual with fitness above a certain threshold). Finally, individuals are often called chromosomes, and represented as vectors of genes that capture their characteristics. This idea is strongly related to how new individuals are constructed: by representing candidates as vectors of independent characteristics, one can build new candidates by combining part of the characteristics of an individual with part of the characteristics of another, or by arbitrarily changing a characteristic of a given individual. These two forms of evolution are called crossover and mutation, respectively, and are the traditional mechanism to build new candidates out of existing ones in genetic algorithms. For further details, we refer the reader to [22].

4.1 Chromosome Representation

In the context of our problem, candidate solutions represent sets of methods from the API of the module being analyzed. We then employ vectors of boolean values as chromosome representation. Let n be the number of methods in the API; the chromosomes in our algorithm will be vectors of size n. For any vector, the i-th position is true if and only if the chromosome contains the i-th method of the API. For example, there are 34 methods in the NCL's API (Table 1), and we enumerated them from 0 to 33. The sufficient set of builders in Fig. 1.1 is characterized by the vector with positions 0, 7 and 25 set to true, and the remaining positions set to false. In this case, the whole search space consists of the 2^{34} possible chromosomes.

4.2 Fitness Function

Given a chromosome representing a set of methods M, our fitness function computes an approximation of the number of bounded objects that can be built using combinations of methods in M. Chromosomes with higher fitness values are estimated to build more objects than those that have smaller fitness values.

Ideally, we would like to explore all the feasible objects within a small bound k, that can be built using the methods of the current chromosome, i.e., $BE(M, k)$. In other words, we need a bounded exhaustive generator for the set of methods. The bound k represents the maximum number of objects that can be created for each class (in Fig. 1, the number of nodes in the NCL objects are bounded by $k = 2$), and the maximum number of primitive values available (for example, integers from 0 to $k - 1$). For this purpose, we developed a prototype modifying the Randoop tool, discussed briefly in Sect. 3.2. First, we altered Randoop to work with a fixed set of primitive values (integers from 0 to $k - 1$). (Normally, Randoop would save primitive values that are returned by the execution of tests, and reuse these values in future tests.) Second, we make Randoop drop sequences of methods that create objects with more than k objects (of any type), to stop it from building objects larger than needed. To achieve this, we canonicalize the objects generated by the execution of each sequence, and we discard the sequence if some object has an index equal or larger than k. Third, we extend Randoop with "global" field extensions, and when the execution of a sequence terminates all the field values of the objects generated by the sequence are added to the field extensions. For example, if Randoop had generated the objects in Fig. 1, then the global field extensions would have the values shown in Fig. 1.3. Our goal is that, given a bound k, when our modified version of

```
(0)  NodeCachingLinkedList()
(7)  addFirst(Object)
(8)  addLast(Object)
(25) removeFirst()
```

Figure 1.4. A set of sufficient but not minimal builders for NCL

```
(0)  NodeCachingLinkedList()
(4)  add(int,Object)
(23) remove(Object)
```

Figure 1.5. Sufficient and minimal builders for NCL with more complex parameters than the ones in Fig. 1.1

Randoop terminates the global field extensions contain all the field values of the bounded exhaustive set of structures with up to k nodes, $BE(M, k)$. The result of the fitness function for the chromosome is the number of field values in the global extensions computed by the tool.

Our rationale for using bounded sets of objects is akin to the small scope hypothesis for bug finding [2]: if one set of methods cannot be used to build small objects that allow to differentiate it from another set of methods, then it is unlikely that these two sets can be distinguished with larger objects. This hypothesis held during our empirical evaluation across all our case studies.

We found that, besides being affected by chance, our tool rarely misses building objects that should add relevant values to the global extensions, when small values for k are employed.

Choosing Better Sets of Builders. In this section, we propose two ways to improve our evolutionary algorithm by tailoring the fitness function to obtain better sets of builders. This is strongly motivated by the way builders are used to build inputs in program analysis. On the one hand, if we have two sufficient set of builders, the set with the smaller number of methods should always be preferred. In this context, there is no reason to include superfluous methods in builders. For example, the builders in Fig. 1.4 can be used to create the same NCL objects as the builders in Fig. 1.1 of Sect. 2 (both sets are sufficient), but they are not minimal since `addLast` is superfluous.

On the other hand, builders with more parameters, or more complex ones, are more taxing on program analysis, as they require more effort to be adequately instantiated. Thus, we define a simple criterion of parameter complexity and adapt our fitness to favor builders with simpler parameters over the more complex ones. For example, both sets of builders in Figs. 1.1 and 1.5 are sufficient and minimal (with 3 routines each), but builders in Fig. 1.5 have more parameters that need to be instantiated. Comparing Figs. 1.1 and 1.5 we can observe that `addFirst` has been replaced by `add`, which has an additional integer parameter, and that `removeFirst` was interchanged with `remove`, which possesses a non-primitive parameter of type Object. Following the criteria explained above, we would like our algorithm to choose the set in Fig. 1.1 over that of Fig. 1.5.

Incorporating these ideas, the fitness function of our approach is defined by:

$$f(M) = \#fieldExt(M) + \left(\frac{w_1 * \left(1 - \frac{\#M}{\#MT}\right) + w_2 * \left(1 - \frac{(\#PP(M) + w_3 * RP(M))}{(\#PP(MT) + w_3 * RP(MT))}\right)}{w_1 + w_2} \right)$$

For a chromosome representing a set M of methods, drawn from the whole set of available methods of the API, MT, the most important part of the fitness for M, is the number of values in the field extensions, $\#fieldExt(M)$, that can be generated using our custom Randoop tool as explained in the previous section. The summand on the right implements the ideas presented in this section. It returns a real value in the interval [0, 1] that is useful to break ties for sets of methods that generate field extensions with the same number of values. In the dividend, the first summand penalizes sets with larger numbers of methods, by computing the quotient of the number of methods in M to the number of methods in MT, and subtracting the result to 1. Constant w_1 ($w_1 \geq 1$) allows us to increase/decrease the weight of this summand with respect to the other summand. The second summand in the dividend penalizes sets of methods with more complex parameters. Similarly to w_1, constant w_2 ($w_2 \geq 1$) serves the purpose of increasing/decreasing the weight of this factor in the sum. Notice that we sum up the parameters differently depending on their types: each primitive parameter adds 1 ($PP(M)$ is the number of primitive parameters in the methods of M), and each reference parameter adds a constant w_3 ($w_3 \geq 1$, $RP(M)$ is the number of reference-typed parameters in the methods of M), which allows us to increase the weight of reference parameters with respect to primitive ones. Intuitively, the whole right-hand summand computes the ratio between the number of parameters of M (with added weight for reference parameters) to the number of (weighted) parameters for MT. The result is then subtracted from 1. Finally, we divide by $w_1 + w_2$ to obtain the desired number in the interval [0, 1].

In our experimental assessment we set $w_1 = 2, w_2 = 1, w_3 = 2$. These values were good enough for our approach to produce sufficient and minimal sets of builders in all our case studies.

It is important to remark that the presented criteria for choosing better builders is based on the kind of program analyses we target (generation of tests cases for parameterized tests, software model checking). New criteria can be defined with other goals in mind, and our approach can be adapted to support them by modifying the fitness function as we did in this section.

4.3 Overall Structure of the Genetic Algorithm

The previously described elements are the constituting parts of the genetic algorithm implementing our approach. A pseudocode of the genetic algorithm is shown in Algorithm 1. Notice that Algorithm 1 follows the general structure of

Algorithm 1. Genetic Algorithm implementing our approach

```
1: pop ← chromosomes with exactly one true gene
2: for i = 1...numEvo do
3:    pop ← keep the popSize fittest chromosomes from pop
4:    for j = 1...cRate ∗ popSize do
5:       c1, c2 ← select two random chromosomes from pop
6:       new ← single point crossover c1, c2
7:       add new to pop
8:    end for
9:    for c ∈ pop do
10:      new ← mutate each gene of c with probability mRate
11:      if new ≠ c then
12:         add new to pop
13:      end if
14:   end for
15: end for
16: result ← fittest chromosome of pop
```

a genetic algorithm. The initial population is generated by producing all the feasible chromosomes with only one available method (vectors with false in all positions except one, set to true) (line 3). Then, it starts to iteratively evolve the population (lines 4–15). At the beginning of each evolution iteration, the algorithm discards some individuals to control population size, by keeping the *popSize* fittest individuals of the current population and discarding the rest (line 5). Then, the algorithm performs single-point crossover on randomly selected individuals (lines 6–10). Crossover is applied a number of times that is proportional to the population size *popSize*, determined by the product of *popSize* and the crossover rate parameter *cRate* ($0 \leq cRate \leq 1$). Then, the algorithm mutates individuals (lines 11–15) by changing the value of each of its genes with probability *mRate* ($0 \leq mRate \leq 1$). Any newly created individual by the crossover and mutation operations are added to the population.

The algorithm stops after *numEvo* evolutions, with *numEvo* a parameter of the algorithm. Notice that, we don't have a target value for our fitness, since an untried set of methods might produce a larger number of field extensions than the algorithm has currently seen. Again, there is a compromise to be made for choosing a good value for *numEvo*: a larger number increases the precision of the algorithm but increases its running time, whereas a smaller number makes it run faster but it might not result in the best set of builders.

As usual, we found a number for the parameters of our algorithm that seems to work well in practice. In our experimental evaluation, we set $numEvo = 20, popSize = 30, cRate = 0.35, mRate = 0.08$ (the last two are the default for the JGap library).

Most of Algorithm 1 is a default evolutionary implementation of the JGap Java library [37]. Notice that, if we take away the complexity of the fitness function, our evolutionary algorithm is rather standard, so it is not surprising that an existing implementation works well for our purposes. Of course, improvements to the evolutionary algorithm, and fine tuning for its parameters (e.g., crossover/mutation rate) might yield faster execution times.

We also implemented a simple multi-threaded version of our approach, that helps improving its performance. Basically, at each iteration we make t copies of the current population, where t is the number of available threads, and evolve each of the population replicas independently of the others. After all the threads have finished, we keep the $100/t$ fittest individuals of the population evolved by each thread, and use them to build the population for the next iteration of the algorithm.

4.4 Reducing the Search Space by Observers Classification

We say a routine is an observer if it never modifies the parameters it takes, and never generates a non-primitive value as a result of its execution. Column Obs? in Table 1 (Sect. 2) indicates whether each NCL method is an observer or not. Clearly, an observer cannot be used to modify nor build new objects, and therefore can never belong to a minimal set of builders. Hence, if we can classify them correctly beforehand, we can remove the observers from the search to significantly reduce the search space, without losing precision. For example, in the NCL API (Table 1) there are 13 observers out of 34 methods, so by removing observers we prune more than one third of the search space.

To detect observers we run another customized Randoop version before our evolutionary algorithm. This time, we check for each method whether it modifies its inputs at each test sequence generated by Randoop involving the method, by canonicalizing the objects before and after execution of the method, and checking if the field values of the objects change after execution. If this is the case, the method is marked as a builder (not an observer). For return values, if in any test sequence generated by Randoop the method returns a non-primitive value, then we mark it as a builder as well. We run this custom Randoop until it generates a large number of scenarios for each method. Ten to twenty seconds was enough for our case studies. At the end of the Randoop execution, methods not marked as builders are considered observers and discarded before invoking the evolutionary algorithm.

Other approaches exist for the detection of pure methods [15,31] (similar to our observers). Note that our evolutionary algorithm is not dependent on the method classification algorithm, so any of them could be useful for our purposes.

5 Experimental Results

In this section, we experimentally assess our approach. The evaluation is based on a benchmark of data structure implementations, including: `NCL` from Apache Collections [36]; `BinaryTree`, `BinomialHeap`, `FibonacciHeap`, `RedBlackTree` taken from [35]; `UnionFind`, an implementation of disjoint sets taken from JGrapht [38]. We also evaluate our technique on components of real software projects such as `Lits` from the implementation of Sat4j [3], taken from [20], which consists of a variable store that monitors when a guess was last made about a value of a variable, and whether listeners are watching the state of that variable; and `Scheduler`, an implementation of a process scheduler taken from [10]. All the experiments were run on 3.4 GHz quad-core Intel Core i7-6700 machines with 8 GB of RAM, running GNU/Linux.

The evaluation consists of two parts. First, we ran our approach (Algorithm 1) on the whole module APIs of the aforementioned classes, to compute sets of builders for each case study. The goal is to assess how good are the builders identified, and the time it takes our approach to compute them. For each case study we ran our approach 5 times. The results are shown in Table 2, including the number of routines in the whole API (#API), a sample of identified builders (some methods might be interchanged in different runs, e.g., `addFirst` and `addLast` in NCL), and the average running time (in seconds) of the 5 runs. We manually inspected the results, and found that the automatically identified sets of builders were in all cases sufficient (all the feasible objects for the structure can be constructed using the builders) and minimal (do not contain superfluous methods). The approach is reasonably efficient, taking about 30 min in the worst case.

The second part of the evaluation regards how helpful are the identified builders in the context of a program analysis, namely, the automated generation of test cases. These objects might be used, for example, as inputs in parameterized unit tests. For the case studies that provide mechanisms to measure the size of objects and to compare objects by equality (i.e., the *size* and *equals* methods of data structures), we generated tests with Randoop using all the methods available in the API (API), and then we generated tests with Randoop using only the builder methods (BLD) identified by our approach in the previous experiment (Table 2). We then compare the number of different objects (No. of Objs.), and the size of the largest object (Max Obj. Size) created by the tests generated from the API, against the tests generated using methods from BLD only. We set three different test generation budgets: 60, 120 and 180 seconds (Budget). The results are summarized in Table 3. In addition, we consider another approach, API+, that involves the generation of tests using the API for a budget that encompasses the test generation budget (Budget) plus the time it takes our approach to identify builders for the corresponding case study. The results show that in the same test budget BLD generates in average 1280% more objects than API. Furthermore, when builders identification time is added to the test generation budget for API (API+), BLD can generate 568% more objects in average (w.r.t API+). In all cases, BLD also generates significantly larger objects than API and API+. In view of these results, it is clear that automated builders identification pays off for the automated generation of structures for stateful classes.

The experiments can be reproduced by following the instructions in the paper website [27]. Furthermore, in the site we experimentally show that the builders identified by our approach can be employed to build efficient drivers for software model checking. We don't show these results here due to space constraints.

Table 2. Builders computation results

	Sample Builders	Time
NCL	NCLinkedList(int)	
	addFirst(Object)	1744
#API: 34	removeFirst()	
UFind	UnionFind()	
	addElement(int)	215
#API: 9	union(int,int)	
FHeap	FibonacciHeap()	
	insert(int)	72
#API: 7	removeMin()	
RBT	TreeMap()	
#API: 8	put(int)	73
BTree	BinTree()	
#API: 7	add(int)	73
BHeap	BinomialHeap()	
#API: 10	insert(int)	121
Lits	Lits()	
#API: 26	getFromPool(int)	
	forgets(int)	1229
	setLevel(int,int)	
	setReason(int)	
Sched.	Schedule()	
#API: 10	addProcess(int)	
	blockProcess()	377
	quantumExpire()	

Table 3. Assessment of using the identified builders (BLD) vs the whole API (API) in test case generation. API+ involves test case generation with the whole API, with budget = (Budget + builders computation time)

	Budget	Max Obj. Size			No. of Objs.		
		API	BLD	API+	API	BLD	API+
NCL	60	8	16	11	1442	42021	13119
#API: 34	120	8	18	11	2423	69017	13247
#BLD: 3	180	9	18	11	3166	91647	13505
UFind	60	8	13	9	3388	34250	8351
#API: 9	120	9	13	9	5180	56418	8574
#BLD: 3	180	9	13	9	6695	74425	9387
FHeap	60	11	15	12	6989	32639	11499
#API: 7	120	12	17	13	11447	54264	17202
#BLD: 3	180	12	17	13	15344	72413	20775
RBT	60	8	15	8	1812	23034	3041
#API: 8	120	8	15	8	2678	35635	3698
#BLD: 2	180	8	15	8	3358	44807	3940
BTree	60	8	15	8	3600	24908	6019
#API: 7	120	8	15	8	5471	39239	7387
#BLD: 2	180	8	15	9	6975	50671	9247
BHeap	60	9	26	10	3874	65915	8076
#API: 10	120	10	29	10	5970	111402	9708
#BLD: 2	180	10	29	11	7638	147260	10606

6 Related Work

As mentioned throughout the paper, the problem of identifying sufficient builders is recurrent in various program analyses, including but not limited to software model checking and test generation. In works like [18,23], in the context of software model checking, and [5,24,32,33], in the context of automated test generation, and just to cite a few, the problem of identifying part of an API and provide it for analysis is present. Typically the problem is dealt with manually.

The use of search-based techniques to solve challenging software engineering problems is an increasingly popular strategy, which has been applied successfully to a number of problems, including test input generation [11], program repair [19], and many others. As far as we are aware of, this is a novel application of evolutionary computation in software engineering. An approach that tackles a related, but different, problem, is that associated with the SUSHI tool [5]. The aim with SUSHI is to feed a genetic algorithm with a *path condition*, produced by a symbolic execution engine, so that an input satisfying the provided path condition can be reproduced using a module's API. This approach assumes that the API (or the subset of relevant methods) is provided, as opposed to our work, that precisely tackles the provision of the restricted API.

Our technique requires a mechanism for identifying *observers*, which we have solved within the work in the paper, resorting to random test generation, and instrumentation for state monitoring. Approaches to the identification of observers, or more precisely *pure methods*, exist in the literature [15,31]. Regarding these lines of work, notice that the focus of our evolutionary algorithm is not the identification of observers, but the construction of minimal and sufficient set of builders. Moreover, our approach is in fact independent of the mechanism used to identify observers/pure methods, and thus could be combined with the works just cited (i.e., replacing our random testing based approach by an alternative one).

7 Conclusions

In this work, we presented an evolutionary algorithm for automatically detecting sets of builders from a module's API. We assessed our algorithm over several case studies from the literature, and found that it is capable of precisely identifying sets of builders that are sufficient and minimal, within reasonable running times. To the best of our knowledge, this is the first work that addresses this problem, which is typically dealt with manually.

We also showed preliminary results indicating that our approach can be exploited by test case generation tools to yield larger and more diverse objects. Other techniques, like software model checking, can benefit as well by using the identified set of builders to automatically construct efficient drivers. More experimentation needs to be done, but given the results in this paper our approach looks very promising.

One of the biggest challenges of this work was the construction of a tool to allow us to generate all the bounded structures, for a given maximum number k of objects, from the methods of the program API. The proposed solution worked well enough for our case studies, but avoiding randomness in the process would be desirable. Using bounded exhaustive generation tools rather than random generation would better fit our purposes [4], but unfortunately none of the tools for bounded exhaustive test generation produce inputs from a module's API. We believe that a promising research direction, that we plan to further explore in future work, is to adapt our presented approach for bounded exhaustive test generation.

Some aspects of our genetic algorithm can be further improved. For instance, a more powerful classification for argument types, in the prioritization of methods according to their complexities, can be defined. Moreover, one may also incorporate other dimensions, such as *code complexity*, to favor simpler methods. We will explore this direction as future work. Also, our genetic algorithm implementation is, for most parts, a default evolutionary implementation of the JGap Java library [37]. Of course, improvements to the evolutionary algorithm, and fine tuning for its parameters (e.g., crossover/mutation rate) might yield faster execution times, so we plan to investigate this further in future work.

References

1. Abad, P., et al.: Improving test generation under rich contracts by tight bounds and incremental SAT solving. In: Sixth IEEE International Conference on Software Testing, Verification and Validation, ICST 2013, Luxembourg, Luxembourg, 18–22 March 2013, pp. 21–30 (2013)
2. Andoni, A., Daniliuc, D., Khurshid, S.: Evaluating the small scope hypothesis. Technical report, MIT Laboratory for Computer Science (2003)
3. Berre, D.L., Parrain, A.: The Sat4j library, release 2.2, system description. J. Satisf. Boolean Model. Comput. **7**, 59–64 (2010)
4. Boyapati, C., Khurshid, S., Marinov, D.: Korat: automated testing based on Java predicates. In: Proceedings of the 2002 ACM SIGSOFT International Symposium on Software Testing and Analysis, ISSTA 2002, pp. 123–133. ACM, New York (2002)
5. Braione, P., Denaro, G., Mattavelli, A., Pezzè, M.: SUSHI: a test generator for programs with complex structured inputs. In: Proceedings of the 40th International Conference on Software Engineering: Companion Proceeedings, ICSE 2018, Gothenburg, Sweden, 27 May–03 June 2018, pp. 21–24. ACM (2018)
6. Calcagno, C., Distefano, D., O'Hearn, P.W., Yang, H.: Compositional shape analysis by means of bi-abduction. J. ACM **58**(6), 26:1–26:66 (2011)
7. Ciupa, I., Leitner, A., Oriol, M., Meyer, B.: ARTOO: adaptive random testing for object-oriented software. In: Proceedings of the 30th International Conference on Software Engineering, ICSE 2008, pp. 71–80. ACM, New York (2008)
8. Claessen, K., Hughes, J.: QuickCheck: a lightweight tool for random testing of haskell programs. In: Proceedings of the Fifth ACM SIGPLAN International Conference on Functional Programming, ICFP 2000, pp. 268–279. ACM, New York(2000)
9. Clarke, E., Kroening, D., Lerda, F.: A tool for checking ANSI-C programs. In: Jensen, K., Podelski, A. (eds.) TACAS 2004. LNCS, vol. 2988, pp. 168–176. Springer, Heidelberg (2004). https://doi.org/10.1007/978-3-540-24730-2_15
10. Do, H., Elbaum, S., Rothermel, G.: Supporting controlled experimentation with testing techniques: an infrastructure and its potential impact. Empirical Softw. Eng. **10**(4), 405–435 (2005)
11. Fraser, G., Arcuri, A.: EvoSuite: automatic test suite generation for object-oriented software. In: Proceedings of the 19th ACM SIGSOFT Symposium and the 13th European Conference on Foundations of Software Engineering, ESEC/FSE 2011, pp. 416–419. ACM, New York (2011)
12. Galeotti, J.P., Rosner, N., López Pombo, C.G., Frias, M.F.: Analysis of invariants for efficient bounded verification. In: Proceedings of the 19th International Symposium on Software Testing and Analysis, ISSTA 2010, pp. 25–36. ACM, New York (2010)
13. Gligoric, M., Gvero, T., Jagannath, V., Khurshid, S., Kuncak, V., Marinov, D.: Test generation through programming in UDITA. In: Proceedings of the 32nd ACM/IEEE International Conference on Software Engineering - Volume 1, ICSE 2010, pp. 225–234. ACM, New York (2010)
14. Goldberg, D.E.: Genetic Algorithms in Search, Optimization and Machine Learning, 1st edn. Addison-Wesley Longman Publishing Co., Inc., Boston (1989)
15. Huang, W., Milanova, A., Dietl, W., Ernst, M.D.: Reim & ReImInfer: checking and inference of reference immutability and method purity. In: Proceedings of the ACM International Conference on Object Oriented Programming Systems Languages and Applications, OOPSLA 2012, pp. 879–896. ACM, New York (2012)

16. Itzhaky, S., Bjørner, N., Reps, T., Sagiv, M., Thakur, A.: Property-directed shape analysis. In: Biere, A., Bloem, R. (eds.) CAV 2014. LNCS, vol. 8559, pp. 35–51. Springer, Cham (2014). https://doi.org/10.1007/978-3-319-08867-9_3
17. Khalek, S.A., Yang, G., Zhang, L., Marinov, D., Khurshid, S.: TestEra: a tool for testing Java programs using alloy specifications. In: Proceedings of the 2011 26th IEEE/ACM International Conference on Automated Software Engineering, ASE 2011, pp. 608–611. IEEE Computer Society, Washington, DC (2011)
18. Khurshid, S., Pasareanu, C.S., Visser, W.: Generalized symbolic execution for model checking and testing. In: Garavel, H., Hatcliff, J. (eds.) TACAS 2003. LNCS, vol. 2619, pp. 553–568. Springer, Heidelberg (2003). https://doi.org/10.1007/3-540-36577-X_40
19. Le Goues, C., Nguyen, T., Forrest, S., Weimer, W.: Genprog: a generic method for automatic software repair. IEEE Trans. Softw. Eng. **38**(1), 54–72 (2012)
20. Loncaric, C., Ernst, M.D., Torlak, E.: Generalized data structure synthesis. In: Proceedings of the 40th International Conference on Software Engineering, ICSE 2018, Gothenburg, Sweden, 27 May–03 June 2018, pp. 958–968 (2018)
21. Meyer, B., Ciupa, I., Leitner, A., Liu, L.L.: Automatic testing of object-oriented software. In: van Leeuwen, J., Italiano, G.F., van der Hoek, W., Meinel, C., Sack, H., Plášil, F. (eds.) SOFSEM 2007. LNCS, vol. 4362, pp. 114–129. Springer, Heidelberg (2007). https://doi.org/10.1007/978-3-540-69507-3_9
22. Michalewicz, Z.: Genetic Algorithms + Data Structures = Evolution Programs, 3rd edn. Springer, Heidelberg (1996). https://doi.org/10.1007/978-3-662-03315-9
23. Nori, A.V., Rajamani, S.K., Tetali, S.D., Thakur, A.V.: The Yogi project: software property checking via static analysis and testing. In: Kowalewski, S., Philippou, A. (eds.) TACAS 2009. LNCS, vol. 5505, pp. 178–181. Springer, Heidelberg (2009). https://doi.org/10.1007/978-3-642-00768-2_17
24. Pacheco, C., Ernst, M.D.: Randoop: feedback-directed random testing for Java. In: Companion to the 22nd ACM SIGPLAN Conference on Object-Oriented Programming Systems and Applications Companion, OOPSLA 2007, pp. 815–816. ACM, New York (2007)
25. Ponzio, P., Aguirre, N., Frias, M.F., Visser, W.: Field-exhaustive testing. In: Proceedings of the 2016 24th ACM SIGSOFT International Symposium on Foundations of Software Engineering, FSE 2016, pp. 908–919. ACM, New York (2016)
26. Ponzio, P., Bengolea, V., Brida, S.G., Scilingo, G., Aguirre, N., Frias, M.: On the effect of object redundancy elimination in randomly testing collection classes. In: Proceedings of the 11th International Workshop on Search-Based Software Testing, SBST 2018, pp. 67–70. ACM, New York (2018)
27. Ponzio, P., Bengolea, V.S., Politano, M., Aguirre, N., Frias, M.F.: Replication package of the article: automatically identifying sufficient object builders from module APIs. https://sites.google.com/view/objectbuildergeneration/
28. Păsăreanu, C.S., Rungta, N.: Symbolic pathfinder: symbolic execution of Java bytecode. In: Proceedings of the IEEE/ACM International Conference on Automated Software Engineering, ASE 2010, pp. 179–180. ACM, New York (2010)
29. Rosner, N., Geldenhuys, J., Aguirre, N., Visser, W., Frias, M.F.: BLISS: improved symbolic execution by bounded lazy initialization with SAT support. IEEE Trans. Softw. Eng. **41**(7), 639–660 (2015)
30. Russell, S., Norvig, P.: Artificial Intelligence: A Modern Approach, 3rd edn. Prentice Hall Press, Upper Saddle River (2009)
31. Sălcianu, A., Rinard, M.: Purity and side effect analysis for Java programs. In: Cousot, R. (ed.) VMCAI 2005. LNCS, vol. 3385, pp. 199–215. Springer, Heidelberg (2005). https://doi.org/10.1007/978-3-540-30579-8_14

32. Tillmann, N., De Halleux, J.: Pex–white box test generation for .NET. In: Beckert, B., Hähnle, R. (eds.) TAP 2008. LNCS, vol. 4966, pp. 134–153. Springer, Heidelberg (2008). https://doi.org/10.1007/978-3-540-79124-9_10
33. Tillmann, N., de Halleux, J., Xie, T.: Parameterized unit testing: theory and practice. In: Proceedings of the 32nd ACM/IEEE International Conference on Software Engineering - Volume 2, ICSE 2010, pp. 483–484. ACM, New York (2010)
34. Visser, W., Mehlitz, P.: Model checking programs with Java PathFinder. In: Godefroid, P. (ed.) SPIN 2005. LNCS, vol. 3639, p. 27. Springer, Heidelberg (2005). https://doi.org/10.1007/11537328_5
35. Visser, W., Păsăreanu, C.S., Pelánek, R.: Test input generation for Java containers using state matching. In: Proceedings of the 2006 International Symposium on Software Testing and Analysis, ISSTA 2006, pp. 37–48. ACM, New York (2006)
36. Website of the Apache Collections library. https://commons.apache.org/proper/commons-collections/
37. Website of the Java Genetic Algorithms Package. http://jgap.sourceforge.net
38. Website of the JGrapht library. https://jgrapht.org/

Author Index

www.ingramcontent.com/pod-product-compliance
Lightning Source LLC
LaVergne TN
LVHW082108200926
848484LV00008B/1928